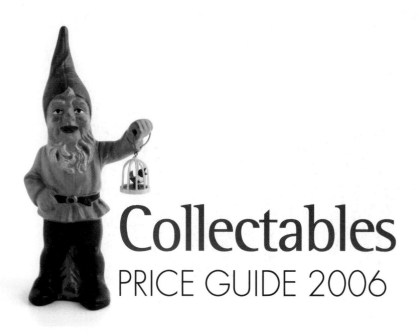

Collectables
PRICE GUIDE 2006

Collectables
PRICE GUIDE 2006

Judith Miller
and Mark Hill

A DORLING KINDERSLEY BOOK

LONDON, NEW YORK,
MELBOURNE, MUNICH AND DELHI

A joint production from DORLING KINDERSLEY
and THE PRICE GUIDE COMPANY

THE PRICE GUIDE COMPANY LIMITED

Publisher Judith Miller

Collectables Specialist Mark Hill

Publishing Manager Julie Brooke

European Consultants Martina Franke, Nicolas Tricaud de Montonnière

Senior Managing Editor Carolyn Madden

Assistant Editor Sara Sturgess

Digital Image Co-ordinator Ellen Sinclair

Sub-editors Jessica Bishop, Dan Dunlavey, Sandra Lange, Alexandra Barr

Design and DTP Tim & Ali Scrivens, TJ Graphics

Photographers Graham Rae, Bruce Boyajian, John McKenzie, Byron Slater, Steve Tanner, Heike Löwenstein, Andy Johnson, Adam Gault

Indexer Hilary Bird

Workflow Consultant Bob Bousfield

Business Advisor Nick Croydon

DORLING KINDERSLEY LIMITED

Publishing Director Jackie Douglas

Managing Art Editor Heather McCarry

Managing Editor Julie Oughton

DTP Designer Adam Walker

Production Elizabeth Warman

Production Manager Sarah Coltman

While every care has been taken in the compilation of this guide, neither the authors nor the publishers accept any liability for any financial or other loss incurred by reliance placed on the information contained in *Collectables Price Guide 2006*

First published in 2005 by
Dorling Kindersley Limited
80 Strand, London WC2R 0RL

A Penguin Company

The Price Guide Company (UK) Ltd
Studio 21, Waterside
44–48 Wharf Road
London N1 7UX
info@thepriceguidecompany.com

2 4 6 8 10 9 7 5 3 1

A CIP catalogue record for this book is available from the British Library.

1 4053 0880 X

Printed and bound in Germany by GGP Media GmbH

Discover more at
www.dk.com

CONTENTS

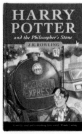

6 | CONTENTS

INTRODUCTION

Welcome to the fourth edition of my Collectables Price Guide, published in association with Dorling Kindersley. As I compile these books each year, I am constantly amazed at the breadth of completely new information that becomes available. Collectors, researchers and my team track down company brochures, price lists, key reference works and, where possible, the actual makers or artists themselves - all in the pursuit of precious pearls of collecting wisdom.

All this new information allows a greater and more accurate understanding of an area, as well as adding great vibrancy to the collectables market. This year we have reflected this by adding even more information than ever before, in the form of extra footnotes and more of our familiar 'Closer Look' features. Over 30 years, I have learnt that knowledge counts for so much when collecting, affecting desirability and prices considerably. With this in mind, we believe that this year's guide will help you stay very much 'top of the tree' in this respect!

We've also taken a generous slice through the world of collecting, covering well over 150 different areas from Beswick to books and from pot lids to Pez. With this much diversity and extra information, I believe this once again makes our price guide the essential collecting companion this year!

Judith Miller.

LIST OF CONSULTANTS

Books
Roddy Newlands
Bloomsbury Auctions, London

Leo Harrison
Biblion, London

Ceramics
Beth Adams
Alfies Antiques Market, London

Nick Ainge
Decoseek.decoware.co.uk

Judith Miller
The Price Guide Company (UK) Ltd

Coins, Banknotes & Bonds
Rick Coleman
Bloomsbury, London

Dolls
Susan Brewer
Britishdollshowcase.co.uk

Glass
Mark Hill
The Price Guide Company (UK) Ltd

Marcus Newhall
Researcher & Collector

Val & Chris Stewart
Cloudglass.com

Dr Graham Cooley
graham.cooley@metalysis.com

Powder Compacts
Sara Hughes
http://mysite.wanadoo-members.co.uk/sara_compacts

Pens & Pencils
Alexander H.I. Crum Ewing
Bloomsbury Auctions, London

Posters
Patrick Bogue
Onslows.co.uk, Dorset

Royal Memorabilia
Andrew Hilton
Special Auction Services, Berkshire

Sporting
Manfred Schotten
Manfred Schotten Antiques, Burford

Tools
Tony Murland
Toolshop Auctions, Needham Market

Toys
Glenn Butler
Wallis & Wallis, East Sussex

We are very grateful to our friends and experts who gave us so much help – Ian Broughton, Sparkle Moore and Sasja of Alfie's Antiques Market, Beverley Adams of Beverley, London, NW8, Ron & Ann Wheeler of Artiusglass.co.uk, Dorothy Sharp at the David Sharp Pottery, Rye, Keith Baker, Oliver Strebbel-Ritter of Transport Collectors Auctions, London, Nigel Wiggins of the Old Hall Club and Peter Chapman and Maurice Flanagan of Zardoz Books, Wiltshire.

HOW TO USE THIS BOOK

HOW TO USE THIS BOOK

Subcategory Heading
Indicates the subcategory of the main category heading and describes the general contents of the page.

A Closer Look at...
Here, we highlight particularly interesting items or show identifying features, pointing out rare or desirable qualities.

The Price Guide
All prices are shown in ranges and give you a "ball park" figure close to what you should expect to pay for a similar item. The great joy of collectables is that there is not a recommended retail price. The price given is not necessarily that which a dealer will pay you. As a general rule, expect to receive approximately 30 per cent less. When selling, pay attention to the dealer or auction house specialist to understand how this may be, and consider that they have to run a business as well as make a living. When buying, listen again. Condition, market forces and location of the place of sale will all affect a price. If no price is available, the letters NPA will be used.

Category Heading
Indicates the general category as listed in the table of contents on pp.5–6.

The Source Code
The image is credited to its source with a code. See the "Key to Illustrations" on pp.576–580 for a full listing of dealers and auction houses.

Collectors' Notes
Provides background information on the designer, factory or make of the piece or style in question.

The Object
All collectables are shown in full colour, which is a vital aid to identification and valuation.

The Caption
Describes the item and can include the maker, model, year of manufacture, size and condition.

Find out more...
To help you seek further information, these boxes list websites, books, and museums where you can find out more.

COLLECTORS' NOTES

- Coca-Cola was invented by Dr. John Pemberton of Atlanta, Georgia in 1886 and was initially marketed as a medicinal pick-me-up called 'Pemberton's French Wine Coca'. The name Coca-Cola was taken from the fact it contained cocaine made from coca leaves and was flavoured with kola nuts.

- The company was sold to Asa Griggs Candler in 1887 who began an aggressive marketing campaign, which accounts for much of the company's success today.

- Magazine advertisements appeared from 1902 and were soon followed by a huge range merchandising including ephemera, trays, signs and clocks, produced for a wide range of countries. Due to the vast selection on the market, collectors tend to specialise in one area such as bottles, signs or tip trays.

- Items from the turn of the 20thC are scarce and tend to be most valuable, though condition is an important factor. Example featuring artwork by popular artists such as Haddon Sundblom, Norman Rockwell or Hamilton King are also sought-after. Becoming familiar with the changing styles of the logo and bottles will help date pieces as well as recognise fakes and reproductions.

A Coca-Cola tip tray, light surface wear to outer edge in a few spots.

1906   *4in (10cm) diam*

£850-950   **JDJ**

A Coca-Cola 'Exhibition Girl' tip tray, a few minuscule chips to outer rim.

1909   *6in (15cm) wide*

£300-400   **JDJ**

A Coca-Cola tip tray, titled "Drink Delicious Coca-Cola", designed by Hamilton King.

1910   *6.25in (16cm) high*

£350-450   **DC**

A Coca-Cola tip tray, light surface crazing to varnish, designed by Hamilton King.

1913   *6in (15cm) wide*

£350-450   **JDJ**

A Coca-Cola tip tray, with slight dimple to lower left and edge wear.

1914   *6in (15cm) wide*

£100-150   **JDJ**

A Coca-Cola tip tray, with small amount of pitting and a few small chips to perimeter.

1916 6in (15cm) wide

£120-180   **JDJ**

A Coca-Cola serving tray, featuring a reclining lady.

Rectangular trays replaced round or oval ones in 1910 and continued for 50 years.

1936
     13.5in (34cm) high

£300-400   **DC**

ADVERTISING

A Coca-Cola Selecto-clock, by Selected Devises Company, Chicago, the painted metal dial in oak case.

16in (40.5cm) wide

£150-200 JDJ

A CLOSER LOOK AT A COCA-COLA CLOCK

These early Baird clocks come in two styles, this figure of eight shape and a simpler round one, known as a 'Gallery' clock.

Edward Baird started producing clock cases in Canada in 1888 and moved to Plattsburg, New York in 1890 when he began making these papier-mâché cases for Coca-Cola.

The 'Ideal Brain Tonic' slogan is early. It was replaced with "Drink Coca-Cola. Delicious. Refreshing.", which is preferred less by collectors.

These clocks typically come with mechanisms made by Seth Thomas.

A Coca-Cola advertising clock, by Baird, captioned 'Relieves Exhaustion-Delicious Refreshing', retaining original interior paper label, both papier-mâché bezels restored, clock face shows some discolouration typical of these clocks, includes pendulum and key.

1893-96   *30.5in (77.5cm) high*

£1,200-1,800 JDJ

A Coca-Cola tin advertising sign, featuring an early cardboard six-pack holder and captioned 'Take Home a Carton', dated, light surface scuffs and scrapes.

1939   *27.5in (70cm) high*

£500-600 JDJ

An early Coca-Cola menu, featuring Hilda Clark.

Actress and singer Hilda Clark first appeared on Coca-Cola advertising in 1899.

1903

£500-600 DC

A 1920s Coca-Cola lithographed metal sign, depicting a six-pack with bottles, Coke-colour contents, some fading to carrier.

The six-bottle pack was introduced in the 1920s, enabling customers to take the refreshing drink home.

13in (33cm) wide

£40-50 TA

A scarce Coca-Cola 'Verbena' die-cut cardboard festoon, complete with original satin ribbon garlands, with one leaf tip broken off and some tears and creases.

1932   *33in (84cm) wide*

£900-1,000 JDJ

A large printed Coca Cola advertisement, from part of a shop festoon.

c1958   *18.5in (47cm) high*

£30-40 DC

FIND OUT MORE...

Petretti's Coca-Cola Collectibles Price Guide, by Allan Petretti, published by Krause Publications, 11th edition, July 2001.

www.cocacola.com, official company website.

COLLECTORS' NOTES

■ Tins reached the height of their popularity between the 1860s and 1930s holding biscuits, tobacco, sweets and other perishables. From the 1890s onwards designs and shapes became more inventive.

■ Many choose to collect by category, with biscuit and sweet tins being the most popular. Look for major manufacturers such as Huntley & Palmer. Household name brands, such as OXO, can also fetch higher value due to cross-market interest with OXO collectors.

■ The style of the artwork can help date a tin. Complex artwork typical of the period is desirable. Early tins from the mid-19th century can be rare. Sporting, aviation, naval or military themes are popular and often fetch higher prices, as can children's themes.

■ A novelty shape can increase the value, especially it if has moving parts. Many were originally designed to be kept and re-used, either decoratively or functionally as storage container or toys.

■ Scratches, dents, rust and flaking all reduce value. A piece in poor condition, even if rare, can be worth less than a more common piece in mint condition. Do not wash tins in water and store them out of direct sunlight.

A Biscuiterie Gauloise lithographed biscuit tin, with scenes of planes, boxing and rugby.

c1910   *7in (18cm) wide*

£100-150   **DH**

A Dunmore lithographed biscuit tin, with scenes of Father Christmas delivering presents.

c1890   *4.5in (11.5cm) wide*

£60-90   **DH**

A 1940s Tavener Rutledge lithographed biscuit tin, with scene of the Queen Mary at Liverpool Princes landing stage.

10in (25.5cm) wide

£50-80   **DH**

A 1930s 'Alice in Wonderland' lithographed biscuit tin, with a scene of the Mad Hatter's tea party.

6in (15cm) wide

£50-80   **DH**

A Huntley & Palmer 'Wallet' lithographed biscuit tin.

c1903   *7in (18cm) wide*

£70-100   **DH**

A Mackintosh's Toffee de Luxe 'Ark' lithographed sweet tin, with pull-out decks.

c1925   *3.5in (9cm) high*

£220-280   **DH**

A William Crawford & Sons biscuit tin, designed by Mabel Lucy Attwell, formed as a cottage with hinged lid.

8.25in (21cm) long

£100-150   **L&T**

A Mackintosh's Toffee de Luxe 'Zoo' lithographed sweet tin, with pull-out section.

This is part of a set of four tins along with the ark tin on this page, and 'Santa's House'. Look out for the rare 'Toffee Shop' tin, featured in last year's edition of this book and worth up to £400.

c1925   *3.5in (9cm) high*

£200-300   **DH**

A Lyon's Assorted Toffieskotch lithographed sweet tin, by E.T. Gee & Son Ltd, in the form of a sergeant of the Queen's Guards.

This tin was also available in other ranks, worth around the same.

c1925   11in (28cm) high

£300-400   **DH**

A 1930s "LK" lithographed sweet tin, in the form of a soldier, possibly Swedish.

8.5in (21.5cm) high

£280-320   **DH**

An unusual Victory V Lozenge sweet tin, modelled as a clock with working movement, the gold-printed case decorated with a scene on the Thames; together with two matching containers.

This is typical of a tin made to keep for decorative reasons after the contents have been eaten. It could easily be displayed on a mantelpiece where one would expect to see a mantel clock and matching garnitures.

14.5in (37cm) high

£150-200   **F**

A Pierrot Gourmond lithographed tin, with rare Pekingese dog image.

c1930   5in (12.5cm) wide

£30-40   **DH**

A rare J.S. Fry & Sons lithographed chocolate tin, in the form of a trunk.

c1900   4in (10cm) wide

£70-100   **DH**

A German Touristen Schokolade lithographed chocolate tin.

c1910   6in (15cm) wide

£120-180   **DH**

A 1930s unmarked lithographed sweet tin, with sporting scenes to outside and tennis scene to lid.

7in (18cm) diam

£80-120   **DH**

A Lovell's RAF Assortment lithographed sweet tin, by G.F. Lovell & Co. Ltd.

c1935   9in (23cm) diam

£220-280   **DH**

A Rowntree's Toffee lithographed sweet tin.

Although plain, the mint condition of this tin, with no damage or wear, makes it valuable.

c1925   4.5in (11.5cm) high

£50-80   **DH**

A Kinema Toffee lithographed sweet tin, by T.W. Parker, with bust of Charlie Chaplin.

c1925   *4.25in (11cm) wide*

£80-120   **DH**

A Lovell's 'Black Pete' liquorice toffee lithographed sweet tin.

c1925   *9.5in (24cm) high*

£80-120   **DH**

A French Negrocao Solubilise Sucre lithographed tin container, for sugar.

c1930   *6.25in (16cm) high*

£30-40   **DH**

A Bisto lithographed tin advertising whistle.

c1920   *1.75in (4.5cm) high*

£25-35   **DH**

A French Negrocao Solubilise Sucre lithographed tin container, for sugar.

This red/brown version is harder to find than the green/blue version above.

c1930   *6.25in (16cm) high*

£40-60   **DH**

A rare Mazawattee Tea lithographed tin, with Alice in Wonderland scene.

In better condition, this tin could be worth up to £650. Mazawattee is known for its complex and very well designed and printed scenes, often involving old ladies drinking tea or images of distant shores where tea is grown. The subject matter is particularly popular.

c1895   *8.5in (21.5cm) high*

£150-250   **DH**

A Colman's 'Naval Ships' lithographed tin container, scenes including 'H.M.S. Dreadnought' and 'Submarine No. A6'.

This is valuable for a number of reasons. Firstly, it was made for Colman's, a collected name, secondly it is in good condition and thirdly, the naval imagery is attractive, complex and of the period.

c1910   *8.25in (21cm) wide*

£180-220   **DH**

An OXO 'Zoo House' lithographed tin container, with 12 card cut-out characters.

c1930   *3.5in (9cm) wide*

£50-80   **DH**

An OXO two-cube sample tin.

This also came in a one-cube tin, which is harder to find and is worth around £35.

c1925   *1.75in (4.5cm) wide*

£15-25   **DH**

A French 'Formodol - Le Meilleur Dentifrice' lithographed tin container.

c1905   *2.5in (6.5cm) wide*

£30-40   **DH**

A 1920s Violette de Parme tooth powder lithographed tin container, retained contents.

3in (8cm) wide

£20-30   **DH**

A 1920s Euthymol Tooth Power lithographed tin container, by Parke Davis & Co.

2.75in (7cm) diam

£15-20   **DH**

A French lithographed cough pastilles tin.

Cocaine was used medicinally from the 1880s onwards due to its local and surface anaesthetic properties – useful for sore throats.

c1935   *3.25in (8cm) wide*

£20-30   **DH**

A CLOSER LOOK AT A SOAP POWDER TIN

Cats are a popular collecting subject and the form is typical for a powder tin.

The design is by Louis Wain, (1860-1939) a notable illustrator known for his cats.

Wain is known for endowing 'character' upon his cats, rather than painting them realistically.

This example is in comparatively poor condition; if it was undamaged it could fetch up to £500.

A Catseye toilet soap powder lithographed tin, by Gospo Ltd London.

c1915   *4.5in (11.5cm) high*

£280-320   **DH**

A 1920s Wilson's Co-Re-Ga lithographed denture fix tin, by Correga Chemical Co.

2.5in (6.5cm) high

£15-20   **DH**

A 1950s Lady Gay lithographed talcum powder tin, by Timothy Whites.

7in (18cm) high

£20-30   **DH**

A 1960s Sindy lithographed talcum powder tin, by Jean Sorelle.

4.75in (12cm) high

£15-20   **DH**

A French Vulcanisateur Méphisto lithographed tin.

c1925   *5in (12.5cm) high*

£60-90   **DH**

An 'Extra Strong Stotherts Seidlitz Powders' advertising lithographed string tin, with hole in lid to pull string through.

c1930   *5.5in (14cm) high*

£25-35   **DH**

A 1920s Anstie's Gold Flake Cigarettes lithographed tin packet sleeve.

      2.75in (7cm) high

£20-30   **DH**

A 1910s 'Minimax Refill' wall-mounted tin receptacle, with black and white pictorial images showing "How To Use Minimax".

Minimax, founded in 1902 in Germany, is still one of the world's leader manufacturers of fire extinguishers. The conical model shown is their most recognisable historic model.

      14in (35.5cm) long

£50-80   **BBR**

A Wild Woodbine Cigarettes lithographed tin sleeve, by W.D. & H.O. Wills, with original pack of cigarettes.

c1910   *2.5in (6.5cm) high*

£20-30   **DH**

A large Dutch lithograph tin, commemorating the Alliance and the end of WWII showing the Chinese, Russian, British and American leaders at the time.

c1945   *9.5in (24cm) high*

£50-80   **DH**

A Charlot Black Russet Extra Cream shoe polish lithographed tin, with image of Charlie Chaplin.

c1920   *1.75in (4.5cm) diam*

£15-25   **DH**

A 1920s lithographed tin cap container, with image of Charlie Chaplin.

      1.5in (4cm) high

£15-25   **DH**

A late 1930s English pictorial lithographed tin cash box, by Burnett Ltd, with four compartments, with original card packaging.

      6in (15cm) wide

£40-60   **DH**

A late 1950s 'Alice in Wonderland' lithographed paint tin, by Page of London.

      20.5in (52cm) wide

£20-30   **DH**

COLLECTORS' NOTES

■ 19th century and early 20th century underwear was constricting and covered much of the body in a close fitting all-in-one suit with buttoned flaps. In 1934, the industry was revolutionized when a designer at the American hosiery and underwear manufacturer S.T. Cooper & Sons developed the world's first 'brief' – and so the underpants that became the legendary 'Y-Front' was born.

■ Similar to the jockstrap, its smaller size and 'masculine support' allowed freedom of movement only previously found with athletic supports. Its name was even based on its inspiration, the 'jock-ey'. Meeting with great success in the US after a short period of disbelief from men and women alike, it was first imported into the UK by department store Simpson's of Piccadilly in 1938.

■ Over 3,000 pairs were being sold a week in the UK when Scottish hosiery and underwear manufacturer Lyle & Scott signed with Coopers to make the Y-Front for the British and European markets. Jockey Y-Fronts were the first underwear to be displayed and advertised prominently in shops – previously all underwear was chosen discreetly, for a shop assistant to then fetch from a back room or counter.

■ From the late 1950s, underwear advertising became more prominent and daring, moving away from a sports or 'activity' focus and towards racy lifestyles. Celebrities such as Bing Crosby, Bob Hope and Rock Hudson appeared in adverts during the 1960s.

■ The 1950s also saw underpants being first advertised as a fashion accessory and by the 1970s, they were also variously marketed as fun, varied and even aspirational – long before Calvin Klein and Mark Wahlberg captured the public imagination in the 1980s. All were also previously un-masculine attributes, showing changing attitudes in society.

■ This is still a growing market. Look for early shop display material, such as signs and 'body forms' used to display underwear. Early examples showing changing attitudes are likely to increase in value as are those endorsed by celebrities, particularly if pictured.

A 1960s Lyle & Scott 'Y-Front Slim Guy – Vented Briefs' advertising shop display card standee.

Not all pants are the same! Different inventions, such as side vents, proliferated along with different shapes as companies tried to dominate the market.

14in (35cm) high

£10-15   **MA**

A 1960s Lyle & Scott 'Y-Front Slim Guy' boxer shorts advertising shop display card standee.

14in (35cm) high

£12-16   **MA**

A 1960s Lyle & Scott 'Y-Front Briefs & Singlets' advertising shop display card standee.

14in (35cm) high

£10-15   **MA**

A 1960s Lyle & Scott 'Y-Front Junior Briefs and Singlets' advertising shop display card standee.

Young boys were often used in advertising instead of men during the 1950s to avoid strict censorship guidelines and promote a wholesome image.

14in (35cm) high

£10-15   **MA**

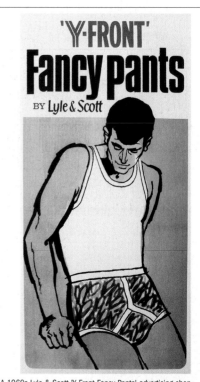

A 1960s Lyle & Scott 'Y-Front Fancy Pants' advertising shop display card standee.

14in (35cm) high

£12-18   **MA**

A Lyle & Scott 'Y-Front shorts put you in great shape' colour photographic advert.

c1967   16.5in (41cm) high

£15-25   **MA**

A Lyle & Scott 'Y-Front sports slips put you in great shape' colour photographic sign.

This style of underwear has recently been re-released.

c1967   16.5in (41cm) high

£15-25   **MA**

A Lyle & Scott Y-Front 'Racers' advertising board.

Advertisements of this type already begin to show underwear in an aspirational way, using ideal physical stereotypes of the day to show the product. The gentleman pictured was a well known model during this period.

c1967   16.5in (42cm) high

£15-25   **MA**

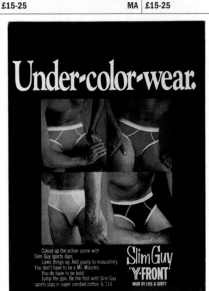

A Lyle & Scott 'Slim Guy Y-Front' photographic advertising sign.

c1967   12.25in (30.5cm) high

£25-30   **MA**

A 1970s Lyle & Scott 'Y-Front Supermesh' advertising board.

18in (45.5cm) high

£22-28   **MA**

A Lyle & Scott 'Y-Front' Christmas advert, depicting four Santas.

c1967   15in (37.5cm) high

£35-40   **MA**

A Lyle & Scott 'Slim Guy Y-Front – Under-color-wear' advertising sign.

This is typical of the advertising promoting underwear as both fun and fashionable, available in different shapes, colours and patterns – previously a very unmasculine consideration.

c1970   12.25in (30.5cm) high

£25-30   **MA**

A 1950s 'Activity Center-front – For men of action!' card advertising sign.

Despite being a British advertisement, note the US spelling of 'centre'. The 'Men of Action' tagline hints at the origins of the 'brief', allowing extra movement.

12.5in (31cm) high

£30-45   MA

A 1950s 'Activity – New! String Fabric' card advertising card sign, with a die-cut grinning model applied over a background showing sports players.

11.5in (29cm) high

£30-45   MA

A 1950s 'Activity – Man Alive!' lithographed underwear advertising card sign.

5in (37.5cm) wide

£30-45   MA

A 1950s 'Activity Fine String Underwear - The Trend's To Activity', advertising card display sign, with a stand-up section of a proud wearer.

13.5in (34cm) high

£30-45   MA

A late 1940s 'Aerborn Stringlet' advertising card sign.

9.5in (24cm) wide

£15-20   MA

A 1970s Lyle & Scott 'Y-Front' plastic shop sign, marked "Made in England".

8in (20cm) wide

£15-25   MA

Are you sure he's dreaming of a white Christmas?

PLEASE STICK
TWIN BRIEF
PACK HERE

Play it both ways this year with
white and bright twin packs from 'Y-FRONT'

A large 1970s 'Y-Front' Christmas shop advertising sign.

This advertisement takes the growing fun and daring associated with Y-Fronts to a new and naughty level. The wording, pose of the 'comfy Casanova' and the position of his homely wife hint strongly at an extra marital affair.

18in (45cm) wide

£35-45   MA

A Franklyn's Fine Shagg 'Good To The End' lithographed tin advertising tray, by the Imperial Tobacco Co.

c1925   16.5in (42cm) wide

£70-90   **DH**

A Wills's Gold Flake Cigarettes lithographed tin advertising tray.

c1925   16in (40.5cm) wide

£70-90   **DH**

A W.D. & H.O. Wills watercolour original artwork, signed to back and with cut-out colour lithographed Capstan packet.

10in (25.5cm) high

£60-70   **VSC**

A 'The Passing Show, Hush!! He's Busy' enamel sign, featuring Lloyd George being looked down upon by politicians including Winston Churchill, some chips, losses and rusting to edges.

28in (71cm) high

£500-700   **ON**

A Huntley & Palmers Biscuits saint's day calendar, for "Reading & Londres".

c1914   3.75in (9.5cm) high

£30-40   **DH**

A 1950s 'Chilk' advert, for a chocolate drink.

£8-12   **GAZE**

A 'Rowntree's Pastilles Buy Here For Quality & Delicious Flavour' enamel advertising sign.

19in (47.5cm) wide

£400-500   **GWRA**

A rare Erdal advertising clock, with two Erdal frogs and logo.

Erdal is an established and recognized brand of shoe polish in Germany. The two frogs are very famous and instantly recognized by the German public.

12.5in (31cm) high

£180-220   **WDL**

A 1930s French Dr Scholl wooden display.

15in (38cm) high

£200-300   **DH**

Four English
Ironstone
Beefeater steak
house plates.

11in (28cm) wide

£15-25

GAZE

A 1930s Vigoral Cocoa advertising mug,
with gilt trim.

3.5in (9cm) high

£15-25

DH

A set of four 1950s Colman's Mustard advertising pots, by
Bourne, Denby.

2in (5cm) high

£5-7

DH

A 1950s Birds Eye dummy
double-sided packaging, for
garden peas/green beans.

5in (12.5cm) wide

£10-15

DH

A Bassett's Jelly Baby dummy
packaging.

c1960   *4in (10cm) wide*

£7-10

DH

Three packets of 1960s airline-branded Marlboro cigarettes.

3.5in (9cm) high

£10-15 each

DH

A Fry's Cocoa tin fold-up
advertising ruler.

c1905   *12in (30.5cm) long*

£80-120   DH

A Fry's Cocoa tin fold-up advertising ruler.

Fry's Cocoa advertising featuring children is more sought-after than other styles.

c1905

12in (30.5cm) long

£180-220

DH

COLLECTORS' NOTES

■ The first manned balloon flight took place in 1783. The balloon was built by the Montgolfier brothers. The 18th and 19th centuries saw a craze for wealthy men to take balloon flights, these always drew a crowd and memorabilia was produced to record the flights.

■ Ferdinand Graf von Zeppelin developed a commercial airship with a rigid hydrogen gas-filled balloon that was capable of transatlantic flights and which saw action in WWI. Following the destruction of the LZ129 Hindenberg in 1937 and the onset of WWII, interest in lighter-than-air flight waned until the late 20th century.

■ Early memorabilia is very scarce and examples that record specific flights are particularly sought-after. Examples from the late 19th and 20th centuries are more affordable.

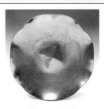

A Creil & Montereau 'Aircraft' plate, with an illustration of an airship.

c1900   8.25in (21cm) diam

£80-120   **ATK**

'Grand Prix De L'Aero Club De L'Atlantique', designed by Wyacauier, printed by Moderne-Beuchet & Vanden Brugge, Nantes.

1925   47in (117.5cm) high

£1,000-1,500   **SWA**

Hans Hildebrant, "Zeppelin-Denkmal für das Deutsche Volk", published by Germania-Verlag, Stuttgart, a history of Count Ferdinand von Zeppelin.

Published on the 25th anniversary of the first successful flight of a Zeppelin.

1925

£150-200   **ATK**

A 'Graf Zeppelin's Weltreise' board game, by Klee.

c1928   12in (30.5cm) wide

£150-250   **DH**

An aluminium fruit dish, with a wavy edge, peak in the middle and a silhouette of the Zeppelin and the trademark name "Zeppelin" stamped into the reverse.

11.5in (29cm) diam

£150-250   **AGI**

A flown Stratosphere Mail Explorer II cover, with "July 12, 1935 Rapid City, S. D. cds." and a "White Lake Nov. 11, 4PM" hand cancel on the face indicating where the balloon landed.

1935

£200-300   **AGI**

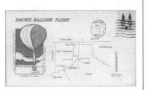

A limited edition Da Vinci Balloon Flight cover, from an edition of 1,000, with a green printed cachet, cancelled with a Las Cruces, NM machine cancel, no marking to indicate that this cover was flown.

1974

£80-120   **AGI**

A Breitling Orbiter 2 flown cover, signed in the centre by pilots Bertrand Piccard and Wim Verstraeten and engineer Andy Elson, the cover cancelled by a Swiss stamp tied by a fancy ballooning cancel.

1998

£50-70   **AGI**

A 'Bisto' ceramic child's bowl, with scene of Louis Blériot.

This bowl depicts the scene of Louis Blériot taking the first recorded flight over a large body of water, when he flew across the English Channel on July 25, 1909.

c1909   9.25in (23.5cm) diam

£200-300   **AL**

An 'Aero Plate' decorative plate, by Higgins & Seiten, New York, commemorating the Hudson-Fulton Centennial Exhibition, glaze flaw at the lower right.

1909   10.5in (26.5cm) diam

£18-22   **AGI**

A 1920s German Aviator Duck bobble headed candy container, made from painted plaster.

6in (15.5cm) high

£30-50   **HH**

A KLM 'De Groote Sprong' lithographed tin.

This tin commemorates the first crossing of the Atlantic by a KLM plane.

c1934   7in (18cm) high

£30-50   **DH**

A 1960s BOAC cup and saucer, by Copeland Spode.

£10-12   **COB**

A 1960s BOAC plate, by Copeland Spode.

8in (20cm) diam

£7-10   **COB**

A CLOSER LOOK AT A PEENEMÜNDE WORKER'S BADGE

The Heeresversuchsstelle (Army Experimental Station) at Peenemünde was the secret German rocket base where the V-1 and V-2 rockets were developed during WWII.

This identification badge would have been worn by a Peenemünder and would have allowed access to the base.

Original badges are rare but reproductions are known. They are shinier and lighter in weight as they are made from different materials. The numbers are also weaker and usually repeat.

Peenemünde is a village on the German island of Usedom on the Peene River, on the easternmost part of the German Baltic coast.

A Peenemünde worker's 'Access' enamelled aluminium badge no. 361, with button back, with a German eagle and swastika in the bottom half below the number.

1937-45

£1,800-2,200   **AGI**

COLLECTORS' NOTES

■ Cutting away the fussiness and ornament of the prevailing Art Nouveau style with its clean lines and extreme modernity, Art Deco revolutionised and dominated Western style from the mid-1920s until WWII.

■ Truly a style that could be enjoyed by all, it was one of the first styles that permeated and affected nearly all levels of society in a wider number of countries than before. Modest suburban houses adopted the look as much as grand and glamorous ballrooms and hotels. This leaves a wide array of items for today's collector, from simple but striking wooden mantel clocks to extravagantly designed suites of furniture.

■ The modern appearance of Art Deco means that it fits well into today's homes. Look for clean lines and minimal surface decoration. Where decoration does appear, it is often geometric or stylised, breaking away

from the traditional representations of patterns found in the 19th and early 20th century.

■ Colours vary from dramatic monochrome black, white and silvers to bright and bold reds, oranges and greens. Consider material as well as form and colour. As technologies developed, new materials such as plastics were used. Aluminium, chrome and enamel are also typical.

■ Themes range from architecture, inspired by the new skyscrapers, to speeding cars and trains and desired luxury, after the deprivations of WWI. Popular areas include lamps, figurines and small personal objects. As well as considering any marks, decoration or materials, always look for correct signs of construction, age or wear, as the look is so popular that reproductions are very common.

A chrome and enamel table lamp, by Electrolier.

15.5in (39.5cm) high

£400-500　　　　**DETC**

A late 1930s Art Deco 'Machine Age' brushed nickel lamp, the shade clips directly on to the bulb.

11in (28cm) high

£300-400　　　　**DETC**

A period copy of a chrome desk lamp, designed by Donald Deskey.

Donald Deskey (1894-1989) created a style within the Art Deco movement known as 'Streamlined Modern'. He favoured aluminium, chrome and bakelite used in a rigidly minimalist, geometric style.

c1935　　　　12in (30.5cm) high

£300-400　　　　**DETC**

A figural alabaster lamp, depicting a naked female figure holding a drape.

17in (43cm) high

£150-250　　　　**DETC**

A wood and Lucite banded conical lampstand.

Transparent plastic Lucite was frequently used from the 1930s-50s, and could be carved and painted. Lucite handbags and bangles from the same period are popular with collectors today.

22in (56cm) high

£150-250　　　　**DETC**

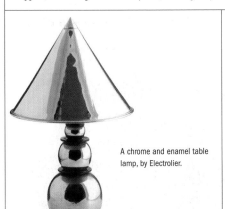

A French Art Deco spelter table lamp, by Fayral, on a two-tier marble base, impressed signature and "Paris France" to reverse.

20.5in (52cm) high

£350-450　　　　**ROS**

A small chrome figural table lamp, in the form of a stylised donkey, with a beaded cord extending from the tail that operates as a switch.

8.5in (21.5cm) long

£300-400　　　　**DETC**

An Art Deco style figure of a prancing nude lady, mounted on a plinth.

13.5in (34.5cm) high

£120-180   **GAZE**

An Art Deco silvered metal and cold painted figure of a female ice skater, on a black marble plinth.

10.25in (26cm) high

£180-220   **ROS**

An Art Deco ivory figure of a young lady, on a round onyx base, chip to base.

7.75in (20cm) high

£350-450   **DN**

An Art Deco style 'Hoop Girl' figure, marked "PK".

This figure is a near copy of Ferdinand Preiss' 'Hoop Girl' designed c1930. An original could be worth over £3,000.

8in (20cm) high

£100-150   **GAZE**

A Goldscheider Art Deco gilt bronze figure of a nude dancer, by P. Philippe, on a hexagonal grey marble base, brass tablet mark to base and signature.

Austrian maker Goldscheider is best known for its Art Deco ceramics, comprising elegant figurines and wall-mounted face masks.

16in (41cm) high

£1,000-1,500   **DN**

A 1930s black finished ceramic figurine of an African lady, the base with impressed marks for "ANZENGRUBER HAND MADE IN AUSTRIA".

Do not confuse these earlier and very popular figurines with the later examples from the 1950s, which tend to be less valuable. Look for better quality materials, more attention to detail and finer, less 1950s stylised modelling.

5.25in (13.5cm) high

£100-150   **PSI**

A 1930s black finished ceramic figurine of a small African boy, with ladybird creeping on his leg.

3.25in (8.5cm) high

£60-80   **PSI**

A 1930s small black ceramic African drummer boy figurine, stamped on the base "ANZENGRUBER", with white glazed drum skin.

4.75in (12cm) high

£60-80   **PSI**

A pair of Art Deco metal and brass stylised sporting figures, in the style of Hagenauer, both upon black vitrolite bases.

Tallest 7in (18cm) high

£180-220   **ROS**

A German ceramic vase, with impressed design of figures in a wheat field, with interior glaze.

1934   *8.5in (21.5cm) high*

£220-280   **DETC**

An Art Deco Weatherby of Hanley jug, cream glazed exterior and pink glazed interior, shape no. 82.

7.25in (18.5cm) high

£15-25   **GAZE**

An Art Deco patinated copper vase, unmarked.

8.25in (21cm) high

£40-60   **WW**

A pair of Art Deco-style hand-painted vases, Czechoslovakian for the French market, the base with printed "Modele Déposé FAÏENCE TCHÉCHOSLOVAQUIE" marks.

8in (20.5cm) high

£20-30   **PSI**

An Art Deco Karlsruhe lidded bowl, lid with handle, marked.

6.75in (17cm) high

£35-45   **WDL**

A pair of Art Deco Czech ceramic deer bookends, some crazing.

6in (15cm) high

£300-400   **DETC**

A pair of French Art Deco ceramic bookends, modelled in the Cubist manner, signed "E. Hadji" and "Made in France".

9.25in (23.5cm) high

£80-120   **DN**

An ABCO lamp, mounted behind an American bisque bust of an Art Deco woman, on a wooden base, dated 1934.

1934   *9in (23cm) high*

£400-500   **DETC**

A 1930s American Seth Thomas mantel clock, with brass accents.

Established in 1813, Seth Thomas is a notable US maker.

11in (28cm) high

£400-500   **DETC**

An Art Deco glass tray with a chrome frame.

Looking at this tray 90 degrees clockwise, you'll note the abstract geometric pattern forms the front or back bumper and wheel of a speeding car.

18in (45.5cm) wide

£150-250   **DETC**

A Waltham Watch Co. clock mechanism mounted in a crystal-bent green and clear glass case, marked "Process Pat. No. 2,024,775".

Waltham is a well-known US maker of watches, pocket watches and clock mechanisms.

15.5in (39.5cm) wide

£400-500   **DETC**

An Art Deco wall plaque, with a scene of deer jumping in a landscape, etched and silvered on black glass.

c1935   24in (61cm) wide

£150-250   **DETC**

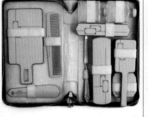

An Art Deco hand-cut celluloid laminated vanity set, in light green over dark green.

15in (38cm) wide

£300-400   **DETC**

A 1930s German Art Deco tin-lined leather hip flask, with two integrated cups.

£200-300   **CVS**

An 1930s American Art Deco Chase 'Pretzelman', whimsical serving piece in polished chrome.

9in (23cm) high

£60-80   **DD**

A musical cigarette dispenser, in the form of a Turk wearing a fez, dispenses cigarettes from the mouth at the push of a button.

Smoking, gambling and drinking paraphernalia underwent a 'make-over' in the 1920s/30s, becoming more witty, amusing and frivolous.

8in (20.5cm) high

£300-400   **DETC**

A 1930s American Art Deco geometric 'Park Ave' set of bridge playing cards, with original box.

3.5in (9cm)

£50-70   **DD**

FIND OUT MORE...

DK Collectors' Guide: Art Deco, by Judith Miller, published by Dorling Kindersley, 2005.

COLLECTORS' NOTES

- Automobilia covers everything from car parts to items relating to automobile associations, repair and garaging and the wide range of ephemera produced in support of car sales. Most collectors focus on one type, such as car mascots, or on one marque such as Ford. More decorative and easy to display items tend to fetch the highest prices, as do items related to luxury makes such as Hispano Suiza and Rolls-Royce.

- Car mascots are perhaps at the apex of collecting, particularly in terms of desirability and price. The most collectables adorned car bonnets from the 1910s to the 1930s. Types include accessory mascots such as animals, characters and figures, manufacturer mascots such as Rolls Royce's legendary 'Spirit of Ecstasy' and advertising mascots such as Michelin's 'Mr Bibendum'.

- Look for figural mascots, which are often designed around themes of speed, strength, satirical humour or good luck. Lively, characterful or dramatic poses are particularly sought-after. Early mascots are usually made from brass or bronze, with alloys coming later. Notable makers include Lalique, Red Ashay, Souest, Bazin and A. & E. Lejeune. Look out for marks as a notable maker can increase value.

- A good level of detail and original plating with good patination increase desirability. Reproductions exist, and watch out for re-plated examples and those that have been over polished. As with much automobilia, mascots from the 1900s-40s are the most desirable, and often valuable, but collectors are turning their attentions towards pieces from the 1950s onwards. As a general rule, look for automobilia by famous marques that represents the glamour and excitement of 20th century motoring, as well as items that are well designed, visually appealing and nostalgic.

A French Max Le Verrier flying bird nickel-plated bronze mascot, with articulated sprung wings, good patina, stamped designer's name, and two foundry socles on the upper body.

3.5in (9cm) high

£220-280　　　　　　**TCA**

A rare 'Aviators' commemorative bronze mascot, depicting the heads of Captain John Alcock and Lieutenant Arthur Whitten Brown, with a deep brown patina.

c1920

£250-300　　　　　　**TCA**

A Rolls-Royce 40/50hp silver-plated nickel on bronze mascot, signed "Charles Sykes" by the feet and engraved "Rolls-Royce Limited Feb 6th 1911" on the base.

This piece has an inscribed date, but its age could also be deduced from the hollow base and lack of under-wing inscriptions – both features of Rolls Royce mascots from this period.

c1914　　　　　　7in (18cm) high

£650-750　　　　　　**TCA**

A rare 1930s Mr Therm chromium-plated brass mascot, sponsored by British Gas.

This mascot was supplied as both a trade gift and a publicity aid during the 1930s.

4.5in (11.5cm) high

£220-280　　　　　　**TCA**

A 1930s French E. Grégoire horse and jockey chromium-plated mascot, display-mounted on a plinth.

5.5in (14cm) high

£180-220　　　　　　**TCA**

An MG leaping tiger half-size chromium-plated mascot, stamped "MG" below the base.

£180-220　　　　　　**TCA**

A 1930s Augustine & Emile Lejeune cobra snake mascot, for Desmo of Birmingham, with nickel-plated finish and "Desmo Copyright" stamped in the side of the base.

7.5in (19cm) high

£200-300　　　　　　**TCA**

AUTOMOBILIA

A 1930s Riley Ski Lady chromium-plated mascot, stamped "Riley Ski Lady' with registered no. 759377 for 1930.

£350-450   **TCA**

A 1930s chrome-plated car mascot, modelled as kneeling flapper girl with her arms outstretched, the screw removed, stamped "12" to base.

6.25in (16cm) high

£300-350   **PSI**

An American chrome-plated moulded angel car mascot, with red Lucite wings, from a Buick 48.

c1955   *8in (20cm) long*

£400-500   **CVS**

A CLOSER LOOK AT FRENCH CAR MASCOT

Introduced in 1919 by the Farman car company, this mascot was designed by French sculptor (1876-1917).

It was produced in two sizes – the slightly larger 6.5in (16.5cm) size was introduced in 1921.

It is stamped 'Finnigans London' - Finnigans were a central London retailer of luxury goods, including luggage and fine car picnic sets.

This mascot was intended as a tribute to Brazilian aviator Alberto Santos-Dumont, hence its name and the theme of Icarus. It is based on a commemorative statue.

An early French Farman 'Conquète de l'Air' small nickel-plated mascot, manufactured by Contenot-Lelièvre, with manufacturer's socle, stamped "Finnigans London – Made in France" and "Colin George".

c1920   *6in (15cm) high*

£350-450   **TCA**

A 1920s nickel-plated winged scarab mascot, with defined feather and beetle detail, display-mounted.

2.5in (6.5cm) high

£200-300   **TCA**

An American Billiken character mascot, probably designed by L.V. Aronson, with indistinct maker's marks and original nickel-plated finish, display-mounted on a radiator cap.

The Billiken is a good luck symbol popularized by illustrator Florence Pretz of Kansas City, MO who received her patent in 1908. It reached the peak of its popularity in 1911 and is closely connected to St Louis University. After 1910, the Aronson Art Metal Works of Newark, NJ (founded 1886) moved from making mascots, lamps, statues and bookends into smoking accessories, eventually becoming the famed Ronson Corp.

c1909-10   *5in (12.5cm) high*

£150-200   **TCA**

An 'Old Bill' car plated brass mascot, in the form of the eponymous hero, edges stamped with copyright and registration number.

WWI cartoon character 'Old Bill' was devised in 1915 by Bruce Bairnsfather (1888-1959) and typified the grumpy demeanour of the British infantryman at war in Europe.

c1918

£180-220   **W&W**

A British Petroleum double-sided pill-shaped globe, by Hailware, with indistinct "8/35" dating code, one side faded, the other almost obliterated, neck with a little nibbling.

1935   16in (40.5cm) high

£300-400   TCA

A 1920s/30s Pratts globe, with signs of ageing.

16in (40.5cm) high

£800,1,000   TCA

A British 1930/40s "National Benzole Mixture" spherical globe, by W.E. Chance & Co Ltd, with signs of ageing.

These globes were placed on top of petrol pumps to advertise petrol companies and were often illuminated at night. They are popular with collectors who want an original pump in their collection, as well as with globe collectors. Reproductions do exist, particularly for Shell, so look for genuine signs of wear and age to the graphics and foot. Handle as many originals as possible as the weight, thickness and type of glass can differ with reproductions.

7in (17.5in) high

£700-800   TCA

A 1930s Russian Oil Products pill-shaped globe, with "ROP" script on four sides, faded and weathered.

16in (40.5cm) high

£550-650   TCA

A "Cleveland Premium" double-sided glass globe, by Hailware, dated "4/63", some fading and neck with a little nibbling.

1963   16in (40.5cm) high

£220-280   TCA

A National Benzole "Premium" diamond-shaped globe, by Hailware, dated "3/78", strip around the centre.

1978   19in (48.5cm) high

£220-280   TCA

A Regent 'Regular' pillow-shaped double-sided glass globe, by Hailware, dated "5/60", neck with a chip and nibbling.

1960   14in (35.5cm) high

£150-250   TCA

A rare early 1930s-40s Regent "Empire Spirit" rectangular globe, a little faded and scratched.

18in (45.5cm) high

£800-1,200   TCA

A Shell glass petrol globe, by Hailware, dated "5/68", with unfaded red graphics and a perfect foot.

1968   17.5in (44.5cm) high

£250-350   TCA

An R.A.C. full member's badge, a pre-1952 example with a king's crown mounted on top of a spoked wheel, replaced enamels.

£40-50   TCA

A 1930s A.A. patrolman's cap badge.

1.5in (4cm) high

£15-25   DH

A car dashboard timepiece, with white enamel dial, in gilt metal case with winding spring below, the dial inscribed "8 DAYS SWISS MADE".

5.5in (14cm) diam

£80-120   GORL

A 'Boa' brass car horn, a few minor dents.

6in (15cm) long

£500-600   AGI

A French patented Burette Blindz no.4 oil can, by J. de la Coux of Paris, in fine condition.

12in (30.5cm) high

£400-500   MUR

An Edwardian workshop oil lamp, designed to be wall-mounted or free-standing, needs cleaning.
c1910

£70-100   TCA

A National Benzole small enamel advertising sign, double-sided with a seal-type "NBC" logo and Mercury logo.

7in (17.5cm) high

£70-100   GWRA

A German poster for 'Automobile Reinicke', a Hamburg car dealer, designed by Anton, printed by 'Plakat Kunst Arno Kypke', linen-backed.

Anton was a local artist who was apprenticed at the Arno Kypke poster agency in Hamburg. He later taught at the High School of Art in Bremen. The strong Art Deco style and large image of the period car makes this appealing and valuable.

c1930   33in (84cm) wide

£700-1,000   CARS

A 1960s Rolls-Royce silver-coloured flask, manufactured by Ruddspeed Ltd., based on the design of the front grille of a Rolls-Royce, registered design no.910435 for 1963.

1963

£120-180   AGI

A 1950s Sadler Pottery 'OKT42' racing car teapot, with printed "Sadler" factory mark to base.

£50-80   ROS

COLLECTORS' NOTES

- Notaphily, the collecting of bank notes, first became popular in the 1960s and grew in the 1970s when it became a separate collecting area from coins.

- Paper notes, however, have been produced in China since the 7th century by merchants who preferred to transport lightweight paper rather than bulkier coins. The first European country to follow China was Sweden in the 1660s.

- Notes are often decorated with vignettes and detailed scenes that are not only decorative but are designed to foil counterfeiters. These vignettes often form the basis of a collection with themes including famous people, wildlife, battles or other historical events. Other collecting themes include special or significant serial numbers, wartime currency or notes from a specific country or time period.

- As most notes were circulated and are therefore worn and soiled, condition has a huge affect on value and uncirculated and therefore mint notes are highly sought after.

An 1840s Bank of Scotland £50 "Promise to Pay", unissued, some light staining.

£30-40 BLO

A Bank of Ireland one pound note, printed in red and black with statues of Hibernia at left and right, heavy circulation, edge splits and few small holes, three heavy hotel stamps at back.
1913

£220-280 BLO

A 1970s Bank of England five pound error note, with J.B. Page governor signature and mirror image of Queen on back.

£50-70 BLO

An enamelled and silvered bronze cigarette case, with engraved design of a Bank of England one pound note, some wear to plating on corners.
c1932

£150-250 BLO

A rare Hong Kong & Shanghai Banking Corp $50 note, hand-signed, heavy creases with pinhole in centre, some initials on back.
1927

£600-700 BLO

A Bank of Japan 200 yen note, with portrait of Fujiwara Kamatari at right, two creases and minor stain at top.
1945

£350-450 BLO

A scarce Bank of Japan 200 Yen note, Provisional issue, black on pale blue with portrait of Takeuchi Sukune at right, two creases.
1945

£800-1,000 BLO

BANK NOTES

A CLOSER LOOK AT AN AMERICAN DOLLAR NOTE

These are fairly hard to come by, especially in such a good state, as most were used and became tatty, dirty and worn out.

This example is extremely crisp. Good condition is critical.

The certificate could be exchanged for silver until as recently as the 1950s. The government put a stop to this when they realised the value of the silver was significantly higher than the note.

The two Dollar silver certificate was available with three different seals - red, black and green. This is a red version.

An American two dollars silver certificate, part of Educational series with group of women and two children, minor ink splashes on bottom corners.

1896

£550-650 BLO

A scarce Seychelles one rupee note, with no major creases but oil stain at left top, small tear at top right.

1928

£250-350 BLO

A Sudanese Seige of Khartoum 100 piastres note, hand-signed by General Gordon.

1884

£500-600 BLO

A Sudanese Seige of Khartoum 2,500 piastres note, with hectograph signature of General Gordon, stamped on back for M.Tito Figari, advocat in Cairo.

£500-600 BLO

An American one dollar silver certificate, part of Educational series with reclining woman and boy at left.

1896

£350-450 BLO

A scarce American two dollars silver certificate, with red seal.

1917

£180-220 BLO

FIND OUT MORE...

International Bank Note Society (IBNS) *General Secretary P.O. BOX 1642, Racine, WI, 53404 USA.*

COLLECTORS' NOTES

■ Barbola was made and sold by Winsor & Newton, British manufacturer of artists' materials such as oil paints. It was aimed at the home hobbyist or crafts-person of the 1930s and was sold in tins. A thick paste, it could be applied to various objects such as mirrors or boxes, then carved and worked into forms and allowed to dry naturally, without the need for a kiln.

■ Due to its thickness and resilience, it allowed higher relief designs than the 'gesso' also marketed at the time. Once dry, it would be painted in pastel colours and then varnished. Floral patterns typical of chintzware of the period by ceramic makers, such as Royal Winton, were the most popular style.

■ Look for complex, intricate patterns that are well modelled and naturalistically painted all over. Dressing table mirrors were one of the most popular objects to decorate. As protrusions were easily damaged, examine surfaces carefully for signs of damage or restoration, looking for cracks or areas of repainting, often showing as slightly differently coloured lines.

A 1930s Barbola ware standing mirror, decorated with green ribbon and flowers.

13.75in (35cm) high

£220-280 FJA

A 1930s English Barbola ware plaster mirror.

11.5in (29.5cm) high

£150-200 FJA

A 1930s English Barbola ware plaster standing mirror.

8.25in (21cm) high

£120-180 FJA

A 1930s Barbola ware toilet mirror, with moulded and painted floral border.

10in (25.5cm) diam

£40-60 B&H

A 1930s Barbola ware standing mirror, with ball feet.

17in (43cm) high

£220-280 FJA

A 1930s Barbola ware mirror, the gilt frame with applied flowers.

10.75in (27cm) high

£100-150 FJA

A 1930s English Barbola ware dressing table mirror on stand.

This example is more valuable due to the revolving frame holding the mirror and the decorated base. The design is also more complex and thicker than others and the mirror is bevelled, the latter being an attractive feature.

13in (33cm) high

£300-350 FJA

A penny farthing bicycle, with sprung leather saddle, finished in white and yellow livery.

£1,800-2,200 LC

A Feho man's bicycle, by Fendt & Hofgärtner, Germany, with pressure pouring wheels, rear wheel-suspension, three course hub circuit and driven by a Cardan shaft.

It is thought that as few as 400 examples of this bicycle were made.

1981

£300-400 ATK

A CLOSER LOOK AT A BICYCLE

Michaux, once erroneously credited with inventing the bicycle, did develop the first bicycle pedal and cranks in 1861.

Typically, this 'boneshaker' has a smaller back wheel, versions with two large front wheels were also made.

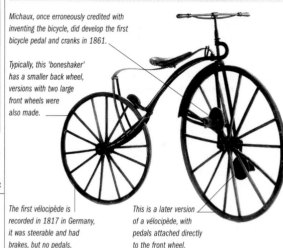

The first vélocipède is recorded in 1817 in Germany, it was steerable and had brakes, but no pedals.

This is a later version of a vélocipède, with pedals attached directly to the front wheel.

An early unmarked 'vélocipède' or 'boneshaker', in the manner of Ernest Michaux, wrought iron frame, wooden spoke wheels with solid iron rims, original leather saddle suspended on large leaf spring, iron pad brake activated by twisting handlebar grip, three-sided pedals, mudguard, with original paint.

c1868   *60in (152cm) high*

£2,200-2,800 ATK

A 19thC 'The Last Lap' woven silk stevengraph, framed and glazed with original mount.

Frame 8.75in (22cm) wide

£400-500 MSA

A bicycling tintype, in a daguerreotype/ambrotype like case.

Frame 3.25in (8.5cm) high

£50-80 PWE

A Doulton Lambeth stoneware ewer, with applied moulded cycling motifs.

8.25in (15cm) high

£450-550 MSA

A Fire Chief lithographed tin bicycle siren, by Ranger Steel Products Corp., in original box.

2.75in (7cm) diam

£20-30 BH

FIND OUT MORE...

The British Cycling Museum, *The Old Station, Camelford, Cornwall.*

The National Cycle Collection, *The Automobile Palace, Temple Street, Llandrindod Wells.* www.cyclemuseum.org.uk

COLLECTORS' NOTES

■ Shares as we understand them today were first issued in the Italian port of Amalfi cAD1000. The first shares that came with certificates were produced in the late 17th century in England and on the continent.

■ Collectable bonds and shares are those made from the turn of the 18th century up to the mid-20th century with older examples usually being the more sought after.

■ Certificates are often decorated with appealing and detailed printed scenes, usually connected to the product or property they represent. The more decorative the share, generally the more desirable.

■ The denomination of the certificate is also an important factor. Higher denominations will be harder to find as fewer were printed and so tend to be more valuable than the same certificate at a lower value.

■ Unlike bank notes, it is relatively easy to find certificates in excellent condition as they were often carefully stored in safes and banks.

An English Clarence Railway Co. certificate for one share, black with impressive blue seal.

1828

£400-500 BLO

A scarce English Forest of Dean Railway Co. certificate for one share, black, very clear embossed seal depicting horse drawing coal wagons.

1826

£1,000-1,500 BLO

An English Hammersmith Bridge Co. certificate for one share, printed on vellum, black, pink seal, very clean condition.

1924

£300-400 BLO

An English Hope Insurance Co. certificate for one £50 share, imprinted revenue stamp.

1807

£180-220 BLO

An English Kent Fire Insurance Office certificate for one £50 share, vignette of prancing horse with fire fighting scenes, printed on vellum.

1802

£400-500 BLO

A scarce English Royal Terrace Pier loan certificate for £100 with 5% interest, green seals.

1845

£300-400 BLO

An English Stanley Gibbons Ltd. debenture for £500, signed by E.S. Gibbons and C.J. Phillips as directors, four page debenture, further signature of Gibbons, UK revenue stamp.

This is one of only 50 certificates issued.

1890

£180-220 BLO

An English West Middlesex Water Works certificate for one share, printed on vellum, black, attached seal.

Only 300 of these early certificates were issued.

1806

£220-280 BLO

An American Alaska-Kotsina Copper Co. certificate for 50,000 shares capital stock, made out to and signed by Oliver P. Hubbard.

1906

£40-60   **BLO**

An American Express Co. share certificate, capital 18,000 shares, signed by Henry Wells, William Fargo and Alexander Holland, adhesive revenue stamp, small cancellation stamp, slight discolouration at bottom left.

1866

£220-280   **BLO**

A CLOSER LOOK AT A CHINESE BOND

This bond is for an unusually high denomination, making it desirable. £1,000 in 1912 is the equivalent to over £60,000 today. £500 Chinese bonds are more common.

Chinese bonds are fairly rare because the Chinese government agreed to convert them back into money during the 1960s. Many individuals chose to cash them in at this time.

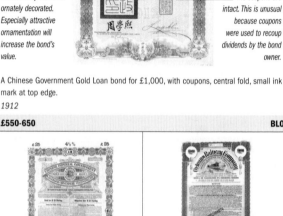

Chinese bonds are particularly appealing because they are often ornately decorated. Especially attractive ornamentation will increase the bond's value.

The coupons are intact. This is unusual because coupons were used to recoup dividends by the bond owner.

A Chinese Government Gold Loan bond for £1,000, with coupons, central fold, small ink mark at top edge.

1912

£550-650   **BLO**

A Kingdom of Bulgaria, 7% Settlement Loan bond for £100, printed by Bradbury Wilkinson & Co., with full coupons.

This appears to be a specimen bond as the serial is No.0000.

1926

£15-20   **BLO**

A Chinese Imperial Government Gold Loan unissued bond for £25, Deutsch-Asiatische Bank issue, with full coupons.

1898

£450-550   **BLO**

A French Orleans Railway Co. specimen bond for £1,000, (Comp. du Chemin de Fer de Paris à Orleans) dated, vignette of river scene, printed by Bradbury Wilkinson & Co., with coupons.

1935

£70-90   **BLO**

A Portuguese Loan bond for £100, coat-of-arms at top, ornate border, text in English and Portuguese, with coupons.

1823

£250-350   **BLO**

A scarce Canadian Stewiacke Valley and Lansdowne Railway, incorporated Novia Scotia, uncancelled £100 first mortgage bond, UK revenue stamp.

1889

£80-120   **BLO**

FIND OUT MORE...

Scripophily: Collecting Bonds and Share Certificates, by Keith Hollender, published by Book Sales, 1985.

www.scripophily.org, the International Bond and Share Society.

COLLECTORS' NOTES

■ Also known as 'pulp fiction' from the pulped paper they were printed on, early paperbacks were derived from the mass-produced, inexpensive periodicals or magazines that boomed in popularity during the 1920s and 1930s.

■ The golden years are between the late 1940s and 1960s, when they were sold inexpensively to a mass, populist market of both men and women. Collectors tend to specialize by genre such as gangster/crime, science fiction and Westerns. Look out for key authors such as Hank Janson and Ben Sarto. Smaller niche areas, such as addiction and delinquency, are also growing in popularity.

■ Today, the words don't matter to collectors as much as the covers, which became more visual in the late 1940s. In the 1950s, both were considered important – some titles were declared obscene and destroyed. Look out for 'dame' covers by Heade, F.W. Perl, or designs that typify the genre.

■ Condition is vital, especially the cover. Creases that damage the image, tears, stains, graffiti and fading all reduce value dramatically. Truly mint or excellent condition examples will command a financial premium. Some titles and editions are rarer than others, the earliest examples are usually more collectable.

James Hadley Chase, "Not Safe To Be Free", published by Robert Hale Ltd.

1959

£3-5   **ZDB**

Norman Deane, "Come Home to Crime", published by Jay Suspense Books.

1959

£3-5   **ZDB**

Blair Edwardes, "The Impatient Miss Blacket", published by James MacMillan.

1947

£20-30   **PCC**

Hank Janson, "Nyloned Avenger", with cover artwork designed by Reginald Heade.

£20-40   **PCC**

Pierre Flammeche, "The Silken Lure", published by Kaywin for The Archer Press Ltd.

Hank Janson, "Silken Menace", published by Top Fiction Ltd.

£30-40   **PCC**

Hank Janson, "Menace", published by Alexander Moring Ltd, with cover artwork by Heade.

1955

£10-15   **PCC**

French sounding names were often used to add 'spice' to a book and hint that good taste may be breached within. France was well-known at the time for its racy and erotic books, permitted by their less stringent obscenity laws.

1951

£30-50   **PCC**

Hank Janson, "This Dame Dies Soon", published by S.D. Frances.

This title was reissued as 'Too Soon To Die', which is worth less.

£30-40   **PCC**

BOOKS

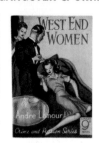

Andre Lamour, "West End Women" from the 'Crime and Passion Series'.
1940s

£12-18   **PCC**

Gypsy Rose Lee, "The Strip-Tease Murders", published by Guild Books.
1953

£3-5   **PCC**

Gene Ross, "This Way For Hell", published by Archer Press Ltd.
1950

£30-50   **PCC**

Ben Sarto, "Miss Otis Throws A Come-Back", published by Modern Fiction Ltd.
1947

£20-30   **PCC**

A CLOSER LOOK AT A PAPERBACK

The cover was designed by Reginald Heade and examples of his work are now highly collectable.

The cover is typical of the genre with a lewd lady exposing herself as she drapes provocatively across the cover.

Roland Vane, "Vice Rackets of Soho", published by Archer Press Ltd.
1951

£40-60   **PCC**

The cover was particularly shocking at the time as the lady is being injected, perhaps with drugs, by the man and the title involves vice.

The pseudonym Roland Vane was re-used on post-war books to cash in on the name's excellent pre-war reputation for similar novels – the author's real name was Ernest McKeag.

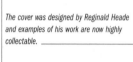

Ben Sarto, "Miss Otis Goes Up", published by Modern Fiction Ltd.

Ben Sarto was the pen name of Frank Dubrez Fawcett (amongst others, who later used this pseudonym) who continued the tales of Miss Otis for seven years, after introducing her in 1946 in 'Miss Otis Comes to Piccadilly'. Generating over 100 novels between 1946 and 1958, at one point he claimed to be writing a book every fortnight!

1947

£20-40   **PCC**

Michael Storme, "Satan Buys A Wreath", published by Archer Press.

Some of Heade's best 'ravished dame' covers appeared on Storme's books. Reginald Heade (1901-57) is known for his extremely well-painted, provocatively posed designs, and his covers usually bear his surname.

1951

£30-50   **PCC**

Edgar Rice Burroughs, "Thuvia, Maid of Mars", A Pinnacle Book, published by Mark Goulden Ltd.

Burroughs is well-known for his Mars and his Tarzan stories.

1975

£8-12   **ZDB**

Neil Gaiman & Kim Newman, "Ghastly Beyond Belief", published by Arrow Books.

1985

£3-5   **PCC**

Edgar Rees Kennedy, "Conquerors of Venus", published by Edwin Self & Co. Ltd.

£8-12   **ZDB**

Kris Luna, "Stella Radium Discharge", published by Curtis Warren Ltd.

Curtis Warren books are collected for their cover artwork, rather than the poor tales within.

1952

£10-15   **ZDB**

Franz Markon, "Spawn of Space", A Scion Science Fiction Novel, published by Scion Ltd.

1951

£10-15   **ZDB**

John E. Muller, "The Mind Makers", first edition published by Badger Books, John Spencer & Co Ltd.

£5-8   **ZDB**

Clark Ashton Smith, "Out of Space & Time", published by Panther Books.

1974

£8-12   **ZDB**

"Supernatural Stories", bi-monthly periodical, published by Badger Books.

The cover is a classic rip-off of the 1954 film 'Creature from the Black Lagoon'.

£12-18   **PCC**

Vargo Statten, "The Avenging Martian", published by Scion Ltd.

Scion was one of the forerunners of science fiction pulp publishing and also one of the best. Later science fiction pulp novels did not enjoy the same popularity with the public as those by Vargo Statten or Volsted Gridban did.

1951

£10-15   **ZDB**

Chuck Adams, "The Hostile Country", first edition, Badger Books, published by John Spencer & Co. Ltd.

£3-5   ZDB

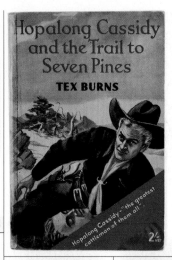

Tex Burns, "Hopalong Cassidy And The Trail To Seven Pines", published by Hodder & Stoughton.

During the 1950s, Westerns became almost as popular as erotic gangster novels, but with a soley male audience who enjoyed their pure action content and tanned, tough but honourable heroes. America's 'Hopalong Cassidy' was shown on BBC TV during the 1940s and their most prolific Western author Lauren Bosworth Paine (known as Mark Carrell, and the world's most prolific novelist, having generated over 900 novels!) also saw his books published in the UK.

1955

£10-15   ZDB

William S. Brady, "Hawk Number Six: Blood Kin", published by Fontana/Collins.

1980

£3-5   ZDB

J.T. Edson, "JT's Ladies Ride Again", published by Corgi Books.

1989

£5-8   ZDB

George G. Gilman, "Adam Steele No.48: Going Back", New English Library, published by Hodder & Stoughton.

1989

£5-8   ZDB

Zane Grey, "Code Of The West", published by Hodder & Stoughton.

1962

£3-5   ZDB

Zane Grey, "The Heritage of the Desert", published by Pan Books.

1953

£3-5   ZDB

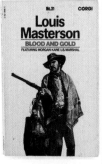

Louis Masterson, "Blood And Gold", published by Corgi Books.

1975

£3-5   ZDB

Hank O'Riley, "Lobo Loot, A Gannet Western".

£5-8   ZDB

Harry Brown, "A Walk In The Sun", published by Ace Books.

1958

£3-5   ZDB

Major-General Walter Dornberger, "V2", published by Panther Books.

1958

£3-5   ZDB

Sven Hassel, "Assignment Gestapo", published by Corgi Books.

1980

£3-5   ZDB

Leo Kessler, "Wotan 21: March Or Die", published by Futura Books.

1985

£5-8   ZDB

Fritz Kirschner, "S.S.", A Digit Books.

Tales involving survival and triumph over brutal atrocities committed by German and Japanese forces were common and popular subjects for nationalistic, populist paperback publishing in the 1950s, as WWII had only ended relatively recently. Cover artwork, such as this example, vividly depicts such atrocities.

1958

£5-8   ZDB

Lee Marks, "Japanese Bushido", A Digit Book, published by Brown Watson Ltd.

1960

£5-8   ZDB

Charles Whiting, "48 Hours to Hammelburg", published by Arrow Books.

1979

£3-5   ZDB

Jon Manchio White with Val Guest, "The Camp on Blood Island", published by Panther Books.

1958

£3-5   ZDB

Roy Winsford, "Against The Gestapo", Digit Books, published by Brown Watson Ltd.

1958

£5-8   ZDB

Ron Goulart, "Vampirella 1: Bloodstalk", published by Sphere Books.

Vampirella is a well known and popular cult character seen in other media such as comics and a 1996 film. Goulart wrote a series of six Vampirella books.

1976

£12-18 PCC

Ron Goulart, "Vampirella 2", published by Sphere Books.

1977

£12-18 PCC

Vern Hansen, "The Grip Of Fear", A Digit Book.

1964

£5-8 ZDB

"More Tales Of Unknown Horror", edited by Peter Haining, published by New English Library, includes "The Night Of The Tiger", by Stephen King.

1979

£3-5 ZDB

H.P. Lovecraft, "The Horror in the Burying Ground", published by Panther Books.

1975

£8-12 ZDB

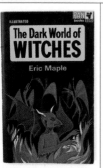

Eric Maple, "The Dark World Of Witches", published by Pan Books.

1965

£3-5 ZDB

Robert Louis Stevenson, "Dr Jekyll And Mr Hyde", published by Pedigree.

1959

£8-12 PCC

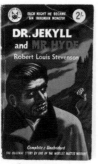

"The Pan Book of Horror Stories", selected by Herbert van Thal, published by Pan Books, 11th printing.

1965

£3-5 ZDB

Dennis Wheatley, "The Devil Rides Out", published by Arrow Books.

This story was filmed in 1968, and starred Christopher Lee.

1959

£3-5 ZDB

Brian Ball, "Space 1999: The Space Guardians", published by Pocket Books.

1975

£3-5　　　　　　　　ZDB

Rafe Bernard, "The Invaders: The Halo Highway", published by Souvenir Press/Corgi Books.

1967

£5-8　　　　　　　　ZDB

Ken Blake, "The Professionals 7: Hiding to Nothing", Sphere Books Ltd.

1982

£3-5　　　　　　　　ZDB

Howard Elson, "Gerry Anderson's Joe 90 in Revenge", published by Armada Paperback.

1969

£5-8　　　　　　　　ZDB

Ian Fleming, "Moonraker", published by Pan Books, rare first paperback edition.

1956

£70-100　　　　　　PCC

Ian Fleming, "Goldfinger", published by Pan Books Ltd.

This is a later reprint of the first paperback edition, but has the same cover as the original – check the publishing date inside as an original first paperback edition can be worth up to 10 times as much.

1962

£5-8　　　　　　　　ZDB

Ian Fleming, "Casino Royale", published by Pan Books.

This is the first edition of the paperback. 1960s paperback editions, also by Pan, tend to be worth under £5.

1955

£70-100　　　　　　PCC

John Garforth, "The Avengers: The Laugh Was On Lazarus", published by Panther Books.

1967

£5-8　　　　　　　　ZDB

David McDaniel, "The Man from Uncle No.9: The Vampire Affair", A Souvenir Press/Four Square Book.

1966

£3-5　　　　　　　　ZDB

BOOKS

Walter Tevis, "The Man Who Fell To Earth", published by Pan Books.

Produced in the same year as the film.

1976

£3-5 ZDB

Alex R. Stuart, "The Devil's Rider", published by New English Library.

1973

£3-5 ZDB

Alex R. Smith, "The Bike From Hell", published by New English Library.

1975

£3-5 ZDB

Mick Norman, "Guardian Angels", published by New English Library.

Biker and hippie stories were popular during the 1970s.

1974

£3-5 ZDB

Maisie Mosco, "Gang Girls", published by New English Library.

1978

£3-5 ZDB

Petra Christian, "Hitch-Hiker", published by New English Library.

1971

£3-5 ZDB

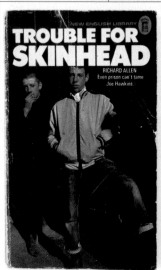

Richard Allen, "Trouble For Skinhead", published by New English Library.

Skinhead/punk is a popular and growing sub-genre that sums up the styles and aspirations of a particular generation and subculture. As this area becomes more popular in general, and as books are comparatively easier to come by and less expensive, it will be interesting to see if popularity and values rise in the future.

1974

£10-15 ZDB

Frank Clews, "The Golden Disc", A Digit Book, published by Brown Watson Ltd.

1963

£3-5 ZDB

Terry Pratchett, "Diggers", published by Corgi Books.

1991

£3-5 ZDB

FIND OUT MORE...

The Mushroom Jungle – A History of Postwar Paperback Publishing, by Steve Holland, published by Zeon Books, 1997.

Huxford's Paperback Value Guide, by Sharon & Bob Huxford, published by Collector Books, 2003.

COLLECTORS' NOTES

■ First editions represent the most original version of a book and the one closest to the author's intent. True first editions are from the first printing, or impression, of the first edition. To identify one, look for the number '1' in the series of numbers on the copyright page.

■ Alternatively, some publishers state clearly it is a first edition, or use letters. Always double-check by looking at the publishing date and comparing it to the year that title was first published.

■ Scarcity and condition are major indicators of value – true 'first' numbers are limited – values usually rise as desirability increases. Dust jackets are very important, particularly with modern titles, values can fall by 50 per cent or more without them.

■ Authors' signatures are a bonus. Dedications less so, unless that person is famous or important. Signed copies of newly published books are now more commonly available.

■ A good tip is to buy (preferably) signed copies of authors nominated for major prizes, like the Booker, before the winner is announced. A notable example illustrated here is Rushdie's Midnight's Children.

■ Fashion is important – Galsworthy and Steinbeck are currently unfashionable. Conversely, Iris Murdoch, Agatha Christie and Ian Fleming are always popular. Books made into films often increase in value as interest surges, if the film is popular.

Douglas Adams, "The Hitch Hiker's Guide to the Galaxy", first hardback edition, original boards, dust jacket.

1979

£250-300   **BLO**

Douglas Adams, "The Restaurant at the End of the Universe", first hardback edition, original boards, dust jacket.

1980

£220-280   **BLO**

Douglas Adams, "Life, The Universe and Everything", first edition, original boards, dust jacket.

1982

£400-500   **BLO**

Martin Amis, "Success", first edition, presentation copy from the author, ownership stamp on front endpaper, original boards, dust jacket.

1978

£120-180   **BLO**

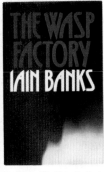

Iain Banks, "The Wasp Factory", first edition, original boards, dust jacket.

This was the author's first book.

1984

£120-180   **BLO**

Julian Barnes, "Flaubert's Parrot", first edition, original boards, dust jacket.

1984

£180-220   **BLO**

Malcolm Bradbury, "Eating People is Wrong", first English edition, original cloth, dust jacket.

1959

£60-90   **BLO**

Anthony Burgess, "A Clockwork Orange", first edition, original cloth, dust jacket.

1962

£700-1,000 BLO

Anita Brookner, "Soundings", first edition, published by Harvill Press.

1997

£8-12 BIB

Raymond Chandler, "Playback", first edition, published by Hamish Hamilton.

This UK version precedes the US first edition.

1958

£70-100 BIB

Leslie Charteris, "Boodle - Stories of the Saint", first edition, original cloth, dust jacket.

1934

£180-220 BLO

Leslie Charteris, "The Saint Sees it Through", first edition, published by Hodder & Stoughton.

1947

£50-70 BIB

Leslie Charteris, "Thanks to the Saint", first edition, published by Hodder & Stoughton.

1958

£45-55 BIB

Bruce Chatwin, "In Patagonia", first edition, original boards, dust jacket.

As well as a specialist at Sotheby's, a journalist and an obsessive collector, Chatwin (1940-89) is best known as a travel writer. This is his best known of seven books, amongst other works.

1977

£250-300 BLO

Arthur C. Clarke, "2001: A Space Odyssey", first edition, original boards, dust jacket.

1968

£250-350 BLO

Bernard Cornwall, "Sharpe's Eagle", first edition, original boards, dust jacket.

This is the author's first Richard Sharpe title.

1981

£220-280 BLO

Bernard Cornwall, "Sharpe's Gold", first edition, original boards, dust jacket.
1981

£100-150 BLO

Bernard Cornwall, "Sharpe's Havoc", first edition, published by Harper Collins.
2002

£15-20 BIB

Bernard Cornwall, "Heretic", first edition, published by Harper Collins, signed by the author.
2003

£18-22 BIB

Colin Dexter, "Last Bus to Woodstock", first edition, dust jacket.

1975

£220-280 BLO

Colin Dexter, "Last Seen Wearing", first edition, original boards, dust jacket.
This features Dexter's famous character Inspector Morse, played on TV by the late John Thaw.
1976

£850-950 BLO

Colin Dexter, "The Dead of Jericho", first edition, original boards, dust jacket.

1981

£300-400 BLO

Fredrick Forsyth, "Avenger", first edition, published by Bantam, signed by the author.
2003

£15-20 BIB

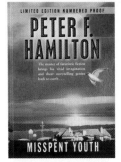

Peter F. Hamilton, "Misspent Youth", first edition, from a limited edition of 841 signed by the author, published by MacMillan.
2002

£15-20 BIB

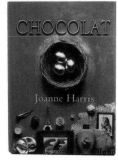

Joanne Harris, "Chocolat", first edition, first printing, published by Doubleday, signed by the author.
1999

£100-150 BIB

Nick Hornby, "About a Boy", first edition, published by Gollancz, signed by the author.

1989

£22-28   **BIB**

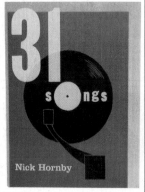

Nick Hornby, "31 Songs", first edition, published by Viking, signed by the author.

2003

£15-25   **BIB**

A CLOSER LOOK AT A MODERN FIRST EDITION BOOK

Highsmith (1921-95) is a noted crime writer who developed the genre considerably. ———

The story was made into a famous film by Alfred Hitchcock in 1951, adding to its popularity.

Highsmith is also famed for creating devious anti-hero Mr Ripley in 1955, played in films by Alain Delon in 1960 and Matt Damon in 1999.

This example is rare and valuable as it is both signed by Highsmith and retains its original dust jacket. ———

Patricia Highsmith, "Stangers on a Train", first edition, New York, signed by the author on title, original cloth, dust jacket.

1950

£1,500-2,000   **BLO**

"Introduction 7, Stories By New Writers", original cloth, dust jacket.

This book includes Kazuo Ishiguro's first appearance in print.

1981

£60-80   **BLO**

Kazuo Ishiguro, "An Artist of the Floating World", first edition, first issue, with Butler and Tanner stated as the printers in title verso, original boards, dust jacket.

This is the author's second novel and winner of the Whitbread Award.

1986

£80-120   **BLO**

Stephen King, "Carrie", first edition, published by Garden City, original boards, dust jacket.

This is King's first novel.

1974

£800-1,200   **BLO**

Stephen King, "Salem's Lot", first English edition, original cloth, dust jacket.

1975

£250-350   **BLO**

Stephen King, "The Shining", first edition, published by Garden City, original boards, dust jacket.

1977

£200-250   **BLO**

Stephen King, "Night Shift", first English edition, dust jacket.
1978

£220-280   **BLO**

Harper Lee, "To Kill a Mockingbird", first English edition, original boards, dust jacket.
1960

£220-280   **BLO**

Gabriel García Márquez, "One Hundred Years of Solitude", first English edition, original boards, dust jackets.
1970

£220-280   **BLO**

Joe Orton, "Entertaining Mr. Sloane", first edition, original board, dust jacket.
1964

£70-100   **BLO**

George Orwell, "Nineteen Eighty-Four", first edition, original cloth, red dust jacket.
1949

£600-800   **BLO**

Chuck Palahniuk, "Diary", first edition, published by Jonathan Cape, signed by the author.

Palahniuk is also the author of "Fight Club", made into a film in 1999, starring Brad Pitt.
2003

£10-15   **BIB**

Tony Parsons, "One More For My Baby", first edition, published by Harper Collins, signed by the author.
2001

£15-20   **BIB**

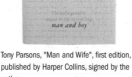

Tony Parsons, "Man and Wife", first edition, published by Harper Collins, signed by the author.
2002

£12-18   **BIB**

Terry Pratchett, "Mort", first edition, original boards, dust jacket.
1987

£250-350   **BLO**

Terry Pratchett, "Equal Rites", first edition, original boards, dust jacket.

1987

£450-550 BLO

A CLOSER LOOK AT A FIRST EDITION

This is the first book published covering Doctor Who's famous arch-enemies, the Daleks.

The story was republished in paperback later by Target – this is an extremely early, original version complete with its dust jacket.

The story is the novelization of the second story from the TV series first season, originally broadcast in 1963.

The author David Whitaker was script editor on the original TV production of this story, as well a number of other Doctor Who stories.

David Whitaker, "Doctor Who", first edition, original cloth, dust jacket.

1964

£500-600 BLO

Anne Rice, "The Mummy", first hardback edition, original boards, dust jacket.

This book was only issued in trade paperback format in the US. Christopher Rice, the author's son, is a well-regarded writer himself, and his first editions may also rise in value in the future if they remain popular.

1989

£100-150 BLO

Salman Rushdie, "Midnight's Children", first English edition, first issue with the American sheets, original cloth-backed boards, dust jacket.

1981

£350-450 BLO

Donna Tartt, "The Little Friend", first edition, published by Bloomsbury, from a signed limited edition of 350.

The book was published simultaneously in the US and the UK, but the author signed books in the UK first.

2002

£80-120 BIB

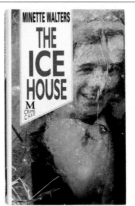

Minette Walters, "The Ice House", first edition, original boards, dust jacket, slightly knocked.

1992

£500-600 BLO

Jeanette Winterson, "Oranges are not the Only Fruit", published by Pandora Press, first edition, very slightly browning to margins, original pictorial wrappers.

1985

£220-280 BLO

COLLECTORS' NOTES

■ As with other books, collectors prefer to buy first editions. Look at the numbers on the inside cover – a '1' in a series of numbers usually means a first edition. Compare the date in the book to the original publishing date to make sure.

■ Authors' signatures add value, as do drawings. Dedications, usually made out if the book is a gift, can reduce the value unless the person is famous – although the personal aspect can be charming.

■ Condition is also important. Doodles and drawings reduce the value dramatically as does a missing dust cover and any damage or wear. Books in fine, excellent or mint condition are more likely to hold their values or rise in the future.

■ Look for classic stories that have entertained many generations of children, or look as if they will continue to entertain in the future as these will be more popular, hence will be in greater demand. Stories made into films also continue to be popular as they revive or further promote interest among a wide audience.

"BB", "The Wayfaring Tree", first edition, published by Hollis & Carter, illustrated by Denys Watkins-Pitchford, signed by author and illustrator.

1945

£80-120 BIB

Maria Bird, "Bill and Ben and The Potato Man", first edition, for Studios 51 Ltd and published by LTA Robinson in the 1950s.

£8-12 SAS

Enid Blyton, "The Circus Of Adventure", paperback, published by Armada.

1966

£3-5 ZDB

Elinor M. Brent-Dyer, "The Chalet Girls In Camp", paperback, published by Armada Paperbacks.

1969

£3-5 ZDB

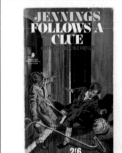

Anthony Buckeridge, "Jennings Follows A Clue", paperback, published by Armada Paperbacks, first published 1967.

£3-5 ZDB

Eoin Colfer, "Artemis Fowl: The Arctic Incident", Penguin first edition.

2002

£8-12 BIB

Zizou Corder, "Lion Boy", first edition, published by Puffin, signed by both authors.

Zizou Corder is the pseudonym of a mother and daughter writing team.

2003

£18-22 BIB

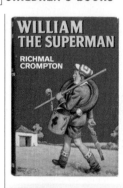

Richmal Crompton, "William the Superman", first edition, original boards, dust jacket.

1968

£180-220   **BLO**

Richmal Crompton, "William and the Masked Ranger", George Newnes first edition.

1966

£80-120   **BIB**

Richmal Crompton, "William and the Pop Singers", first edition, published by George Newnes.

1965

£80-120   **BIB**

Richmal Crompton, "William's Treasure Trove", first edition, published by George Newnes.

1962

£80-120   **BIB**

A CLOSER LOOK AT DAHL'S "THE GREMLINS"

This was Dahl's first children's book – it was never reprinted and is very rare.

These Gremlins were personifications of inexplicable problems experienced with WWII planes – Dahl was an ex-RAF pilot.

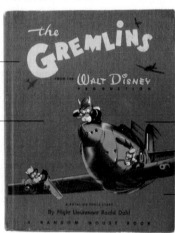

It was produced for Disney, and contains illustrations by Walt Disney Productions, making it desirable across that collecting market too.

A film to be made by Disney was planned, but it was cancelled.

Roald Dahl, "The Gremlins", first edition, published by Random House, New York.

1943

£2,000-3,000   **BRB**

Richmal Crompton, "William and the Space Animal", paperback, Merlin Books, published by Paul Hamlyn.

As well as the ever-popular William, the story of a space monster would have been exciting to a child of the 1960s, when outer space was a thrilling and popular subject.

1967

£3-5   **ZDB**

"Dan Dare, Pilot of the Future", published by Juvenile Productions Ltd., with realistic pop-up pictures, with pencil annotations from Christmas 1953.

1953   10.5in (26.5cm) wide

£60-80   **GAZE**

Jane Eayre Fryer, "The Mary Frances Cook Book", or "Adventures Among the Kitchen People", published by Harrap & Co., illustrations by Margaret G. Hayes and Jane Allen Boyer.

£100-150   **BIB**

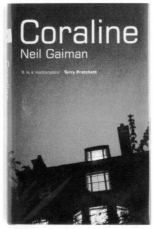

Neil Gaiman, "Coraline", first edition, published by Bloomsbury, signed by the author at Harrods, London, with a line drawing.
2002

£70-100 BIB

Neil Gaiman, "The Wolves in the Walls", first edition, published by Bloomsbury.
2003

£20-30 BIB

Captain W.E. Johns, "Wings – Wings A Book of Flying Adventures", first edition, published by John Hamilton.
1931

£120-180 BLO

Captain W.E. Johns, "Biggles in Africa", first edition, published by the Oxford University Press.
1936

£280-320 BLO

Captain W.E. Johns, "Biggles takes a Holiday", first edition, published by Hodder & Stoughton.
1949

£60-80 BIB

Captain W.E. Johns, "Sergeant Bigglesworth C.I.D.", paperback, by Hodder & Stoughton.
1954

£3-5 ZDB

Captain. W.E. Johns, "Biggles and the Plane That Disappeared", first edition, published by Hodder & Stoughton.
1963

£150-200 BIB

Captain W.E. Johns, "Biggles Looks Back", first edition, published by Hodder & Stoughton.
1965

£80-120 BIB

Captain W.E. Johns, "Biggles Flies North", paperback, published by Armada.
1966

£3-5 ZDB

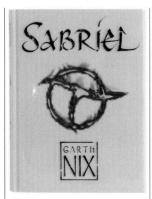

Garth Nix, "Sabriel", first edition, published by Harper Collins.

1995

£10-20 BIB

Philip Pullman, "The Subtle Knife", first US edition, with dust jacket, published by Alfred A. Knopf Inc., signed by the author.

1997

£120-180 BIB

Philip Pullman, "The Amber Spyglass", Scholastic first edition, second issue.

2000

£40-50 BIB

Frank Richards, "Billy Bunter Afloat", first edition, published by Cassell.

1957

£40-60 BIB

Frank Richards, "Thanks to Bunter", first edition, published by Cassell.

1964

£60-80 BIB

Frank Richards, "Lord Billy Bunter", first edition, published by Cassell.

1956

£60-80 BIB

Frank Richards, "Bunter's Last Fling", first edition, published by Cassell.

This was the 38th and final Bunter book.

1965

£50-70 BIB

Frank Richards, "Billy Bunter and the Secret Enemy", Pocket Merlins paperback, published by Paul Hamlyn.

1968

£3-5 ZDB

A CLOSER LOOK AT A HARRY POTTER BOOK

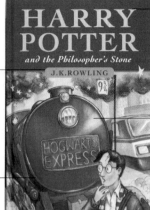

Only 500 of this true first hardback edition of Rowling's first book were printed, at a time when Rowling was unknown.

This is in unread condition with no fading or damage, making it rarer still. This first print run was issued without a dust jacket.

Many were sent to libraries, or abroad, meaning that they were stamped or worn through use.

Scholastic published the first US edition as "Harry Potter and The Sorcerer's Stone". The first print run is identified by its purple covers and $16.95 retail price. It can now fetch up to £1,500.

J.K. Rowling, "Harry Potter and the Prisoner of Azkaban", first edition, first issue, original pictorial boards, dust jacket.

This is the first issue with the copyright reading 'Joanne Rowling' (rather than J.K. Rowling) and dropped text on page 7.

1999

£500-700 BLO

J.K. Rowling, "Harry Potter and the Philosopher's Stone", first edition, original pictorial boards.
1997

£12,000-18,000 BLO

Dr. Seuss, "The Cat in the Hat", first American edition, published by Random House, New York.
1957

£4,500-5,500 BRB

Dr. Seuss, "One Fish Two Fish Red Fish Blue Fish", first edition, published by Random House, New York, in first-issue dust jacket listing no other books.
1960

£500-700 BRB

Dr. Seuss, "Fox in Socks", first American edition, published by Beginner's Books, New York.
1965

£700-1,000 BRB

G.E. Studdy, "The Bonzooloo Book", London, colour pictorial bands, 12 colour plates, other illustrations.
c1928

£200-300 FRE

G.P. Taylor, "Shadowmancer", first edition, Finland, from an edition of 2,500 privately printed for the author, signed by the author and with wizard's hat motif, unread with typographical error "right s" on title page.
2002

£600-800 BLO

A German porcelain reservist tankard, with hand-painted decoration of scenes of military life, the handle with unusual relief.

9.25in (23cm) high

£150-200   **WDL**

A Jugendstil Merkelbach stoneware beer tankard, decorated with enamelled four figures and "Allweil fidel" ('always lively'), a flat stannous lid with engraving, unmarked.

7.25in (18cm) high

£40-60   **WDL**

A CLOSER LOOK AT A BEER STEIN

Stein comes from the German word Steinzeugkrug, meaning stoneware jug or tankard, but has come to mean any vessel for drinking beer that has a hinged lid and handle.

Lids were added to mugs when a law was passed in Germany in the 15thC requiring all food and drink containers to be covered to prevent the spread of disease by insects. This stein has a stepped pewter lid with a large and very detailed artilleryman on top and an eagle thumbpiece.

Steins were traditionally made with stoneware bodies and pewter lids and hinges, but examples can be found in a range of materials.

Regimental steins developed after the Franco-Prussian war (1840-71), when reservists commemorated their military active duty with a customised stein with the decoration often depicting a training or combat scene.

A German porcelain reservist beer stein, hand-painted on pre-printed lines, unusually painted stepped base, paint slightly rubbed, inscribed "7. Comp. Königl. Sächs. Inftr. Regt. Prinz Georg No. 106, Leipzig 1898-1900".

10.75in (27cm) high

£220-280   **WDL**

A T.G. Green tankard, for the Bass-Worthington group, with remains of label.

T.G. Green are perhaps better known for their Cornish ware range of blue and white striped homewares.

5.75in (14.5cm) high

£10-15   **GAZE**

A 'Tuborg 1903' ceramic hanging plaque, for Tuborg beer.

8.75in (22cm) high

£40-50   **TAB**

An Ind Coope's enamelled tin advertising ashtray.

c1910   5.25in (13.5cm) diam

£50-70   **DH**

A 'Worthington Pale Ale' perfume bottle, by Jago & Jerome, containing 'Jasmine' perfume.

c1930   3in (7.5cm) high

£15-25   **DH**

BREWERIANA & DRINKING

A Friary Meux's Treble Gold lithographed tin advertising tray.

c1955   13.5in (34.5cm) high

£15-25   **DH**

A Whitbread's enamelled tin advertising tray.

c1930   12.15in (31cm) wide

£60-80   **DH**

A Guinness Brewery, Dublin guide book.

c1939   7in (18cm) high

£10-15   **DH**

A postcard of the Guinness Festival of Britain clock at Great Yarmouth.

c1951   5.5in (14cm) high

£1-2   **DH**

A 1950s Miss Berger lithographed tin advertising standee.

18.25in (46.5cm) high

£40-50   **DH**

A set of six Guinness buttons, each of the six domed glass buttons with reverse-cut and painted Guinness character decoration.

Each 0.5in (1.5cm) diam

£60-80   **F**

A rare mechanical device for moving barrels.

£20-30   **MUR**

A Farmars publicans' slide rule, boxwood, in fine condition.

13.5in (34.5cm) long

£120-180   **MUR**

A set of three 1950s Guinness printed card advertising darts flights.

3.5in (9cm) high

£4-6   **DH**

COLLECTORS' NOTES

■ Photography became more popular during the 1840s. Cameras of the time usually had wooden bodies with brass or other metal fittings. Early 'wet plate' cameras from the 1840s-1880s are often highly desirable, particularly if rigid, sliding boxes. Bellows were developed c1851. Brass lenses are common, and most have a glass back plate to compose the picture and wooden holders for the photographic plates.

■ Most wooden cameras found on the market today will be 'dry plate' folding cameras dating from the 1880s-1920s. Look for a good quality construction and manufacturers' names, such as Watson, Lancaster and Sanderson. An original case and accessories adds value, as does use of other materials, such as teak.

■ Leica cameras, by Leitz of Wetzlar, Germany, are the most collectable 35mm cameras. The first was developed in 1913 and they are still made today. Screw lens mounts were used 1930-54, with bayonet lens mounts used thereafter, on the 'M' series. Condition is

absolutely paramount to collectors, with wear, scratches, scuffs, dents and broken mechanisms reducing value considerably, depending on the degree of damage.

■ All Leica cameras are numbered, and this gives the model and year of manufacture. Look for unusual engravings, such as 'Luftwaffe Eigentum' (Property of the Luftwaffe), but be aware that fakes are numerous as originals usually fetch high values. Variations in colour, form or original use add value and accessories such as lenses can have high individual values.

■ Subminiature, 'detective' and unusually shaped cameras are highly collectable, and can offer a more affordable and 'fun' entry into the market. Condition again is key, particularly for plastic examples and more modern cameras. Other names such as Canon, Zeiss Ikon and Voigtlander are also collectable, with rare models or lenses fetching higher prices. Kodak's 'Box Brownies' were made in vast numbers and are generally of low value.

A Lancaster & Son of Birmingham '1898 Instantograph' camera, with Lancaster brass lens f=10 and two wooden backs.
c1900
£200-300 ATK

A Thornton Pickard Imperial Triple Extension camera, with mahogany frame, unmarked brass lens, and Thornton-Pickard roller-blind shutter, with four wooden double backs.
1904-26
£120-180 ATK

A Sanderson half-plate field camera, with brass and mahogany body, Ross No. 2 Wide Angle Symmetric 4in lens and Thornton Pickard roller blind shutter.
c1898
£220-280 ATK

An unmarked mahogany plate camera, with petrol-coloured bellows and a Zeiss Tessar 1:4.5, f=21cm lens.
11.25in (28cm) long
£70-100 WDL

A Watson Alpha quarter-plate camera, with mahogany body, black bellows, Beck Isostigmar f=6.3 8.25in lens, set in a Bausch & Lomb shutter and with maker's label "W. Watson & Sons, London Made for H. Carette, Paris", focusing back replaced.
£100-150 EG

A 'Mars' wooden magazine box camera , by Emile Wünsche of Dresden, brass lens with rotating diaphragm.
1895
£500-600 ATK

A German Ernemann Ermanox camera, with Ernostar f=1.8 8.5cm lens, Vertex f=4.5 6cm lens and accessories, instructions and maker's fitted leather case.
c1925
£500-600 EG

A CLOSER LOOK AT A LEICA CAMERA

Only 984 Leica 'Reporter' cameras were ever made – it has a film capacity of 250 exposures.

Look out for the version with an electric motor drive – only 29 examples were made and it can fetch £30,000 or more.

This is from the first series of only 246 cameras, modelled after the Leica III.

This is in black (top plate and bottom plate) – look out for the extremely rare model with chrome top and base plates.

A Leica 'Reporter' 250 FF camera, serial no. 135642, with Elmar 3.5/5 cm lens.

1934

£6,500-7,500   **ATK**

A Leica chrome IIIa camera, synchronised, with Summar f=2/5cm lens and lens cap.

1935

£180-220   **ATK**

A Leica IIIb camera, with Leitz Summar f=2 5cm lens, in brown leather case.

1938   *5.5in (14cm) w*

£200-250   **GORL**

A rare Leica IIIa 'Monté en Sarre' camera, fitted with an Elmar 3.5/5cm lens, original invoice and with maker's case.

Part of Leica's production was moved to Sarre in 1949-51 to avoid high French tax duties. Around 500 IIIa models were produced, engraved 'Monté en Sarre' and retailed for the French market.

1950

£1,500-2,500   **ATK**

A Leica IIIf 35mm camera with 'Red-Dial', with Summaron f=3.5 3.5 cm lens.

The IIIf was the first Leica to have flash synchronisation. Look out for the Canadian model, which can be worth up to five times more.

1952-53

£120-180   **EG**

A Leica IG camera, long shutter speed, with Elmar 3.5/5cm lens and 5cm finder, knob damaged, dent behind rewind knob.

1958

£250-350   **ATK**

A Leica M3 camera, with Summicron 2/50 lens, and lens cap.

1960

£1,000-1,500   **ATK**

A Canon Pellix camera, with Canon FL 1.2/58 lens, Canon lens cap, incorrect diaphragm.

£60-90   ATK

A 1950s Kiku 16 miniature camera, complete with box, case and extra yellow filter.

Camera 2.25in (6cm) wide

£80-120   EPO

A Nikon FM2 N camera, with instructions, papers and box.

1990

£150-250   ATK

A rare transparent demonstration model Polaroid Autofocus 660.

£150-250   ATK

A Voigtländer Bessamatic CS camera, with Color-Skopar 2.8/50 lens, exposure meter working.

1966

£120-180   ATK

A Zeiss Ikon Kolibri camera, with Novar 4.5/5cm lens and Telma shutter, lacks foot.

1928

£150-200   ATK

A Zeiss Ikon Contax I camera, version four with Tessar 2.8/5cm lens, marked "A" for conversion or modification by Zeiss Ikon.

1933

£200-300   ATK

An early Zeiss Contarex I camera, with Planar 2/50 lens and exposure meter filter secured.

1962

£350-450   ATK

A Zeiss Ikon Contarex I camera, with Biogon 4.5/21 lens and viewfinder 435 for 21mm.

1964

£500-600   ATK

A Japanese Rokuoh-Sha machine-gun camera, by Konishiroku Kogaku, taking single 35mm pictures, with Hexar 4.5/75 lens, working spring motor drive, shutter releases, with accessories and spare parts, in original wooden box.

These cumbersome cameras are scarce, especially in complete condition with their boxes. They were use to train machine gunners and the idea is said to have been copied from the 1915 British 'Hythe' machine gun camera used in WWI.

1943

£1,000-1,500   **ATK**

A E.R.A.C. Mercury I brown Bakelite pistol camera, by the E.R.A.C. Selling Co. Ltd., London, invented by H. Covill & H Steward.

c1931

£450-550   **ATK**

An extremely rare Holly red Bakelite box camera, by Allgäuer Kamerawerkstätte Gomag, Pfronten, with Gomar 4.5/85 lens.

1950

£350-450   **ATK**

A Coronet Midget olive green plastic subminiature camera.

The red, green and blue colours are more desirable than brown or black.

1935   0.75in (2cm) high

£120-180   **ATK**

A Swiss Concava AG Tessina Automatic 35mm wrist-mounted camera, with Tessinon 2.8/25 lens, in original box with wrist strap.

1960   0.75in (2cm) wide

£250-350   **ATK**

A Kodak Peer 100 pocket camera, in shape of a cigarette box, lacks release, with original box.

1976

£150-250   **ATK**

A Fotodisc chrome-plated,full-metal subminiature camera, by the American Safety Razor Corp. of New York.

As this lacks both its serial number and photodisc, it is possibly a prototype.

c1960   1in (24cm) high

£500-600   **ATK**

An American Magic Introduction Co. Photoret 'pocket watch' subminiature camera, engraved "A Magazine Snap-Shot Camera".

1894   0.5in (1.5cm) h

£450-550   **ATK**

A Mickey Mouse camera, the lens marked "Copyright Walt Disney Prod.", with f=25 1:9 lens.

1956

£40-60   **ATK**

COLLECTORS' NOTES

■ Edna Best (1900-74) began her film career in 1921 and grew to be one of the most popular actresses in the 1920s and '30s. She is best remembered for her role as the mother in Alfred Hitchcock's first version of 'The Man Who Knew Too Much', filmed in 1934. From the early 1930s to 1940 she worked in Hollywood, after moving there with her husband.

■ Although she did not design the bright Art Deco ceramics by the Pearl Pottery of Hanley, Staffordshire, she did lend her name to them, thereby creating an early instance of 'celebrity endorsement' in homewares.

■ Following the fashion of the day, they are hand-painted in bright colours with geometric, stylised patterns somewhat similar to Clarice Cliff's work. Look for those that also follow Art Deco forms as these are often more desirable. Most of the pieces produced were teawares, other items such as vases are scarcer.

An Edna Best Art Pottery round teapot.
c1930 — 7.75in (19.5cm) high
£150-200 NAI

A 1930s Edna Best Art Pottery milk jug.
3.25in (8.5cm) high
£40-50 NAI

A 1930s Edna Best Art Pottery teapot.
6.5in (16.5cm) high
£150-200 NAI

An Edna Best Art Pottery low teapot.
c1930 — 4.25in (10.5cm) high
£150-200 NAI

A 1930s Edna Best Art Pottery coffee can and saucer.
4.25in (10.5cm) diam
£40-60 NAI

An Edna Best Art Pottery for Lawley's vase, with two-ring handles.
c1930 — 9in (23cm) high
£200-250 NAI

CERAMICS

COLLECTORS' NOTES

■ The Beswick pottery was founded at Loughton, Staffordshire in 1894. Although animal figures were produced in the 1900s, they only formed a larger part of production from the 1930s.

■ In 1939, skilled animal modeller Arthur Gredington joined, and went on to design most of Beswick's vast range of animals, many produced well into the 1990s. Other modellers of note include Colin Melbourne, known for his CM range and his wildfowl, Graham Tongue, Albert Hallam and Alan Maslankowski, who also designed Royal Doulton figurines.

■ Collectors tend to focus on one type of animal, with cattle being one of the most popular, particularly among farmers, butchers and countryside lovers. Prices, particularly for rare variations or models, have rocketed recently, especially for those produced for short periods of time, or that went out of production

decades ago, such as after 1969 when the range was rationalized.

■ Also consider the animal itself, as large, visually impressive bulls tend to be slightly more desirable than cows, but both are usually more desirable than smaller calves. Modern limited editions, even from the late 1990s can be valuable too, particularly if the edition was produced a small numbers.

■ Most figures are found in a gloss finish, the matt finish usually having been produced for shorter periods of time, as it was less popular. This means some matt pieces can be more valuable today.

■ Colourways that depart from the normal add value too. Roan and Rockinghorse grey are usually more valuable than brown. Always examine protruding parts such as ears and legs for damage as this, or restoration, lowers appeal and thus value considerably.

A Beswick 'Limousin Cow', 3075B, from a limited edition of 656 for the Beswick Collectors' Club.

1998   5in (13cm) long

£220-280   **GORW**

A Beswick 'Limousin Bull', 2463B, from a limited edition of 653 for the Beswick Collectors' Club, designed by Alan Maslankowski.

1998   5in (13cm) long

£300-400   **GORW**

A Beswick 'Highland Bull' gloss figure, 2008, designed by Arthur Gredington.

1985-89   5in (13cm) long

£180-220   **GORW**

A Beswick 'Dairy Shorthorn Ch. Eaton Wild Eyes, 91st', 1510, designed by Arthur Gredington.

1957-73   4.75in (12cm) long

£1,000-1,500   **GORW**

A Beswick 'Dairy Shorthorn Ch. Gwersylt, Lord, Oxford, 74th', 1504, designed by Arthur Gredington.

1957-73   5in (13cm) long

£900-1,000   **GORW**

A Beswick 'Polled Hereford Bull', 2549A, designed in 1975 by Graham Tongue.

1977-97   5in (13cm) high

£150-200   **GORW**

A Beswick 'Hereford Bull' gloss figure, 1363A, designed by Arthur Gredington.

This gloss version with his horns protruding from behind his ears is worth up to three times more than the later version with horns set flush with his ears.

Until 1997   8.5in (11cm) high

£150-200   **GORW**

CERAMICS

A Beswick 'Guernsey Ch. Sabrina's Sir Richmond 14th' gloss figure, 1451, designed by Colin Melbourne, with restored ear.

1956-89   *4.75in (12cm) high*

£150-200   **GORW**

A CLOSER LOOK AT A BESWICK ANIMAL

Look out for model number 899 with the horns pointing upwards, it was the first version and was produced in 1941 only.

Examine the horns closely for signs of damage or repair.

The roan and white version of this model (948) is the most sought-after variation and rarely comes on to the market.

This is a good example of a desirable model that has risen above the book price recently, doubling in value since 2000.

A Beswick 'Hereford Cow', 948, designed by Arthur Gredington.

1941-c1957   *5in (13cm) high*

£450-550   **GORW**

A Beswick 'Ayrshire Ch. Ickham Bessie', 1350, designed by Arthur Gredington.

1954-90   *5in (13cm) long*

£200-250   **GORW**

A Beswick 'Jersey Ch. Dunsley Coy Boy' gloss figure, 1422, designed by Arthur Gredington.

1956-97   *4.75in (12cm) high*

£100-150   **GORW**

A Beswick 'Charolais Cow' gloss figure, 3075A.

Look out for the rare matt finish, produced for the first two years of production only, which can be worth around 25 per cent more.

1988-97   *5in (13cm) long*

£150-200   **GORW**

A Beswick 'Charolais Bull' gloss figure, 2463A, designed in 1973 by Alan Maslankowski.

1979-97   *5in (13cm) long*

£150-200   **GORW**

A Beswick 'Aberdeen Angus Cow' gloss figure, 1563, designed by Arthur Gredington, with unusual grey hooves.

The matt version can be worth around 25 per cent more than the gloss version.

1959-89   *4.25in (11cm) high*

£180-220   **GORW**

A Beswick 'Aberdeen Angus Cow' gloss figure, 1563, designed by Arthur Gredington, with a restored foot.

1959-89   *4.25in (11cm) high*

£150-200   **GORW**

A Beswick 'Aberdeen Angus Bull', 1562, designed by Arthur Gredington.

This model was approved by the panel of judges for the Breed Society.

1958-89   4.75in (12cm) high

£180-220   GORW

A Beswick 'Black Galloway Cow', 4113B.

£180-220   GORW

A Beswick 'Friesian Ch. Coddington Hilt Bar' gloss figure, 1439A, designed by Arthur Gredington.

1956-97   4.75in (12cm) high

£120-180   GORW

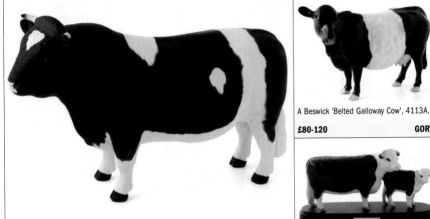

A Beswick 'Belted Galloway Cow', 4113A.

£80-120   GORW

A Beswick 'Friesian Bull Ch. Coddington Hilt Bar' matt figure, 1439A, designed by Arthur Gredington.

This is the scarcer matt version of the gloss model also shown on this page. It was produced for a shorter period of 1985-89, and can be worth up to 40 per cent more.

4.75in (12cm) high

£200-300   GORW

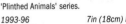

A Beswick 'Hereford Cow and Calf' on plinth, 1360 and 1827C, from the 'Plinthed Animals' series.

1993-96   7in (18cm) high

£180-220   GORW

A Beswick 'Charolais Cow and Calf' on plinth, 3075 and 1827B, the calf modelled by Arthur Gredington.

1993-96   6in (15cm) high

£180-220   GORW

A Beswick 'Jersey 'Ch. Newton Tinkle' and 'Jersey Calf', 1345 and 1249D, both designed by Arthur Gredington.

These models were also released on a wooden plinth as part of the 'Plinthed Animals' series between 1993 and 1997. They would have fetched more on the plinth.

1954-97

£80-120   GORW

A Beswick 'Dairy Shorthorn Calf', 1406B, designed by Arthur Gredington.

1956-75   *3in (7.5cm) high*

£350-450   **GORW**

A Beswick 'Hereford Calf', 1406B, designed by Arthur Gredington.

1956-75   *3in (7.5cm) high*

£150-200   **GORW**

A Beswick 'Hereford Calf', 901B, designed by Arthur Gredington, with restored back leg.

Look for the more valuable roan and white colourway and the early, open-mouthed version.

To 1957   *4in (10cm) high*

£60-80   **GORW**

A Beswick 'Ayrshire Calf' gloss figure, 1249B, designed in 1952 by Arthur Gredington.

The gloss re-issue from 1985-90 is worth around 15 per cent less.

1956-75

£120-180   **GORW**

A Beswick 'Guernsey Calf' gloss figure, 1249A, designed by Arthur Gredington, with restored ears.

1985-89   *2.75in (7cm) high*

£50-70   **GORW**

A Beswick 'Limousin Calf', 1827E, designed by Arthur Gredington and from a limited edition of 711 for the Beswick Collectors' Club.

1998   *3in (7.5cm) long*

£200-300   **GORW**

A Beswick 'Charolais Calf' gloss figure, 1827B, designed by Arthur Gredington.

1985-97   *3in (7.5cm) long*

£100-150   **GORW**

A Beswick 'Aberdeen Angus Calf', 1827A, designed by Arthur Gredington.

1985-89   *3in (7.5cm) long*

£280-320   **GORW**

A Beswick 'Aberdeen Angus Calf', 1406A, designed by Arthur Gredington.

1956-75   *3in (7.5cm) high*

£250-350   **GORW**

A large Beswick 'Mallard Duck', 1518, from the 'Peter Scott Wildfowl' series, designed by Arthur Gredington.

Although this the largest size is the most valuable, look out for the first version of the smallest size, at 4.5in (11.5cm) long, as this is worth around 20-30 per cent less than this one, but more than other sizes.

1958-71   6.5in (16.5cm) long

£150-200   **GORW**

A Beswick 'Goosander', 1525, from the 'Peter Scott Wildfowl' series, designed by Colin Melbourne.

1958-71   4.75in (12cm) long

£180-220   **GORW**

A Beswick 'Shelduck', 1527, from the 'Peter Scott Wildfowl' series, designed by Colin Melbourne.

1958-71   4in (10cm) long

£100-150   **GORW**

A Beswick 'Smew Duck', 1522, from the 'Peter Scott Wildfowl' series, designed by Colin Melbourne.

1958-71   3in (7.5cm) long

£100-150   **GORW**

A Beswick 'Teal Duck', 1529, from the 'Peter Scott Wildfowl' collection, designed by Colin Melbourne.

1958-71   2.75in (7cm) long

£100-150   **GORW**

A Beswick 'Mandarin Duck', 1519, from the 'Peter Scott Wildfowl' series, designed by Arthur Gredington.

1958-71

£120-180   **GORW**

A Beswick 'Song Thrush' gloss figure, 2308, designed by Albert Hallam.

The matte finish is worth around 50 per cent less.

£100-150   **GORW**

A Beswick 'Gamecock', 2059, designed by Arthur Gredington.

Examine the tailfeathers and beak of this upright and proud bird, as they are prone to breakage.

1966-75   9.5in (24cm) high

£600-800   **CHEF**

A Beswick 'Small Owl', 1420, designed by Colin Melbourne, with sgraffito-type detailing, artist's initials and factory paper label to underside.

The stylization of the form and features is typical of the look of the 1950s, when this 'contemporary' range of animals was released. Many are rare and desirable today, but are disliked as much as loved for their modern appearance.

1956-65   5in (13cm) high

£150-200   **ROS**

CERAMICS

A Beswick 'Mounted Indian' gloss figure, 1391, designed by Mr. Orwell.

1955-90   8.5in (21.5cm) high

£400-500   PSA

A CLOSER LOOK AT A BESWICK HORSE FIGURE

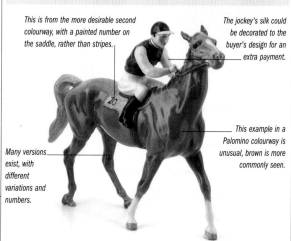

This is from the more desirable second colourway, with a painted number on the saddle, rather than stripes.

The jockey's silk could be decorated to the buyer's design for an extra payment.

Many versions exist, with different variations and numbers.

This example in a Palomino colourway is unusual, brown is more commonly seen.

A rare Beswick 'Racehorse And Jockey' figure, 1037, designed by Arthur Gredington, colourway two with Palomino horse.

£2,500-3,000   PSA

A Beswick 'Canadian Mounted Cowboy', 1377, designed by Mr. Orwell.

This large and impressive figurine has cross-market appeal, making it more desirable and hence valuable.

1955-73   8.75in (22cm) high

£1,500-2,000   PSA

A Beswick 'Huntsman Standing', 1501, in brown, with six foxhounds and a fox.

Earlier, more valuable, gloss hounds date from 1941-69 and have thicker tails and legs. Look out for this Huntsman in Rockinghorse grey as it can fetch up to six times more than this colourway.

1957-95

Huntsman 8.25in (21cm) high

£600-700   BRI

A Beswick 'Fox Standing' gloss figure, MN1440, with four gloss foxhounds, 2264, 2262, and 941.

1956-97

Fox 2.5in (6.5cm) high

£200-300   PSA

A Beswick 'Zebra' gloss figure, 845B, designed by Arthur Gredington.

The earlier version with black stripes on a tan body is rarer and more desirable, worth up to three times more than this version.

To 1969   7.25in (18.5cm) high

£120-180   PSA

A Beswick 'Small Giraffe' gloss figure, 853, in a realistic colourway, designed by Arthur Gredington.

1940-75   7in (18cm) high

£80-120   PSA

A Beswick 'Donkey' matt figure, 1364B, designed by Mr. Orwell.

Although this matt finish is desirable, look out for the ultra-rare earlier version, produced in 1955 only with its tail hanging free from the hind leg. This was presumably discontinued as the tail was prone to damage. It was also easier to manufacture with the tail attached to the leg.

1987-89   4.75in (12cm) high

£20-40   PSA

A Beswick vase, shape 1649, designed by Albert Hallam.

c1960-65   *8in (20.5cm) high*

£60-80   **NPC**

A Beswick vase, shape 1653, designed by Albert Hallam.

c1959-66   *10.5in (27cm) high*

£70-90   **NPC**

A Beswick vase, shape 1402, designed by Colin Melbourne.

c1956   *7.25in (18.5cm) high*

£30-50   **NPC**

A Beswick vase, model 128M, moulded with rose flowers and a bird, moulded and printed marks.

A Beswick vase, shape 1357, designed by Albert Hallam in 1954.

c1957-62   *8in (20.5cm) high*

£60-80   **NPC**

11.5in (29cm) high

£100-150   **WW**

A 1930s Beswick yellow and mottled glazed jug, no.177/2.

8.75in (22cm) high

£25-35   **GAZE**

A 1930s Beswick vase, with blue, orange and yellow glazes.

7.5in (19cm) high

£40-60   **GAZE**

A 1930s Beswick green and mottled glazed jug, no.177/2.

8in (20cm) high

£25-35   **GAZE**

FIND OUT MORE...

The Charlton Standard Catalogue Of Beswick Animals, *published by The Charlton Press, 2004.*

CERAMICS

COLLECTORS' NOTES

■ Bing & Grøndahl was formed in Copenhagen, Denmark in 1853 by artist Frederick Grøndahl and brothers Jacob and Meyer Bing. Initially, they produced fine quality porcelain tableware. Figures were introduced in c1895.

■ Pieces are typically decorated in soft, pale colours such as grey, blue, brown and white and are glossily overglazed. The factory's mark is based on Copenhagen's coat of arms and features three towers over the company's initials. If the mark is scratched through, this indicates a second.

■ Figures have always been collectable, although ranges produced for long periods of time tend to be less popular with collectors. Early examples, those produced for a short period of time and large or complex models are sought-after, as are those with unusual variations.

A CLOSER LOOK AT A BING & GRØNDAHL FIGURINE

Henning Seidelin (1904-87) was a Danish industrial designer who worked in a number of media including metalware and ceramics.

This figure is still in production but is large and complex, as well as being very charming and an appealing Danish subject.

Fellow Dane, Hans Christian Anderson is a popular subject with collectors, as are figures inspired by his fairy tales.

2005 is the 200th anniversary of Anderson's birth and this is likely to increase interest in him.

A Bing & Grøndahl 'Hans Christian Anderson' porcelain model, no. 2037, designed by Henning Seidelin.

9in (23cm) high

£200-300 | **LOB**

A Bing & Grøndahl 'Who is Calling?' porcelain figurine, no. 2251, designed by Michaela Ahlman.

6in (15cm) high

£70-90 | **LOB**

A Bing & Grøndahl porcelain figurine of a boy with a crab at his toes, no. 1870, designed by Ingeborg Plockross Irminger. c1980

8in (20cm) high

£70-100 | **LOB**

A Bing & Grøndahl 'Girl Sitting' porcelain figuring, no. 1879, designed by Ingeborg Plockross Irminger.

7in (18cm) high

£120-180 | **LOB**

A Bing & Grøndahl porcelain model of a couple dancing, no. 2385, designed by Claire Weiss.

8in (20cm) high

£80-120 | **LOB**

A Bing & Grøndahl porcelain figurine of a terrier, no. 1998, designed by Dahl-Jensen.

6.75in (17cm) long

£150-200 | **LOB**

COLLECTORS' NOTES

■ The Brannam Pottery was founded in 1847 by Thomas Brannam in Barnstable, Devon and is still in production today. Along with many other 19th century potteries, such as Doulton, it initially made utility wares such as tiles and piping. In 1879, the pottery's most notable chapter began when Charles Brannam, Thomas' artistic son, who also worked at the pottery, eventually persuaded his father to allow him to design and produce art pottery.

■ The new range became very successful and in 1882, London department store Liberty & Co. became their sole agent. Grotesque and 'fantastical' animal designs, ranging from birds to dragons, were produced to much

acclaim into the 1930s. When Charles Brannam died in 1937, artistic direction was lost and the company moved into plainer domestic wares, which are not as desirable or as sort after today.

■ Marks vary widely and can include the name 'Royal Barum Ware' registered in 1886, but in general, early marks are usually signed in script, often with a date. Initials usually indicate the skilled designers John Dewdney or William Baron. Large and visually appealing pieces, such as vases, tend to fetch the highest sums, but always look for typical designs and ideally the animal forms, for which the pottery became so well known.

A C.H. Brannam sgraffito jug, the pouring lip in the form of a fish, sgraffito decoration in cream and blue against terracotta, incised marks and dated "1898".

1898   12in (30cm) high

£280-320   **GORL**

A C.H. Brannam cream and blue glazed vase, of globe and shaft form with three bird panels, incised marks and dated "1888".

1888   11in (28cm) high

£250-300   **GORL**

A pair of C.H. Brannam vases, with three handles, painted with scenes of Dutchmen running by the waterside, on blue ground.

A large C.H. Brannam three-handled vase, decorated with sgraffito fish and pond flowers against a pitted ground, dated "1902", restored.

1902   7in (18cm) high

£220-280   **GORL**

A pair of C.H. Brannam novelty spill vases, modelled as a heron beside bamboo shoots.

9.5in (24cm) high

£150-200   **GORL**

11in (28cm) high

£300-400   **B&H**

A C.H. Brannam for Liberty & Co. tyg, decorated with a fish in sgraffito, incised monogram and impressed mark.

6in (15cm) diam

£80-120   **GORL**

A C.H. Brannam novelty chamberstick, modelled as a griffin holding a flowerhead, marked "Rd 44561" and dated.

1912   7in (18cm) high

£180-220   **GORL**

A C.H. Brannam puffin jug, with all-over green glaze, impressed marks.

6.5in (16.5cm) high

£100-150   **GORL**

A C.H. Brannam four-piece wash set, each with a simple orange and white ground, impressed marks.

Large bowl 15in (38cm) diam

£40-60   **GORL**

CERAMICS

COLLECTORS' NOTES

■ Briglin was founded in 1948 in Crawford St, Mayfair, London by Brigitte Goldschmidt (later Appleby) and Eileen Lewenstein. Its hand-thrown, hand-decorated pots were highly successful, with their wares being stocked by Heal's and Peter Jones.

■ Earthy tones dominate and blue and cream glazes are also common. Patterns tend to be stylized representations of flowers or leaves, or simple geometric patterns. Most patterns are marked out in the underlying clay, using a wax-resist process, or by scoring the design into the body of the piece.

■ The pottery closed in 1990 and over the past few years collecting interest and values have grown rapidly. Look for larger pieces, those with all-over glazes or designs displaying a sympathetic combination of glaze and unfinished clay. Consider shapes carefully as unusual examples can fetch a premium. Vases and bowls tend to be more desirable than animal shapes or kitchen pieces.

A Briglin Pottery matte black glazed vase, decorated with white glazed flowers, stamped "BRIGLIN".

9.5in (24cm) high

£60-90   **GC**

A 1960s Briglin Pottery cylinder vase, with unusual geometric sgrafitto decoration, the base impressed "BRIGLIN".

5.5in (14cm) high

£20-30   **AGR**

A Briglin Pottery brown glazed vase, with wax-resist technique pattern of leaves, stamped "BRIGLIN".

7.75in (19.5cm) high

£40-60   **GC**

A 1970s Briglin Pottery small light blue and white glazed vase, with thistle pattern marked out using wax-resist and scoring.

5in (12.5cm) high

£30-50   **GC**

A Briglin Pottery black matte glazed vase, with carved recessed areas highlighted with applied white glaze and white glazed interior, stamped "BRIGLIN ENGLAND".

6in (15cm) high

£50-80   **GC**

A Briglin Pottery green and silver black lustre vase, with matte finish, base stamped "BRIGLIN ENGLAND".

8.75in (22cm) high

£100-150   **GC**

A Briglin Pottery gloss glazed baluster vase, with round Briglin paper label, also stamped "PJ", with white glazed interior.

The "PJ" may stand for Chelsea department store Peter Jones, who stocked Briglin's wares during the 1960s.

10.5in (26.5cm) high

£60-90   **GC**

An unusual 1960s Briglin Pottery small vase, with wasp neck and sgrafitto decoration.

5.75in (14.5cm) high

£20-30   **AGR**

A 1980s Briglin small vase, with attenuated neck and sgraffito decoration, with cobalt oxide and white glaze.

4in (10cm) high

£20-30   **AGR**

A CLOSER LOOK AT A BRIGLIN POTTERY VASE

This flower pattern is commonly found on Briglin Pottery.

The interior of the neck is glazed white, showing attention to detail.

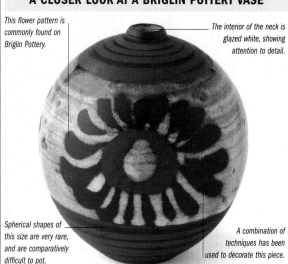

Spherical shapes of this size are very rare, and are comparatively difficult to pot.

A combination of techniques has been used to decorate this piece.

An unusual Briglin spherical vase, with wax-resist flower pattern.

4in (10cm) high

£30-40   **GROB**

A Briglin Pottery small cup, with swirling pattern in natural rough clay, the base stamped "BRIGLIN ENGLAND".

4in (10cm) high

£7-10   **GROB**

A Briglin Pottery large tankard, with striped wax-resist decoration, stamped "BRIGLIN".

5in (12.5cm) high

£15-18   **GROB**

A Briglin Pottery tall cylindrical jug, with swirling natural clay pattern.

10in (25.5cm) high

£40-60   **GROB**

A Briglin Pottery sgrafitto decorated milk jug, with unusually simple pattern.

3.25in (8cm) high

£10-15   **AGR**

A 1970s/80s Briglin-designed tile, on a Carter blank.

Like many smaller potteries, Briglin did not make its own tiles. The tile producer's name is usually moulded into the back.

£20-30   **AGR**

A Burleigh Ware jug, the handle in the form of a squirrel.

The Central Pottery was founded in Hanley, Staffordshire in 1851. It was renamed the 'Burleigh Pottery' by Frederick Burgess and William Leigh who acquired it in 1862. As well as other wares, it is known for its colourful jugs made in the 1920s and 30s, often decorated with animal and natural scenes and primarily in beige-yellow colours. Charlotte Rhead also worked there as a designer between 1926 and 1931. The pottery continues today.

c1930   7in (18cm) high

£40-50   **TCM**

A CLOSER LOOK AT A BURLEIGH WARE CACTUS POT

The form was designed by Earnest Bailey with the colours chosen by Harold Bennett – they designed all of Burleigh's 1950s modernist pieces.

The cactus is another typical 1950s motif. Such house plants were popular with a new generation of home-makers.

The colours, modern form and decoration such as polka dots are all typical of the 1950s.

This range was not a commercial success so was made for only a short period, making examples scarce today.

A rare Burleigh Ware Cactus series preserve pot.

c1958   4.25in (11cm) high

£28-32   **NPC**

A 1930s Burleigh Ware jug, the handle in the form of a squirrel.

7in (18cm) high

£40-50   **GAZE**

A 1930s Burleigh Ware jug, the handle in the form of parrot.

7.5in (19cm) high

£40-60   **GAZE**

A 1930s Burleigh Ware wheatsheaf and rabbit jug.

7in (18cm) high

£50-80   **GAZE**

A Burleigh Ware vase, with a leaf design, printed marks and number.

5.25in (13.5cm) high

£40-60   **TCM**

A Burleigh Verona Ware charger, moulded design of grazing deer and stylized flowers and glazed in green with brown highlights, unsigned.

c1969   15.75in (40cm) diam

£70-100   **GORL**

COLLECTORS' NOTES

- Wiltshaw and Robinson established the Carlton Works in Stoke on Trent in 1890 and used the trade name Carlton Ware from 1894. The company name became Carlton Ware in 1958.

- Inspired by Wedgwood's successful 'Fairyland' lustre range, the company began producing its own richly decorated lustre range, with a variety of patterns on different coloured grounds, in 1925. The patterns were often influenced by oriental chinoiserie or ancient Egypt, birds were also a popular theme.

- The 1930s saw the introduction of a moulded range of practical tableware decorated with a wide range of flowers, fruit and vegetables usually in greens, yellows and pinks. This range was produced in large amounts until the late 1950s and is still affordable today, although rare variations of colour and decoration are sought-after.

- The 1960s saw simpler shapes and decoration, often two-tone exemplified by the 'Orbit' range, influenced by the Space Race. Facing financial difficulties due to the recession, the company introduced the Walking Ware range designed by husband and wife team Roger Mitchell and Danka Napiorkoska. The range's popularity helped secure the company and lead to number of variations such as 'Running' and 'Jumping'.

- The company changed hands a number of times in the 1980s before being bought by Francis Joseph in 1997.

A Carlton Ware 'Devil's Copse' pattern vase and flower frog, no.3817, printed and painted marks.

7.75in (20cm) diam

£280-320   **WW**

A Carlton Ware 'Sketching Bird' pattern conical bowl, with printed mark.

9.25in (23.5cm) diam

£600-700   **WW**

A Carlton Ware 'Barge' pattern bowl, no.2519, in blue lustre glaze.

The 'Barge' pattern is harder to find than some of the other Chinoiserie patterns.

9in (23cm) diam

£100-150   **CA**

A Carlton Ware 'Paradise Bird and Tree' bowl, no. 151, in yellow glaze.

9in (23cm) diam

£180-220   **CA**

A Carlton Ware 'Chinese Dragon' pattern vase, no.3656, printed and painted marks.

6.75in (17cm) high

£220-280   **WW**

A Carlton Ware 'Paradise Bird and Tree With Cloud' pattern vase, no.3144, printed and painted marks.

6in (15.5cm) high

£400-500   **WW**

An early Carlton Ware vase, impressed "294".

11.75in (30cm) high

£300-400   **BEV**

A pair of Carlton Ware Rouge Royal candlesticks.

£40-50   **GAZE**

CERAMICS

A Carlton Ware green-glazed salad bowl and pair of servers, marked "Registered Australian Design".

£30-50 GAZE

A Carlton Ware cabbage leaf and lobster salad bowl and servers.

The Public Health service banned the red paint used to decorate these lobsters in 1976 due to its high lead content.

8.75in (22cm) wide

£100-150 BAD

An Art Deco Carlton Ware pear sugar caster.

c1930 5.5in (14cm) high

£60-80 BAD

A Carlton Ware 'Fruits' condiment set.

9in (23cm) wide

£25-35 GAZE

A 1930s Carlton Ware 'Cottage' pattern jam pot.

This jam pot will appeal to collectors of cottage ware as well as Carlton ware.

5in (12.5cm) high

£100-150 BEV

A Carlton Ware pen holder, with moulded bird decoration.

Carlton Ware produced pen holders for a number of pen companies but are perhaps best known for those made for Parker Pens. Items such as this appeal to both Carlton Ware and pen collectors.

7in (17.5cm) wide

£100-150 BAD

A Carlton Ware toast rack, printed marks including "Registered Australian Design".

6.5in (16.5cm) wide

£18-22 GAZE

A Carlton Ware triple candleholder.

7.5in (19cm) wide

£35-45 NPC

A 1960s Carlton Ware 'Orbit' pattern dish, with two compartments.

£25-35 NPC

A 1950s Carlton Ware square plate, with abstract turquoise and black decoration.

7in (18cm) wide

£15-25 NPC

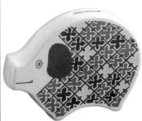

A 1960s Carlton Ware 'Flatback' series pig money box.

6in (15cm) long

£40-50 FD

A Carlton Ware 'Bug-Eye' series snail money box.

c1965 *5in (12.5cm) long*

£50-60 FD

A 1960s Carlton Ware 'Flatback' series Noah's Ark money box.

7in (18cm) wide

£40-50 FD

A Carlton Ware 'Walking Ware' teacup, with feet in blue shoes, walking.

4.25in (11cm) high

£25-35 CHS

A Carlton Ware 'Walking Ware' sugar bowl, with feet in yellow shoes, standing, printed marks.

5.5in (14cm) high

£40-60 CHS

A limited edition Carlton Ware 'The Pigeon Fancier' character jug, from an edition of 500.

£30-40 GAZE

A late 1970s Carlton Ware 'Denim' range salt and pepper shaker.

£30-40 NPC

A late 1970s Carlton Ware 'Denim' range teapot.

This range was a commercial disaster for Carlton Ware – especially in America where it was thought to have homosexual connotations. It contributed to the closure of the company.

£60-80

9in (23cm) high

NPC

A J. Meir & Son chintz jug, with registered design mark.

Typical of early chintz patterns, this jug has panels of decoration with space between the flowers and more muted colours. Later examples have brightly coloured patterns with tightly packed flowers.

c1866   8.5in (22cm) high

£100-150   **BAD**

A Royal Winton 'Royalty' pattern cup and saucer.

c1930   saucer 5.75in (14.5cm) diam

£40-60   **BAD**

A 1930s Royal Winton 'Hazel' pattern milk jug.

8.5in (11cm) high

£80-120   **BAD**

A Royal Winton 'Mecca' foot warmer, pattern no.1094, with marks.

When Queen Mary visited the Winton factory in 1913 she was presented with one of these foot warmers.

10in (26cm) high

£150-200   **SWO**

A 1950s Royal Winton 'Marion' pattern candy box.

5in (13cm) long

£150-200   **BAD**

An early 1950s Royal Winton 'Julia' pattern butter dish.

6in (16cm) wide

£150-200   **BAD**

A 1940s/50s Royal Winton 'Somerset' pattern basket.

This basket is desirable as the pattern covers the majority of the basket with the exception of the inside of the handle.

12.25in (31cm) wide

£150-200   **BAD**

A Royal Winton 'Richmond' pattern trefoil dish.

8in (20cm) wide

£100-150   **BAD**

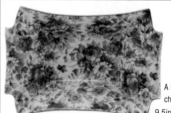

A Royal Winton chintz dish.

9.5in (15cm) wide

£70-100   **BAD**

COLLECTORS' NOTES

■ Clarice Cliff was born in Tunstall, Staffordshire, in 1899 and, in a region dominated by the potteries, joined a local company in 1912. In 1916 she moved to A.J Wilkinson's where she was soon promoted to a more influential and artistic position. In 1925, managing director Colley Shorter gave Cliff her own studio at the newly purchased Newport Pottery.

■ This pottery had a large stock of defective blank wares, many in old-fashioned shapes. Cliff covered them in brightly coloured and thickly applied patterns, to hide the faults. The new range was given the name 'Bizarre' and was launched in 1928 to great success. The 'Crocus' pattern was particularly popular.

■ The 'Fantasque' line, consisting of similar wares to the 'Bizarre' range, was launched in 1928. As both lines developed, the patterns moved away from the typically Art Deco, simple geometric designs to become more elaborate, abstract and bold, particularly in the 'Fantasque' range.

■ As public tastes changed, the Fantasque name was phased out in 1934, with Bizarre following a year later, although pieces with those backstamps continued to leave the factory. When production restarted after WWII, Cliff, by now art director, continued to design, but not with the success of previous years. When Shorter, by now Cliff's husband, died in 1963 she sold the pottery to rival Midwinter.

■ Items that display a pattern well, such as large plates, jugs and vases are popular. Look for thickly painted wares with visible brushstrokes and black outlines, as these typify early Cliff and are very desirable. Distinctly Art Deco patterns and forms are also favoured by collectors, whilst designs in muted colours, or those that are not typical of Cliff, receive less attention.

■ Many patterns were produced in a range of colourways so look out for rare variations: orange is a common colour whilst blue and purple are often rarer and more valuable.

A Clarice Cliff Fantasque Bizarre toast rack.

1929-34   6.5in (16.5cm) diam

£300-400   **BEV**

A CLOSER LOOK AT A CLARICE CLIFF PRESERVE POT

Due to its early date, this pot will probably have been hand-painted by either Cliff herself or Gladys Scarlett who was the first decorator to work with Cliff.

This early mark with a hand-painted "Bizarre" was only used in 1928 before being replaced with a stamped mark.

Typical of the earliest ware, this pot has a relatively simple geometric pattern. It also has visibly hand-painted decoration.

The Newport Pottery mark denotes a blank taken from the pottery's unused old stock.

An early Clarice Cliff Bizarre preserve pot, with chromed lid, Newport Pottery mark and hand-painted "Bizarre".

c1928   8cm high

£250-300   **NAI**

A rare Clarice Cliff 'Bobbins' pattern Bizarre biscuit barrel, moulded with lug handles, slight flaking to orange enamel, printed marks.

c1931-33   6.75in (17cm) wide

£550-650   **B**

A Clarice Cliff Fantasque Bizarre 'Canterbury Bells' pattern pot.

1932-33   3in (7.5cm) diam

£300-400   **BEV**

A Clarice Cliff 'Blue Chintz' pattern bowl.

c1932   7.5in (19cm) diam

£280-320   **GORL**

A Clarice Cliff Bizarre 'Crocus' pattern 14-piece part Tankard coffee set.

The most popular design produced by Clarice Cliff, the Crocus pattern was introduced in 1928 and, with the exception of the war years, was made until 1963. It was produced in a number of colourways.

Pot 7in (18cm) high

£1,200-1,800 **GORL**

A Clarice Cliff Bizarre 'Crocus' pattern Bon Jour preserve pot and cover.

1928-63 4.25in (10.5cm) high

£300-400 **BEV**

A Clarice Cliff Fantasque 'Melon' pattern beehive honey pot.

c1930-32 3.75in (9.5cm) high

£180-220 **GORW**

A Clarice Cliff Bizarre 'My Garden Flame' pattern pedestal bowl, "AF" printed marks to underside.

c1934-41 8in (20cm) high

£100-150 **ROS**

An A.J. Wilkinson 'Orange' pattern Daffodil shape grapefruit dish, designed by Dolly Cliff, marked "Wilkinson, England Honeyglaze Handpainted".

Clarice Cliff's sister Dolly worked as a designer at A.J. Wilkinson at the same time as her.

7in (17.5cm) wide

£30-40 **NAI**

A Clarice Cliff Fantasque Bizarre 'Pastel Autumn' pattern fern pot, printed marks, introduced in 1934.

3in (7.5cm) high

£220-280 **WW**

A Clarice Cliff Bizarre 'Pastel Autumn' pattern Conical coffee set.

1932 Pot 7in (18cm) high

£2,800-3,200 **GORL**

A Clarice Cliff Bizarre 'Pink Pearls' pattern sugar sifter, printed mark.

This is a variation of Rhodanthe with an alternative colourway.

1934-37 5.5in (14cm) high

£200-300 **WW**

A 1930s Clarice Cliff Fantasque 'Red Trees & House' Conical jug.

6.25in (16cm) high

£800-1,200 **BEV**

A Clarice Cliff 'Tree and Gate' pattern preserve pot, cover glued.

4.25in (11cm) wide

£700-800   **GORL**

A Clarice Cliff honeyglaze and blue oval meat plate, with matching tureen and cover, gilded with sailing boats.

£25-35   **GORW**

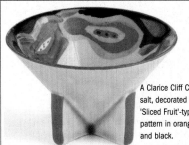

A Clarice Cliff Conical salt, decorated with 'Sliced Fruit'-type pattern in orange, blue and black.

2.75in (7cm) high

£150-250   **GORL**

A Clarice Cliff Bizarre 'Secrets' pattern charger.

1933-37

10.75in (27cm) diam

£700-900   **BEV**

A Clarice Cliff Bizarre 'Sliced Fruit' pattern preserve pot and cover, printed mark.

c1930   3.5in (9cm) high

£180-220   **WW**

A Clarice Cliff Bizarre 'Viscaria' pattern Liner vase, shape no.469, with printed mark, introduced in 1934

8.25in (21cm) high

£450-550   **WW**

A 1930s Clarice Cliff 'Water Lily' planter, shape no.973.

This was the best selling shape in this range.

8.75in (22cm) wide

£60-80   **GAZE**

A Clarice Cliff circular Bon Jour cream jug, painted with a concentric design in brown, yellow and grey, and a similar sugar bowl.

2.5in (6.5cm) diam

£80-120   **GORL**

A Clarice Cliff Biarritz plate, with abstract design of orange flowers and lines, impressed date.

1935   9in (23cm) wide

£100-150   **GORL**

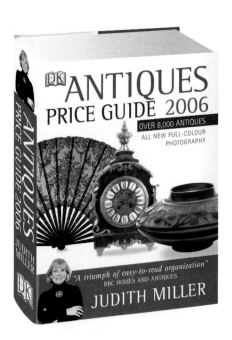

A Gray's Pottery lampbase, probably designed by Susie Cooper, pattern no.9677, printed clipper mark.

8in (20cm) high

£180-220 WW

A Gray's Pottery platter, designed by Susie Cooper, pattern no.2866, painted with flowers, liner mark.

14.5in (37cm) wide

£12-18 WW

A Gray's Pottery coffee can and saucer, designed by Susie Cooper, pattern no.8330, printed liner mark.

2.75in (7cm) high

£180-220 WW

Two of a set of six Susie Cooper Productions dinner plates, retailed by Ingwald Nielsen, Oslo, pattern no.E316, printed and painted marks, minor paint wear, two shown.

10in (25.5cm) diam

£650-750 (SET) WW

A Susie Cooper Productions 'Black Pom and Tango Terrier' lemonade jug, printed in colours printed mark, hairlines to rim, crazing.

9.5in (24cm) high

£80-120 WW

A Susie Cooper studio ware 'Acorn' pattern jug, in the Kestral shape, signed and dated.

1932 *6.25in (16cm) high*

£80-120 SWO

A Susie Cooper Pottery 'Seagull' pattern side plate, with printed marks.

c1935 *7in (17.5cm) diam*

£250-350 WW

A 1950s Susie Cooper bone china cup and saucer, with spiral decoration.

5in (13cm) diam

£30-40 BAD

An Adderley bone china coffee cup and saucer, with gilt rim.

saucer 5in (12.5cm) diam

£15-25   **JL**

An Aynsley cup and saucer, with gilt rim.

c1920   *saucer 4.5in (11cm) diam*

£30-40   **JL**

A Bing & Grøndahl cup and saucer, with a shaped seagull handle and gilt highlights, marked "108b".

saucer 4.75in (12cm) diam

£50-70   **JL**

A Bromfield cup and saucer, the cup with painted marks, the deep saucer with impressed marks, dated.

1879   *saucer 5.25in (13cm) diam*

£40-50   **JL**

A Carltonware moulded trio set, with hand-painted decoration and decorative flower handle to tea cup.

A Carltonware Moderne shape cup and saucer, with solid wavy rectangular handle in gilt.

saucer 5in (13cm) diam

£40-60   **BEV**

plate 5.5in (14cm) diam

£60-80   **JL**

A New Chelsea 'May Time' pattern cup and saucer, with hand-coloured printed decoration and gilt trim.

c1935   *saucer 5.5in (14cm) diam*

£35-45   **JL**

A Co-Operative Wholesale Society Limited 'Balmoral' china cup and saucer, with floral decoration and gilt trim.

c1960s   *saucer 5.5in (14cm) diam*

£18-22   **JL**

A Royal Doulton octagonal coffee cup and saucer, with mottled malachite green decoration.

c1935   *saucer 4.5in (11cm) diam*

£15-25   **JL**

A Royal Doulton cup and saucer, in blue and white with gilt decoration.

1914   *saucer 7.5in (19cm) diam*

£70-90   **BAD**

A Royal Doulton 'Felicity' pattern D450 trio set, with an unusual cup, dated.

1934   *plate 7.5in (19cm) diam*

£50-70   **BAD**

A 1930s Royal Doulton De Lux cup and saucer, with a bold mint green and black design on a white ground.

saucer 5.5in (14cm) diam

£70-90   **BAD**

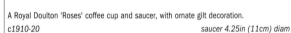

A 1980s Habitat 'Othello' pattern cup and saucer, with printed marks.

saucer 6in (15cm) diam

£12-18   **CHS**

A Royal Doulton 'Roses' coffee cup and saucer, with ornate gilt decoration.

c1910-20   *saucer 4.25in (11cm) diam*

£70-90   **BAD**

A German Hutschenreuther cup and saucer, with painted floral and moulded decoration.

saucer 4.75in (12cm) diam

£25-35   **JL**

A Jadson & Gosling trio set, hand decorated with blue bands and gilt decoration.

c1920   *plate 6in (15cm) diam*

£50-70   **JL**

A German Krautheim coffee cup and saucer, with floral painted decoration and gilt rim, marked "scene H".

saucer 4.5in (11cm) diam

£35-45   **JL**

A Court China trio set, by William Lowe, with hand painted and gilt decoration.

c1930   *plate 6in (15cm) diam*

£30-40   **JL**

A Melba bone china trio, with floral decoration.

6in (15cm) diam

£15-25 **BAD**

A Paragon China small cup and saucer, decorated in colours with budgerigars within a turquoise border.

1930

£40-50 **SAS**

A Paragon China trio set, with hand painted decoration and gilt rim.

c1904 *plate 7in (17.5cm) diam*

£45-55 **JL**

A Royal Paragon floral trio set, with gilt trim.

plate 6. 75in (17cm) diam

£60-80 **BAD**

A Royal Paragon trio set, with mint green, pale blue and gilt floral decoration.

plate 6.5in (16.5cm) diam

£40-60 **BAD**

A Paragon Apple Blossom trio set, with a gilt edge and a six-point star mark.

plate 4.75in (12cm) wide

£70-90 **BAD**

A Royal Paragon cup and saucer, with flower-shaped handle and foxglove and gilt decoration.

saucer 5.5in (14cm) diam

£60-80 **BAD**

A Royal Paragon trio set, the reverse inscribed "Replica of Service made for HM The Queen".

£50-60 **SAS**

A 1960s Ridgway's Royal Vale cup and saucer with octagonal cup, with heavy gilt decoration.

saucer 6.5in (16cm) diam

£20-30 **JL**

A CLOSER LOOK AT A SHELLEY TRIO

The 'Mode' shape was designed by Eric Slater in 1930 and was a radical departure from Shelley's previous traditionally 'Victorian' designs.

The Art Deco shape combines perfectly with the stylized Art Deco decoration.

This impractical solid tea cup handle proved unpopular with the public and was replaced with the 'Eve' shape cup with a cut-out handle in 1932.

Despite being produced for only a few years, over 30 patterns were used on this shape – 'Blue Iris' is one of the most commonly found.

A Shelley Mode 'Blue Iris' trio, comprising cup, saucer and side plate, pattern 11850 printed and painted marks.

1930-32

cup 3in (7.5cm) high

£250-350

WW

A Rosenthal coffee cup and saucer, with coloured and gilt decoration, embossed, marked "Vera".

saucer 4.25in (10.5cm) diam

£25-35

JL

A Sampson Smith yellow trio set, printed floral decoration and gilt rim, marked "Old Royal China".

c1930

plate 7in (17.5cm) diam

£30-40

JL

A Sampson Smith green and gilt trio set, hand-painted over transfers with flowers, marked "Old Royal China est 1846".

c1930

plate 6in (15cm) diam

£35-45

JL

A Shelley Mode 'Orange Block' trio comprising cup, saucer and side plate, pattern number 11792, with printed and painted marks.

c1932

cup 3.25in (8cm) high

£200-300

WW

A Spode Copeland cup and saucer, with gild rim, marked "Ryde".

1953

saucer 4.75in (12cm) diam

£30-40

JL

A Spode Copeland trio set, comprised of a coffee cup, tea cup and saucer, hand-painted over transfer and gilt trim, the cups c1851-1885, the saucer c1891.

saucer 5.5in (14cm) diam

£60-80

JL

CERAMICS

An English hand-painted bone china trio set.

plate 6in (15cm) wide

£30-40   **JL**

A paisley pattern coffee cup and saucer, with gilt rim, marked "Made in Czechoslovakia".

saucer 4.5in (11cm) diam

£35-45   **JL**

A Victorian trio set, hand-painted over transfers with pink flowers among leaves.

plate 6in (15cm) diam

£40-60   **JL**

A hand-painted trio set, with orange floral decoration.

plate 6in (15cm) wide

£40-50   **JL**

A late Victorian hand-painted teacup and saucer, with orange and gilt decoration and embossed decoration.

saucer 5.5in (14cm) diam

£25-35   **JL**

An English bone china trio set, with shaped octagonal plate and printed and hand-coloured decoration.

plate 6.5in (16cm) diam

£25-35   **JL**

A moulded cup and saucer, the cup with a printed scene titled "Past Church Paignton".

saucer 5.25in (13cm) diam

£20-30   **JL**

A hand-painted coffee cup and saucer, unmarked.

saucer 4.5in (11cm) diam

£25-35   **JL**

A Victorian hand-painted cup and saucer, with gilt rim.

saucer 5.5in (14cm) diam

£45-55   **JL**

COLLECTORS' NOTES

■ Production of pottery began at Denby in 1809, two years after William Bourne saw the opportunities presented by the discovery of a seam of clay nearby. William's son Joseph ran the pottery, now known as the 'Joseph Bourne' pottery, which soon built up a reputation for its salt-glazed stoneware jars and bottles in subdued colours.

■ The range grew by the 1920s to incorporate functional domestic wares such as dishes, jelly moulds and hot water bottles as well as decorative wares such as vases and bowls. All such decorative wares were stamped 'Danesby Ware'. In 1931, Norman Wood joined and revolutionised production methods enabling brighter glazes to be used.

■ The main designer at this time was Albert Colledge. Others included Alice Teichtner, from the Wiener Werkstatte, and Donald Gilbert, who joined in 1934 and increased Denby's decorative output. During the 1950s, production changed to focus on tableware, for which they are still well known today.

■ 1950 also saw the arrival of Albert Colledge's son, Glyn (1922-2000), and the renaming of hand-decorated 'Danesby Ware' to 'Glyn Ware' in honour of his arrival. Look out for his designs including the 'Glynbourne' range and particularly those signed by him. His earliest designs are inscribed with his signature, later examples until the 1970s are signed with a brush.

A Denby pale green 'Gretna' pattern cigar ashtray, designed by Alice Teichtner, with printed marks to base.

8in (20.5cm) diam

£50-70　　　　**PSI**

A Denby large beige bowl, designed by Alice Teichtner, with printed script Denby mark to base, "AT" monogram and "W.T.L & S 1937" mark.

11.5in (29.5cm) diam

£80-120　　　　**PSI**

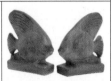

A pair of Denby Danesby Ware book ends, modelled as angel fish, covered in a pastel blue glaze, printed mark.

6.75in (17cm) high

£100-150　　　　**WW**

A Denby pale green 'Gretna' pattern vase, designed by Alice Teichtner, with printed marks to base.

1937-38 8.5in (22cm) high

£120-150　　　　**PSI**

A 1930s Denby Orient Ware hand-decorated three-handled vase, script printed mark to base.

Orient Ware, with its recognisable matte blue and brown decoration, became a popular range of giftware during the 1930s. The gloss glaze version is known as 'Electric Blue' and was introduced in 1925.

7.25in (18.5cm) high

£40-60　　　　**PSI**

A 1930s Denby stoneware 'Sylvan Pastel Mushroom Group', designed by Donald Gilbert, design no.SP12.

7in (17.5cm) high

£350-450　　　　**WW**

A Denby 'Danesby Ware' large stoneware single-handled vase, printed mark.

12in (30.5cm) high

£80-120　　　　**WW**

A 1950s Denby Stoneware hand-painted 'Hazlewood' pattern snack dish, with curling sides, designed by Glyn Colledge.

12.25in (31cm) long

£30-40   AGR

A mid-1950s Denby burgundy-striped 'Hazlewood' pattern stoneware posy basket, designed by Glyn Colledge.

5.5in (14cm) wide

£30-40   AGR

A Denby 'Burlington' pattern stoneware ovoid vase, with flared neck.

The Burlington range was introduced in the late 1950s and designed by Albert Colledge, in collaboration with his son Glyn, and was unlike his usual style. Contemporary at the time, its clean lines and black and white decoration were typical of the period.

11.5in (29.5cm) high

£35-45   AGR

A Denby 'Burlington' pattern stoneware tapering vase.

8.25in (21cm) high

£30-40   AGR

A Denby 'Cloisonné' pattern hand-painted triangular dish, designed by Glyn Colledge.

Other patterns feature wine glasses, hearts and stripes.

c1957   *6.75in (17cm) wide*

£60-80   AGR

A Bourne Denby hand-painted vase, designed by Glyn Colledge, with printed Bourne Denby and Glyn Colledge marks to base.

8.5in (21.5cm) high

£35-45   GROB

A Denby 'Arabesque' pattern tankard, designed by Gill Pemberton, unmarked.

'Arabesque' revolutionised tableware and became a highly popular pattern, being produced between 1960 and 1984. It was exported to the US, where it is known as 'Samarkand'.

c1965   *5.25in (13.5cm) high*

£10-12   GROB

FIND OUT MORE...

Denby Pottery 1809-1997, *by Irene & Gordon Hopwood, published by Richard Dennis Publications, 1997.*

CERAMICS

COLLECTORS' NOTES

- The first Doulton figurines as we know them were launched in 1913 by Royal Doulton's Art Director Charles Noke, although Doulton had made figurines during the 19th century.

- Over 4,000 different models and colour variations are known. Each colour variation has its own 'HN' number and a figure may have been produced in a number of different colourways, each often worth a different amount.

- Many choose to collect by type such as 'fair ladies', children or literary and historical characters. Certain modellers are known for certain types of figurine, such as Harradine and his fair ladies.

- Ranges such as the 'Dickens' series also prove popular, but some figurines will be rarer and more valuable than others. Figurines only produced before WWII are rare and tend to be very valuable, as are those produced for short periods of time.

- Figurines produced for long periods like 'The Balloon Man', or those that are still in production today tend to be less valuable or desirable. Condition is directly related to value. Chips and cracks reduce value considerably. Examine all examples carefully.

A Royal Doulton 'The Parson's Daughter' figurine, HN564, designed by Harry Tittensor.

1923-49   9.5in (24cm) high

£100-150   **L&T**

A Royal Doulton 'Victorian Lady' figurine, HN728, designed by Leslie Harradine.

There are 15 different colourways of 'Victorian Lady' known.

1925-52   7.75in (20cm) high

£120-180   **L&T**

A Royal Doulton 'Sweet Anne' figurine, HN1330, designed by Leslie Harradine.

1929-49 7.25in (18.5cm) high

£70-100   **L&T**

A Royal Doulton 'Miss Demure' figurine, HN1402, designed by Leslie Harradine.

1930-75   7.5in (19cm) high

£50-80   **L&T**

A Royal Doulton 'Parson's Daughter' figurine, number HN1356, designed by Harry Tittensor.

1929-38   5.75in (14.5cm) high

£300-400   **DN**

A Royal Doulton 'Pantalettes' figurine, HN1412, designed by Leslie Harradine.

1930-49 7.75in (20cm) high

£120-180   **L&T**

A Royal Doulton 'Chloe' figurine, HN1470, designed by Leslie Harradine.

1931-49   5.5in (14cm) high

£100-150   **L&T**

A Royal Doulton 'Janet' figurine, HN1537, designed by Leslie Harradine.

1932-95   6.25in (16cm) high

£30-40   **L&T**

A Royal Doulton 'Daydreams' figurine, HN1732, designed by Leslie Harradine.

1935-49   5.5in (14cm) high

£40-60   **L&T**

A CLOSER LOOK AT A FAIR LADY

Leslie Harradine is well known for his fair ladies, which are sought-after by many collectors.

'Camille' was produced for a comparatively short period around WWII, making her scarcer than others.

She was produced in three different colourways – look out for the pink and cream variation, which is even more desirable.

She is one of the most valuable colourways, with hand-painted flowers on her dress.

A Royal Doulton 'Margery' figurine, HN1413, designed by Leslie Harradine.

1930-49   11in (28cm) high

£150-250   **SWO**

A Royal Doulton 'Top O'The Hill' figurine, HN1833, designed by Leslie Harradine.

1937-71   7in (18cm) high

£60-90   **L&T**

A Royal Doulton 'Camille' figurine, HN1648, designed by Leslie Harradine.

1935-49   6.5in (16.5cm) high

£200-300   **L&T**

A Royal Doulton 'Autumn Breezes' figurine, HN1913, designed by Leslie Harradine.

Earlier versions of this figurine have two feet showing, later examples have only one, as here.

1939-71   7.5in (19cm) high

£50-80   **L&T**

A Royal Doulton 'Lady Charmian' figurine, HN1949, designed by Leslie Harradine.

1940-75   8in (20cm) high

£50-80   **L&T**

A Royal Doulton 'The Ermine Coat' figurine, HN1981, designed by Leslie Harradine.

1945-67   6.75in (17cm) high

£70-100   **L&T**

A Royal Doulton 'Memories' figurine, HN2030, designed by Leslie Harradine.

1949-59
6in (15cm) high

£80-120　　　**L&T**

A Royal Doulton 'Judith' figurine, HN2089, designed by Leslie Harradine.

1952-59　　*7in (18cm) high*

£80-120　　　**L&T**

A Royal Doulton 'Hostess of Williamsburg' figurine, HN2209, designed by Margaret Davies, from the Figures of Williamsburg series.

1960-83 7.25in (18.5cm) high

£50-70　　　**L&T**

A Royal Doulton 'Melanie' figurine, HN2271, designed by Margaret Davies.

1965-81   7.75in (20cm) high

£50-80　　　**L&T**

A Royal Doulton 'Katrina' figurine, HN2327, designed by Margaret Davies.

1965-69   7.5in (19cm) high

£80-120　　　**L&T**

A Royal Doulton 'The Ballerina' figurine, HN2116, designed by Margaret Davies.

1953-73   7.25in (18.5cm) high

£70-100　　　**L&T**

A Royal Doulton 'Hilary' figurine, HN2335, designed by Margaret Davies.

1967-81 7.25in (18.5cm) high

£30-50　　　**L&T**

A Royal Doulton 'Loretta' figurine, HN2337, designed by Margaret Davies.

1966-81   7.75in (20cm) high

£30-40　　　**L&T**

A Royal Doulton 'Masquerade' figurine, HN2251, designed by Margaret Davies.

1960-65　　　　　*8.5in (21.5cm) high*

£100-150　　　**L&T**

A Royal Doulton 'My Love' figurine, HN2339, designed by Margaret Davies.	A Royal Doulton 'Simone' figurine, HN2378, designed by Margaret Davies.	A Royal Doulton 'Fiona' figurine, HN2694, designed by Margaret Davies.	A Royal Doulton 'Pensive Moments' figurine, HN2704, designed by Margaret Davies.
1969-96 6.25in (16cm) high	*1971-81 7.25in (18.5cm) high*	*1974-81 7.5in (19cm) high*	*1975-81 5in (13cm) high*
£50-70 L&T	**£40-60** L&T	**£40-60** L&T	**£50-80** L&T

	A Royal Doulton red 'Julia' figurine, HN2705, designed by Margaret Davies.	A Royal Doulton 'Veneta' figurine, HN2722, designed by Bill Harper.
	1975-90 7.5in (19cm) high	*1974-81 8in (20cm) high*
	£40-60 L&T	**£40-60** L&T

A Royal Doulton red 'Eliza' figurine, HN2543, with painted flowers, designed by Eric Griffiths, from the Haute Ensemble series.	A Royal Doulton 'Clarinda' figurine, HN2724, designed by Bill Harper.	A Royal Doulton 'Kate' figurine, HN2789, designed by Margaret Davies.
1974-79 11.75in (30cm) high	*1975-81 8.5in (21.5cm) high*	*1978-87 7.5in (19cm) high*
£100-150 L&T	**£50-70** L&T	**£40-60** L&T

CERAMICS

A Royal Doulton 'Greta' figurine, HN1485, designed by Leslie Harradine.

1931-53   5.5in (14cm) high

£120-180   **L&T**

A Royal Doulton 'Tootles' figurine, HN1680, designed by Leslie Harradine.

1935-75   4.75in (12cm) high

£15-25   **L&T**

A Royal Doulton 'Cassim' figurine, HN1231, designed by Leslie Harradine.

1927-38   3in (7.5cm) high

£450-550   **WW**

A Royal Doulton 'Little Boy Blue' figurine, HN2062, designed by Leslie Harradine, from the Nursery Rhymes series.

1950-73   5.5in (14cm) high

£50-70   **L&T**

A Royal Doulton 'Baby Bunting' figurine, HN2108, designed by Margaret Davies.

1953-59   5.25in (13cm) high

£100-150   **L&T**

A Royal Doulton 'Pillow Fight' figurine, HN2270, designed by Margaret Davies.

1965-69   5in (13cm) high

£60-90   **L&T**

A Royal Doulton 'Belle' figurine, HN2340, designed by Margaret Davies.

1968-88   4.5in (11.5cm) high

£20-30   **L&T**

A Royal Doulton 'River Boy' figurine, HN2128, designed by Margaret Davies.

1962-75   4in (10cm) high

£50-80   **L&T**

A Royal Doulton 'Alice' figurine, HN2158, designed by Margaret Davies.

1960-81   5in (13cm) high

£30-50   **L&T**

A Royal Doulton 'Georgina' figurine, HN2377, designed by Margaret Davies, from the Kate Greenaway series.

There are 18 characters in the Kate Greenaway series.

1981-86 5.75in (14.5cm) high

£70-100   **L&T**

A Royal Doulton 'Francine' figurine, HN2422, designed by J. Bromley.

Another variation exists with the bird's tail pointing up. It is worth roughly the same as this variation.

1972-onwards 5in (13cm) high

£60-90   **L&T**

A Royal Doulton 'Carrie' figurine, HN2800, designed by Margaret Davies, from the Kate Greenaway series.

1976-81   6in (15cm) high

£70-100   **L&T**

A Royal Doulton 'Lucy' figurine, HN2863, designed by Margaret Davies, from the Kate Greenaway series.

1980-84   6in (15cm) high

£70-100   **L&T**

A Royal Doulton 'Sleepy Darling' figurine, HN2953, designed by Polly Parsons, from the Royal Doulton International Collectors Club series.

1981   7.25in (18.5cm) high

£50-80   **L&T**

A Royal Doulton 'Tom' figurine, HN2864, designed by Margaret Davies, from the Kate Greenaway series.

1978-81 5.75in (14.5cm) high

£100-150   **L&T**

A Royal Doulton 'Hope' figurine, HN3061, designed by S. Mitchell, from the NSPCC Charity series.

Hope was produced, along with Faith and Charity, in a limited edition of 9,500 of each figure for Lawleys By Post.

1984   8.25in (21cm) high

£100-150   **L&T**

A Royal Doulton 'Faith' figurine, HN3082, designed by Eric Griffiths, from the NSPCC Charity series.

1986   8.5in (21.5cm) high

£50-80   **L&T**

A Royal Doulton 'Charity' figurine, HN3087, designed by Eric Griffiths, from the NSPCC Charity series.

1987   8.5in (21.5cm) high

£80-100   **L&T**

A Royal Doulton 'The Old Balloon Seller' figurine, HN1315, designed by Leslie Harradine.

7.5in (19cm) high

£80-120   **SWO**

A Royal Doulton 'The Cobbler' figurine, HN1706, designed by Charles Noke.

1935-69   8.25in (21cm) high

£120-180   **L&T**

A Royal Doulton 'Calumet' figurine, HN689, designed by Charles Noke.

1935-49   6.75in (17cm) high

£250-450   **SWO**

A Royal Doulton 'Carpet Seller' figurine, HN1464A, designed by Leslie Harradine.

The earlier version, produced from 1929, has an open outstretched (and easily damaged!) hand. It is harder to find and can be worth up to 20 per cent more. The model pictured was withdrawn in 1969.

9in (23cm) high

£120-180   **L&T**

A Royal Doulton 'The Milkmaid' figurine, HN2057A, designed by Leslie Harradine.

The blue, red and white version of this model is known as 'The Jersey Milkmaid' and can be worth up to 25 per cent more, as it was only produced during the 1950s.

1975-81   6.5in (16.5cm) high

£60-80   **L&T**

A Royal Doulton 'The Orange Lady' figurine, HN1759, designed by Leslie Harradine.

1936-75   8.75in (22cm) high

£80-120   **L&T**

A Royal Doulton 'The Balloon Man' figurine, HN1954, designed by Leslie Harradine.

1940-   7.25in (18.5cm) high

£70-100   **L&T**

A Royal Doulton 'Fortune Teller' figurine, HN2159, designed by Leslie Harradine.

1955-67   6.5in (16.5cm) high

£150-200   **L&T**

A Royal Doulton 'Silversmith of Williamsburg' figurine, HN2208, designed by Margaret Davies.

1960-83   6.5in (16cm) high

£70-100   **L&T**

A Royal Doulton 'Pickwick' figurine, HN556, designed by Leslie Harradine.

1923-39   7in (18cm) high

£180-220   **SWO**

A Royal Doulton 'Micawber' figurine, HN557, designed by Leslie Harradine, from the Dickens series.

There are 24 characters to collect from the Dickens series.

1923-39   7in (18cm) high

£180-220   **SWO**

A Royal Doulton 'Sir Walter Raleigh' figurine, HN2015, designed by Leslie Harradine.

1948-55   11.75in (30cm) high

£250-350   **SWO**

A Royal Doulton 'Frodo' figurine, HN2912, designed by David Lyttleton, from the Middle Earth series.

Thanks to the popular films, interest in and values of the Middle Earth series have grown.

1980-84   4.5in (11.5cm) high

£100-150   **PSA**

A Royal Doulton 'Legolas' figurine, HN2917, designed by David Lyttleton, from the Middle Earth series.

1981-84   6.25in (16cm) high

£80-120   **PSA**

A Royal Doulton 'Florence Nightingale' figurine, HN3144, designed by Polly Parsons.

This was produced in a limited edition of 5,000 for Lawleys By Post in 1988.

1988   8.25in (21cm) high

£150-250   **L&T**

A CLOSER LOOK AT A JESTER

Celebrated modeller Noke was fascinated by the theatre and is also noted for his character studies of which this is an excellent example.

It was made before World War II, when comparatively fewer examples were made, some estimates say fewer than 2,000.

All variations of The Jester are scarce and valuable, however those in more muted colourways were less popular at the time and tend to be more valuable.

It was produced between 1918-36, but this example can be dated more precisely as modellers' names were dropped from the bases in c1930.

A rare Royal Doulton 'The Jester' figurine, HN308, in black and lavender suit, designed by Charles Noke and signed "CJ Noke".

1918-c1930   10.25in (26cm) high

£3,000-4,000   **PSA**

CERAMICS

A Royal Doulton 'Seated Bulldog' figure, DA228, in fawn with white top hat and tails, boxed with certificate.

£70-100   PSA

A limited edition Royal Doulton 'Bulldog' figure, DA228, in white with a black top hat and tails, boxed with certificate.

£80-120   PSA

A Royal Doulton 'Character Dog Playing With A Ball' figure, HN1103.

£35-45   PSA

A Royal Doulton 'Pekinese Puppy Seated' figure, HN832, minor scratches to glaze.

£150-200   PSA

A Royal Doulton 'Horse Head Tucked Leg Up' brown gloss figure, DA51.

£40-50   PSA

An early Royal Doulton trial piece matt horse, marked "Property of Royal Doulton Not For Sale" and signed by J.A.J. Brown.

8in (20cm) high

£400-500   PSA

A rare Royal Doulton 'Seated Red Setter' figure, HN976, with collar, in an unlisted flambé glaze.

Doulton's flambé glaze was developed from an appreciation of the Chinese 'sang de bouef' glaze. Working with modeller Charles Noke, chemist Bernard Moore developed a modern version that was used on a number of Noke's figures. It is a popular finish with collectors today. This model was not recorded in a flambé.

£600-700   PSA

A Royal Doulton 'Spirit Of The Wild' brown matt figure, DA183, on wooden plinth.

£60-80   PSA

A Royal Doulton 'Connoisseur Fresian Bull' black and white matt figure, DA23, on wooden plinth.

£150-200   PSA

A Royal Doulton 'Bayeux Tapestry' series jug.

4in (10cm) high

£80-120 GORW

A rare Royal Doulton 'Aldin's Dogs' series water jug, with a Cecil Aldin character scene, some crazing.

Illustrator Cecil Aldin (1870-1935) was renowned for his illustrations of mischievous dogs, which Doulton used to form a series.

1926-46 *5in (13cm) high*

£300-400 PSA

A pair of Royal Doulton Dickens ware candlesticks, featuring 'Alfred Jingle' and 'Barnaby Rudge'.

6.5in (16cm) high

£180-220 SAS

A Royal Doulton 'Gibson Girls' series rack plate, light nip to rim.

9.5in (24cm) diam

£80-120 PSA

A Royal Doulton 'Golfing' series vase.

2.25in (5.5cm) high

£70-90 GORW

A Royal Doulton 'Jackdaw Of Rheims' series oval bowl.

10.5in (27cm) long

£70-90 PSA

A Royal Doulton 'Under The Greenwood Tree' series water jug.

5.5in (14cm) high

£100-150 PSA

A Royal Doulton David Souter 'Kateroo' mug, restored.

2.75in (7cm) high

£50-80 PSA

CERAMICS

A Doulton Lambeth stoneware jug, impressed marks to base.

7in (18cm) high

£80-120 GAZE

A Doulton Lambeth 'Merry Monks' jar and cover.

£60-80 GORW

A Doulton Lambeth tobacco jar and cover, by George Tinworth, decorated with a pipe-smoking mouse.

George Tinworth (1843-1913) studied at the Lambeth School of Art and then the Royal Academy School before being employed by Royal Doulton in 1867 where he spent the rest of his career. He was best known for his terracotta sculptures and produced a terracotta relief for the Doulton building.

6.75in (17cm) high

£700-800 GORW

A pair of Doulton Lambeth faïence vases, of waisted form, initialled "MW" and "EJG".

8.25in (21cm) high

£350-450 GORL

A pair of Royal Doulton stoneware vases.

12.5in (32cm) high

£150-200 GORL

A Royal Doulton 'Bird of Paradise' hand painted plate, D 4602, printed marks.

£18-22 GAZE

A 1930s Royal Doulton white-glazed vase, with heavy base to prevent movement on ship, base with "O.S.N.Co. 165" imprint.

The logo on the vase is for the Orient Shipping Line and was created by designer Edward McKnight Kauffer (1890-1954), famous for his posters for London Transport and Shell Oil as well as theatre costume, exhibition designs, murals, book illustrations and textiles.

6.75in (17cm) high

£60-80 RETC

A Royal Doulton 'Marriage Day/After Marriage' salt-glazed reversible miniature jug, no. X895.

3.5in (9cm) high

£200-300 SWO

A Royal Doulton 'Toby' stoneware figure, impressed marks.

6in (15cm) high

£500-600 WW

A bisque ring stand, in the form of a hand.

This would have been used as a ring stand, with rings being placed on the fingers and in the 'sleeve' tray.

A L'Amour China hand-painted vase, in the form of a pair of cupped hands.

5.25in (13.5cm) high

£15-25   DAC

A small purple-tinted vase/bowl, in the form of a pair of cupped hands.

6.25in (16cm) long

£15-20   DAC

4in (10cm) high

£10-15   DAC

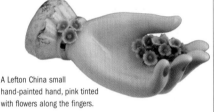

A Lefton China small hand-painted hand, pink tinted with flowers along the fingers.

5.5in (14cm) long

£10-15   DAC

A ceramic pair of hands, holding a flower bedecked shoe, unmarked.

Hand-shaped vessels were popular from the 1930s-60s as ladies' dressing table accessories and were used to store and display small items such as earrings, rings or small posies of flowers. Many were made in Japan during the late 1940s and 1950s, usually from the familiar glazed white bisque. Look for large, more finely modelled examples and especially those with intricate decoration, such as the flowers on this example. Always examine tips and details carefully as they were prone to breakage and repair.

A gold painted vase, in the form of a pair of hands holding a fan, probably Japanese.

7in (18cm) high

£20-30   DAC

£18-22   DAC

6.75in (17cm) high

DAC

A ceramic hand holding a goblet, with applied flowers, base stamped JAPAN.

5.25in (13.5cm) high

£10-15   DAC

A compote, held by a hand, with printed decoration of roses.

Dish 7in (18cm) diam

£15-25   DAC

A Royal Japan hand-painted hand and cornucopia vase.

6in (15cm) high

£10-15   DAC

COLLECTORS' NOTES

■ First released in 1935, Goebel's 'Hummel' figurines were inspired by drawings of children by a nun, Sister Berta Hummel. Since then, over 500 different figurines have been modelled. Examine marks on the base to help you identify the name and the period in which that particular piece was made.

■ 'Crown' marks and marks with a large bee motif denote early examples, which are amongst the most valuable. Over time from 1950, the bee becomes smaller in size and moves inside the V shape. After 1964, the bee motif was dropped in favour of text, a large 'G' dominating the mark from 1972.

■ As well as early examples from the 1930s-50s, also look for variations in colour of certain parts of clothing. These variations can be sought-after and fetch higher prices. Larger examples above the 6in size are also more valuable.

■ Dates shown here relate to the time period each piece was produced in, using its mark to help date it. Note that some designs are still in production today.

■ Condition is a vital indicator to value. The ceramic chips and cracks easily, so examine figurines carefully for damage or repair, which reduces value. Also take care not to bruise figurines against each other when on display.

A Hummel 'Girl with Nosegay' figure, No. 239A.

This figurine, along with 'Girl With Doll' also on this page and 'Boy With Horse' were released and traditionally sold together from the 1960s as the 'Children Trio' set.

1979-91   3.5in (9cm) high

£15-25   **AAC**

A Hummel 'Girl with Doll' figure, No.239B.
1991-99   3.5in (9cm) high
£10-15   **AAC**

A Hummel 'Birthday Candle' candleholder, No.440, exclusive special edition for the Hummel Collectors' Club.
1983   5.5in (14cm) high
£40-60   **AAC**

A Hummel 'Doll Bath' figure, No. 319, with 1960s smooth finish.

Look out for the ultra-rare early examples with a 'full bee' mark which can fetch up to £1,200 or more.

1964-72 5.25in (13.5cm) high
£70-100   **AAC**

A Hummel 'Little Sweeper' figure, No. 171.
1958-72   4.5in (11.5cm) high
£30-50   **AAC**

A Hummel 'Just Resting' figure, No. 112, with a cracked corner and a three-line mark.
c1964-72 3.75in (9.5cm) high
£30-50   **ERI**

A Hummel 'Smiling Through' figure, No. 408/0, exclusive special edition only for members of the Hummel Collectors' Club.
1983   4.75in (12cm) high
£70-100   **AAC**

A Hummel 'Soldier Boy' figure, No. 332, with red medal, crazing.

The medal on the figure's cap changed from red to blue during the 'Three Line Mark' period. Examples from this period can have either colour, but the red is more desirable.

1964-72   6in (15cm) high

£50-80   **AAC**

A Hummel 'Doctor' figure, No.127.

The more valuable early examples have the figure's feet extending over the edge of the base, a feature changed due to easy breakage.

1958-72   4.75in (12cm) high

£30-50   **AAC**

A Hummel 'Postman' figure, No. 119, crazing.

1958-72   4.75in (12cm) high

£40-60   **AAC**

A Hummel 'Boots' figure, No. 143/0.

1972-79   5.5in (14cm) high

£30-50   **AAC**

A Hummel 'Brother' figure, No. 95, marked "Germany" in black, no decimal.

The earliest, and most valuable, figurines have a blue coat and can fetch up to £200.

1940-59   5.5in (14cm) high

£15-25   **AAC**

A Hummel 'For Father' figure, No. 87, crazing.

Look at the colour of the radishes – if they are green or orange, the value can exceed £500.

1958-72   5.5in (14cm) high

£30-50   **AAC**

A Hummel 'Boy with Toothache' figure, No. 217, marked with an incised circle and "Germany" in black, damaged.

1958-72   5.5in (14cm) high

£30-50   **AAC**

A Hummel 'March Winds' figure, No. 43, underbase crazing.

1958-72   5in (12.5cm) high

£30-40   **AAC**

A Hummel 'I'm Here' figure, No. 478.

1989-91   3in (7.5cm) high

£20-30   **AAC**

CERAMICS

A Hummel 'Sweet Music' figure, No. 186, with doughnut-shaped base, marked "Germany" in black.

Look out for striped slippers, only found with the early Crown mark, as this rare variation can be worth five times more.

1947-59 5.25in (13.5cm) high

£70-100   **AAC**

A Hummel 'Little Cellist' figure, No. 89/I, crazing.

1958-72   6in (15cm) high

£40-60   **AAC**

A CLOSER LOOK AT A HUMMEL FIGURINE

'Little Fiddler' was from the first range of 46 Hummels produced.

Rare, pale-coloured 'doll' faces can be worth up to £1,500 or more, and are very early in date.

This example is so valuable as it is large; the standard 6in size is worth around £50-70.

It is undamaged, with no chips or cracks.

A large Hummel 'Little Fiddler' figure, No. 2/II.

1972-79   11in (28cm) high

£180-220   **AAC**

A Hummel 'Happy Days' figure, No. 150/2/0.

1972-79
                    4.25in (11cm) high

£30-50   **AAC**

A Hummel 'Happiness' figure, No. 86, incised crown mark and marked "U.S. Zone Germany" in black.

This figurine was modelled in 1938, but the combination of the early Crown mark and the 'US Zone Germany' mark means it can be dated to a four year period of production.

1946-50   4.75in (12cm) high

£80-120   **AAC**

A Hummel 'Serenade' figure, No. 85/0.

1972-79   4.75in (12cm) high

£30-40   **AAC**

A Hummel 'Little Tooter' figure, No. 214H, paint flake.

Although not obvious, this figure comes from Hummel's nativity set.

1964-72   4in (10cm) high

£30-50   **AAC**

A bust of Sister M.I. Hummel, Hu 3, special edition No. 3 for the Goebel Collectors Club, some crazing, with box.

1972-79 5.75in (14.5cm) high

£20-30   **AAC**

A Hummel 'Flower Madonna' figure, No. 10/I, with closed halo, marked with an incised circle and "Western Germany" in green, lower part crazing.

Examples with 'open' haloes, where the Madonna's hair shows, date from before the mid-1950s and usually fetch more. Also look out for colour variations such as royal blue and beiges.

c1955-59   9.25in (23.5cm) high

£100-150   **AAC**

A Hummel 'Heavenly Protection' figure, No. 88/I.

1972-79   6.25in (17cm) high

£80-120   **AAC**

A Hummel 'Adoration' figure, No. 23/I.

1958-72   6.25in (16cm) high

£80-120   **AAC**

A Hummel 'Worship' figure, No. 84/0.

1958-72   5in (12.5cm) high

£40-60   **AAC**

A Hummel 'Girl with Fir Tree' candleholder, No. 116, crazing.

1958-72   3.5in (9cm) high

£12-18   **AAC**

A Hummel 'Infant Jesus' figure, No. 214A.

As with all figures numbered 214, they form part of the Hummel nativity set.

1964-72   3.5in (9cm) wide

£12-18   **AAC**

A Hummel 'Herald Angels' candleholder, No. 37, with high candleholder, incised circle, marked "Western Germany" in black.

A taller candleholder is found on older versions of this piece.

1958-72   4in (10cm) wide

£70-100   **AAC**

FIND OUT MORE...

Luckey's Hummel Figurines & Plates Price Guide – 12th Edition, by Carl F. Luckey and Dean A. Genth, published by Krause Publications, 2003.

No.1 Price Guide to Hummel Figurines, Plates and More, by Robert L. Miller, published by Portfolio Press, 2003.

CERAMICS

COLLECTORS' NOTES

■ The Iden Pottery was founded by Dennis Townsend after he left the Rye Pottery in 1959. As its success grew, the pottery moved from the nearby village of Iden into larger premises in the town of Rye in 1966.

■ The pottery is known for its hand decorated stonewares. The glazes tend to be colourful with graduated effects. Use of the wax-resist technique is common. Patterns tend to echo those of Rye or are made up of geometric shapes, often in bands.

■ The business was very successful but closed in 2000 with Townsend now producing individual studio pieces via the David Sharp Pottery. The export market has long been an important one for the pottery and Harrods and Heal's have also stocked their wares.

■ All marks include a motif made up of Townsend's initials. The earliest were inscribed into the clay, while later marks are stamped in ink. Two typical marks are shown below. Look out for small gaps in the circle from 1974; a further 'gap' was added each year. Hence two gaps would indicate a date of 1975.

■ After 1978, the wording appeared in upper and lower case, rather than all in upper case. Marks on pieces made for retailers usually include the retailer's name. Look out for dishes, which display their patterns well. Larger pieces and those with complex colourful patterns tend to fetch the highest prices.

An Iden Pottery wax-resist technique glazed waisted vase, with printed mark to base.

1965-72 4.25in (10.5cm) high

£10-15   **AGR**

An Iden Pottery wax-resist technique glazed small vase, with printed mark to base.

1965-70   4.5in (11.5cm) high

£20-30   **AGR**

An Iden Pottery wax-resist technique glazed beaker or cylindrical vase, with blue dots and printed mark to base.

1965-72   4.25in (11cm) high

£20-25   **AGR**

An early Iden Pottery glazed small vase, with a green lancleate pattern with red dots and printed marks to base.

This was the first printed mark and was used from c1959 until c1965.

1959-62   3.75in (9.5cm) high

£15-25   **AGR**

An Iden Pottery wax-resist technique glazed vase, with printed marks to base.

This printed mark was used from 1965-78.

1965-70   4in (10cm) high

£15-25   **AGR**

An Iden Pottery speckled unglazed brown and white glazed dropper bottle, marked "IDEN POTTERY" and "Hand Made Sussex England".

6.25in (16cm) high

£15-25   **GC**

An Iden Pottery wax-resist plate, with capital letter "IDEN POTTERY RYE SUSSEX" mark with triangular logo.

c1973   8in (20.5cm) diam

£30-40   **AGR**

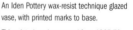

CERAMICS

COLLECTORS' NOTES

■ Founded in 1953 in Almacera near Valencia, Spain, by three brothers, Lladró has made over 4,000 designs since its inception. Over 1,200 are still available, with figurines being retired annually. The Nao company was established in 1968 as part of the Lladró group.

■ Look on the base for marks, as fakes are known. Pieces from the 1950s are rare and usually have incised marks. Standardized impressed and incised marks were used from c1960. From 1971 the familiar blue stamp was used, but lacked the accent over the 'o' until 1974, when the version still used today was introduced.

■ Pastel colours are typical, usually in a high gloss glaze. A matte glaze is scarcer and often fetches higher prices. A third finish, similar to the earthy

tones of stoneware, is known as 'Gres', and is often used for large pieces.

■ Early pre-production pieces have a plain creamy finish and are sought after and valuable, as are early pieces from the 1950s-70s. Limited editions, popular designs that have been retired, or that were only produced for a short period of time, usually fetch higher values due to their comparative rarity.

■ Also look for large or complex mouldings but always examine protruding parts carefully for damage or repair, as this reduces value considerably.

■ Consider the facial expression, which should be full of character and individuality, something Lladró is known for. Lladró never use black to mark out eyes, brows and lids, a fact that can help identify fakes.

A Lladró 'After School' figure, no.5705, designed by Salvador Debón.

1990-93   10in (25.5cm) high

£80-120   **AAC**

A Lladró 'Dreamer' figure, no.5008, designed by Francisco Catalá.

1978-99   10in (25.5cm) high

£70-100   **AAC**

A Lladró Nao 'Girl with Poodle, Hands Behind Her' figure.

9.25in (23.5cm) high

£40-60   **AAC**

A Lladró 'Girl with Hat in Front' figure.

9in (23cm) high

£30-50   **AAC**

A Lladró Nao 'Girl Running with Puppy' figure, no.1027.

1987-Current   6.25in (16cm) high

£30-50   **AAC**

A Lladró 'Spring is Here' figure, no.5223.

1984-Current   6.75in (17cm) high

£60-80   **AAC**

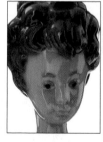

A Lladró 'Garden Classic' figure, no.7617, an 'event' figure, designed by Juan Huerta.

1991   9in (22cm) high

£120-180   **AAC**

A Lladró Nao 'Girl with Violin' figure, no.1034.

1987-Current   7.5in (19cm) high

£50-70   **AAC**

A Lladró Nao 'Girl with Cello' figure, no.1035.

1987-Current   7.5in (19cm) high

£40-60   **AAC**

A Lladró 'Girl with Turkey' figure, no.4569, designed by Fulgencio García.

1969-81   5.5in (14cm) high

£80-120   **AAC**

A Lladró 'Boy with Pails' figure, no.4811, designed by Salvador Furió.

1972-88   8.5in (21cm) high

£70-100   **AAC**

A Lladró 'Winter' boy and dog figure, no.5220, designed by Juan Huerta.

1984-2001 8.5in (21cm) high

£70-100   **AAC**

A Lladró 'Bird Watcher' figure, no.4730, designed by Vicente Martínez.

1970-85   6.5in (16cm) long

£120-180   **AAC**

A Lladró 'Puppy Love' figure, no.1127, designed by Vicente Martínez.

1971-96   10.5in (26cm) high

£150-250   **AAC**

A Lladró 'Good Night' figure, no.5449, designed by Juan Huerta.

1987-91   8.5in (21cm) high

£70-100   **AAC**

A Lladró 'Children at Play' figure, no.5304, designed by Regino Torrijos.

1985-90 11.25in (28.5cm) high

£150-250   **AAC**

CERAMICS

A Lladró 'Aranjuez Little Lady' figure, no.4879, designed by Vicente Martínez.

1974-96   12.5in (32cm) high

£120-180   **AAC**

A Lladró 'Evita' figure, no. 5212, designed by José Puche.

1984-98   7.25in (18cm) high

£70-100   **AAC**

A Lladró 'Trying on a Straw-Hat' figure, no.5011, designed by Francisco Catalá.

1978-98   10.5in (26cm) high

£70-100   **AAC**

A Lladró 'Ingenue' figure, no.5487, designed by José Puche.

1988-91   8in (20cm) high

£40-60   **AAC**

A Lladró 'Quixote Standing Up' figure, no.4854, with matte finish, designed by Salvador Furió.

Popular Spanish character, Don Quixote was produced in a number of different poses with different values. This figurine displays the sought-after elongation typical of Lladró designs.

A Lladró 'Buenas Noches' (Good Night) figure, no.5449, designed by Juan Huerta.

1987-91   8.5in (21cm) high

£120-180   **AAC**

1973-91   12in (30cm) high

£70-100   **AAC**

A Lladró 'Shepherdess with Rooster' figure, no.4677, designed by Juan Huerta.

Look for the matte version, also retired in 1991, as it can be worth half as much again.

1969-91 7.75in (19.5cm) high

£30-50   **AAC**

A Lladró 'Countryman' figure, no.4664, designed by Salvador Furió.

1969-79   11.75in (30cm) high

£120-180   **AAC**

A Lladró 'Japanese Girl Decorating' figure, no.4840, designed by Vicente Martínez.

1973-97   7.5in (19cm) high

£50-70   **AAC**

A Lladró 'Eskimo Playing With Bear' figure, no.1195, with matte finish, designed by Juan Huerta.

1972-91   *4.75in (12cm) high*

£40-60   **AAC**

A Lladró 'Pekinese Sitting' figure, no.4641, designed by Salvador Furió.

1969-85   *6in (15cm) high*

£100-150   **AAC**

A Lladró 'It Wasn't Me!' figure, no.7672G, Collector's Society piece, designed by Antonio Ramos.

1998   *4in (10cm) high*

£120-180   **AAC**

A CLOSER LOOK AT A LLADRÓ FIGURINE

A Lladró 'Kitty Confrontation' figure, no.1442, designed by Juan Huerta.

1983-91   *3.5in (9cm) wide*

£80-120   **AAC**

This figure was designed by Juan Huerta, one of Lladró's most celebrated sculptors.

He is known for his children and animals that incorporate a 'story' into the design.

The series was only produced between 1978 and 1981, making it comparatively scarce today.

This was part of the 'Painful Animals' series of six wounded animal figurines – collectors like to collect an entire series.

A Lladró 'Koala Love' figure, no.5461G, designed by Antonio Ramos.

1988-93   *8.5in (21cm) high*

£100-150   **AAC**

A Lladró 'Painful Kangaroo' figure, no.5023, designed by Juan Huerta.

1978-81   *7in (18cm) high*

£220-280   **AAC**

A Lladró 'Swan with Wings Spread' figure, no.5231, designed by Francisco Catalá.

1984-91   *7.5in (19cm) high*

£70-100   **AAC**

FIND OUT MORE...

Collecting Lladró: Identification & Price Guide, by Peggy Whiteneck, published by Krause, 2003.

Lladró Authorised Reference Guide, by Lladró, published by Lladró US Inc, 2000.

CERAMICS

COLLECTORS' NOTES

■ What is now known as the Lomonosov Porcelain Factory was founded in St Petersburg in 1744, initially to produce porcelain for the Russian royal household. During the reign of Catherine The Great it was known as The Imperial Porcelain Factory, becoming the State Porcelain Works after the Revolution in 1917. Later it was renamed Lomonosov after the founder of the Russian Academy of Science.

■ Figurines produced in the late 20th century are becoming more desirable to collectors and prices are rising. A large variety of animals were produced with bears, closely tied in with Russian folklore and legend, being particularly favoured. All are hand-painted with smooth, glossy glazed finishes. Sizes range from very small to very large examples, often in dramatic poses.

■ Often now known as the 'Sevrès of Russia', the factory is still producing today. Look closely at the mark on the base as this can help with dating. Most desirable are earlier figurines. Green, black or blue stamped marks generally date from the 1930s-1960s.

■ However, most collectors will find printed marks in red, dating from the late 1960s onwards. Examples marked "MADE IN USSR" are sought-after, dating from before the 1980s when Russia went into turmoil as Communism was over thrown. Later examples from after the late 1980s onwards are marked "MADE IN RUSSIA". Beware of "Russia" marks that have been altered to look like more valuable, earlier "USSR" marks.

A 1950s Lomonosov she-bear figure, with "Made in the USSR" mark, no longer in production.

6.25in (16cm) high

£70-90   **DSC**

A Lomonosov inkwell, in the form of two bear cubs playing, with "Made in the USSR" stamp, lacks liner under the lid, out of production.

5in (13cm) high

£80-100   **DSC**

A 1950s Lomonosov bear cub figure, with "Made in the USSR" stamp.

Earlier pieces were more 'bumpy' than later smoother examples.

5in (12.5cm) high

£15-20   **DSC**

A 1970s Lomonosov bear cub figure, with "Made in the USSR" stamp.

5.75in (14.5cm) high

£15-20   **DSC**

A 1950s Lomonosov lion and hare figure, with "Made in the USSR" stamp.

The theme of this figurine is taken from a popular Russian folk tale. It is no longer produced.

5in (13cm) high

£80-100   **DSC**

A Lomonosov large 'Misha' mascot figure, with "Made in the USSR" stamp.

Misha was the official mascot of the 1980s Olympic Games, held in Moscow.

4.25in (11cm) high

£40-50   **DSC**

A 1970s Lomonosov seated lion cub figure, with "Made in the USSR" stamp.

4in (10cm) high

£25-30   **DSC**

CERAMICS

A 1970s Lomonosov reclining lion cub figure, with "Made in the USSR" stamp.

5in (13cm) wide

£25-30   DSC

A 1960s Lomonosov crouching snow lynx figure, with "Made in the USSR" stamp.

5in (13cm) long

£25-30   DSC

A 1970s Lomonosov seated fox figure, with "Made in the USSR" stamp.

4.25in (11cm) high

£25-30   DSC

A 1960s/70s Lomonosov Afgan hound figure, with "Made in the USSR" stamp.

6in (15.5cm) high

£30-35   DSC

A late 1960s Lomonosov small wren figure, with "Made in the USSR" stamp.

2.25in (6cm) long

£18-22   DSC

A 1990s Lomonosov seated hedgehog figure, with "Made in Russia" stamp.

3in (7.5cm) high

£10-15   DSC

A late 1980s Lomonosov small seated grey rabbit figure, with "Made in the USSR" sticker.

£10-15   DSC

A late 1960s Lomonosov seated rabbit figure, with "Made in USSR" stamp.

2.25in (6cm) long

£15-20   DSC

A late 1960s Lomonosov badge figure, with "Made in the USSR" stamp.

4.75in (12cm) long

£15-20   DSC

FIND OUT MORE...

250 Years of Lomonosov Porcelain Manufacture at St Petersburg 1744-1994, by Galina Agarkova & Nataliya Petrova, published Palgrave Macmillan, 2002.

CERAMICS

COLLECTORS' NOTES

■ W.R. Midwinter was founded in 1910, moving to Burslem, Staffordshire in 1914. Art Deco style tableware such as tea sets dominated production until WWII saw the closure of much of the factory.

■ Midwinter's turning point came in the late 1940s, when the factory began to modernise. By 1950, Roy Midwinter had risen through the company to become Sales and Design Director and he encouraged new, young designer Jessie Tait, who had joined in 1946, to develop her designs.

■ Modern patterns began to replace the stylized floral designs dominant at the time, but traditional shapes were still used. Roy Midwinter visited the US in 1952, and saw the innovative modern designs by potters such as Raymond Loewy and Russell Wright and was inspired to move the company along these lines.

■ The result was the 'Stylecraft' shape and range, launched in 1953, with a variety of modern patterns

designed by Tait. Some were hand-painted. This was followed by the 'Fashion' range in 1955, which saw even more modern and clean-lined shapes being introduced. The ranges were targeted at, and became popular with, young homemakers.

■ Look for patterns that sum up the style and feeling of the day as these are usually the most popular. Period textiles were often an inspiration. Abstract patterns and highly stylized floral, fruiting or foliate designs are typical, usually executed in bright colours. More traditional floral designs tend to be less sought-after.

■ Characteristic pieces that combine a typically modern shape with a modern pattern are ideal. Tea cups and saucers and plates are common and worth less than items such as vases, teapots and coffee pots, which are harder to find, and complex items such as cake stands. Look out for designs by notable designers Terence Conran and Hugh Casson, as these are also popular.

A 1950s Midwinter Pottery Stylecraft tea set for six, designed by Jessie Tait, decorated with roses.

£50-70   **GOR**

A Midwinter Pottery Fashion shape 'Cannes' pattern coffee set, designed by Hugh Casson.
1960   *8in (20cm) high*
£280-320   **GGRT**

A 1960s Midwinter Pottery Fashion shape 'Homespun' pattern coffee set, designed by Jessie Tait.

7.5in (19cm) high

£220-280   **GGRT**

A Midwinter Pottery Fashion shape 'Whispering Grass' pattern cup and saucer, designed by Jessie Tait.

1960   *saucer 6.25in (16cm) diam*
£45-55   **GGRT**

A Midwinter Pottery Fashion shape 'Zambesi' early morning teapot.
This is both a desirable shape and pattern.
c1956   *5in (13cm) high*
£120-180   **AGR**

A Midwinter Pottery Fashion shape 'Whispering Grass' pattern coffee pot, designed by Jessie Tait.
1960   *7.5in (19cm) high*
£100-150   **GGRT**

A Midwinter Pottery Fashion shape 'Graphic' pattern trio, designed by Jessie Tait.

1964 (17.5cm) diam
£15-25   **GGRT**

A Midwinter Pottery 'Mosaic' pattern bowl, designed by Jessie Tait.

1960   4in (10cm) high

£100-150   **GGRT**

A Midwinter Pottery 'Mosaic' pattern cake stand, designed by Jessie Tait.

1960   3.75in (24cm) wide

£100-150   **GGRT**

A Midwinter Pottery 'Mosaic' pattern hors d'oeuvres dish, designed by Jessie Tait.

1960   6.75in (17.5cm) wide

£60-80   **GGRT**

A Midwinter Pottery 'Mosaic' pattern celery vase, designed by Jessie Tait.

Unlike many, this pattern is textured, with impressed lines created by the mould. The decoration is sponged on, so can vary in depth of colour and placement.

1960   6.75in (17cm) high

£320-380   **GGRT**

A Midwinter Pottery 'Mosaic' pattern Long Tom buffet tray, designed by Jessie Tait.

1960   22.25in (56.5cm) long

£220-280   **GGRT**

A Midwinter Pottery Fashion shape 'Chequers' plate, designed by Terence Conran.

1957   8.75in (22cm) diam

£60-80   **GGRT**

A Midwinter Pottery 'Flower Mist' pattern plate, designed by Jessie Tait.

This were made for the American market with a speckled background, which was not very popular in England. The pattern reflects contemporary textile designs.

1956   9.75in (25cm) diam

£70-100   **GGRT**

A Midwinter Fashion shape 'Rose' plate.

6in (15.5cm) wide

£5-8   **GROB**

CERAMICS

A Midwinter Pottery Stylecraft Modern Shape plate, with printed hatched blue pattern.

7.5in (19cm) wide

£10-15   **GROB**

A Midwinter Pottery royal blue Fashion shape sauce boat.

4.5in (11.5cm) high

£15-18   **GROB**

A CLOSER LOOK AT A MIDWINTER VASE

Vases are more scarce and sought-after than other shapes such as plates or cups and saucers.

Jessie Tait had learned tube-lining in 1945 when she worked as a decorator under Charlotte Rhead at H.J. Wood in Burslem. Rhead is famous for her tube-lined designs.

The pattern is not printed like 'Zambesi', but is raised to the touch – black slip has been trailed onto the white body in a process known as 'tube-lining'.

As well as the pattern, Tait unusually also designed the shape. In 1956 she designed ten vase and flask shapes, the only ones she designed for Midwinter.

A Midwinter Pottery 'Tonga' vase, designed by Jessie Tait, covered in tube-lined black lines, printed mark.

c1956   7in (17.5cm) high

£220-280   **WW**

A late 1950s Midwinter Pottery 'Stubble' pattern vase, designed by Jessie Tait.

9in (23cm) high

£250-350   **PC**

A late 1950s Midwinter Pottery 'Bands and Dots' pattern small vase, designed by Jessie Tait.

6.75in (17.5cm) high

£320-380   **GGRT**

A pair of late 1950s Midwinter Pottery 'Bands and Dots' pattern tube-lined studio vases, designed by Jessie Tait.

£400-600   **PC**

A late 1950s Midwinter Pottery 'Banded' pattern carafe, designed by Jessie Tait.

11.25in (28.5cm) high

£300-500   **PC**

A Midwinter figure, 'Madonna', with stamped marks.

10.75in (27cm) high

£70-100   **WW**

COLLECTORS' NOTES

■ Myott, Son & Co. Ltd was founded by Ashley Myott in 1898 in Staffordshire, expanding in the late 1920s to form the 'Alexander Potteries'. At this time, they also expanded their traditional tableware range to include hand-painted decorative wares in the new Art Deco style. It is this range that interests collectors most.

■ Decorators followed a pattern guide but as each is hand-painted, differences do occur meaning each piece is effectively unique. Red paint is very rare, with 'autumnal' oranges and browns being more common, along with greens and blues. Decorators did not sign or date their work.

■ A gold stamped mark was used 1930-42, and this Art Deco period is the most desirable one. The printed number is the pattern number. Impressed marks relate to a part of the production process.

■ Some pieces are marked 'B.A.G. Co. Ltd' indicating that they were made for British American Glass for export. 'BAG' pieces are often more finely painted and there may have been exclusive BAG patterns.

■ A fire at the Myott factory in 1949 destroyed all records and pattern books making it hard for collectors to find out more. This may explain why interest in and values for Myott have not risen as much as for its contemporary Clarice Cliff. However, this is changing rapidly.

■ Shape and pattern are the main indicators to value. Beaky jugs (with long beak-like spouts) are sought after, often fetching £2,000-3,500. 'Wedge' and 'Cone' or 'Owl' vases are also prized and can be worth £1,000-1,500 each. Condition is important – brown and orange paints flake easier than other colours and reduces value considerably on common pieces.

A Myott hand-painted medium 'Pinchtop' jug, pattern no.8974.

The 'Pinchtop' is also known as 'Persian'. This is an unusual colourway – very light blue is a rare shade.

7.25in (18.5cm) high

£80-100   NAI

£180-250   NAI

A Myott hand-painted large 'Pinchtop' jug, pattern no.8678.

These jugs were also available in sets of three. It is very rare to find a pattern that combines floral and geometric decoration.

8in (20cm) high

A Myott hand-painted large 'Pinchtop' jug, pattern no.H8301.

This common pattern was copied by Wade Heath.

8in (20cm) high

£30-50   NAI

A Myott hand-painted 'Balloon Tree' pattern small 'Pinchtop' jug, pattern no.1143FO.

£80-120   NAI

A Myott hand-painted small 'Pinchtop' jug, pattern no.H8319.

£40-60   NAI

A Myott hand-painted large 'Pinchtop' jug, pattern no.H8339.

8in (20cm) high

£70-100   NAI

A Myott hand-painted large 'Pinchtop' jug, pattern no.2682F.

8in (20cm) high

£80-120   NAI

CERAMICS

A Myott hand-painted large 'Squareneck' jug, pattern no.860.

Jugs were available in three different sizes, from small to large. Small sizes are usually worth around 30-40% less than large.

8.75in (22.5cm) high

£80-100   NAI

A Myott hand-painted 'Squareneck' jug, pattern no.8951, decorated with coloured chrysanthemums.

8.5in (21.5cm) high

£200-300   NAI

A Myott hand-painted small 'Squareneck' jug, pattern no.H8696.

7.5in (19cm) high

£80-120   NAI

A Myott hand-painted medium 'Squareneck' jug, pattern no.8697.

8.75in (22cm) high

£80-120   NAI

A Myott hand-painted medium 'Squareneck' jug, pattern no.8695.

8.25in (21cm) high

£200-300   NAI

A Myott hand-painted medium 'Squareneck' jug, un-numbered pattern decorated with sunrays.

8.25in (21cm) high

£120-200   NAI

A Myott hand-painted medium 'Squareneck' jug, pattern no.8940.

It is rare to find this pattern on a Squareneck jug, it is more commonly found on a castle vase.

8.25in (21cm) high

£200-300   NAI

A CLOSER LOOK AT A MYOTT JUG

The pattern uses the shape of the jug well, and it is in excellent condition with no flaking or damage.

This pattern is also found with a pink dress, which is rarer and can be worth up to £250-300.

This is one of the few known official pattern names, as it is printed on the base, with many others having been made up by collectors.

As most users are right-handed, the main decoration is on the side with the handle on the right. The decoration in the back is less complex.

A Myott hand-painted 'Sweet Seventeen' pattern medium 'Squareneck' jug, pattern no.8971 decorated with a woman wearing a green dress.

8.25in (21cm) high

£200-250   NAI

A Myott hand-painted 'Danté' jug, pattern no.9814.

9in (22.5cm) high

£120-180　　　**NAI**

A Myott hand-painted large 'Danté' jug, pattern no.BG25, decorated with berries and leaves.

9in (22.5cm) high

£80-120　　　**NAI**

A Myott hand-painted small 'Trumpet' jug, pattern no.P9638.

£80-120　　　**NAI**

A Myott hand-painted medium 'Trumpet' jug, pattern no.P9637, Reg'd design mark 779152 for late 1932.

7.75in (19.5cm) high

£120-150　　　**NAI**

A Myott hand-painted 'Scroll' jug, un-numbered, with "B.A.G." and Myott markings.

£300-500　　　**NAI**

A Myott hand-painted 'Classic' jug, pattern no.8692.

7.75in (19.5cm) high

£100-150　　　**NAI**

A Myott hand-painted large 'Conical' jug, pattern no.8496, with embossed decoration of blue chrysanthemums.

8in (20cm) high

£120-180　　　**NAI**

A Myott hand-painted 'Bowtie' jug, pattern 9767.

This is a common pattern, the high value is due to the lack of flakes commonly found on red and brown paintwork.

8.75in (22cm) high

£180-220　　　**NAI**

A Myott hand-painted 'Bowtie' jug, pattern no.9747.

8.75in (22cm) high

£280-320　　　**NAI**

CERAMICS

A Myott hand-painted 'Fan' vase, pattern no.6888.

8.25in (21cm) high

£100-150 NAI

A Myott hand-painted 'Fan' vase, pattern no.8599.

8.25in (21cm) high

£300-350 NAI

A Myott hand-painted 'Fan' vase, pattern no.8517.

Originally produced for Christmas 1933, this is one of Myott's most common patterns.

8.25in (21cm) high

£200-250 NAI

A rare Myott hand-painted 'Moderne' vase.

This shape is also known as Pyramid or Finger.

8.75in (22cm) high

£300-400 NAI

A rare Myott hand-painted 'Moderne' vase, pattern no.8940.

This is a very rare pattern on this shape.

8.25in (21cm) high

£500-800 NAI

A Myott hand-painted 'Castle' vase, pattern no.8940.

8.75in (22cm) high

£300-400 NAI

A rare Myott hand-painted 'Square' vase, pattern no.9143, with frog.

7in (18cm) high

£250-350 NAI

A Myott hand-painted 'Square' vase, scales pattern, not numbered.

7in (18cm) high

£150-250 NAI

A Myott hand-painted 'Bowtie' vase, pattern no.9761, marked with Reg'd design mark 789318 for 1934.

8.5in (21.5cm) high

£250-350 NAI

A Myott hand-painted 'Diamond' vase, pattern no.8515, with frog.

6in (15.5cm) high

£100-150   **NAI**

A Myott hand-painted 'Overflow' vase, pattern no.P9652, marked with Reg'd design no.779153 for late 1932.

6.75in (17cm) high

£300-350   **NAI**

A CLOSER LOOK AT A MYOTT VASE

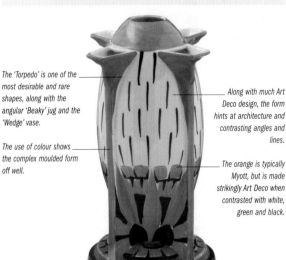

The 'Torpedo' is one of the most desirable and rare shapes, along with the angular 'Beaky' jug and the 'Wedge' vase.

The use of colour shows the complex moulded form off well.

Along with much Art Deco design, the form hints at architecture and contrasting angles and lines.

The orange is typically Myott, but is made strikingly Art Deco when contrasted with white, green and black.

A Myott hand-painted 'Torpedo' vase, pattern no.8981.

8.75in (22cm) high

£700-1,000   **NAI**

A Myott hand-painted 'Fluted' vase, pattern no.HW93 painted with flowers and brown sponged decoration, with flared lip.

8.75in (22.5cm) high

£80-120   **NAI**

A Myott hand-painted 'Plain' vase, pattern no.P9764.

7.25in (18.5cm) high

£80-100   **NAI**

A Myott hand-painted 'Top Hat' vase, pattern no.P9566, with frog, marked "B.A.G. Co. Ltd" and "CP" painters monogram, lacks Myott mark.

If the frog is missing, the price is reduced by £30-50.

8.5in (21.5cm) high

£180-220   **NAI**

A rare Myott hand-painted 'Onion' or 'Bulbous' vase, pattern no.HW94, with slight flared body, and green sponged decoration.

8.5in (21.5cm) high

£120-180   **NAI**

A Myott hand-painted large bowl, pattern no.H2086.

9in (23cm) diam

£50-70   **NAI**

A Myott hand-painted medium bowl, pattern no.P9532.

8in (20.5cm) diam

£40-60   **NAI**

A Myott hand-painted medium bowl, pattern no.8072.

8in (20.5cm) diam

£40-60   **NAI**

A Myott hand-painted small bowl, pattern no.P9531, with rare decoration of oranges.

7in (18cm) diam

£30-50   **NAI**

A Myott hand-painted trug, pattern no.P9602.

13.5in (34cm) wide

£280-320   **NAI**

A rare Myott chevron dish/fruit bowl, with rounded feet.

12in (30.5cm) high

£80-120   **NAI**

A Myott hand-painted beaker, pattern no.9375.

4.5in (11.5cm) high

£30-50   **NAI**

A Myott hand-painted beaker, pattern no.H8286.

4.5in (10.5cm) high

£30-40   **NAI**

A Myott hand-painted powder box.

5in (13cm) diam

£30-50   **NAI**

FIND OUT MORE...

The Mystery of Myott *by Anne Myott & Philip Pollitt, privately published, 2003.*

www.myottcollectorsclub.co.uk

COLLECTORS' NOTES

■ Carter & Co. Pottery of Poole began producing domestic ware in 1921, through their subsidiary company, Carter, Stabler & Adams.

■ Truda Adams was a key designer. Her pieces were typically hand-painted with geometric or floral designs on pale backgrounds. Impressed shape numbers and painted letters for the pattern name are often found. Her stylised geometric pieces, large examples and items with animals are desirable.

■ After WWII, Alfred Burgess Read became chief designer. He worked with painter Ruth Pavely and thrower Guy Sydenham to create hand-thrown and decorated pieces, which are effectively unique.

■ The Swedish-inspired 1950s Contemporary range, with bold stripes and wavy lines, is very desirable today.

A Poole Pottery hand-thrown 'LE' pattern vase, decorated by Nicola Massarella, the unusual elaborate design with grey birds.

6.5in (16.5cm) high

£50-80   **C**

A 1930s Poole Pottery hand-thrown 'AT Abstract Deco' pattern vase.

4in (10cm) high

£120-180   **C**

A 1930s Poole Pottery hand-thrown 'Leo The Lion' pattern pot, decorated by Myrtle Bond, shape 986.

4in (10cm) high

£50-£80   **C**

A Poole Pottery hand-thrown 'YE Abstract Yellow' pattern vase, shape 443, with a red body.

7in (18cm) high

£180-£220   **C**

A Poole Pottery hand-thrown 'TY' pattern vase, shape 401, with a red body and two handles.

4.5in (11.5cm) high

£180-220   **C**

A Poole Pottery hand-thrown 'PH' grey and black pattern vase, shape 199.

6in (15cm) high

£200-300   **C**

A Poole Pottery hand-thrown 'CS' pattern step-handled vase, shape 995, painted by Anne Hatchard from a design by Truda Carter, red earthenware body.

Geometrically stylised Art Deco floral or foliate designs on unusual shapes tend to fetch a premium amongst collectors.

1928-34   9in (23cm) high

£800-1,200   **C**

CERAMICS

A Poole Pottery 'Persian Deer' pattern plate, painted by Betty Gooby.

c1950s   *10in (25.5cm) diam*

£100-150   **C**

A Poole Pottery 'BN' pattern plate, shape 413, painted by Hilda Trim.

c1930s   *8in (20cm) diam*

£30-50   **C**

A Poole Pottery hand-thrown 'AQ Abstract Floral' pattern bowl, painted by Anne Hatchard.

13.5in (34.5cm) diam

£200-250   **C**

A Poole Pottery hand-thrown 'RH' abstract floral pattern plate, on a red body.

9in (23cm) diam

£80-120   **C**

A 1930s Poole Pottery 'UG' pink floral pattern vase, shape 335, decorated by Marian Heath.

6in (15cm) high

£200-300   **C**

A 1930s Poole Pottery hand-thrown 'AT Abstract Deco' jug.

4in (10cm) high

£120-180   **C**

A Poole Pottery perfume bottle, with original label for W. H. Smiths, The Square, Bournemouth.

£20-30   **C**

A 1930s Poole Pottery small biscuit barrel, shape 926, with a matching lid, sprayed in pastel yellow.

£30-50   **C**

A single 1930s Poole Pottery 'Elephant' bookend, No. 813, designed by Harold Brownsword, finished in a pale grey glaze.

£120-180   **C**

A Poole Pottery 'PRP' pattern plate, in the 'Bracken' colourway.

c1953-54   13in (33cm) diam

£180-220   NPC

A Poole Pottery 'Freeform' low bowl, shape 676, painted by Gwen Haskins, in the 'PRP' pattern.

c1953-54

£80-120   C

A Poole Pottery FF plate, painted by Gwen Haskins in 'PLT' pattern.

c1959-67   13in (33cm) diam

£180-220   NPC

A Poole Pottery cucumber dish, painted in the 'Contemporary' TNC design, designed by Alfred Read.

16in (40.5cm) wide

£120-180   C

A Poole Pottery 'PF' pattern dish, shape 338.

The long, slim form with its upwardly curving side was made for display on narrow 1930s window sills.

17.25in (44cm) wide

£70-100   NPC

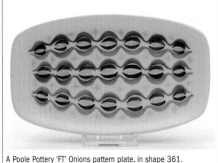

A Poole Pottery 'FT' Onions pattern plate, in shape 361.

c1957   7in (18cm) wide

£30-40   NPC

A 1950s Poole Pottery 'Slits' pattern shaped dish.

£30-40   NPC

A Poole Pottery 'YHP' design carafe, shape 690.

10in (25.5cm) high

£50-80   C

A Poole 'Contemporary' vase, painted by Iris Downtow in the 'PRP' pattern, designed by Alfred Read.

7in (18cm) high

£80-120   NPC

A CLOSER LOOK AT A POOLE POTTERY VASE

The modern shape and pattern are typical of Read's innovative 'Contemporary' range launched in 1953 that reflected the spirit of the 1950s.

At over 15in (38cm), this example is extremely large, making it more valuable.

The charcoal grey, Purbeck and lime colour combination is harder to find than others.

The carafe's clean-lined shape, numbered 698, had been used before and works well with the linear pattern.

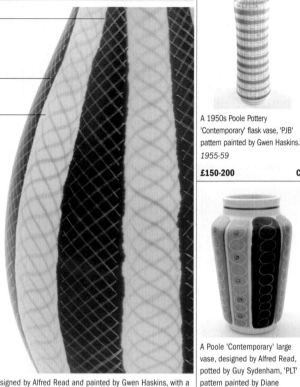

A Poole 'Contemporary' large carafe, designed by Alfred Read and painted by Gwen Haskins, with a pre-1959 back stamp.

c1954-59   15.25in (39cm) high

£350-400   **NPC**

A 1950s Poole Pottery 'Contemporary' flask vase, 'PJB' pattern painted by Gwen Haskins. 1955-59

£150-200   **C**

A Poole 'Contemporary' large vase, designed by Alfred Read, potted by Guy Sydenham, 'PLT' pattern painted by Diane Holloway.

c1953-54   8.75in (22cm) high

£200-300   **NPC**

A Poole Pottery 'Contemporary' large egg-cup shaped pot, shape 721, 'HOL' pattern painted by Gwen Haskins.

9in (23cm) high

£300-400   **C**

A Poole Pottery 'PF Butterfly' pattern vase, in shape 653 designed by Alfred Read, potted by Guy Sydenham and designed by Ruth Pavely in 1957.

c1958

£150-200   **NPC**

A Poole mushroom posy vase, in 'PRP' pattern with Bracken colourway, painted by Diane Holloway.

5in (13cm) diam

£20-30   **NPC**

A Poole 'FF' pattern 'Tea for Two' set.

Teapot 8in (20cm) wide

£80-120   **NPC**

COLLECTORS' NOTES

■ Robert Jefferson succeeded Alfred Read as chief designer at Poole Pottery in 1958. He developed kitchen wares and set up studios producing artistic pieces, employing painter Tony Morris in 1963.

■ The studio's handmade and decorated pieces formed the new 'Delphis Collection', launched in 1963, using bright natural or abstract designs. From 1966 the Delphis name was applied to mass-produced pieces, with bright glazes. These do not have the word 'Studio' in the backstamp and are less desirable.

■ In 1970, a similar range with a grainier texture, 'Aegean', was introduced. Both ranges were phased out in 1980 and are becoming popular with collectors as prices for 1930s and 1950s Poole soar. Early Studio pieces are still the most desirable.

A Poole Pottery Delphis charger, painted with a scorpion in black and purple, printed and painted marks.

Delphis is the Greek word for 'dolphin', and is the logo of the factory.

13.75in (35cm) diam

£180-220   **WW**

A Poole Pottery Delphis charger, shape number 5, by Cynthia Bennett, printed and painted marks.

13.75in (35cm) diam

£50-80   **WW**

A Poole Pottery Delphis deep dish, painted by Carol Cutler in an abstract red and dark blue design.

c1969-75   11in (28cm) diam

£50-80   **C**

A Poole Pottery Delphis plate, painted in an abstract floral design.

8in (20cm) diam

£30-40   **C**

A Poole Pottery Delphis plate, painted by Jean Millership, in an abstract circle and spoke design.

c1966-69   8in (20cm) diam

£70-100   **C**

A Poole Pottery Delphis plate, painted by Susan Allen in a starburst red and orange design.

8in (20cm) diam

£70-100   **C**

A Poole Pottery Delphis deep bowl, shape 57, painted in a multitude of colours.

11in (28cm) diam

£150-200   **C**

A Poole Pottery Delphis small pin tray, painted by Jean Millership in the abstract yellow and black design.

£30-40   **C**

CERAMICS

A Poole Pottery Delphis 'Abstract Floral' pattern hand-thrown vase, shape 85.

16in (40.5cm) high

£200-300 C

A Poole Pottery Delphis vase, shape number 85, by Loretta Leigh, printed and painted marks.

15.75in (40cm) high

£180-220 WW

A Poole Pottery Delphis cushion vase, shape 90, possibly by Shirley Campbell, painted in the abstract wheel design on a green background.

c1966-69

£120-180 C

A Poole Pottery Delphis cushion vase, shape 90, painted by Angela Wyburgh with a brown design on white ground with a magnolia back and a blue stamp.

c1968 *8in (20cm) high*

£150-200 C

A Poole Pottery Delphis bowl, shape 40, decorated by Janet Laird (1969-74) with an abstract petal design against a bold orange ground, with painted artist's monogram.

10.5in (27cm) wide

£180-220 GORL

A Poole Pottery Aegean wall plate, decorated by Diana Davis, with a full-rigged galleon on a turbulent sea, in russet, brown and yellow tones, impressed marks and painted "D.Davis".

12.5in (32cm) diam

£100-150 DN

A Poole Pottery Aegean wall plate, decorated with black outline of a tree, and splashes of bright orange, against a speckled ground, impressed "Poole England" and stamped "Aegean".

12.5in (32cm) diam

£100-150 DN

A Poole Pottery Aegean wall plate, a collaboration between Leslie Elsden and Jane Brewer, decorated with an owl perched on a tree stump, flanked by foliage and a sun, stamped mark with dolphin, and "Aegean by Leslie Elsden" and "design by J. Brewer".

c1973 *13.75in (35cm) diam*

£180-220 DN

A Poole Pottery Aegean 'Catapult' pattern vase, shape 85, in an unusual pale blue.

16in (40.5cm) high

£150-200 C

A CLOSER LOOK AT A POOLE DISH

This is a one-off, unique 'Studio' piece. It is thus earlier and rarer than other examples in standard production.

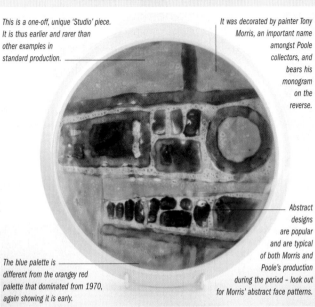

It was decorated by painter Tony Morris, an important name amongst Poole collectors, and bears his monogram on the reverse.

A limited edition Poole Pottery Medieval Calendar plate for July, designed by Tony Morris.

c1974　　13in (33cm) diam

£80-120　　　　**C**

Abstract designs are popular and are typical of both Morris and Poole's production during the period - look out for Morris' abstract face patterns.

The blue palette is different from the orangey red palette that dominated from 1970, again showing it is early.

A Poole Pottery Medieval Calendar plate for March, designed by Tony Morris and painted by S. M. Allen, from a limited edition of 1,000.

A Poole Studio dish, No. 47, with a decorated inner of turquoise and blue on a white ground, and with impressed Studio mark and Tony Morris monogram to back.

11in (28cm) diam

£2,000-2,500　　　　**C**

c1973　　13in (33cm) diam

£80-120　　　　**C**

A Poole Pottery plate, with unusual sgraffito design showing a racing yacht and three sailors on a stormy sea.

8in (20cm) diam

£50-80　　**C**

A Poole Pottery Atlantis Gourd pot, A52, by Jennie Haigh with deep carving and glazing to exterior.

The Atlantis range was introduced in 1972 and withdrawn in 1977. Guy Sydenham was part of the team that worked on its development.

4in (10cm) high

£200-300　　　　**C**

A Poole Pottery Ionian heavy charger, carved, glazed and finished by Jane Brewer, with a signature to reverse and "Cottage in Forest".

The Ionian range, developed by Julia Wills, was only produced during 1974 and 1975.

c1974　　17in (42cm) diam

£300-500　　　　**C**

A limited edition Poole Pottery Eclipse plate.

This limited edition was designed by Alan Clarke to commemorate the total eclipse of the sun in 1999 and uses Poole's famed 'Living Glaze' technique.

14in (35.5cm) diam

£80-120　　　　**C**

FIND OUT MORE...

Poole Pottery by Leslie Hayward and edited by Paul Atterbury, published by Richard Dennis Publications, 2002.

Collecting Poole Pottery by Robert Prescott Walker, published by Kevin Francis Publishing, 2001.

CERAMICS

A large Bernard Rooke vase, modelled with birds amongst foliage, incised "BR".

Bernard Rooke (b.1938) founded his pottery in South London in 1960. Using coils and blocks of clay, most pieces had a sculptural form. Vases and lampbases were common due to their functionality and popularity. In 1967, the pottery moved to larger premises in East Anglia where it continues to run today under the guidance of Rooke and his son. As well as his familiar designs, a feeling for natural motifs inspired by the surrounding landscape influenced designs.

12.25in (31cm) high

£120-180   **WW**

A Bernard Rooke lamp base, with abstract forms and applied abstract slabs, stamped "ROOKE".

8in (20.5cm) high

£50-70   **AGC**

A Bernard Rooke specimen vase, with numerous holes, in the form of leaves, in brown and green matte glazes, hand signed "B.R."

8in (20cm) high

£50-80   **GC**

A 1980s Bernard Rooke squat vase, with frogs and lily pad moulded and applied designs, hand inscribed to base "B.R."

6.25in (16cm) wide

£50-70   **GC**

A Bernard Rooke small vase, with moulded abstract patterns, top half glazed beige.

Earlier Rooke pieces are typified by a rougher feel and appearance to the clay and form.

c1968-1972   5.25in (13.5cm) high

£30-50   **GC**

A Bernard Rooke stoneware vase, impressed marks.

7in (17.5cm) high

£70-100   **WW**

A Bernard Rooke Studio ceramic biscuit barrel, with cane handle, inscribed "B.R." to base.

4.75in (12cm) high

£30-40   **GAZE**

A Bernard Rooke stoneware lampbase, covered in a blue glaze, impressed "ROOKE".

9in (23cm) high

£100-150   **WW**

A large Bernard Rooke lampbase, impressed "ROOKE".

13.5in (34cm) high

£60-90   **WW**

CERAMICS

COLLECTORS' NOTES

- Royal Copenhagen was founded in 1775 under the patronage of Queen Juliane Marie of Denmark. Frantz Henrich Müller devoted years to unravelling the secret of making hard paste porcelain, which was known to only a very few European factories at the time.

- 'Blue Fluted' – the first dinner service made by Royal Copenhagen – remains the most popular line today. The company was known primarily for well-decorated blue and white wares for most of its early history.

- From the 1950s, luminaries such as Henning Koppel helped to secure Royal Copenhagen's reputation for being at the forefront of the Scandinavian design movement, which influenced global ceramic design.

- The 'Fajence' range of tin-glazed earthenware is popular with collectors today, as are the human and animal figurines designed by Lotte Benter, Knud Kyhn and others.

A large Royal Copenhagen 'Baca' 'Fayence' vase, designed by Nils Thorsson.

7.5in (19cm) high

£40-60　　　**NPC**

A Royal Copenhagen 'Baca' 'Fayence' vase, designed by Nils Thorsson.

5in (12.5cm) high

£22-28　　　**NPC**

A Royal Copenhagen 'Baca' 'Fayence' square section vase, designed by Johanne Gerber, with stylized bird decoration.

9in (23cm) high

£50-80　　　**GAZE**

A Royal Copenhagen 'Fayence' vase.

11in (28cm) high

£40-60　　　**GAZE**

A Royal Copenhagen 'Fayence' vase, the hand-decorated design by Nils Thorsson, marked "870/3740".

6.25in (16cm) high

£40-60　　　**GAZE**

A Royal Copenhagen 'Fayence' vase, designed by Nils Thorsson, with birds and fishes.

7.25in (18.5cm) wide

£50-60　　　**FD**

A Royal Copenhagen 'Fayence' vase, designed by Johanne Gerber, marked "780" over "3181".

7.5in (19cm) high

£70-90   **FD**

A Royal Copenhagen 'Fayence' vase, designed by Kari Christensen, with "KC" cypher, marked "427" over "3114".

8.5in (21.5cm) high

£70-90   **FD**

A CLOSER LOOK AT A ROYAL COPENHAGEN LAMP BASE

Nils Thorsson (1898-1975) became interested in ceramics at an early age and was apprenticed to leading artist Christian Joachim in 1912.

'Fayence' (faience) is a type of earthenware which is tin-glazed to make it impervious to water. It was developed in France in the 16thC.

Lamp bases like this piece were made and sold in smaller numbers than vases, making this a relatively scarce example of Thorsson's work today.

The large size and shape of this lamp makes it desirable to collectors.

A large Royal Copenhagen 'Fayence' lamp base, designed by Nils Thorsson.

11.5in (29cm) high

£100-150   **FD**

A Royal Copenhagen Aluminia 'Fayence' vase, with "CK" backstamp.

11.5in (29cm) high

£70-100   **GAZE**

A Royal Copenhagen lamp base, designed by Ellen Malmer.

11.5in (29cm) high

£40-60   **FD**

A Royal Copenhagen 'Fayence' wall hanging salt pot, with wooden lid.

£8-12   **GAZE**

A CLOSER LOOK AT A ROYAL COPENHAGEN FIGURINE

Between 1911 and 1914 Lotte Benter designed a range of figures featuring girls in national or peasant dress, including 'Girl from Bornholm' also on this page.

Part of a series of nine, this porcelain group is very collectable thanks to its charm and patriotic subject matter.

Amager is a Danish island in the Øresund and Copenhagen lies partly on it.

The group displays the typically muted colours of Royal Copenhagen.

A Royal Copenhagen 'Girl From Bornholm' porcelain model, no.1323, designed by Lotte Benter.

c1988   8.5in (22cm) high

£150-200   **LOB**

A Royal Copenhagen 'Amager Girls' porcelain model, no.1316, designed by Lotte Benter.

6.75in (17cm) high

£250-350   **LOB**

A Royal Copenhagen 'Woman Knitting' porcelain model, no.1323, designed by Lotte Benter.

c1994   7in (18cm) high

£180-220   **LOB**

A Royal Copenhagen porcelain model of a girl with a doll, no.1938, designed by Ade Bonfils.

5in (13cm) high

£180-220   **LOB**

A Royal Copenhagen porcelain model of a girl with a calf, no.779.

c1975   6.75in (17cm) high

£150-200   **LOB**

A Royal Copenhagen porcelain dish with a mermaid, no.3231, designed by Hans H. Hansen.

c1965   6in (15cm) diam

£60-70   **LOB**

A Royal Copenhagen stoneware model of a bear, designed by Knud Kyhn.

3.5in (9cm) long

£30-40   **LOB**

A Royal Copenhagen stoneware model of a bear, designed by Knud Kyhn.

Kyhn (1880-1969) was a Danish sculptor and painter, well known for his interest in nature and animals. He produced a number of animal figures for Royal Copenhagen as well as Bing & Grøndahl.

4in (10cm) long

£30-40   **LOB**

A Royal Copenhagen porcelain model of a kingfisher, no.1769, designed by Peter Herold.

Herold (1879-1920) designed a number of avian figurines for Royal Copenhagen, which were produced between 1910 and 1924.

8.5in (11cm) high

£100-150   **LOB**

A Royal Copenhagen porcelain model of a sea lion, no.1441, designed by Th. Madsen.

c1980

£50-70   **LOB**

A Royal Copenhagen porcelain model of a polar bear walking, no.320, by Carl J. Bonnesen.

Carl Johan Bonnesen (1868-1933) was well known for his depictions of animals and primitive historical scenes in metal and ceramics. One of his designs stands on top of the Carlsberg brewery in Denmark.

7in (18cm) long

£60-70   **LOB**

A Royal Copenhagen porcelain model of a fawn, no.20183.

c1935   4in (10cm) long

£35-45   **LOB**

A Royal Copenhagen porcelain model of a cock, with its head up, no.1126, designed by Chr. Thomsen.

4.25in (11cm) high

£70-100   **LOB**

A Royal Copenhagen porcelain dish with a crab, no.3131, designed by Jorgen Balslov.

6.25in (16cm) diam

£70-100   **LOB**

A Royal Crown Derby 'Dappled Quail' paperweight, with gold stopper, designed by Louise Adams.

1999

£40-60   **PSA**

A Royal Crown Derby 'Puffin' paperweight, with gold stopper and box.

1996

£50-70   **PSA**

A Royal Crown Derby 'Bee Eater Bird' paperweight, with gold stopper and box.

£50-70   **PSA**

A Royal Crown Derby 'Rough Collie' paperweight, with gold stopper and box.

£80-120   **PSA**

A Royal Crown Derby 'Fort', from the Treasures of Childhood series, boxed.

£40-60   **PSA**

A Royal Crown Derby 'Train', from the Treasures of Childhood Series, boxed.

£50-70   **PSA**

A Royal Crown Derby porcelain model of an Egyptian cat, boxed.

1986   *8.5in (21.5cm) high*

£100-150   **CA**

A Royal Crown Derby porcelain model of an Siamese cat, boxed.

1986   *8.5in (21.5cm) high*

£120-180   **CA**

CERAMICS

COLLECTORS' NOTES

- Pottery has been produced in and around Rye since the Middle Ages. Names of notable potteries include Cadborough and Bellevue, both of which merged in 1890 to form what is now known as the Rye Pottery.

- Early 20th century styles were avant garde, following the fashionable Art Deco look of the day. After WWII, the pottery was taken over by brothers Walter (Wally) and Jack Cole who took this avant garde nature further with modern styles typical of the 1950s.

- They trained a number of apprentices, many of whom, like Dennis Townsend of Iden, left to set up their own potteries in the area. The potter David Sharp (1932-93) is one of the most notable names.

- Sharp worked for Rye from 1947 for six years, before undertaking his national service. After returning and finding Rye had become less studio-oriented, Sharp left to form his own company, 'Cinque Port Pottery', with

his friend George Gray in 1956.

- The business was a success, becoming 'Cinque Ports Pottery Ltd' in the early 1960s. In 1964, Gray left and set up in new premises at The Monastery, taking the name with him.

- Gray's business continued in the 1980s, primarily producing more commercial domestic ware. Sharp set up the David Sharp Pottery and, after a shaky start, gained fame with his hand-painted house name plaques, novelty animals and unique studio pieces. The pottery still operates today, selling new and old pieces.

- Look for patterns typical of the period, such as stripes, zigzags and 'atomic' motifs. 'Filament' and similar complex patterns also tend to be popular, as do the earlier studio pieces of the 1950s and 1960s. Collectors focus on the work of Sharp and pieces identified as being by him are desirable, so always examine marks.

A Rye Pottery bowl, of elliptical form, painted with black stripes, impressed mark.

8in (20cm) wide

£120-180   **WW**

A Rye Pottery bowl, of elliptical form with pink stripes, printed mark.

7.75in (19.5cm) wide

£180-220   **WW**

A late 1950s Rye Pottery flattened tapering pillow vase, thrown by David Sharp, with printed and impressed marks.

The impressed capital 'D' near the printed mark shows that Sharp was responsible for throwing this piece. This mark was first used in 1957, however Sharp left the pottery in 1956 meaning that this piece was thrown in 1956 and decorated in 1957.

1956-57

£40-60   **AGR**

7.5in (19cm) high

A Rye Pottery bowl, with printed marks.

9.25in (23.5cm) diam

£80-120   **CHS**

A 1950s Rye Pottery vase, with printed marks to base.

5.5in (14cm) high

£30-40   **CHS**

A Rye Pottery bulbous vase.

The style of the shape and decoration place this piece at around 1960.

c1960   5.5in (14cm) high

£50-80   **AGR**

A 1960s Rye Pottery 'Filament' pattern dish.

4.75in (12cm) diam

£15-25 **AGR**

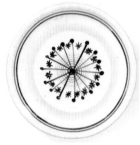

A Rye Pottery 'Galaxy' pattern bowl, impressed "J" for Jim Elliot, mark for 1956 on red clay.

c1956 9in (22.75cm) high

£80-120 **GGRT**

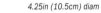

An early Rye Pottery 'Cigar' pattern pin dish, thrown by David Sharp, with impressed and printed marks to base.

This mark was used 1954-56.

A Rye Pottery butter dish, with stylized starburst design with a yellow border.

1957-59 3.25in (8.5cm) diam

£15-25 **AGR**

An early Rye Pottery butter dish, decorated with the early star design, and early stamped mark to base.

1949-52 3.25in (8cm) diam

£20-30 **AGR**

1954-56 4.25in (10.5cm) diam

£30-40 **AGR**

A Rye Pottery jug, with vertical green stripes.

4.5in (11.5cm) high

£30-40 **GROB**

Two Rye Pottery 'Mosaic' pattern tankards, printed marks.

4.5in (11.5cm) high

£40-60 each **CHS**

An unusual Rye Pottery robin on a circular base, marked on the base "RYE".

3.25in (8.5cm) high

£30-40 **GROB**

A Cinque Ports Pottery jug, with printed marks.

10in (25cm) high

£10-20　　　　　　　　**GAZE**

A Cinque Ports Pottery footed vase, finely painted by David Sharp, with green, blue and black bands and hatching.

1960-64　　　*4in (10cm) high*

£30-40　　　　　　　　**AGR**

A Cinque Ports Pottery small dropper bottle, painted by David Sharp.

1956-60　　　*4.25in (10.5cm) high*

£30-40　　　　　　　　**AGR**

A Cinque Ports Pottery, The Monastery waisted vase, with hand-painted red and black swirling decoration and printed mark to base.

3.75in (9.5cm) high

£15-20　　　　　　　　**AGR**

A Cinque Ports Pottery, The Monastery baluster vase, with cream ground and hand-painted green and brown foliate design.

10.5in (26.5cm) high

£30-40　　　　　　　　**GC**

A Cinque Ports Pottery, The Monastery vase, with white glaze with wax resist black and brown swirls.

This pattern has become increasingly hard to find due to attention from collectors.

8.5in (21.5cm) high

£30-50　　　　　　　　**GC**

A Cinque Ports Pottery, The Monastery baluster vase, with light brown glaze and incised but glazed swirling designs.

10.5in (26.5cm) high

£30-50　　　　　　　　**GC**

A David Sharp Pottery green/blue bowl, with stylized 'star burst' interior, and signed on the base by Sharp.

c1970

£20-30

2.25in (6cm) high

AGR

COLLECTORS' NOTES

- Two of the most important and dominant factories in Scandinavian ceramic design are Sweden's Gustavsberg and Finland's Arabia. Both followed the Scandinavian trend of employing talented designers. Gustavsberg was led by Wilhelm Kage and his successor Stig Lindberg, who introduced modern forms combined with bright, stylized geometric patterns. Arabia's key designer was Kaj Franck.

- Some of the smaller factories can provide a comparatively inexpensive entry route into the collecting field. Consider Saxbo and Upsala Ekeby, among others. Pieces were designed to be functional – kitchenware from the 1950s and '60s is readily available today, but does not usually fetch as much as more decorative wares such as vases or dishes.

- Clean-lined, modern forms are typical, and are often asymmetric free form, emphasising a handmade appearance. Decoration varies between muted designs in deep, strong colours and brightly coloured, joyful transfer-printed or hand-painted patterns. Nature was a key inspiration in terms of form, decoration and often colour.

- The Scandinavian look inspired other potteries such as Rye and Poole in England. It also contributed towards the growth of the global studio pottery movement during the late 20th century.

- Always look for the hallmarks of Scandinavian design and try to buy pieces by a factory's key designers, as these are most likely to appreciate in value.

A 1950s Rorstrand 'Rubus' range vase, designed by Gunnar Nylund.

Nylund (b.1904) was Art Director at Rorstrand from 1931-58.

9in (22.5cm) high

£30-40   GAZE

A small 1950s Rorstrand 'Rubus' range vase, designed by Gunnar Nylund.

3.25in (8.5cm) high

£15-25   GAZE

A 1960s Arabia vase, with striped and square decoration, with printed marks including "5-64".

7in (17.5cm) high

£40-50   GROB

An Upsala Ekeby vase, with sgraffito decoration.

10.5in (26.5cm) high

£10-15   GAZE

A 1960s Danish Conny Walther unglazed studio vase, impressed "CW" monogram to base.

6.5in (17cm) high

£150-200   RWA

A Rorstrand pottery bottle vase, designed by Carl Harry Stahlane, with incised factory marks and initials to the base.

13.5in (34cm) high

£180-220   ROS

A Gustavsberg yellow glazed asymmetric vase, designed by Stig Lindberg, model number 261, mark and label to base.

c1950   7in (18cm) high

£150-200   GAZE

A 1930s Danish Bode Willumsen studio vase, decorated in relief with a leaping stag and seated horse.

3.5in (9cm) high

£110-130   RWA

A 1950s/60s Danish Conny Walther squat vase, with matt and high-fired glaze decoration.

3.5in (9cm) high

£100-120 RWA

A Rorstrand green and black vase, designed by Irma Claesson, with painted marks and initials, crazed.

7in (18cm) high

£50-80 TCM

A Royal Copenhagen bottle vase, with a peacock design, printed and painted marks.

5.5in (14cm) high

£40-60 TCM

A 1950s/60s Finnish Kupittaan Savi blue ground studio vase, with green and black stylized vine decoration and brown spots in slip.

Kupittaan Savi was founded in 1712 and was the oldest pottery in Finland. Focusing on bricks and industrial products, production of domestic ware only began in 1915 and had trailed off by the 1930s. It continued, albeit on a smaller but successful scale, until the factory's demise in 1969.

9.25in (23.5cm) wide

£150-250 FD

A 1960s Danish Palshus vase, by Annelise and Per Linnermann-Schmidt, with incised design.

£80-100 RWA

A Danish Knabstrup square vase, designed by Erik Reiff, with leaf-pattern design.

c1965-77 9.75in (24.5cm) high

£80-120 RWA

A 1960s Danish Soholm hand-painted pottery vase, stamped "Handmade in Soholm Denmark".

8.5in (21.5cm) high

£12-18 GAZE

A 1960s Swedish Niitsjo stoneware cylindrical vase, probably designed by Thomas Stengus, painted "Niitsjo Sweden 7117" and stamped "Thomas Stengus".

£8-12 GAZE

A Norwegian Figgjo Flint 'Saga' pattern tapered vase, with flared rim and printed marks.

10.25in (26cm) high

£20-25 TCM

An Upsala Ekeby Keramic oval dish, with abstract geometric design, designed by Mari Simmulson, with impressed marks.

Estonian designer Simmulson (1911-?) worked for Uppsala Ekeby from 1949-72. The design here is very similar to those by Stig Lindberg for Gustavsberg, where Simmulson had worked from 1945-49.

11.5in (29cm) long

£70-100 **TCM**

A Stig Lindberg studio ceramic bowl, with artist's cypher and marked "Sweden P/46-3".

As well as having an abstract linear design typical of Lindberg's designs, the organically curving linear form, inspired by a leaf, is typical of Scandinavian design at the time. A similar example can be found in the Victoria & Albert Museum collection.

A Danish long dish, with an abstract design, printed marks.

12.5in (32cm) long

£50-70 **TCM**

c1950 9.5in (24cm) wide

£150-250 **FD**

A 1960s Upsala Ekeby studio ceramic shallow bowl, designed by Sven-Erik Skawonius, stamped "UE Sweden 9037 SES" to reverse.

8.5in (22cm) diam

£8-12 **GAZE**

A Rorstrand dish, designed by Sylvia Leuchovious, signed "W R WW SWEDEN" and "S-L 8-1" to reverse.

7.5in (19cm) diam

£20-30 **GAZE**

A Rorstrand hand-painted Sgrafo Modern plate, with printed marks.

5.5in (14cm) diam

£30-40 **TCM**

A 1950s Rorstrand 'Florita' square dish.

8.5in (22cm) wide

£10-12 **GROB**

A square dish by Stig Lindberg, depicting a maiden in a high tower, painted marks and designer's label.

6.25in (16cm) wide

£50-70 **TCM**

A Rorstrand Sgrafo Modern footed bowl, with moulded foot, wavy rim and impressed marks.

5.5in (14cm) wide

£70-100 **TCM**

CERAMICS

A Gustavsberg wall plaque of three figures on an elephant, designed by Lisa Larson, stamped "LISA L".

£50-80   **GAZE**

A 1960s Rorstrand wall plaque, designed by Olle Alberius, with incised marks.

Alberius (b.1926), designed for Rorstrand from 1963-71.

12.5in (32cm) wide

£180-220   **TCM**

A Nymølle 'Donna Elvira' large oval display plate, designed by Bjørn Wiinblad, printed signature to reverse.

1954

£45-55   **GAZE**

A Bing & Grøndhal snail wall plaque.

5.75in (14.5cm) diam

£22-28   **FD**

A Norwegian Figgjo Flint 'Saga' pattern silk screened plaque, marked "Saga norske design".

Note the similarity in style to Bjørn Wiinblad's designs. Flint makes more use of colour and symmetry.

6.25in (16cm) long

£8-12   **GROB**

A Rorstrand "Bayleaves" storage jar, with wooden lid.

3.5in (9cm) high

£8-12   **GROB**

A 1950s Ganiopta Swedish stylized bird dish, signed to the base and with red foil label.

13in (33cm) long

£35-45   **GAZE**

A Rorstrand lidded ovenware dish, with printed marks.

5.75in (14.5cm) wide

£20-25   **TCM**

An Arabia jug, designed by Kaj Franck, with a green stylized cat design.

4in (10.5cm) high

£20-30   **MHT**

FIND OUT MORE...

Scandinavian Ceramics & Glass in the Twentieth Century, *by Jennifer Opie, published by V&A Publications, 2001.*

Scandinavian Design, *by Charlotte & Peter Fiell, published by Taschen, 2002.*

COLLECTORS' NOTES

- The Shelley Pottery began life as Wileman & Co., when Joseph Ball Shelley went into partnership with Henry Wileman at the Foley China Works of Fenton in Staffordshire in 1827. The Shelley name was in use by 1910, but it was not until 1925 that the factory became known by that name.

- Their ceramics were executed in bone china or earthenware, with patterns being hand-painted or applied by lithographic transfer. Designers included the notable Frederick Rhead, Walter Slater and Eric Slater. Hilda Cowham, who joined in 1925, and Mabel Lucie Attwell, who joined in 1926, are known for their nursery ware.

- Shelley is very well known for its Art Deco tea wares. Look for an Art Deco shape, such as Vogue, Eve or Mode, combined with a geometric or Art Deco stylized floral or foliate pattern. Cups and saucers are a strong collecting area – over 50 patterns were produced in the Vogue and Mode shapes and over 200 for the Regent shape, so there is plenty to collect.

- The Shelley factory continued production until 1966 when it was taken over by Allied English Potteries, who themselves became part of the Doulton Group in 1971. Marks can help date pieces, with the word Foley last being used in marks c1916. Most marks are printed in green with the word Shelley inside a shield.

A Shelley Regent shape coffee set for six, including a coffee jug, sugar bowl and milk jug.

Although the shape was introduced in 1932 and continued until the 1960s, this service was manufactured for two years only, starting in 1935, and combines a good Art Deco shape and pattern.

1935-37   *pot 7.5in (19cm) high*

£250-350   **CA**

A Shelley Regent shape 'Brown Swirls' pattern tea set for six, including two large side plates, a slop bowl and sugar bowl.

c1936

      pot 8in (20cm) high

£250-350   **CA**

A Shelley Vogue shape part tea service for six, including a cake plate, printed factory mark, painted "11741".

1930-c1933

£1,500-2,000   **L&T**

A Shelley Princess shape cup and saucer, with stylised flowers in oranges and brown, marked "12227".

c1934

£70-90   **BAD**

A Shelley Vogue shape trio set, with green rings, marked "11959".

1930-c1933   *plate 6.75in (17cm) wide*

£200-300   **BEV**

A Shelley Mabel Lucie Attwell cup and saucer, with a copyright design.

Beware of the many fakes on the market. Designs that scratch off easily, weaker colours and date marks before 1926, when Attwell joined Shelley, indicate reproductions or fakes.

c1930   *saucer 5.5in (14cm) diam*

£150-200   **BEV**

A Shelley Dainty shape nut or sweet dish, decorated with roses and a gilt rim.

4.25in (11cm) wide

£25-35   **BAD**

CERAMICS

A Shelley Dainty shape rectangular dish, marked "Rd 272101".

5in (13cm) wide

£25-35 **BAD**

An unusual Shelley Ludlow shape hand-painted nut dish, with geometric design similar to 'Sunray'.

c1930 *4in (10cm) wide*

£35-45 **BAD**

A CLOSER LOOK AT A SHELLEY FIGURINE

The style of this figure is typical of Attwell, with its rounded face, pudgy body and bright, appealing colours.

These figures were produced for children as part of Mabel Lucie Attwell's range of nursery ware, which is popular with collectors today.

These figurines are rare – other charming characters can also be found

Like all her nursery ware, this piece is marked with Attwell's name, but beware of modern reproductions by considering marks, colours and quality.

A Shelley Nursery 'I's Shy' figure, designed by Mabel Lucie Attwell, model no.LA.9, printed mark and facsimile signature.

6in (15.5cm) high

£1,200-1,800 **WW**

A Shelley lustred bowl, designed by Walter Slater.

Walter Slater took over from Frederick Rhead as Art Director in 1905 and remained until 1937, contributing many designs.

c1930 *9.5in (24cm) diam*

£220-280 **BEV**

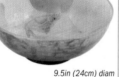

A Shelley Harmony ware waisted vase, with dripping bands of orange and green.

The Harmony ware range was introduced in 1932. Even though it was moulded, it was meant to give the impression of hand-thrown pieces. Drip and banded designs are typical.

c1932 *8.25in (21cm) high*

£100-150 **BEV**

A pair of 1930s Shelley Harmony ware vases, with streaked glaze effects in shades of green, grey, orange and yellow.

8in (20.5cm) high

£80-120 **GORL**

A pair of 1930s Shelley Harmony ware vases, of waisted form.

4.75in (12cm) high

£50-70 **GORW**

A Shelley 'Groom' figure, designed by Mabel Lucie Attwell.

6in (15.5cm) high

£220-280 **WW**

A 1980s Aldermaston Pottery dish, made by Nicola Werner, with painted and impressed marks.

Aldermaston was founded in 1955 by Alan Caiger-Smith and Geoffrey Eastop and is known both for its tin glazes and as a training ground for new potters.

7in (17.5cm) diam

£30-40   AGR

A 1970s Aldermaston Pottery jug, with typical hand-painted stylized leaf design.

9.25in (23.5cm) high

£50-80   AGR

An early 1960s Ambleside Pottery small vase, with sgrafitto decoration.

5in (12.5cm) high

£15-25   AGR

A 1950s early Ambleside Pottery tankard, with slipware and sgrafitto decoration, signed "Cook" to the base, with thumbpiece to handle.

5.25in (13.5cm) high

£30-40   AGR

An Arklow Pottery studio ware plate, with tan and black glaze.

Arklow Pottery is best known for its domestic tableware. It was founded in 1934 in Arklow, County Wicklow in the Republic of Ireland and was eventually taken over by Noritake in the 1990s. The company ran into financial difficulties and liquidators were called in in August 1998. Production ceased in April 1999.

£8-12   GAZE

A Bewlyn Pottery dish, painted in blue with a Classical scene.

Bewlyn was based in Bonchurch on the Isle of Wight.

11.5in (29.5cm) long

£20-30   AGR

A Gordon Baldwin studio pottery abstract piece, signed "G.B. 1971".

Gordon Baldwin (b.1932) has been working with ceramics since the 1950s. Unlike his contemporaries, he has moved from pure sculpture to an exploration of the vessel. He counts the Dada and abstract artist and sculptor Jean Arp, and a Welsh beach, among his inspirations – all can be seen in this piece in terms of its form and colour.

21.25in (54cm) wide

1971

£250-350   GAZE

CERAMICS

A Michael Cardew earthenware cider flagon, covered in a greenish-yellow and reddish-brown glaze with applied iron-brown decoration, retaining tap, impressed Winchcombe pottery seal and MC seal.

Cardew (1901-83) studied under Bernard Leach from the early 1920s before setting up the Winchcombe Pottery in 1926. In 1939 he left to set up a new pottery in Wenford Bridge, Cornwall. His work is loved for its glazes and he is also remembered for his pottery instruction book, as well as his work in Africa.

c1930   14.5in (37cm) high

£180-220   **ROS**

A Carn Pottery plaque, by John Beusmans, with galleon decoration, printed mark and pencil signature.

11.5in (29cm) wide

£70-100   **WW**

A CLOSER LOOK AT CARN POTTERY

Carn pieces are slip-cast, using liquid clay and a mould.

Fans are a hallmark Carn shape and are much sought-after by collectors.

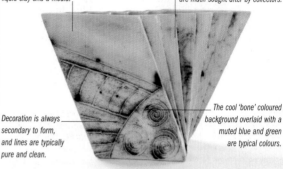

Decoration is always secondary to form, and lines are typically pure and clean.

The cool 'bone' coloured background overlaid with a muted blue and green are typical colours.

A 1970s Carn Pottery of Penzance fan vase, with low-relief moulded patterns of geometric and floral patterns to either side.

Carn Pottery was founded by John Beusmans in 1971. Most pieces are small and light in weight. Look out for Carn cats, which are highly collectable.

6.75in (17cm) wide

£15-25   **AGR**

A Carn Pottery 'Maze' wall plaque, by John Beusmans, printed mark and pencil signature.

9.25in (23.5cm) diam

£80-120   **WW**

A Celtic Pottery wall plate, with bird design.

4.75in (25cm) diam

£15-25   **GAZE**

A 1960s Kenneth Clark Pottery moulded shallow dish, designed by Clark's wife Ann Wynn-Reeves, decorated with a yellow duck.

6.75in (17cm) long

£30-40   **AGR**

An Everett Pottery tea caddy, by Ray Everett, with bamboo handle and beige glaze.

Ray Everett initially worked for Rye Potteries.

5.5in (14cm) high

£30-50   **AGR**

A David Frith ovoid stoneware jar and cover, covered in mottled brown glaze, with applied fish scale type decoration, impressed pottery mark.

David Frith (b.1943) founded his pottery, which became known as the Brookhouse Pottery, in 1963 in North Wales. An active member of the Craft Potter's Association, he has become famous for his fine decoration and superb glazes.

11.75in (30cm) high

£80-120 **ROS**

An Annette Fuchs footed bowl, with a rich blue glaze and handwritten paper label to base reading "ANNETTE FUCHS 1969".

1969 *3.5in (9cm) high*

£30-50 **AGR**

A 1970s Hastings Pottery triangular dish, decorated in blue with stylized peacock pattern, the base with impressed mark of two fish.

6.75in (17cm) long

£15-20 **AGR**

A Holkham Pottery blue circular solifleur vase on base, or hollow sculptural object, with pottery stamped mark to base.

c1980 *5.5in (14cm) high*

£25-35 **AGR**

A late 1970s Honiton Studio Pottery squat baluster vase, with brown and beige glazed decoration.

Although the Honiton Pottery mass-produced functional and decorative wares, the appearance of this piece is very different from their standard production run.

4.25in (10.5cm) high

£20-30 **AGR**

A 1970s Louis Hudson brown glazed tall lampbase, with moulded oval and semi-circular decoration.

The Louis Hudson pottery was founded in Trethevy in 1971. Reflecting traditional Cornish textures and colours, earlier works from the 1970s are becoming popular. Pieces featuring the heavy geometric or the 'rune' or 'heiroglyphic-like' mouldings are much sought-after. Large decorative pieces, such as lamp bases and vases, are currently more popular than utilitarian kitchenware, made from around 1980. Hudson left to become a truck driver in 1983. The company became Presingoll in 1998 and is now based in Bodmin.

11.75in (30cm) high

£60-80 **GC**

A Louis Hudson vase, with greeny grey glazes and moulded banded runic designs.

8in (20cm) high

£30-40 **GC**

CERAMICS

A Louis Hudson green and brown glazed runic/hieroglyphic moulded lampbase.

7.75in (19.5cm) high

£60-90   GC

A Louis Hudson wheel vase, with green glaze and brown moulded decoration, oval opening, reverse with diamond pattern in circle.

5.25in (13.5cm) high

£35-45   GC

A Louis Hudson small candleholder, with wide lip, with brown, unglazed rim.

This is one of the most commonly found shapes.

4in (10cm) high

£10-15   GC

A Jersey Pottery large double-drum tall vase, with printed mark.

11.25in (28.5cm) high

£60-90   GC

A 1960s Langley lampbase, the hand-painted pattern designed by Glyn Colledge.

7.75in (19.5cm) high

£50-80   GC

A Langley large vase, pattern designed by Glyn Colledge, with painted "CP" mark to base.

Denby acquired Lovatt & Lovatt, who made Langley, in 1959, explaining how Colledge (1922-2000) came to design Langley pieces.

10.25in (26cm) high

£100-150   GC

A David Leach celadon vase, of shallow foot and everted rim with curved fluted decoration to the exterior, impressed "DL" seal and Lowerdown pottery mark.

Part of the important Leach dynasty of potters, David learnt from Shoji Hamada. He founded the Aylesford Pottery in 1955, which became known for its stoneware and fine porcelain, the latter often having fine carving and a deep celadon green glaze.

5.25in (13.5cm) high

£180-220   ROS

A David Leach stoneware vase, painted with a willow tree on celadon glaze, impressed "DL" seal mark, firing crack.

6in (15cm) high

£100-150   WW

A 1980s Llanbrynmair, Powys, Wales tankard, by Michael Mosse, decorated with a sgrafitto gremlin.

Mosse worked at the Aldermaston Pottery with Alan Caiger-Smith from 1976-78.

6.25in (16cm) high

£20-30   AGR

A Llangollen, Wales ovoid green glazed vase, with printed mark to base.

8in (20.5cm) high

£35-45   GC

A 1970s John Maltby Studio pottery pedestal tankard, with signature and label.

John Maltby (b.1932) originally trained as an artist, before learning potting under David Leach at Lowerdown Pottery in Devon in 1962. In 1964, he founded his own pottery near Crediton, making one-off pieces and domestic wares. His pieces often bear naive, stylized forms and decoration inspired by Picasso, as is seen here. Examples of his works are in the Victoria & Albert Museum, London.

6in (15cm) high

£300-500   GAZE

A John Maltby stoneware pot and cover, stamped seal mark.

From c1976, Maltby concentrated purely on unique pieces which are typified by their contrasting areas of light and dark glazes as is seen in this example.

£220-280   WW

A Milland Pottery brown vase, with banded foliate sgrafitto decoration and printed windmill mark to base, also inscribed by hand "RM 18.6.51".

1951   8in (20cm) high

£20-30   PSI

A Prinknash blue and white striped vase, with flared rim, the base stamped "PRINKNASH".

9in (23cm) high

£30-50   PSI

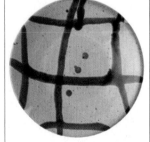

A Phil Rogers stoneware dish, impressed seal mark.

10.5in (27cm) diam

£100-150   WW

CERAMICS

A 1970s Shelf Pottery vase, with flattened lobes and wheel/flower pattern.

Although a gold label was used, Halifax-based Shelf Pottery pieces are often not marked, but can be recognized from the diagonally cut base and brown felt on the base. As well as lamps and vases, they made a range of animals, all with a creamy glaze and areas of unglazed clay.

8.75in (22cm) high

£15-25   **GC**

A Shelf Pottery tapering rectangular vase, with moulded sunburst pattern in brown, unfinished clay.

6.75in (17cm) high

£15-25   **GC**

A Shelf Pottery globe vase, with pierced circular motifs and shapes on the rim, and moulded 'fluting', cream and brown glaze.

4in (10cm) high

£10-15   **GC**

A Shelf Pottery snail money box, cream glaze.

3.75in (9.5cm) high

£10-15   **GC**

A Peter Smith Studio Pottery rough-form charger, brown and cream glazed, "PS" marks to base.

Peter Smith founded the Bojewyan Pottery near Penzance in 1974.

12.5in (32cm) diam

£70-100   **GAZE**

An Angus Suttie Studio pottery abstract piece, with paper label "Angus Made Me".

6.25in (16cm) wide

£50-80   **GAZE**

A Marianne De Trey Studio pottery pedestal bowl, personal impressed seal, pink glazes.

Marianne de Trey (b.1913) studied textile design at the Royal College of Art. She learnt how to pot from her American husband, Sam Haile, and moved back to the UK in 1944. In 1947, she and her husband took over Shinner's Bridge Pottery in Dartington. Known for her domestic wares, since 1985 she has concentrated on unique pieces in porcelain. Among other public collections, the Victoria & Albert Museum contains examples of her work.

5.5in (14cm) high

£100-150   **GAZE**

A rare 1920s Batchelder salesman's tile sample board, with plain and decorated tiles mounted in a metal frame, stencilled "124, BATCHELDER TILES LOS ANGELES".

Successful American ceramicist and Arts & Crafts designer Ernest Batchelder (1875 - 1957) was perhaps best known for his ceramic tiles and coined the phrase "No two tiles are the same".

13.5in (34cm) high

£1,200-1,800   **DRA**

A CLOSER LOOK AT A WILLIAM DE MORGAN TILE

William de Morgan (1839-1917) was a prolific, pioneering member of the Arts & Crafts movement.

In 1888, de Morgan established his own pottery at Sands End, Fulham, where some of his finest works were produced.

He was particularly well known for his tiles and specialised in their production from 1882.

This example shows de Morgan's typically rich shades of gold, ruby red and greens.

A pair of William de Morgan tiles, from the early Fulham period and with Sands End Pottery impressed marks.

Each 6in (15cm) wide

£400-500   **GAZE**

A T. & R. Boote Art Nouveau-style green tile, with stylized curling leaf and flower decoration.

c1900   5in (15cm) wide

£30-40   **AGR**

A California tile table top, the two tiles painted with a scene after Cecil Aldin, mounted on a wrought-iron base, chip to one edge of one and hairline from one to the other.

16.5in (42cm) wide

£150-250   **DRA**

An early 1960s printed tile, designed by Dorin Court, from the 'Rustic Peasants' series, on a Carter blank.

The humour, monochromatic design and style is similar to that of Danish designer Bjørn Wiinblad.

5in (15cm) wide

£12-18   **AGR**

A rare William de Morgan 'Persian' tile, small chip to edge.

6in (16cm) wide

£250-350   **PSA**

A 1950s polychrome stencil printed tile, by Dunsmore, decorated with a lamb, on a Minton blank.

5in (15cm) wide

£20-40   **AGR**

A Minton Hollins hand-painted tile, decorated with a design by W.B. Simpson.

c1885   8in (20cm) wide

£120-180   **AGR**

A Minton 'Stag & Doe in Pasture' pattern tile, designed by William Wise, from the 'Animals of the Farm' series.

Three Mosaic nursery rhyme-themed tiles, decorated in cuerda seca, mounted in a Arts & Crafts frame, stamped marks.

Roughly translating as 'dry rope', the cuerda seca method outlines the decoration with a mixture of manganese and grease to prevent the different coloured glazes mixing.

A 1950s Packard & Ord 'Pilgrim's Progress' hand-painted tile.

c1879   5in (15cm) wide

£60-80   **AGR**

Each 4.5in (11.5cm) wide

£400-500   **DRA**

4.25in (10.5cm) wide

£15-20   **AGR**

A Packard & Ord 'King Lear' hand-painted tile, designed by R. Leeper, from the 'Shakespearean Characters' series, on a Pilkington blank.

The small monogram in the bottom right identifies this as Packard & Ord.

A Poole Pottery Carter tile, depicting rabbits and grass, in a decorative frame.

A set of four Poole Pottery Carter tiles, designed by Cecil Aldin and featuring four different designs of dogs, in original box.

c1953   5in (15cm) wide

£20-40   **AGR**

c1953

£30-50   **C**

£120-180   **C**

A 1960s Ann Wynn Reeves tile, decorated with a design of chairs, on an H.&R. Johnson blank.

A 1960s Ann Wynn Reeves tile, decorated with design of a train or truck, on an H. & R. Johnson blank.

A 1950s Richards tile, screen-printed with a 'Homemaker' style design.

This pattern was inspired by the success of Ridgway's Homemaker pattern. The design is subtly different and the printing is of poorer quality and is over, rather than under, the glaze as is found on Homemaker.

5in (15cm) wide

£20-25   **AGR**

5in (15cm) wide

£20-25   **AGR**

5in (15cm) wide

£15-20   **AGR**

A CLOSER LOOK AT A SET OF WEDGWOOD TILES

A 1950s polychrome stencil printed tile, designed by E.E. Strickland in the 1920s, with a scene of rabbits from the 'Farmyard' series, on a Carter blank.

5in (15cm) wide

£30-50   **AGR**

As well as the polychrome versions seen here, this series was also produced in monochrome browns and blues.

The tiles were designed by Thomas Allen, who oversaw Wedgwood's tile production in the late 19thC.

This tile was made using the dust-pressed method, patented by William Boulton in 1863. It used dust clay that was pressed into one or more copper plates perforated with the desired pattern.

A set of 12 tiles were designed for the series.

Four Josiah Wedgwood, Etruria tiles, with scenes from Shakespeare's 'A Midsummer Night's Dream', including Puck, Bottom, Lysander and Hermia, marked "65413" in ink of the reverse.

c1880-90   *Each 6in (15cm) wide*

£500-600   **GAZE**

A 1950s polychrome stencil tile, designed by Reginald Till, from the 'English Countryside' series, on a Carter blank.

5in (15cm) wide

£40-60   **AGR**

A Villeroy & Bosch 'Acapulco' pattern tile trivet.

8in (20.5cm) wide

£18-22   **GROB**

A Wedgwood 'Old English' tile, designed by Helen J.A. Miles, with underglaze dust pressed technique print of the 'April' scene from the 'Months' series.

c1890   *5in (15cm) wide*

£80-100   **AGR**

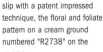

A Wedgwood tile, decorated in slip with a patent impressed technique, the floral and foliate pattern on a cream ground numbered "R2738" on the reverse.

c1880   *5in (15cm) wide*

£25-35   **AGR**

A 1960s Italian printed tile, of a stylized teenager's head.

This pattern is usually found on dressing table sets.

6in (15.5cm) wide

£12-15   **GROB**

COLLECTORS' NOTES

- Tremaen was founded by artist Paul Ellery in Marazion, Cornwall, in 1965. Forms and decoration are unusual and hand-executed. The pottery saw enough success to see it gain 12 employees and move to larger premises in Newlyn in 1967.

- Despite its continued success, Ellery preferred to paint and left the pottery in 1988. Earlier, larger pieces or those with typical painterly glazes and moulded, runic style patterning, tend to be the most desirable.

- Tremar was founded by husband and wife Roger and Doreen Birkett in Tremar, near Liskeard in 1962. Production was aimed at the tourist market and included hand-thrown utilitarian items such as bottles and vases.

- Success led to expansion to three sites. Production methods changed to moulded items during the 1970s, allowing commercial production of a wider range of 'collectable' items. These included animals, boats, houses and a popular series of public houses that preceded ceramic model companies such as David Winter.

- Glazes tend to be in muted greeny beiges, with moulded relief decoration showing the colour of the underlying clay. Many pieces are stamped, but the colour and form is highly recognizable. Falling sales led to the pottery's closure in 1983. Both companies are being reappraised by collectors, with Tremaen pieces currently being of greater interest, and in many cases, value.

A CLOSER LOOK AT A TREMAEN LAMPBASE

A Tremaen tapered lamp base, with runic moulded symbols and browny-orange glazes.

11.5in (29cm) high

£100-150　　　　　　　　**GC**

The unusual form is typical of early Tremaen, being based on pebbles found on the Cornish coast.

The piece is marked with an impressed stamp and the texture is like coastal rock.

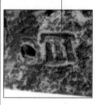

The large size gives dramatic impact, making it more desirable.

The moulded abstract geometric pattern, almost akin to hieroglyphics, is a typical feature.

A Tremaen pebble-form lampbase, designed by Paul Ellery.
c1967

12.5in (32cm) high

£120-180　　　　　　　　**GC**

A Tremaen square section vase, with white glazed interior.

6in (15.5cm) high

£15-25　　　**GC**

A Tremaen pebble-form flower 'frog', glazed in greens, yellows and creams.

The painterly and liberal use of glazes is another hallmark of Ellery's early designs.

5.75in (14.5cm) wide

£10-15　　　**GC**

A Tremar lampbase with two handles, with moulded, unglazed stylized landscape.

9.75in (25cm) high

£60-90　　　**GC**

A Tremar green glazed vase, with stylized tree/floral motif with mushrooms beneath, with "TREMAR UK" stamp.

6in (15cm) high

£15-20   **GC**

A Tremar cylindrical vase, with double-flower moulded unglazed motif, with "TREMAR UK" stamp.

6.75in (17cm) high

£7-10   **GC**

A Tremar whisky bottle, with cork stopper.

10in (25.5cm) high

£10-15   **GC**

A Tremar 'Honey' lidded pot, with unglazed moulded and raised design, lacks spoon.

4.25in (11cm) high

£7-10   **GC**

A Tremar salt cellar, with turned wooden spoon, and leather hanging loop.

5in (12.5cm) high

£10-15   **GC**

A Tremar 'Flowers' flattened oval vase with impressed flower and wording, green glaze, with "TREMAR UK" impressed stamp.

£10-15   **GC**

A Tremar 'The Pig And Whistle' house-shaped money box, with "TREMAR UK" stamp to base.

6in (15.5cm) high

£15-25   **GC**

A Tremar 'The Miners' Arms' money box, cream glazed with brown unglazed moulded and raised detailing.

6.5in (16.5cm) wide

£15-25   **GC**

A Tremar cat-shaped money box, with green glaze, and brown eyes, base stamped "TREMAR UK".

7in (18cm) long

£15-20   **GC**

CERAMICS

COLLECTORS' NOTES

■ Troika was founded in 1963 at the Wells Pottery, St Ives by sculptor and painter Lesley Illsley, potter Benny Sirota and architect Jan Thompson, who left in 1965. Illsley focused on shapes, while Sirota focused on surface decoration, which was inspired by the work of artist Paul Klee, Aztec designs and Scandinavian ceramics of the period.

■ The first pieces were domestic, such as teapots, mugs and vases. Glazes on these early pieces tended to be shiny, rather than matte. Marks include the name 'St Ives', used from 1963-70. The earliest pieces bear a linear 'trident in a box' shaped mark, which was used until 1967.

■ The 1960s saw rapid and strong growth, with sales spurred on by the local tourist industry and interest from London department stores Heal's, Liberty and Selfridges. In 1970, the pottery expanded, moving to new premises in Newlyn.

■ New shapes were designed and introduced and, by 1974, most pieces were matte and textured. Marks also changed, and the 'St Ives' name was dropped. 'Newlyn' itself never appears in any mark, so all marks that do not mention 'St Ives' will date from 1970 onwards.

■ Large, sculptural pieces or those in shapes characteristic of Troika such as 'doublebase', 'coffin' and 'wheel' vases, are the most sought-after.

■ Look for decorators' monograms, as the work of certain decorators can be more desirable. Dates shown here represent the working dates of decorators where known, or a date range based on the mark.

■ Troika closed in 1983 due to a drop in tourist levels and less expensive foreign imports. Over the past five years, collecting interest has grown, resulting in prices up to around £2,000-4,000 for large, rare and highly characteristic pieces such as masks.

An early Troika Pottery flask, with impressed Trident mark.

1963-67   7in (17.5cm) high

£650-750   **WW**

A rare early Troika St Ives Pottery flask, with bronze glazed sides and stylized blue glazed flower head and leaf design to one side and embossed disk to the other, impressed trident mark to base.

1963-67   6.5in (16.5cm) high

£550-650   **B&H**

A Troika Pottery flask, by Anne Lewis, the white ground with a blue painted Aztec star design to either side.

1967-72   6.5in (16.5cm) high

£550-650   **B&H**

A Troika Pottery medium 'wheel' lamp base, by Sally Bart, with textured ground and embossed stylised Aztec helmet and geometric designs to either side.

c1975   8.25in (21cm) high

£200-300   **B&H**

A Troika Pottery large 'wheel' lampbase, with painted marks.

1970-83   13.75in (35cm) high

£1,000-1,500   **WW**

A Troika Pottery 'wheel' vase, decorated by Ann Jones, with painted "Troika" mark and "AJ" monogram, restored top rim.

1976-77   *6.75in (17cm) high*

£250-350   **WW**

A CLOSER LOOK AT A TROIKA WHEEL VASE

The wheel vase is one of Troika's best-known and most typical shapes.

Avril Bennett worked at the factory from 1971-79 and was Head Decorator.

The clearly demarcated geometric design is desirable as it is both attractive and unusual.

At nearly 13in (33cm) diameter, it is an unusually large size.

A Troika Pottery large 'wheel' vase, decorated by Avril Bennett, with painted marks.

1971-79   *12.75in (32.5cm) high*

£1,500-2,000   **WW**

A Troika Pottery 'wheel' vase, with painted marks.

7.75in (19.5cm) high

£350-450   **WW**

A Troika Pottery 'wheel' vase, with painted marks to base.

6.5in (16.5cm) high

£220-280   **WW**

A Troika Pottery 'wheel' vase, with painted "Troika Cornwall" mark and "CC" monogram.

1970-83   *6.5in (16.5cm) high*

£250-350   **WW**

A Troika Pottery small 'wheel' vase, mottled blue with abstract design upon both sides, marked "Troika" with initials to underside.

1970-83   *4.5in (11.5cm) high*

£120-180   **ROS**

A Troika Pottery 'wheel' vase, both sides with geometric patterns, factory marks to base.

6.5in (16.5cm) high

£180-220   **SWO**

A Troika Pottery 'wheel' vase, by Alison Brigden, with painted "Troika Cornwall" mark and "AB" monogram.

Brigden was promoted to Troika's Head Decorator in 1981.

1976-83   *7.75in (19.5cm) high*

£400-500   **WW**

CERAMICS

A Troika Pottery 'rectangle' vase, decorated by Ann Jones, with painted mark and artist's monogram to base.

1976-77   *12.5in (32cm) high*

£350-450   **WW**

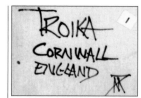

A Troika Pottery large 'rectangle' vase, with mottled green ground and each side decorated with a small cluster of disks, with unknown monogram.

The style of the painted marks show this vase dates from 1970-83. As the painter's monogram is as yet unidentified, it may date from the early 1980s when Troika employed young students on a government work training scheme, or may be by a 1970s decorator who has not yet been identified.

1970-83   *12.25in (31cm) high*

£280-320   **B&H**

A rare Troika Pottery 'rectangle' vase, painted with geometric repeats and with painted "Troika St Ives" mark.

This is rare and early, bearing both a St Ives mark and a glossy rather than a matte glaze.

1964-70   *5.25in (13.5cm) high*

£280-320   **WW**

A Troika Pottery 'coffin' vase, with geometric designs to the front and rear and inscribed decoration to the sides.

     6.75in (17cm) high

£80-120   **SWO**

A Troika Pottery 'slab' vase, decorated by Avril Bennett, painted marks.

1973-79   *7in (17.5cm) high*

£350-450   **WW**

A Troika Pottery 'rectangle' vase, initialled "JF", probably decorated by Jane Fitzgerald.

1977-83   *8in (20.5cm) high*

£100-150   **GORL**

An early Troika Pottery 'slab' vase, decorated with blue medallion motif, stamped "Troika St Ives England".

1964-70   *4.5in (11.5cm) high*

£120-180   **WW**

A Troika Pottery lampbase, with painted "Cornwall Troika" mark to base.

1970-83   *8.75in (22cm) high*

£220-280   **WW**

CERAMICS

A Troika Pottery bronze glazed dish, by Penny Black, probably retailed by Heal's, painted mark "Troika England" and "PB" monogram.

1970-76   *4.75in (12cm) wide*

£120-180   **WW**

A Troika Pottery ashtray, by Alison Brigden, of square form decorated with bronze-glazed centre and pale brown domino embossed border.

1976-83   *6.25in (16cm) diam*

£280-320   **B&H**

A Troika St Ives Pottery shallow dish, by Honor Curtis, of square form, with raised sides, plain white glaze and bronze glazed central disk.

1966-70   *5in (12.5cm) diam*

£220-280   **B&H**

A Troika Pottery cube, painted with bronze roundels on white, stamped "Troika St Ives England".

1964-70   *3.25in (8cm) high*

£280-320   **WW**

A Troika cube vase, painted by Sylvia Valance, with painted "Troika St Ives" mark and painter's monogram.

1967-69   *3.25in (8cm) high*

£120-180   **GAZE**

An early Troika Pottery marmalade pot, decorated by Marilyn Pascoe, with impressed designs, covered in a dark burnished finish, with Troika pottery mark and initials "MP" to underside.

1970-74

£120-180   **ROS**

A Troika Pottery square dish, painted mark "Troika Cornwall" and artist's monogram.

1970-83   *7.75in (20cm) wide*

£350-450   **WW**

A rare Troika Pottery tile, with painted and incised design, and painted "Troika" mark.

Troika tiles were an early product made at St Ives. Floor tiles were discontinued a couple of years after the pottery was founded, although other tiles were made throughout the St Ives period.

1963-c1967   *5.5in (14cm) wide*

£450-550   **WW**

CERAMICS

An early Troika St Ives Pottery D-plate, of rounded square form, with stylized flower head and leaf design in blues and black, with moulded trident mark to the base.

1963-67   *7.5in (19cm) diam*

£400-500   **B&H**

A rare early Troika St Ives Pottery wall plaque, with purple, blue and green glazes and raised textured abstract design.

Wall plaques are among the most sought after of Troika's shapes, as well as being some of the earliest objects made. Most have the trident mark and each is effectively unique. Large examples can fetch extremely high prices, as can those made by the founders.

1963-70   *7.75in (19.5cm) wide*

£1,200-1,800   **B&H**

A rare Troika St Ives D-plate, of rounded square form, having embossed flower head and leaf designs with blue and bronze glaze, with impressed trident mark to base.

1963-67   *7in (18cm) diam*

£450-550   **B&H**

A rare early Troika St Ives charger, by Honor Curtis, of circular form decorated with embossed geometric flower head and leaf designs and raised edge.

Chargers are an uncommon shape for Troika.

1966-70   *9in (23cm) diam*

£500-600   **B&H**

An early Troika St Ives circular plate, with painted geometric blue band with raised edge.

These plates were often sold with double eggcups. Note the similarity in design to the eggcup over the page.

c1965-70   *7in (18cm) diam*

£150-200   **B&H**

A Troika Pottery cylinder vase by Marilyn Pascoe, with painted marks.

1970-74   *14.25in (36.5cm) high*

£220-280   **WW**

A Troika Pottery cylinder vase, painted mark "Troika St Ives England" and artist's monogram.

1964-70   *6in (15cm) high*

£120-180   **WW**

A Troika cylindrical vase, with painted mark, chips.

1970-83   *4.5in (11.5cm) high*

£250-300   **WW**

A Troika Pottery 'doublebase' vase, with beige ground and geometric patterns.

1970-83   14in (35cm) high

£700-800   **BRI**

A Troika Pottery 'doublebase' lampshade, by Ann Jones, with painted "Troika Cornwall" mark and "AJ" monogram.

A Troika Pottery 'doublebase' vase, modelled in low relief, with painted marks.

1970-83   14in (35.5cm) high

£1,200-1,800   **WW**

1976-77   14in (35.5cm) high

£600-1,000   **WW**

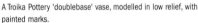

A Troika Pottery double egg cup and tray, stamped "Troika St Ives England".

Introduced at the request of department store Heal's, eggcups were made in large quantities, but only sold for a short period of time.

c1965   6.75in (17cm) diam

£250-300   **WW**

A Troika Pottery spice jar, painted by Alison Brigden, with textured panels depicting abstract motifs, blue funnel with white interior and with painted Troika mark and initials "AB".

1976-83   6in (15cm) high

£150-200   **ROS**

A Troika Pottery mug, stamped "Troika St Ives England".

1964-70   5in (12.5cm) high

£80-120   **WW**

FIND OUT MORE...

Troika Ceramics of Cornwall by George Perrott, published by Gemini Publications Ltd, 2003.

A J.H. Cope & Co. wall mask, of a lady in a large feathered hat.

c1934   12in (30.5cm) wide

£180-220   **BEV**

A CLOSER LOOK AT A WALL POCKET

Royal Doulton wall pockets are generally hard to find, 'Old Charley' is a particularly scarce example.

Wall pockets were only produced for a short amount of time during WWII, which would account for their limited production.

'Old Charley' was designed by Charles Noke, who is well known for his reintroduction of figurines to the Royal Doulton range.

This is the only known colourway for this wall mask.

A rare Royal Doulton 'Old Charley' wall pocket, D6110, designed by Charles Noke.

c1940-41   7.25in (18.5cm) high

£700-800   **PSA**

A rare Royal Doulton 'Jester' wall pocket, D6111, designed by Charles Noke.

c1940-41

£600-700   **PSA**

A small Goebel pottery wall mask of a young woman, with blonde hair, very small chip to base.

5in (12.5cm) long

£50-70   **CA**

A rare Goldscheider wall mask.

c1925-8   8.5in (21.5cm) high

£800-900   **SCG**

A 1950s Austrian 'Keramic' Art Deco mask.

8.5in (21.5cm) high

£80-120   **GEW**

A 1930s Czech Art Deco wall mask, of Marlene Dietrich.

8in (20.5cm) high

£180-220   **GEW**

A German pottery mask, the stylized face with craquelure glaze, unmarked.

6in (15.5cm) high

£180-220   **WW**

A CLOSER LOOK AT A ROYAL WORCESTER DINNER SERVICE

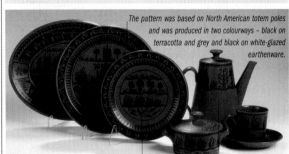

The pattern was based on North American totem poles and was produced in two colourways - black on terracotta and grey and black on white-glazed earthenware.

A Royal Worcester large ovoid vase, with scroll side handles, decorated with flowers on a blush ground, shape '1969'.

c1899   12in (30.5cm) high

£350-450   **WW**

Royal Worcester commissioned artist Robert 'Scottie' Wilson (1890-1972) to design this dinner service pattern in the early 1960s.

He is well known for his Primitive Style of art featuring stylized floral and fauna and his work was owned by Pablo Picasso. It is also included in the Tate Gallery and the Metropolitan Museum, New York.

Perhaps due to its high cost, the pattern was unsuccessful and was retired in 1965. The design, however, was much admired and it has become a popular with collectors on both sides of the Atlantic.

An early 1960s Royal Worcester 'Cheltenham' pattern part tea, coffee and dinner service, designed by Scottie Wilson, approximately 90 pieces, printed factory marks.

£1,500-2,000   **L&T**

A Royal Worcester globular vase, with a moulded mouth, the body decorated with flowers on an ivory ground, puce mark.

c1884   9in (23cm) high

£250-300   **WW**

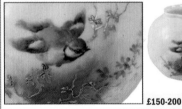

A Grainger & Co. Worcester globular vase, painted with a blue tit on gilded branches.

2.5in (6.5cm) high

£150-200   **SAS**

A Royal Worcester pot pourri centrepiece, of Etruscan shape, on pedestal base, date code.

1895   10in (25.5cm) diam

£220-280   **GORL**

A Royal Worcester centrepiece shell dish, with scalloped rim, on entwined dolphin stem, date code.

1878

8.25in (21cm) wide

£180-220   **GORL**

A pair of trumpet vases, after Royal Worcester, each painted with a similar large floral spray, sprigs and an insect against a pale yellow ground.

7.75in (19.5cm) high

£120-180   **GORL**

CERAMICS

A Royal Worcester 'Blue Lagoon' conical candle extinguisher, boxed.

c2001   3.25in (8.5cm) high

£30-40   **GAZE**

A CLOSER LOOK AT A ROYAL WORCESTER CANDLE EXTINGUISHER

Royal Worcester have almost continuously produced candle extinguishers since 1850. This particular snuffer was introduced in the 1870s.

With the advent of electricity at the end of the 19thC, snuffers began to become obsolete and later examples were produced for decoration rather than function.

Snuffers were usually available singularly or as a pair, often with a matching stand. They are often decorative and amusing.

Despite heavy use, the vulnerable hands and hat rim have survived in good condition with no damage. This increases the desirability.

A Royal Worcester blush ivory 'Granny Snow' candle extinguisher.

This model was produced in cream-coloured Parian as well as this blush and was available in two sizes.

c1903   3in (7.5cm) high

£250-300   **GCL**

A Royal Worcester blush ivory 'The Monk' candle snuffer.

c1899   4in (10cm) high

£200-250   **GCL**

A Royal Worcester 'India' figure, by Freda G. Doughty, no.3071.

Doughty worked as a modeller at Royal Worcester from 1930 to 1963 and is best known for her models of children, often based on those she knew. Although considered old fashioned by some, her designs were extremely popular with the public and were produced for a long period of time.

3.25in (8cm) high

£150-200   **WW**

A Royal Worcester 'Friday's Child' porcelain figurine, modelled by Freda G. Doughty, no.RW3261.

c1950   7in (18cm) high

£150-200   **DN**

A Royal Worcester 'Thursday's Child' porcelain figurine, modelled by Freda G. Doughty, no.RW3260.

6.5in (16.5cm) high

£150-200   **DN**

Two Royal Worcester figures, 'Monday's Child' and 'Saturday's Child', modelled by Freda G. Doughty, hairline crack to first, with printed marks.

£80-120   **WW**

FIND OUT MORE...

Royal Worcester Figurines, by Anthony Cast, John Edwards, published by Charlton Press, February , 2005.

A pair of Baron ware Barnstable vases, incised marks to base.

William Leonard Baron (1863-1937) worked at Doulton, Lambeth until 1884 when he moved to Brannam Pottery. He establish his own pottery in 1893 where he produced motto wares, puzzle jugs and art pottery. A fierce rivalry developed between him and his former employers Brannam. Following his death the pottery was sold to Brannam in the late 1930s.

A prototype Lorna Bailey 'Ginger Rogers' figure, in blue and black outfit.

After her father bought the assets of Wood & Sons in the late 1990s, Bailey began designing new pieces in the style of early Clarice Cliff, which proved a great hit. Prototypes such as this afford a premium with collectors.

8.75in (22cm) high

£200-300   PSA

A limited edition Lorna Bailey Art Deco 'Wendy' figure, from an edition of 100, with certificate.

8.5in (21.5cm) high

£70-100   PSA

5.5in (14cm) high

£15-25   GAZE

A modern Belleek flower-encrusted vase.

8.5in (21.5cm) high

£180-220   DN

A Bretby comical bulldog figure, modelled with bandaged paw in a sling, impressed marks and inscribed "After The".

9.5in (24cm) high

£100-150   WW

A pair of Burmantoft yellow-glazed vases, impressed marks to underside.

8.5in (21.5cm) high

£300-400   ROS

A 1920s Bursley Ware 'Baghdad' pattern hand-painted bowl, designed by Frederick Rhead, with printed marks to base.

Frederick Rhead (1856-1933) became Art Director at Wood & Sons in 1912 and persuaded the owner to purchase the adjacent Crown Pottery, which was renamed Bursley Ltd. in 1920. Rhead designed a number of art ware ranges including Sylvan, Amstel, Benares and Merton. His daughter Charlotte also produced a number of designs for them.

9.5in (24cm) diam

£200-250   PSI

CERAMICS

A 1940s Bursley Ware bowl, by Charlotte Rhead, with tube-lined decoration, painted marks to base.

The Bursley Ware name was revived by Wood's in 1942 and was given to the range of tube-lined pieces Rhead designed for them.

11in (28cm) diam

£100-150   **ROS**

A West German Carstens Bauhaus-style ceramic jug, with brown ring glazed design.

Carstens closed in 1984.

7.75in (19.5cm) high

£5-10   **GAZE**

A Cobridge Stoneware 'Autumn's Dawn' vase, by Carole Mellor and another artist.

10.25in (26cm) high

£120-180   **BEL**

A Coronet ware Pixie 'The Apple Picker' jug.

Parrott & Co., the makers of Coronet ware, merged with Burgess & Leigh c1939.

c1930   *8in (20cm) high*

£50-70   **GAZE**

A Stella Crofts stoneware group, modelled as a family of tigers, etched "Stella R Crofts May 1925".

Potter Stella Crofts studied at the Central School of Arts and Crafts and the Royal College of Art. She was known for her naturalist models of animals and birds, which were reproduced in slip-cast earthenware.

c1925   *8.75in (22cm) wide*

£800-1,000   **WW**

A Crown Devon lustre tapered vase, decorated in an Oriental dragon pattern on orange ground, marked "2078".

This design is very similar to Carltonware's Oriental 'Royale' range, which was inspired by the success of Wedgwood's Fairyland Lustre.

9.75in (25cm) high

£180-220   **PSA**

A Crown Devon 'Memphis' vase, shape CM10, designed by Colin Melborne, printed mark, facsimile signature.

8.75in (22.5cm) diam

£60-80   **WW**

A 1930s Crown Devon Lustrine fruit bowl, painted with a galleon in colours and gilt, on pedestal base.

10.25in (26cm) wide

£35-45 GORL

A CLOSER LOOK AT A CROWN DUCAL CHARGER

Charlotte Rhead (1885-1947) was the fourth child of pottery designer Frederick Rhead and, together with some of her siblings, joined the family trade.

Rhead joined Wardle & Co. in c1901 producing tube-line decorated pieces, a technique she had learnt from her father. It was to become her trademark.

In 1932, Rhead joined A.G. Richardson and designed wares for the Crown Ducal range that included nurserywares and tablewares as well as tube-lined pieces.

Compared to some of her contemporaries, Charlotte Rhead pieces are still affordable. This may change in the future.

A Crown Ducal 'Hydrangea' pattern charger, by Charlotte Rhead, no.3797, tubeline decorated with hydrangea printed mark, facsimile signature.

c1935 12.5in (32cm) diam

£250-350 WW

A Crown Ducal vase, painted with a stylised tree and coloured leaves against a honey glazed ground.

10in (25.5cm) high

£100-150 GORL

A Crown Ducal three-piece novelty tea set, modelled as three black cats.

Pot 10in (25.5cm) long

£150-200 CA

A Crown Ducal vase and matching bowl.

Vase 9in (23cm) high

£30-40 GAZE

A Crown Ducal black and blue glazed 'coffee for two' set, with printed marks, chip to coffee pot base.

Coffee 7in (18cm) high

£10-20 GAZE

A Crown Ducal drip glazed green mottled vase, with printed marks.

3.75in (9.5cm) high

£20-30 RETC

CERAMICS

A pair of Crown Staffordshire cockatoos.

9.75in (25cm) high

£100-150   PSA

A 20thC Delft figure of standing bull, with blue floral design, restored horns, missing ear.

7.5in (19cm) long

£150-200   BRI

A crested china model of a battleship bearing the crest of Manchester.

4.75in (12cm) long

£20-30   GAZE

An unmarked china model of a dog bearing the crest of Cheltenham.

2.25in (5.5cm) high

£4-6   GAZE

An Arcadian china model of Tommy Atkins, bearing the crest of Caistor-on-Sea and the lyrics of a patriotic song.

3.75in (9.5cm) high

£70-100   GAZE

A Carlton china 'Fums Up' model of a man bearing the crest of St Ives.

'Fums up' (thumbs up) was a WWI figure made as a charm to provide encouragement during the war.

3.5in (9cm) high

£8-12   GAZE

A Spode for Hayter & Stickland of Winchester 'Cardinal Beaufort's Candlestick', crested with the arms of St. Goss Hospital.

6in (15cm) high

£50-70   SAS

A Waterfall crested china model of an ambulance bearing the crest of York.

3.5in (1.5in) long

£20-30   GAZE

A Gouda pottery jardinière, painted with flowers, printed marks.

7.5in (19cm) high

£120-180   WW

A Gouda pottery vase, painted with a bird, painted marks.

6.25in (16cm) high

£220-280 WW

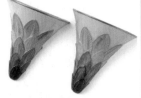

A pair of Grays Pottery Art Deco wall pockets, one restored.

8.5in (21.5cm) high

£20-30 GAZE

A Habitat 'Monaco' pattern milk jug, with printed marks.

3.25in (8cm) high

£12-18 CHS

An Hungarian Herend figure of a girl riding a goose.

Herend was established by Vince Stingl in the village of Herend in 1826. It was taken over by Mór Fischer in 1836 who turned production towards more decorative wares, which proved popular with the Hungarian aristocracy. The pottery continues to produce high quality hand-painted figures and decorative wares today.

8in (20cm) high

£120-180 PSA

Three comical rabbit figurines, possibly by Lippelsdorf, Germany, unmarked.

3.75in (9.5cm) high

£40-50 WDL

A Martin Brothers lidded pot, inscribed marks to base "Martin Bros, London and Southall 12 1892", restored.

£120-180 GAZE

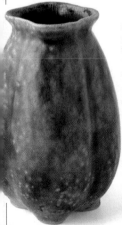

A Martin Brothers studio pottery vase, inscribed marks to base "Martin Bros. Southall 13-37".

The four Martin brothers established their pottery in Fulham, London in 1837, moving to Southall, Middlesex in 1877. Perhaps best known for their sought-after 'grotesque' bird-jars, they also produced a range of Arts and Crafts vessels, typically stoneware in a palette of muted salt-glazed colours, often with incised sgraffito decoration.

6.25in (16cm) high

£200-300 GAZE

A Minton blue transfer-printed jug, with pewter lid, paper label to base.

c1880 *7in (18cm) high*

£40-60 GAZE

CERAMICS

A lustre plate by Bernard Moore, with a design after Hals' 'The Laughing Cavalier'.

c1904   8.5in (21.5cm) diam

£400-500   **TCS**

A CLOSER LOOK AT A MINTON'S JARDINIÈRE

Minton's Secessionist line was designed by Marc-Léon Solon, who was Art Director of the company from 1900-10.

Bright, dramatic colours, such as this rich red, formed the palette.

Forms are typically simple, so that they do not compete with the decoration.

Tube-lining was often used to ensure the different colours did not bleed into each other.

A Minton's Secessionist jardinière, with tube-lined foliate decoration, No. 72.

Charlotte Rhead, perhaps the best known exponent of tube-lining was taught by her father, Frederick Rhead, who had been an assistant to Solon at Sèvres, before he came to Minton's.

8in (20cm) diam

£350-450   **GAZE**

A Pilkington 'Royal Lancastrian' lustre glazed vase.

6in (15cm) high

£150-200   **PSA**

A Pilkington 'Royal Lancastrian' large blue-glazed vase.

11.75in (30cm) high

£60-80   **GAZE**

A Portmeirion 'Cypher' pattern salt-glazed coffee pot.

The matte salt glaze creates a much finer effect, giving more definition to the moulded design than gloss or other finishes.

1963   12.5in (31.5cm) high

£60-80   **AGR**

A Portmeirion 'Totem' pattern cobalt blue cheese dish and base.

It is hard to find this blue colourway in good condition as the glaze is prone to fading through washing.

£12-18   **GAZE**

A Radford Tavern jug, with moulded and painted decoration.

4.75in (12cm) high

£5-7   **GAZE**

CERAMICS

A 1930s Pearl Pottery Royal Bourbon ware jug, painted with butterfly and flowers.

7in (18cm) high

£40-60   **GAZE**

A Royal Dux elephant, with trunk in salute.

10.25in (26cm) high

£40-60   **PSA**

A Shorter & Sons two-handled vase, of waisted cylindrical form.

7.5in (19cm) high

£18-22   **GAZE**

A Shorter & Sons moulded and painted jug, with blackberry design.

5.5in (14cm) high

£20-30   **GAZE**

A 20thC Sitzendorf equestrian model, the underside with factory mark and inscribed "Royal Horse Guards The Blues 1815", minor damage.

15in (38cm) high

£200-300   **DN**

A Staffordshire Pottery figure of Lord Roberts, inscribed "Roberts" on the base, the details picked out in copper lustre.

13.5in (34.5cm) high

£60-80   **W&W**

A J.M.W. & Sons Hanley Art Deco jug, painted with birds and berries.

6in (15cm) high

£50-70   **GAZE**

A Spode porcelain 'Hydra' jug, iron-red mark, painted pattern no.3620, some rubbing to gilding.

c1821   *8in (20.5cm) high*

£300-400   **DN**

A Wemyss candlestick, impressed "RH and S" mark.

12in (30cm) high

£180-220   **L&T**

CERAMICS

A late 19thC Minton glazed parian model of a gardener, in green and cream glazes.

9.75in (25cm) long

£100-150   **ROS**

A Wemyss 'Jazzy' pattern cylindrical tankard, painted marks "Wemyss 217".

7in (17.5cm) high

£180-220   **L&T**

A 1930s Arthur Wood 'To London' jug.

7in (18cm) high

£40-60   **GAZE**

A large Wemyss goblet vase, impressed mark, printed Thomas Goode mark.

The Scottish Wemyss pottery was established by Robert Methven Heron in 1822 and was named after the Wemyss family who were early patrons. Pieces are often decorated with bright, bold decoration of flowers - typically roses, fruit or birds. Thomas Goode was the sole distributor in England and commissioned some pieces himself.

11.5in (29.5cm) high

£250-350   **L&T**

A late 19thC Belgian pottery figure of a lady seated at a spinning wheel.

8.5in (22cm) high

£80-120   **CHEF**

A 1930s Japanese hand-painted moulded green dog or goblin candle holder, his tail as a handle, the base printed "FOREIGN" and impressed "1838".

5in (13cm) high

£15-25   **PSI**

A 19thC pottery Toby jug, modelled as a seated ruddy faced gentleman holding a mug of beer.

9.5in (24cm) high

£220-280   **ROW**

A 19thC silver lustre mask jug, decorated with three grotesque male masks.

5.5in (14cm) high

£80-120   **ROW**

A Continental pottery group of a standing harlequin and a flapper, signed "J. Meier".

11in (28cm) high

£80-120   **CA**

A CLOSER LOOK AT A POPEYE TOY

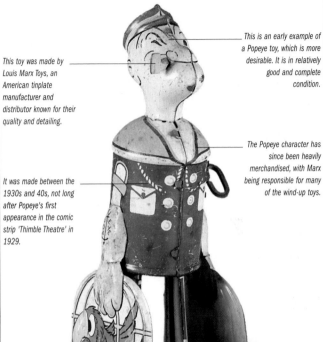

This toy was made by Louis Marx Toys, an American tinplate manufacturer and distributor known for their quality and detailing.

This is an early example of a Popeye toy, which is more desirable. It is in relatively good and complete condition.

It was made between the 1930s and 40s, not long after Popeye's first appearance in the comic strip 'Thimble Theatre' in 1929.

The Popeye character has since been heavily merchandised, with Marx being responsible for many of the wind-up toys.

A 1950s Gundikins 'Popeye' plush and soft vinyl-headed doll, with card feet and original tag, signs of wear and discolouration.

9in (23cm) high

£20-30 **WAC**

A 1950s Gundikins 'Olive Oyl' plush and soft vinyl doll, with card feet, so she can stand, and original tag.

8.5in (21.5cm) high

£20-30 **WAC**

A 1930s/40s American Louis Marx 'Popeye' wind-up toy, carrying parrot cages at his side, fading and small abrasions to toy, mechanism working.

8.5in (21.50cm) high

£120-180 **JDJ**

A pair of Japanese Woolikin 'Popeye' and 'Olive' Oyl dolls, by F.W. Woolnough, with vinyl heads.

12.5in (32cm) high

£70-100 **SOTT**

A Gund Mfg. Co. 'Olive Oyl' hand puppet, with original bow.

9.75in (25cm) high

£20-30 **SOTT**

An Aladdin Industries 'Popeye' lunchbox and Thermos flask, with embossed detailing.

1980   8in (20.5cm) wide

£40-50 **STC**

A 'Popeye' lithographed tinplate dime register bank.

c1929-30   2.5in (6.5cm) high

£40-50 **SOTT**

A 1960s 'Official Batman Batplane' friction-powered plastic toy, marked "©National Periodical Publications Inc. 1976", boxed.

Box 5in (12.5cm) wide

£40-60 **GAZE**

An Aurora Comic Scenes 'Bat-Man' assembled model kit, marked "©1974 National Publications Inc".

£80-120 **NOR**

A 'Superman' 204-piece jigsaw puzzle, by APC.

c1974 5.5in (14cm) high

£8-12 **BH**

A 'Batman and Robin' Society Charter Member's pin, in original packaging.

c1966 3.25in (8.5cm) diam

£15-25 **BH**

A Toy Biz 'Superman' figurine, with Kryptonite ring that makes the figure fall over.

Superman figures are not common, especially those that are a good likeness.

c1989 10in (25.5cm) high

£40-60 **NOR**

A printed card packet of Mr. Bubbles 'Super Friends' bubble bath.

c1984 9.75in (25cm) high

£8-12 **BH**

A 'Super Friends' Thermos flask, by Aladdin Industries.

6.5in (16.5cm) high

£6-8 **BH**

A 'Dudley Do-Right' printed glass, from the Pepsi Collector's Series.

5in (12.5cm) high

£4-6 **BH**

A 'Flub-a-Dub' soft vinyl and cloth hand puppet.

A character on the Howdy Doody show, Flub-a-Dub was an amalgamation of eight different animals. It is one of the hardest characters from the show to find.

9.5in (24cm) high

£30-40 **SOTT**

A 1980s plastic 'Pac-Man' gum ball dispenser, by Superior Toy & Mfg Co.

5.75in (14.5cm) high

£10-15 **WAC**

A CLOSER LOOK AT A HOWDY DOODY COOKIE JAR

Purinton Pottery was formed in 1936 in Wellesville, Ohio and produced a range of dinner and casualwares. They made a range of items for other companies including Taylor, Smith & Taylor, for whom they made this cookie jar and a similar money bank.

This cookie jar is an early example, costing $3-4 in 1953. Reproductions do exist so ensure you are buying from a reliable source.

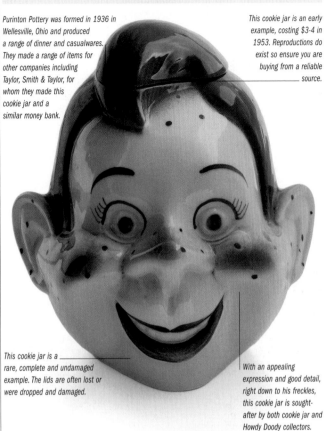

An American Louis Marx 'Porky the Pig' wind-up tin toy, with vibrating action and spinning umbrella above, marked "USA. © 1939 Leon Schlesinger", soiling and abrasions.

c1939   *8in (20cm) high*

£100-150 **JDJ**

This cookie jar is a rare, complete and undamaged example. The lids are often lost or were dropped and damaged.

With an appealing expression and good detail, right down to his freckles, this cookie jar is sought-after by both cookie jar and Howdy Doody collectors.

A very rare Howdy Doody cookie jar, by Purinton. *c1953*   *7.75in (19.5cm) high*

£250-350 **SOTT**

A Rocky printed glass, from the Pepsi Collector's Series.

5in (12.5cm) high

£4-6 **BH**

An Aladdin Character Kits 'Ronald McDonald – Sheriff of Cactus Canyon' lunchbox, with plastic flask.

c1982   *8.25in (21cm) wide*

£20-40 **NOR**

A 1970s Woody Woodpecker flashlight, by the Dyno Mdse. Corp.

3.5in (9cm) high

£8-12 **BH**

A Woodstock painted plaster nodder, marked "made in Korea".

c1972   *3.75in (9.5cm) high*

£15-25 **HH**

COINS

COLLECTORS' NOTES

■ Coin collecting is the oldest of the numismatic fields. The sheer range of types available can seem daunting to a new collector.

■ It is advisable to concentrate on one area such as the ancient world, commemoratives, error coins, or examples from one specific period and place.

■ When buying commemorative issues, take the edition number into account. Those released in large numbers will appreciate less than strictly limited issues.

■ Beware of facsimile collectors coins, which are common. Although not necessarily made to deceive, it can be hard to tell them from the genuine article.

■ As condition is very important, coins should be handled as little as possible. Always hold coins by the edges, and invest in a good quality album and mounts to display and store your collection.

■ Resist the temptation to clean coins – collectors generally prefer coins with an 'original' appearance. Cleaning might reduce values by half or more.

A CLOSER LOOK AT A POST-TREATY NOBLE

The noble was initially introduced during the reign of Edward III. This is an early example from that period.

The coin was worth approximately 6s 8d. It is a high denomination, making it rarer than lower denominations

The other side depicts Edward the III in a boat, rooting the noble in its historical context and adding appeal.

Although fairly difficult to come by, a hoard of around 130-140 nobles was found in Belgium around five years ago. This increased the number coming to market in the UK.

A post-treaty noble of Calais mint, minted by Edward III, with flag at stern, pellet at centre and around fleurs-de-lys, extremely fine. *1327-44*

£1,200-1,800   **BLO**

A long cross Penny, minted by Aethelred II, extra pellet in one quarter and with usual Danegeld chopmarks, very fine condition. *978-1016*

£400-500   **BLO**

A quatrefoil-type penny of York, minted by Cnut, in very fine condition. *1016-35*

£200-300   **BLO**

A scarce penny of Winchester, minted by Edward the Confessor, facing right wearing a pelleted helmet, two small annulets in one quarter, in very fine condition. *1042-66*

£300-400   **BLO**

A rare class II groat of London, minted by Richard II, the reverse with bar above second 'N' of London, in very fine condition.

£750-850   **BLO**

A rosette-mascle issue groat of Calais, minted by Henry VI, the reverse with plain cross, toned and in extremely fine condition. *1422-26*

£220-280   **BLO**

A scarce groat, minted by Philip & Mary, with a few light scratches, toned, in extremely fine condition.
1554-58

£250-350 BLO

A fifth issue shilling, minted by Elizabeth I, obverse scratches in field, in very fine condition.
1558-1602

£250-350 BLO

A scarce fifth issue angel, minted by Elizabeth I, in good condition.
1558-1602

£1,500-2,000 BLO

A first coinage shilling, minted by James I, second bust, with mid-grey tones, light marks in fields, in extremely fine condition.

£250-350 BLO

A third bust Crown, minted by Charles II, toned, very fine condition.
1672

£180-220 BLO

A rare Commonwealth crown, with 1656/4 overdate, with the usual weakly struck centres, lightly toned, the overdate particularly clear, in very fine condition.

1654

£1,200-1,800 BLO

A scarce first busts half-crown, minted by William & Mary, caul and interior frosted, pearls, with superb tones, in extremely fine condition.

1689

£700-800 BLO

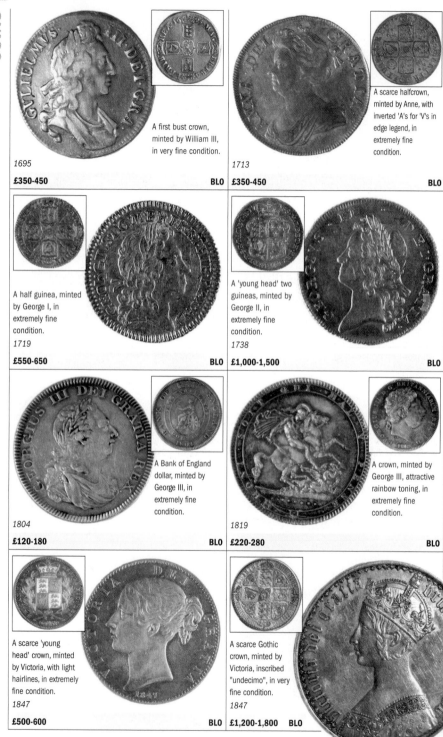

A first bust crown, minted by William III, in very fine condition.

1695

£350-450 BLO

A scarce halfcrown, minted by Anne, with inverted 'A's for 'V's in edge legend, in extremely fine condition.

1713

£350-450 BLO

A half guinea, minted by George I, in extremely fine condition.

1719

£550-650 BLO

A 'young head' two guineas, minted by George II, in extremely fine condition.

1738

£1,000-1,500 BLO

A Bank of England dollar, minted by George III, in extremely fine condition.

1804

£120-180 BLO

A crown, minted by George III, attractive rainbow toning, in extremely fine condition.

1819

£220-280 BLO

A scarce 'young head' crown, minted by Victoria, with light hairlines, in extremely fine condition.

1847

£500-600 BLO

A scarce Gothic crown, minted by Victoria, inscribed "undecimo", in very fine condition.

1847

£1,200-1,800 BLO

A CLOSER LOOK AT A DUTCH GULDEN

The gulden has been struck by machine.

This is in remarkable condition for its age. It is one of the finest known examples to come to market.

The coin has a rainbow sheen to the surface. Collectors favour good colouring as it is an indication that the coin has not been cleaned. A cleaned coin can be worth 50 per cent less.

The reverse depicts the coat of arms of William I of the Netherlands.

A rare Dutch gulden, virtually as struck with super rainbow tones and proof-like fields.

1820

£800-1,000   BLO

An American trade dollar, some light marks, in extremely fine condition.

1874

£120-180   BLO

An Australian shilling, in extremely fine condition.

1911

£80-120   BLO

A scarce Austrian thaler, of Vienna mint, as struck with attractive toning.

1829

£180-220   BLO

A rare 1800s Belgian gilt bronze franc, date indistinct, superb proof fields, with small toned area on reverse.

£80-120   BLO

A German States gulden, Baden, almost as struck, with light grey and rainbow tones.

1838

£80-120   BLO

An unusual Irish first Harp issue groat, minted by Henry VIII, with "H.I." for Henry and Jane Seymour, double-striking of obverse legend, in very fine condition.

1509-c1536

£70-100   BLO

A scarce Irish shilling, minted by Mary, in fine condition.

1553-58

£550-650   BLO

An Irish shilling, minted by Philip & Mary, usual weak portraits for this issue, in very fine condition.

1555

£550-650   BLO

An Italian chios, minted in Venice, anonymous contemporary copy of an Andrea Dandolo zecchino.

Andrea Dandolo was doge of Venice from 1342-54.

£220-280   BLO

An Italian gold zecchino, minted in Venice, with portrait of Gerolamo Pruili, in very fine condition.

1559-67

£100-150   BLO

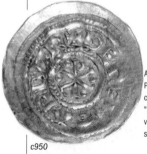

An Italian silver denaro, minted in Padua, with "Derengarivir" around chi-ro symbol, the reverse with "Papiaci" and "Potianarei", virtually as struck, some weak strike.

c950

£500-600   BLO

A scarce Swiss five francs coin, with light edge and field marks, in extremely fine condition.

1890

£80-120   BLO

A rare Vietnamese silver tien, minted in Annam, in extremely fine condition.

1848-83

£80-120   BLO

A scarce Swiss Cantons half thaler, minted in Zurich, city view with bridge in foreground, in extremely fine condition, attractive rainbow tones.

1720

£180-220   BLO

FIND OUT MORE...

'Standard Catalog of World Coins', *by Chester L. Krause & Clifford Mishler, published by Krause Publications.*

COLLECTORS' NOTES

■ Rarity and condition are crucial to value, the latter particularly so for people who collect for investment rather than for pleasure. The examples in this section are in particularly fine condition, as indicated by their high value.

■ Independent third-party companies such as Comics Guaranty LLC will grade the condition of a comic for a fee. The lower the number the poorer the condition.

■ The first issue of a title is usually the most desirable, with values dropping considerably even for the second issue. Other sought-after issues feature the first appearance, 'origin' or death of a character.

■ Golden Age (1938-c1955) comics continue to be popular and are generally the most valuable, with Superman and Batman the most sought-after.

■ Spider-Man is probably the most desirable Silver Age (c1956-c1969) character. Other Marvel titles of that period are currently more popular than titles from the other big publisher DC Comics.

■ Comics continue to be a source of material for Hollywood and a number of films released in 2005 including: Batman Begins, Superman, and the Fantastic Four. This should increase interest in the original comics.

"Action Comics", No.2, Jul. 1938, published by DC Comics, very good to fair condition (5), off-white pages, with cover artwork by Leo E. O'Mealia, featuring the second appearance of Superman.

The number in brackets is the grading given by Comics Guaranty LLC (CGC) for this particular example.

£7,000-9,000   MC

"Adventure Comics", No.48, Mar. 1940, published by DC Comics, very fine condition (8), off-white to white pages, with cover artwork by Bernard Bailey, featuring the first appearance of Hourman.

£8,000-10,000   MC

"The Amazing Spider-Man", No.14, Jul. 1964, published by Marvel Comics, near mint condition (9.4), off-white to white pages, featuring the first appearance of the Green Goblin.

£4,500-5,500   MC

"The Amazing Spider-Man", No.5, Oct. 1963, published by Marvel Comics, near mint condition (9.4), off-white to white pages, with cover artwork by Steve Ditko, featuring an appearance by Dr. Doom.

£5,500-6,500   MC

"The Amazing Spider-Man", No.121, Jun. 1973, published by Marvel Comics, near mint condition (9.4), off-white to white pages, featuring the death of Gwen Stacey by the Green Goblin.

£450-550   MC

A CLOSER LOOK AT A COMIC

The All Star title was created for the first superhero group, The Justice Society of America.

The title changed to 'All Star Western' from the 58th issue and the Justice Society was retired.

The Green Lantern figure on the cover was cut-and-pasted from the cover of 'All American' comic, issue 16.

The dramatic cover artwork, with its bold use of colour, makes this a striking example of a Golden Age comic.

"The Amazing Spider-Man", No.100, near mint condition (9.4), off-white pages.

£350-450   MC

"All Star Comics", No.2, Fall 1940, published by DC Comics, near mint condition (9.2), off-white to white pages.

£10,000-15,000   MC

"The Avengers", No.1, Sep. 1963, published by Marvel Comics, very fine condition (7.5), featuring the origin and first appearance of The Avengers.

£800-1,200   **MC**

"Batman", No.11, Jun/Jul 1942, published by DC Comics, very good to fair condition (5), off-white to white pages, featuring a classic Joker cover by Jerry Robinson.

£700-1,000   **MC**

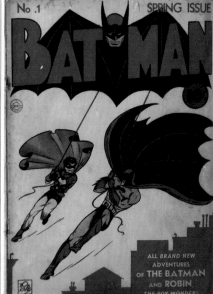

"Batman", No.1, Spring 1940, published by DC Comics, very good condition (3.5), cream to off-white pages, featuring the origin of Batman and the first appearance of the Joker and Catwoman.

£6,000-8,000   **MC**

"Batman", No.20, Dec. 1943/Jan. 1944, published by DC Comics, very fine to near mint condition (9), off-white pages, featuring the first appearance of the Batmobile on the cover.

£1,200-1,800   **MC**

"Batman", No.3, Fall, 1940, published by DC Comics, very fine condition (8), off-white to white pages, featuring the first appearance of Catwoman in costume, with cover artwork by Bob Kane and Sheldon Moldoff.

£3,000-4,000   **MC**

"Captain America Comics", No.1, Mar. 1941, published by Marvel Comics, fine condition (6), featuring the origin and first appearance of Captain America, with cover artwork featuring Adolf Hitler by Joe Simon.

£4,000-6,000   **MC**

"Captain Marvel Jr.", No.29, Apr 1945, published by Fawcett Publications, mint condition (9.9), with double cover.

£5,500-6,500   **MC**

A CLOSER LOOK AT A DETECTIVE COMIC

Issue 27 of Detective Comic saw the first appearance of the ever popular Batman.

Despite the relatively poor condition of this example, its rarity makes it desirable in virtually any state.

'The Batman' was created by artist Bob Kane, who took inspiration from Zorro, Leonardo da Vinci and the horror film 'The Bat-man', together with writer Bill Finger who is rarely credited.

"Detective Comics", No.27, May 1939, National Periodical Publications, good condition (2.5).

£20,000-25,000   **MC**

A CLOSER LOOK AT A FANTASTIC FOUR COMIC

The Fantastic Four was Marvel Comics answer to DC Comics popular superhero team, the Justice Society of America.

The team was created by legendary writer Stan Lee and artist Jack Kirby just as Lee was considering leaving the industry.

Unusually for the time, the Fantastic Four had no secret identities and, initially, often appeared without costume. They were also far from infallible and displayed very human traits, common with many of Lee's creations.

The latest film version of the franchise, due for released in 2005, is likely to increase interest in the comics.

"The Fantastic Four", No.1, Nov. 1961, published by Marvel Comics, very fine condition (8.5), off-white pages.

£15,000-20,000   MC

"Doctor Strange", No.169, Jun. 1968, published by Marvel Comics, near mint condition (9.6), white pages.

£400-500   MC

"The Fantastic Four", No.112, Jul. 1971, published by Marvel Comics, near mint condition (9.2), white pages, with date stamp to the front cover.

£180-220   MC

"The Fantastic Four", No.12, Mar. 1963, published by Marvel Comics, fine condition (6), off-white pages.

£350-450   MC

"The Human Torch", No.3, Winter 1940, published by Timely/Marvel Comics, very fine to near mint condition (9), off-white pages.

£4,000-6,000   MC

"The Incredible Hulk", No.1, May 1962, published by Marvel Comics, fine to very fine condition (7), off-white to white pages.

In this first issue, the Hulk is grey but due to printing problems, his colour was changed to green in issue two, although the grey Hulk briefly appeared again later in the series.

£3,000-4,000   MC

"The Incredible Hulk", No.4, Nov. 1962, published by Marvel Comics, very fine condition (7.5), cream to off-white pages.

£450-550   MC

"The Incredible Hulk", No.6, Mar. 1963, published by Marvel Comics, very fine condition (8.5).

£1,000-1,500   MC

A CLOSER LOOK AT A MARVEL COMIC

This was the first and only issue of this title, which became Marvel Mystery Comics from issue two.

Most copies of this issue were over-printed with 'November'; this version retains the original 'October'.

It features the first proper appearance and origin of Namor, the Sub-Mariner and the first appearance of the Human Torch.

This example comes from the collection of Hollywood actor Nicolas Cage, a well-known comic book fan. This adds to the value.

"Marvel Comics", No.1, Oct. 1939, published by Timely Comics, very good to fair condition (5).

£25,000-35,000   MC

"The Silver Surfer", No.2, Oct. 1968, published by Marvel Comics, near mint condition (9.6), off-white to white pages.

£650-750   MC

"Superman", No.1, Summer, 1939, published by DC Comics, very fine condition (8), restored.

Superman gained his own title one year after his first appearance and was the first superhero to do so.

£12,000-18,000   MC

"Superman", No. 8, Jan./Feb. 1941, published by Marvel Comics, very fine condition, (7.5), cream pages.

£1,000-1,400   MC

"Tales of Suspense", No. 59, Nov. 1964, published by Marvel Comics, near mint condition (9.4), off-white to white pages, features Silver Age Captain America's first solo story.

£800-1,200   MC

"The X-Men", No.2, Nov. 1963, published by Marvel Comics, very fine condition (8.5), off-white pages.

£800-1,200   MC

"The X-Men", No.12, Jul. 1965, published by Marvel Comics, very fine condition (8.5), cream-off-white pages, featuring the origin of Professor X.

£150-250   MC

"X-Men Giant Size", No.1, Summer 1975, published by Marvel Comics, near mint condition (9.4), white pages, featuring the first appearance of the new X-Men lineup.

£700-1,000   MC

"Adventures Into Terror", No.10, Jun. 1950, published by Atlas Comics, near mint condition (9.2), white pages.

£300-400   MC

"Chamber of Chills", No.15, Jan 1953, published by Harvey Publications, near mint condition (9.4).

£400-500   MC

"Chilling Tales", No.13, Dec. 1952, Youthful Publications, very fine to near mint condition (9), with cover art by Matt Fox.

£550-650   MC

"The Crypt of Terror", No.18, Jun./Jul. 1950, published by E.C. Comics, very fine to near mint condition (9).

£1,000-1,500   MC

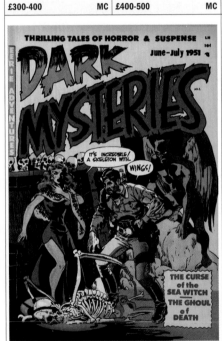

"Dark Mysteries", No.16, Feb. 1954, published by Master/Merit Publications, very fine condition (8), off-white to white pages.

£300-400   MC

"Dark Mysteries", No.1, Jun./Jul. 1951, published by Master Publications, near mint condition (9.2), off-white pages.

£1,800-2,200   MC

"Fantastic Fears", No.7, May 1953, published by Ajax/Farrell Publications, very fine condition (8.5), off-white to white pages.

£350-450   MC

"The Haunt of Fear", No.6, Mar./Apr. 1951, published by Fawcett Publications, near mint condition (9.6).

£800-1,200   MC

"The Haunt of Fear", No.12, Apr. 1952, published by E.C. Comics, near mint condition (9.2).

£500-600   MC

"Haunted Thrills", No.4, Dec. 1952, published by Ajax/Farrell Publications, very fine to near mint condition (9), white pages.

£450-550   **MC**

"Out of the Shadows", No.8, Apr. 1953, published by Standard Comics, very fine condition (8.5).

£650-750   **MC**

"Shock SuspenStories", No.8, Apr./May 1953, published by E.C. Comics, near mint condition (9.6).

£1,000-1,500   **MC**

"Strange Suspense Stories", No.1, Jun. 1952, Fawcett Publications, very fine to near mint condition (9).

£600-700   **MC**

A CLOSER LOOK AT A MARVEL COMIC

Whilst the popularity of superhero comics slumped in the 1950s, horror titles were in great demand.

E.C Comics, run by Will Gaines, produced some of the best horror comics of the period. Companies such as Star Publications, owned by L.B. Cole, also specialized in horror titles.

This example has typically lurid and shocking cover artwork by owner, L.B. Cole, who believed a striking cover was more important than the content.

The horrific nature of these graphically illustrated comics contributed to the creation of the Comic Code Authority in 1954, which changed the industry as a whole.

"Startling Terror Tales", No.11, Jul. 1952, published by Star Publications, near mint condition (9.2).

£3,500-4,500   **MC**

"Tales From The Crypt", No.30, Jun./Jul. 1952, published by E.C. Comics, near mint condition (9.4), off-white pages.

£800-1,200   **MC**

"The Thing!", No.7, Aug. 1952, very fine condition (8), off-white pages.

£550-650   **MC**

"This Magazine is Haunted", No.7, Oct. 1952, published by Fawcett Publications, near mint condition (9.2), graded, white pages.

£700-900   **MC**

A CLOSER LOOK AT A SCI-FI COMIC

Planet Comics was the first original science fiction comic title released. Previous examples re-used material from newspaper strips.

The cover art work is by Lou Fine and acclaimed American comic artist Will Eisner.

Issue one features the first appearance and origin of Auro, Lord of Jupiter.

Its provenance together with its extremely fine condition adds to the value of this rare comic.

"Planet Comics", No.1, Jan. 1940, published by Fiction House Magazines, near mint condition (9.4), off-white pages,

Provenance: from the collection of Nicolas Cage.

£20,000-25,000   MC

"Weird Fantasy", No.9, Sep./Oct. 1951, published by E.C. Comics, near mint condition (9.2).

£450-550   MC

"Weird Fantasy", No.15, Sep./Oct. 1953, published by E.C. Comics, near mint condition (9.4).

£1,500-2,000   MC

"Weird Science", No.10, Nov./Dec. 1951, published by E.C. Comics, very fine to near mint condition (9).

£350-450   MC

"Weird Science-Fantasy", No.29, Jun. 1955, published by E.C. Comics, near mint condition (9.4), off-white to white, featuring cover artwork by Frank Frazetta.

£4,000-5,000   MC

"Weird Science", No.19, May/Jun. 1953, published by E.C. Comics, near mint condition (9.4).

£1,000-1,500   MC

"Weird Science", No.20, Jul./Aug. 1953, published by E.C. Comics, near mint condition (9.4), white pages.

£1,000-1,500   MC

COMICS

"Brenda Starr", Vol.2 No.8, May 1949, published by Superior Comics, near mint condition (9.2), off-white to white pages.

£1,200-1,800 MC

"Crimes By Women", No.1, Jun. 1948, published by Fox Features Syndicate, near mint condition (9.2), off-white to white, featuring the true story of Bonnie Parker (Bonnie and Clyde).

Crime comics of the late 1940s and 1950s often featured scenes of torture and violence against women. Many were cited in 'Seduction of the Innocent' by Fredric Wertham in 1953, which asserted that crime comics encouraged children to delinquency. The book contributed to the introduction of the Comic Code Authority in 1954.

£2,500-3,500 MC

"Crime Detective Comics", Vol.1 No.1, Mar. 1948, published by Miller Periodicals, near mint condition (9.6), off-white pages, featuring true police cases.

£700-900 MC

"Crime Does Not Pay", No.24, Nov. 1942, published by Comic House, very fine condition (8.5), off-white pages, featuring the first appearance of Mr. Crime.

£2,500-3,500 MC

"Detective Picture Stories", No.1, Dec. 1936, published by Comics Magazine Company, fine condition (6.5).

£1,500-2,000 MC

"Little Dot", No.1, Sep. 1953, published by Harvey Publications, very fine condition (7.5).

£2,000-2,500 MC

"Mad", No.4, Apr./May 1953, published by E.C. Comics, near mint condition (9.4), off-white to white pages.

£1,000-1,500 MC

"Mad", No.5, Jun./Jul. 1953, published by E.C. Comics, near mint condition (9.2).

£2,000-2,500 MC

"Sgt. Fury and His Howling Commandos", No.1, May 1963, published by Marvel Comics, fine condition (6.5), off-white to white pages.

£250-350 MC

FIND OUT MORE...

Official Overstreet Comic Book Price Guide, by Robert M. Overstreet, published by House of Collectibles, 2004, 34th edition.

A CLOSER LOOK AT A COMMEMORATIVE PARIANWARE BUST

Arthur Balfour (1848-1930) was prime minister from 1902-05.

Parian is a semi-matt type of porcelain made with feldspar that was often used to make replicas of ancient sculptures and marble models.

An unusual George Kinloch commemorative earthenware mug, printed with a named portrait inscribed with detail of his flight from the country and subsequent representation of Dundee, restored.

George Kinloch MP, fled Scotland after protesting against the Peterloo massacre. He returned after he was pardoned and became MP of Dundee.

1832   4in (10cm) high

£100-150   **SAS**

A Lord Brougham commemorative pink lustre earthenware jug, with a named portrait of Lord Brougham and inscribed "Reform" in a cartouche.

Henry Brougham, 1st Baron Brougham and Vaux (1778-1868) was Lord Chancellor from 1830–34 and brought about a number of reforms including the abolition of slavery.

1832   5.5in (14cm) high

£180-220   **SAS**

Commemorative pieces of Balfour are hard to find.

Robinson & Leadbeater were based in Stoke-on-Trent and specialized in parianware, particularly portrait busts such as this.

An Arthur Balfour commemorative white parian portrait bust, by Robinson and Leadbeater.

8in (20cm) high

£200-300   **SAS**

A rare Earl of Iddesleigh memorial plate, registered design no. for 1895.

Stafford Henry Northcote, 1st Earl of Iddesleigh (1818-87) held, among other offices, Foreign Secretary (1886–87).

9in (23cm) diam

£20-40   **GAZE**

A Continental Irish Home Rule commemorative spill holder, possibly by Schäfer & Vader, modelled as a frightened figure in a boat entitled 'It's all up now'.

Inspiration for this piece probably came from a cartoon of the period depicting a politician cast adrift in a dinghy.

c1920

£100-150   **SAS**

A Paragon Neville Chamberlain commemorative plate, titled 'Chamberlain the Peacemaker', the reverse inscribed.

1938

£70-100   **SAS**

COMMEMORATIVES

A Winston Churchill commemorative pottery jug, with a named portrait of Winston Churchill, lined in yellow and brown.

c1940   8.25in (20.5cm) high

£120-180   **SAS**

A Royal Doulton Winston Churchill commemorative tankard, the base marked "for a thousand years, men say, this was their finest hour".

c1940-42   5.75in (14.5cm) high

£100-150   **H&G**

A Grays Winston Churchill commemorative earthenware lustre trim jug.

c1940-42   3.75in (9.5cm) high

£80-100   **H&G**

A Bakelite Winston Churchill commemorative portrait plaque.

These early plastic plaques were made in a variety of sizes.

c1940-42   5in (12.5cm) diam

£60-80   **H&G**

A Kent Winston Churchill & Franklin Delano Roosevelt earthenware plate, commemorating the union between the US and Britain during WWII.

c1942-45   8.75in (22cm) diam

£80-120   **H&G**

A Winston Churchill commemorative money bank, titled 'Save for Victory' on the back.

c1940-45
4.25in (11cm) high

£50-60   **H&G**

A WWII 'Victory in Europe' commemorative wooden tankard, with metal bands and plaque reading "Made from battleships of Britain", and with a Churchill quote from his VE Day broadcast "Advance Britannia, long live the cause of freedom".

c1945   4.5in (11.5cm) high

£60-70   **H&G**

An Ashmor 'Winston Churchill' painted ceramic figurine, number 13 in the series.

11.25in (28.5cm) high

£180-220   **W&W**

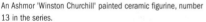

A Burleigh Ware 'Winston Churchill' character jug.
1965   *5.25in (13cm) high*

£80-120   **SAS**

A Copeland Winston Churchill commemorative jug, with inscribed portrait oval of Winston Churchill and on the reverse a bulldog upon the globe.

6.75in (17cm) high

£150-200   **SAS**

A limited edition Spode in memoriam 'The Churchill Plate', from an edition of 5,000, boxed.
1965

£40-60   **SAS**

A Spitting Image Margaret Thatcher mug, designed by Fluck & Law, to commemorate Thatcher's second election victory.
c1983   *4.5in (11.5cm) high*

£70-90   **H&G**

A Winston Churchill metal pin.

1in (2.5cm) long

£10-15   **LG**

A limited edition Paragon China Winston Churchill cigar box, from an edition of 500, to commemorate Churchill's birth.
1974   *10in (25.5cm) wide*

£120-180   **W&W**

A Drostdy Ware Independence of Rhodesia commemorative mug, made for the Friends of Rhodesia, printed with a sepia portrait of Ian Douglas Smith.
c1965

£50-80   **H&G**

An earthenware mug, commemorating the 10th Anniversary of Rhodesian independence, with image of Ian Douglas Smith.

c1975   *3.5in (9cm) high*

£30-50   **H&G**

A set of six Danbury Mint Horatio Nelson tankards, on Wedgwood Queen's Ware.

£150-200   **W&W**

A CLOSER LOOK AT A NELSON COMMEMORATIVE TYG

This three-handled cup commemorates the centenary of the death of Horatio Nelson (1758-1805).

Nelson memorabilia was highly collectable even during his own lifetime and early pieces are very difficult to obtain. Even pieces made well after his death are sought after.

2005 was the 200th anniversary of the Battle of Trafalgar, where Nelson lost his life. This should increase interest in him and help prices to rise.

Copeland is adesirable maker and its pieces are more likely to retain or increase their value.

A cast spelter candlestick in the form of Nelson's column, cast mark "Regd No 783811 Made in England", for 1933.

10.75in (27.5cm) high

£100-150   **W&W**

A Royal Doulton Horatio Nelson centenary commemorative stoneware spill vase, with a portrait cartouche of Nelson.

1905   5.5in (13.5cm) high

£500-600   **SAS**

A Copeland for Goode 'Subscriber's Copy' pottery tyg, decorated in colours with portrait of Nelson, ships and Britannia, inscribed and lined in gilt.

c1905   6in (15cm) high

£1,200-1,800   **SAS**

A scarce Aller Vale pottery three-handled cup, with shallow relief figure of a soldier, inscribed "South Africa 1899-1900" and "God Bless you Tommy Atkins, here's your country's love to you", stamped "Aller Vale" to the base.

£180-220   **W&W**

A Lord Roberts and Boer War commemorative beaker, by RAH. & SAL. Plant.

c1900   4.5in (11.5cm) high

£80-120   **H&G**

A Transvaal china pottery mug, by Foley, with a named portrait of Baden-Powell, the reverse inscribed in black for the siege and relief of Mafeking with dates.

1900

£180-220   **SAS**

A Boer War commemorative mug, by J.G. & M., London, with scrolls either side reading "Union is Strength" and "Peace with Honour". *3.25in (8.5cm) high*	A Boer War souvenir pipe, the bowl carved with portraits of Lords Bobs & 'Oom Paul', marked "Boer War 1899-1902".	Two Boer War carved bone napkin rings, one with "Vader van Tobie St Helena 1902, the other "St Helena 1902", the inscriptions heightened in black, with crenellated edges.
£120-180 **W&W**	**£80-120** **W&W**	**£60-80** **W&W**

A MacIntyre globular match holder, with printed scene of a soldier, the reverse inscribed with verse by Rudyard Kipling.	A WWI silvered copper cigarette box, with a Caton Woodville relief scene of British troops overrunning a German gun, together with the Allies and patriotic inscription by Rudyard Kipling. *8in (20.5cm) long*	A WWI commemorative faïence plaque moulded with the heads of seven Allied servicemen inscribed "Les, 7 Peches Capitaux de L'Allemagne". *14.5in (36cm) wide*
£50-60 **SAS**	**£40-60** **W&W**	**£150-200** **SAS**

A Paragon World War II plate, decorated with St. George slaying the dragon, the reverse inscribed and dated.

Paragon is well known for its commemorative wares, with fine quality bodies and decoration. This hand-decorated piece is unusual as it is similar in style to majolica pottery.

1941

£350-450   **SAS**

COMMEMORATIVES

A Robinson & Leadbeater commemorative white parian portrait bust, of pianist Frédéric-François Chopin, on named base.

7.75in (19.5cm) high

£80-120 SAS

A Hastings souvenir octagonal pottery plate, printed in black and enamelled in colours with named views.

£40-60 SAS

A commemorative agriculture-related pottery plate, the centre decorated with a plough within an Imari-style border.

c1840

£20-30 SAS

An 1851 Great Exhibition porcelain mug, printed in grey with a named and dated view of the Crystal Palace.

3.25in (8cm) high

£80-120 SAS

A Staffordshire pottery figure, depicting the minister in his pulpit.

c1860   11.25in (28cm) high

£120-180 SAS

A Charles Dickens in memoriam tile trivet.

c1870   6.25in (16cm) wide

£100-150 H&G

A Paragon Malcolm Campbell commemorative trio set, decorated with blue birds in flight, the reverse of each inscribed and dated.

Released to commemorate Campbell breaking the World Land Speed record in his car 'Bluebird'.

1932

£80-120 SAS

A Minton plate, enamelled with initials "HS" surmounted by a coronet, the reverse with indistinct impressed mark.

c1880   9.75in (24.5cm) diam

£200-300 SAS

A small Grand Tour gilt metal mounted purse, the front set with four miniature pictures.

2.25in (5.5cm) wide

£70-100 CA

A Paragon bone china mug, made to commemorate the Festival of Britain.

c1951   4in (10cm) high

£200-300   **H&G**

A Festival of Britain commemorative aluminium teapot, with bakelite handle and knop, marked "Swan Brand" and "2 Cups".

1951   4in (10cm) high

£15-25   **DH**

A Festival of Britain commemorative copper eggcup, with applied enamel logo.

1951   1.5in (4cm) high

£15-20   **DH**

A Festival of Britain commemorative brass ashtray.

1951   3.5in (9cm) high

£15-25   **DH**

A Festival of Britain commemorative chrome tea caddy spoon.

1951   3in (7.5cm) long

£7-10   **DH**

A Poole pottery plate, possibly decorated by Jean Best, commemorating the Festival of Britain.

c1951   10in (25.5cm) diam

£70-100   **C**

A Festival of Britain London Children's concert programme.

1951   10in (25.5cm) high

£4-5   **DH**

Four Festival of Britain bus tickets.

1951   4in (10cm) high

£1-2 each   **DH**

COLLECTORS' NOTES

- Vintage fashion is popular with both established collectors and casual buyers wanting to create an unusual look. Something can be found for every budget. Clothing made by the top fashion houses tends to attract the highest prices, but interesting and stylish items can be picked up for as little as £5.

- An appealing area of collecting is 1960s fashion. Clothes often fall into one of two categories – the stark, geometric, space age look of Andre Courreges or the multicoloured, ethnic, hippie style.

- The 1970s saw a diversity of styles including highly patterned clothes inspired by ethnic and peasant dress, brightly coloured spandex disco outfits and everyday wear such as tank tops and flares. Clothes

by high profile designers, such as Ossie Clark and Yves Saint Laurent, are very desirable, as are unnamed pieces that are typical of the period, or sum up a specific look, such as late 1970s punk.

- Clothes dating from the 1980s, once considered tasteless and hugely unfashionable, have again found favour with a rapidly increasing number of enthusiasts. Bold glitzy designs, 'power suits' and ra-ra skirts were all popular, as was newly fashionable sportswear by makers such as Nike. Labels were important to the style-conscious 1980s lady and items by well known designers also tend to command a premium today. Look out for Vivienne Westwood, Karl Lagerfeld, Georgio Armani and Gianni Versace.

An early Ceil Chapman beaded and sequined black dress.

Ceil Chapman was one of a Marilyn Monroe's favourite designers.

£550-650　　　　　**MA**

A CLOSER LOOK AT A GUNNE SAX DRESS

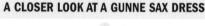

Gunne Sax of San Francisco made dresses to designs by Jessica McClintock, who joined in 1969. _____

The successful style launched many imitators, which are less desirable, as are Gunne Sax's designs from the 1980s onwards

Gunne Sax produced many successful and popular styles, including 'granny dresses', dresses inspired by Victorian and Edwardian styles, and prairie-style dresses like this one. _____

Cotton was a typical material, and beige and browns typical colours – both echo the roots of the revivalist style.

An early to mid-1970s Gunne Sax 'prairie' style dress, cotton with cotton lace detailing and string-like soutache detailing.

49.5in (126cm) long

£120-180　　　　　**NOR**

A 1980s purple Contempo Casuals cotton and lycra dress, with rigid wired base, pulling in towards the legs.

The Contempo Casuals chain of over 200 stores became part of Wet Seal Inc (founded 1962) in 1995, as the 'forward looking' teen fashion sister brand to Wet Seal. In 2001, the brand disappeared with all stores being renamed Wet Seal. This dress retains its original price tag for $108, so would have been expensive in its day.

31in (79cm) long

£80-120　　　　　**NOR**

An Estelle of Jackson Heights, New York, couture dress, the flesh-coloured silk catsuit covered with regular pieces of silver-coloured fabric and diamanté set straps and neckline.

c1968　　49.5in (126cm) long

£70-100　　　　　**NOR**

A 1960s/70s Lanvin polyester shift dress, with belt and geometric abstract print.

40.5in (103cm) long

£50-80   **NOR**

A Lanvin printed polyester chemise, with belt, in green, blue and black.

c1969   *42in (107cm) long*

£40-60   **NOR**

A CLOSER LOOK AT A JEANNE LANVIN TROUSER DRESS

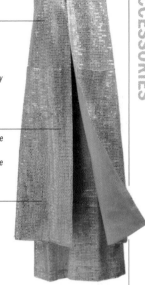

The shimmering exterior is made of silver-coloured reflective fabric tape sewn into a woven wool form in horizontal bands.

The form and material exemplifies the 'space-age' look of the late 1960s championed by Andre Courreges, Pierre Cardin and Paco Rabanne, and inspired by man's ventures into outer space.

It has a white label reading 'Lanvin 22 Faubourg St Honore PARIS', meaning it may be an haute couture piece sold in the boutique and made to order.

It was designed by the house of Lanvin's designer at the time, Jules-Francois Crahay, who joined in 1963 and remained there until 1984.

A late 1960s Jeanne Lanvin sleeveless trouser dress, with sleeveless coat ensemble, lined with beige wool felt.

51.25in (130cm) long

£300-400   **NOR**

An early 1970s Lanvin block-printed silk chemise, with belt.

Jeanne Lanvin (1867-1946) founded the first haute couture house in France in 1909. Her hallmark designs were the robes de style, with small waists and full skirts, based on 18thC designs. Numerous designers worked for the house, including Giorgio Armani.

42.5in (108cm) long

£50-80   **NOR**

A 1960s 'Waste Basket Boutique' polka dot disposable paper dress, by Mars of Asheville NC.

The Pop Art movement, led by Andy Warhol, led to the use of new materials such as paper. Aimed at being disposable, designs were mass produced and aimed at the mass market.

54in (137cm) long

£40-60   **NOR**

A Lilly Pulitzer 'The Lilly' pink and yellow sleeveless shift dress.

41in (104cm) long

£60-80   **NOR**

COSTUME & ACCESSORIES

A 1970s Lilly Pulitzer 'The Lilly' blue printed floral cotton sleeveless dress, with applied knitted cotton flowers.

39.75in (101cm) long

£30-40   **NOR**

A CLOSER LOOK AT A LILLY PULITZER DRESS

Her name is always incorporated into the design of authentic examples

Her hallmark shift dresses are typically sleeveless

The original was made by Pulitzer's own dress maker and included lining and lace seam beadings around the neck and pocket. Pulitzer continued this attention to detail throughout her career.

As well as being fashionable during the 1960s, the bright floral colours were originally made to conceal orange juice stains as Pulitzer first developed the dress as a uniform for her orange juice stall attendants.

A 1960s Lilly Pulitzer yellow and green sleeveless dress.

When Pulitzer's old school friend Jackie Kennedy began wearing her designs, she shot to fame and her look became popular across the US.

39.5in (100cm) long

£40-60   **NOR**

A Saks Fifth Avenue black and white banded silk sack dress, possibly 1960s, with vertical flat 'ruff' to front.

Starting in 1911, this famous department store carried native and European designs, but closed its couture and custom design department in the 1970s.

91.5in (94cm) long

£15-20   **NOR**

A 1960s 'Malcolm Starr Couture' printed cotton dress, with border of glass jewels.

53.5in (136cm) long

£30-40   **NOR**

A 1980s navy polyester cocktail dress, by Collections, decorated with gold-coloured polka dots, size 5-6.

£20-30   **BR**

A 1980s American white knitted cotton dress, by Leslie Fay, with multi-coloured geometric design, US size 8.

£8-12   **BR**

A 1960s Mod-style corduroy mini-dress, by Full Circle.

33.5in (85cm) long

£20-30   **NOR**

An American turquoise dress, by International Ladies Garments Workers Union, with ruffled neckline and cuffs.

£12-18   **BR**

A 1940s Hawaiian 'Mun' printed silk dress, by Liberty House, Honolulu and Waikiki, size small.

£300-400   **MA**

A 1940s Pake Mud printed Rayon dress, by the Liberty House, Waikiki, size 10.

£500-700   **MA**

An Ondine of California printed pink, green and black tartan sleeveless dress, with black faceted buttons.

38.25in (97cm) long

£30-40   **NOR**

A 1960s polyester bandana print dress, with elasticated cinched waist and flowing sleeves.

51.5in (131cm) long

£20-40   **NOR**

A 1960s printed velvet harlequin-style gown.

70.75in (150cm) long

£30-50   **NOR**

A black polyester dress, with ruffled neck, cuffs and skirt, decorated with small flower design, size 42.

£10-15   **BR**

A 1930s black gown, with rhinestone and sequin decoration.

£300-400   **MA**

A long red gingham dress, with white collar and cuffs.

£10-15 BR

A green evening dress, with matching brocade coat with three-quarter length sleeves.

£8-16 BR

A printed polyester and silk dress, decorated with Art Nouveau ladies' heads.

The 1960s looked back to the Art Nouveau style for inspiration, but updated it in the bright, psychedelic colours typical of the period. Here the whiplash motif, clouds and flowing tresses of hair, as well as the skirt length are given a truly 1960s makeover. Note the ruff neck, which also copies Victorian style.

£40-60 NOR

A long blue evening dress, with attached overcoat, and beaded detailing.

£15-20 BR

A late 1960s metallic thread lace dress.

The overall shape, use of metallic thread and the length of the skirt recall the flapper dresses of the 1920s.

35.5in (90cm) long

£12-18 NOR

A 1960s flesh-coloured crepé and silk dress, with plastic sequins.

39.75in (101cm) long

£20-30 NOR

A late 1960s psychedelic-coloured sequin and silk crepé net dress, unlabelled.

35.5in (90cm) long

£30-40 NOR

A 1960s border print lurex dress, with button-through top.

39.25in (100cm) long

£25-35 NOR

An acetate sack dress, with psychedelic mushroom print.

37.5in (95cm) long

£25-35 NOR

A short yellow dress, with zippered back and bold floral design.

£10-15   BR

A 1960s printed cotton dress, decorated with Tudor-type figures, unlabelled.

36.25in (92cm) long

£15-25   NOR

A 1960s handmade blue and green embroidered flower mini dress.

31.5in (80cm) long

£50-80   NOR

A 1960s abstract print cotton sleeveless shift dress.

39in (99cm) long

£10-15   NOR

A Papillon blue and black geometric printed cotton sleeveless dress.

The design of this dress either resembles a Folk Art rug or the geometric prints of Emilio Pucci, who would have been a popular, and expensive, designer name at the time this dress was made.

57in (145cm) long

£25-35   NOR

A pink and black printed white cotton dress, with printed, stylized ruffs and button-down front.

36.25in (92cm) long

£25-35   NOR

A mohair tunic dress, with frayed hem.

£7-9   BR

A 1960s black suede and white leather sleeveless dress, unlabelled.

The style of this dress almost mimics those of Andre Courrèges.

39.75in (101cm) long

£60-90   NOR

A 1960s black silk and rhinestone inlaid Mod dress, with retro 1920s styling.

34.25in (87cm) long

£40-60   NOR

A black and white chequered woven wool coat dress, unlabelled.

40.5in (103cm) long

£60-90   NOR

A 1960s Bergdorf Goodman silk trouser suit, with blue and brown 'Maurice' signature floral print.

trousers 41.75in (106cm) long

£45-55 NOR

A Bogart of Texas red suede-look velvet hot pants and vest suit, with red polyester polka dot blouse.

vest 28in (71cm) long

£35-45 NOR

A 1980s Contempo Casuals ochre cotton and lycra two-piece suit, with rigid wired base, pulling in towards the legs.

£80-120 NOR

A late 1960s Leslie Fay Original gold lamé snakeskin effect two-piece trouser suit.

Founded in 1947, Leslie Fay was popular due to its affordable yet appealing designs. Aimed at the middle-aged, it is not known for avant-garde design. Joan Leslie and David Warren are also associated with the brand.

jacket 29.25in (74cm) long

£30-50 NOR

A printed cotton one-piece pant suit, with Aztec designs in bands and card and plastic green belt with card buckle.

52.25in (133cm) long

£15-25 NOR

A 1970s/80s Yves Saint Laurent 'Rive Gauche' red woollen jacket, with black and white piping.

Yves Saint Laurent's 'Rive Gauche' ready-to-wear brand was established in 1966. The combination of structured form and strong, powerful colours evoke the 1980s, a decade of power dressing for women.

26.25in (67cm) long

£60-90 NOR

A 1960s Shulman Furs of Philadelphia leopard skin fur coat, with black mink fur trim.

30.25in (77cm) long

£800-1,200 PC

A 1960s Sandy Chrysler faux fur sleeveless coat.

56.75in (144cm) long

£50-80 NOR

A 1960s Domani Knits woven wool and cotton sleeveless jacket, with bands of geometric, almost Aztec designs and metallic lion-head buckle fastening.

41.75in (106cm) long

£20-30 NOR

A 1960s faux leopard skin sleeveless coat, by Young Generation.

Despite the terrible associations with real fur, fake fur is making a comeback on the catwalks.

43.75in (111cm) long

£50-80   NOR

A gold and blue paisley lamé coat, with side fastenings, unlabelled.

56.25in (143cm) long

£40-60   NOR

A 1960s suede 'alpine look' cape and matching apron, with applied flowers, unlabelled.

31.5in (80cm) long

£100-150   NOR

A 1960s/70s purple and black suede hippie cape.

28.75in (73cm) long

£50-80   NOR

A 1960s/70s embroidered green suede poncho, unlabelled.

31.75in (81cm) long

£50-80   NOR

A long leather jacket, with popper fastenings, lacks label.

£30-40   BR

An early 1960s all hand-embroidered sweater jacket, with triangular designs.

19.75in (50cm) long

£25-35   NOR

A Peter Max signature design unisex reversible jumper, the reverse with yellow stripes on red background.

The design, colour, form and material scream the 1980s. Peter Max became famous in the 1960s for his way-out psychedelic designs known as 'Cosmic 60s'. His fondness for bright colours and skill at visually encapsulating the changing styles of an age continued through his career.

c1989   26in (66cm) long

£20-30   NOR

A ladies' knitted jumper, by Crochetta, Malta, with applied fabric and shell decoration.

£10-20   BR

A ladies' knitted acrylic and nylon jumper, by Destiny.

£10-15   BR

A ladies' knitted jumper, by Jessica at Sears.

£8-12   BR

A ladies' printed sweatshirt, by Les Modes, Minique, Canada.

£12-18   BR

A ladies' knitted jumper, by Mirere, metallic thread geometric decoration, size medium.

£6-9   BR

A ladies' knitted jumper, by Nonpareil, with sequinned decoration, size medium.

£8-12   BR

A ladies' knitted jumper, by Normandy, USA, size large.

£15-20   BR

A ladies' paisley pattern tunic, with zippered back.

£3-5   BR

A ladies' polyester sweatshirt, by Northern Spirit, size small.

£12-18   BR

A ladies' knitted jumper, lacks label.

£6-8   BR

A 1960s Mascot by Trude of California mohair silk and cotton sleeveless top, with Mondrianesque design.

22.5in (57cm) long

£30-40   **NOR**

A Western-style ladies' shirt, by Karman, size 12.

£8-12   **BR**

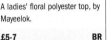

A ladies' floral polyester top, by Mayeelok.

£5-7   **BR**

A polyester shirt, by Pant Man.

£4-6   **BR**

A Perfection by Roxanne printed polyester blouse.

£12-18   **NOR**

A ladies' polyester top, with metallic thread decoration, size large.

£10-15   **BR**

A ladies' brown shirt, decorated with orange flowers, lacks label.

£5-7   **BR**

A ladies' shirt, with floral decoration, lacks label.

£7-9   **BR**

A 1960s brown suede and woven wool hippie top and matching cape, with woven wool tie and bobbles.

28.75in (73cm) long

£80-120   **NOR**

A ladies' Western-style shirt, by Zazie, London, with red gingham check panel and cuffs.

£4-6   **BR**

A 1960s Italian 'Mod' woven knit Maxi skirt.

43.75in (111cm) long

£15-25   **NOR**

A 1960s Prestige of Boston 'flower power' printed velvet skirt.

£20-30   **NOR**

A 1960s long skirt, with floral decoration on a black ground.

£7-9   **BR**

A long striped skirt, with pink decoration and long side split.

£5-7   **BR**

A long blue skirt, with floral decoration and elasticated waistband.

£5-7   **BR**

A 1950s long black skirt, with applied patchwork decoration of a basket of balls of wool.

£3-5   **BR**

A 1950s Mexican hand-painted cotton full skirt, with design of a Mexican native, highlighted with applied sequins.

£120-180   **MA**

A 1950s Mexican handpainted full skirt, with design of a chief among cacti, with natives and pyramids in the background.

£120-180   **MA**

A 1950s black felt gilt skirt, with applied design of leopard fur and glitter decoration, gold-coloured chain belt.

£200-300   **MA**

A 1950s turquoise-blue full circle skirt, with applied glitter and felt decoration of a car at traffic lights.

The condition of the glitter and the appliqué felt decoration is excellent. This, twinned with the stylish motifs, typical of the period, add value.

£150-200   **MA**

A 1980s black and pink net lace layered skirt, by Honey, waist 25in.

£8-12   **BR**

A denim skirt, with indistinct label, size 11.

£6-9   **BR**

A 1970s 'Lick Me' blue printed cotton wraparound skirt.

This print incorporates a slightly naughty version of the now famous Smiley face developed by American artist Harvey Ball in 1963 and popularised during the 1970s.

26in (66cm) long

£15-25   **NOR**

A printed skirt, lacks label, size 44.

£4-6   **BR**

An A-line skirt, with chevron design, lacks label, size 32.

£8-10   **GR**

A pair of multicoloured floral culottes.

£5-7   **BR**

A pair of 1960s psychedelic printed cotton hip-hugger jeans, unlabelled.

39in (99cm) long

£30-40   **NOR**

A pair of 1960s psychedelic flower printed trousers.

37in (94cm) long

£15-25   **NOR**

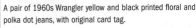

A pair of 1960s Wrangler yellow and black printed floral and polka dot jeans, with original card tag.

It is rare to find jeans like these in such immaculate condition and with their original tag.

£30-40   **NOR**

A 1960s Emilio Pucci for Formfit Rogers polyester slip, with EPFR monogram.

EPFR designs were by Emilio Pucci, but all FormFit Rogers pieces were intended as underwear and were mass-produced.

20.75in (53cm) long

£50-70   **NOR**

A 1970s Emilio Pucci for Formfit Rogers chemise, with EPFR monogram, pink white and black design with border print.

34.25in (87cm) long

£70-100   **NOR**

A 1970s Emilio Pucci for Formfit Rogers four-piece lingerie set, made from nylon, Lycra and Spandex, comprising two sets of knickers, a bra and a sleeveless 'baby doll' tunic, all with EPFR monogram within the printed design.

£100-150   **NOR**

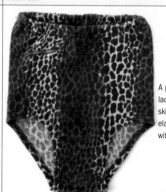

A 1950s leopard skin print bra, unmarked.

£30-50   **SM**

A pair of 1950s lady's leopard skin print elasticated pants, with zip fastener.

11in (28cm) long

£70-90   **SM**

A 1950s Vanity Fair leopard print girdle, with attached suspenders, size 6.

14.5in (37cm) long

£60-90   **SM**

A Rosy white lace waist girdle, with original tags, size 42.

14in (35.5cm) long

£80-120   **SM**

A pair of 1950s 'Good Fairy' nylon pants, with applied fabric and nylon fairy and rhinestones.

11.75in (30cm) wide

£50-80   **SM**

A CLOSER LOOK AT A GOTLOP SUIT

M.S. Gotlop Ltd were a fine quality central London civil, naval and military tailors who first appeared in London listings in 1896.

Based at 49 Whitehall, London, the company changed their name to Lidgett & Sons in 1955 with official records existing until 1969. It is likely that this suit was made around the early 1960s when the Lidgetts may have still liked to use the heritage 'Gotlop' name in their labels.

The long length, fitted, high buttoning, double-breasted design was typical of the 'Mod' look of the 1960s, influenced by Victorian and even Georgian styles.

The pinstripe suit is made from heavy, worsted wool, a quality cloth.

The trousers are cut at a very unusual angle, to point towards the toe-cap of a shoe with the creases falling above the laces and giving the impression of matching spats.

A 1970s denim two-piece trouser suit.

Jacket 23.5in (60cm) long

£50-80   NOR

A blue worsted wool pinstripe suit by 'Gotlop'. 1960-65

35.5in (90.5cm) long

£80-120   NOR

A pair of early 1970s printed cotton 'stars and stripes' hip hugger low-cut jeans, with period stars waistcoat.

This highly patriotic and celebratory clothing was produced in the same decade as the US Bicentenary.

Trousers 35in (89cm) long

£70-100   NOR

A pair of 1970s 'VOTE' printed cotton trousers, in red, white and blue.

40.25in (102cm) long

£60-90   NOR

A late 1970s 'Superfly' style black wool and leather men's coat.

The fit and style of this coat is similar those worn by hip, funky anti-hero 'Priest', played by Ron O'Neal in the 1972 film 'Superfly'.

£40-60   NOR

A 1970s Ponzi of Phillipsburg, NJ tuxedo, with velvet collar, satin trim, with shirt, dress trousers with satin band, and velvet bow tie.

30.75in (78cm) long

£80-120   NOR

A 1960s cobalt blue crushed velvet smoking/dinner jacket, with silk lapels and trim and single button fastening.

34.75in (88cm) long

£70-100   NOR

COSTUME & ACCESSORIES

A CLOSER LOOK AT A JOE NAMATH SHIRT

Charismatic baseball player Joe Namath (b.1943) was renowned for his off-pitch social excesses, earning him the nickname 'Broadway Joe'.

His endorsements continued to give him a source of income after his playing years – as well as the Arrow brand shirts, he was spokesman for Dingo boots.

A 1970s Arrow 'Joe Namath' printed polyester shirt.

Namath's road room-mate once observed that being around a 25-year-old Namath was 'like travelling with a Beatle'.

Made during the Disco era, this shirt, with its pointed wing collars and all-over print, would have been very fashionable.

The design shows Arrow advertisements designed by J.C. Leyendecker from the 1920s and '30s, harking back to the historic heritage of the company, which was founded in 1851.

32in (81cm) long

£30-40   **NOR**

A 1960s batik-style printed cotton jacket, made in Hong Kong, with small lapels.

£30-50   **NOR**

A 1970s batik-style handprinted cotton men's jacket, made in Great Britain for a retailer in Bermuda.

34in (81cm) long

£50-80   **NOR**

A 1960s/70s Mexican burnt leather and suede poncho.

The horse head design is burnt into the leather with a thin hot rod.

41in (104cm) long

£80-120   **NOR**

A 1970s Malber International, Hong Kong multicoloured suede men's jacket.

£30-40   **BR**

A men's short suede jacket, by Lee, lacks label.

£30-40   **BR**

A 1970s Canadian Jeno de Paris men's cropped leather jacket.

£20-30   **BR**

COLLECTORS' NOTES

■ Also known as 'Aloha' shirts, colourful Hawaiian shirts have become immensely collectable over the past 20 years, the best fetching hundreds of dollars or more. The mid-1930s to the mid-1950s is considered the 'golden age' of production and examples from this period are the most sought-after due to the quality of their colour and design. During this period most were made in rayon, which despite being hot to wear, retains the vibrancy of its colours very well, unlike cotton which fades. The very best rayon shirts have a silky feel, which earned them the nickname, 'silkies' and is different from much modern rayon.

■ Certain brand names, designers and designs are more popular than others. Look out for Kamehama (founded 1936) and Cisco Champion Kahanamoku.

■ Reproductions exist in their millions, so examine labels and cloth for signs of age and wear. Famous wearers of Hawaiian shirts dating from the golden age when they were first popular include Dwight D. Eisenhower, Harry Truman on the front of 'Time' magazine in 1951, and Elvis Presley in 1961's 'Blue Hawaii'. Tom Selleck's TV character, private detective 'Magnum' was also known for his fondness for such garments in the 1980s.

A 1950s printed Hawaiian shirt, by Champion, Kahanamoku, made by Cisco.

£300-500 MA

A Champion Kahanamoku Hawaiian shirt, with leaf print.

A shirt of the same design was worn by movie idol Montgomery Clift in the film 'From Here to Eternity' in 1953.

c1940

£300-500 CVS

A 1950s Kilohana printed Hawaiian shirt, size medium.

£150-200 CVS

A late 1930s Hawaiian shirt, by G. H. Gurupo, Tokyo, with Mount Fuji Japanese print, size XLarge.

This shirt is very rare because of the extra large size.

£280-320 CVS

A 1960s American printed polyester Dashiki.

Early Afro-American Dashikis, printed on natural fabrics using traditional batik methods, are more desirable than later polyester versions.

28.75in (73cm) long

£15-25 NOR

A 1980s Michael Jackson printed cotton short-sleeved shirt.
28.75 (73cm) long

£50-80 NOR

A 1940s N. Turk wool and cotton western-style shirt, size medium.

£220-280 CVS

FIND OUT MORE...

The Hawaiian Shirt: Its Art & History, by Thomas Steele, published by Abbeville Press, 1984.

COSTUME & ACCESSORIES

A men's cotton work shirt, by Red Kap, USA, with applied patches.

£5-8   BR

A cotton and polyester men's work shirt, by Buckeye.

£8-12   BR

A men's cotton work shirt, by Red Kap, with applied patches.

£7-10   BR

An olive military shirt, label marked "96-100" and "1972".

£15-25   BR

A Canadian Army olive green jacket.

£15-25   BR

A men's printed cotton Army jacket.

The fashion for army-style combat clothing, particularly in camouflage colours, has led to army surplus shops becoming popular shopping destinations – particularly for less formal, non-combat bomber jackets such as these.

£30-50   BR

A men's wool checked jacket, with "Canadian Camper Coat by the Bell Shirt Co.", with mohair and nylon.

£20-30   BR

A men's checked wool shirt, by Pioneer, with knitted cotton waistband.

£20-30   BR

A men's checked cotton shirt, by Romano, Canada, size 16-16 1/2 large.

£10-15   BR

A men's checked shirt, by Bridgeport, Canada.

£7-10   BR

A CLOSER LOOK AT A COWICHAN SWEATER

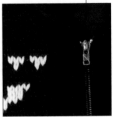

Authentic Cowichan sweaters are hand-knitted by women in the Cowichan Valley, Vancouver Island, Canada, so each one is unique.

These sweaters are highly collected. The design should always be considered – shooting motifs are fairly common, a skull-and-crossbones design can be worth over £120, and a shark around £200!

The zipper has a 'flash' meaning this example can be dated to the 1950s or '60s.

Colours should be natural, such as brown or white, black is rare.

A men's knitted Cowichan-style sweater, with eagle decoration, lacks label.

£60-90   **BR**

A knitted men's college sweater, by Clover, with applied "OL" patch and "Clover 100% Pure Virgin Wool" label, size small.

£15-20   **BR**

A knitted men's college cardigan, with applied "St Francis Xavier CYO Circuit Champions 1965" patch, lacks label.

£30-40   **BR**

A men's knitted Cowichan-style sweater, by Kingsway Simpson-Sears, with stitched decoration of a hunter and a bird, size medium 38-40.

£30-40   **BR**

A men's knitted Cowichan-style sweater, with geometric decoration, lacks label.

£30-40   **BR**

A men's knitted Cowichan-style sweater, with geometric decoration, lacks label.

£30-40   **BR**

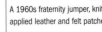

A 1960s fraternity jumper, knitted wool with applied leather and felt patches, large size.

£70-100   **MA**

A Levi's denim blouse jacket, with 'Big E' red tab.

The woven red and white Levi's trademark tab was introduced in 1936. Until 1971, all the letters in LEVI'S were in capitals, afterwards, the E became a lower case 'e'. Any labels with a 'Big E' will date from before 1971.

£50-80   BR

A Lee denim blouse jacket, size 40 large.

£70-100   BR

A pair of Levi's 501 denim jeans, size W30, L36, post 1971.

£50-80   BR

A Wrangler denim jacket, with Stars & Stripes patch and metal studs, size 38.

£40-60   BR

A pair of Levi's denim jeans, size 32.

1971-83

£50-80   BR

A pair of Lee Rider denim jeans, with 'Union Made' label.

Levi's are not the only collectable name in vintage jeans – vintage Lee and Wrangler are also sought-after, although less so. Look out in particular for their 'Cowboy' brand – a 1940s jacket can fetch up to £4,000 or more! Lee Rider jeans were introduced in 1924 in a 13 ounce denim, at the time Levi's were produced in a 10 ounce fabric, making these Riders 'more durable'.

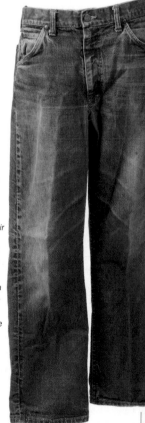

A pair of Levi's 501 'red line' jeans, size W32 L33.

Levi's denims are considered 'vintage' and collectable if they date from before 1983. Apart from the 'E' in the label, another good way to help identify vintage Levi products is to turn them inside out. Jeans produced before 1983 can be identified by a thin 'red line' sewn into the selvage (the edge of the material) at the seam.

£50-80   BR

A pair of late 1960s Lee Riders jeans, size 32.

£80-120   BR

£180-220   BR

A Nike nylon jacket, size large.

£10-15   **BR**

An Adidas blue sweatshirt, marked "Made in Canada", size large.

£10-15   **BR**

A Nike black sweatshirt, size large.

£7-10   **BR**

A Ralph Lauren pink polo shirt.

Certain shades of colours are no longer produced, making them sought-after. Vintage examples are also often made of better quality cottons.

£4-6   **BR**

A Nike red t-shirt.

£3-5   **BR**

A Menasha Re. Dept. baseball t-shirt, with "Sport-T by Stedman" label.

£5-8   **BR**

A Nike blue t-shirt, with applied stripes at shoulders, size XL.

£5-8   **BR**

A black mesh American Football shirt.

£7-10   **BR**

A 'Five Star' v-neck t-shirt, by Trumark, size M.

£5-8   **BR**

A Nike navy vest, with white transfer decoration.

£7-10   **BR**

A large embroidered handbag, with a beige ground, decorated with roses and fringes, silver-plated clasp.

c1915 *11.5in (29cm) long*

£80-120 **WDL**

A 1950s gold-painted straw and wicker handbag, with black velvet panel, woven wool poodle, glued sequins, yellow gold silk lining and label for "Midas of Miami".

8.25in (21cm) wide

£200-250 **SM**

A 1950s wicker shopping bag, with applied red felt with hand sewn woollen poodles with inset rhinestone eyes.

12.5in (32cm) wide

£80-120 **MA**

A 1950s fish-shaped plastic-covered wire handbag, with fabric-lined interior.

15.25in (38.5cm) long

£250-300 **SM**

An Enid Collins 'By The Roadside' printed and plastic jewelled handbag, interior marked with Collins logo and "Copyright The Original Collins of Texas".

Enid Collins opened her handbag shop in Medina, Texas in 1959 and produced bags in two main styles – a wooden box bag and a canvas bucket bag. They were decorated by hand with kitsch, glitzy motifs with paint, sequins and rhinestones. Do-it-yourself kits were also sold. Many designs had titles, which were printed on the bags, together with the Enid Collins' signature. The company was bought out by the Tandy Leather Corporation in 1970.

10.75in (27.5cm) wide

£50-60 **NOR**

A 1960s clear vinyl handbag, with internal design of silk flowers and perspex handle.

13in (33cm) wide

£20-40 **MA**

A 1960s wooden box bag, with hand-painted 'dining doggies' scene, the interior with mirror and reading "Collectors Item by Gary Jolie Dalas Decorated for you Made in Hong Kong".

6.25in (16cm) wide

£15-25 **NOR**

A 1960s red plush hand-painted bag, with 'doggie' scene.

7.75in (19.5cm) high

£20-40 **NOR**

A 1960s Enid Collins 'Do-Drop In' plastic jewelled and printed handbag.

10.5in (27cm) wide

£30-40 **NOR**

A 1960s vinyl bag, with coloured matchbook design and vinyl interior.

£20-30   NOR

A 1960s Mod box bag, with wooden body, white vinyl and gold bosses, label to red fabric interior "Handmade in British Hong Kong".

7in (18cm) wide

£30-40   NOR

A 1960s/70s box 'Wonder Bag', decorated with applied painted canvas daisies.

10in (25.5cm) wide

£25-35   NOR

The original Jerry Terrence 'Waste Basket' 'For Your Personal Trash' handbag, with faux fur panel.

13.75in (35cm) high

£60-70   SM

A green leather satchel, with applied car design.

£8-12   BR

A patchwork bag, decorated with a scene of a musician.

£18-22   BR

A CLOSER LOOK AT A CHANEL QUILTED PURSE

Together with the Hermès Kelly bag, this is one of the most iconic bags ever made. It was Karl Lagerfeld who increased the size of the Chanel Logo and the thickness of the chain.

Although popular when first released, it did not reach iconic status until the 1980s when it was adopted by the label-hungry buyer obsessed with ostentation.

The original quilted bag is called the '2.55' after the date it was designed by Coco Chanel - February 1955.

Coco Chanel preferred understated black, but the quilted bag has since been produced in a huge range of colours, fabrics and patterns and in 2005, the 20th anniversary year, even as a man's bag.

A Chanel quilted leather purse, in pebble textured leather, with single signature chain strap, open back pocket, interior zip pocket, gold embossed "CHANEL" logo inside with signature zipper pull and all hardware marked "Chanel".

As this bag is widely faked, check the bag is correctly marked and that the construction and material is of suitably high quality.

8.5in (21.5cm) wide

£400-500   FRE

COSTUME & ACCESSORIES

A Fun Ship Holidays travel bag.

£7-14   **BR**

A Canadian Fun Finders Tours travel bag.

£10-15   **BR**

A Canadian Leo's Travel Ltd, Edmonton travel bag.

£12-14   **BR**

A Vacances Esprit travel bag.

£8-12   **BR**

A Trafalgar's Europe and Britain travel bag.

£8-12   **BR**

A pair of 1960s Taj of India shocking pink silk shoes, with clear soles.

10.25in (26cm) long

£100-150   **SM**

A pair of flower power printed silk shoes, by 'Schiaparelli Paris & New York'.

9.5in (24cm) long

£20-30   **NOR**

A pair of Da Venci black satin and fur/plush high heeled shoes, with their original hatbox-shaped box.

£80-120   **SM**

A pair of 1950s black suedette high heeled shoes, with black bakelite heels and bow, with applied metal 'coins'.

£180-220   **SM**

A pair of 1970s large orange fading through to clear plastic frames, the arm marked "Frame Hong Kong", with shaped arms and face.

6.25in (16cm) wide

£20-40   **BB**

A pair of large, mock tortoiseshell gent's frames, the arms stamped "Zyloware U.S.A. 5 1/2" and set into the fronts.

6in (15cm) wide

£20-30   **BB**

A pair of 1960s clear plastic and fabric laminated sunglasses.

5.75in (14.5cm) wide

£120-180   **VE**

A pair of brown striated pearlized 'wood effect' frames, by Fathaway, with chromed metal inserts, the arms marked "Fathaway 5 1/2".

5.25in (13.5cm) wide

A pair of 1950s French hand-carved mock tortoiseshell plastic 'mask' sunglasses.

6.25in (16cm) wide

£350-450   **VE**

£18-22   **BB**

A pair of 1950s black and white laminated plastic frames.

£20-30   **BB**

A pair of grey pearlized lady's frames, with heart-shaped metal inserts, with shaped tips of the arms.

£18-22   **BB**

A pair of metal bronze coloured frames, the arms marked "HUD US 5 1/2".

5in (13cm) wide

£15-20   **BB**

A 1960s psychedelic purple and orange silk tie.

£6-8   BR

An American hand-painted silk tie, by Towncraft Deluxe Cravats, decorated with two swordfish.

£7-10   BR

A gentleman's tie, made to a 1950s design from unused 1950s 'Showgirl' tie silk.

5.25in (13.25cm) long

£120-180   CVS

A hand-painted 'Bold Look' silk tie, by Currie.

£7-9   BR

A polyester tie, by Cartier, with geometric design.

£2-3   BR

A Canadian hand-painted silk tie, by Rembrandt, with a decoration of a peacock.

£10-15   BR

A silk tie, by Bluestone, with floral decorative panel.

£7-10   BR

A blue polyester tie, decorated with Classical lamp, unmarked.

£4-6   BR

A psychedelic floral cotton tie, made in England.

£4-6   BR

A pair of 1940s apple juice cast phenolic and white dice cufflinks.

Face: 0.75in (2cm) wide

£20-40 **PC**

A pair of 1930s/40s bakelite dice cufflinks, unmarked.

0.5in (1cm) wide

£60-80 **CVS**

A pair of late 1960s/early 1970s faceted plastic and gold-coloured cufflinks.

0.75in (2cm) diam

£8-12 **DTC**

A pair of 1920s/30s 14ct rose gold Egyptian motif cufflinks, with green painted paste scarab and sarcophagus and ankh-shaped links, unmarked.

Scarab 1.25in (3cm) long

£100-150 **BB**

A pair of mid-20thC Kreisler Craft gold-filled cufflinks, with reversible pearlized brown and green roller rolling cylindrical 'bars'.

0.75in (2.25cm) wide

£10-15 **BB**

A pair of 1950s Mexican silver cufflinks, set with turquoise, with abstract metal pattern.

1in (2.5cm) wide

£70-100 **CVS**

A pair of 1950s white metal cufflinks, with pink plastic cabochon stones.

1.5in (4cm) wide

£25-35 **CVS**

A 1970s Swank chrome tie clip bar and cufflinks set, in mint plush box.

£6-8 **BB**

A pair of 1960s metal cufflinks, in original box.

1in (2.5cm) diam

£12-18 **DTC**

COLLECTORS' NOTES

■ Named pieces continue to rise in popularity and value, particularly those by Trifari, Coro, Haskell, Joseff and others. Many people buy to wear, so even unsigned pieces can fetch high prices if the look is fashionable.

■ Well-made pieces from the 1930s-1940s using better quality materials are also increasing in value, particularly if named. Names are often found stamped on the back. Learning how to recognise makers' styles and marks can help with dating.

■ Trifari is one of the most collectable names. It was founded in New York in 1918 by Gustavo Trifari and Leo F. Krussman, with Carl Fishel joining in 1929. This led to the 'TKF' stamped mark.

■ Jaunty, novelty shapes abound, as do floral or foliate designs – particularly pins. Large, brightly coloured, complex examples with glittering rhinestones are the most desirable. Look out for designs worn by Hollywood stars from the 1930s-1960s.

A 1950s Trifari pin, in the form of a parrot on a branch, with red rhinestone inset eyes.

1.25in (3cm) high

£40-60   **CRIS**

A 1950s Trifari owl pin.

1.25in (3cm) high

£40-60   **CRIS**

A 1950s Trifari dog pin, with green enamel body and inset rhinestone ears.

1.25in (3cm) high

£50-80   **CRIS**

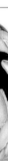

A 1950s Trifari flapping duckling pin.

1.25in (3cm) high

£40-60   **CRIS**

A 1950s Trifari penguin pin.

Penguins are a comparatively rare animal for Trifari pins.

1.25in (3cm) high

£50-80   **CRIS**

A 1950s Trifari teddy bear pin, with 'faux fur' texture, red enamel and rhinestone inset paws.

The teddy bear pin is relatively scarce. It also appeals to teddy bear collectors, often meaning values are higher.

1.25in (3cm) high

£50-80   **CRIS**

Three 1950s Trifari butterfly pins, with 'plique à jour' coloured glass set in gilt frames.

2in (5cm) wide

£40-60 each   **CRIS**

A CLOSER LOOK AT A TRIFARI PIN

This pin was designed by Frenchman Alfred Philippe, Trifari's chief designer from 1930-68, whose designs helped to make Trifari successful.

It is made from vermeil – gold-plated sterling silver – showing it was made during the 1940s and is thus highly collectable.

The design was inspired by the explosion of romantic and historical movies during the 1930s-50s.

Large cabochons are typical of these designs – later reissues from the 1980s are of lesser quality and are less collectable.

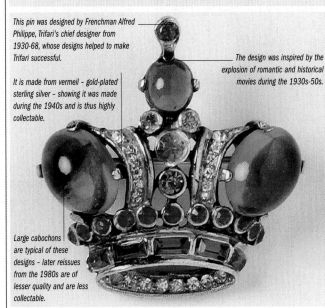

A 1940s Trifari vermeil crown pin, designed by Alfred Phillippe, with prong-set green glass cabochons, blue baguettes and blue, ruby red, and clear rhinestones, slight wear to gold-plating.

1.25in (3cm) high

£120-180　　　　　　　　　　　　　　　　　**PC**

A pair of 1960s Trifari gold-plated and pierced 'sponge' earrings, with their original Trifari tag.

0.75in (2.25cm) diam

£15-25　　　　　　　　**TR**

A pair of mid-1950s Trifari pierced gold-plated pendant fruit earrings.

1.5in (4cm) long

£30-50　　　　　　**CRIS**

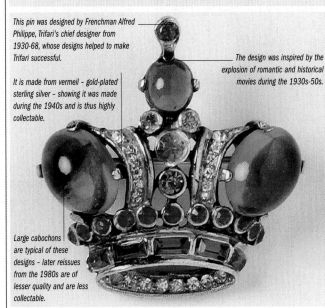

Four late 1950s Trifari small fruit pins, comprising an apple, a pineapple, a bunch of grapes and a pear, in matte finish silver and gold alloy.

Largest 1in (2.5cm) long

£15-25 each　　　　　　**CRIS**

A 1950s Trifari 'retro' flower pin, of pierced silver alloy with pear, navette and round clear rhinestones.

1.5in (4cm) diam

£30-50　　　　　　**ABAA**

A 1950s Trifari leaves and berries pin, of matte finish gold alloy, with elongated faux pearls.

4in (10cm) long

£50-80　　　　　　**CRIS**

A 1950s Trifari gilt and simulated pearl and rhinestone pin.

4in (10.5cm) long

£50-80　　　　　　**CRIS**

An early 1970s Trifari faux fabric black bow-tie pin, designed by Diane Love.

3in (7cm) wide

£40-60　　　　　　**TR**

COSTUME JEWELLERY

A late 1950s Coro 'space age' pin, of polished and textured white metal, with a round metal cabochon centre.

2.25in (5.75cm) diam

£20-30 MILLB

A late 1950s Coro 'space age' pin, of gold-tone metal, with clear and ruby red crystal rhinestones.

2.25in (5.75cm) diam

£12-18 MILLB

A late 1940s/early 1950s Coro vermeil flower-head pin, with clear crystal rhinestones.

2in (5cm) diam

£30-50 MILLB

A pair of 1950s Coro floral motif earrings, of antiqued goldwash metal, with faux baroque pearls and red crystal rhinestones.

1.25in (3.25cm) long

£30-50 MILLB

A pair of Coro floral motif earrings, in gold-tone metal with pink, aquamarine and citrine crystal navettes.

1945-50 *1in (2.5cm) long*

£15-20 MILLB

A pair of Coro floral earrings, with pale pink plastic petals and aurora borealis crystal rhinestone centres.

c1955 *2.5in (6.25cm) long*

£15-20 MILLB

A mid-1950s Coro floral bracelet and earrings, with white plastic petals and gold-tone metal centres with pale green and blue and clear crystal rhinestones.

Coro was founded in New York in 1919 and continues to produce affordable costume jewellery today on a massive scale. This provides collectors with enormous scope and variety. Look out for their higher end 'Corocraft' name and their 'Duette' pins, made from three detachable pieces.

bracelet 6in (15.25cm) long

£30-50 MILLB

A 1950s Coro Victorian-style love token pin, of gold-tone cast metal in the form of a hand proffering a rose.

2.5in (6.25cm) long

£30-50 JJ

A 1960s/70s Coro belt, with silver-tone metal chain and antiqued, mottled silver-tone inverted shield pendant.

Designs derived from African or ethnic forms were very popular in the 1960s and '70s.

chain 30in (76cm) long

£20-30 MILLB

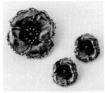

A 1960s ART gilt and silver flower pin and earring set.

pin 2in (5cm) diam

£30-40 JJ

A 1960s/70s Les Bernard clown with umbrella pin, of gold-tone cast metal with red, black and white enamelling.

2in (5cm) long

£20-30 JJ

A CLOSER LOOK AT A CHOKER

Cristobal Balenciaga (1895-1972) was an influential Spanish couturier working in Paris – he launched his couture range in 1919.

This is an haute couture piece, made only to order, so very few examples would have been made.

The very simple lines and colours are aimed to complement the classical elegance of his clothing designs.

The black glass imitating jet and inset turquoise give the choker a 19thC appeal, brought into the 1960s by the simple, modern lines.

A Balenciaga couture choker, with four interwoven strands of faceted black glass beads and gilt metal clasp with turquoise glass cabochons and clear rhinestones.

c1960 *16.25in (41.5cm) long*

£1,200-1,800 SUM

A 1970s Marcel Boucher turtle pin, of textured gold-tone metal casting with clear crystal rhinestone highlights.

1.5in (3.75cm) long

£20-30 JJ

A 1960s Alice Caviness raspberry and leaf pin, of textured gold-tone metal with pavé-set faux ruby cabochons.

2.75in (7cm) long

£40-60 ABIJ

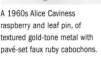

A 1960s Alice Caviness necklace and matching bracelet, of rhodium-plated metal, set with graduated rows of lavender, pink and black rhinestones.

necklace 16.5in (42cm) long

£280-320 ABIJ

A 1960s Alice Caviness necklace and matching bracelet, of japanned metal with olivine and ruby glass cabochons and prong-set aurora borealis, blue and green rhinestones.

necklace 16in (40.5cm) long

£220-280 ABIJ

A pair of 1980s Karl Lagerfeld earrings, in the form of 'Louis-style' bérgère armchairs, in gold-washed metal with clear crystal beads to the sides.

1.25in (3cm) long

£40-60   **JJ**

A 1960s Marvella leaf and buds pin, of gold- and silver-tone metal, with faux pearls and pavé-set clear crystal rhinestones.

1.75in (4.5cm) long

£30-50   **ABIJ**

A CLOSER LOOK AT A PAIR OF MIRIAM HASKELL EARRINGS

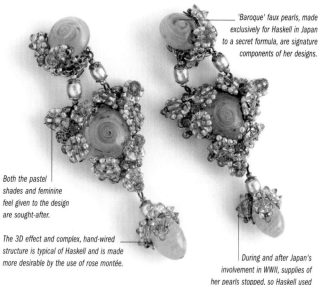

'Baroque' faux pearls, made exclusively for Haskell in Japan to a secret formula, are signature components of her designs.

Both the pastel shades and feminine feel given to the design are sought-after.

The 3D effect and complex, hand-wired structure is typical of Haskell and is made more desirable by the use of rose montée.

During and after Japan's involvement in WWII, supplies of her pearls stopped, so Haskell used French glass cabochons instead.

A rare pair of 1950s Miriam Haskell earrings.

If the extremely rare matching necklace could be found, the set could be worth over £2,000!

4in (10cm) long

£400-600   **BY**

A Kramer bracelet and earrings set, with gilt metal clasps and links and clear and textured white glass beads.

1958-62

bracelet 7in (17.75cm) long

£30-40   **MILLB**

A 1960s/70s Judy Lee floral burst pin and matching earrings, of gold-tone filigree, with navette-cut clear and topaz and round-cut ruby and grey-green rhinestones.

pin 2.75in (7cm) diam

£30-50   **ABIJ**

A 1960s Lisner necklace, with gold-tone metal chain and castings, set with Rivoli cabochons and clear crystal rhinestones.

16in (40.5cm) long

£100-150   **JJ**

A Monet flower pin, with stalk, centre and petal borders of gold-plated metal, the petal surface strands of base metal with white enamelling.

c1965-75   *2in (5cm) long*

£15-25   **MILLB**

A 1960s Robert butterfly pin, of gilt metal with black poured glass body and blue and green enamel wings.

1.75in (4.5cm) wide

£30-40   **JJ**

A 1950s Robert bird-on-umbrella pin, of gilt metal casting with red, brown, pink and green enamelling.

2.5in (6.25cm) high

£30-40   **JJ**

A pre-1960s Volupté open bangle, of gold-tone metal, the inner band of wire mesh, the outer band pierced and chased with arabesque patterns.

3in (7.5cm) wide

£40-60   **JJ**

A pair of 1940s Weiss strawberry earrings, with ruby crystal beads and emerald crystal rhinestones in japanned metal settings.

1in (2.5cm) long

£40-60   **JJ**

A pair of 1950s Weiss fleur-de-lys earrings, of antique gold-tone cast metal, with pale green round and dark green navette crystal rhinestones.

1in (2.5cm) long

£15-20   **MILLB**

A pair of 1960s Whiting & Davis pendant snake's head earrings, in punched and engraved silver plate.

1.75in (4.5cm) long

£15-20   **ABIJ**

A 1940s Weiss 'jack-in-the-box' pin, of gilt metal with red and black enamelling and clear and emerald rhinestones.

2in (5cm) high

£50-80   **JJ**

A 1960s Whiting & Davis silver-plated coiled snake bangle, with expandable mesh wrist band and solid punched and engraved head.

12in (30.5cm) long

£30-40   **JJ**

An early 1950s Whiting & Davis bracelet, with gold-plated links and safety chain and ruby red glass cabochons.

7.5in (19cm) long

£30-40   **ABIJ**

COSTUME JEWELLERY

A 1950s unsigned toucan pin, of gilt cast metal with blue, green and red enamelling and ruby glass cabochon eyes.

2.25in (5.75cm) long

£10-15 CRIS

A 1950s unsigned crested bird-on-a-branch pin, of gold-tone metal with black enamelling and clear crystal rhinestones.

3in (7.5cm) long

£10-15 CRIS

A 1960s unsigned stylized humming bird pin, of gold-plated cats metal with turquoise Lucite rings and aquamarine crystal rhinestone eyes.

3.25in (8.25cm) long

£30-40 CRIS

A 1950s unsigned humming bird pin, of gilt cast metal set with clear and ruby rhinestones and pavé-set turquoise crystal cabochons.

2.5in (6.25cm) long

£15-20 CRIS

A 1950s unsigned peacock pin, of gilt cast metal with black enamelling and polychrome and clear crystal rhinestones.

2.5in (6.5cm) long

£20-30 CRIS

A 1940s unsigned pair of sterling enamel and inset diamanté 'Patriotic' pins, in the form of sailor bunnies.

During WWII, much jewellery was produced in the red, white and blue colours of the American flag, as well as in patriotic forms such as the US flag or sailors.

1.75in (4.5cm) high

£70-100 BY

A 1960s unsigned caliph pin, of gold-tone cast metal with black enamelling, aquamarine and turquoise glass cabochons, round and baguette clear rhinestones and a faux pearl.

2.75in (7cm) long

£40-60 CRIS

A 1930s unsigned painted lead pin, in the form of a snake charmer boy, with trembling snake.

2.25in (5.5cm) high

£30-50 BY

A 1930s dark blue schooner pin, with chrome-plated base metal sails and mast.

2in (5cm) long

£30-40 ABAA

A 1960s-70s unsigned pair of handbag earrings, with gold-tone metal castings and white enamelling with 'Organic Modernism' amoeboid pattern.

1.5in (3.75cm) long

£70-100   **LB**

A pair of 1950s German fruit earrings, with red glass and red bead strawberries, green glass leaves, japanned metal stalks and yellow crystal rhinestones.

1.25in (3.25cm) long

£40-60   **BY**

An early 1920s French 'fruit salad' vase-of-flowers pin, with polychrome French carved glass and clear crystal rhinestones on a sterling silver casting.

2in (5cm) high

£100-150   **CRIS**

A 1950s fruit pin, with two glass apples with applied tiny glass beads in red and green, with three green glass leaves and single yellow diamanté, stamped on the reverse "MADE IN WEST GERMANY".

2in (5cm) wide

£30-40   **BY**

A late 1920s/early 1930s brown pin, of scrolling geometric form encrusted with clear rhinestones.

2.5in (6cm) wide

£20-30   **ABAA**

A 1920s dark brown stylized shoe-shape pin, encrusted with clear rhinestones.

2.5in (6cm) long

£20-30   **ABAA**

A 1920s black stylized scrolling leaf pin, with a row of clear rhinestones.

1.5in (4cm) long

£20-30   **ABAA**

A 1930s jade green and black stylized feather pin, with gold edging, incised linear decoration and clear rhinestones.

2.75in (7cm) long

£50-80   **ABAA**

An early 1930s Egyptian-revival motif pin, iridescent pink, red and taupe with a small, central mauve cabochon.

3in (8cm) long

£50-80   **ABAA**

COSTUME JEWELLERY

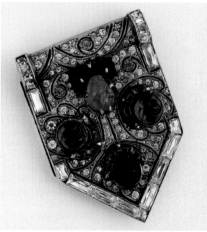

A 1940s unsigned pin, of vermeil sterling silver, with a large aquamarine paste stone and emerald, sapphire, ruby and aquamarine crystal rhinestones.

4in (10cm) long

£70-100 **CRIS**

A 1920s unsigned shield pin, of sterling silver with faceted and baguette clear crystal rhinestones, and ruby, sapphire and emerald glass stones.

2in (5cm) long

£120-180 **BY**

A 1960s unsigned, Byzantine-style floral pin, of gilt cast metal set with clear crystal rhinestones and faux pearls.

4in (10cm) long

£40-60 **CRIS**

A 1960s unsigned Maltese Cross pin, with scrolling forms of filigree gold wire set with faux baroque pearls and clear rhinestones.

2.5in (6.5cm) wide

£30-40 **CRIS**

A 1950s unsigned pin, with faux pearl berries, emerald green glass leaves and a mottled jade green glass fruit drop.

2in (5cm) long

£30-50 **ECLEC**

An unsigned entwined snakes pin, in brass with a large jade green plastic stone and four jade green drops.

c1915-20 *2.5in (6.25cm) long*

£120-180 **CGPC**

A 1960s unsigned pair of French earrings, in gold-tone metal, with green and white enamelling, clear crystal rhinestones and French jet cabochons.

1.25in (3.25cm) long

£20-30 **CRIS**

A 1950s unsigned pair of star motif earrings, in silver set with bands of round-cut aquamarine crystal rhinestones.

1.25in (3.25cm) diam

£30-40 **CRIS**

A 1960s unsigned pair of oval earrings, with filigree gilt metal castings and matrix faux turquoise centres.

1in (2.5cm) long

£15-20 **CRIS**

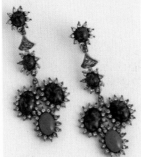

A late 1920s/early 1930s pair of black pendant-hoop clip earrings, encrusted with clear rhinestones and tiny faux pearls.

2.75in (7cm) long

£20-30 ABAA

A 1960s unsigned pair of 'Jewels of India' earrings, with starburst drops, of silver-tone metal set with faux lapis and faux coral cabochons and clear crystal rhinestones.

3in (7.5cm) long

£40-60 CRIS

A pair of unsigned leaf motif earrings, in hand-beaten white metal with wire wraps.

c1960s   *2.5in (6.5cm) long*

£60-90 PC

A 1930s unsigned necklace and pair of pendant earrings, with faceted rock crystal beads and drops and rock crystal spacers.

necklace 16in (41cm) long

£80-120 BY

A 1920s/30s necklace, with silver links set with clear crystal rhinestones and faceted ruby glass shield motifs.

14in (36cm) long

£70-100 ECLEC

A 1920s unsigned necklace, with bunches of grapes of ruby red glass beads alternated with hoops of clear glass.

16.25in (42cm) long

£70-100 ECLEC

An unsigned fruit garland necklace, with poured glass leaves and orange and lemon glass bead fruits.

c1930s   16.25in (42cm) long

£70-100 ECLEC

An unsigned glass necklace, with pale green, blue, red, black, lilac and coffee glass beads.

c1930s   15.25in (39cm) long

£40-60 ECLEC

A 1920s unsigned faux coral woven bead necklace, with two small rings inset with diamanté near the pendant.

16.5in (42cm) long closed

£120-180 BY

A 1920s/30s Czechoslovakian quadruple-pendant necklace, of gilt metal with round-, oval- and square-cut red glass beads and stones.

pendant 8.5in (22cm) long

£150-200   **ECLEC**

A 1960s/70s unsigned pendant necklace and earrings, of gold-plated metal with mottled green glass cabochons.

necklace 14.75in (38cm) long

£40-60   **ECLEC**

A 1920s French floral motif bar pin, with carved blue glass and clear crystal rhinestones on a silver casting.

2.5in (6.5cm) long

£70-100   **CRIS**

An 1930s French Art Deco necklace, of matte finish gold-plated metal, with triangular sections of black enamelling, unsigned.

17in (43cm) long

£350-400   **CRIS**

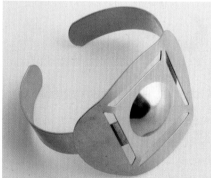

A 1960s/70s unsigned Scandinavian pendant necklace, with red plastic neckband and graduated and articulated discs of polished steel.

Pendant 6.25in (16cm) long

£1,000-1,500   **LB**

An early 1970s unsigned Pop Art open bangle, of gold-tone metal with a shield ornament, stylistically a pastiche of Classical Greco-Roman forms.

3.5in (9cm) wide

£20-30   **MILLB**

COLLECTORS' NOTES

■ Colour, form and date are the main indicators of value for the bakelite and plastic jewellery, which saw its heyday during the 1920s and 30s. Becoming popular by adding a much needed and affordable shot of glamour during the Great Depression, it was produced in a riot of bright and bold colours. The brighter or more numerous the colours, the more desirable a piece is likely to be.

■ Consider the form, as this can help you date and value a piece. Forms tended to be plainer and more geometric in the late 1920s, with figurative and animal pins, and more outrageous, novelty designs appearing in the 1930s. Dangling components and an inherent humour and wit also add value, as do sporting themes, including golf and riding.

■ Also examine decoration – the plastics used were ideally suited to carving. Hand carved items are the most desirable and the heavier and the more intricate the design, the better. Similarly, pieces that are decorated all over, rather than in panels, are more sought-after. The material also counts. Transparent 'apple juice' bakelite, a form of Lucite is one of the most sought after and can be carved and painted, adding yet more value.

■ In its day, bakelite jewellery was stocked by many leading fashionable department stores such as Harrods and Macy's, but after WWII, less expensive plastics were introduced and quality and desirability began to decline. However, the 'Pop' period of the 1960s is fast becoming a popular area, when even leading couturiers re-examined plastic. Look for styling typical of the day and bright colours – pieces can still be found for under £40.

■ Reproductions of classic pieces do exist, but materials and therefore colours tend to be different. Reproduction and often feel lighter in weight. Gently feel around pieces with your finger nail and examine them closely as scratches and cracks, particularly if deep, can be hard to repair and devalue a piece considerably.

A 1940s orange basketweave carved bakelite bangle.

6in (8.5cm) diam

£100-150   BB

A red 'over-dye' 'creamed corn' bakelite bangle, engraved with flowers.

3in (7.5cm) diam

£60-80   EVL

A carnelian red bakelite bangle, the outside edges heavily carved with a swirling, stylised, foliate design.

3.5in (9cm) diam

£100-200   EVL

A brown bakelite imitation wood bangle, carved all over with a leaf design and unusually pierced.

3.25in (8cm) diam

£60-80   EVL

A 1940s jade green bakelite bangle, carved with flowers.

This piece is worth less than others as the design is very simple, appears on two panels only and may have been carved on a machine. It is also thinner and is less visually appealing than other examples.

3in (7.5cm) diam

£40-50   EVL

A hand carved jade green bakelite bangle, with inset daisy on a panel of leaves and a carved twist design.

3.25in (8cm) diam

£80-120   EVL

A late 1920s hand carved geometric black bakelite bangle.

3.5in (9cm) diam

£300-400   EVL

COSTUME JEWELLERY

A well carved yellow bakelite bangle, with alternating 'twisting' panels of plain, floral and foliate decoration.

3in (7.5cm) diam

£80-120 EVL

An Art Deco style 'apple juice' bakelite bangle, reverse carved with grass-like decoration, with black painted inner rim surfaces.

3.25in (8.5cm) diam

£300-400 EVL

A CLOSER LOOK AT A BAKELITE BANGLE

This type of bracelet is known as a 'bowtie' due to the bowtie shapes, made here with the yellowy-orange plastic.

They are comparatively rare and hard to find, as well as being very popular with collectors, making them valuable.

Look out for multi-coloured examples using more than two colours – the more colours the more valuable the bangle will be.

Individual sections of bakelite are assembled to form the bangle – examine the entire bangle as cracks will devalue a piece considerably.

An orange and 'creamed corn' 'bow tie' bangle.

3.5in (9cm) diam

£800-1,200 EVL

A laminated coloured bakelite and wood striped bangle.

3in (7.5cm) diam

£70-100 EVL

A 1930s green and yellow mottled cast phenolic hinged bracelet, with two applied carved Scottie dogs.

3in (7.5cm) wide

£150-200 BY

A 1950s pearlized fleck and black fleck curling reeded plastic bangle, with sprung hinge.

3.25in (8cm) diam

£15-25 BB

A contemporary Corian 'granite effect' bangle, by Barry Spector.

Corian is a blend of natural products and pure acrylic polymer and is made by DuPont in a wide range of mottled, stone-like colours.

c2000

3.75in (9.5cm) diam

£60-80 BB

A 'Bambi' fawn 'creamed corn' and painted bakelite pin.

This characterful pin was probably released around the same time as the Disney film.

c1942   3.25in (8.5cm) high

£80-120   **EVL**

A CLOSER LOOK AT A BAKELITE PIN

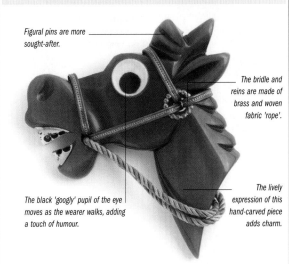

Figural pins are more sought-after.

The bridle and reins are made of brass and woven fabric 'rope'.

The black 'googly' pupil of the eye moves as the wearer walks, adding a touch of humour.

The lively expression of this hand-carved piece adds charm.

A burgundy red cast phenolic horse brooch, with fabric rope and metal harness and bridle.

2.75in (7cm) high

£300-400   **EVL**

A carved wood and green bakelite leaping gazelle pin.

It is uncommon to find bakelite jewellery where the wood part is mounted onto the bakelite part – the other way around is much more common.

2.25in (6cm) high

£150-200   **EVL**

A carved yellow marbled bakelite pin, in the shape of a chess 'knight'.

2.75 (7cm) high

£50-70   **EVL**

A 1930s green bakelite figural pin, showing a Chinese man pulling a rickshaw.

2.75in (7cm) wide

£80-120   **EVL**

A 1930s carved jet black bakelite swordfish pin.

This is both an unusual colour and subject matter, almost resembling hardstone jet popular in the Victorian era. Fish and animals are sought-after subjects.

4in (10cm) wide

£150-200   **EVL**

A carved and painted yellow bakelite dagger-shaped pin, the painted black grip decorated with wire and pressed brass.

3.25in (8cm) diam

£70-100   **EVL**

An 'apple juice' bakelite fruit dangling bar pin.

3.25in (8cm) high

£100-150   **EVL**

A dangling bunch of cherries pin, with plastic leaves and plastic-covered string, in excellent condition.

3.5in (9cm) high

£150-200   EVL

A rare orangy-red 'over-dye' hunting theme dangling pin, with hunting horn, boot, cap and rhinestone inlaid horseshoe.

Dangling pins are much sought-after, especially when themed. Check the condition carefully as repairs or replaced parts reduce the value.

3.25in (8cm) high

£200-250   EVL

A 1930s/40s celluloid 'school' themed pin, with dangling slate, painted bakelite pencil and book.

2in (5cm) wide

£50-70   BB

An 'apple juice' bakelite bar pin, with reverse-carved and painted bakelite flowers, with laminated shaped yellow bakelite ends.

2.75in (7cm) long

£100-150   EVL

A well carved 'apple juice' bakelite Swan pin.

This comparatively complex pin is carved from both the front and the back and is pierced. Furthermore, white paint applied to the back gives the watery swirls their 'depth' and the swan its 'body'.

2.75in (7cm) wide

£150-200   EVL

A heavily carved large yellow bakelite flower pin.

It's the large size – almost the same diameter as a bangle – and the excellent level of hand carving that makes this pin desirable and valuable.

3.25in (8cm) diam

£120-180   EVL

A reverse-carved amber Lucite starfish-shaped pin, carved with a frondy leaf to imitate real amber jewellery.

3.25in (8.5cm) diam

£70-100   EVL

A red carved wreath pin, carved all over with a stylized foliate pattern.

2in (5cm) diam

£40-50   EVL

A very rare brown bakelite-on-silver metal golf clubs and bag shaped pin.

This is an extremely rare pin – it is unusual for ladies' jewellery to have a golf theme, although more ladies were playing golf in the 1920s and 1930s.

3in (7.5cm) high

£150-200   EVL

A contemporary Lea Stein plastic brooch, in the form of a dappled cat with reflective eyes and ears.

4in (10cm) long

£40-50 AGO

A 1970s vintage Lea Stein brooch, in the form of an elephant with black tusk and ear.

Lea Stein (b.1931) began making rhodoid jewellery in the late 1960s. Her 'vintage' period dated from then until 1981 when her company closed. In 1988 she began making jewellery again and continues to do so today.

2.75in (7cm) long

£40-50 AGO

A contemporary Lea Stein plastic brooch, in the form of a red tortoise, with glittering patterned shell.

3in (7.5cm) length

£40-50 AGO

A contemporary Lea Stein plastic brooch, in the form of a purple poodle.

2.5in (5cm) long

£40-50 AGO

A late 1990s Lea Stein 'Panther' brooch, made of mottled brown and orange laminated rhodoid.

4in (10cm) wide.

£60-70 CRIS

A vintage Art Deco-style Lea Stein brooch, in the form of a bird.

Here Stein strongly harks back to the Art Deco period – not only in the geometric design and bright colours, but also by visually imitating 'shagreen' a luxury material widely used in the 1920s and 1930s.

4.25in (11cm) long

£40-50 AGO

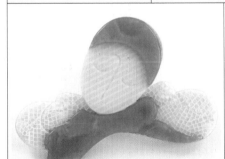

A contemporary Lea Stein plastic brooch, in the form of a 1920s flapper, with imitation mother-of-pearl collar.

2.25in (6cm) long

£40-50 AGO

An early 1980s Lea Stein full 'Colorette' pin, made of dark blue, ice blue, black and faux pearl laminated rhodoid.

The word 'Colorette' relates to the full, circular fan behind the head.

2in (5.5cm) diam

£60-70 CRIS

COSTUME JEWELLERY

A pair of 1930s injected cream and brown bakelite clip loop earrings.

Loop 1.5in (4cm) diam

£80-120   **BB**

A pair of 1960s Pop Art black and green clip earrings, with injection moulded green dot.

2.5in (6.5cm) high

£80-120   **BB**

A pair of early 1970s large Pop Art straw boater pendant earrings, unsigned, in candy striped plastic and goldtone base metal.

3.5in (9cm) long

£8-12   **MILLB**

A pair of mid- to late 1960s Pop Art plastic 'flower power' earrings, unsigned, with semi-translucent petals and opaque deep purple centres.

1.5in (4cm) diam

£10-15   **MILLB**

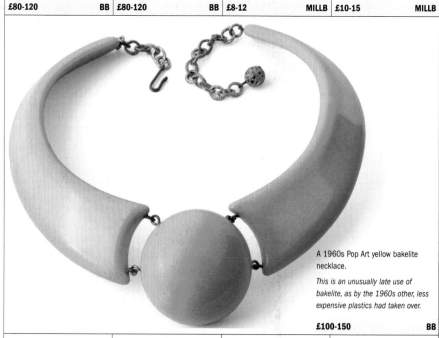

A 1960s Pop Art yellow bakelite necklace.

This is an unusually late use of bakelite, as by the 1960s other, less expensive plastics had taken over.

£100-150   **BB**

A 'creamed corn' and black bakelite articulated necklace.

7in (17.5cm) diam

£60-80   **BB**

A 1960s/70s Lanvin 'Space Age' necklace, with black and red plastic pendant.

Along with other notable designers, Lanvin explored the futuristic space theme that dominated haute couture during the late 1960s.

Pendant 3in (8cm) diam

£120-150   **LB**

An early 1970s unsigned Pop Art belt, with candy coloured plastic and goldtone metal links and a long disc pendant.

40in (101.5cm) long

£10-15   **MILLB**

Six 1960s clear and coloured laminated Lucite fashion rings.

1.25in (3cm) high

£25-35 each   **DTC**

FIND OUT MORE...

DK Collectors' Guide: Costume Jewellery, by Judith Miller, published by Dorling Kindersley, 2003.

COLLECTORS' NOTES

■ Type, date, condition and rarity are the main gauges of value for Disneyana. Many of the items found by collectors are children's toys, which were usually thoroughly play-worn. As a result, mint condition toys, especially if they retain their original box, will fetch a considerable premium over those that have been played with.

■ Memorabilia dating from the 1930s is generally the most sought-after and valuable. When trying to date Disneyana, look first at the shape and design of a character or item as some characters were only made at certain times, and others changed over time – Mickey Mouse is typical of this. Although he is one of the most popular characters, he is not the rarest and rare characters can fetch higher values.

■ Markings are also important. George Borgfeldt's name will generally date an item to the 1930s, as he was the first to receive a license to produce Disney's characters, in 1930. Legendary salesman and marketer Kay Kamen is another early name. He signed a deal with Disney in 1933 that was cut short by Kamen's death in a plane crash in 1949.

■ Before c1939, licensed items were marked 'Walt Disney Enterprises', or 'Walter E. Disney'. Licensed items made in the UK could also be marked 'Walt Disney Mickey Mouse Ltd'. From the 1940s onwards, items were marked 'Walt Disney Productions'. Other marks usually indicate unlicensed or later products.

■ From the 1930s to the 1960s, many unlicensed products were made outside the US. Many of these came from Germany, followed by Japan from the late 1940s. Early examples from the 1930s are often desirable and valuable, and those from the 1950s can represent an affordable alternative to collecting period pieces. Many collectors prefer licensed products.

■ As items from the 1930s-1950s become more scarce, collectors are increasingly looking to later decades. Now may be the time to buy, although always aim to go for memorabilia in mint condition. Similarly, paper ephemera from the primary vintage period, such as cards, badges and paper, is possibly still undervalued.

■ Small limited editions based on characters from recent Disney classics such as The Lion King are currently hot property.

An early 1930s German hand-painted ceramic Mickey Mouse figure, marked "820 1/2".

2.25in (5.5cm) high

£20-30 GAZE

A Japanese painted ceramic Mickey Mouse figure, stamped "Mickey Mouse" on his front, "MADE IN JAPAN" and "Walt E. Disney" on the back.

4in (10cm) high

£40-60 PWE

A CLOSER LOOK AT A MICKEY MOUSE FIGURE

Mickey has become more 'juvenile' over the years, changing his appearance considerably. This helps to date earlier examples.

His head is smaller, less rounded and more rodent-like than today's Mickey.

This Mickey has a wide smiling mouth with teeth - a scary feature that appears on some very early licensed and unlicensed products including this figurine.

Differences between this Mickey and later incarnations include the tail, longer legs and arms, big hands and striped trousers.

A 1930s German large hand-painted plaster Mickey Mouse, cracked at the legs and re-glued, moulded "1234 GESCH" on back of stand.

7.75in (19.5cm) high

£750-850 AMJ

A 1950s 'Mickey Mouse' collapsible plastic Maxi Puppet, by Kohner, marked "© Walt Disney Productions".

5.5in (14cm) high

£15-20 SOTT

A 1970s Mickey Mouse Club 'Minnie Mouse' soft toy, with Mickey Mouse Club badge, faded body, one eye missing.

11in (28cm) high

£15-20 GAZE

A 1950s Schuco clockwork Donald Duck tinplate toy, movement in working order, some wear.

Donald Duck first appeared in the Silly Symphony cartoon "The Wise Little Hen" in 1934. Audiences appreciated his characteristic short fuse and during the 1940s he starred in more broadcast cartoons than Disney's 'golden boy' Mickey Mouse.

£200-300   **LAN**

A 1950s Donald Duck ceramic money bank, with "Japan" foil label.

5.5in (14cm) high

£20-30   **SOTT**

A late 1930s American Seiberling Latex moulded rubber Happy dwarf, marked "© Walt Disney".

5.5in (14cm) high

£50-70   **PWE**

An American Ideal composition Pinocchio, loosely strung, light soiling to clothing, some crazing to rear of head and split under left ear.

13in (33cm) high

£150-250   **JDJ**

A late 1930s American Seiberling Latex moulded rubber Doc dwarf, by Seiberling Latex and marked "© Walt Disney".

6in (15cm) high

£35-45   **PWE**

A Japanese Flower ceramic figure, from "Bambi", marked "Disney Japan".

3in (7.5cm) high

£8-12   **SOTT**

A Britain's Pluto No.18H lead figure.

Pluto's curling tail has been broken, which is a common ailment. A complete set of five Britain's Disney characters, including Mickey, Donald, Goofy and Pluto, may fetch £2,000.

£40-50   **GAZE**

A Bambi lithographed die-cut wooden figure, marked "© W.D.P.".

c1942   *6in (15cm) high*

£18-22   **SOTT**

A 1940s Mickey Mouse and Donald Duck fire truck rubber toy, by Sun Rubber Co. USA, marked "© Walt Disney Productions".

In 1944, the Sun Rubber Co. also produced a Mickey Mouse gas mask with Walt Disney's full approval, in case of inland attack after the bombing of Pearl Harbour. Few survived and today they are very rare.

6.5in (16.5cm) long

£40-50 SOTT

A 1940s Donald Duck and Pluto rubber toy car, by Sun Rubber Co. USA, marked "© Walt Disney Productions".

6.5in (16.5cm) long

£50-70 SOTT

A 1960s Walt Disney Club toy car, made in Hong Kong for S.S. Kruesge, marked "© Walt Disney Productions".

5.75in (14.5cm) high

£10-15 SOTT

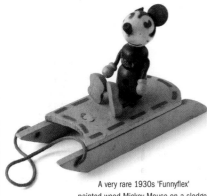

A very rare 1930s 'Funnyflex' painted wood Mickey Mouse on a sledge, with remains of transfer reading "Mickey Mouse Corp by Walt Disney", one ear detached.

6in (15cm) long

£800-1,200 PWE

A Fisher Price Mickey Mouse 'Puddle Jumper' wooden pull-along toy, with lithographed paper covering.

As you pull the toy along, the back of the car wobbles and makes a noise. It is hard to find the paper on this pull-along toy in such bright, intact and unspoilt condition.

1953-56 *6.5in (16.5cm) long*

£100-150 SOTT

A 1950s Fisher Price Donald Duck lithographed paper-on-card and wood pull-along toy drummer.

7.5in (19cm) long

£180-220 SOTT

A 1950s/60s Japanese TM Modern Toys battery operated tinplate Mickey Mouse on a buggy, with original box.

8in (20cm) long

£100-150 W&W

An American Louis Marx wind-up tinplate and celluloid 'Disney Dipsy Car', with Donald Duck, marked "Walt Disney Prod", mint and boxed.

c1950 *6in (15cm) long*

£400-500 PWE

A 1950s Japanese Line Mar Toys wind-up tinplate 'Mechanical Pluto The Drum Major', marked 'Walt Disney Productions', mint and boxed.

6.5in (16.5cm) high

£250-350 PWE

A Japanese Pluto bean bag toy, with painted rubber head, marked "© Walt Disney Productions".

7in (18cm) wide

£8-12   **SOTT**

A 1950s Japanese lithographed tin Thumper friction toy, from "Bambi", made by Line Mar Toys, marked "© W.D.P.".

3in (7.5cm) long

£25-35   **SOTT**

A 1950s Japanese lithographed tin Flower friction toy, from "Bambi", made by Line Mar Toys, marked "© W.D.P.".

3in (7.5cm) long

£20-30   **SOTT**

A Mickey Mouse wood and printed paper acrobat toy.

It is hard to find these simply made, delicate toys in this intact and bright condition as they are so easily damaged through play.

8in (20cm) high

£40-50   **SOTT**

A rare 1950s celluloid Mickey and Minnie Mouse see-saw toy, both figures marked, "Japan" at hip, stamped, "Made in Japan" on bottom of tin base.

£400-500   **JDJ**

A Donald Duck lithographed tin paint box, by Transorgron Co. Inc., marked "Walt Disney Enterprises".

c1946

£20-30   **SOTT**

A 1960s Mickey Mouse Drawing Tutor, by Welsotoys, no. 9/99, lithographed tinplate, marked "©Walt Disney Productions Ltd".

Box 19.25in (49cm) wide

£25-35   **GAZE**

A 1950s 'Mickey Mouse' lithographed card kaleidoscope, marked "© Walt Disney Production".

7.75in (19.5cm) long

£35-45   **SOTT**

A 1950s American lithographed tin sand pail, by J. Chein, decorated with Mickey Mouse scene, marked "© Walt Disney Productions".

4.25in (11cm) high

£40-50   **SOTT**

A Minnie Mouse vinyl purse, marked "© Walt Disney Productions".

c1958   4.25in (11cm) wide

£18-22   **SOTT**

A 1990s Disney's 'Wonderful World of Reading' school book backpack.

This backpack advertises the popular children's bookclub run by Disney, promoting the reading of classic tales for children.

£4-5   **BR**

A 1930s Snow White and the Seven Dwarfs child's scarf, marked "W.D.E." for Walt Disney Enterprises.

19in (48.5cm) wide

£20-30   **SOTT**

A 1930s fringed silk scarf, with printed design of Mickey catching a football, unmarked.

8.5in (21.5cm) wide

£20-30   **SOTT**

A 1950s pair of Mickey Mouse socks.

10.5in (26.5cm) long

£6-8   **BH**

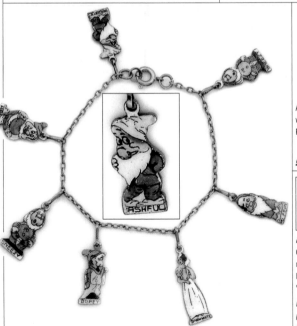

A 1930s novelty base metal charm bracelet, featuring Snow White and the Seven Dwarfs as enamelled charms.

7in (18cm) long

£150-200   **WW**

A 'Snow White' and 'Dopey' child's wristwatch, marked "© Walt Disney Productions".

1in (2.5cm) diam

£60-85   **SOTT**

A 'Mickey Mouse Globetrotters' membership badge, by Kay Kamen Ltd, marked "Eat Freihofers Perfect Loaf".

Bread advertising was often tied in to popular characters. This badge would have been produced shortly after 1933, the worst year of the Depression.

c1934   1.25in (3cm) diam

£40-50   **SOTT**

A Walt Disney Pluto plastic clock, by the Allied Manufacturing Company, marked "Walt Disney Productions", mint and boxed.

Box 10.5in (26.5cm) high

£150-250   PWE

A Mickey Mouse bakelite alarm clock, by US Time Ingersoll, marked "© W.D.P."

c1940   4in (10cm) high

£22-28   JDJ

A 1950s Minnie Mouse alarm clock, by Bradley, Germany, marked "© Walt Disney Productions".

4.5in (11.5cm) diam

£15-20   JDJ

A German Waechtersbach Donald Duck ceramic clock, marked "© Walt Disney Productions", on a metal base.

9in (23cm) high

£60-80   PWE

An early Mickey and Minnie Mouse reverse-painted glass tray, signed on lower right, "A GEORGES GAPIN, VIEN, AMICHLEMENT, E.SEVRE", paint worn in places.

16in (40.50cm) long

£60-80   JDJ

A 1950s Donald Duck Chocolate Syrup lithographed tin can, by Atlantic Syrup Refining Corp., marked "©Walt Disney Productions", unused.

4.5in (11.5cm) high

£15-20   BH

A Snow White and the Seven Dwarves milk glass child's cereal bowl, by Vitrock, marked "W.D. Ent.".

£40-50   SOTT

A pair of Mickey and Minnie Mouse painted cast plastic napkin rings, marked "W.D.P"

3in (7.5cm) high

£20-30   SOTT

A 1950s Mickey Mouse painted ceramic ashtray, with Mickey playing the saxophone, marked "Made In Japan".

3in (7.5cm) high

£80-120   PWE

A 1950s Three Little Pigs ceramic ashtray, stamped on the bottom "Made in Japan © WALT DISNEY".

3.25in (8.5cm) high

£80-120   PWE

DISNEYANA

A J. Chein Snow White and the Seven Dwarfs electric 78rpm child's record player, marked "PortoFonic", with lithographed tin base.

14in (35.5cm) diam

£70-100 JDJ

A 'Mickey Mouse' portable 33 or 45rpm child's turntable, manufactured by General Electric, USA, model RP 3122 B, in a plastic case.

c1970

£80-120 ATK

A CLOSER LOOK AT DISNEY STATIONERY

Disposable and easily used functional items such as children's writing paper can be extremely rare today, despite the large amount originally made – and this is in excellent, bright condition.

It is very rare to find Horace Horsecollar accompanying Mickey and Minnie as he was a short-lived character. He first appeared in the 1929 film 'The Plow Boy' and he was soon replaced by Goofy.

Horace was not created by Disney himself but, after appearing as a supporting character, appeared in stories of his own.

Mickey and Minnie both have 'pie-section' eyes indicating a comparatively early date.

Horace Horsecollar can be distinguished from Mickey's other horse Tanglefoot as he walks upright.

An 1930s Walt Disney child's writing paper and envelope, with rare image of Horace Horsecollar.

5.75in (14.5cm) high

£10-15 SOTT

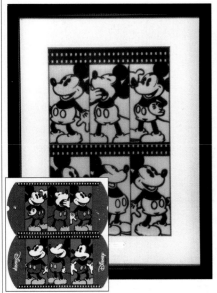

An original Disney Studios Mickey Mouse printing plate, with two original gift box samples, in original frame.

£80-120 ATK

A "Walt Disney presents The Jungle Book" 7in mini-LP and 24 page book, LLP319, from Disneyland Records.

1977

£7-10 GAZE

A Walt Disney World souvenir book.

1972   11in (28cm) wide

£10-15 BH

"The Art of Walt Disney: From Mickey Mouse to the Magic Kingdom", 1970s American advertising poster.

40in (101cm) high

£70-90 CL

DOLLS

A 1950s Pedigree hard plastic walking doll, marked "Lulu" and "22".

Pedigree was founded by the Lines Brothers in 1919 and began making composition dolls in the 1930s. In the 1950s they turned to hard plastic dolls and it is these that are so sought-after by collectors today.

22in (56cm) high

A 1950s Pedigree clockwork 'Walker' hard plastic doll, with Tri-ang key.

14in (35.5cm) high

A 1950s Pedigree 'Knee Joint' hard plastic doll.

She has the same face as the Saucy Walker doll. Her knee joints allow her to sit in a chair and also kneel to pray.

22in (56cm) high

£100-150   **GAZE** | £60-80   **DSC** | £70-100   **DSC**

A Pedigree hard plastic doll, shoes marked "Cinderella Size 1", in original box.

14.5in (37cm) high

A 1950s Pedigree 'Saucy Walker' hard plastic doll, with 'flirty' eyes and two teeth, with unjointed knees.

This doll has the same face as The Pretty Peepers doll also on this page, and her head turns as she 'walks' Knee bend examples are more valuable.

21in (53.5cm) high

£70-100   **GAZE** | £60-80   **DSC** | **DSC**

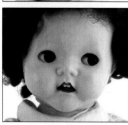

A 1950s Pedigree 'Little Princess' hard plastic doll.

A rare 1950s Pedigree 'Pretty Peepers' hard plastic doll, with jointed knees.

This doll has a plastic plate in her chest which, when pressed, alters the colour of her eyes and their position from left to centre to right. They are hard to find in this condition.

22in (56cm) high

Based on Princess Anne, this doll was released in the Coronation year, 1953. Her clothes were designed by Norman Hartnell, the Queen's designer but tend to disintegrate, making them rare. An example without clothes would be worth up to £70.

14in (35.5cm) high

£200-250   **DSC** | £100-150   **DSC**

A 1950s Roddy smiley-faced hard plastic doll.

The company that became known as 'Roddy' in the 1950s was founded in 1948. This example has a slightly less common face. She has plastic eyelashes, which are typical of Roddy. Earlier Roddy dolls had tin eyes.

10in (25.5cm) high

£30-40   **DSC**

A Roddy hard plastic walking doll, boxed.

Box 4.25in (11cm) high

£12-18   **GAZE**

A 1950s Roddy walker pouty-faced hard plastic doll, with turning head mechanism and moulded shoes.

The hands with 'thumbs-up' are typical of Roddy. Check the back of the head and lips for paint wear. The moulded shoes are also a typical feature of many Roddy dolls.

12in (30.5cm) high

£30-40   **DSC**

A Roddy Maori hard plastic doll and baby, with quill skirt and feather cloak.

14in (35.5cm) high

£30-40   **GAZE**

A 1950s Roddy 'Topsy' hard plastic doll, with moulded "Roddy Made in England" mark.

This was also made as a white baby, but as less black dolls were made, they are usually more valuable. The unusual name comes from the hairstyle.

9in (23cm) high

£30-40   **DSC**

A 1950s Tudor Rose straight-legged hard plastic boy doll.

The less valuable white version of this doll is worth approximately £10, but values for Tudor Rose are rising.

8in (20cm) high

£10-15   **DSC**

A 1950s Tudor Rose 'Blondy Blueyes' hard plastic doll, by Rosedale Associated Manufacturing Ltd, with unusual moulded clothes and walking action, boxed.

7in (18cm) high

£20-30   **DSC**

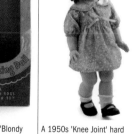

A 1950s 'Knee Joint' hard plastic doll, by Rosebud.

17in (43cm) high

£60-80   **DSC**

A late 1950s Rosebud 'Knee Joint' hard plastic doll, with vinyl head.

Late 1950s hard plastic dolls with vinyl heads are known as 'Transitionals' - the vinyl allowed hair to be rooted directly into the scalp rather than being a glued on wig. It was too expensive for all the machinery to be changed as soon as vinyl was introduced, so the new heads were used with old-fashioned style bodies and limbs.

17in (43cm) high

£40-60   **DSC**

A 1980s Peggy Nisbet 'Sarah Ferguson Bride' vinyl doll, with original box.

Peggy Nisbet made her first doll in 1953, to celebrate the coronation of Queen Elizabeth II. Many of her highly detailed dolls are drawn from history, such as Henry VIII and his six wives and the 'Cries of London' series of Victorian dolls. In the 1980s she made a series of Royal dolls, which are popular with collectors. The company became 'House of Nisbet' in the mid-1970s and teddy bears began to take precedence. Although Nisbet herself died in 1985, her dolls were produced until 1999. Mint and complete condition is essential.

16in (10.5cm) high

£60-80   **DSC**

A CLOSER LOOK AT A PEGGY NISBET DOLL

The head and neck are fixed, giving Diana's characteristic look, and her hair is in its original style.

She retains her original box, showing an original price tag of £24.99 at famous London toy store Hamley's.

She is complete with train, veil, necklace and bouquet, which are all in mint condition

As they were expensive, most of these dolls were sold to collectors, so it is not hard to find mint and boxed examples.

A 1980s Peggy Nisbet 'My Princess' Diana, Princess of Wales vinyl doll.

16in (40.5cm) high

£60-80   **DSC**

A 1980s Peggy Nisbet 'Prince William Toddler Sailor Suit' vinyl doll, with "PN" monogram on back of neck, mint with original box.

18in (45.5cm) high

£60-80   **DSC**

A mid-to late 1980s Peggy Nisbet 'Prince Harry Baby Sun Suit' vinyl doll, mint with original box.

As this doll has the same face as the Prince William doll, it can often be difficult to tell them apart.

18in (45.5cm) high

£60-80   **DSC**

A 1970s Peggy Nisbet 'Queen Victoria' vinyl doll.

7in (18cm) high

£15-25   **DSC**

A 1970s Peggy Nisbet 'Nefertiti' vinyl doll, with enamelled and gilt-decorated metal head dress.

The weighty head dress makes this delicate doll top heavy and unable to stand without support.

8in (20cm) high

£20-30   **DSC**

A 1970s Peggy Nisbet 'Dolls Seller' vinyl doll.

7in (18cm) high

£15-20   **DSC**

A Pedigree Sindy 'Ballerina' doll, mint with original box.

This doll was only made for one year making it scarce. In played-with condition and lacking the box, she would be worth up to £30 if she retained her dress. Sindy was introduced in 1963 and as with Barbie, features help to date her. In 1968 she gained eye lashes, a new side-parted hairstyle and a twist waist, and in 1970 a ball-jointed neck and extra joints at the elbows and knees. By the middle of the decade she had moveable wrists and could point her toes. Despite disappearing in 1997, she reappeared in 1999 under the 'Vivid Imaginations' company.

1985

£70-100 DSC

A Pedigree Sindy 'Starlight' doll, mint in box.

This doll has the new Sindy face. The following year, the brand was taken over by Hasbro.

1986

Box 13.5in (34cm) high

£60-80 DSC

An early 1980s Pedigree Sindy 'Space Fantasy' doll, with original clothing and shoes.

This was the only Pedigree Sindy made with pink hair.

11in (28cm) high

£60-80 DSC

A Pedigree Sindy 'Sweet Dreams' doll, with original nightdress.

This was the only Sindy to be produced with painted sleeping eyes.

1979

£15-20 DSC

A 1980s Dutch Fleur doll.

Fleur was the Dutch version of Sindy and had the same body.

11in (28cm) high

£15-25 DSC

A 1960s Palitoy Tiny Tears vinyl doll.

Palitoy Tiny Tears was introduced in 1965 and is beloved of many nostalgic for their childhood. They are also becoming increasingly sought-after by collectors, particularly in clean condition with their original outfits which came in blue and pink. The bib tends to get detached from the outfit and washing fades the logo. Bibs in good condition are hard to find.

16in (40.5cm) high

£40-60 DSC

A 1980s Palitoy 'Tiny Tears' vinyl doll.

16in (40.5cm) high

£40-50 DSC

A 1980s Palitoy Teeny Weeny Tiny Tears vinyl doll, in mint condition with original box.

Complete but without the original box, she would be worth up to £30.

8in (20cm) high

£60-80   **DSC**

A 1980s French Miro-Meccano 'Tinnie' vinyl doll, in mint condition with original box.

This is the French version of Tiny Tears.

16in (40.5cm) high

£30-40   **DSC**

A Pedigree 'First Love' vinyl doll, mint in original box.

She was brought out to rival 'Tiny Tears' and proved successful for 10 years. In played-with but complete condition she can fetch up to £25.

c1977   16in (40.5cm) high

£60-80   **DSC**

A Pedigree 'Alice in Wonderland' vinyl doll, in mint condition with original box.

These dolls use a Sindy type body, and are desirable to Sindy collectors. The appealing box makes them highly collectable.

1978   11in (28cm) high

£40-60   **DSC**

A Pedigree 'Snow White' vinyl doll, in mint condition with original box.

1978   11in (28cm) high

£40-60   **DSC**

A 1980s Pedigree 'Matilda' vinyl doll, in mint condition with original box.

7in (18cm) high

£15-20   **DSC**

A 1980s Pedigree Grocer's shop with vinyl doll, in mint condition with original box.

This is part of a series, each in a different shop.

£15-25   **DSC**

A 1980s Hornby Flower Fairies 'Sweet Pea' vinyl doll, in mint condition with original box.

£15-25   **DSC**

A 1980s Hornby Flower Fairies 'Self-Heal Pixie' vinyl doll.

This pixie was usually sold with a fairy, the single boxed versions are much rarer.

Box 9.75in (25cm) high

£15-20   **DSC**

A 1970s Burbank 'Victoria Rose' vinyl doll, with soft body and legs.

Burbank were a short-lived company. As well as the soft body and legs, Victorian styles are typical.

22in (56cm) high

£15-25   **DSC**

A 1960s Amanda Jane Ltd 'Amanda Jane' vinyl doll, with sleepy eyes, in mint condition with original box.

These are commonly copied, but copies are of poorer quality and often have shorter legs. Eyes were painted, not sleepy, from the 1970s onwards.

8in (20cm) high

£15-25   **DSC**

A CLOSER LOOK AT A MORMIT DOLL

These dolls, launched 1945-46, used a heavy, rubbery PVC allowing them to be bathed – an innovation in an age of non-water resistant composition and painted dolls.

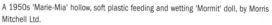

The limbs have a push-fit joint, allowing them to be taken apart and drained after bathing.

She is in mint condition with her box and feeding bottle, which are rare.

The coloured dyes used were not 'fast', so can fade or brown in sunlight or due to excessive handling. This one has an excellent complexion with original hair, rouged cheeks and red lips.

A 1950s 'Marie-Mia' hollow, soft plastic feeding and wetting 'Mormit' doll, by Morris Mitchell Ltd.

Founder F.G. Mitchell named the dolls 'Marie' with the second name being those of his five daughters, here 'Mia'.

11in (28cm) high

£50-70   **DSC**

A 1960s Chiltern (H.G. Stone) vinyl girl doll, with tight curl 'Saran' rough textured honey coloured hair, in mint condition with original box.

12in (30.5cm) high

£20-30   **DSC**

A 1970s Flair 'Daisy Longlegs' vinyl doll, designed by Mary Quant, with walking/dancing action.

Quant also designed a range of costumes, which help to determine value. Outfits like this example are rare. There was also a smaller version at 11in high.

15in (38cm) high

£15-25   **DSC**

A 1960s Roddy tennis girl vinyl doll, with Saran hair, in mint condition with original box.

15in (38cm) high

£40-50   **DSC**

A 1960s Rosebud 'Bride' vinyl doll, lacks shoes and veil.

Complete she would be worth up to £40.

15in (38cm) high

£15-25   **DSC**

A 1930s hand-painted bisque doll, with googly-eyes and a preying mantis on its head, moveable arms.

6.25in (16cm) high

£25-35   RP

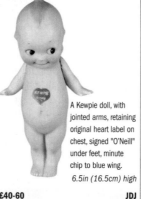

A Kewpie doll, with jointed arms, retaining original heart label on chest, signed "O'Neill" under feet, minute chip to blue wing.

6.5in (16.5cm) high

£40-60   JDJ

A Kewpie doll, wearing a painted moulded Prussian helmet, with outstretched hands.

2.75in (7cm) high

£120-180   JDJ

A rare German Kewpie soldier doll, with moulded clothing, helmet and gun, partial paper label on chest, some damage.

Kewpie was designed by US illustrator Rose O'Neill in 1909. The first dolls were made from around 1912, primarily in Germany but also in the US and Japan, with the craze lasting into the 1920s. Licensed Kewpies are the most desirable, especially if large or in different poses or 'clothes' - look for O'Neill's name on the base of the foot, star-shaped hands or heart-shaped or circular labels.

3.75in (9.5cm) high

£180-220   JDJ

A Kewpie 'Action' doll.
c1910   5in (12.5cm) high

£300-350   BEJ

A large seated Kewpie doll, playing a mandolin, with original paper label, repair to stem of mandolin.

4in (10cm) high

£60-80   JDJ

A Kewpie Governor doll, sitting in a wicker chair, with folded arms, marked "C" in a circle on bottom of chair.

£120-180   JDJ

A large Kewpie Thinker doll, signed on bottom.

4.5in (11.5cm) high

£120-180   JDJ

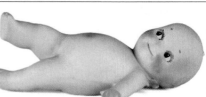

A Kewpie Blunderboo doll, minute chip to hair tip.

4.5in (11.5cm) high

£120-180   JDJ

A Heinrich Handwerck PK doll, with brown sleeping eyes, pierced ears, open mouth with four teeth, the head stamped "109/11 3/4", some wear.

c1900   22in (55cm) high

£400-500   **LAN**

A Hertel, Schwab & Co. PK girl doll, 98/12, with flirty eyes, some damage to eye lids.

20in (50cm) high

£300-400   **LAN**

A rare Armand Marseille Asian doll, with closed mouth, stamped "353 2 3/4-3 1/2".

A Hertel, Schwab & Co. PK character baby doll, 152/2, with sleeping eyes, open mouth with tongue and two teeth, mohair wig, on a baby body.

c1912   11.25in (28cm) high

£350-450   **LAN**

Examine the back of bisque dolls' heads to check for marks identifying the maker and the mould number. Look for well painted features and examine the bisque carefully for cracks or damage. Clean bisque is also sought after, as are large dolls and unusual nationalities, which are generally rarer.

17.25in (43cm) high

£500-600   **LAN**

A Wagner & Zetzsche bisque shoulder head doll, with blue sleep eyes, open mouth, four teeth, jointed body with composition arms.

25in (63.5cm) high

£180-220   **W&W**

A small French bisque doll, with composition body.

9in (23cm) high

£80-120   **ROS**

A German painted bisque boy doll.

c1920   5in (12.5cm) high

£200-300   **BEJ**

A pair of stone bisque children, with jointed arms and hand-painted details.

c1920   5in (12.5cm) high

£80-100   **BEJ**

A set of early 1900s bisque 'pudding' dolls.

These miniature hand-painted, simply moulded dolls were often put in Christmas puddings as favours.

1.25in (3cm) high

£4-5 each   **DSC**

A 'Madam Hendron' composition doll, by Universal Talking Toys Co., featuring a spring-driven mechanism concealed in its body, with original dress and two cylinders.

c1922   26in (65cm) high

£300-400   **ATK**

An Italian composition 'Flirty' child doll, dressed in bright clothing with a straw hat.

c1930

£120-140   **BEJ**

A CLOSER LOOK AT A CORONATION DOLL

Her well-painted face is in excellent condition as is her hairstyle, which retains its original, tight curls and hairnet.

She has a disc-playing mechanism in her stomach that makes her sing the National Anthem and recite a poem about the coronation.

She is in mint condition with all her clothes including her fur-trimmed coronation robe, sash, instructions and the original card box she was mailed in.

She was released at the time of the coronation of Queen Elizabeth II to help girls celebrate.

A 'Queen Elizabeth' speaking/singing composition doll, by Mark Payne Ltd, with original box.

c1953   26in (66cm) high

£400-600   **DSC**

A 1940s composition girl doll, probably by Roddy, all original.

18in (45.5cm) high

£60-80   **DSC**

A 1950s Rosebud fairy painted composition doll, with original outfit, wand and box.

7in (18cm) high

£30-40   **DSC**

A 1940s composition boy doll, by Diamond Tile Company, with soft body.

15.5in (39.5cm) high

£30-40   **DSC**

A late 19thC sailor boy doll, with cloth body, hand-painted face and composition head, "VH" mark at the back of the head, a few scratches to the face.

9in (23cm) high

£40-60   **EPO**

A Norah Wellings 'Jolly Toddler' doll, with original clothes and box.

c1930 17in (43cm) high

£350-400 BEJ

A 1930s Norah Wellings 'Queen Mary' sailor doll.

This doll is more desirable because it has the name of a well-known ship on the cap.

10in (25.5cm) high

£80-120 BEJ

A 1950s Lupino Lane doll, by Dean's Rag Book of London, with dog-tooth check suit and printed facial features.

This doll is modelled after the 1930s music hall star Lupino Lane, who is best known for the song 'The Lambeth Walk' from the musical 'Me and My Girl'.

c1939 11.5in (29cm) high

£150-250 TCT

A very rare Steiff British policeman poseable doll, with accurate blue felt uniform, his velvet face with boot button eyes, stitched and printed detail.

It's the early date, condition, subject matter and great rarity that make this doll as valuable as it is.

c1910 18in (46cm) high

£1,200-1,800 F

A 1950s Chad Valley 'George' fabric doll, with felt clothes and hat, label to foot.

12in (30.5cm) high

£200-300 TCT

A 1930s/40s Chad Valley fabric doll, the painted head with eyes looking to the side, label to foot.

18in (45.5cm) high

£50-70 GAZE

A Lenci cloth doll, arms jointed at the shoulders.

24in (61cm) high

£180-220 GORL

A 1930s fabric half doll, with painted features and blonde mohair wig, unmarked.

11.25in (28.5cm) high

£35-45 GAZE

EARLY COMPUTERS

COLLECTORS' NOTES

■ Technology has developed in leaps and bounds over the past few decades and those with an eye for nostalgia or for collecting important, classic technologies have begun to consider early computers.

■ Many collectors usually use their computers, to play original games that are no longer available, except possibly on emulators. As such, examples must be in working condition and be as complete as possible to fetch the higher values.

■ Look out for models from the 1970s-early 1990s that are considered landmarks of their time. Mass produced and highly successful models such as Sinclair's Spectrum range are usually of lower value as so many survive today.

■ Certain models are rarer than others. Accessories such as games and power packs are also often sought-after.

■ A single year shown represents the year of introduction, a range gives the years of production.

An Acorn Archimedes A410 home computer.

Despite being at least twice as fast as the – then current – Atari ST and Amiga models, the Archimedes was expensive and saw little success outside of British schools.

1987-89   19in (48.5cm) w

£15-20   **PC**

An Apple IIe (European Model) home computer.

This model was the updated version of the II+, the 'e' standing for 'enhanced'.

1983-93   17in (43cm) wide

£15-25   **PC**

An Apple Mac Classic home computer.

The Classic was the cut-down successor to the Mac SE, with limited features for a budget market, and was thus rather underspecified compared to its siblings.

1990-92

£30-50   **PC**

A Commodore Amiga A-500+ home computer.

1986   18in (45.5cm) wide

£6-9   **PC**

An Atari 400 home computer, with touch-sensitive keypad and built-in tape drive.

1979-82   13in (33cm) wide

£20-30   **PC**

A Commodore Amiga A1000 home computer and keyboard.

Despite being a high-spec machine, the high price made it unpopular outside of the UK.

1985-87   17.5in (44.5cm) wide

£30-50   **PC**

A Commodore CDTV home computer.

This was designed as a home entertainment system, but was unpopular due to its high cost and lack of software.

1990-93   17in (43cm) wide

£40-60   **PC**

A Memotech MTX 512 home computer.

c1983 19in (48cm) wide

£20-30   **PC**

A New Brain AD home computer, by Grundy Business Systems Ltd, with one line, 16 character screen.

An earlier model 'A' existed, without a screen. Neither were highly successful as, perhaps put off by the poor keyboard, the trade press noted that it was not a good games or business machine.

1982   *10.75in (27cm) wide*

£80-120   **PC**

A Research Machines 380Z professional computer, with 32K RAM, a 5.25in double disc system and keyboard.

These computers were made primarily for use in schools and cost over £1,800 + VAT.

c1982 19.5in (49.5cm) wide

£20-30   **PC**

A Sinclair ZX Spectrum+ home computer.

c1984 12.5in (31.5cm) wide

£20-30   **PC**

A Sinclair Spectrum ZX 48K home computer, in fitted carrying case with power pack, manual, tape deck and games.

The 16K version is hard to find and can be worth up to twice the value of the 48K version.

1982-84   *8.5in (21.5cm) wide*

£30-40   **PC**

A TRS-80 colour 2 home computer, by Tandy Radio Shack.

c1982 15in (37cm) wide

£20-30   **PC**

A Sinclair ZX Spectrum +3 home computer.

c1987   *17in (43cm) wide*

£30-50   **PC**

12 issues of 'Popular Electronics' magazine from 1975, including the January edition which showcased the introduction of one of the first mini-computers, the 'Altair 8800' - an event that prompted Bill Gates to found Microsoft five months later.

1975

£280-320   **ATK**

A 1947 Esquire Girl calendar, unsigned artwork, with original mailing envelope.

In 1946, Vargas and Esquire ended their collaboration and Vargas went on to produce his own pinup calendar in 1948. In the meantime, Esquire released this uncredited calendar using unsigned Vargas artwork.

£50-70   **HH**

A CLOSER LOOK AT AN ESQUIRE MAGAZINE PINUP CALENDAR

Alberto Vargas (1896-1982) started drawing fashion illustrations before being commissioned to paint the Ziegfield Follies in 1919. He worked with them for 12 years.

In 1939 he joined Esquire magazine, producing a centre spread. These were collected into the 'Varga Girl' calendars.

The illustrations proved particularly popular with the US armed forces overseas and the designs were copied onto jackets and aircraft nose cones.

Playing to the soldiers over seas, Vargas has illustrated this lady in an army cap from the Signal Corp.

A 1945 Esquire magazine pinup calendar, with artwork by Alberto Vargas and verses by Phil Stack.

12.25in (31cm) high

£50-70   **HH**

A 1948 Varga 'The Varga Girl' calendar, with original mailing envelope, in mint condition, with verses by Earl Wilson.

As Esquire magazine had trademarked the name 'Varga Girls' they were able to continue to publish artwork under that name even though their association with Albert Vargas had ended.

12.25in (31cm) high

£60-80   **HH**

A 'Garden of Eden' poster, artwork by Benito Jacovitti (1923-1997).

Jacovitti is probably the best known Italian satirical cartoonist. His first cartoons appeared in 1939 and his recognizable style is typically absurd, bizarre and often risqué.

25.25in (65cm) high

£20-30   **CL**

An Italian erotic poster, designed by Benito Jacovitti, copyright Club Anni Trenta, Genova.

1977

£60-90   **CL**

A 1950s 'Bust with Humor' small pamphlet, with drawings of various breast types, shapes and names, such as 'Sunnyside Up', 'Loaded 38s', and the rather unfortunate 'Olives' and 'Sandbags'.

4in (10cm) high

£12-18   **HH**

Gretchen Edgren, "The Playboy Book – 40 Years of Pictorial History", first UK edition, published by Mitchell Beazley.

1994

£50-70   **GAZE**

A late 19thC erotic transformation picture with musical movement and clockwork drive, with two scenes, the Swiss cylinder musical mechanism playing one melody.

£280-320   ATK

A Club Trocadero, Chicago matchbook, the matches with printed images of burlesques, unused.

2in (5cm) high

£20-25   SM

A 'Beautiful Girls' theatre lounge matchbook, from the 'Burlesque Lounge' Dallas, the cover and interior printed with naked showgirls, the cover with embossed bosoms.

2in (5cm) high

£15-20   SM

A pair of 1950s terry cotton hand towels, by Cannon, made in the USA, titled 'Boss' and 'Slave', each with a dog, the eyes set with metal studs.

18in (45.5cm) long

£25-35   SM

A 'Glamour Girls' bone china pintray, of a naughty bride, gilt trim on scalloped edge.

4.5in (11.5cm) wide

£25-35   MA

A 1950s Adderley bone china transfer-printed 'glamour girl' ashtray.

5in (12.5cm) wide

£20-30   MA

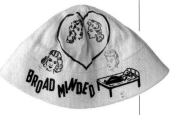

A 1950s cotton 'Broad Minded' hat, with applied cloth patches, made in Japan.

12in (30.5cm) wide

£40-60   SM

COLLECTORS' NOTES

■ Style and design in terms of shape, pattern and colour are of primary importance to most collectors and interior decorators. Pieces by notable designers or factories will fetch more than unnamed items, although a known designer is not always necessary. The 1950s look, even hinted at with a single object, can be acquired without resorting to famous designers or spending large sums of money.

■ Look for rounded, asymmetric and organic forms. Clean-lined kidney and tulip shapes that show patterns off to their best are typical. Angled, spindly legs with ball feet can be found on furniture and other small furnishing items. All are quintessentially modern and represent a stylistic break from the 1940s and traditional designs of previous periods.

■ Patterns are stylized and modern in appearance, ranging from atomic designs to zebra prints, playing cards, polka dots, ballerinas and even pin-up girls.

Parisian and foreign scenes showed a yearning for prosperity, travel and glamour. Colours tend to be bright and cheerful, appealing to the young, and pastel shades are particularly prevalent. The 1950s saw the birth of the teenager and rock 'n' roll, leading to a fashion for related motifs.

■ Many new materials appeared during this period, such as Formica and different plastics. The early part of the decade saw surplus wartime aluminium being used frequently for domestic products. All these materials allowed for new forms to be made inexpensively.

■ Always consider condition, as many mass-produced pieces were not made to last long. As a result, some can be rare as most examples have long since been broken and discarded. When fashions changed, many 1950s artifacts were stored carelessly, if they were kept at all. In all cases, always aim to collect pieces that fulfil as many of the style criteria as possible.

A 1950s vase, with impressed marks and serial number.

8.25in (21cm) high

£10-15   **TCM**

An H.J. Wood Ltd 'Piazza ware' vase.

As well as the stylized design and colours, the curving asymmetric form and rim is archetypally 1950s.

c1957   9.5in (24cm) high

£30-50   **NPC**

A Hornsea Pottery 'Coastline' pattern sugar bowl.

c1955   3.25in (8.5cm) high

£18-22   **AGR**

A Hornsea Pottery 'Elegance' pattern milk jug, sugar bowl and another bowl, designed by John Clappison.

This pattern was also available with a white interior.

c1955-c1959

jug 4.25in (11cm) high

£60-80   **AGR**

A 1950s J. & G. Meakin transfer and hand-coloured decorated plate.

Meakin ceramics currently have lower values than those by companies such as Midwinter, but this may change as more collectors turn their attention to Meakin's 1950s designs.

10in (25.5cm) diam

£15-20   **PSI**

A 1950s Gouda shallow dish, with floral design, printed "Paima Flora Gouda Holland", some crazing.

8in (20.5cm) long

£10-15   **TCM**

An H.J. Wood Ltd 'Piazza' ware lidded butter dish, marked "845 BM" and "R".

6.5in (16.5cm) wide

£20-25   **FD**

A 1950s French tall hand-painted black asymmetric vase, with impressed and painted marks to base.

16in (40.5cm) high

£40-60   PSI

A ceramic 'tiki' mug, in the shape of an Easter Island head, marked "Japan".

Tiki mugs were popular Hawaiian souvenirs during the 1950s and 1960s and were used in 'tiki bars'. Reproductions are sold today, but are usually of poorer quality and not marked "Japan".

6.5in (14cm) high

£25-35   SM

A ceramic 'tiki' mug, marked "Orchids of Hawaii" and "Japan".

6in (15cm) high

£22-28   SM

A ceramic 'tiki' mug, with a tropical lady, marked "Orchids of Hawaii" and "Japan".

7in (18cm) high

£22-28   SM

A 1950s ceramic lady head vase, with umbrella.

6in (15cm) high

£40-50   DAC

A 1950s ceramic lady head vase, with green hood, praying hands and ceramic eyelashes.

Always examine the cowl of these vases as they are easily damaged. The more common version, with just one or no hands, is less valuable.

5.75in (14.5cm) high

£60-90   MA

A 1950s West German painted ceramic gnome, holding a plastic bird in a cage, the base printed "W.Germany /1".

8.25in (21cm) high

£15-25   PC

A 1950s/60s Italian Raymor ceramic cat, marked "1529 Italy".

The market for Raymor and similar Italian ceramics of the 1950s and 1960s is in its infancy but is growing, with values likely to escalate. Look out for figurative pieces, sculptures or large cylindrical or square rectangular vases. Many share the same colours and impressed 'runic' motifs. Always avoid damaged examples.

15.25in (38.5cm) long

£180-220   FD

A 1950s or 1950s-style studio pottery figure of a dachshund, chipped.

Note the similarity of the pattern and colours to some of the 'Contemporary' range patterns produced by Poole Pottery during the 1950s.

6in (15cm) long

£30-40   BRI

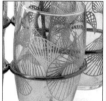

A 1950s set of conical glasses in a wire frame, with transfer-printed designs of a native islander beating a drum.

Large glasses are more sought-after and valuable than sets of smaller shot glasses.

14.5in (37cm) wide

£50-70   **PWE**

A 1950s 'Stars 'n' Stripes' lemonade set, in bent wire holder.

Glasses screen-printed with colourful designs were produced in vast quantities during the 1950s and 60s. Many were contained in wire stands such as this example. As they were inexpensive at the time and used heavily, many sets are incomplete, which lowers their value considerably. Avoid buying examples that show wear to gilt trim or the transfer. Look out for rock 'n' roll and exotic themes, which fetch more, with scantily clad 'pin-up' girl patterns topping the bill.

17in (43cm) wide

£80-120   **MA**

A 1950s set of six screen-printed tumblers, in wire holder.

6.75in (17cm) high

£40-50   **MA**

A 1950s set of six multicoloured screen-printed tumblers, with stylized dancing tribesmen.

5in (12.5cm) high

£40-50   **MA**

A 1950s set of four screen-printed tumblers, with rare top hat and cane design.

5.5in (12.5cm) high

£20-30   **MA**

A pair of tomato juice glasses, with printed decoration.

3.75in (9.5cm) high

£2-3   **BH**

Two 1950s printed 'Ubangi' glasses.

7in (17.5cm) high

£60-80   **CVS**

One of a set of four 1950s printed 'Hi Fi' record album glasses.

5in (12.5cm) high

£60-80 (SET)   **MI**

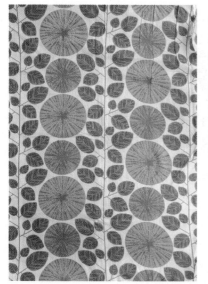

A length of 1950s Swedish fabric, with a stylized foliate design.

144in (366cm) long

£60-70   **FD**

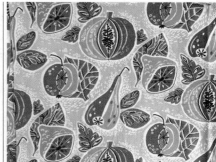

A length of 1950s English bark cloth, printed with a design of stylized fruit.

144in (366cm) long

£20-30   **FD**

A length of 1950s cotton fabric, with embroidered silk trees, converted to curtains.

144in (366cm) long

£30-40   **FD**

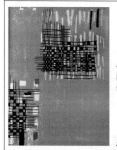

A framed panel of 'Quarto' pattern fabric, by Lucienne Day for Heals.

35.75in (91cm) high

£30-40   **GAZE**

A pair of 'Plantation' printed curtains, by Lucienne Day.

Lucienne Day (b.1917) is one of Britain's most influential 20thC textile designers. Bringing a new vitality into people's homes, she became known for her abstract designs.

c1958   *84in (213cm) l.*

£80-120   **GAZE**

A small folding table, by Arnold Designs Ltd.

The angled spindle legs, curving form and stylized bull shout the 1950s, when flat-packed occasional furniture such as this became widespread. Arnold Designs of Chalford, near Stroud in Gloucestershire, were known for making giftware, furniture and household goods and employed 25 people by 1972.

20in (51cm) long

£10-15   **GAZE**

A 1950s/60s kidney or boomerang-shaped laminated wood occasional table.

The kidney-shaped table was a fashionable 1950s favourite, representing a rounded visual departure from the hard angles of utility furniture. It was also practical, as it could fit around the arm of a sofa.

21in (53cm) long

£10-15   **GAZE**

A 1950s red-painted metal desk light.

£30-40   **GAZE**

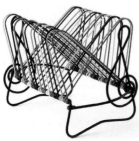

A 1950s plastic-coated wire 78rpm record stand, with treble clef motif.

13.75in (35cm) wide

£60-80   **MA**

A 1950s pink embossed and printed 'My Favourite Tunes' record holder, by Ponytail.

7.5in (19cm) high

£20-30   **MA**

A 1950s Max Bill ceramic kitchen wall clock, with timer.

Max Bill (1908-94) studied under Walter Gropius at the Bauhaus from 1927-29 before becoming a prolific architect, artist and designer. He is also known for a small series of simple clocks, of which this is one. The pastel blue colour and curving lines are very much of the period.

c1954   10.5in (27cm) long

£600-700   **SK**

A CLOSER LOOK AT A COFFEE MACHINE

This coffee machine was designed by Giordano Robbiati of Milan in the late 1940s. A patent was granted in the US in 1951.

It is made from aluminium, which was used extensively for domestic objects in the 1940s, partly due to a fondness for new materials and partly to use up surplus wartime stocks.

Its space age design is the epitome of 'modern' and was arguably way ahead of its time.

Made until the early 1980s, vintage models like this one are highly sought-after by collectors of modern design. It also has a legendary ability to make excellent coffee.

A Brevetti Robbiati 'Atomic' aluminium stove-top espresso coffee machine, with original jug.

c1951   8.25in (21cm) high

£200-300   **SWO**

A 1950s 'Mexican playing guitar' novelty bottle opener, with detachable guitar bottle opener, attached to the stand with a magnet.

7in (18cm) high

£8-12   **MA**

A 1950s American Oster chrome and black bakelite 'Airjet' tabletop hairdryer, with original box and instructions.

The futuristic Oster Airjet was introduced in 1949.

c1950   8.5in (22cm) high

£18-22   **NOR**

A 1950s ceramic Las Vegas dice-shaped lighter and ashtray set, stamped "Japan".

2.5in (6.5cm) wide

£50-70   **SM**

COLLECTORS' NOTES

■ As with the 1950s, consider form, pattern and colour when looking at 1960s and 1970s memorabilia. Always aim to buy items that fulfil as many of the criteria as possible. Colour and pattern are perhaps the most important as they are so characteristic of the age. Bright, acid and often clashing colours dominate, designs explode in psychedelic or 'flower power' patterns. The themes of 'love' and 'peace' recur.

■ The Art Nouveau style of the 1900s also made a comeback, but with a new palette and often with chunkier forms around the sinuous 'whiplash' design. Look out for textiles, which add a notable period touch to any room. Leading names include Heal's of London and Marimekko of Finland.

■ Materials developed too, particularly plastic, which was used heavily for furniture until the petrol crisis of the mid-1970s intervened. Plastic was closely related to an important theme running since the 1950s, that of outer space and the future. As with the 1950s, Sixties style ran through the home, from kitchenware to designer furniture to clothing. As nostalgia is so important to the general market away from notable names, aim to buy brands or designs that inspire fond memories.

A 1960s screen printed 'LOVE' drinking glass.

5.75in (14.5cm) high

£8-12   **NOR**

A 1960s 'flower power' printed drinking glass, marked "Georges Briard".

Georges Briard was a New York based importer and retailer of decorative and functional glassware.

5.75in (14.5cm) high

£8-12   **NOR**

A set of four Ravenhead screen-printed glass tumblers, probably designed by Alexander Hardie Williamson, in original box.

Printed glasses by designers such as the prolific Alexander Hardie-Williamson are becoming more sought-after, particularly in their original box.

c1965   4.75in (12cm) high

£20-30   **DTC**

A 1970s screen printed enamelled fondue set, on a stand with a spirit burner.

8in (20cm) high

£20-30   **MTS**

An early 1970s saucepan, with a bright stylized floral design and blue lid.

Kitchenware became more 'fun' and colourful during the 1960s as formal dining declined in popularity, being replaced with dining informally in the kitchen.

7in (18cm) diam

£15-20   **MTS**

A Norwegian enamelled kettle, with white stylized leaf pattern.

7.75in (19.5cm) high

£7-10   **GAZE**

A Royal Tudor Ware 'Fiesta' coffee set, by Barker Bros of Staffordshire, comprising a coffee pot, sugar bowl, milk jug and six cups and saucers.

This design was released in the early 1960s and was influenced by Enid Seeney's Homemaker pattern, as can be seen from the design, pattern and colour.

pot 9in (23cm) high

£60-80   **FD**

A Fiesta plastic snack set, made in Spain by Transplastic S.A., in original box.

8.25in (21cm) high

£20-30   **MTS**

A length of 'Fandango' pattern fabric, designed by Maija Isola for Marimekko.

Isola worked for Marimekko from 1951-87 and her designs are among the most familiar Marimekko products, her most notable being 'Unikko' from 1964. The Fandango design is still available today.

1963   116.75in (210cm) long

£25-35   **GAZE**

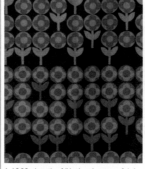

A 1960s length of 'Verdune' pattern fabric, designed by Peter Hall for Heal's.

£30-40   **GAZE**

A length of 1970s 'flower power' material.

£15-20   **GAZE**

A length of heavy cotton fabric, by Heal & Son, in mint condition.

c1964   144in (366cm) long

£100-150   **FD**

A pair of 'Watergarden' pattern curtains, designed by David Bartle for Heal's.

£25-35   **GAZE**

A pair of 'Shimma' pattern fabric curtains, by Natalie Gibson for Conran Fabrics.

This was available in different colours and an example is in the collection of the Victoria & Albert Museum, London.

c1967

£12-18   **GAZE**

A pair of 1960s 'Naxos' Op Art-style pattern fabric curtains, designed by Bernard Warde.

100in (254cm) wide

£60-70   **FD**

A 1960s Peter Max designed inflatable plastic cushion, with printed psychedelic design.

Disposable inflatable furniture in new synthetic materials was extremely popular during the 1960s. The most famous example is Zanotta's inflatable PVC 'Blow' armchair. Peter Max (b.1937) is a noted US designer who works in the highly recognisable 'Cosmic 60s' psychedelic style.

11.75in (30cm) wide

£20-30   **NOR**

A 1970s 'LOVE' inflatable plastic coathanger.

15in (38cm) wide

£18-22   **MTS**

A 1960s 'flower power' printed tin document storage box.

10.25in (26cm) high

£20-30   **NOR**

An Ohio Art 'flower power' printed metal lunchbox.

c1970   9in (23cm) wide

£25-35   **NOR**

A CLOSER LOOK AT A MARGARET KEANE PRINT

Big eyed, often weepy waif-like children, such as this girl, are typical of Keane's style – the style was so successful that it was widely copied.

1960s prints have seen a rapid rise in popularity and value recently, led by the globally known Vladimir Tretchikoff and followed by J.H. Lynch.

Initially thought to be by Walter Keane (1915-2000), the original paintings were in fact painted by his wife Margaret and their origins were the subject of a US court case in 1986, which Margaret won.

Colour prints are more common, black and white is comparatively rare. They were all sold inexpensively in great quantities, but usually thrown away when the style went out of fashion.

A 1960s Keane 'big-eyed' girl and dog black and white print, designed by Margaret Keane.

Margaret Keane is still a successful artist today and owns a gallery in San Francisco, selling her new works.

frame 25.5in (65cm) high

A 1960s teenager's printed plastic singles record holder, with retractable handles.

8.5in (21.5cm) high

£25-35   **MA**

£60-80   **NOR**

A 1960s vinyl hanging shoe rack, with printed musical decoration.

This example is in mint condition, which is very hard to find as the majority were torn or soiled through use.

31.25in (79.5cm) long

£70-100   **MA**

A 1960s 'Peace' 'flower power' printed tile trivet.

9.5in (24.5cm) long

£5-7   **NOR**

A 1970s cheeseboard and knife, with an inset tile panel.

11.75in (30cm) wide

£10-15   **MTS**

A 1970s Lord Kitchener printed mirror.

13.75in (35cm) high

£15-25   **MTS**

A 1960s German Salvest plastic clock.

4.25in (11cm) diam

£25-35 MTS

A Panasonic blue Toot-a-Loop radio.

When closed this radio could be worn around a wrist like a bangle. Produced in a number of colours, lime green, lilac and mauve are the rarest.

c1972 6in (15cm) diam

£50-60 MTS

A 1960s/70s stool, with white single-button seat and brushed aluminium base.

17.75in (45cm) high

£30-50 GAZE

A 1960s pink and chrome standing 'UFO' circular heater.

£7-10 GAZE

A CLOSER LOOK AT A LORD KITCHENER PLATE

'I was Lord Kitchener's Valet' was a famous London shop in the 1960s, selling vintage clothes, regimental uniforms and modern products, usually incorporating similar imagery and the Union Jack.

Images from WWI such as Lord Kitchener were in vogue again during the 1960s, after a period of intense distaste. The Union Jack was a symbol of 'Swinging London', which was given a boost when Britain won the World Cup in 1966.

The shop used the logo seen on this plate, with Kitchener superimposed in a 'pop art' manner over the Union Jack.

Patronised by celebrities like Jimi Hendrix, and representing an 'alternative' street style, the first shop was on Portobello Road and was followed by shops in Chelsea and Soho.

A small 1960s Lord Kitchener plate, marked "I was Lord Kitchener's Valet" to the back.

4.75in (12cm) diam

£40-60 MTS

A 1960s RCA clock radio.

9.5in (24cm) wide

£40-50 MTS

A Fornasetti cylindrical table lamp base, with leaf design.

Largely ignored in his day, Piero Fornasetti was one of the most prolific designers of the 1950s and '60s. His work is undergoing a revival in popularity today, particularly his ceramics and furniture, the latter in collaboration with Gio Ponti. His style leans heavily on Classical architectural motifs as well as suns, faces, stars and playing cards, usually executed in black and gold.

£60-80 GAZE

An Italian yellow and black plastic standard ashtray, the black section pulling off.

21.25in (54cm) high

£10-15 GAZE

A 1970s orange plastic and chrome table lighter.

5.5in (14cm) high

£10-15   **DTC**

A Shattaline cast resin paperweight, made in Scotland.

This was retailed along with a series of lamps, which can fetch up to £40-50 with their original shade.

c1968   3in (7.5cm) high

£10-15   **DTC**

A 1970s Circle of Friends telephone and address book.

6.25in (16cm) diam

£10-15   **MTS**

A Mary Quant pastel crayon set.

Fashion designer Mary Quant's name was attached to a variety of objects during the 1960s.

4.25in (11cm) wide

£18-22   **MTS**

A 1960's psychedelic box of Peter John matches.

Note the attention to detail in the differently coloured match heads.

£12-18   **GAZE**

A 1960s Russian giraffe figure, marked "Made in the USSR' on the base.

The value of these figures depends of the decoration – circles are more common but flowers or fruit can be worth up to £60-80.

9.5in (24.5cm) high

£30-40   **DSC**

COLLECTORS' NOTES

■ The market in props and costumes from films and TV shows began in earnest during the 1990s. High profile acquisitions by restaurant chains such as Planet Hollywood demonstrated to the studios that these items have value and generate interest even after cinema runs have ended. What was previously discarded or recycled is now traded across the globe.

■ Props are generally designed with a very specific use in mind and, if they are to feature prominently in the foreground, they are likely to be more detailed and better made than items used in the background. Weapons used by lead characters will be more carefully constructed than those carried by extras, and this will be reflected in the price.

■ It is important to be sure of the authenticity of a prop or piece of costume. Look out for the identifying tags that are used by many of the major studios, such as names on a collar. The more characteristic the item is of the film or character, or the more prominent the scene it appeared in affects value.

■ Fluctuations in the market are frequent. There can be a sudden clamour for memorabilia when a production is first shown, so it can be a good idea to wait until the publicity has subsided for an opportunity to buy at more realistic prices.

■ Some of the most dramatic price rises occur when a production is badly received on its initial release only to become a cult phenomenon later on.

A copy of 'The Single Parent's Handbook' from "About A Boy", mounted with stills from the movie showing the book.

2002   *20.5in (52cm) wide*

£300-400   **PSL**

A varsity-style crew jacket and badge from "The Abyss", with patches for 'Benthic Petroleum', the 'U.S.S. Montana' and the 'US Navy SEALs' and an 'I survived the toughest shoot in history' badge, size large.

The badges were made by crew members after shooting to commemorate Cameron's notoriously rigorous style of filmmaking.

1989

£150-250   **PSL**

A prop miniature book from "The Affair of the Necklace", with faux ivory cover and brass clasp, seen carried by a prostitute heading to the Cardinal's quarters.

2001   *4in (10cm) high*

£35-45   **PSL**

An Adrian Brody chair back from "The Affair of the Necklace", some signs of use.

2001   *21in (54cm) wide*

£35-45   **PSL**

A prop Greek sling shot stone from "Alexander", the painted rubber projectile with star symbol to top.

2004   *3in (7cm) high*

£7-9   **PSL**

A prop library scroll from "Alexander", used as set dressing.

2004   *13.5in (34cm)*

£15-25   **PSL**

A rare prop 'Weyland Yatani' plastic mug from "Alien", with blue corporate logo to one side.

1978   *3.5in (9cm) high*

£400-500   **PSL**

A CLOSER LOOK AT A PROP FROM "ALIEN"

These boots can be seen when Dallas and his crew leave their ship, the Nostromo, to investigate the distress call from the crashed alien ship.

The heavyweight boots were custom-made from grey painted rubber, which has been given a distressed look.

Released over 25 years ago, it is unusual for props from "Alien" to come on the market.

They have the character's name "Dallas" handwritten on the inside of the tongue.

A pair of prop spacesuit boots from "Alien", worn by Dallas (Tom Skerritt).

1978

£1,000-1,500   **PSL**

A prop hand grenade from "Alien Resurrection", used by General Perez (Dan Hedaya), the soft rubber prop painted blue with yellow stripes and two working LEDs, lacks pin section, some paint worn.

1997   *3in (8cm) high*

£150-200   **PSL**

Three souvenir plastic cups from the "Alien War" attraction.

The Alien War attraction was situated in the basement of the Trocadero Centre off Piccadilly Circus, London and ran from 1993 to 1996. 'Colonial Marines' would guide people through darkened corridors where 'Aliens' would then appear at opportune moments to terrify the paying guests.

8in (21 cm) high

£15-20 each   **PSL**

A 'Tall Oaks Band Camp' polo shirt from "American Pie 2", made by Jerzees, with camp emblem of an oak leaf on the chest 'Tall Oaks' and 'Band Camp' underneath, child's size large.

2001

£60-80   **PSL**

A 'Guard Dog Security' sew on patch from "Armed and Dangerous".

1986

4in (10cm) diam

£8-12   **PSL**

FILM & TV

A mini legal pad from "Austin Powers in Goldmember", by Roaring Spring, used by Mini Me (Verne Troyer), the first eight pages filled with various Austin Powers doodles and scribbles.

2002   *5.25in (13.5cm) high*

£200-300   **PSL**

An alien head appliance from "Babylon 5", worn by Andreas Katsulas as G'kar, the Narn Regime ambassador, made of reinforced foam rubber painted with coloured patches and dark coloured spots, with evidence of glue inside, small sections of the paint flaked off.

1994-98

£600-700   **PSL**

A shooting schedule from "Babylon 5", for the season one episode 'Babylon Squared', consisting of 14 A4 pages, signed by Michael O'Hare (Lt Cmdr Jeffrey Sinclair) and dated 1/31/94.

£150-200   **PSL**

A launch bay technicians jumpsuit from the original "Battlestar Galactica" TV series, the cotton jumpsuit with reflective silver taping down both arms and legs and an elasticated waist, embroidered emblem on the left hand side of the chest.

c1980   *size 42*

£350-450   **PSL**

A prop UV bomb from "Blade II", the resin prop painted in black, silver and bronze.

2002   *3in (8cm) high*

£400-500   **PSL**

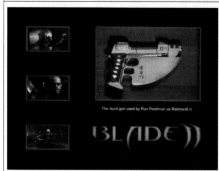

A stunt gun from "Blade II", used by Reinhardt (Ron Perlman), made from hard rubber, the highly detailed prop with Chinese symbols on the blade and on the barrel, mounted, framed and glazed.

2002   *33.5in (85cm) wide*

£1,200-1,800   **PSL**

A prop 'Sunnydale Rockets' padded cushion from "Buffy the Vampire Slayer", with a letter of authenticity.

The 'Sunnydale Rockets' was the name of the college football team, though there is little mention of them throughout the series. Its lack of air-time has become an in-joke among fans.

1999-2000   *13.5in (34cm) wide*

£300-400   **PSL**

A 'MOO' badge from "Buffy the Vampire Slayer", used in the season three episode 'Gingerbread'.

MOO stands for Mothers Opposing the Occult.

c1998   *2.5in (6.5cm) diam*

£100-150   **PSL**

A prop 'Chicago Evening Star' newspaper display from "Chicago", mounted, framed and glazed.

2002   *33in (83cm) high*

£600-700   **PSL**

A CLOSER LOOK AT A BUFFY THE VAMPIRE SLAYER PROP

This weapon was used by Buffy (Sarah Michelle Geller) during the show's first season.

The hunga munga is a traditional African throwing knife or iron that often had symbolic or ritualistic uses.

A clip of the character holding the weapon is seen in the opening titles through seasons one and two.

The prop is made of solid metal meaning it would have been made for close-up shots rather than action scenes where a safer, rubber version would have be used.

A prop hunga munga weapon from "Buffy the Vampire Slayer", made from solid metal with distressed effect, mounted framed and glazed.

A prop data card from "Cleopatra 2525", used by Drack (Glen Drake) in the season two episode 'Noir or Never', adapted from a Zippo lighter with a lime green Perspex casing.

c2001   *3in (7cm) wide*

£70-90   **PSL**

c1997   *35in (89cm) high*

£2,000-2,500   **PSL**

A pair of Gucci frameless glasses from "Collateral", worn by Max (Jamie Foxx), with fake blood on one lens, the other cracked, together with a black hard case labelled by the prop department and a Dreamworks Studio certificate of authenticity.

There would have been a number of pairs of glasses used throughout the film. This damaged pair was used after the car crash scene.

2004

£300-400   **PSL**

A prop leather wallet from "Collateral", used by Vincent (Tom Cruise), containing a number of fake credit cards and plastic store cards as well as 'Motion Picture Money', some scuff marks.

2004   *4.5in (11cm) wide*

£500-600   **PSL**

A digital press pack for "Daredevil", containing a DVD with photographs and production notes, and a small booklet also with production notes.

2003

£25-35   **PSL**

FILM & TV

A stunt throwing star from "Daredevil", used by Bullseye (Colin Farrell), mounted, framed and glazed.

2003   20.5in (52cm) wide

£700-800   **PSL**

A Max Guevara wanted poster from "Dark Angel", used in the season one episode 'Blah Blah Woof Woof', mounted, framed and glazed.

c2000   27.5in (70cm) wide

£180-220   **PSL**

A prop 'Hell's Kitchen' cork coaster and a paper napkin from "Dawson's Creek", printed with the restaurant logo in black.

Hell's Kitchen was one of the focal points of the show and a regular meeting point for the main characters.

Coaster 6in (14cm) high

£10-15   **PSL**

A prop bank note from "Dinotopia", printed with "100 Motion Picture Money" and with a dinosaur's head.

2002   8in (20cm) wide

£8-12   **PSL**

A Disney Channel promotional jacket, size XXL.

£70-100   **PSL**

A piece of concept artwork from "Dune", titled "Dune, Guilsman - Front & side elevations" and produced by Don Post Studios, Inc.

The character is incorrectly called a 'Guilsman', rather than 'Guildsman'. This design does not appear to have been recreated on the screen.

c1984   17in (44cm) high

£500-600   **PSL**

A crew gift organizer from "Elizabeth", the black nylon zip-up case containing an organizer with a colour postcard of Elizabeth I on the cover.

1998   12in (30cm) high

£15-20   **PSL**

Madonna's Brooch worn in

EVITA

A set of medical scrubs from "ER", worn by Dr. Mark Greene (Anthony Edwards), with 'Costume Collection' tag.

1994-2002

£200-300   **PSL**

A custom-made brooch from "Evita", worn by Eva Peron (Madonna), the flower-shaped brooch set with ruby red and clear stones, mounted, framed and glazed.

1996   18in (46cm) wide

£800-1,200   **PSL**

A police codpiece from "The Fifth Element", made from vacuum-formed plastic, painted bronze with black distressing.

1997 9.75in (25cm) long

£35-45 PSL

A tie from "Frasier", worn by Kelsey Grammer in the title role, with maker's label 'Metropolitan View' and handwritten notation by the costume department "F124B, IV".

1993-2004

£60-80 PSL

A crew jacket from "The Full Monty", made by Carhartt and customised with the film title over the breast pocket, size 48.

1997

£100-150 PSL

A prop appearance generator from "Galaxy Quest", cast from resin with holographic film in the centre.

1999 3in (8cm) diam

£50-60 PSL

A limited edition "Get Carter" script, signed by screenwriter and author Mike Hodges, from an edition of 500, with the original film title "Carter's the Name".

£150-200 PSL

A crew fob watch from "Harry Potter and the Philosopher's Stone", engraved "Harry Potter Cast and Crew 2001", with original presentation box.

c2001

£400-500 PSL

A London premiere crew zip-up top from "Harry Potter and the Prisoner of Azkaban", size medium.

2004

£80-120 PSL

A prop clan MacLeod battle banner from "Highlander", mounted, framed and glazed.

1986 46in (117cm) wide

£450-550 PSL

Two prop Christmas presents from "How The Grinch Stole Christmas".

Largest 12in (30.5cm) wide

£35-45 PSL

FILM & TV

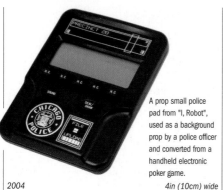

A prop small police pad from "I, Robot", used as a background prop by a police officer and converted from a handheld electronic poker game.

2004   *4in (10cm) wide*

£25-35   **PSL**

A prop Chicago Police cap badge from "I, Robot", made from resin.

2004
        2.5in (6cm) high

£150-200   **PSL**

A European premier party menu for "King Arthur".

2004   *8in (21cm) wide*

£7-9   **PSL**

A CLOSER LOOK AT A 'I-ROBOT' PROP

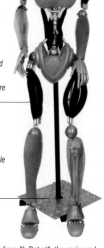

These robots are an iconic and integral part of the film and its storyline.

Although many of the robots on the screen were computer generated, a number of real-life models would have been made for close-ups and publicity.

The muscles in the robots arms and legs are based on McKibben's air muscles, used in robots manufacture today.

The custom built stand is a desirable feature, meaning the otherwise unwieldy prop can be more easily displayed.

A full-size NS5 articulated robot from "I, Robot", the resin and fibreglass and metal prop with bright red LED in the chest and white LED in the skull, on custom-made stand.

2004   *74.75in (190cm) high*

£7,000-9,000   **PSL**

A prop dagger from "King Arthur", used by Galahad (Hugh Dancy), the painted resin giving the effect of a metal blade and leather bound handle with animal head design, with a black leather sheath.

2004   *6.5in (42cm) long*

£400-500   **PSL**

A stunt pistol from "The Last Samurai", used by Nathan Algren (Tom Cruise), made from hard rubber painted to look like metal and wood, mounted, framed and glazed, together with a letter from the film's weapons coordinator.

2003   *28in (71cm) wide*

£1,500-2,000   **PSL**

A prop 'Daily Planet' newspaper from "Lois & Clark: The New Adventures Of Superman, used in the pilot episode.

1993   *23in (58cm) high*

£200-300   **PSL**

The gun used by Carrie Anne Moss as Trinity in

MATRIX RELOADED   *MATRIX REVOLUTIONS*

A prop Beretta handgun from "The Matrix Reloaded" and "The Matrix Revolutions", used by Trinity (Carrie Anne Moss), the highly detailed rubber weapon with serial number and manufacturer's details clearly visible, mounted, framed and glazed together with a letter of authenticity from the productions weapons coordinator.

Ian McKellan's ticket to the VIP after premiere party for "The Lord of the Rings: The Return of the King", mounted with a signed photograph of the actor as Gandalf, framed and glazed.

2003   *12in (53cm) wide*

£400-500   **PSL**

2003   *23in (59cm) wide*

£2,000-2,500   **PSL**

MATRIX REVOLUTIONS

A rare Sentinel eye display from "The Matrix Revolutions", made from painted hard black rubber, mounted framed and glazed.

It is very rare to find any original props from the Matrix films.

2003   *22in (56cm) wide*

£300-400   **PSL**

A crew hooded top from "Meet the Parents", size XL.

2000

£35-45   **PSL**

A prop 'Precrime' ID card and strap from "Minority Report", with image of John Anderton (Tom Cruise), produced for the film but not used.

The Precrime ID card was made well into the production process of the film but was never used as 'retinal scans' featured throughout, thus making it redundant.

2002   *3.5in (9cm) wide*

£700-800   **PSL**

A crew black fleece jacket from "The Mummy", size medium.

c1999

£100-150   **PSL**

A prop Isabel and Jesse wedding photo from "Roswell", seen in the season three episode 'A Tale of Two Parties'.

c2002   *12in (31cm) high*

£60-80   **PSL**

A prison uniform from "The Shawshank Redemption", comprising of striped cotton shirt and blue jeans, the shirt prisoner number across the chest.

1994

£200-300   **PSL**

A pair of prop 'sync device' clone goggles from "The Sixth Day", the painted black metal glasses in original plastic prop storage box.

2000   *7in (18cm) long*

£300-400   **PSL**

A rare prop marine smart grenade from "Space: Above and Beyond", made from plastic and metal, painted dark grey, silver and black.

1995-96   *6in (15.5cm) long*

£180-220   **PSL**

A 'Spice Force 5' sew-on patch from "Spice World".

'Spice Force 5' was a spoof sci-fi adventure that featured in the film.

1997   *3in (8cm) diam*

£7-10   **PSL**

A promotional cap from "Spider-Man".

2002

£10-15   **PSL**

A Mobile Infantry sergeant's cap from "Starship Troopers", worn by Career Sergeant Zim (Clancy Brown), with Infantry insignia on the front and "Zim" written inside.

1997

£300-400   **PSL**

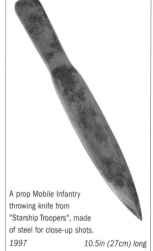

A prop Mobile Infantry throwing knife from "Starship Troopers", made of steel for close-up shots.

1997   *10.5in (27cm) long*

£220-280   **PSL**

A prop alien tool from "Star Trek: The Next Generation", used in the season six episode 'The Quality of Life' as an Exocomp's tool, and reused in the Voyager season four episode 'Random Thoughts', made from part of a Romulan rifle, the main resin body with a metal end and plastic nodules at the top.

c1992   *10in (25.5cm) long*

£800-1,200   **PSL**

A spatial trajector device from "Star Trek: The Next Generation", used in the Voyager season three episode 'The Dauphin' and reused in the Voyager season one episode 'Prime Factors', made from black painted resin with a transparent orange plastic section, one metal decoration peeling off.

c1989   *8in (20cm) high*

£700-1,000   **PSL**

A CLOSER LOOK AT A STAR TREK PROP

This style of weapon was used in approximately three episodes of The Next Generation and was a common sight on Deep Space Nine.

It has come from the private collection of the prop maker on the show and is in near mint condition.

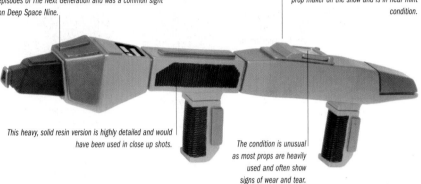

This heavy, solid resin version is highly detailed and would have been used in close up shots.

The condition is unusual as most props are heavily used and often show signs of wear and tear.

A prop type III phaser rifle, from "Star Trek: The Next Generation" and "Star Trek: Deep Space Nine", made from resin sprayed grey and black, with a transparent green insert on top.

25in (64cm) long

£1,000-1,500 **PSL**

A production-used script from "Star Trek: Deep Space Nine", for season four episode 'Our Man Bashir', the blue-coloured cover signed by script writer Robert Gillan.
1995

£150-200 **PSL**

A crew fleece top from "Star Wars Episode II: Attack of the Clones", with "Star Wars Episode II" and "Props & Models Australia 2000" embroidered on the chest, size small.
c2000

£150-200 **PSL**

A de-assimilation neural link control box from "Star Trek: The Next Generation", used on Locutus of Borg (Patrick Stewart) by Data (Brent Spiner) in the season four episode 'Best of Both Worlds, part II', the custom made, light-up prop made from resin and plastic with two metal connectors on top where the links were attached.
c1990 *4.5in (11cm) high*

£700-900 **PSL**

A Cyberdyne tool box from "Terminator 3: The Rise Of The Machines", made from hard rubber painted grey with blue sections and a "Cyber Research Systems" label on one side.
21.5in (54cm) wide

£200-300 **PSL**

A prop small keypad from "Thunderbirds", made from black plastic and silver-painted resin with a plastic screen and numerical keypad.
2004 *7in (12cm) wide*

£25-35 **PSL**

A prop Thunderbirds 4 access box from "Thunderbirds", made from blue-painted metal labelled "T4, Access 3094-R, For Sequential Routine Checks Refer To Onboard Manual 0923/4 V5".

2004   *5.5in (14cm) wide*

£35-45   **PSL**

A pair of sunglasses from "2 Fast 2 Furious", worn by Monica Fuentes (Eva Mendes), mounted, framed and glazed.

2003   *21in (53cm) wide*

£250-350   **PSL**

A cast and crew screening invitation for "Troy", dated May 16th 2004.

8.5in (21cm) high

£7-9   **PSL**

A 'Stop Animal Testing' crew T-shirt from "Twelve Monkeys", size large, in worn condition.

The cast and crew wore animal-themed T-shirts during the production of this film.

1995

£60-70   **PSL**

A prop silver vampire bullet from "Underworld", mounted, framed and glazed.

2003   *18in (46cm) wide*

£180-220   **PSL**

An ornate vampire-killing stake from "Van Helsing", made from wood-effect resin with silver-coloured decoration.

2004   *23in (59cm) long*

£300-400   **PSL**

A 'Die! Bug Die!' bug spray can from "The X-Files", used in the season three episode 'War of the Coprophages'.

c1995   *8in (20cm) high*

£80-120   **PSL**

A prop helmet from "Xena: Warrior Princess", worn by Xena (Lucy Lawless) in the season six episode 'Return of the Valkyrie', made of soft silver-painted leather with hard rubber decorations, labelled "Xena".

c2000

£800-900   **PSL**

An Amazonian necklace from "Xena: Warrior Princess", the leather and suede necklace decorated with coloured beads and silver painted stones.

8in (20cm) wide

£40-60   **PSL**

A red crew T-shirt from "The X-Files", printed with the X-Files logo on the front, "Season 9" underneath and "Want it" on the back, size XL.

These were given to crew members by Robert Patrick who played Special Agent John Doggett in season nine.

c2001

£60-80 PSL

A prop camping blanket and strap from "X-Men 2", with applied logo badge for "Xavier's School For Gifted Youngsters".

2002

£200-300 PSL

A prop vehicle license plate from "The X-Files", used in the season two episode 'Little Green Men' on Dana Scully's jeep.

c1994 12in (30.5cm) wide

£150-200 PSL

A prop missile launching system panel and hard drive from "xXx", with moulded resin hard drive and spray painted acrylic, launching system panel, lacking a light-up panel.

2002 12in (30cm) wide

£400-500 PSL

A sweatshirt and pants from "X-Men", each with the 'X' logo patch with "Xavier's School For Gifted Youngsters", mounted, framed and glazed together with a Fox Studios certificate of authenticity.

2000 39.5in (100cm)

£350-450 PSL

COLLECTORS' NOTES

■ The successful return of Doctor Who in 2005 has meant that the profile of cult films and TV series has risen again. Coupled with the nostalgia for all things 1970s and 80s, this has resulted in an increased desire for film and TV toys and memorabilia from that period.

■ Early examples are usually the most sought-after and often the hardest to find, particularly in good and complete condition, as few would have been made. The original box and any instructions or certificates will also be desirable.

■ While Doctor Who is riding high in the popularity charts, large amounts of toys are being released onto the market. When buying modern examples, look for well-known manufacturers and good quality materials and construction, as these are more likely to hold their value. Limited editions are also a good bet, but only if the number really is limited, ideally to under 1,000.

■ As of 2005 there are no new series of Star Trek in production and it will be interesting to see how this affects the market for the toys and memorabilia. The early Mego figures for the original series continue to be sought-after, but later examples, particularly for the last series may suffer.

■ As numerous shows and films are being reinvented for the next generation, nostalgia for the originals often increases, bringing with it a demand for vintage memorabilia. Cult film series, such as Star Wars and James Bond, remain extremely popular, with older pieces tending to attract the most interest.

■ In the long run, pieces from an unpopular period may prove a good investment as production may be limited and few will have been bought, making them scarce in later years. A new audience may be more appreciative and the toys could become sought-after.

David Banks, "Doctor Who The New Adventures – Iceberg", published by Virgin Publishing.

1993

£6-8   TP

Terrance Dicks, "Doctor Who – The Five Doctors", published by Target, 20th Anniversary special edition.

1983   *7in (18cm) high*

£4-6   TP

Paul Cornell, "Doctor Who The Missing Adventures – Goth Opera", published by Virgin Publishing.

This was the first title in Virgin's Missing Adventures series, featuring 'lost' stories of the Doctor's adventures that took place in between episodes of the TV series.

1994

£7-10   TP

Howe, Stammers and Walker, "Doctor Who – The Handbook: The Seventh Doctor", published by Virgin Publishing.

1998

£7-10   TP

Stephen Marley, "Doctor Who The Missing Adventures – Managra", published by Virgin Publishing.

1995

£6-8   TP

Jim Mortimer, "Doctor Who The New Adventures – Parasite", published by Virgin Publishing.

1994

£8-10   TP

Jim Mortimer, "Doctor Who The New Adventures – Blood Heat", published by Virgin Publishing.

1993

£6-8   TP

Howe, Stammers and Walker, "Doctor Who - The Sixties" annual, published by Virgin Publishing.

1992   *12in (30.5cm) high*

£20-30   **TP**

Howe and Stammers, "Doctor Who - Companions" book, published by Virgin Publishing.

1995   *12in (30.5cm) high*

£20-30   **TP**

Nigel Robinson, "Doctor Who The New Adventures - Birthright", published by Virgin Publishing.

1993

£6-8   **TP**

A Doctor Who "The Pescatons" audio CD, by Silva Screen.

1991   *5.5in (14cm) wide*

£15-25   **TP**

Nigel Robinson, "Doctor Who The New Adventures - Timewyrm: Apocalypse", published by Virgin Publishing.

1991

£7-10   **TP**

Gary Russell, "Doctor Who The Missing Adventures - Invasion of the Cat-People", published by Virgin Publishing.

1995

£7-10   **TP**

A Doctor Who mobile phone cover, for a Nokia 3310.

6.75in (17.25cm) high

£10-15   **TP**

A Doctor Who 'Sonic Screwdriver' ballpoint pen.

c2001   *5in (12.5cm) long*

£10-15   **TP**

A Doctor Who pewter Dalek keyring.

c2001   *1.5in (4cm) high*

£3-5   **TP**

A Doctor Who pewter TARDIS keyring.

c2001   1.5in (4cm) high

£4-5   **TP**

A Doctor Who Dalek-shaped pewter bottle stopper.

c2002   1.5in (4cm) high

£10-15   **TP**

A Doctor Who 'Cyberman Attacking' figure, by Media Collectables.

c2002   Figure 2in (5cm) high

£6-8   **TP**

A CLOSER LOOK AT A DALEK TOY

A Doctor 'The Mysterious Daleks' black battery-operated figure, by Marx Toys, with eyepiece and weapons, in excellent condition, the box with some graffiti and one indentation.

c1964

£180-220   **GAZE**

As these toys made to be played with and usually were, the delicate eyepiece and weapons are often damaged or missing, and the box also is often missing.

Daleks were one of the first characters from the series to be recreated as toys.

Palitoy and Marx also made Dalek toys, but this is usually considered the most sought-after.

The Daleks were recently voted most evil villains in recent UK survey, and much to fans delight, they have returned in the new series of Doctor Who.

A Dr Who 'War of the Daleks' game, by Denys Fisher.

c1975   Box 19.5in (49.5cm) w

£35-45   **GAZE**

A Codeg (Cowan de Groot) 'Mechanical Dalek' blue plastic figure, 'Strong Clockwork with Realistic Action', with two weapons, lacks eyepiece, toy marked "©BBCTV 1965", box incorrectly marked "Black".

c1965   Box 5.25in (13.5cm) high

£400-500   **GAZE**

An A-Team 'Mr T' action figure, by Galoob, boxed.

Box 15in (38cm) high

£30-40   **GAZE**

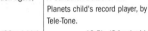

A Canadian Battle of the Planets child's record player, by Tele-Tone.

13.5in (34cm) wide

£50-70   **NOR**

A very rare Japanese Official Universal Studios 'Creature From The Black Lagoon' tin and plastic toy, mint & boxed.

c1991   9in (23cm) high

£180-220   **NOR**

A 1960s Bonanza lithographed tin mug, made in Hong Kong.

It is rare to find Bonanza memorabilia that includes an image of Pernell Roberts, who played Adam Cartwight in the series and left in the sixth season.

3.5in (9cm) wide

£7-10   **BH**

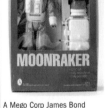

A Mego Corp James Bond Moonraker fully poseable figure, in original box.

c1979   Box 13.5in (34.5cm) high

£70-100   **F**

An American 'James Bond 007 Secret Agent' game, by MB Games.

c1964   19in (48cm) wide

£60-80   **NOR**

An early James Bond 007 Thunderball game, by Milton Bradley, made in Australia.

Box 19in (48.5cm) wide

£30-50   **GAZE**

A James Bond "007 Best 4" picture sleeve, OH-27, from United Artists Records.

c1964

£20-30   **GAZE**

A James Bond 'Jaws' action figure, made in Hong Kong, marked "©1979 Eon Productions".

c1979   13in (33cm) high

£5-8   **GAZE**

A Japanese James Bond "From Russian with Love" soundtrack 45rpm, BS-7019, from King Stereo, featuring the 'Kiss-Theme' from Niagara on the B-side.
c1963

£7-10   GAZE

A Timpo 'Captain Scarlet' plastic figure.

2.25in (5.5cm) high

£12-18   GAZE

An LJN E.T. The Extra-Terrestrial poseable toy, mint and boxed.

11in (27.5cm) high

£18-22   NOR

A Flash Gordon medals and insignia set, by Larami Corp.
c1980   *7in (18cm) high*

£7-10   NOR

A Green Hornet LP record.

12in (32cm) wide

£15-25   NOR

An Aladdin ET lunchbox.
c1982   *8.25in (21cm) wide*

£60-80   NOR

A Record Guild of America 'Flash Gordon' story record.
These story records were cut out from cereal boxes, and it rare to find a two-sided version.

6.75in (17cm) diam

£20-30   NOR

A 'Ming The Merciless' plastic poseable doll, by King Features Syndicate
c1976   *10in (25.5cm) high*

£30-40   NOR

Brandon Keith, "The Green Hornet and the Case of the Disappearing Doctor", illustrated by Larry Pellini, published by the Whitman Publishing Company.
1966   *8in (20cm) high*

£20-30   NOR

A Knight Rider metal lunchbox, by Thermos.

c1982   *8.5in (21.5cm) wide*

£10-15   **BH**

A Lassie the Wonder Dog 'Timmy' grey cotton outfit, by Wings, size 10.

£40-60   **NOR**

A King Seeley Thermos Mork & Mindy lunchbox.

This appeals to Robby the Robot collectors too, as he also features on the lunchbox.

c1979   *9in (23cm) wide*

£30-40   **NOR**

A 'Mork & Mindy ' plastic Mork Eggship, marked "©1979 Paramount Pictures Corp.", with removable Mork figure.

Egg 4.25in (11cm) high

£8-12   **NOR**

A Lost In Space 'Robby the Robot' battery powered robot, manufactured by Remco Industries, marked "©Space Productions".

The character of Robby the Robot first appeared in the film 'Forbidden Planet' in 1956 and was designed by prop maker Robert Kinoshita. The robot suit was altered slightly and was used in the TV series 'Lost in Space' as Robot B-9. Robby went on to appear in a number of other films and shows including 'Mork & Mindy'. This Remco robot was also produced in blue and red colourway.

c1966   *11.75in (30cm) high*

£150-250   **NOR**

A PPC Mork poseable figure in costume.

c1979   *9.5in (24.5cm) high*

£15-20   **NOR**

An Our Gang 'Darla' carded action figure, by Mego Corp.

c1975   *9in (23cm) high*

£40-50   **NOR**

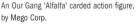

An Our Gang 'Alfalfa' carded action figure, by Mego Corp.

c1975   *9in (23cm) high*

£30-40   **NOR**

FILM & TV

An Our Gang 'Mickey' carded action figure, by Mego Corp.

c1975 *9in (23cm) high*

£50-70 **NOR**

A Planet of The Apes plush, plastic and furry hand puppet.

9.75in (25cm) high

£40-50 **NOR**

A United Artists Corp Rocky figurine, mint in bubble pack and card.

8.5in (22cm) high

£8-12 **NOR**

An unopened box of Planet of the Apes bubble gum cards.

c1967 *7.5in (19cm) high*

£80-120 **NOR**

A signed Warrick Davis publicity postcard.

6in (15cm) high

£7-10 **LCA**

A signed Kenny Baker (R2-D2) 'Star Wars' publicity postcard.

6in (15cm) wide

£10-15 **LCA**

A signed Caroline Blakiston (Mon Mothma) 'Return of the Jedi' publicity postcard.

6in (15cm) high

£6-8 **LCA**

A signed Ian McDiarmid (Emperor Palpatine) 'Return of the Jedi' publicity postcard.

6in (15cm) high

£10-15 **LCA**

A signed Jeremy Bulloch (Boba Fett) Return of the Jedi' publicity postcard.

6in (15cm) high

£10-15 **LCA**

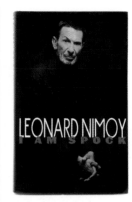

A signed Brian Blessed (Boss Nass) 'Star Wars: Episode I – The Phantom Menace' publicity postcard, as Boss Nass.

6in (15cm) high

£7-10 LCA

Leonard Nimoy, "I Am Spock", first edition published by Century, London, signed by the author.

1995

£70-100 PSL

A Star Trek 'Klingon' carded action figure, by Mego Corp, on 'six-face' card.

This was one of the first figures by Mego and is commonly found.

c1974 Card 9in (23cm) high

£15-25 NOR

Released five years after the original figures, Mego produced a range of smaller figures to complement the first Star Trek movie hoping to emulate the massive success of Kenner and their 3in Star Wars action figures.

c1979 box 9in (23cm) high

£70-100 W&W

Three unusual Mego Corp 'Star Trek: The Motion Picture' figures, in original packaging, comprising Spock, Kirk and Willard Decker.

"TV Century 21 Annual", published by City Magazines Ltd., featuring Stingray, Fireball XL5 and Lady Penelope.

1965 15.5in (39.5cm) high

£12-18 GAZE

A CLOSER LOOK AT A STAR TREK FIGURE

Released one year after the first figures, the Aliens series comprised of four alien characters, Neptunian, Gorn, The Keeper and Cheron.

While none of these new figures were exact replicas of aliens seen on the screen, the Neptunian was entirely created by Mego.

Look for examples that are on a 14-back card, which are much rarer than the 10-back card.

This second series of figures is rarer than the original series, a further four aliens were released, which are considerably harder to find.

A Star Trek Aliens 'Neptunian' carded action figure, by Mego Corp.

c1975

£100-150 NOR

FILM & TV

A limited edition whimsical 'Wizard of Oz' lidded jar, by Rick Wisecarver, from an edition of 30, signed "Rick Wisecarver No-28-95", incised "The Wizard of Oz" on the rear and "Copyrights G931-0999 Roseville Ohio" on the base.

16.5in (42cm) long

£220-280 **BEL**

A very rare card, cast iron and tinplate Scarecrow from The Wizard of Oz jigger, the dancing printed card figure moves up and down as a record is played, base moulded 'PAT.FEB.11-19'.

c1940 *7.5in (19cm) high*

£200-300 **PWE**

A mint Aladdin 'Wild Bill Hickock' vacuum bottle, with original box.

c1955 *6.5in (16cm) high*

£40-60 **NOR**

A mint Aladdin 'Zorro' vacuum bottle, with original box.

c1955 *6.5in (16cm) high*

£60-80 **NOR**

A Mego Corp Emerald City playset, with Wizard figure, Emerald City, tree, plastic-covered card throne, spinning crystal ball, lacks some parts, but shows very few signs of wear, boxed and complete.

The Wizard of Oz range was particularly successful for Mego, with well-modelled and detailed figures. They were produced in large numbers and are generally easy to find loose but boxed examples are scarce. Three playsets were produced - Munchkinland, Emerald City and Wicked Witch Castle, which is the rarest. Although it is often thought that the Wizard figure was only available with this playset, he could be bought individually. Singularly boxed examples are extremely rare.

Box 14.75in (37.5cm) wide

£180-220 **NOR**

Four Mego Corp Wizard of Oz figures.

These figures came with a range of accessories that are often lost, complete examples are worth over twice as much. The Dorothy figure, which came with a small Toto figure is scarce as are the four diminutive Munchkin figures.

8.25in (21cm) high

£10-15 each **NOR**

A Venetian glass St Marks lion, awarded at the Venice Film Festival during the 1960s.

18in (45.5cm) wide

£80-120 **GAZE**

COLLECTORS' NOTES

■ Carnival glass is the name given in the 1960s to the colourful, press-moulded glass produced in the US and Europe from around 1905-7. It was inspired by Tiffany's iridescent glass, fashionable but expensive at the time. After being inexpensively made in mechanical presses, pieces were sprayed with metallic salts to give them their iridescence.

■ The 'Prime' period of production was from c1910-c1925, with the late 1920s and 1930s being of secondary interest to collectors. Notable factories include Fenton (est.1904), Northwood (1888-1925) who became Dugan & Diamond, and Imperial (est.1903) in the US, Sowerby in the UK, and Brockwitz in Germany. After the 1920s, US production declined in favour of other countries.

■ Prices vary widely from around £10-15 up to a £1,000 or more for the best and rarest pieces. Most pieces can be easily found for £50-150, providing excellent variety. When collecting, consider four main areas – shape,

pattern, colour and iridescence. Certain shapes such as plates are scarcer than ruffled bowls, for example, and can fetch a premium.

■ Consider the pattern. Sometimes a combination of pattern and form is rare, some are scarcer than others in general and so command premium. Patterns can also help identify a manufacturer, and although manufacturers produced seemingly identical patterns, there are usually small differences that distinguish them. Pattern variants can make for an interesting collection.

■ To examine the base colour, hold it up against strong light to see which colour it is. Marigold is one of the most common colours with opalescent colours and red, launched in 1920 by Fenton, being generally scarcer. The base colour should be strong. Iridescence should also be strong, with a shimmering quality ranging from deep to light colours across the entire surface. Pieces with excellent levels of iridescence are sought-after.

A Fenton 'Heart & Vine' pattern blue Carnival glass plate.

This large plate is very scarce and is most valuable in this colour.

9.5in (24cm) diam

£400-500   **GL**

A Northwood 'Peacocks on a Fence' pattern green Carnival glass plate.

This pattern breaks the usual rule that plates are the rarest shape, as while plates are scarce, the pie-crust and ruffled edge bowls are rarer in this pattern.

9.5in (24cm) diam

£350-450   **GL**

A Fenton 'Sailboats' blue Carnival glass plate.

The plate is very rare in this colour, a bowl in this pattern may fetch around £30-40. Look out for the ultra-rare red.

6.25in (16cm) high

£250-350   **GL**

A very rare 'Rose Show' pattern blue Carnival glass plate.

Only found on bowls and a plate, this pattern was only produced in small quantities, making it hard to find today.

9.5in (24.5cm) diam

£800-900   **GL**

An Imperial 'Open Rose' pattern purple Carnival glass bowl, with panelled pattern on the outside of the bowl and excellent iridescence.

7in (18cm) diam

£60-80   **GL**

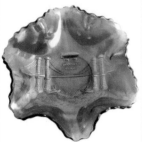

A Diamond Glass Company 'Brooklyn Bridge' pattern Carnival Glass souvenir ruffled bowl.

This bowl is only known in marigold. Look out for the rare example without the lettering under the Zeppelin. During the 1920s and 30s these German airships ferried passengers and mail between Europe and New York and Brazil until the Hindenburg disaster in 1937 ended their viability as a form of transport.

c1930   9in (23cm) diam

£120-180   **GL**

A CLOSER LOOK AT A CARNIVAL GLASS PLATE

Large plates are rare in the majority of Carnival glass patterns, but there are a few exceptions.

Although the iridescence on this example is good, those with better iridescence can fetch up to £3,000-4,000.

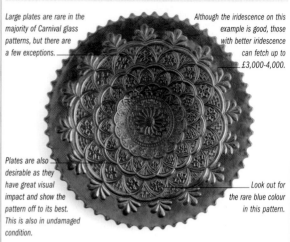

Plates are also desirable as they have great visual impact and show the pattern off to its best. This is also in undamaged condition.

Look out for the rare blue colour in this pattern.

A Dugan 'Persian Garden' pattern large amethyst Carnival glass chop plate.

13in (32.5cm) diam

£1,500-2,500   **GL**

An Imperial 'Scroll Embossed' pattern purple Carnival glass bowl.

This is a very common pattern, but this one is made rarer as it has a fluted exterior. Plain examples are more common and worth less.

7.25in (18cm) diam

£60-80   **GL**

A Northwood 'Poppy' pattern ice blue Carnival glass oval pickle dish.

8.5in (21.5cm) diam

£250-350   **GL**

A Fenton 'Kittens' pattern small blue Carnival glass child's cereal bowl.

This pattern was aimed at children and has become very popular with collectors.

c1920   3.75in (9.5cm) diam

£150-250   **GL**

A Fenton 'Open Edge Basketweave' pattern red Carnival glass hat-shaped bowl.

5.75in (14.5cm) wide

£120-180   **GL**

A Northwood 'Wild Rose' pattern marigold Carnival glass footed bowl.

7.75in (19.5cm) diam

£60-80   **GL**

A Dugan or Diamond Glass 'Double Stem Rose' pattern Celeste blue Carnival glass ruffled bowl.

1916-c1926   *4.5in (11.5cm) high*

£250-350   **GL**

A Northwood 'Beaded Cable' pattern aqua opalescent Carnival glass rose bowl.

4.25in (10.5cm) high

£150-200   **GL**

A Northwood 'Peacock at the Fountain' pattern marigold Carnival glass compote, with excellent iridescence and applied clear glass foot.

6in (15.5cm) high

£350-450   **GL**

A Northwood 'Grapes & Cable Banded' pattern green Carnival glass hatpin holder.

The moulded 'ring' around the upper part identifies this as a scarce variant of the very common 'Grape & Cable' pattern by Northwood. The shape and colour add to this piece's desirability.

7in (17.5cm) high

£150-250   **GL**

An Imperial 'Tiger Lily' pattern purple Carnival glass water beaker.

This pattern is 'intaglio', meaning the pattern is set into the piece rather than protruding from it. It is only found on a water set, the pitcher and the blue colour being much sought-after.

4.25in (11cm) high

£50-70   **GL**

An Imperial 'Grapes' pattern purple Carnival glass water bottle.

This is slightly scarcer, but not always more valuable than, the decanter also shown here. It was made from the same mould as the decanter but with the lip flared out.

8.75in (22cm) high

£150-200   **GL**

A rare Fenton 'Kittens' pattern blue Carnival glass child's cup.

2.25in (5.5cm) high

£200-250   **GL**

An Imperial 'Grapes' pattern purple Carnival glass water decanter with stopper.

12in (30.5cm) high

£180-220   **GL**

FIND OUT MORE...

The Standard Encyclopaedia of Carnival Glass, *by Bill Edwards & Mike Carwile, published by Collector Books, 2002.*

The Pocket Guide to Carnival Glass, *by Monica Lynn Clements & Patricia Roser Clements, published by Schiffer Books, 2001.*

COLLECTORS' NOTES

■ Chance Brothers was created when William Chance joined his brother Robert, who had bought a factory at Smethwick near Birmingham in 1832. They initially focused on producing industrial and optical glass, only moving into domestic wares in the 1920s.

■ During the 1920s and 1930s, glass was mass produced using pressing techniques. The range included ovenware. In 1951, Chance launched its Fiesta range, made from thin and lightweight glass sheets, transfer or screen-printed with a pattern. The glass plate was then placed on a mould and heated until it sagged into the form.

■ Shapes were simple and modern, complementing the the modern patterns such as 'Swirl' and 'Night Sky'. Fiestaware was a great success and was produced into the 1980s. As so much was made, avoid buying examples with chips or worn decoration or trim.

■ Handkerchief vases were produced in their thousands from the 1950s. They were based on Venini's 'fazzoletto', produced in Murano and originally designed around 1949. Here, a printed glass plate was balanced on a cylinder. As the plate was heated, it sagged into a random but similar shape. The exterior printed surface is easy to scratch, so examine examples carefully.

■ The two most common sizes are the large at 7in (18cm) high, and the small at 4in (10cm) high. The oversized version is the rarest, followed by the medium size. Printed polka dot. Chequered and banded patterns are commonly found. Those in bright, acid colours typical of the 1960s tend to be the most desirable and valuable. Unprinted, transparent examples are generally worth slightly less than printed ones.

A 1960s Chance aqua and green pinstriped handkerchief vase.

4in (10cm) high

£30-40　　　　　　　　**MHT**

A 1960s Chance large black and white pinstriped handkerchief vase.

7in (18cm) high

£80-90　　　　　　　　**MHT**

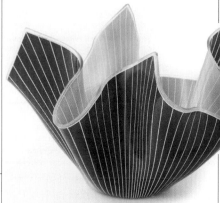

A 1960s Chance large red and white pinstriped handkerchief vase.

7in (18cm) high

RETC

A 1960s Chance yellow banded handkerchief vase.

4in (10cm) high

£35-45　　　　　　　　**MHT**

£70-90

A 1970s Chance graduated blue handkerchief vase, with original Chance oval sticker.

4in (10cm) high

£35-45　　　　　　　　**MHT**

A 1960s Chance amber hammered-effect Aqualux handkerchief vase.

4in (10cm) high

£30-35　　　　　　　　**MHT**

A 1960s Chance green bark effect handkerchief vase.

Some handkerchief vases were made using industrial or domestic glass. This type of textured glass was also used in door panels.

4in (10cm) high

£30-35　　　　　　　　**MHT**

A 1960s Chance dark green polka dot handkerchief vase.

4in (10cm) high

£40-45 RETC

A 1960s Chance white lattice handkerchief vase.

4in (10cm) high

£35-40 MHT

A Chance Fiestaware 'Giraffe' decanter, in the 'Swirl' pattern designed by Lady Margaret Casson, with gilt rim and glasses.

1955-c1965

Decanter 12.5in (31.5cm) high

£50-70 REN

A Chance Fiestaware 'Giraffe' carafe, in the 'Calypto' pattern designed by Michael Harris.

Michael Harris went on to found Mdina Glass on Malta in 1968 and then Isle of Wight Studio Glass in 1972.

c1959 11.5in (29cm) high

£60-80 MHT

A Chance Fiestaware 'Lace' pattern rectangular dish.

This was one of the first two Fiestaware patterns designed.

c1951 13in (33cm) wide

£30-40 MHT

A Chance Fiestware oval platter, in the 'Swirl' pattern designed by Lady Margaret Casson, with gilt rim.

c1955 14in(35.5cm) long

£55-60 MHT

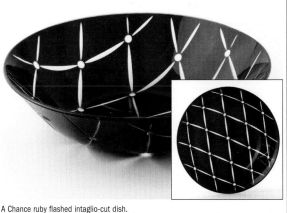

A Chance ruby flashed intaglio-cut dish.

These early ruby-flashed pieces are hard to find. They are produced by plating or casing clear glass with ruby glass, which is then cut back to reveal the underlying clear glass.

c1953 8.75in (22cm) wide

£60-80 RETC

GLASS

COLLECTORS' NOTES

■ Cloud glass is a decorative form of hand or mechanically pressed coloured glass, containing coloured, wispy swirls. The swirls are created by adding trails of dark coloured glass to a lighter coloured glass base. When the mass of glass is pressed into shape in a mould, the characteristic trails are formed. As this trailing is random, the patterns created are unique to each piece.

■ The idea was developed by George Davidson & Co, of Gateshead, England, and was introduced from 1923 with production ending by WWII. Some colours were however produced into the 1950s. Other companies also produced cloud glass, such as Sowerby and Jobling of England, Walther and Brockwitz of Germany, and Reich of the Czech Republic, but they were not as prolific.

■ Values vary according to a combination of shape, colour and patterning. Complex, large shapes, or those made up of different pieces or made for shorter periods of time are more valuable. Look for a good variation of cloud-like wispy trailing, evenly spread across the piece. Colours should be strong. Some colours are rarer and so are more valuable than others. For Davidson, amber is the most common, red the rarest.

■ Colours were produced at different times, helping to date pieces to a period. Davidson's colours include purple (1923-34) amber (1928-57), blue (1925-34), green (1934-41), orange (1933-35) and red (1929-32). Shapes were also produced in specific periods and comparing the two can sometimes narrow a period down.

A Davidson purple cloud glass flower bowl set, with stand, pattern no.699C.

A Davidson purple cloud glass parfait, pattern no.1.

Note the unusual, broad trailing on this example known as 'Ribbon Cloud', which is not as popular with many collectors, but is quite rare.

1923-34 5.25in (13.5cm) high

£25-35   **STE**

A Davidson cloud glass celery vase, pattern no.283.

Although the shape was produced from 1912-42, this pattern was only made in cloud glass in the 1920s.

1923-30   7in (17.5cm) high

£40-60   **STE**

The price is comparatively low as this set is not deemed particularly attractive by collectors.

1923-34   10in (25.5cm) diam

£50-60   **STE**

A Davidson matt finish purple cloud glass flower bowl set, with frog and stand, pattern no.1910MD.

This piece is made more unusual as it is matt to both sides, not just the underside.

1923-34   8in (20cm) diam

£50-60   **STE**

A very rare Davidson purple cloud glass number 269 dish.

This is one of Davidson's most long-lived patterns, registered in 1908 and produced into the 1960s. Very few pieces were made in Cloud Glass, making this example rare.

1923-34   5in (13cm) wide

£40-60   **STE**

A rare Davidson purple cloud glass sugar bowl, pattern no.283.

1923-34   7in (18cm) wide

£70-90   **STE**

A Sowerby purple cloud glass bowl, with remains of a label.

1965-70   7in (18cm) wide

£10-15   **STE**

A Davidson amber cloud glass vase, pattern no. 34SVF.

This vase with a flared rim, as here, is rarer than the same shape with a smaller, unflared rim.

1934-42   *6in (15cm) high*

£30-40   **STE**

A very rare Davidson amber cloud glass Tutankhamun bulb bowl.

This shape, designed in 1922, had a very limited run and is usually found in black. It was made in amber cloud glass from 1928. Tutankhamun's tomb was discovered in 1922, sparking off 'Egypt-o-mania' in design.

1928-30   *6in (15cm) wide*

£80-100   **STE**

A Davidson amber cloud glass no.1 size cigarette box, for 70 cigarettes.

These were made in three sizes.

1931-42   6.25in (16cm) wide

£30-40   **STE**

A Davidson amber cloud glass rose bowl, pattern no.10/1910.

The top section was moulded in a modified ashtray mould.

1935-c1957   12in (30cm) diam

£25-35   **STE**

A rare J.A. Jobling amber cloud glass flower bowl, with registered no.795794 for 1935.

Jobling is known for making pressed glass and Pyrex and did not produce much cloud glass. Its cloud glass was made by machine whereas Davidson's was hand-pressed. The line was not successful so was quickly abandoned.

1935-38   *6in (15.5cm) diam*

£60-80   **STE**

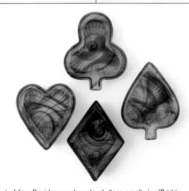

A Davidson amber cloud glass vase, with frog, pattern no.278.

1928-37   7in (18cm) high

£40-60   **STE**

A Davidson amber cloud glass parfait, pattern no.1.

1928-42   5.5in (14cm) high

£15-20   **STE**

A set of four Davidson amber cloud glass small-size 'Bridge Ashtrays', pattern nos 29, 30, 31, 32.

With their original box, these could be worth up to £200-300.

1933-39   *Club 2.25in (6cm) wide*

£70-90   **STE**

A Davidson blue cloud glass faceted 'Column Vase', with flared rim, pattern no.279D.

1928-34   7in (17.5cm) high

£40-60   **STE**

A pair of Davidson blue cloud glass tall candlesticks, pattern no.283.

1925-34   7.5in (19cm) high

£50-70   **STE**

A Davidson blue cloud glass no.2 cigarette box, for 50 cigarettes.

1931-34   3.5in (9cm) wide

£30-50   **STE**

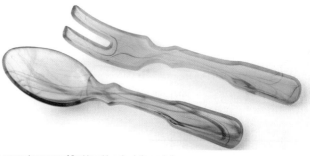

A Davidson blue cloud glass vase, pattern no.277.

Smaller 10in and 16in versions of this vase are available. Very few examples are found in cloud glass, making this rare. It was also made in purple.

1925-34   18in (45.5cm) high

£550-650   **STE**

An extremely rare set of Davidson blue cloud glass salad servers.

Glass salad servers were introduced in 1923, but these are currently the only known cloud glass examples.

1925-34   9in (23cm) long

£200-300   **STE**

A rare Davidson orange cloud glass cylindrical vase, pattern no.712.

1933-35   8in (20cm) high

£150-200   **STE**

A very rare Davidson 'modified' orange cloud glass flower dome and bowl, pattern no.1910D.

Only around 50 orange flower domes were ever made in this size.

1933-35   11in (28cm) diam

£250-300   **STE**

A Davidson 'modified' orange cloud glass flower bowl and frog, pattern no.732.

Davidson produced two types of orange cloud glass, this 'modified' colour is the later version.

1933-35   8in (20cm) wide

£80-100   **STE**

A Davidson unmodified orange cloud glass faceted 'Column Vase', pattern no.279.

This is often thought to be 'yellow' cloud glass but is actually an early attempt at orange.

c1933   10in (25.5cm) high

£250-300   **STE**

A Davidson red 'Ora' cloud glass flower set, pattern no.700D.

1929-32   11.5in (29cm) wide

£400-500   **STE**

A CLOSER LOOK AT A DAVIDSON CLOUD GLASS TRINKET SET

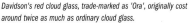

Davidson's red cloud glass, trade-marked as 'Ora', originally cost around twice as much as ordinary cloud glass.

Their red cloud glass is actually amber or purple cloud glass enamelled to one side with red. It had to be fired again after enamelling and the enamel rubs off easily.

Red is the rarest colour for cloud glass and, despite high hopes, it was unpopular due to its cost and flaking enamel. It was only produced for three years.

This set is missing a pin dish and small pot, a complete set could be worth £1,500-2,000.

A Davidson red cloud glass part trinket set, pattern no.283, with original label to tray.

Fakes are known so look for an original label or traces of a label to identify it.

1929-31   18.25in (35cm) wide

£800-1,200   **STE**

A Davidson green cloud glass flower bowl, pattern no.204R.

1934-40   12in (30.5cm) diam

£60-70   **STE**

An unusual Davidson green cloud glass vase, pattern no.34 SVG.

1934-41   7in (18cm) high

£50-70   **STE**

A Davidson green cloud glass vase, with turned in rim, pattern no.294.

This shape was made 1931-36 and green was made 1934-41, making this piece easy to date.

1934-36   6in (15cm) high

£10-15   **STE**

A Davidson Topaz-Briar cloud glass fan vase, pattern no.296.

1957-61   5in (13cm) high

£60-80   **STE**

A German Walther violet cloud glass KDG powder bowl.

Walther produced cloud glass from around 1932-39. Violet is popular, sepia is more common. Opposite to Davidson, amber is rare.

1932-39   4in (10cm) diam

£60-80   **STE**

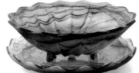

A German Walther violet cloud glass Zentrum cress strainer and dish.

1935-39   8.5in (22cm) diam

£80-120   **STE**

A German Walther Prismem violet cloud glass flower bowl.

Walther sold its cloud glass under the trade name Oralit.

1932-39   9.75in (24.5cm) diam

£70-100   **STE**

A German Walther lilac cloud glass plate.

1932-39   12.25in (31cm) diam

£80-120   **STE**

A German Walther pink cloud glass bowl.

1935-39   5.25in (13.5cm) wide

£40-50   **STE**

A German Walther 'malachit' cloud glass 'Lotos' vase.

1935-39   5.75in (14.5cm) high

£100-120   **STE**

A 1920s/30s Reich grey cloud glass 'Viktoria' vase, pattern no.4857.

Grey cloud glass is hard to come by.

8in (20cm) high

£250-300   **STE**

A Walther sepia cloud glass 'Lotos' vase, with Oralit label.

Sepia is the most common colour for Walther cloud glass.

1932-1939   18cm high

£70-90   **STE**

FIND OUT MORE...

www.cloudglass.com

Davidson Glass – A History, *by Chris & Val Stewart, 2005.*

GLASS

COLLECTORS' NOTES

- Ronald Stennett-Willson founded King's Lynn Glass in King's Lynn, Norfolk in 1967. Before this, Stennett-Willson had worked for J. Wuidart & Co., a UK importer of Scandinavian glass, and been a Reader in Industrial Glass at the Royal College of Art, London.

- The factory produced high quality tableware and decorative ware in line with the popular Scandinavian style. Forms were clean and modern, relying on the colour and clarity of the glass, which ranged from cool icy blues to strong purples.

- The successful factory was acquired by Wedgwood in 1969. It continued to use Stennett-Willson's designs as well as commissioning new designs until his retirement in 1979. In 1982, Wedgwood acquired a controlling 50

per cent stake in Dartington Glass, which was then acquired by Caithness in 1988. The King's Lynn factory was closed in 1992.

- The many candleholders produced, such as the instantly recognisable 'Sheringham', form the core of many collections. The range, size and colour count towards value. Vases are also popular, as are the numerous animal paperweights, which are at the most affordable and varied end of their production.

- As simple form and colour are so important to the design, always aim to buy pieces in immaculate condition. Chips, especially to the rim, cracks and internal liming reduce the appeal and desirability of a piece, as well as the value.

A 1970s Wedgwood 'Sheringham' topaz candlestick, design RSW13-2, by Ronald Stennett-Willson, with two discs.

5.5in (14cm) high

£25-35   **NPC**

A 1970s Wedgwood 'Sheringham' amethyst candlestick, design RSW13-2, by Ronald Stennett-Willson, with two discs.

5.5in (14cm) high

£25-35   **NPC**

A 1970s Wedgwood 'Sheringham' amethyst candlestick, design RSW13-1, by Ronald Stennett-Willson, with single disc and applied boss.

Look out for inset Wedgwood ceramic plaques, celebrating events such as the Queen's silver jubilee in 1977. Amethyst glass was a popular colour for commemorating Royal events.

5.5in (14cm) high

£15-20   **NPC**

A King's Lynn blue glass display vase, designed by Ronald Stennett-Willson, with heavy foot and straight stem and original Lynn paper label.

5in (12.5cm) high

£80-100   **GC**

A 1970s Wedgwood blue textured candleholder or posy vase, design RSW58, by Ronald Stennett-Willson, with "Wedgwood England" acid stamp to base.

4.25in (11cm) high

£30-35   **MHT**

A Wedgwood light blue textured tumbler, design RSW128-13, designed by Ronald Stennett-Willson, with moulded flame motifs.

These were sold in boxed pairs.

c1969   *5in (13cm) high*

£15-20   **GC**

A Wedgwood 'Squat Vase', design RSW110, by Ronald Stennett-Willson, with heavy cased clear glass base and pink mottled white internal layer.

c1969   *5in (13cm) high*

£60-90   **GC**

GLASS

A very rare Wedgwood heavily cased blue 'ariel' vase, designed by Ronald Stennett-Willson, with internal elliptical bubble patterns.

This is part of a series of unique vases produced under Stennett-Willson's guidance during the late 1970s, shortly before his retirement from Wedgwood. The complex 'ariel' process used was similar to that developed by Orrefors around 1937 where a pattern was sandblasted onto a piece before it was cased, resulting in trapped air bubbles forming the design. Many have natural motifs such as leaves.

c1975-78   *4in (10cm) high*

£300-400   GC

A Wedgwood 'Galaxy' faceted glass paperweight, design RSW14, by Ronald Stennett-Willson, with two controlled opaque blue internal bubbles.

This was one of the first paperweights designed by Stennett-Willson for Wedgwood in 1970. They were discontinued in 1973, making them hard to find today, particularly in undamaged condition.

1970-73   *4in (10cm) high*

£50-70   GC

A Wedgwood topaz and clear glass decanter, design RSW43, by Ronald Stennett-Willson, with clear stopper with three controlled internal bubbles.

11.75in (30cm) high

£60-80   GC

A Wedgwood whiskey decanter, design RSW60, by Ronald Stennett-Willson, with heavy moulded dimpled base.

This was originally designed for King's Lynn Glass in 1967, and was produced until the early 1970s.

c1970   *10in (25cm) high*

£35-45   GC

A 1970s Wedgwood white cased pear paperweight, design RSW231, by Ronald Stennett-Willson, with acid-etched Wedgwood mark to base and paper label.

4.75in (12cm) high

£35-45   GC

A 1970s Wedgwood black and white cased panda paperweight, design SG421.

3.5in (9cm) high

£45-55   GC

FIND OUT MORE...

Wedgwood Glass, by Susan Tobin, 2001, ISBN: 0-9580234-0-9.

COLLECTORS' NOTES

■ Mdina was founded on Malta in 1968 by Michael Harris (1933-94) who had been a tutor in glass at the Royal College of Art, London. Colours are instantly recognisable as the rich blues, greens, sands and browns of the Mediterranean landscape around the factory. The glass also tends to be thickly rendered.

■ Pieces are typically free blown, with Harris taking the studio glass movement to a new commercial level. Harris left in 1972, and early pieces produced when Harris was at Mdina fetch a considerable premium. Look for his hallmark 'Fish' vases, which are one of his most popular shapes with collectors today. Rounded vase and dish forms are also typical shapes.

■ Souvenir hunting tourists preferred smaller, less expensive examples. Pieces were also exported to Germany, the UK and the US among other countries. Larger pieces command a premium as fewer were made. Most examples are signed 'Mdina' in script on the base, but look for those signed with Harris' signature as these are extremely rare.

■ Later examples from the 1980s onwards are currently less sought-after but, as with all Mdina glass, are growing in desirability and value. Pieces dated or signed by Joseph Said and subsequent owner, can also fetch comparatively high prices. Oranges, pinks and white are all signs of later pieces produced into the 1980s after Harris left.

A CLOSER LOOK AT A MDINA 'FISH' VASE

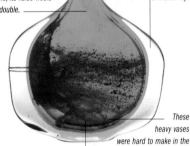

The rounded, organic form is typical of Harris' early pieces, if it were signed by Harris with his name, its value would nearly double.

This 'axe-head' shape is known as a 'Fish' vase with the clear parts being like the 'wings' of a manta ray.

These heavy vases were hard to make in the early days of the factory, with Harris being one of a very few who were competent enough.

It is unusual to find an example that has been 'double-cased', with a blue outline under the clear glass.

A Mdina 'Fish' vase, heavily cased in clear glass with internal swirls and cut with two facets on one side, signed "Michael Harris, Mdina Glass, Malta" on the base.

c1970   8.75in (22cm) high

£300-500   **GROB**

A rare Mdina 'Fish' vase, designed and made by Michael Harris, cased in clear glass.

Very few of these were made in this large size by Harris at this time.

c1970   11.5in (29cm) high

£300-400   **ART**

A 1980s Mdina blue 'Fish' vase, unsigned.

The green spidery internal patterning combined with the general 'squared off' shape with a thin, elongated neck show this to be a late example. Note that early examples tend to be in the earlier colourways including browns, amethyst and mottled, rather than striated, greens.

8.25in (21cm) high

£80-120   **NPC**

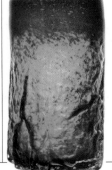

A Mdina large mould-blown textured vase, of square section with dropped-in circular neck and polished pontil mark.

The texture and polished, lens-like pontil mark means these pieces are often mistaken for Whitefriars. This large size is very rare.

8.75in (22.5cm) high

£80-120   **GC**

A Mdina vase, signed and dated "Mdina Glass 1974".

Dated examples such as this are more desirable among collectors than undated.

6.75in (17cm) high

£50-80 NPC

A Mdina blue and green glass vase, with two pulled handles, signed "Mdina" on the base.

6in (15cm) high

£30-50 NPC

A 1970s Mdina gourd-shaped vase, signed "Mdina" on the base.

8in (20cm) high

£40-60 NPC

A Mdina goblet, with 'craggy' trailed knop and clear stem and foot.

7.5in (19cm) high

£70-90 NPC

A Mdina green and blue swirl pattern vase, signed "Mdina" on the base.

5.5in (14cm) high

£30-50 GAZE

A Mdina glass ball paperweight, signed "Mdina" on the base.

5in (13cm) high

£15-20 GAZE

A Mdina tortoiseshell-coloured textured cylindrical vase.

8in (20cm) high

£30-50 NPC

A Mdina orange-amber glass vase, overlaid with randomly applied blue-green straps.

6in (15cm) high

£30-40 GAZE

A 1980s Mdina pink mottled vase, with applied blue trails, with Maltese cross stamped logo.

5in (12.5cm) high

£50-70 JL

COLLECTORS' NOTES

■ After leaving Malta in 1972, Michael Harris founded a second island factory near Ventnor, Isle of Wight. Initial ranges are currently the most desirable and tended to have coloured swirling or cloud-like patterns such as 'Pink & Blue Swirls' or 'Blue Aurene'.

■ The factory's major commercial breakthrough came in 1978-79 with the 'Azurene' range, with silver and gold leaf applied to the surface. Developed by Harris and Royal College of Art student William Walker, it was exported all over the world. Black is the most common base glass colour, others, such as white, are rarer.

■ Look for a stamped 'flame' mark on the base that indicates production was between c1974 and c1982. A flat, polished base indicates a date after 1982. Labels can help to date a piece, with a triangular black label being used in the 1980s and a black or gold square sticker from the 1990s.

■ Pieces signed by Harris with his name command a substantial premium, as do large examples. Short-lived 1980s and 1990s ranges tend to be more collectable and valuable today than ranges that were more popular at the time, as fewer examples exist.

■ After Harris' death in 1994, production was continued by his wife and two sons. The factory is still producing today, under the expertise of one of his two sons, Timothy, and his wife. As with Mdina glass, examples are increasing in desirability and value.

An Isle of Wight Studio Glass 'Pink & Blue Swirls' vase, with impressed 'flame' pontil mark.

c1974-c1980   5.75in (14.5cm) high

£60-80   **GC**

A Isle of Wight Studio Glass 'Pink & Blue Swirls' vase, with impressed 'flame' pontil mark.

c1974-78   3.5in (9cm) high

£30-50   **TGM**

An Isle of Wight Studio Glass 'Pink & Blue Swirls' perfume bottle, with impressed 'flame' pontil mark.

Perfume bottles of this period and shape always have clear stoppers.

c1974-c1980   6.25in (16cm) high

£50-70   **PC**

An Isle of Wight Studio Glass brown streaked vase, with an impressed 'coach-bolt' prunt to the base.

A plain applied concave 'prunt' covering the broken pontil mark is a rare feature of early Isle of Wight examples made in 1973 only.

1973   4in (10cm) high

£40-60   **ART**

An Isle of Wight Studio Glass 'Blue Aurene' type cylinder vase.

1973-82   9.5in (24cm) high

£80-120   **GC**

A Isle of Wight Studio Glass 'Blue Aurene' perfume flask, with impressed 'flame' pontil mark.

1973-82   3.75in (9.5cm) high

£60-80   **PC**

An early Isle of Wight Studio Glass 'Black Azurene' cylindrical vase, with polished base and black triangular sticker.

1978-82   7.5in (19cm) high

£40-60   **EAB**

An Isle of Wight Studio Glass 'Pink Azurene' vase, with impressed 'flame' pontil mark.

The Azurene range was made with different base glass colours. Seen without light shining it, the surface effect is similar to the black one also on this page.

c1979-87   7.5in (19cm) high

£40-60   **TGM**

An Isle of Wight Studio Glass 'Poppy' vase, from the 'Meadow Garden' range with polished base.

This shape was issued in 1987 only, although the range was one of their most popular.

1987   9in (23cm) high

£50-70   **TGM**

A 1980s Isle of Wight Studio Glass spherical glass vase, from the 'Meadow Garden' range, with polished base and triangular black label.

This shape was only made in this prolific range in 1986-88 only.

1986-88   6in (15.5cm) h

£50-80   **TGM**

A very rare Isle of Wight Studio Glass 'Allsorts' perfume bottle, from the 'New Bon Bon' range, with deep gold-coloured ground and iridescent green and blue spots, signed on the base "Michael Harris Isle of Wight Glass".

This shape was only produced in this colourway in 1989. Its rarity is tripled as it is signed by Michael Harris.

1989   3.75in (9.5cm) high

£120-180   **TGM**

An Isle of Wight Studio Glass small 'Satin & Silk' vase, with polished base and triangular sticker.

1988-91   5in (13cm) high

£20-25   **TGM**

An Isle of Wight Studio Glass pink and white swirled bowl or ashtray, with impressed 'flame' pontil mark.

c1980   4.25in (10.5cm) wide

£20-40   **TGM**

An Isle of Wight Studio Glass for Kerry Glass 'Peat' vase, with reversed, impressed 'flame' pontil mark.

This was part of a range produced by Kerry Glass in Ireland, but designed by Isle of Wight Studio Glass.

1980-82   5.25in (13.5cm) high

£40-50   **TGM**

A scarce Isle of Wight Studio Glass goblet, designed and made by Timothy Harris, with applied abstract rod of coloured glass fused into stem.

1992-93   5.5in (14cm) high

£60-80   **MHT**

COLLECTORS' NOTES

■ The Venetian island of Murano has been a centre of glass production since the 14thC. The 1950s saw a renaissance of the island's industry via the adoption of modern design principles and a huge range of colours.

■ Figurines of clowns and other novelties are mostly produced on a large scale for the tourist market. These items generally have little value on the secondary market due to the quantity produced.

■ Beware of glass offered as 'Murano style', which will probably have been made in workshops in Asia or South America.

■ Damage will of course devalue a piece of Murano glass. Even minor losses such as 'flea bites' or tiny rim chips will have an adverse affect on most pieces.

■ Collectors pay the highest prices for glass blown by, or at least under the supervision of, well-known glassmasters or designers such as Ercole Barovier, Carlo Scarpa and Fulvio Bianconi. Company names to watch out for include Venini, Fratelli Toso and the innovative Seguso Vetri d'Arte.

■ Murano glassblowers use a wide variety of techniques and forms, including murrines, air bubbles and a method of casing glass known as 'sommerso', which translates as 'submerged'.

■ Value is dependant on many variables including size, colour and rarity. Generally, more complex or demanding designs by well-known manufacturers will be more valuable.

A Murano sommerso vase, in four colours.

c1955   6.25in (16cm) high

£60-80   **NPC**

A 1960s Murano large flared rim vase, light amber glass encasing green.

13.75in (35cm) high

£35-45   **GAZE**

A Seguso Vetri d'Arte sommerso vase, pale violet, blue and green cased glass, with vertical ribbing.

c1970   7.5in (18.5cm) high

£220-280   **VZ**

An Anfora sommerso orange and cased clear glass vase, by Andrea Zilio, with trapped air bubbles and gold leaf inclusions and signed to the base "Anfora, Murano '04".

2004   18.5in (47cm) high

£300-400   **VET**

An Arte Nuova Murano clear, blue and light yellow sommerso vase, in the style of Flavio Poli, with maker's label "ARTE NUOVA MURANO GRAND PRIZE ... World Fair Brussels 1958".

c1958   7in (18cm) high

£70-100   **VZ**

A Seguso Vetri d'Arte sommerso vase, designed by Flavio Poli, with burgundy glass cased in yellow and clear glass.

Flavio Poli is one of the earliest and most successful designers working with the sommerso technique. In 1954, he won the prestigious Compasso D'Oro award for his sommerso designs. As here, forms tend to be sculptural and rounded. Look out for larger examples such as his elliptical 'Valva' vases.

c1958   5.75in (14.5cm)

£80-120   **VZ**

A Barovier & Toso vase, designed by Ercole Barovier, clear glass spiralling with overlaid dark-red and cobalt-blue canes, with original paper label to base.

c1966   *10.3in (25.8cm) high*

£350-450   **VZ**

A Seguso Vetri d'Arte sommerso vase, designed by Flavio Poli, teardrop shape with angled neck.

c1955   *9.25in (23.5cm) high*

£300-400   **VZ**

A Seguso Vetri d'Arte sommerso vase, designed by Flavio Poli, in grey-green, clear and rosé-flashed glass.

c1958   *7.75in (19.5cm) high*

£250-350   **VZ**

A Venini vase, the bulbous body with controlled trails of large air bubbles and narrow flared neck, marked on the base "Venini Murano ITALIA".

c1950   *10.25in (25.5cm) high*

£350-450   **VZ**

A Barovier & Toso 'Efeso' vase, designed by Ercole Barovier, with pale and dark blue powder inclusions and irregular internal glass bubbles.

c1964   *6.5in (16.5cm)*

£450-550   **VZ**

A Venini opaline vase, made to a 1930 design by Napoleone Martinuzzi, with thick horizontal ribbing, signed "Venini 94 Carlo Scarpa" on the base.

1994   *11.75in (29.5cm) high*

£350-450   **VZ**

A Vistosi Memphis glass vase, designed by Ettore Sottsass, white glass applied with red and green dots.

8.75in (22cm) high

£550-650   **WW**

A 1930s Murano vase, the body of spiralling vertical canes, with zanfirico rods, with applied blue rim, mounted on a hollow base.

7.25in (18.5cm) high

£150-250   **KAU**

A late 20thC Venini vase, of flattened ovoid form with 'Scotsasi' tartan pattern, with clear plastic label and engraved "Venini Italia".

8.75in (22cm) high

£350-450   **ROS**

A Venini & C. handled vase, designed by Vittorio Zecchin, with ruby-red body, two applied handles, marked "Venini Murano ITALIA" on base.

c1925   *5.5in (14cm) high*

£120-180   **VZ**

A Seguso Vetri d'Arte vase, designed by Mario Pinzoni, in chrysoberyl (alexandrite) glass.

c1955   *8.5in (21.5cm) high*

£200-300   **VZ**

A Venini clear and red glass stem vase, incised marks to base reading "Venini Italia 14.10.59".

c1959   *7in (18cm) high*

£35-45   **GAZE**

An opaque pink and opaline footed tall vase, possibly Seguso, with tall, elongated neck.

17in (43cm) high

£60-70   **RETC**

A Venini & C. vase, with arched rim, cased clear and cyclamen-red glass turning turquoise-blue towards rim.

c1952   *10.75in (27.5cm) high*

£250-350   **VZ**

A CLOSER LOOK AT A MURANO VASE

This vase is by the renowned Fratelli Toso factory, famous for its murrine designs, which used coloured 'tiles' of glass.

The murrines are intended to look like the glass shades found on Tiffany lamps.

Rather than using lead, as on a real Tiffany lamp, the iridescent black areas are actually glass and part of the murrine itself.

This style of murrine was designed around the 1960s-70s, when Tiffany lamps became popular collectors pieces, so that the look could be offered to clients who liked the Tiffany design.

The coloured strands are formed from diagonal rods laid onto the vase and are known as 'pietini'.

A rare Fratelli Toso 'Tiffany' murrine and opaque white and coloured strand pietini vase, designed and made by Vittorio Ferro.

1960-70   5.5in (14cm) high

£1,500-2,000   **PC**

A Venini 'Grenadine' glass vase, designed by Gianni Versace, the clear glass with blue panels with turquoise, yellow and red murrines, engraved "Venini Gianni Versace 1988/57".

1988   9.75in (25cm) high

£400-500   **ROS**

A Venini Murano large glass vase, attributed to Alessandro Mendini, clear cased with applied vertical canes in turquoise, red and blue, with label and engraved "Venini 80" to underside.

1980   15.5in (39.5cm) high

£350-450   **ROS**

A very rare Fratelli Toso 'field flower' and 'grass' murrine vase, designed and made by Vittorio Ferro.

1950-70   6.25in (16cm) high

£1,500-2,000   **PC**

A Murano ruby red lobed bowl, with internal trails of bubbles.

c1965   5.5in (14cm) diam

£12-18   **NPC**

A 1950s Seguso glass ashtray, in red, blue and turquoise.

5in (13cm) wide

£45-55   **P&I**

A Venini 'corroso' bowl, designed by Carlo Scarpa, marked on base "Venini Murano".

Corroso glass was developed at Venini in the early 1930s. The 'frosted' or 'veined' effect is gained by applying a wax resist and then acid to the exterior.

c1936   2.75in (7cm) wide

£100-150   **VZ**

A Venini bowl, designed by Carlo Scarpa, with trails of internal air bubbles and gold inclusions.

c1940   2.75in (7cm) wide

£80-120   **VZ**

A 1950s Murano turquoise trefoil bowl, with silver foil and coloured inclusions.

5.25in (13.5cm) diam

£25-35   **AG**

A Murano opaline green cased glass ashtray, with pulled rim.

7in (18cm) high

£40-50   **RETC**

A Seguso Vetri d'Arte ashtray, the opening in the form of a rosette, signed "Seguso V. d'Arte", and with "Seguso Vetri d'Arte Murano Made in Italy" label with handwritten number "13152".

c1970   *8.75in (22cm) diam*

£300-400   **VZ**

A Seguso Vetri d'Arte bowl, with "Seguso Murano Made in Italy" label.

c1960   *3.5in (9cm) wide*

£120-180   **VZ**

A Venini 'corroso' bowl, designed by Carlo Scarpa, in clear and turquoise-blue cased glass, frosted from the base upwards.

c1940   *7.75in (19.5cm) wide*

£120-180   **VZ**

A Seguso Vetri d'Arte bowl, in dark-blue and turquoise cased iridescent glass.

c1965   *2.75in (7cm) high*

£180-220   **VZ**

A Venini & C. small honey-coloured glass dish, with trails of regular air bubble inclusions, marked on base "Venini Murano ITALIA".

c1960   *4.5in (11.5cm) diam*

£80-120   **VZ**

A Murano green glass lobed bowl, with four coloured openings.

                          6.25in (16cm) diam

£20-40   **NPC**

A CLOSER LOOK AT A MURANO VASE

Yoichi Ohira is a respected glass designer who combines Murano glass with Japanese ceramic forms and styles.

The piece uses glass canes typical of Murano and the form resembles a tea bowl.

This is made with the 'incalmo' process, where two separate 'vessels' are made in different types of glass and joined while still hot.

Its simple lines and form are accentuated by the separately applied rim and solid colour foot.

A 1980s De Majo bowl, designed by Yoichi Ohira.

5in (12.5cm) high

£200-300   **VET**

A Seguso Vetri d'Arte bowl, with flared rim and applied hollow foot, the black glass cased in opaque white, light green and clear glass, with "Seguso Murano Made in Italy" label and handwritten lot number.

The form of this bowl echoes those produced in Murano in the early 16thC, but with modern colours.

c1960   7.75in (19.5cm) diam

£200-300   **VZ**

A Venini 'fazzoletto' vase, designed by Fulvio Bianconi, clear glass with vertical band inclusions in opaque lobster-red and purplish-black.

The fazzoletto or handkerchief vase was developed by Fulvio Bianconi and Paolo Venini around 1947. Millions of copies have been made by other factories, mainly for the tourist market. Large examples and authentic Venini pieces fetch the most. Look for a delicacy and complexity of form, or an acid etched "Venini Murano Italia" signature, denoting a piece made before 1960.

c1950   4.25in (10.5cm) high

£100-150   **VZ**

A Venini 'fazzoletto' vase, designed by Fulvio Bianconi, marked "Venini murano ITALIA" on base.

c1950   3.75in (9.5cm) high

£150-250   **VZ**

GLASS

A Murano art glass bowl, red and pale blue, encased in clear glass.

18.5in (47cm) wide

£20-30 **GAZE**

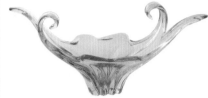

A Murano yellow and green tinted glass 'splash' bowl.

19in (48cm) wide

£20-40 **GAZE**

A 1960s Seguso sommerso orange and green glass vase, with curving leaf-like rim.

14.25in (36cm) wide

£150-200 **RETC**

A Venini bowl, designed by Napoleone Martinuzzi, the deep moulded shape with ribbed rosette pattern in the centre and flared rim.

c1930 *19in (47.5cm) diam*

£120-180 **VZ**

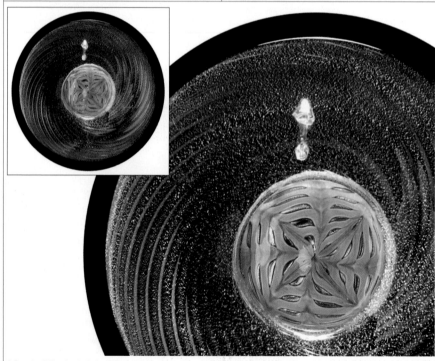

A Barovier & Toso bowl, designed by Angelo Barovier, with gold-foil inclusions in a spiral pulton, clear-glass centre with opaque pink and purple lattice work.

c1974 *14.5in (37cm) diam*

£300-400 **VZ**

A Murano glass display piece, of two geese in flight, mounted on an oval sommerso glass base.

c1960   *8in (20cm) high*

£20-30   **GAZE**

A pair of 1950s Murano sommerso glass swans, in cranberry glass with air bubbles encased in clear glass, standing on bubbly 'rocky' plinths.

               6.25in (16cm) high

£80-120   **AG**

A Seguso Vetri D'Arte fish, designed by Mario Pinzoni.

c1965   *12.75in (32.5cm) long*

£100-150   **VZ**

A Murano glass clown ornament.

Popular tourist pieces, clowns have been produced in great numbers for decades. Larger sizes fetch more, as do those with complex and more finely applied details.

£20-30   **GAZE**

A Venini Murano incalmo glass decanter, designed by Gio Ponti, with stopper, engraved "Venini Italia 83" to underside.

1983   *14.25in (36cm) high*

£280-320   **ROS**

A Venini 'Acrobat' figure, the design attributed to Fulvio Bianconi, in white and black glass, depicted in a handstand, unsigned.

              15in (38cm) high

£400-500   **ROS**

GLASS

A Venini glass pepper, designed by Napoleone Martinuzzi, with applied green stalk, unsigned.

c1930   *4in (10cm) diam*

£350-450   VZ

A Salviati amber and dark green decorative pear, with "Salviati & C. Made in Italy" label.

c1965   *7.75in (19.5cm) high*

£150-200   VZ

A Seguso Vetri d'Arte sommerso vessel, designed by Flavio Poli.

c1965   *2.5in (15cm) high*

£280-320   VZ

A Murano glass tall, yellow, four sided obelisk, unmarked but possibly by Venini, with black, reflective base.

17in (43cm) high

£150-250   PSI

A 1950s Murano sommerso glass green and amber cased lamp base.

11in (28cm) high

£40-50   NPC

A Fratelli Toso cup, with millefiori-style murrine and applied pulled scroll handle.

c1910   *1.5in (4cm) high*

£70-100   VZ

COLLECTORS' NOTES

■ Holmegaard was founded in Zealand, Denmark in 1825. From the 1830s, it produced bottles and pressed glass, including tableware. A second glassworks was built at Kastrup in 1847. It was sold in 1873 to allow for expansion of Holmegaard, although the Kastrup factory continued with its own glass production.

■ Holmegaard's first notable modern designer was Jacob Bang (1899-1965) who joined in 1927. He left in 1941 and joined Kastrup in 1957 where he worked until his death. His designs tend to be classical and restrained, with minimal surface decoration.

■ The second notable designer was Per Lütken, who joined in 1942 and is known for his asymmetric, organic and flowing designs that sum up the aesthetic of the 1950s and 1960s. Curving bud-like or teardrop forms are typical, as are 'pulled' rims. Colours tend to be cool,

classical greys or blues and pieces have heavy walls.

■ Apart from the stylistic appearance, Lütken's designs are often recognisable from the inscription on the base which includes his initials and a date. His tend to be among the most consistently popular Holmegaard designs today. In 1965, the Kastrup factory was merged with Holmegaard to enable production to be expanded.

■ Also highly desirable is Lütken's cheerful 'Carnaby' range, which is the polar opposite of his usual aesthetic, being brightly coloured and geometric in shape. This mould-blown series is similar to the 'Palet' range produced by Holmegaard & Kastrup and designed by Jacob Bang's son, Michael, between 1968 and 1976. The bright pillar box red is the most typical colour and all have a 'plastic'-like appearance.

A Holmegaard smoke grey bubble vase, designed by Per Lütken and signed "HOLMEGAARD PL 1958".

1958   3.5in (9cm) high

£4-6   **NPC**

A Holmegaard heart-shaped aqua blue 'Minuet' vase, designed by Per Lütken, with original label.

c1955   4.25in (11cm) high

£60-80   **NPC**

A Holmegaard capri blue 'Provence' bowl, designed by Per Lütken.

This was made in a similar way to Lütken's earlier small bowls with heavy bodies. Although larger, it used the same amount of glass so was more cost effective, but its thin body made it more vulnerable to damage.

c1962   7in (18cm) diam

£50-60   **NPC**

A rare Holmegaard tall aqua blue glass vase, designed by Per Lütken, with slender neck.

A similar shape was designed by Paul Kedelv for Flygsfors, and used by Whitefriars (with a bubbled base). Flygsfors uses the white, clear and coloured glass typical of that range. It is sometimes known as the 'dog bone', because of its shape.

c1955   11in (28cm) high

£60-80   **NPC**

A Holmegaard aqua blue glass bowl, designed by Per Lütken and signed on the base.

c1955   6in (15.5cm) d.

£30-40   **GAZE**

A Holmegaard vase, designed by Per Lütken, signed "Holmegaard PL" on the base.

1960   9in (23cm) high

£70-80   **NPC**

GLASS

A Holmegaard smoke grey glass cylinder vase, designed by Per Lütken and signed on the base.

1969   7in (18cm) high

£40-60   **NPC**

A CLOSER LOOK AT A HOLMEGAARD VASE

Pulled or everted rims and parts are a typical feature of many of Lütken's designs.

The organic, budlike-form is typical of Lütken's asymmetric designs during the 1950s and of the influence of nature on Scandinavian designers.

The small hole is created by inserting a pin into the bubble of molten glass. As air escapes, the hole opens wider and a randomly sized cavity opens up.

The walls are heavy, with a green glass element being cased in clear glass, and then manipulated with tools while still hot.

A Holmegaard Smoke grey glass dish, designed by Per Lütken, with heavy walls, signed on the base.

1959   8.5in (11cm) diam

£12-18   **NPC**

A Holmegaard 'Abstraction' vase, designed by Per Lütken, signed "HOLMEGAARD 19 PL 58" to the base.

1958   7in (18cm) high

£70-100   **GAZE**

A 1940s Holmegaard vase, designed by Per Lütken, with early bold signature.

6in (15cm) wide

£50-70   **NPC**

A large Holmgaard handkerchief-like clear glass vase.

£50-80   **GAZE**

A Holmegaard sapphire blue cylinder vase, designed by Per Lütken and signed.

1965   9in (23cm) high

£45-55   **NPC**

GLASS

An unusually large Holmegaard red glass stepped and tapering vase, with flared rim.

A Holmegaard deep amber glass 'Gulvase', designed by Otto Brauer.

c1960   11.5in (29cm) high

£40-60   **NPC**

A Holmegaard large sapphire blue glass vase.

11.5in (29cm) high

£35-45   **NPC**

11in (28cm) high

£60-80   **NPC**

A 1960s Holmegaard large tricorn vase, blue encasing green glass, with a flared rim, signed on the base with Holmegaard marks.

The combination of coloured glass is highly unusual for Holmegaard and recalls Muranese designs. However, the pulled rim and thick walls echo the designs of Per Lütken.

14.5in (37cm) high

£20-30   **GAZE**

A Holmegaard seven-piece water or lemonade set.

c1957-65

£35-45   **NPC**

A set of six Holmegaard beakers, five with original labels.

£40-60   **NPC**

A 1970s Holmegaard neck glass, designed by Christer Holmgren, with original box.

Christel and Christer Holmgren established their design studio in Denmark in 1971. Designed to hang around the neck, this weighted glass freed the hands of the drinker to 'smoke, eat, shake hands, or even hold another drink'.

3.5in (9cm) high

£30-40   **NPC**

A Holmegaard glass clock, white with green glass applied decoration.

11in (28cm) diam

£20-40   GAZE

A group of 1970s Holmegaard red cased 'Gulvase' bottle vases, designed by Otto Brauer.

These were based on a design by Per Lütken from 1958.

c1962   Left: 17.75in (45cm) high

£350-550

c1962   Middle: 13.75in (35cm) high

£300-400

c1962   Right: 19.75in (50cm) high

£550-750   **EOH**

A Kastrup & Holmegaard red cased 'Carnaby' line vase, designed by Michael Bang in the 1960s.

11.75in (30cm) high

£300-500   **EOH**

A Holmegaard blue bottle vase, with globe stopper.

21.5in (55cm) high inc stopper

£450-650   **EOH**

A Kastrup large grey glass floor vase, designed by Jacob Bang, with internal white casing.

17.5in (44.5cm) high

£100-120   **GC**

A Kastrup blue glass vase, designed by Jacob Bang, with paper label.

8.25in (21cm) high

£70-80   **GC**

A Kastrup green glass vase, designed by Jacob Bang.

6in (15cm) high

£60-70   **GC**

A Kastrup smokey grey tapering vase, designed by Jacob Bang.

10.25in (26cm) high

£60-70   **GC**

A smokey grey tapering vase, possibly design by Jacob E. Bang for Kastrup.

£120-180   **EOH**

COLLECTORS' NOTES

■ Riihimäki (known as Riihimaën Lasi Oy from 1937) was founded in 1910 in Finland and initially produced container, industrial and domestic glass. The innovative factory held competitions to employ new designers in the 1930s and 1940s.

■ Helena Tynell joined in 1946, Nanny Still in 1949 and Tamara Aladin in 1959. Aimo Okkolin had already joined the factory in 1937, and these names dominated design into the 1960s. A style based around clean-lined geometric form with little surface decoration typifies their production. Colours tend to be jewel-like, bright and rich, and some are more desirable that others.

■ The designs reflecting the 'Pop' style of the age. They employed a manufacturing process, which used moulds to ensure consistency of form and colour. Aladin is known for her geometric forms, usually incorporating flanges. Pieces showing numerous strong geometrical or curving parts in rich colours tend to be the most desirable and valuable.

■ Initial secondary market interest came from those interested in Scandinavian and interior design, primarily as the designs sit so well within modern interiors. Over the past few years, collecting interest has grown, as has an understanding of Scandinavian glass. Always avoid chipped, cracked or scratched examples as the purity of colour and form so typical of Scandinavian glass is disrupted.

A Riihimaën Lasi Oy cased green glass cylindrical vase, designed by Aimo Okkolin.

c1970   7in (18.5cm) high

£20-30   **GC**

A Riihimaën Lasi Oy cased green glass waisted vase, designed by Aimo Okkolin.

c1970   7in (18.5cm) high

£15-25   **NPC**

A Riihimaën Lasi Oy cased green glass vase, designed by Nanny Still.

c1976   9.75in (25cm) high

£25-35   **NPC**

A Riihimaën Lasi Oy green vase, designed by Helena Tynell.

7in (18cm) high

£45-55   **NPC**

A Riihimaën Lasi Oy green geometric 'Disc' vase, designed by Tamara Aladin.

11in (28cm) high

£40-60   **NPC**

A Riihimaën Lasi Oy olive green stepped vase, designed by Tamara Aladin.

11in (28cm) high

£30-50   **NPC**

A Riihimaën Lasi Oy green vase, designed by Tamara Aladin.

c1976   9.75in (25cm) high

£20-30   **NPC**

A CLOSER LOOK AT A RIIHIMÄKI VASE

This is known as the 'Pablo' vase, perhaps due to its 'Cubist' style lines that bring to mind Picasso's paintings.

As with all Riihimäki pieces, it has been made in a mould to ensure consistency of form and colour.

It was designed by Erkkitapio Siiroinen and is very unusual in blue.

Such sharply angled protrusions are comparatively uncommon in Riihimaki's designs.

A rare Riihimaën Lasi Oy vase, designed by Erkkitapio Siiroinen.
c1968   8in (20cm) high
£70-90   NPC

A Riihimaën Lasi Oy 'Pompadour' vase, designed by Nanny Still.
c1968   9in (23cm) high
£30-40   NPC

A Riihimaën Lasi Oy blue 'Pompadour'-style vase, designed by Nanny Still.
6.25in (16cm) high
£18-22   NPC

A Riihimaën Lasi Oy blue vase, designed by Helena Tynell.
8.25in (21cm) high
£35-45   NPC

A 1960s Riihimaën Lasi Oy blue 'Tuulikki' vase, designed by Tamara Aladin.
7.5in (19cm) high
£25-35   NPC

A Riihimaën Lasi Oy octagonal bottle vase, designed by Nanny Still, with knobbly decoration and label.
7in (18cm) high
£60-70   NPC

A Riihimaën Lasi Oy blue-grey vase, designed by Helena Tynell.
8.25in (21cm) high
£25-35   NPC

A Riihimaën Lasi Oy smoky blue-grey vase, designed by Nanny Still.
1960-70   25in (63cm) high
£20-30   NPC

A Riihimaën Lasi Oy red vase, designed by Nanny Still.

9.75in (25cm) high

£25-30   NPC

A Riihimaën Lasi Oy red glass vase, designed by Tamara Aladin.

c1965   8in (20cm) high

£25-35   NPC

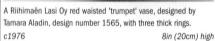

A Riihamaën Lasi Oy red 'Tuulikki' vase, designed by Tamara Aladin.

c1976   8in (20cm) high

£25-30   NPC

A Riihimaën Lasi Oy red waisted 'trumpet' vase, designed by Tamara Aladin, design number 1565, with three thick rings.

c1976   8in (20cm) high

£35-45   NPC

A Riihimaën Lasi Oy tobacco brown vase, designed by Nanny Still.

11in (28cm) high

£25-35   NPC

A Riihimaën Lasi Oy turquoise 'lantern-style' vase, designed by Tamara Aladin.

9.75in (25cm) high

£30-40   NPC

A Riihimaën Lasi Oy blue vase, designed by Tamara Aladin.

25in (63.5cm) high

£25-35   NPC

COLLECTORS' NOTES

■ Iittala was founded in Finland in 1881. As with many other Scandinavian factories, it initially produced domestic glass, such as bottles and traditional tableware. Designs became more modern with a series of competitions in the 1930s that resulted in leading designers, such as Alvar Aalto, joining.

■ Between 1947 and 1954, this escalated further, pushing Iittala to become a cutting edge glass company employing leading designers, such as Gunnel Nyman, Tapio Wirkkala, Timo Sarpaneva and Kaj Franck. Designs were often executed in clear glass and were inspired by the Scandinavian landscape, so incorporated the texture or appearance of bark and ice. These tend to be the most sought-after designs today. Look for good levels of texture and examples free of damage.

An Iittala tripod candle or taper holder, designed by Tapio Wirkkala.

2.75in (7cm) high

£15-25   **NPC**

An Iittala candle holder, possibly designed by Timo Sarpaneva.

3.5in (9cm) diam

£10-15   **NPC**

An Iittala 'Iceberg' vase, designed by Tapio Wirkkala, unusually marked with full signature and serial marks rather than unsigned or initialed "TW".

This design is typical of Wirkkala's interest in the Scandinavian environment and natural textures such as ice or bark.

6.25in (16cm) high

£60-70   **NPC**

An Iittala cushion vase, designed by Timo Sarpaneva, with label.

5in (12.5cm) high

£20-30   **NPC**

A group of three Iittala 'Festivo' candlesticks, designed by Timo Sarpaneva.

Typical of the fashion for textured glass in the 1960s, the popularity of this design endured well into the 1980s. The texture was created by pouring the hot glass into a wooden mould, which burnt each time, altering the texture. This process was initially created for the textured Finlandia range, of which Festivo was a spin-off.

c1968   Largest 7.25in (18.5cm) high

£50-70   **NPC**

An Iittala bamboo beaker.

4.75in (12cm) high

£10-15   **NPC**

An Iittala 'Savoy' clear glass vase, designed by Alvar Aalto.

6in (15cm) high

£60-80   **NPC**

COLLECTORS' NOTES

- Kosta was founded in 1742 and Boda in 1864, both in Sweden. Like most factories they began to focus on design during the 1920s and 1930s. Always overshadowed by rival Orrefors, their fortunes changed when Vicke Lindstrand joined as Art Director in 1950, from Orrefors.

- Lindstrand is known for his modern designs, from curving, organic forms to those incorporating internal threading or cut or engraved designs. Goran Warff was employed from 1964-74, and then again from 1985, and often designed sculptural forms.

- Kosta, Afors and Boda formed an alliance in 1964, becoming Kosta Boda in 1976. Since then, all pieces produced have been under this brand. Bertil Vallien joined Afors in 1964 and transformed the company. He is known for his richly coloured designs, often with mottled, matte surfaces, which are popular with collectors today. In 1990, the company merged with Orrefors to become Orrefors Kosta Boda.

A 1950s Kosta organic, near circular dish, designed by Vicke Lindstrand, with small internal bubbles and marked "Kosta".

8in (20cm) wide

£60-80   **NPC**

A Kosta bowl, designed by Ernest Gordon, with sand-blasted panels cut with deep ovals, the base incised "E. Gordon Kosta GS4014".

Ernest Gordon worked briefly at Kosta with eminent designer Vicke Lindstrand between 1953 and 1955. He then joined Afors in Sweden, where he worked as a designer until the early 1960s. He is known for his cut glass designs in the dominant, organic, often asymmetric, styles of the period as shown here.

c1954   *9.5in (24.5cm) wide*

£350-450   **PSI**

A Kosta clear glass knobbly candleholder, designed by Goran Warff.

c1970

£12-18   **NPC**

A Kosta Boda bowl, designed by Kjell Engman, mottled purple decoration with a matt translucent body, signed "KOSTA BODA 58891 K.Engman".

4in (10cm) high

£20-30   **GAZE**

A 1980s Kosta Boda pink vase, designed by Kjell Engman, with leaf motif.

7.5in (19cm) high

£30-40   **NPC**

A Boda handmade vase, designed by Bertil Vallien, the green body with applied decoration signed "BODA B.VALLIEN ATELJE277" on the base.

6.75in (17cm) high

£80-120   **GAZE**

A Kosta Boda 'Points of View' sculpture, by Bertil Vallien, etched for presentation and signed, on a black stand.

1998

£80-120   **NPC**

A pair of Kosta clear cut-glass candlesticks, one with remains of sticker, etched "Kosta 06202".

11in (28cm) high

£30-50   **GAZE**

COLLECTORS' NOTES

■ Orrefors was founded in Sweden in 1898 and initially produced bottles and tableware. It became globally renowned in the 1920s and 1930s for its engraved and innovative 'graal' and 'aerial' designs by Knut Bergvist, Simon Gate and Edward Hald.

■ From the 1930s until 1950, Vicke Lindstrand took the company forward with his engraved designs. Other notable designers include Sven Palmqvist, Nils Landberg and Ingeborg Lundin. Orrefor's reputation for innovative processes was continued with 'Kraka', 'Ravenna' and 'Fuga' ranges. In 1990, it merged with the Kosta Boda and Afors group and still produces today within the 'Royal Scandinavia' group.

An Orrefors 'Polaris' bowl.

6.25in (16cm) wide

£25-35　　　　　　　　　　　　　**NPC**

An Orrefors light blue dish, with thickly rendered, lobed design.

6.25in (16cm) wide

£25-35　　　　　　　　　　　　　**NPC**

An Orrefors small red asymmetric footed bowl, the interior with marbled effect, the foot in clear glass, the base incised "Orrefors PU3297/21".

2.75in (7cm) high

£50-80　　　　　　　　　　　　　**PSI**

An Orrefors 'Selena' bowl, designed by Sven Palmquist, with engraved decoration inspired by Uppsala Ekeby.

Orrefors are well known for their engraving, particularly that designed by Edward Hald and Simon Gate during the 1930s. Palmqvist worked at Orrefors from 1928-71 and studied under Gate.

c1950　　　　　　　　　8in (20cm) diam

£50-60　　　　　　　　　　　　　**NPC**

A Orrefors blue 'Fuga' bowl, marked "Fuga ORREFORS".

The Fuga range was manufactured with centrifugal forces, which forced the glass into the mould to form a consistently thick bowl shape. The process was developed by Sven Palmqvist during the 1940s, and introduced in 1954.

c1955　　　　　　8in (20cm) diam

£20-30　　　　　　　　　　**GAZE**

An Orrefors blue cased glass vase, designed by Sven Palmqvist, inscribed "Orrefors DW 3591/15" on the base.

c1960　　　　　9in (23cm) high

£40-60　　　　　　　　**GAZE**

A Orrefors clear cylindrical vase, with white stripe decoration and frosted base.

6.75in (17cm) high

£30-40　　　　　　　　　　　　　**NPC**

An Orrefors blue free-blown decanter, with applied clear glass foot and leaf-shaped pressed stopper, the body with extensive liming from water to the interior.

The liming reduces the value considerably. If it were not limed, it would be worth up to £50-80.

12.5in (32cm) high

£20-30　　　　　　　　　　　**GC**

A CLOSER LOOK AT AN EKENAS DISPLAY PIECE

The amber glass block has been hewn or carved and then engraved by hand with a design of three naked ladies on the front and back, creating perspective.

The rough carving has been utilized as part of the design, forming the illusion of the entrance to a cave.

It has been signed by the artist with the designer's name and a serial number probably containing a date.

The lady on the front has been engraved with the reflective base of the piece in mind, so that she appears to sit on the floor.

A unique John Orwar Lake amber glass display piece, signed on the left "J. O. LAKE EKENAS SWEDEN 508.68;710.68".

Ekenas was founded in Sweden in 1917 and closed in 1976. Little is known about the factory, although some smaller factory-made pieces have come to light. John Orwar Lake (b.1921) was their Chief Designer from 1953-76. He was joined by Michael Bang briefly during the 1960s.

1968   9in (23cm) widest

£100-200   **BY**

A Flygsfors 'Coquille' amethyst and clear glass bowl, with pulled rim.

c1963

£20-30   **NPC**

An Alsterfors red vase, designed by Per Ström.

6in (15cm) high

£15-20   **NPC**

A pair of Ekenas blue bubbled glass cylindrical vases, designed by John Orwar Lake, one with original label.

c1960   6in (15cm) high

£40-60   **GAZE**

An Alsterfors moulded, textured vase, designed by Per Ström, etched "P Ström 68" on the base.

1968   10in (25cm) high

£25-30   **GC**

A Flygsfors 'Coquille' clear cased amethyst bowl, with undulating rim.

c1963 10.5in (27cm) wide

£15-25 **NPC**

A Gullaskruf green vase, designed by Kjell Blomberg, with J. Wuidart & Co. label.

Wuidart was a London-based importer of Scandinavian glass and design. Ronald Stennett-Willson, founder of King's Lynn Glass (later Wedgwood Glass), was sales manager at Wuidart from 1951-64.

c1960 6.25in (16cm) diam

£40-60 **GROB**

A CLOSER LOOK AT A FLYGSFORS DISH

The 'Coquille' range was designed by Paul Kedelv, who worked at Flygsfors between 1949 and 1956 after working for Orrefors and, briefly, Nuutajärvi.

It is typified by freeform shapes with pulled rims, loosely inspired by seashells, as the name suggests.

Launched in 1952, it was immensely popular, selling into the 1960s in the US as well as throughout Europe.

Early colours were opaque white glass with either blue, green, red or purple glass, which was then cased in clear glass.

A Flygsfors 'Coquille' amethyst and clear asymmetrical glass bowl.

1952-c1964 6.25in (16cm) wide

£20-30 **NPC**

A Gullaskruf tall blue floor bottle, designed by Arthur Percy, with bulbous base and attenuated flaring neck.

Arthur Percy worked as a designer for Gullaskruf between 1951 and 1965.

c1960 19in (48cm) high

£80-100 **GC**

A clear globular vase, designed by Benny Motzfeldt, with bubbles and metallic oxide inclusions, acid-etched "PLUS BM NORWAY".

Benny Motzfeldt (1909-95) worked at the Norwegian Hadeland factory as part of its design team from 1955-67, as well as Ransfjord later on. After this period he set up his own glass studio to produce primarily one-off pieces. He became one of Norway's most important studio glass artists.

c1970 6in (15cm) diam

£80-120 **GROB**

A Nuutajävi Nötsjo red and green speckled vase, by Oiva Toikka, on a white ground, with engraved signature to underside.

6.5in (16.5cm) high

£180-220 **ROS**

FIND OUT MORE...

Collector's Guides: 20th Century Glass, by Judith Miller, published by DK, 2004.

20th Century Factory Glass, by Leslie Jackson, published by Mitchell Beazley, 2000.

Scandinavian Ceramics & Glass in the 20th Century, by Jennifer Opie, Victoria & Albert Museum, 1989.

COLLECTORS' NOTES

■ In 1965, the Rudolfova Hut, Hermanova Hut, Libochovice, Rosice and other glassworks were incorporated into Sklo Union, the national glass manufactory. The name 'Royal Bohemia' or 'Bohemia Glass' is often applied as these names are found on labels applied by importers and exporters.

■ All examples here are made from pressed glass. Communist Czechoslovakia developed its own unique design ethic from the 1940s onwards. Although made on a factory basis, production standards were very high and were inextricably linked with design, in line with the Industrial design movement.

■ Many highly skilled designers, such as Frantisek Vizner and Adolf Matura are now well known. However others have remained unrecognized outside Czechoslovakia, due to a continuing shortage of information, often leading to erroneous attributions.

■ Many of the modern designs were produced for very long periods, primarily from the 1950s-80s. The dates of introduction of some shapes are known, as indicated. Some shapes were designed before WWII and the moulds reused after the war, making it hard to date pieces. It is estimated that in 1965, half the moulds being used in Sklo Union factories were of pre-war origin.

■ Charity shops and collectors fairs often have examples and prices are still comparatively affordable. Due to trade sanctions and taxes a great many designs and examples did not make it to the West at all, so were sold within Communist states, where they may be more common.

■ Designers and factories, as well as dates, can only be identified from company brochures and records or trade journals, many in German or Czech. Some information may never be found. As more information is researched and published, already growing interest from collectors in this fascinating, colourful and characterful glass is sure to boom.

A Sklo Union clear glass cylindrical vase, with vertical wavy textured pattern.

9in (23cm) high

£30-40   **GC**

A Sklo Union clear glass cylindrical vase, designed by Frantisek Vizner, with clear glass moulded concave prunts or lenses, retaining original importers silver foil and black "Royal Bohemia" label.

11in (28cm) high

£50-70   **GC**

A Sklo Union clear glass cylindrical vase, produced at the Hermanova Glassworks to a design by Frantisek Peceny, with all-round moulded design in the form of a Chinese dragon's head, made from 1972.

Peceny (b.1920) began work as a designer at Hermanova in the mid-1940s after studying at the Institute of Applied Arts in Prague. As well as his industrial designs, he is renowned for his improvements to the design and related production of pressed glass.

8in (20.5cm) high

£40-60   **GC**

A Sklo Union small clear glass cylindrical vase, with moulded stylized flowers with concave centres.

6in (15.5cm) high

£10-15   **GC**

A Sklo Union clear glass square section vase, produced at the Rosice Glassworks to a design by Vladislav Urban, made from 1967.

This design was also produced in light blue and amber. It is also found in low rectangular bowls, ashtrays and candlesticks.

9.75in (25cm) high

£30-50   **GC**

A Sklo Union clear glass square section candlestick, produced at the Rosice Glassworks to a Vladislav Urban design, with moulded geometric design, made from 1967.

3in (7.5cm) high

£10-15   GC

A Sklo Union dark green vase, in an Art Deco style, designed c1925.

This is a typical example of a shape and mould being in use for decades after it was designed.

10in (25.5cm) high

£35-45   GC

A Sklo Union tapering green glass vase, designed by Vaclav Hanus, with alternating stylized leaf like design.

8in (20.5cm) high

£30-50   GC

A Sklo Union green fluted tapering cylinder vase, with flared disc rim, produced at the the Rudolfova Glassworks to a Rudolf Jurnikl design, made from 1964.

This is pattern no.13157 and can also be found in amber. Smaller candleholders can also be found, which are pattern no.13155.

8in (20cm) high

£30-35   GC

A Sklo Union green glass vase, with moulded convex teardrop shapes to the bottom half and curving 'cut out' rim.

9.75in (25cm) high

£30-50   GC

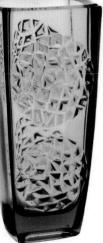

A Sklo Union tall green glass vase, made at the Rudolfova Glassworks to a Rudolf Jurnikl design, with two circular areas of moulded raised, hobnail-like designs to each side, made from 1964.

This design can be found in a number of different shapes, sizes and colours, including orange, purple and light blue. Jurnikl (b.1928) worked in glass design for nearly 30 years and arrived as a designer at Rudolfova in 1960. He became one of the most experienced pressed glass designers, winning many prizes including the gold medal at the International Exhibition of Industrial Design in 1973.

£35-55   GC

A Sklo Union yellow glass tapering cylindrical vase, with moulded hobnail-like, pyramidal prunts.

8in (20.5cm) high

£20-30   GC

A Sklo Union amber glass, square section vase, with high relief-moulded geometric pattern.

7in (17.5cm) high

£30-50   MHC

A Sklo Union graduated red, amber and yellow glass vase, with bulbous body and linear pattern.

6.25in (16cm) high

£35-55   **GC**

A CLOSER LOOK AT A SKLO UNION VASE

This vase was designed in 1940 by Rudolf Schrötter for the Rudolfova Glassworks based in Teplice, Czechoslovakia.

This design was produced in great numbers from the 1940s into the 1970s, meaning examples can be found comparatively easily today – always look for those in perfect condition.

The machine-cut base with a 'bird bath' like depression is typical of the pressed glass produced by these factories at this time.

It can be found in a variety of jewel-like colours including green and amber. The oval 'lenses' give an interesting optical effect.

A 1940s-70s Sklo Union bullet-shaped glass vase, with moulded oval shapes to each of the four sides.

7.75in (19.5cm) high

£15-25   **GC**

A Sklo Union ashtray, produced at the Rudolfova Glassworks to a Rudolf Jurnikl design, with circular area of moulded raised, hobnail-like design on the underside, made from 1964.

6in (15cm) wide

£10-20   **GC**

A Sklo Union blue glass, tapered vase, with geometric diamond-shaped moulded patterns changing to fan shapes near the rim.

This is a pre-WWII shape that remained in production for over 40 years.

16in (5cm) high

£25-35   **GC**

A Sklo Union light blue glass vase, shape number 13227/13, produced at the Rudolfova Glassworks to a Rudolf Jurnikl design, with a circular area of moulded raised, hobnail-like design to each side, made from 1964.

7in (17.5cm) high

£30-40   **GC**

A Sklo Union lilac glass vase, with stepped, 'festooned' moulded pattern.

This is another pre-WWII shape that remained in production for over 40 years.

8in (20cm) high

£25-35   **GC**

COLLECTORS' NOTES

- The contemporary glass movement for spheres and orbs developed in the late 20th century from the creation of art glass marbles and paperweights by contemporary glass artists, mainly in the US. From functional objects has sprung a new, exciting and dynamic art glass movement. Spheres tend to be larger than marbles, with the tag 'orb' being reserved for the largest examples.

- The designs are not painted on the interior or exterior of the sphere, but are contained within the sphere, being carefully hand-worked in hot, coloured glass and most often in more than one layer. The glass designs are then encased in a top layer of clear borosilicate 'crystal' glass.

- Spheres really need to be handled and viewed in person, as this is the best way to appreciate the intricate detail within and myriad reflections and magnifications caused by the curving surface. The skill involved in their creation shows how far the studio glass movement has progressed since the late 1960s.

- Names to look out for include Paul Stankard, Jesse Taj, David Salazar, Dinah Hulet, Rolf & Genie Wald and Josh Simpson. New artists come to the field every year, each bringing their own style and skill, making this a vibrant and ever-changing market. Prices are currently comparatively affordable for such detailed, unique works.

- Watch out for new young makers, examining their work and comparing it to established names. Many artists make their own murrines, which are also known as 'milli', 'millefiori' or 'murrini'. Some artists such as Jesse Taj and David Strobel sell their murrines for others to incorporate into their own designs.

- As well as established marble collectors, a new younger audience has been attracted to the market. Images from cartoons and popular and sub-cultures are often included, making this art form highly relevant to today. Spheres are intricate, easy to display and offer great variety. Values should increase as the market grows.

A Jerry Kelly sphere, with rake-pull patterns around circular set-ups of individual murrines also made by Kelly, signed "JK05".

2005   *1.5in (4cm) diam*

£40-60   **BGL**

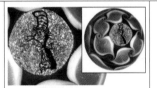

A Jerry Kelly 'Cat In The Hat' sphere, with rake pull forms around a central internal foil decal of Dr Seuss' 'Cat in The Hat', signed "JK2005".

'Rake pull' designs are created by dragging the molten glass into a shaped and swirling pattern with a tool.

2005   *1.5in (4cm) diam*

£60-80   **BGL**

A Rajesh Kommiene 'Reverse Rake' sphere, with layer of rake pulled blue quatrefoils, signed "RK 04".

2004   *2in (5cm) diam*

£70-100   **BGL**

A Rajesh Kommiene sphere, with internal iridescent swirl core and rake pulled upper layer in a band and floral motifs.

2004   *2in (5cm) diam*

£80-120   **BGL**

A Jerry Kelly 'Bob Marley' sphere, the 'front' with swirls around an internal printed foil decal of Bob Marley, the 'back' with rake pulls surrounding a murrine of a Rastafarian lion with flag.

Kelly has been involved with lamp working since 1993 and is renowned for his attention to detail and is attracted by the variety and challenge offered by marble making.

2.5in (6.5cm) diam

£80-120   **BGL**

A prototype David Salazar 'Irises' sphere, signed "DP Salazar".

This unique piece was used to practice the iris pattern before execution on the larger 'Night Sky' piece also shown on this page. Salazar's white ground marbles and spheres are very rare.

2004   1.75in (4.5cm) diam

£150-250   **BGL**

A John Kobuki 'Flower' sphere, signed in kanji.

Kobuki began working in glass in the mid-1990s. His style is typified by floral or seabed designs encased in clear glass that magnifies the internal design in a similar way to a paperweight.

2005   2in (5cm) diam

£30-40   **BGL**

A rare David Salazar experimental 'Irises Over Night Sky', signed "DPSG 6103 1-X".

This combination of a core of blue and yellow swirls and an outer layer of irises was inspired by two of Vincent Van Gogh's most famous paintings. Salazar has been involved in hot glass for over 26 years, and worked as an apprentice at the legendary Lundberg Studios in California in 1972. His love of nature and marine life is apparent in all his works.

3.5in (9cm) diam

£550-650   **BGL**

A Christopher Rice 'Butterfly with Flower' sphere, with rake pull back, signed "CYK".

Also known as 'Pan', Rice began working in glass in 1999 and works with pinwheel, vortex and natural motifs.

2005   2.25in (5.5cm) diam

£100-150   **BGL**

A Christopher Rice 'Butterfly' sphere, signed "C Rice 05".

2005   1.5in (4cm) diam

£15-25   **BGL**

A Steve Hitt 'Cedar Trees' sphere, containing butterfly and flower murrines made by Hitt over a layer of cedar trees and a layer of the sky and moon, signed "SH 03".

2003   2in (5cm) diam

£70-100   **BGL**

A large Cathy Richardson Aquarium sphere, signed "Richardson 2002".

Richardson (b.1949) attended Pilchuck Glass School in 1991 and worked at the Corning Glass Studio from 1996-2000.

2002

£200-300   **BGL**

A Christopher Rice 'Frog' sphere, with applied lampwork frog over a sphere with concave swirling interior.

2005

1.5in (4cm) diam

£20-30   **BGL**

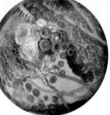

A CLOSER LOOK AT A PAUL STANKARD ORB

Stankard is the world's leading paperweight artist – his work is sold by top galleries. It can be found in over 20 public collections including the Metropolitan Museum of Art and The Corning Museum of Glass in New York, the Victoria & Albert Museum, London and the Museum of American Glass, New Jersey.

He is inspired by his love of nature and botany – each individual component is made from glass worked with a hot torch, with the artist concentrating on correct colour, form and detail.

The glass assemblage is then encased in a layer of clear glass, which magnifies certain areas as it is viewed and gives the impression of a moment of living nature trapped in time and glass.

As well as an intricate and accurate visual appearance, Stankard's work considers deeper mystical and poetic themes of the progress of life and nature, involving seeds, flowers, fertility, root systems and decay.

A limited edition Paul Stankard large glass orb, one-of-one from the Whitman Botanial series, with internal cased lampwork design of a honeycomb, two bees, moss, flowers and lilies.

Stankard (b.1943) began working with glass around 1961. In 1969 he focused on paperweights, after initially making lampworked animals. During the 1970s, his floral and botanical subject weights, inspired by 19thC French works and friend Francis Whittemore, met with great success. In 1982, he began making a series of botanical obelisks, known as 'Botanicals'. Orbs and spheres are a comparatively new area, only begun in the last few years.

2004   4.25in (11cm) diam

£4,000-5,000   **BGL**

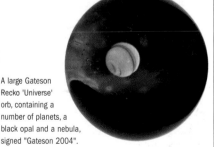

A large Gateson Recko 'Universe' orb, containing a number of planets, a black opal and a nebula, signed "Gateson 2004".

This is the largest 'Universe' orb made to date, taking many days to create. The incredible internal 'space' effect can only be properly appreciated by handling the orb and viewing it from different angles.

2004   3.5in (9cm) diam

£700-800   **BGL**

A limited edition Josh Simpson 'Planet' sphere, together with a selection of the murrines used, signed "Simpson AP14 2003".

Renowned glass artist Simpson is well known for his fantastical 'Inhabited' planet paperweights, as well as other blue glassworks depicting the Mexican night sky.

2003   2.75in (7cm) diam

£120-180   **BGL**

GLASS

A Dustin Morell 'Vortex' sphere, with rake pull reverse design, signed "DKM 2004".

Complex to make, vortex spheres give the impression that the very centre of the internal concave vortex is deeper than the corresponding outside surface of the sphere itself.

2004   2.25in (5.5cm) diam

£60-80   **BGL**

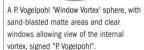

A Dustin Morell 'Vortex' sphere, the reverse with randomly shaped coloured design, signed "DKM 2004".

2004   2.25in (5.5cm) diam

£50-60   **BGL**

A P. Vogelpohl 'Window Vortex' sphere, with sand-blasted matte areas and clear windows allowing view of the internal vortex, signed "P. Vogelpohl".

2.25in (5.5cm) diam

£70-100   **BGL**

A David Strobel 'Murrini' double-sided sphere, the front with a flat field of orange and yellow stars under a clear dome, the reverse with hemispherical field of many complex murrines, including flying skulls, celtic crosses, jellyfish, Egyptian eyes and a rainbow and clouds over mushrooms, signed "DS04".

Strobel began working in glass in 1991 and has become well known for his complex murrine designs, begun in 1998.

2.25in (6cm) diam

£80-120   **BGL**

A Douglas Sweet 'Fantasy Orb', with sand-blasted areas and clear circular panels showing a set-up of millefiori rods, signed "Sweet".

2005   2in (5cm) diam

£40-60   **BGL**

A Dinah Hulet 'Embellished' lampworked sphere.

Hulet has worked with glass for over 30 years and is one of the best known established studio glass artists working with mosaic glass and spheres.

2005   2in (5cm) diam

£100-150   **BGL**

A Mark Matthews 'Windmill Variations' graal sphere, from a series of black and white spheres with various geometric designs, signed to the base "Matthews 2002".

2002   2.75in (7cm) diam

£700-1,000   **BGL**

FIND OUT MORE...

Contemporary Marbles & Related Art Glass, by Mark Block, *published by Schiffer Book, 2001.*

The Encyclopedia of Modern Marbles, Spheres, and Orbs, by *Mark Block, published by Schiffer Books, 2005.*

A limited edition Wendy Besett 'Stillness Night' orb, signed "W Besett C 03 2/4".

2003

2.5in (6.5cm) diam

£150-200   **BGL**

COLLECTORS' NOTES

- Whitefriars was founded in central London in the 17th century. It was acquired by James Powell in 1834 and was known as 'Powell & Sons' until 1962 when its name reverted back to Whitefriars. In 1923 the factory moved to Wealdstone, Middlesex.

- Famous for its ecclesiastical stained glass, which provided invaluable experience when making coloured decorative glassware, the factory saw peaks in popularity from 1910s-30s and from the 1950s-70s. The factory closed in 1980 due to financial problems caused by a harsh economic climate.

- Today, most collectors focus on post-WWII ranges and it is for these pieces that values have risen sharply over the past decade. The key designer during this period is Geoffrey Baxter, who joined in 1954 and remained with the company until its closure in 1980.

- Whitefriars both moved with, and reflected the fashions and styles of, the times. Shapes varied from organic, asymmetric and flowing styles to the simple, clean-lined and modern style of the 1950s and 60s. The clarity and form of the glass was often more important than surface decoration. For both styles, Scandinavian glass of the period was a strong influence.

- 1967 saw the arrival of Baxter's innovative 'Textured' range, which is perhaps the most popular amongst today's collectors. Moulds with internal protrusions were used to make textured glass, often in outlandish and avant-garde shapes in the bright, psychedelic colours of the day.

- Consider the form as certain shapes are rarer or more desirable than others. Colour counts towards value considerably. The 'TV' vase is common in tangerine, but rarer in aubergine. Meadow green tends to be a comparatively scarce colour, especially in the sought-after 'Banjo' vase.

- Larger pieces are generally more valuable than smaller pieces. For textured pieces, avoid low levels of texture variation indicating a worn mould, or flattened areas that indicate polished-away damage – both reduce value.

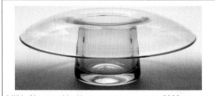

A Whitefriars sapphire blue posy vase, pattern no.8993.

c1945   6.25in (16cm) diam

£10-15   **NPC**

A Whitefriars sapphire blue vase, from the Wealdstone range.

5.5in (14cm) high

£50-60   **RETC**

A Whitefriars amber pillow-shaped lobed vase, pattern no.9376, designed by James Hogan.

This is typical of Hogan's designs, which tended to be influenced by Scandinavian designs, with their organic lobed forms rendered in thick glass.

c1940   8.25in (21cm) high

£70-90   **GROB**

A Whitefriars ruby red Ribbon Ware footed fruit dish, pattern no.8901, designed by Barnaby Powell.

Look out for examples with the trailing and bowl in two different colours as these are rarer and more valuable.

c1950   8in (20cm) diam

£70-80   **GROB**

A Whitefriars/ Powell & Sons amber decanter, possibly designed by Harry Powell.

c1930   10in (25cm) high

£60-80   **GC**

A Whitefriars kingfisher blue jug.

With the six matching beakers, this could be worth £85-90.

9in (23cm) high

£30-40   **NPC**

GLASS

A Whitefriars arctic blue tapering vase, pattern no.9495, designed by Geoffrey Baxter.

This was one of Baxter's first designs for Whitefriars.

c1957   8in (20cm) high

£40-60   **RETC**

A very rare Whitefriars 'Lichen' cased vase, designed by Geoffrey Baxter.

This colour combination is very rare, using the colour pewter streaked with green.

c1974   6.75in (17cm) high

£200-250   **GC**

A CLOSER LOOK AT A WHITEFRIARS VASE

Rather than a single colour, as is usual, this vase has a pinky-orange cased glass base and a blue glass main body.

Surviving examples are extremely rare with only a handful known to collectors. A similar single colour vase would be worth under £100.

Although this vase is darker and the colours less delineated than other known examples, it is larger.

The combination of colours was incompatible, leading to examples breaking down in the furnace.

A very rare Whitefriars 'Evening Sky' tapered vase, designed by Geoffrey Baxter.

c1957   10.25in (26cm) high

£700-900   **GC**

A Whitefriars green and clear cased vase.

c1965   7.25in (18.5cm) high

£30-40   **MHT**

A Whitefriars kingfisher blue 'Lips' or 'Beak' vase, pattern no.9556 designed by Geoffrey Baxter.

Again, note the similarity of this design to the work of Per Lütken for Holmegaard, specifically his organic and flowing 'Beak' vase from c1954.

c1960   7.75in (19.5cm) high

£20-30   **RETC**

A Whitefriars kingfisher blue and clear cased ribbed 'Eight Way' bud vase, designed by Geoffrey Baxter.

c1969   8.5in (21cm) high

£35-40   **GC**

A Whitefriars green and clear cased vase.

c1967   6.75in (17cm) wide

£30-40   **RETC**

A Whitefriars blue cased trefoil dish, with moulded foot, pattern no.9516, designed by Geoffrey Baxter.

A Whitefriars sapphire blue ashtray, with controlled internal bubbles, pattern no.9099.

c1960   5in (12.5cm) diam

£10-15   **RETC**

A Whitefriars sea green vase, with lobed base and internal large bubbles, pattern no.9286, designed by William Wilson.

c1952   7.5in (19cm) high

£40-50   **MHT**

A Whitefriars brown streaked Knobbly vase, pattern no.9844, designed by William Wilson and Harry Dyer.

c1964   5in (13cm) high

£30-40   **RETC**

A Whitefriars flint and green streaked Knobbly vase, pattern no.9842, designed by William Wilson and Harry Dyer.

c1964   7in (17.5cm) high

£70-100   **ROS**

A Whitefriars amethyst vase from the 'Blown Soda' range, designed by Geoffrey Baxter.

c1963 7in (18cm) high

£70-90   **RETC**

A Whitefriars indigo vase from the 'Blown Soda' range, designed by Geoffrey Baxter.

This is a rare large size. Note the similarities to Ronald Stennett-Willson's floor vases for King's Lynn, however the size is smaller, the glass is thinner and the colours are different.

c1963   8in (20cm) high

£120-160   **GC**

A Whitefriars midnight grey tapered vase from the 'Blown Soda' range, pattern no.9553, designed by Geoffrey Baxter.

c1965   4.5in (11.5cm)

£15-25   **NPC**

A Whitefriars ruby red barrel vase from the 'Blown Soda' range, pattern no.9596, designed by Geoffrey Baxter.

c1963   9.5in (24cm) high

£40-50   **GC**

A Whitefriars ruby red vase from the 'Blown Soda' range, pattern no.9607, designed by Geoffrey Baxter.

c1963   7.5in (19cm) high

£10-15   **RETC**

A Whitefriars large tangerine bark log vase, pattern no. 9691, designed by Geoffrey Baxter.

c1969   *9in (23cm) high*

£60-80   **TCS**

A Whitefriars large ruby red bark log vase, pattern no. 9691, designed by Geoffrey Baxter.

c1967   *9in (23cm) high*

£60-80   **TCS**

A Whitefriars medium-sized cinnamon brown bark log vase, pattern no. 9690, designed by Geoffrey Baxter.

c1967   *7in (18cm) high*

£20-30   **TCS**

A Whitefriars large willow brown bark log vase, pattern no.9691 designed by Geoffrey Baxter.

c1967   *9in (23cm) high*

£60-80   **TCS**

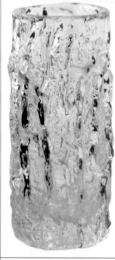

A Whitefriars large flint grey bark log vase, pattern no. 9691, designed by Geoffrey Baxter.

This is a scarce colourway. Look out for the largest cylinder bark-textured vases, with tapered bases, as these are very rare, having been produced for only three months around 1969.

c1967   *9in (23cm) high*

£70-100   **TCS**

A Whitefriars 'Glacier' bark-textured lead crystal decanter, pattern number M145, designed by Geoffrey Baxter, with original circular textured stopper.

c1972   *13in (33cm) high*

£50-70   **GC**

A set of six Whitefriars 'Glacier' bark-textured lead crystal whisky tumblers, in original box, pattern no.M31, designed by Geoffrey Baxter.

c1969   *Box 11.5in (29cm) wide*

£50-80   **WW**

A Whitefriars indigo textured 'Cucumber' vase, pattern no.9679, designed by Geoffrey Baxter, with Whitefriars paper label.

c1967

11.5in (29cm) high

£150-200   **WW**

A Whitefriars kingfisher blue 'Coffin' vase, pattern no.9686, designed by Geoffrey Baxter.

c1967   5in (13cm) high

£60-70   **NPC**

A CLOSER LOOK AT A WHITEFRIARS VASE

Along with the Banjo vase, this is one of Baxter's most characteristic designs.

Kingfisher blue is an unusual and more desirable colour than others such as tangerine, for example.

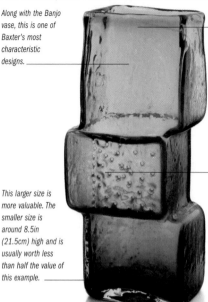

This larger size is more valuable. The smaller size is around 8.5in (21.5cm) high and is usually worth less than half the value of this example.

The level of texture is very good – less textured pieces are less desirable.

A Whitefriars ruby red 'Coffin' vase, pattern no.9686, designed by Geoffrey Baxter.

c1967   5.5in (13.5cm) high

£60-70   **NPC**

A Whitefriars kingfisher blue 'Drunken Bricklayer' vase, pattern no.9672, designed by Geoffrey Baxter.

This shows Baxter's interest in the landscape around him for inspiration. Here manmade objects such as piled bricks inspired him over more natural textures and forms.

c1967   13.25in (33.5cm) high

£800-1,200   **WW**

A Whitefriars willow 'Drunken Bricklayer' vase, pattern no.9673, designed by Geoffrey Baxter.

c1967   13in (33cm) high

£200-300   **WW**

A Whitefriars willow 'TV' or 'Concentric Circles' vase, pattern no.9677, designed by Geoffrey Baxter.

c1969   7in (18cm) high

£150-200   **WW**

A Whitefriars indigo textured 'Mobile Phone' vase, pattern no.9679 designed by Geoffrey Baxter.

c1965   10in (25.5cm) high

£300-400   **ROS**

FIND OUT MORE...

Whitefriars Glass, *by Lesley Jackson, published by Richard Dennis, 1996.*

Whitefriars Glass website – *www.whitefriars.org*

A Brierley clear glass urn-shaped display vase, designed by Constance Spry, with thickly rendered twisted decoration.

Constance Spry (1886-1960) was a noted and innovative florist, who also wrote about and taught floristry. She encouraged people to create arrangements with foliage and flowers from hedgerows and wastelands as well as from tended gardens. She also designed a range of ceramic and glass holders for her arrangements.

c1960   7.5in (19cm) high

£80-90   **GC**

A Brierley clear glass solifleur or candlestick, designed by Constance Spry, with acid-etched "Brierley Constance Spry" mark to base and broken pontil.

10.5in (26.5cm) high

£70-90   **GC**

A German Op Art lead crystal vase, by Ichendorf Bleikristall, with maker's silver sticker.

6.5in (16.5cm) high

£40-50   **FD**

A Jones & Co. green glass vase, with a bark texture finish.

This is often mistaken for Whitefriars, but was actually produced by Jones & Co. of Birmingham and manufactured in Sweden. The glass is thinner and Whitefriars did not produce this pattern or this shape.

c1969   8in (20cm) high

£15-20   **NPC**

A Joseph Lucas polished metal and green glass centrepiece, with cast marks.

12.5in (32cm) diam

£450-550   **WW**

A Sherdley 'Festival' pattern Conical tumbler, the pattern designed by Alexander Hardie Williamson.

c1959   4.75in (12cm) high

£4-5   **EWC**

A Val St Lambert square green and clear dish, designed by Leon Ledru, with diagonal polished away green casing, etched "L.L."

4.25in (11cm) wide

£100-150   **RETC**

A yellow Walsh Walsh 'Pompeian' baluster glass vase.

Recognisable by its many internal bubbles and shapes, the Pompeian range was released in 1929 in a number of colours. Look out for pink and amethyst, as these are scarcer.

c1930   9.5in (24cm) high

£120-140   **GC**

A Walsh Walsh Venetian revival dessert dish and plate, or comport and dish.

The light bubbles and iridescence were intended to look like ancient, Roman glass. This was the polar opposite of the modern glass designed by Clyne Farquharson at the same time, showing Walsh Walsh's range.

c1935

£70-100   RETC

A German Walther clear and green glass stem vase, with label.

6.5in (16.5cm) high

£12-18   GAZE

A Webb clear glass vase, decorated with moulded rounded prunts and "Webb England" acid stamp to base.

6.75in (17cm) high

£15-25   GAZE

A WMF (Württembergische Metallwarenfabrik) Ikora glass bowl.
c1930   9.25in (23cm) diam

£150-200   VZ

A heavy green art glass jug, with iridescent finish.

7.25in (18.5cm) high

£50-70   GAZE

A 1960s vaseline glass solifleur vase, possibly from Murano.

8.75in (22cm) high

£25-35   GROB

An Italian-style glass fish ornament.
12.5in (32cm) long

£8-12   GAZE

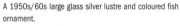

A large coloured glass fish ornament.
20.5in (52cm) long

£6-8   GAZE

A 1950s/60s large glass silver lustre and coloured fish ornament.

These commonly seen Italian fish underwent a revival in fashion some years ago. This now appears to have been a temporary re-appreciation. Silver lustre examples are rarer than the shoals of the more common coloured blotchy examples. Look for larger examples and unusual poses or colours as these remain the most desirable.

21.5in (55cm) long

£35-45   GAZE

COLLECTORS' NOTES

- Holiday memorabilia continues to be popular on both sides of the Atlantic, with Hallowe'en and Christmas examples the most commonly sought after.

- German pieces, dating from before WWII, are usually the earliest and most desirable and, as such, command the highest prices.

- America also started producing its own examples in the 1920s with production carrying through to today. Pieces from the 1950s and later are typically plastic.

- Many of the early pieces were made of easily damaged materials such as pulped cardboard or lithographed tin, so condition has a great effect on value.

- Celluloid memorabilia started to appear from Japan in the 1930s and became an increasingly prolific producer.

- As earlier pieces become less accessible to new collectors, later, plastic examples from the 1960s onwards are becoming more sought-after and prices are starting to rise.

- Look for Halloween jack-o-lanterns, particularly double-sided or two-tone versions, as well as black cats and witches.

- Santa Claus is the most commonly found Christmas character, following by Christmas trees, snowmen and snowbabies.

A 1920s German Hallowe'en 'Betty Boop'-style pumpkin hanging display piece, of moulded and painted card.

The Betty Boop style character face is very rare.

9.75in (25cm) high

£40-60   HH

A 1920s German Hallowe'en black memorabilia pumpkin, of moulded and painted card.

This subject matter is very rare and unusual, and appeals to black memorabilia collectors as well as Hallowe'en collectors.

10.25in (26cm) high

£150-200   HH

A 1930s Hallowe'en articulated creeping cat hanging display piece, of printed die-cut card.

13.5in (34cm) long

£20-25   HH

A 1920s German painted and moulded card Hallowe'en hanging display plaque of a witch on a broomstick.

13in (33cm) wide

£40-60   HH

An American Hallowe'en printed and cut card hanging display piece of a witch with devilish pumpkin, by Dennison.

Very few of these were made, making this piece rare.

20.5in (52cm) high

£15-25   HH

A German 'Happy Hallowe'en' colour printed card table top decoration of a girl making a potion, some water stains.

4.75in (12cm) high

£15-25   HH

A German 'Happy Hallowe'en' printed card table top decoration of a girl with an owl and a cat.

4.75in (12cm) high

£25-35   HH

A 1930s/40s American Hallowe'en printed and die-cut card articulated skeleton, by H.E. Lehr.

22.75in (58cm) high

£15-25   HH

A 1950s/60s Hallowe'en plastic lamp, of a witch holding a pumpkin.

These lamps have become popular, with demand and thus prices rising over the past two years.

14.5in (37cm) high

£10-20   **HH**

A 1950s/60s Hallowe'en plastic lamp, of a pumpkin emanating from a frying pan.

9in (23cm) high

£10-20   **HH**

A 1920s German Hallowe'en papier-mâché jack-o-lantern.

The airbrushed highlights, colour and smiling face are scarce and desirable, hence its higher price. It also retains its original paper insert.

5in (12.50cm) high

£400-600   **JDJ**

A 1920s German papier-mâché jack-o-lantern, with original printed paper insert.

This shape with a hat is very rare, as is the larger size.

6in (15cm) high

£150-200   **HH**

An American printed tinplate candy holder, with whistle/noisemaker nose, by the US Metal Toy Co.

3.75in (9.5cm) high

£15-25   **HH**

A 1960s black and orange plastic pumpkin lolly holder.

3in (7.5cm) high

£28-32   **HH**

A 1940s/50s Japanese Hallowe'en finger-operated concertina toy, of wood and printed card, back of card printed "JAPAN".

Card 4.25in (11cm) high

£25-35   **HH**

A complete American printed canvas 'Witch Party' game, by The Saalfield Publishing Co. of Akron, Ohio.

The aim of the game, a variation of 'pin the tail on the donkey', is to pin small cut-out canvas pumpkins on the white space while blindfolded!

c1913   17in (43cm) wide

£60-80   **HH**

A 1950s RCA Victor Walt Disney Production 'Trick or Treat' storybook, and two 78rpm records.

7.5in (19cm) high

£8-16   **HH**

A sitting Santa Claus candy container, with papier-mâché face, red crêpe paper coat, cotton batting beard, hair and other trim, blue crêpe paper hands, and black crêpe paper boots, some dustiness.

18in (45.50cm) high

£650-750 | **JDJ**

A CLOSER LOOK AT A SANTA

Schoenhut, founded in Philadelphia in 1872 and closed by 1935, is a sought-after American maker.

It is very large in size at 11in (28cm) high and is in excellent condition with only a little in-painting.

It is known for its wooden and composition toys, which are well made – other roly-ploy figures are also known.

It is very early in date for Christmas memorabilia produced in the US, most was produced in Germany at this time.

An early Schoenhut Santa Claus composition roly-poly, retaining partial label on base. c1920

11in (28cm) high

£800-1,000 | **JDJ**

A 1920s/30s card, felt and material Santa Claus figure.

9in (23cm) high

£70-100 | **HH**

A German Santa Claus hollow bisque figure, with lantern, marked "Germany".

This shape is extremely rare and is not listed in any of the Santa and Snowbaby reference books.

3in (7.5cm) high

£40-50 | **HH**

An American Santa Claus-on-skis die-cast metal figure, marked "Made in USA".

£25-35 | **BH**

An 1940s/50s American 'King Santa' plastic lamp and money bank, by Harett Gilmar of New York, with coin slot in back of shoulders, in mint condition.

7in (18cm) high

£20-30 | **HH**

A 1940s/50s West German large flock-covered Santa Claus, with bobbing head, faux fur beard and interior printed with a design of flowers and marked "Container made in West Germany".

13.5in (34cm) high

£50-60 | **HH**

A 1950s West German Santa Claus candy holder, the card-bodied figure with bobble head and rare gold glitter decoration.

9in (23cm) high

£40-50 | **HH**

A 1920s German Santa Claus moulded, printed and embossed card standee, with silver glitter details.

9.75in (25cm) high

£35-45 HH

A 1920s German papier-mâché snowman decoration.

7in (18cm) high

£20-30 HH

A 1950s snowman white plastic lamp, with green Christmas tree.

The Christmas tree is often missing or broken, and values are greatly reduced, making complete examples rare.

7.5in (19cm) high

£30-40 HH

A 1950s/60s snowman white plastic candy holder, with removable pipe.

Look out for the rare orange Hallowe'en variation, shown on page 357 of the 'DK Collectibles Price Guide 2005' by Judith Miller with Mark Hill, which can fetch up to £50.

2004 5.25in (13.5cm) high

£10-15 HH

A 1950s/60s snowman lolly holder, in blue, red and white plastic, on silver plastic skis.

5.5in (14cm) high

£20-30 HH

A 1960s American friction-driven push-along snowman on a pumpkin, by Fun World Inc.

£20-25 HH

A 'Hi-Ho Santa' pull-along toy-on-wheels, of red, green and tan plastic.

This combination of colours is hard to find.

9.75in (25cm) high

£60-90 HH

A 1950s Santa on cart plastic candy container, with no damage.

9.5in (24cm) long

£35-45 HH

A 1950s Christmas clown and drum, of yellow red and green plastic.

This is a rare shape, with a detailed form and moving wheels. It is rarest in Hallowe'en colouring such as orange, with examples in similar condition fetching up to £280.

8in (20cm) high

£100-150 HH

A 1950s small plastic nativity scene.

A 'Christmas Cat' painted bisque cake decoration, the double bass with gold glitter.

1.75in (4.5cm) high

£8-12 LG

A rare pair of 1930s hand-made skiers, with plaster heads, woven wool bodies, metal skis and wooden poles with paper discs.

5.5in (14cm) high

£70-90 HH

These decorations are growing in popularity. This example has palm trees, which is a desirable feature.

7in (18cm) wide

£6-8 HH

A 1950s plastic nativity scene, with silver glitter highlights, in mint condition with original box and price.

5.5in (14cm) high

£8-12 HH

A late 20thC Christmas musical display, of angels in front of an altar, made in Hong Kong.

This example is desirable as it has a musical movement.

4.75in (12cm) wide

£5-7 HH

A 1950s Japanese Christmas bell, with foil and plaster over a card base and moulded papier-mâché Santa and embossed card candle and holly decal to reverse, stamped "Made in Japan".

3.75in (9.5cm) high

£20-40 HH

A 1950s/60s Christmas tree, with plastic fronds over paper-coverd wire.

This resembles the first artificial Christmas trees, made in Germany in the 1880s, of painted goose feathers on wire branches.

11.75in (30cm) high

£10-15 HH

A 1950s plastic Christmas tree, with faux snow, glass baubles and wooden base.

13.5in (34cm) high

£20-30 HH

A set of four 1950s Japanese Relco Creation Christmas candleholders, with climbing Santas, in original box, each printed "Made in Japan".

Candleholder 3.25in (8cm) high

£10-20 HH

COLLECTORS' NOTES

■ After its 'accidental' discovery in 1913, stainless steel was first promoted for wider domestic use at the 1934 'Ideal Home Exhibition' by J.&J. Wiggin Ltd, under the name 'Olde Hall'. In 1928 William Wiggin made a toast rack, which is said to be the world's first item of stainless steel tableware, followed by a teapot in 1930. Some pre-WWII designs were by Harold Stabler, but they were expensive to manufacture and were not continued when production resumed after the war.

■ In 1955, the company appointed Robert Welch as consultant designer and the company's modern and durable products really began to take off, as did British metalware design. During the 1960s and 70s, it was one of the most popular wedding presents and was sold all over the world.

■ Values vary depending on range and date, with early, pre-WWII items and Welch's designs tending to be the most sought-after. Look at the base as marks can help date a piece. 'Olde Hall' was used from 1928-59, when the 'e' in 'Olde' was dropped. 'Ye Olde Hall' marks are very rare, being used in 1934 and 1935 only. 'Old Hall' was used from 1959 until 1984, when the company closed due to competition from Far Eastern imports.

■ Pieces can still be found in charity shops, car boot sales and general auctions as the market is comparatively new. As so many examples exist, avoid buying examples with scratches, dents or missing parts. Always consider the design and form above all and learn how to recognise scarce pieces by joining a club (see page 352). Other makers include Viners, (whom Gerald Benney designed for) although these are not as popular as Old Hall, which attracts a thriving and growing band of collectors.

An Olde Hall stainless steel one-pint 'Cottage' hot water jug, with 'Staycool' handle, and registered design number 828398 for 1938.

1938-59   6in (15cm) high

£30-40   **GC**

An Olde Hall spherical stainless steel one and a half-pint 'Cottage' teapot, with 'Staycool' handle, and registered design number 828398 for 1938.

1938-59   5in (13cm) high

£30-40   **GC**

A Firth Staybrite Ye Olde Hall Quality one and a quarter-pint plain 'Warwick' hot water jug.

All marks containing 'Staybrite' of 'Firth Staybrite' are pre-war.

c1935   5.75in (14.5cm) high

£30-40   **GC**

A 1960s Old Hall stainless steel two-pint 'Connaught' teapot, registered design number 879702 for 1956.

4.5in (11.5cm) high

£15-20   **GC**

A 1970s Old Hall stainless steel one and three-quarter pint 'Savoy' hot water jug, registered design number 928745 for 1966.

6.5in (16.5cm) high

£10-15   **GC**

A 1960s Old Hall one pint 'Campden' coffee set, designed by Robert Welch, with wooden handles and finials.

Designed in 1957, these were used together, one being for coffee, the other for hot milk. Look out for the low sugar bowl, made from the same tooling as the pot, but simply 'cut down'.

7in (18cm) high

£50-60   **FD**

KITCHENALIA & DOMESTIC

A 1970s Old Hall stainless steel half-pint sauceboat, designed by Robert Welch.

A matching tray was also available.

9in (22.5cm) long

£8-12 **GROB**

A 1960s Old Hall stainless steel half-pint tankard, with foot.

4in (10cm) high

£15-20 **GROB**

A CLOSER LOOK AT AN OLD HALL TEA SET

This set was designed in 1964 by Robert Welch, who was employed as consultant designer from 1955, and won a Design Award in 1965.

The spouts are integral with the body, and were moulded using the 'lost wax' casting technique, giving a smooth finish all round.

The modern, clean-lined Alveston range is the most collectable and desirable range produced by Old Hall.

The one and three-quarter-pint hot water jug is harder to find than the teapot as fewer were made.

An Old Hall stainless steel one and three-quarter-pint 'Alveston' tea set, comprising tea pot, hot water jug, milk jug and sugar bowl.

c1962

£200-300 **ADE**

A 1960s Old Hall stainless steel ice bucket and tongs, designed by Robert Welch.

5in (13cm) high

£20-30 **GAZE**

A pair of 1960s Viners stainless steel salt and pepper shakers.

4in (10cm) high

£18-22 **GROB**

A pair of 1970s Old Hall candle holders, with Whitefriars 'Ruby' blown Soda range shades designed by Geoffrey Baxter.

8.25in (21cm) high

£15-25 **GROB**

A 1950s Olde Hall lidded honey pot, with sliding lid attached to hinged handle and registered number 627169 for 1949.

3.5in (9cm) diam

£15-20 **GC**

A set of six 1960s Viners stainless steel 'Studio' pattern grapefruit spoons, designed by Gerald Benney, in original box.

10in (25.5cm) long

£70-90 **GC**

FIND OUT MORE...

The Old Hall Club – www.oldhallclub.co.uk.

A Catalogue for the Collector, by Michael Bennett, published by The Old Hall Club, available via the above website.

A Gaydon Melmex blue mug, by British Industrial Plastics.

British Industrial Plastics Ltd established a design research department in 1952, to encourage the use of robust, cost-efficient plastics such as melamine in table- and dinnerware. They produced designs for a number of companies' ranges including Gaydon's Melmex and Ranton's Melaware. Melamine takes dyes very well and ranges were produced in many colours. Wares in pastel colours are usually from the 1950s, brighter examples are later. Prices are still affordable but are rising. Despite being marketed as unbreakable, melamine with damage should be avoided.

3.5in (9cm) high

£5-7   GROB

A Gaydon Melmex red mug, by British Industrial Plastics, with high handle.

The mug is a less commonly found shape.

3.5in (9cm) high

£5-7   GC

A 1960s Melaware orange tea cup and saucer, by Ranton & Co.

6.25in (16cm) diam

£5-7   GROB

A Gaydon Melmex pastel green milk jug, by British Industrial Plastics.

2.75in (7cm) high

£4-6   GROB

A Melaware grey eggcup, by Ranton & Co, in the shape of a top hat.

1.75in (4.5cm) high

£4-6   GROB

A 1960s Midwinter 'Modern' Melamine pastel green bowl, unmarked.

3in (7.5cm) high

£6-8   GROB

A Melaware pastel blue and white two-part dish, by Ranton & Co.

11.25in (28.5cm) wide

£12-15   GROB

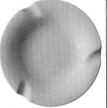

A Gaydon Melmex yellow and cream cruet set, by British Industrial Plastics.

This set should also include a stainless steel mustard 'dab'.

Tray 7in (18cm) long

£5-7   GC

A Gaydon Melmex pastel yellow ashtray, by British Industrial Plastics.

Also made in grey, this uncommon shape is often found damaged.

5in (13cm) diam

£6-8   GROB

Two circular copper jelly or cake moulds.

c1859   10in (25cm) diam

£100-150   **ATK**

A Purina 'Cow Chow' milk scale, by Chatillion, with brass front and twin needles.

A very early copper baking tin, in form of a jumping fish.

c1800   11in (29cm) long

£25-35   **ATK**

17in (43.5cm) high

£50-70   **EG**

A 19thC Danish iron, with turned wooden handle.

5.25in (13.5cm) long

£80-120   **ATK**

A mechanical apple peeler, by Goodell, in very good condition.

A wood and brass coffee grinder, the crank lever engraved with "Roseta Petrascheck", hinged lid and drawers with brass knob.

c1880   10.5in (26cm) high

£180-220   **WDL**

£80-120   **MUR**

A beech spinning wheel, stained in red, with adjustable parts and remains of some flax, missing footboard.

50in (125cm) high

£20-30   **WDL**

A 1940s Bakelite, wood, chrome and metal desk fan, by Ventaxia, reg'd no.s 442469, 429958.

13.5in (34cm) high

£80-120   **PSI**

An American Art Nouveau-style tabletop fan.

£20-30   **GAZE**

An American 'Heart-Shaped Toaster Universal E 9411', by Landers, Frary & Clark, New Britain, CT, nickel-plated case with ivory bakelite handles and feet.

1929

£300-400   **ATK**

A Dutch turnover toaster, by Huza, nickel-plated metal, with white bakelite knobs.

Pulling down the flaps causes the toast to turn over.

c1930

£40-60   **ATK**

A countertop fan-scale, by The Standard Computing Scale Co., Detroit, with sliding weight and hopper, lacking back glass.

27in (68.5cm) wide

£45-55   **EG**

A bulldog curling iron heater, by the American Electric Heater Co., Detroit, with nickelled dog and slate base.

c1915

6in (15cm) wide

£60-100   **EG**

An Elkington 'Pride' silver-plated teapot, designed by David Mellor, "53722" stamping to base.

David Mellor (b.1930) is a silversmith and designer specialising in cutlery and other tablewares. His classic 'Pride' range, designed for Walker & Hall in 1954 is still in production today. He was commissioned by the British government to design cutlery, which included the 1966 'Thrift' range of standard that was used in all their canteens.

A Walker & Hall 'Fanfare' silver-plated teapot, designed by David Mellor, stamped "53725" to base.

9.5in (24cm) long

£70-100   **RETC**

c1960   *9in (23cm) long*

£80-120   **RETC**

A Deakin & Francis silver ashtray, with gilt wash textured rim, and Birmingham hallmarks for 1971.

1971   *4in (10cm) diam*

£120-140   **MHT**

A set of six 1960s Viners stainless steel 'Empire' shape knives, forks and spoons.

Knives 8.25in (21cm) high

£80-120   **GC**

A quite rare Elkington or Walker & Hall set of cutlery, from the Pride range, designed by David Mellor, knife with ivorine handle.

Both companies were licensed to make the Pride range.

c1955   *Knife 8.25in (21cm) long*

£10-15 each   **RETC**

A Pyrex Gaiety casserole dish, on warmer stand, in unused condition with original box and packaging.

Corning Glass first released the heat-resistant glass Pyrex in 1924. It became particularly popular when the opaque version was produced in the 1950s with a wide range of patterns and decoration. It was made in the US and in the UK by J. A. Jobling of Sunderland under license. Other companies, such as Phoenix Glass, made their own version of heat resistant oven-to-table glass ware. Vintage pieces are still usable, but don't put them in the dishwasher as this can fade the colours and decoration.

Box 13.75in (35cm) wide

£15-25   **MA**

A 1950s Pyrex vegetable dish, on warmer stand, with hunting scene transfer.

12.5in (31.5cm) wide

£12-18   **MA**

A Pyrex tumbler, with yellow holder, and original box, holder marked "Registered 881736" for 1956.

5in (12.5cm) high

£10-15   **MA**

A Grenadier Phoenix red sprayed Pyrex-type lidded dish, reg'd design 872873.

9in (23cm) wide

£10-15   **GROB**

A Pyrex sauceboat and underplate, sprayed apple green.

Plate 8in (20cm) long

£8-10   **GROB**

A Phoenix milk glass beaker, with transfer-printed rose, in a plastic holder.

4.5in (11.5cm) high

£6-8   **GROB**

A 1970s Stelton red plastic vacuum jug.

11.75in (30cm) high

£6-8   **GAZE**

A Homepride Flour 'Fred' parmesan cheese or herb shaker, by Spillers.

4.25in (11cm) high

£4-5   **L**

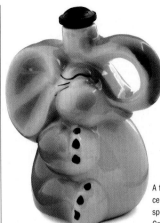

A fat elephant ceramics laundry sprinkler, by Cardinal China.

A white poodle ceramic laundry sprinkler.

8.5in (22.5cm) high

£60-80   **DAC**

A yellow clothes peg shaped ceramic laundry sprinkler.

8.75in (22cm) high

£80-120   **DAC**

As the demand for ceramic and glass sprinklers rise, together with prices, collectors' interest in plastic sprinklers is beginning to grow.

6.75in (17cm) high

£220-280   **DAC**

A 1960s Japanese iron-shaped ceramic laundry sprinkler, with scene of girl and boy farmers, with "Tilso Japan Hand-painted" label to base.

7in (18cm) high

£100-150   **DAC**

A Granforest hand-painted ceramic cookie jar, with handle.

£10-15   **BH**

A glass decanter, with printed striped decoration and an 'E-Z Por' pink plastic pourer.

10.5in (26.5cm) high

£8-12   **BH**

A painted and frosted glass syrup pourer, decorated with a rooster.

5.5in (14cm) high

£4-6   **BH**

A set of four painted tin kitchen canisters, with Bakelite knobs.

Largest 7.5in (19cm) high

£12-18   **BH**

A pair of American hand-painted ceramic salt and pepper shakers, by Holt-Howard. c1962

3.5in (9cm) high

£4-5   **BH**

COLLECTORS' NOTES

■ Marble collectors divide vintage collectable marbles into two distinct types; handmade marbles and machine-made marbles. Handmade marbles were produced primarily in Germany from c1860-1920. Machine-made marbles were primarily produced in the US after M.F. Christensen developed a marble-making machine in 1905. In the 1950s-60s Far Eastern and South American marbles such as 'cats eyes' took over.

■ Handmade marbles can be identified by the presence of the remains of a 'pontil' where the marble was broken off from the glass rod and formed into a sphere. These are traditionally the most valuable and sought-after, but have recently fallen slightly behind the best machine-made marbles in popularity.

■ Value is primarily indicated by type. Swirls are the most commonly found type, with marbles categorised by the pattern, style and colours. Some are rare. Look for symmetry in design, bright colours and large sizes. More unusual marbles such as the opaque Indians and 'sulphides', with their internal white forms, are also worth looking out for.

■ Machine-made marbles have no pontil and grew enormously in popularity during the 1920s eclipsing, and then replacing, German exports. The short-lived Christensen Agate Company produced some of the most colourful and collectable marbles in this sector of the market. Other notable names include the Peltier Glass Company and Akro Agate, who became the largest US producer until their closure in 1951.

■ Condition is more important with machine-made marbles than older handmades. Marbles in truly mint condition can sell for up to double the value of marbles with wear such as 'hit' marks, chips and scuffing, especially if they obscure any internal pattern. All marbles shown here are in mint or near-to-mint condition. Restoration can usually be felt as it alters the shape. 'Eye appeal' is also a very important consideration, but factors that appeal to one collector may not appeal to another, making it a matter for personal taste.

A handmade swirl-type 360-degree 'Indian' marble.

Indians have opaque black bases, 'swirl type' examples have strands that run unbroken from pole to pole. Here the bands run all over the marble, which is highly prized, unlike the more common 'panelled' example on the following page. Yellow and white are the most common colours, red being rarer with oxblood being the rarest.

c1860-1920

0.5in (1.5cm) diam

£80-120   **AB**

A handmade End of the Day 'Joseph's Coat' swirl marble.

'End of the Day' refers to the construction of the marble, using stretched flecks of left-over glass instead of rods. 'Joseph's Coat' marbles have closely packed coloured strands of bands just beneath the surface with little clear glass showing in between them.

c1860-1920   0.75in (2cm) diam

£100-150   **AB**

A handmade 'Solid Core' swirl marble.

c1860-1920

0.75in (2cm) diam

£6-8   **AB**

A handmade End of the Day 'Onionskin' marble.

Red, blue and green stripes are more common colours and the more colours present, the rarer and more desirable the marble.

c1860-1920   1.25in (3cm) diam

£60-80   **AB**

A handmade 'Mist' marble.

This type has a translucent or transparent base with translucent or transparent coloured strands. Blue and green are the most commonly found colours.

c1860-1920   0.5in (1.5cm) diam

£20-30   **AB**

A handmade End of the Day 'Joseph's Coat' marble.

Note the very clear, and slightly protruding, pontil mark on the left hand side of this marble. The patterning is unusual and attractive.

c1860-1920   0.5in (1.5cm) diam

£40-60   **AB**

A handmade swirl-type 'Banded Opaque' marble.

c1860-1920   0.75in (2cm) diam

£70-100   **AB**

MARBLES

A handmade 'Latticinio Core' swirl marble.

These are the most common types of handmade marble, but look out for blue core threads, which are rarer than white.

c1860-1920   0.75in (2cm) diam

£6-8   AB

A handmade 'Banded' Lutz marble.

A 'Banded' Lutz has two sets of single-coloured bands, which are made of finely ground copper.

c1860-1920   0.75in (2cm) diam

£50-70   AB

A handmade 'Divided Core' swirl marble, the core with four bands.

The core of this type is formed with three or more separately coloured bands, with clear glass between.

c1860-1920   0.75in (2cm) diam

£15-20   AB

A 'Solid Core (lobed)' swirl marble.

c1860-1920   0.75in (2cm) diam

£8-12   AB

A German handmade 'Sparkler' marble.

c1860-1920
         0.75in (2cm) diam

£8-12   AB

A Christensen Agate Company 'Hand-gathered' marble.

A handmade 'Indian' marble.

c1860-1920
         0.75in (2cm) diam

£40-50   AB

The Christensen Agate Co. was founded in 1925 and the 'hand-gathered' swirls are their earliest marbles. They can be recognised by their slightly irregular shape and '9' and 'tail' shapes at alternate poles, which are also very rare. There are also a range of four to five different colours, which are unique to this company, again helping with identification.

c1927   0.5in (1.5cm) diam

£100-150   AB

A handmade 'Confetti' marble.

Confetti marbles are transparent with internal flecks of colour. They always have one pontil mark. A coloured base glass is very rare.

c1860-1920   0.5in (1.5cm) diam

£50-70   AB

An American Transitional 'Leighton Ground Pontil' marble.

These marbles are reputed to have been made by James Leighton & Company in Ohio during the late 1890s. Most contain an 'oxblood' colour as here, which triples or quadruples the value. These have a single pontil with the swirling pattern forming a '9' shape at the opposite pole. Some of these marbles have also been found in Lauscha, Germany, opening up discussion as to their precise origins.

c1897   0.75in (2cm) diam

£200-250   AB

A Christensen Agate Company 'Swirl' marble.

Swirls are the most common marble made by the Christensen Agate Company and can be found in a great many different and typically bright colours.

c1927-29   0.75in (2cm) diam

£10-15   **AB**

A CLOSER LOOK AT A MARBLE

Christensen Agate made marbles for two years only, from around 1927 until 1929, and their marbles are among the most desirable and collectable machine-made marbles.

This example has five different colours, the maximum number of colours known on a Christensen Agate swirl and a rare feature.

Christensen Agate is also known for its bright colours, which never blended together when mixed, remaining distinctly separate.

The complex and detailed random patterning is intense and the colour combination is strong, making this even more desirable.

A Christensen Agate Company 'Exotic' swirl marble.

1927-29   0.5in (1.5cm) diam

£200-300   **AB**

A 1920s/30s American Peltier Glass Company 'National Line Rainbo Tiger' marble.

National Line Rainbo marbles are among the most collectable of Peltier's output. Collectors have given their colourful marbles names based around their colours, as here. They can be differentiated from the similar Miller swirls as they have two seams.

0.75in (2cm) diam

£20-30   **AB**

A Vitro Agate Company 'Sweet Pea Patch' marble.

0.75in (2cm) diam

£7-10   **AB**

An Akro Agate Company 'Swirl Oxblood' marble.

c1930-45   0.5in (1.5cm) diam

£8-12   **AB**

A 1920s/30s Peltier Glass Company 'National Line Rainbo Zebra' marble.

0.75in (2cm) diam

£7-10   **AB**

A Christensen Agate Company 'Moonie' marble.

0.75in (2cm) diam

£60-80   **AB**

A Christensen Agate Company 'Flame Swirl' marble.

Flame Swirls, where the stripes appear in rows (or opposing rows) almost like the flames on a 'hot-rod' car of the 1950s are rare. The colours and pattern affect value, with this example being highly desirable.

c1927-29   0.5in (1.5cm) diam

£100-150   **AB**

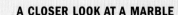

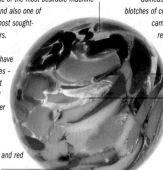

A CLOSER LOOK AT A MARBLE

The Guinea is one of the most desirable machine-made marbles and also one of the rarest and most sought-after by collectors.

Guineas always have transparent bases – clear is the most commonly found colour with amber and blue being much rarer. The rarest are the legendary green and red coloured bases.

Guineas have stretched flecks or blotches of coloured glass – the name came about as workers were reminded of the colours on guinea cocks running around the factory yard.

The rarest variation is the Guinea Cobra, which has colours inside as well as on the outside like standard Guineas.

A rare Christensen Agate Company 'Guinea Cobra' marble.

Reproductions of Guineas are being made, so if in doubt compare to an original or seek professional advice.

c1927-29   0.75in (2cm) diam

£200-300   **AB**

An Akro Agate Company 'Carnelian Oxblood' marble.

Carnelian marbles are very rare. 'Oxblood' refers to the opaque deep rust red-coloured glass with black filaments.

0.75in (2cm) diam

£60-80   **AB**

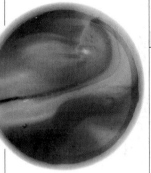

An Akro Agate Company 'Carnelian' marble.

c1930s   0.75in (2cm) diam

£12-18   **AB**

A Christensen Agate Company 'Striped Transparent' marble.

This type of marble can be recognised by the stripes predominately confined to or only on one side of the marble – electric colours, as here, are more valuable. The base, transparent on this type, can also be opaque in which case the marble is known as a 'Striped Opaque'.

c1927-1929   0.5in (1.5cm) diam

£150-250   **AB**

A Christensen Agate Company 'Slag' marble.

c1927-29   0.5in (1.5cm) diam

£8-12   **AB**

A Vitro Agate Company '8-Finger Ribbon' marble.

0.75in (2cm) diam

£12-18   **AB**

An Alley Agate Company 'Flame Swirl' marble.

1929-49   0.75in (2cm) diam

£20-30   **AB**

FIND OUT MORE...

www.marblecollecting.com

Marbles: Identification & Price Guide, by Robert Block, published by Schiffer Publishing, 2002.

COLLECTORS' NOTES

■ Forerunners of the moving images we watch today at the cinema, optical toys developed throughout the 18th and 19thC, catering to a growing public fascination with moving images.

■ The first magic lanterns were produced in the 17thC. By the late Victorian period they were a staple of sideshows and fairs everywhere. Showmen would compete to put on the most lavish spectacle.

■ Magic lanterns were generally lit by small paraffin lamps and will usually have a funnel or chimney at the top, designed to allow the fumes to escape.

■ Many of these pre-cinema toys were discarded or stored carelessly in attics once they were no longer fashionable, falling into disrepair. Examples in good original condition can be hard to find today.

■ Stereoscopes reached the peak of their popularity during the later half of the 19thC. They create the illusion of depth by displaying two slightly different views of the same scene, one tailored to each eye.

■ The wood used to make stereoscopic viewers was often very thin, and the paper slides were very fragile. Slides are very much in demand today.

A German Ernemann wood-bodied stereoscopic viewer.

Glass or card stereoscopic slides would be inserted into the back plate and viewed through the focusing lenses. Look for decoratively shaped examples in fine woods as these are worth more.

1907   7in (18cm) wide

£250-350   **ATK**

A German Wurzelholz stereoscopic viewer and 116 stereocards, the cards including including 21 'tissue' cards of France, 32 cards of views of Switzerland by W. England, and others.

c1905   7in (18cm) wide

£200-300   **ATK**

A French P.H. Suchard Art Nouveau-style printed tinplate stereoscopic viewer, together with ten stereocards.

c1910   Cards 2.75in (7cm) wide

£150-250   **ATK**

A 'La Taxiphote' mahogany tabletop stereoviewer, for stereoscopic slides in magazines, with nickel fittings, and 12 filled magazines containing over 250 slides.

The interior of the box contains a revolving metal rack system to hold the glass slides. Turning the knob on the side revolves the slides, with the upper knobs focusing the eyepiece. A ground glass plate at the back allows light in to illuminate the slides. Further slides are contained in the base. These most commonly contain 'tourist' views of different countries.

c1915   19.5in (49cm) high

£750-850   **ATK**

A black painted wooden stereographoscope, with a carved floral pattern and six stereocards.

The main lens was used for viewing prints or photographs, the lower dual lenses for stereoscopic cards. Larger and more decorative examples in fine woods command higher prices.

c1880

£100-150   **ATK**

A carte-de-visite graphoscope, of ebonised wood with carved foliate decoration, with some splits to top edge.

c1880   5.5in (14cm) high

£80-120   **EG**

A rare J.T. Chapman of Manchester mahogany and brass magic lantern, with slide carrier and gas light burner.

c1890   21in (53.5cm) high

£600-700   ATK

An English large professional 'triunnial' magic lantern, the mahogany body with brass lenses and fittings, three original gas burners and accessories, unmarked, chimney replaced.

Triunnial magic lanterns are very rare, this example is of very fine quality, although the chimney has been replaced and is smaller than usual. Using three separate images, the operator could fade between different scenes to tell a story.

c1885   35in (89cm) high

£8,000-12,000   ATK

An extremely rare French 'Aubert Brevete' magic lantern, for round picture discs, with one hand-painted circular slide, lacks burner.

c1880   14.75in (27cm) high

£500-600   ATK

A rare French 'Perfectionnée' Lampascope magic lantern, by Aubert, Paris, with brown body and original chrome burner.

c1870   17.5in (44cm) high

£250-350   ATK

An American 'Sciopticon' magic lantern, by The Pettibone Bros. Mfg. Co. Inc. of Cincinnati, Ohio, with rotating holder for ten slides, box and instruction sheet, electrified, chimney replaced.

c1895   22in (56cm) high

£1,500-2,000   ATK

A German magic lantern, by Georg Carette & Co., with burner, 33 circular glass slides and six mechanical slides.

c1900   10.25in (26cm) high

£120-180   ATK

A small magic lantern for 1.7in-slides, with 12 slides and burner, in a wooden box.

These often contained slides of educational themes or children's tales and were used as toys. The condition of the components and completeness dictates value.

c1890   7in (17cm) high

£150-200   ATK

An unusual American 'Comiscope' magic lantern, by Remington-Morse of New York & Chicago, with a cardboard projector in its original box.

This is a very late date for a magic lantern.

1942   9in (23cm) wide

£80-120   ATK

An American floor-standing metal-bodied mutoscope, by the International Mutoscope Corp. of Long Island City, NY, with original mutoscope reel no.7.365 showing an acrobatic dancer, lacks key for cash box.

Herman Casler patented the 'Mutoscope' in 1897. They soon became popular attractions at seaside resorts or other tourist destinations. The viewer would insert money to watch a titillating, amusing or otherwise entertaining show created by photographic cards flipping at speed to create an illusion of movement.

c1920   *75in (191cm) high*

£800-1,200   **ATK**

An American mutoscope peep show, by the American Mutoscope & Biograph Co. of New York, with an original Mutoscope reel no. 16T showing a dressed dancer, with repainted exterior and replaced locks.

c1925   *56in (144cm) high*

£800-1,200   **ATK**

An American coin-operated 'Artist's Models in 3D' floor standing viewer which, for five cents, shows for a full 90 seconds variously posed 'artist's models' in full colour, with 18 transparencies.

c1958

£600-700   **ATK**

A Japanese 'Cinema Revue' celluloid toy, with key-wound musical movement and moving pictures, and revolving 'merry-go-round' on top.

c1950   *9.5in (24cm) high*

£120-180   **ATK**

A CLOSER LOOK AT AN OPTICAL TOY

The Filoscope was invented by Henry W. Short and patented on 3rd November 1898.

Short worked as a cameraman for British film pioneers including Robert Paul and Bert Ayres and is known for his work with early cinema.

Handheld and containing a revolving reel of single photographic shots, it was operated by flicking each card past a thumb, creating the sense of movement.

Bridging optical toys with moving images and real cinema further, Short used shots from real films on his Filoscope reels, of which 12 titles are known.

A British 'Filoscope', manufactured under license from the Mutoscope & Biograph Syndicate, Ltd. for the UK, fitted with 'The Cuddle' flip-film roll.

1898   *10in (25.5cm) wide*

£280-320   **ATK**

A French Zoetrope 'Les Images Vivantes', with a cardboard body, 11 double-sided black-and-white and colour paper strips, on a varnished wooden stand.

c1910   10.5in (28cm) high

£400-500   **ATK**

A London Stereoscopic & Photographic Co.'Wheel of Life', with a cast-iron base, tin drum, 12 one-sided colour strips and 12 bottom discs with colour motifs.

11.75in (37.5cm) high

£650-750   **ATK**

An early French 'Ombres Chinoises' shadow theatre, by Saussine, Paris, in original box with coloured lithograph scene, cut-out stage with red curtain decor and transparent screen, an assortment of cut- and un-cut figures, an original sheet by Pellerin & Cie, Épinal, cover illustrated by B. Condert.

c1860

£1,200-1,800   **ATK**

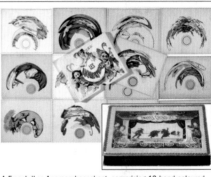

A French 'Les Anamorphoses' set, comprising 13 hand-coloured lithographic anamorphic views about French Royals, with folder.

Anamorphic views look like semi-circles of colour until viewed through an upright, cylindrical mirror, which corrects the distortions in the printed image, allowing a face or figure to be viewed. One of the most famous anamorphic views is the skull in Holbein's 1533 painting 'The Ambassadors' in the National Gallery, London.

c1852   7in (19.5cm) high

£500-600   **ATK**

A pair of Barr and Stroud military issue binoculars, with leather carrying case, marked "7xCF41".

c1940

£70-100   **ROS**

An extremely rare 1870s French chromolithograph advertising fan, with magic lantern scenery, showing clowns presenting a magic lantern show and other activities, stamped "Brasserie Vetzel".

15.5in (39cm) high

£900-1,000   **ATK**

COLLECTORS' NOTES

- The first 'golden age' of the paperweight was from 1845-50 with production centred in France. Major factories included Clichy, Baccarat and Saint Louis. Typical designs included lamp worked flowers and often complex 'set-ups' of cut millefiori canes, millefiori being the Italian word for 'a thousand flowers'. The base or 'ground' could be coloured or comprise of a number of random canes made from twisted white strands and clear glass known as 'muslin'.

- Although paperweights continued to be produced, the next major period of production is from the mid-to late 20th century, when Scotland and the US became of greater importance. Names such as Paul Ysart, Caithness, Charles Kaziun, Paul Stankard and John Deacons led developments, based on 19th century examples, with a more modern slant. Historic French houses such as Baccarat and Saint Louis continue to produce today and their work is much sought-after.

- Look for complex set-ups and large or very small miniature sizes. The work of notable names is worth looking out for, especially if they have ceased production such as Paul Ysart (now dead) and William Manson, who has changed his career. Many either sign their work on the base or include 'signature canes' showing their initials.

A French Saint Louis limited edition paperweight, from a limited edition of 400, signed and dated "SL 1976".

1976   3.25in (8cm) diam

£300-400   **BGD**

A French Saint Louis paperweight, signed and dated "SL 1975".

Saint Louis was founded in Alsace, France in 1767 and its work is typified by a single flowers or fruit, often on swirling, white strand grounds. Millefiori is often combined with these two motifs.

1975   3in (8cm) diam

£350-450   **BGD**

A French Saint Louis paperweight, signed and dated 1970.

1970   3.25in (8cm) diam

£120-180   **BGD**

A French Saint Louis paperweight, signed and dated "SL 1970".

1970

3.25in (8cm) diam

£400-500   **BGD**

A French Saint Louis commemorative paperweight, with 'Bicentenaire de la Révolution' inscription to reverse and a small central set-up of millefiori carrying the dates "1789" and "1989".

1989   2.75in (7cm) diam

£120-180   **BGD**

A French Saint Louis scrambled millefiori paperweight, the central cane with a silhouette of a camel.

2in (5cm) diam

£400-500   **BGD**

A limited edition Baccarat paperweight, from an edition of 100, signed and dated "B 1994".

1994   3.5in (9cm) diam

£500-600   **BGD**

A French Baccarat 'Prince Albert's Bird of Paradise' paperweight, signed and dated "B 1997".

1997   3.25in (8.5cm) diam

£650-750   **BGD**

A limited edition French Baccarat paperweight, from an edition of 300, signed and dated "B 1977".

1977   3in (7.5cm) diam

£550-650   **BGD**

A Scottish Perthshire paperweight, with three millefiori and 'silhouette' canes of animals, signed and dated "P 1975".

Silhouette canes show animals in black against a white background, often with extra coloured details around them.

1975   2.75in (7cm) diam

£220-280   **BGD**

A Scottish Perthshire paperweight, shaped as an ornate star.

2in (5cm) diam

£60-80   **BGD**

A Scottish John Deacons paperweight, signed and dated "JD 2004".

2004   3.5in (9cm) diam

£150-200   **BGD**

An Italian Seguso paperweight, signed "Seguso F... 1995".

1995   3.25in (8cm) diam

£40-50   **NOR**

A Scottish Paul Ysart paperweight, with a four-leafed clover over a cloudy amber ground.

Paul Ysart's paperweights are highly desirable and he is considered the 'father' of Scottish paperweight making. He worked for Scotland's Moncrieff Glassworks from the 1930s until 1963 when he joined Caithness Glass. From 1970 until 1982 he produced under his own name. Look out for those with animal motifs in particular.

c1975   5in (7.5cm) diam

£300-400   **BGD**

A French Val Saint Lambert paperweight, with polychrome marbled decoration pulled into a swirling star shape.

4in (10cm) diam

£80-120   **BGD**

A French commemorative sulphide paperweight, with profile of Benjamin Franklin.

3in (7.5cm) diam

£120-180   **BGD**

COLLECTORS' NOTES

- Waterman, Parker, Montblanc and Dunhill Namiki are the most sought after brands, with early, metal-covered pens tending to be the most desirable. The best of Dunhill's 1930s maki-e lacquer models occupy the very high end of the market.

- In the past, collectors tended to concentrate on pens produced in their own country, probably driven by nostalgia. As the market matures and prices rise, collectors are looking further afield. For example, England's brightly coloured and highly useable Conway Stewarts are now proving popular on both sides of the Atlantic.

- As many collectors use their pens, condition and completeness is very important. Replaceable parts such as nibs and clips should be original and cracked or chipped examples should be avoided.

- Before the ballpoint became universal, fountain pens were mass-produced, even those with gold nibs. The vast majority are worth under £20, however they can make good writing instruments and are useful for budding repairmen (or women) to practice on.

- Modern limited editions are often produced in large numbers and, as they are often bought for investment, are kept in pristine condition. This makes used examples undesirable. Values for these are unlikely to rise significantly and collectors should look for early examples, such as Parker's Spanish Treasure and Hall of Independence or those from small editions.

An American Conklin Endura ringtop lever-filler pen, sapphire blue Pyroxlin plastic with Conklin Endura fine nib, in Conklin card box, excellent condition.
c1930-32

£40-60　　　　　　　　　　　　　　　　**BLO**

An American Conklin ringtop lever-filler pen, cream and black celluloid with Conklin Toledo fine nib, in excellent condition, teeth marks on the cap.
c1931

£40-60　　　　　　　　　　　　　　　　**BLO**

A 1930s English Curzons Summit lever-filler pen, blue and bronze marble celluloid with Summit 14ct gold medium nib, a rare colour, in very good condition.

£50-70　　　　　　　　　　　　　　　　**BLO**

A limited edition Delta Colosseum lever-filler pen, from an edition of 1,926, marbled yellow celluloid with Delta 18ct gold medium nib, mint condition complete with box and papers.
1997

£150-200　　　　　　　　　　　　　　　**BLO**

A Mabie Todd & Co. Blackbird 5277 Self-Filler pen, red celluloid lever-filler with Blackbird nib, in excellent condition.
c1950

£20-30　　　　　　　　　　　　　　　　**BLO**

A rare 1920s English MacNiven & Cameron self-filler pen, chequer-design black hard rubber lever-filler with shaped Waverley 14ct nib, in excellent to near mint condition.

£60-80　　　　　　　　　　　　　　　　**BLO**

An extremely rare 1930s Scottish MacNiven & Cameron Waverley pen set, green and black 'tiger-striped' celluloid with Robert Burns clip and shaped Waverley 14ct nib, with matching pencil, and presentation box.

£220-280　　　　　　　　　　　　　　　**BLO**

A CLOSER LOOK AT A MONTBLANC SAFETY PEN

The Montblanc Pen Company started as The Simplo Filler Pen Company in c1906. This model was made from 1920 to 1928.

Black is the most common colour for this model, red and mottled red and black hard rubber versions do exist but are considerably rarer.

Montblanc made this model in a number of sizes from '00' to '12'. The '2' size is the most common, with the smallest and largest being more scarce.

The early models were named 'Diplomat' or 'Rouge et Noir' after the black body and the red 'star' in the cap crown.

A very rare German Montblanc Rouge et Noir 12 M pen, smooth black hard rubber safety filler with Rouge et Noir barrel imprint and Simplo Pen Co. 12 nib, barrel stamp slightly worn, otherwise in very good condition, an unusual nib.
c1920

£3,000-4,000   **BLO**

A rare German Simplo 'Diplomat' 4 safety pen, mottled red and black hard rubber with 'Diplomat' barrel imprint and Warranted 4 14ct nib, and white metal accommodation clip modelled as a monkey, lacks iridium nib tip and cap lip possibly shortened.
1912-28

£320-380   **BLO**

A rare German Simplo safety pen, wave-chased black hard rubber with white cap dome and Gustav Gruber Wien and Sunny Pen barrel imprints and Simplo-style Warranted 2 14ct nib, some polishing.
c1913-15

£70-100   **BLO**

A rare German Montblanc Rouge et Noir 2M safety pen, for the Italian market, smooth black hard rubber, with floral decorated gold-filled bands, 18ct rolled gold Montblanc accommodation clip and 14ct 2 fine-flexible nib, cap possibly replaced or repaired.
1920-23

£220-280   **BLO**

A German Montblanc 1-M safety pen, smooth black hard rubber with Simplo 1 fine nib, in excellent condition.

1920-25

£70-100   **BLO**

A very rare German Montblanc yellow-metal safety pen, with engine-turned and plain panels and Montblanc 2 medium nib, marked "585" on the clip and signed "Mont Blanc", barrel threads replaced with black hard rubber, otherwise in excellent condition.
1925-28

£1,000-1,500   **BLO**

A rare German Montblanc III A-F, Azurite plastic blue push button-filler pen, with later Mont Blanc 14ct 2 nib, tassie and blind cap oxidised, engraved name, in good condition.

The conservative German pen market traditionally favoured pens in plain solid colours such as black and red. Examples in other colours, such as this blue marbled Montblanc, will attract a premium.

1932-34

£350-450   **BLO**

A rare German Montblanc 322 EF pen, pearl and black marbled celluloid button-filler with Warranted 'a' nib, barrel slightly amberized, lightly engraved name.

1935-38

£350-450 BLO

A Danish Montblanc 30 Masterpiece pen, black celluloid with 4810 M fine nib, minor brassing otherwise in excellent condition.

Montblanc maintained a factory in Denmark during WWII and due to shortages in parts and materials, produced models such as this example, that were outside the normal catalogue.

1935-46

£250-350 BLO

A rare 1930s German Montblanc 72S PIX pencil, chased black hard rubber with alternating columns of engine-turned barley and hatched design, with some brown discolouration otherwise in very good condition.

£100-150 BLO

A rare and unusual Danish Montblanc gold-plated [242] pen, with engine-turned 12-sided faceted overlay signed "Mont-Blanc" around the cap top, and Montblanc 14ct 585 fine nib, light wear to plating, mostly towards the clip.

Produced at the tail-end of WWII when metals would have been in short supply, this gold-plated pen is rare.

1944-54

£220-280 BLO

A Montblanc 144 Meisterstück pen, black celluloid piston filler with two-colour 4810 nib, in good condition with loose cap bands.

1949-60

£70-100 BLO

A rare German Montblanc Masterpiece 146 pen, green-striped and visible celluloid with two-colour 4810 14ct medium nib, light brassing, clip screw discoloured, turning knob replaced.

Despite some discolouration and a replaced part, this pen is made of a variation of the usual celluloid, making it desirable to collectors.

c1949

£300-400 BLO

A German Montblanc 142 F pen, silver pearl striated piston-filler with Montblanc two-colour 4810 14ct nib, discoloured.

1952-58

£150-250 BLO

A rare 1950s Spanish Montblanc 440 pen, cinnamon pearl-lined piston-filler with yellow ink-window, Montblanc cap band and Montblanc 14ct medium nib, excellent condition.

1950s

£220-280 BLO

A very rare English Montblanc 9ct gold Masterpiece 149 pen, fine barley overlay, by S.J. Rose, with 18ct 'tri-colour' 4810 fine nib, windmill crest engraved on cap, mechanism stuck, London hallmark for 1972.

Montblanc did not produce their own gold-covered version of the 149 until c1982, so while this customized version by jewellers S.J. Rose is not an 'official' model, it is still sought-after by collectors.

£800-1,000 BLO

A German Montblanc M-N 22 pencil, pearl and black marbled celluloid, in excellent condition.

1935-38

£100-150 BLO

A Moore 94A Maniflex pen, silver-brown and black striated celluloid lever-filler with grey cap top, gold-filled trim and Moore Life-Maniflex nib, in excellent condition.

1939-46

£80-120 BLO

An American Parker Maxima Vacumatic pen, silver pearl celluloid with pearl section, metal Speedline-filler, and two-colour Arrow fine nib, in excellent condition.

1938

£50-70 BLO

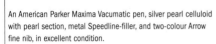

A Canadian Parker Senior Maxima Vacumatic pen, jet celluloid metal Speedline-filler, with medium oblique gold Arrow nib, in good to very good condition.

1940

£120-180 BLO

An American Parker Slender Maxima Blue-Diamond Vacumatic pen, burgundy pearl laminated celluloid, with aluminium Speedline-filler, and two-colour Arrow fine-firm nib, in excellent or near mint condition.

The Blue Diamond on the clip denotes Parker's Lifetime guarantee.

1939

£120-180 BLO

An American Parker Senior Maxima Blue-Diamond Vacumatic pen, gold pearl laminated celluloid aluminium Speedline-filler with two-colour Parker Arrow fine nib, near mint and exceptionally clean.

1940

£180-220 BLO

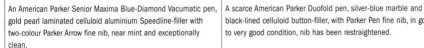

A scarce American Parker Duofold pen, silver-blue marble and black-lined celluloid button-filler, with Parker Pen fine nib, in good to very good condition, nib has been restraightened.

1941

£60-80 BLO

An American Parker Duofold Vacumatic pen, silver-red marble and black-lined celluloid aluminium Speedline-filler with Parker Pen medium-fine nib, in excellent condition.

1941

£60-80 BLO

An American Parker Major Blue-Diamond Vacumatic pen, azure blue pearl laminated celluloid with lucite Speedline-filler, gold-filled 'wedding ring' band and gold Arrow nib, in good to very good condition, an unusual variation.

1942

£60-80 BLO

A CLOSER LOOK AT A LIMITED EDITION PARKER

This limited edition was made to commemorate the wedding of Prince Charles and Lady Diana Spencer on July 29th, 1981.

The pen is based on the standard model 105 and can be differentiated by the engraved plaque on the barrel and the top of the cap is engraved with the Prince of Wales' feathers.

It is limited to only 1,000 pieces, a relatively low number for a limited edition. This means pieces are more likely to hold their value.

Collectors look for limited editions that retain all their boxes and paperwork, which will usually include a numbered certificate of authenticity.

A limited edition English Parker 'Royal Wedding' 105 pen, from an edition of 1,000, rolled gold 'royal oak' finish with medium 14ct 585 nib, in original presentation box with card outer, guarantee and certificate of authenticity, in mint condition.

1981

£250-350   **BLO**

A scarce American Parker Slender Maxima Blue-Diamond Vacumatic pen, jet laminated celluloid with lucite Speedline-filler, gold-filled 'wedding ring' cap band and two-colour Arrow medium nib, good condition.

1942

£60-80   **BLO**

An American Parker Major Blue-Diamond Vacumatic pen, azure blue pearl laminated celluloid, with lucite Speedline-filler, and gold Arrow fine nib, near mint condition.

1946

£50-70   **BLO**

A late 1950s American Parker 61 Custom pen, black with Insignia design cap and fine nib, in unused condition.

£30-50   **BLO**

A 1960s English Parker 61 Custom Insignia pen, all rolled gold with Insignia design and medium nib, in fair to good condition with light dents and dings from use.

£40-60   **BLO**

A 1960s English Parker 61 Heirloom pen, rage red with pink and green gold-filled rainbow cap, medium nib and hard box, in excellent to near mint condition.

£40-50   **BLO**

A 1970s English Parker 61 Custom Insignia pen, all rolled gold with Insignia design and fine nib, in black and white Polka dot Parker 61 box, in mint condition.

£40-50   **BLO**

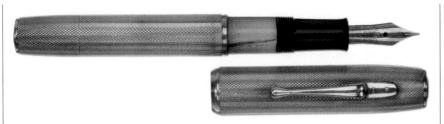

A German Pelikan 100 pen, piston-filler with 14ct solid gold overlay, with Pelikan symbol on cap top, small crack in ink window.
c1935

£500-700   **ATK**

A 1930s Japanese Platinum maki-e lacquer balance piston-filler pen, decorated with gold and silver taka maki-e Japanese coins on a kuro-nuri (black volcanic) lacquer ground.
The tactile textured finish of the background is very unusual.

£800-1,000   **BLO**

A 1970s Sheaffer Nostalgia pen, vermeil filigree overlaid cartridge-filler marked ".925", with fine 14K nib, in excellent condition.
This pen is inspired by the attractive filigree overlaid pens of the early 20thC. Vermeil is gold-plated silver.

£250-300   **BLO**

A German Soennecken S13 pen, pearl and black lined marbled celluloid button-filler with chrome trim and medium-oblique Soennecken nib, in excellent condition.

c1947

£100-150   **BLO**

A German Soennecken 304 pen, lapis lazuli blue celluloid button-filler with fine Soennecken nib, in very good condition.

c1933

£150-200   **BLO**

A German Soennecken 222 Extra pen, turquoise green 'lizard' celluloid piston-filler with medium Soennecken nib, in near mint condition.
c1952

£180-220   **BLO**

A German Soennecken 111 Superior pen, silver-grey herringbone celluloid piston-filler with medium-oblique Soennecken nib, in mint condition.
c1954

£200-250   **BLO**

An English Stephens No.106 lever-filler pen, blue and bronze marble with Stephens 106 medium-oblique nib, lacks two fins on feed, otherwise in very good condition.

Writing styles of the time mean that many vintage pens have fine nibs, which are not always suitable for modern writers. Oblique and broad nibs are sought-after, even if fitted in relatively common pens.
c1937

£70-100   **BLO**

An English Summit Savoy button-filler pen, blue and black 'lizardskin' celluloid with Warranted 2 nib, some brassing on clip, blindcap lacks bezel.

c1937

£20-30   **BLO**

A CLOSER LOOK AT A WATERMAN'S LEVER-FILLER

'L.E.C.' stands for Lower End Covered, meaning a fully overlaid barrel; the 'Hand Engraved Vine' is often seen on this version.

Before the introduction of plastics to pen production, the use of precious metals and jewels was the only way to add 'colour' to the plain black or red hard rubber bodies.

Waterman's comprehensive numbering code describes the model. '5' in the hundreds column indicates a solid gold model, '5' in the tens column indicates a lever-filler and '2' in the units column is the size of the pen. The '1/2' indicates a slender, but full-length pen.

Engraved initials, names or presentation inscription will generally devalue a pen, though light engravings can be removed.

A rare American Waterman's 552 1/2 L.E.C. 'Hand Engraved Vine' pen, marked "14kt" on the rose-gold cap, barrel, clip and lever, with Waterman's 2 fine nib, in very good condition with lightly engraved name.

1924-27

£300-400 | **BLO**

A late 1940s Eversharp 'Sixty-Four' duo set, black lever-filler with 14ct gold cap and matching pencil, in fitted gift box.

Based on the 'Fifth Avenue' range, the 'Sixty-Four' was so called because the pen retailed at $64. It also tied into the 'Take it or Leave it' quiz show with the '$64 Question' catch phrase, that Eversharp sponsored.

£80-120 | **ATK**

A late 1930s English Unique lever-filler pen, rose and black 'lizard' celluloid with large Warranted 2 medium nib, in good to very good condition.

£40-60 | **BLO**

An American Waterman's 0552 1/2 'Basketweave' pen, gold-filled filigree overlay with Clip-Cap and Waterman's 2 medium-fine nib, in good to very good condition, two initials.

1923-27

£60-80 | **BLO**

An American Waterman's 55 pen, smooth black hard rubber with Ideal 5 fine nib, light surface scratches otherwise excellent/near mint.

1923-27

£100-150 | **BLO**

A rare American Waterman's 554 'Basketweave' pen, green-gold cap and barrel filigree, clip and lever, marked "14kt", with Waterman's 4 medium nib, in very good condition.

1924-27

£400-600 | **BLO**

An American Waterman's 452 'Basketweave' pen, marked "Sterling" on the cap, barrel and Clip-Cap, with Waterman's 2 medium nib, in good to very good condition.

1924-27

£180-220 | **BLO**

A 1920s American Waterman's 'Pansy Panel' gold overlaid pencil, marked "14K", with matching clip, three initials and in near mint condition, nozzle/mechanism needs reconnecting.

£60-80 | **BLO**

A 1920s Canadian Waterman's 51V Ripple pen, red and black hard rubber with Waterman's Ideal Canada 1 medium fine nib, lacks clip, otherwise very good condition.

This is an extremely rare short model, with a small no.1 sized nib.

£100-150 | **BLO**

An American Waterman's [028]52 pen, smooth black hard rubber with broad gold-filled bands at each end and 18ct gold-filled Clip Cap and Waterman's Reg US 2 fine nib, very good condition.

This rare model was first offered in the 1925 catalogue as a 55-size. It is very rare to find in others sizes.

1925-27

£100-150 | **BLO**

A 1920s American Waterman's 452 'Basketweave' pen, marked "Sterling" on cap, barrel, Clip-Cap and lever, with Waterman's 2 Canada medium nib, engraved with three fancy initials.

£180-200 | **BLO**

An American Waterman's 52 Cardinal pen, red hard rubber with Waterman's Ideal 2 fine nib, in very good to excellent condition.

1928-30

£100-150 | **BLO**

A 1920s American Waterman's 0552 1/2 V [L.E.C.] 'Pansy' pen set, gold-filled ringtop lever-filler with Waterman's Reg US 2 nib and matching pencil, engraved Gothic initials on each.

£80-120 | **ATK**

A limited edition Waterman Edson Signé Boucheron pen, from an edition of 3,741, with overlaid 18ct gold filigree by Boucheron, with medium nib, boxed, in mint condition.

c1996

£250-300 | **BLO**

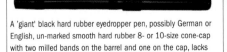

A 'giant' black hard rubber eyedropper pen, possibly German or English, un-marked smooth hard rubber 8- or 10-size cone-cap with two milled bands on the barrel and one on the cap, lacks nib, cap lip repaired, otherwise excellent or near mint condition.

c1915-20   *8.25in (21cm) long*

£60-100 | **BLO**

FIND OUT MORE...

Fountain Pens of the World, by Andreas Lambrou, published by Philip Wilson Publishers, 1995.

The Fountain Pen: A Collector's Companion, by Alexander Crum Ewing, published by Running Press, 1997.

The Writing Equipment Society, www.wesoc.co.uk

The Pen Collectors of America, www.pencollectors.com

COLLECTORS' NOTES

- The mechanical propelling pencil was first patented in 1822 by Sampson Mordan and John Isaac Hawkins and became known as the 'Everpointed' pencil. Hawkins sold his share of the rights to Mordan in 1823, who in turn sold them to a wealthy, successful stationer called Gabriel Riddle. With Riddle's financial support, Mordan was able to build his company into the 19th century success story it was.

- Mordan and Riddle's partnership ended in 1837. Pieces made 1823-37, and particularly before 1825, are scarce and desirable. Many bear an 'SM GR' hallmark and 'S.MORDAN & COs PATENT' wording. Pieces bearing 'S.MORDAN & CO MAKERS & PATENTEES' date from around 1838 until the 1850s-1860s when 'S.MORDAN & CO MAKERS' was used. From the 1860s onwards 'S.MORDAN & CO' was used.

- Mordan worked under Joseph Bramah, who patented a way of cutting quills mechanically in 1809, producing small quill nibs to be fitted into holders with a swivelling clamp. Bramah's patent expired in 1824, and holders were made well into the 1850s, and even beyond on a lesser scale. For both types, look for early examples, ornate decoration and fine materials such as ivory and precious metals. Marked examples are also more desirable. Avoid those with damage or missing parts as these are hard to repair.

A Bramah-type penholder, with agate shaft and gold fittings formed as leaves and set with turquoises.

These precious metal and hardstone holders are scarce. Those with collars covering repairs to the shaft or those that are shorter, due to damage, are worth around 50 per cent less.

c1840	6.25in (16cm) long
£700-1,000	**PC**

A rare Mordan silver Bramah-type penholder, the grip stamped "S.MORDAN'S IMPROV'D", with ring collar and hobnail terminal.

This is likely to have been made after Bramah's patent expired in 1825 as the only improvement seems to be the way the nib retracts into the holder to protect the nib.

	3.25in (8cm) long
£150-250	**BLO**

A Mordan double-ended silver pen and pencil, with reeded body, sliding ring grips and friction fit pen holder, marked "S.MORDAN &Co MAKERS & PATENTEES".

c1840	3.5in (9cm) long
£120-180	**BLO**

A Georgian silver quill 'presentation' or 'prize' pen, with later Bramah-type holder and London hallmarks for "IR" for 1804.

This would originally have had an integral silver nib but was modified, perhaps due to heavy use, after 1825. Presentation pens were costly and usually given as prizes. They sometimes bear inscriptions relating to the event.

1804	9in (23cm) long
£300-500	**BLO**

A Bramah-type penholder, with a carved ivory shaft, the holder stamped "S.MORDAN'S IMPROV'D".

c1830	6in (15.5cm) long
£80-120	**BLO**

A very rare Mordan pen and pencil combination, the ivory shaft stamped "S.MORDAN & Co. MAKERS & PATENTEES", the Bramah-type pen holder stamped "BRAMAH PATENT", with sliding ring.

c1820-1830	7in (18cm) long
£400-600	**PC**

A Mordan for Lund silver pen and reeded pencil combination, decorated shaped sliders, stamped "LUND - CORNHILL LONDON", with "SM" hallmarks for London, 1857.

Based in Cornhill, London, Lund was a stationer and retailer of fine, often mechanical objects, such as corkscrews.

1857	3.5in (9cm) long
£100-150	**BLO**

A CLOSER LOOK AT A MORDAN PENCIL

Three colours of cast gold are used, pink, green and yellow – these were complex and expensive to produce.

Only a handful are known to collectors, making them extremely rare.

It is inset with seed pearls and small ruby cabochons.

The hand engraved gold plated shaft has a split, showing it may have been damaged and shortened slightly.

A small Mordan pencil, with gold shaft engraved with scrolling vines, the screw-off terminal set with seed pearls and rubies in a flowering vine pattern, the slider set with two rubies and pink gold fleur-de-lys, and pink and yellow gold end set with rubies, with fleur-de-lys in pink gold, marked "S.MORDAN & CO."

c1860 2in (5cm) long

£500-700 **PC**

A very rare "S.MORDAN & CO'S PATENT" silver pencil, with "SM*G R" hallmarks for London, 1825, and crown-like terminal.

This is an early example with a Sampson Mordan and Gabriel Riddle hallmark.

1825 4in (10cm) long

£200-300 **BLO**

An "S.MORDAN & CO MAKERS" silver pencil, with alternating columns of fine barley and line-and-dot, bloodstone-set terminal screwing off to reveal lead storage, "SM" hallmarks for London, 1848.

1848 4in (10cm) long closed

£80-120 **BLO**

A rare "S.MORDAN & CO" silver pencil, with "SM" hallmarks for London 1859, engraved with script presentation engraving "H.T. Lister", and with large screw-off agate set acanthus leaf terminal revealing lead storage.

This pattern is rare. The heavy terminal is similar to the capital of a classical architectural column.

1859 4in (10cm) long

£120-180 **BLO**

An 1830s "S.MORDAN & Co MAKERS & PATENTEES" silver pencil, with reeded body and citrine-set terminal.

3.5in (9cm) long closed

£70-100 **BLO**

An "S.MORDAN & CO. MAKERS" 18ct gold pencil, with fine barley shaft and bloodstone-set terminal with two engraved initials, screwing off to reveal lead storage, slider with carved flower and leaf motifs.

As well as the fact it is 18ct gold, it is in mint condition, which is a very rare attribute for such a functional and expensive object.

c1845 3.25in (8.5cm) long

£200-300 **BLO**

A miniature pencil and penknife, modelled as a musket with mahogany stock.

Novelty shaped pencils were popular during the second half of the 19thC. Look for those made by Mordan, especially in the forms of animals, guns, swords and other items such as boats.

c1880 3.5in (9cm) long

£50-80 **BLO**

An ivory Lund pencil, stamped "LUND PATENTEE LONDON", with rotating spiralling silver collar to propel the lead.

c1840 3.75in (9.5cm) long

£50-70 **BLO**

FIND OUT MORE...

Victorian Pencils: Tools to Jewels, *by Deborah Crosby, published by Schiffer Publishing, 1998.*

An English Wells & Lambe travelling writing case, the interior stamped "Wells & Lambe Manufacturers to the Queen", covered in green morocco leather.

c1840   9.5in (24cm) wide

£300-400   **BLO**

A rare French travelling writing set, with loops for ruler, seal, paper, pen, pencil, a wafer case and various accessories, the ends folding-out with a glass inkwell and a pounce pot with brass caps.

c1850   11.5in (29cm) wide

£500-600   **BLO**

A globe inkwell, with 12 coloured gores on brass sphere, markings in English, hinged cover and inner cover, and glass ink bottle.

1.75in (4.5cm) diam

£80-120   **EG**

A very rare 1950s English Parker Quink black Bakelite ink station, with central covered reservoir for Quink dispenser, some lettering missing paint.

7in (18cm) wide

£80-120   **BLO**

An early English Mabie Todd & Co counter-top display case, with two lift-out trays, repainted MTCo decal and plinth base, lacks inner trays and plaques from tray edges.

c1910   16.25in (41.5cm) high

£450-550   **BLO**

A rare 1920s English Mabie Todd & Co. 'Swan Pens' notepad holder, brass with sprung clamp titled in red with a black swan, on four dimpled feet, in excellent condition.

7in (17.5cm) high

£80-120   **BLO**

A German 'Kann Dir die Hand nicht geben' (I can't take your hand) humourous 'inky hand' postcard.

£10-15   **BLO**

A rare and early English Waterman's catalogue, with lithographed, embossed and gold-printed covers, 24pp printed in black and white and illustrations.

c1915   8in (20cm) high

£600-800   **BLO**

A celluloid alligator paperknife, 'swallowing' a black man-headed pencil.

7in (18cm) long

£30-40   **SOTT**

COLLECTORS' NOTES

- Commercial perfumeries boomed in the early years of the 20thC and devised many ingenious marketing and packaging ploys to increase sales of their products.

- Bottles often echo the name of the perfume they contain. Cherigan's 1929 fragrance 'Chance' featured a glass horseshoe on the bottle.

- Collectors will pay more for bottles full of perfume and complete with as much original packaging as possible. Many will even purchase empty packaging in order to reunite it with a stray bottle.

- Bottles with screw tops that have plastic linings can be dated to the 1960s or later. Those with rubber, cork or other linings will probably be older than this.

- One of the most prolific perfumers of the 20thC was Elsa Schiaparelli, an Italian who opened a successful Paris fashion house in 1929. The bottle for 'Shocking', released in 1936, was the first in the form of a female torso – a design since revived by Jean Paul Gaultier.

- A big name will not necessarily fetch a big price. Limited editions and scents that sold badly will be harder to find and therefore are often worth more.

- Perfume bottle enthusiasts might organise their collections by designer, company, fragrance or form. Much of the appeal of these bottles lies in the variety of materials used in their design. Glass, silver, fabric, ceramic, wood and bakelite were all used, often in combination.

A 'Blue Grass' by Elizabeth Arden "Merry Christmas Stocking" holiday gift set, the stocking holding a miniature bottle, with label, in plastic display, introduced in 1934.

'Blue Grass' is Arden's best-selling fragrance.

c1950s   1.75in (4.5cm) high

£150-250   **RDL**

A 1930s 'Carnation' by Elizabeth Arden special miniature perfume bottle, the bottle with interior blown flower and hang tag in original window box.

4in (10cm) high

£600-700   **RDL**

A 1960s Avon perfume bottle, in the shape of a soda siphon, unmarked.

7.5in (19cm) high

£15-25   **LB**

A 1930s 'Evening in Paris' by Bourjois blue bakelite owl-shaped perfume bottle and holder.

4in (10cm) high

£80-100   **LC**

A 1930s 'Evening in Paris' by Bourjois perfume bottle.

4.5in (11.5cm) high

£50-70   **LB**

A 1930s 'Evening in Paris' by Bourjois perfume bottle, in a novelty presentation case shaped as the Eiffel Tower.

2in (5cm) high

£100-150   **LB**

A late 1930s/early 1940s Cardinal 'Tantalux' presentation set, containing 'Bouquet', 'Chypre' and 'Gardenia', in the form of a tantalus with lock.

Also made as a twin set with screw-down top and lock.

4.5in (11.5cm) wide

£80-120   **TDG**

A 'Perfume Hypnotic' by Hattie Carnegie miniature perfume bottle, designed by Tommi Parzinger, with paper label, sealed.

c1946   *2in (5cm) high*

£200-300   **RDL**

A 'Les Pois de Senteur de Chez Moi' by Caron perfume bottle, designed by Baccarat, boxed, introduced in 1947.

4.75in (12cm) high

£220-280   **LB**

A 'Chance' by Cherigan perfume bottle, with applied glass horseshoe and black glass stopper, introduced in 1929.

3.25in (8cm) high

£450-550   **RDL**

A 1940s 'Dashing' by Lilly Dache perfume bottle, in faux ivory, with glass interior, on silk base with cover, lacking stopper.

Successful milliner and designer Lilly Dache introduced her two perfumes, 'Dashing' and 'Drifting', in 1941. She was advised by her husband, who had worked for Coty.

7.5in (19cm) high

£600-800   **RDL**

A 1940s 'Pink' by De Raymond holiday presentation bottle, with a glass bottle and fluorescent plastic Christmas tree, with plastic display box.

5in (12.5cm) high

£400-500   **RDL**

A 1950s 'Miss Dior' by Christian Dior perfume bottle, with label, introduced in 1947.

5.25in (13.5cm) high

£100-150   **LB**

A 1910s 'Illusion' by Drallé perfume bottle, with box and papers.

Drallé perfumes were packaged in wooden cases.

3.5in (9cm) high

£60-90   **LB**

A 1920s Fragonard presentation set of perfume solids, containing 'Supreme', '5' and 'Xmas', in wooden containers with labels and box.

containers 1in (2.5cm) high

£200-300   **RDL**

A 'Rose' by Gabilla perfume bottle, bottle by Baccarat, engraved "ABA" on stopper, introduced in 1912.

2.75in (7cm) high

£180-220   **LB**

A 'La Vierge Folle' by Gabilla perfume bottle, designed by Baccarat, introduced in 1912.

2.75in (7cm) high

£180-220 LB

A 'Cajolerie' by Gilot perfume bottle, with original box, introduced in 1930.

box 3.5in (9cm) high

£40-60 TDG

A 1950s '21' by Goya perfume gift set, with two different bottles.

The playful period graphics on this box make it a desirable example.

larger bottle 2.75in (7cm) high

£80-120 LB

A 1950s 'Gardenia' by Goya small perfume bottle.

1.5in (4cm) high

£15-25 LB

A 'Gardenia' by Goya perfume bottle, with original box, introduced in 1952.

'Gardenia' bottles were made with varying numbers of rings and collectors often seek to acquire one of each of example.

2.5in (6.5cm) high

£20-40 LB

A 'Contes Choisis' by Marcel Guerlain perfume bottle, by Depinoix, with sepia stain and label, introduced in 1926.

3.5in (9cm) high

£700-900 RDL

A limited edition 'Tropiques' by Lancôme perfume bottle, by Jean Sala, with label, in deluxe display box.

1944 *4.75in (11.5cm) high*

£600-700 RDL

A 1900s 'Violettes Prince Albert' by Oriza L. Legrand perfume bottle, old factory bottle.

4in (10cm) high

£60-90 LB

A 'La Saison des Fleurs' by Lionceau presentation set of perfume solids, in bakelite containers with moulded scent names, boxed.

c1936 *dice 0.75in (2cm) high*

£150-200 RDL

PERFUME BOTTLES

A 'Femme Divine' by Loulette perfume bottle, made by Depinoix to a Julien Viard design, with pink enamel and grey stain, minor flaw, introduced in 1926.

3.75in (9.5cm) high

£300-400 RDL

A 'Bouquet de Papillons' by Lubin perfume bottle, by Depinoix, introduced in 1919.

3in (7.5cm) high c1935

£300-400 RDL

A 'Nuit de Long Champ' by Lubin perfume bottle.

6.5in (15cm) high

£120-180 LB

A 'Prince Douka' by Marquay perfume bottle, with jewelled fabric cape and neck label, with box, introduced in 1956.

This bottle was sold with a range of differently coloured capes.

4in (10cm) high

£300-400 RDL

A 1950s Mary Chess 'Perfume Gallery' complete presentation of six perfumes, the bottles shaped as chess pieces, with chessboard box.

box 3.25in (8cm) wide

£600-700 RDL

A 1920s 'Princess Maria' by Prince Matchabelli perfume bottle, stencilled "France".

2.5in (6.5cm) high

£300-400 RDL

A 1960s 'Chantrelle' by Max Factor perfume bottle.

This example was probably a promotional Christmas design. 'Chantrelle' was one of the most popular Max Factor perfumes – it was a well known design and there are many variations on the cat theme. The glass dome echoes Schiaparelli's earlier designs.

6in (15cm) high

£30-40 LB

A 'Habinita' by Molinard perfume bottle, with box, introduced in 1925.

3in (7.5cm) high

£120-180 LB

A 'Muguet' by Molinard tester perfume bottle, sealed, introduced in 1928.

3.5in (9cm) high

£100-200 RDL

A 1930s 'Oeillet' perfume bottle, possibly by Arys, with "Vrai Parfum Oeillet" label.

7in (18cm) high

£70-100   **TDG**

A set of 'Bouquet' by Ota perfume bottles, in the form of pearls, each with a stopper to the base, in display box with label, one stained pearl, introduced in 1929.

box 6in (15cm) high

£500-700   **RDL**

A 1900s 'Extrait des Fleurs' perfume bottle, retailed by Parfymeri F. Pauli of Stockholm, probably French, with original box.

4in (10cm) high

£30-40   **LB**

A 1900s 'Bouquet Marie-Louise' by Ed Pinaud perfume bottle, with label and box.

4.5in (11.5cm) high

£300-400   **RDL**

A 'Parfum Pompeia' by L.T. Piver perfume bottle, with label, seal and box.

c1924   *4.5in (11.5cm) high*

£300-400   **RDL**

A 'Carnet de Bal' by Revillon perfume bottle, with gold label attached to neck.

c1937   *3.5in (9cm) high*

£80-120   **LB**

An 'Amour Daria' by Revillon perfume bottle, introduced in 1935.

4.25in (11cm) high

£80-120   **LB**

A 'Coeur Joie' by Nina Ricci perfume bottle, with box, introduced in 1946.

4in (10cm) high

£180-220   **LB**

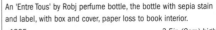

An 'Entre Tous' by Robj perfume bottle, the bottle with sepia stain and label, with box and cover, paper loss to book interior.

c1925   *3.5in (9cm) high*

£600-800   **RDL**

PERFUME BOTTLES

An 'Aladin' by Rosine perfume bottle, in cast metal with chain handle and faux ivory stopper, introduced in 1919.

2.5in (6.5cm) high

£200-300 **RDL**

A 1930s Saturday Night Lotion' bottle, with gold label, embossed "ASJ", probably English.

5in (13cm) high

£20-30 **LB**

A 'Mischief' by Saville perfume bottle, in a bakelite novelty egg-shaped presentation case, introduced in 1935.

2.5in (6.5cm) high

£120-180 **LB**

A 'Shocking You' by Schiaparelli perfume bottle, in novelty cigarette carton style box.

box 4in (10cm) high

£40-60 **TDG**

A CLOSER LOOK AT A PERFUME BOTTLE

One of Schiaparelli's best known perfumes, introduced in 1936.

This bottle was designed by Eleanore Fini after a bust sent by Mae West for Schiaparelli to fit her clothes to.

Schiaparelli was the first to use the term 'shocking pink' and the colour became her trademark .

Her 1949 perfume, Zut, was sold in a bottle shaped as a woman's lower torso, forming a whole with this bottle.

A 1930s 'Shocking' by Schiaparelli perfume bottle, in a domed presentation case, with box.

dome 4in (10cm) high

£220-280 **LB**

A 'Sleeping' by Schiaparelli perfume bottle, introduced in 1938.

6.25in (16cm) high

£200-300 **LB**

A 'Sleeping' by Schiaparelli miniature perfume bottle, with plastic screw cap in the form of a flame and full banner label, introduced in 1938.

3.25in (8cm) high

£60-80 **RDL**

A 'Success Fou' by Schiaparelli perfume bottle, the bottle with enamelled and gilt detail and foil label in heart-shaped display box, including advertisement affixed to interior.

1953 *2.5in (6.5cm) high*

£250-350 **RDL**

A CLOSER LOOK AT A PERFUME BOTTLE

A 'Zut' by Schiaparelli perfume bottle, the bottle with gold details, in silk-lined box, wear to box exterior, introduced in 1948.

5in (12.5cm) high

£300-400   **RDL**

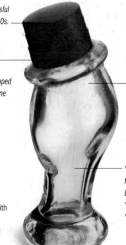

Parisian Suzy was a successful milliner in the 1930s and 40s.

The normal size bottle, designed by Baccarat and produced in crystal, was topped with a stopper shaped as one of Suzy's hats.

A rare 'Ecarlate Suzy' by Suzy miniature perfume bottle, the glass bottle with plastic screw cap in the form of a hat, introduced in 1939.

The standard bottle was made in three sizes.

'Ecarlate Suzy' was her first perfume, followed by 'Golden Laughter', 'Bandbox' and 'Madrigal'.

1.75in (4.5cm) high

£800-1,000   **RDL**

A 'Zut' by Schiaparelli perfume bottle, the bottle with gold details, sealed and labelled, with waist sash and suede drawstring pouch, introduced in 1948.

3.75in (9.5cm) high

£400-600   **RDL**

A 'Ze Zan' by Tuvache perfume bottle, in gilt glass with wooden screw cap, on wooden stand with gold-glazed ceramic display cover.

1947   *4.25in (10.5cm) high*

£1,200-1,800   **RDL**

A 1930s 'Golliwogg' by Vigny perfume bottle, the clear glass bottle forming the head, with plastic screw cap collar and box, tied to hang as a Christmas ornament.

2in (5cm) high

£300-400   **RDL**

A 'Le Chick-Chick' by Vigny perfume bottle, with gold-coloured detail and yellow metal stopper cover, introduced in 1923.

3.5in (9cm) high

£800-1,000   **RDL**

A 'Pourpre d'Automne' by Violet perfume bottle, by Lucien Gaillard, with painted detail, some paint loss, introduced in 1922.

3.75in (8.5cm) high

£400-500   **RDL**

A 1930s 'Antilope' by Weil perfume bottle, with engraved "W" on stopper.

6in (15cm) high

£50-70   **LB**

COLLECTORS' NOTES

■ Pez were invented by Viennese confectioner Eduard Haas III in 1927. Sold in tins, the peppermint flavoured sweets were aimed at the adult market in Austria as a breath freshener. In 1948, Oskar Uxa designed a new dispenser shaped like a cigarette lighter, these are known as 'regulars' today.

■ The company expanded into the US in 1952 and while initially unsuccessful, the addition of character heads into the dispensers and new fruit-flavoured sweets aimed at the children proved a great marketing ploy.

■ The first ranges included Santa Claus, Space Trooper and Popeye and have since expanded to include animals, people (but rarely real-life personalities), cartoon and film characters and holiday-themed dispensers. Companies and organisations, such as Zielpunkt, eBay, Nivea, and the rare Sparefroh, have also commissioned promotional dispensers over the years. With such a range, many have cross-over appeal.

■ Many characters have been continually produced, with a number of redesigns and variations appearing, and collectors often try to collect the whole set. In general, early examples, lacking the feet which were added in 1987, are more desirable and, unusually, the plain 'regulars' from the early 1950s are some of the most sought-after.

■ With such a strong collectors' market, Pez now produce a range of dispensers and other merchandise aimed directly at collectors.

An early 1960s Walt Disney's 'Donald Duck' Pez dispenser, with die-cut stem and without feet.

This is one of five dispensers made with a die-cut stem, the Easter Bunny is the most sought after at approximately £300.

4.25in (11cm) high

£70-100　　　　　**DMI**

An early 1960s Walt Disney's 'Pluto' Pez dispenser, first version with movable ears and without feet.

4in (10cm) high

£15-20　　　　　**DMI**

A mid-1960s Walt Disney 'Lil' Bad Wolf' Pez dispenser, without feet.

3.75in (9.5cm) high

£15-25　　　　　**DMI**

A late 1960s Walt Disney's 'Baloo' Pez dispenser, from "The Jungle Book", with blue-grey head and without feet.

4in (10cm) high

£12-22　　　　　**DMI**

A late 1970s Walt Disney's 'Thumper' Pez dispenser, from 'Bambi', without feet.

Look for the rare variation that has a copyright symbol together with "WDP" on the head, it could be worth up to £100.

4in (10cm) high

£30-50　　　　　**DMI**

A late 1980s Walt Disney's 'Goofy' Pez dispenser, with green hat and with feet.

4.5in (11.5cm) high

£1-2　　　　　**DMI**

A 1990s Walt Disney's 'Duck Nephew' Pez character dispenser, with feet.

c1990　　　　4in (10cm) high

£3-5　　　　　**DMI**

A CLOSER LOOK AT A PEZ DISPENSER

This is one of five dispensers that were produced with a die-cut design cut into the stem, the others were Casper, Donald Duck, Mickey Mouse and the Easter Bunny.

The character of Bozo the Clown was created by Alan W. Livingston in 1946 and a TV show was released in 1949. The rights to the character were bought by Larry Harmon in 1956, who then expanded the franchise considerably.

A late 1990s 'Asterix the Gaul' Pez character dispenser, from the reissue series.

The original series, made without feet, was released in the mid-1970s, but not in the US, making it very rare there. It can be worth up to £1,200.

At £200-300, the Easter Bunny version is the most valuable of this range.

Like most of these five, a solid version of Bozo was also made. Unusually the solid version is slightly more valuable.

A 'Popeye' Pez dispenser, with applied hat and plain face and without feet.

4.5in (11.5cm) high

An early 1960s Bozo the Clown Pez dispenser, with die-cut stem.

4.25in (11cm) high

5in (12.5cm) high

£40-60 DMI	**£2-4** DMI	**£70-100** DMI

A late 1980s 'Papa Smurf' Pez dispenser, from the first Smurfs' series, with thin feet.

4in (10cm) high

A 'Batman' Pez dispenser, blue mask version with short ears and with feet.

4.25in (11cm) high

An 'R2-D2' Pez dispenser, from the third Star Wars series.

2002   4.5in (11cm) high

An 'E.T.' Pez dispenser, manufactured to coincide with the 2002 reissue of the Steven Spielberg film.

2002   4in (10cm) high

£3-6 DMI	**£6-8** DMI	**£1-2** DMI	**£1-2** DMI

PEZ DISPENSERS

A 'Lamb' Pez dispenser, from
the Merry Music Makers series,
without feet.

An 'Easter Bunny' Pez
dispenser, with fat ears and
without feet.

c1970   *4.25in (11cm) high*

£15-20   **DMI**

A 1990s 'Easter Bunny' Pez
dispenser, version 'D' with long
ears and plain nose.

4.75in (12cm) high

£1-2   **DMI**

A 'Lamb' Pez dispenser, from
the Merry Music Makers series,
without feet.

c1985   *4in (10cm) high*

£12-18   **DMI**

A 1980s 'Chick in Egg' Pez
dispenser, the thick plastic
shell with saw-blade points.

4.75in (12cm) high

£2-4   **DMI**

A 1980s 'Jack-o-Lantern' Pez
dispenser, with die-cut face
and with feet.

4.25in (11cm) high

£6-8   **DMI**

A Japanese 'Jack-o-Lantern' Pez
dispenser, with a blue-tinted
crystal head.

4.5in (11.5cm) high

£2-3   **DMI**

An early 1970s 'Angel' Pez
dispenser, with yellow hair and
feet.

4.75in (12cm) high

£25-35   **DMI**

A 'Santa Claus' Pez dispenser,
an unusual colourway with a
tan face and white hat.

4.5in (11.5cm) high

£4-5   **DMI**

A 1950s 'Santa Claus' full body Pez dispenser.

*Santa Claus dispensers are perennially popular and have been
made continually since the 1950s. This is the first version and the
most desirable. Examples made from the 1970s are very common.*

3.75in (9.5cm) high

£80-120   **DMI**

An early 1970s 'Policeman' Pez dispenser, from the Pez Pals series.

4in (10cm) high

£30-40 **DMI**

An African American 'Bride' Pez dispenser, from the Pez Pals series, with feet.

4.25in (11cm) high

£7-10 **DMI**

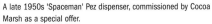

A late 1950s 'Spaceman' Pez dispenser, commissioned by Cocoa Marsh as a special offer.

The version lacking the 'Cocoa Marsh' on the stem is worth about 15 per cent less.

4.5in (11.5cm) high

£100-150 **DMI**

An African American 'Groom' Pez dispenser, from the Pez Pals series, with feet.

The early version without feet is very rare and can be worth £200-300.

4.5in (11.5cm) high

£5-8 **DMI**

An early 1980s 'Indian' Pez dispenser, from the Merry Music Maker series.

Merry Music Makers feature a whistle on the back of the head of the dispenser and were introduced in the early 1980s. The owl is the rarest version and can be worth over £1,000.

5in (12.5cm) high

£12-18 **DMI**

A 'Bubbleman' yellow neon Pez dispenser, with feet.

1998 4.25in (11cm) high

£2-4 **DMI**

A mid-1990s 'BP' Pez dispenser, from the Pez Pals series with BP 'body parts'.

4.5in (11.5cm) high

£5-8 **DMI**

An early 1980s 'Koala' Pez dispenser, from the Merry Music Maker series, with feet.

4in (10cm) high

£5-8 **DMI**

A mid-1970s 'Rooster' Pez dispenser, with white face and red crop and comb.

White is the most common colour for the 'Rooster'.

4.5in (11.5cm) high

£20-30 **DMI**

A 1990s 'Icee Bear' Pez dispenser.

4.5in (11.5cm) high

£3-4   DMI

A 'Crystal Ball' Pez dispenser on stand, with blue stars.

Produced for a mail-in offer, the first 2,500 were made with silver stars instead of blue stars but there is not a great deal of difference in value at the moment.

2002   5in (12.5cm) high

£12-18   DMI

A limited edition 'Nivea Truck' promotional Pez dispenser, from an edition of 10,000, commissioned by Nivea and made available at the European Nivea Fun Fest.

2003   4in (10cm) long

£5-10   DMI

A 'Smiley' promotional Pez dispenser, commissioned by the Austrian supermarket chain Zielpunkt, depicting their mascot, complete in original packaging.

1999   8.5in (21.5cm) high

£5-8   DMI

A Euro 2004 promotional Pez dispenser, to commemorate Sweden's participation in the finals, complete in original packaging.

2004   8.5in (21.5cm) high

£15-20   DMI

An 'LSU Tigers' baseball promotional Pez dispenser.

4in (10cm) high

£12-18   DMI

A 'Metro Stars' Hockey Pez dispenser.

4in (10cm) high

£12-18   DMI

An 'eBay' Pez dispenser, commissioned by and sold through eBay.

Pez produced 5,000 dispensers for eBay in yellow, blue, red and green colourways, which were sold online in 2000, and are worth approximately the same.

2000   4.5in (11.5cm) high

£8-12   DMI

A 'Silver Glow' Pez regular dispenser, made to commemorate the opening of a new Pez factory in Hungary.

1991   3.5in (9cm) high

£15-20   DMI

FIND OUT MORE...

Collector's Guide to Pez, by Shawn Peterson, published by Krause Publications, 2nd edition, 2003.
The Museum of Pez Memorabilia, 214 California Drive, Burlingame, California, 94010, USA.
www.pezcentral.com
www.pezcollectors.com

'Dartmouth Winter Carnival' Canadian tourism poster, designed by Ostberg.

1939   *34in (85cm) high*

£1,200-1,800   **SWA**

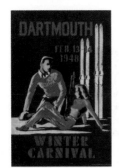

'Dartmouth Winter Carnival', Canadian tourism poster, designed by Gish.

1948   *33.25in (83cm) high*

£1,800-2,200   **SWA**

'Nice/Beuil', French tourism poster, designed by Jean Gabriel Domergue.

c1935   *39.5in (99cm) high*

£450-550   **SWA**

'Japan XI Olympic Winter Games', Japanese tourism poster, designed by Yosuke Kamekura (1915-97).

1972   *40.75in (102cm) high*

£500-600   **SWA**

'Sun Valley / "Round House"', American ski poster designed by D.S.

Ski posters have become sought-after due to their bold and visually appealing imagery that combines the romance of foreign destinations with the excitement and fashions of the winter sport. Sun Valley, Idaho was created by Averell Harriman (Chairman of Union Pacific Railroad) as a destination resort to encourage people to ride the railroad out west.

                    40in (100cm) high

£1,700-2,000   **SWA**

'Engelberg/Trübsee', Swiss tourism poster, designed by Herbert Matter (1907-84).

1936   *28.75in (72cm) high*

£1,500-2,000   **SWA**

'St. Moritz', Swiss tourism poster, designed by Walter Herdeg (1908-95).

1934   *39.75in (99cm) high*

£500-600   **SWA**

'St. Moritz', Swiss tourism poster, designed by Walter Herdeg.

1934   *40in (100cm) high*

£1,200-1,800   **SWA**

'USA, Psychedelic Travel', 1970s American tourism poster.

39in (100cm) high

£50-60 CL

'See America, Welcome to Montana', 1980s American tourism poster, designed by J.H. Rothstein.

28in (71cm) high

£80-120 CL

'Visit Washington State', 1960s American tourism poster, designed by Harry Bonath.

1964   29in (73cm) high

£300-400 CL

'New York Loves You', 1970s American tourism poster showing famous singer Lena Horne wearing an 'I Love NY' badge, photograph by Richard Avedon.

36in (91cm) high

£80-120 CL

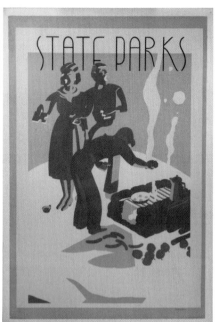

'State Parks', 1930s American tourist poster, designed by Dorothy Waugh.

41in (104cm) high

£300-500 CL

'Mexico', 1950s Mexican tourism poster, designed by Espert.

37in (94cm) high

£150-250 CL

'Deutschland', 1920s German tourism poster designed by Friedel Dzubas.

39in (100cm) high

£650-750   **CL**

A CLOSER LOOK AT A TRAVEL POSTER

Hohlwein (1879-1934) was one of Germany's most notable poster artists, known for his WWI designs and use of bold, colours.

This poster was designed as part of a series of four, advertising Munich Zoo in 1911, the others show a flamingo, eagles and panthers.

Hohlwein was an animal lover and a hunter and often used animals in his designs.

This was the first in the series as the image was also used to advertise the opening of the zoo on August 1st 1911.

'Zoologischer Garten München', designed by Ludwig Hohlwein (1874-1949), printed by G. Schuh, Munich.

1911   *46.75in (117cm) high*

£700-1,000   **SWA**

'Germany, Spring in Wiesbaden', 1930s German tourism poster.

33in (80cm) high

£250-350   **CL**

'Baden-Baden', 1960s German tourism poster, by an unknown designer.

33in (82.5cm) high

£180-220   **SWA**

'Saint Aubin', 1930s French tourism poster, designed by A. Galland.

39in (99cm) high

£220-280   **CL**

'Mont St. Michel', 1950s French tourism poster, designed by E. Thollander.

37in (34cm) high

£70-100   **CL**

Saison d'Été Menton', 1950s French tourism poster, designed by F. Ferrie.

39in (100cm) high

£350-450   **CL**

'Egypt', 1950s Egyptian tourism poster, designed by M. Azmy.

39in (99cm) high

£150-250   **CL**

'Egypt', 1950s Egyptian tourism poster, designed by Ihap Hulusi.

Ihap Hulusi studied under German graphic designer Ludwig Hohlwein until 1925. He was one of the earliest, and best known, Turkish graphic designers until the 1960s. He is well known for his travel posters.

39in (99cm) high

£250-350   **CL**

'Finland', 1930s Finnish tourism poster, designed by Bade.

39in (100cm) high

£200-300   **CL**

'Visit India, Kashmir', 1930s Indian tourism poster.

39in (100cm) high

£150-250   **CL**

'Centro Turistico Giovanile', 1950s Italian tourism poster.

39in (100cm) high

£150-250   **CL**

'Poland, Fishing in the Mazurian Lakeland', 1960s Polish tourism poster, designed by Slomczyinski.

39in (100cm) high

£120-180   **CL**

'Ribatejo, Portugal', 1950s Portuguese tourism poster, designed by Gustavo Fontoura.

39in (100cm) high

£100-150   **CL**

'Scotland's Wonderland by MacBraynes Steamers', designed by E.C. Le Cadell, printed by McCorquodale, small losses, tears and pinholes to margin, fold.

40.25in (102cm) high

£300-400   **ON**

COLLECTORS' NOTES

- Pre-1950s Airline posters evoke an era when air travel was an exciting and glamorous novelty. The designs were often stylish and innovative, reflecting the cutting-edge world of flight and making them particularly popular with today's collectors. 1930s posters featuring Art Deco artwork and notable airlines can command high prices, although examples by unknown designers can be worth less.

- Air travel had become more common by the 1950s and posters from that period tend to emphasis speed and convenience over glamour. Bold lines, geometric shapes and flat colours remained predominant.

- Posters for well-known airline companies, such as Pan Am, British Overseas Airways Corporation (BOAC)

and Air France, tend to attract a premium due to the size of their following, as do designs featuring appealing locations.

- Posters were produced to be used and were often printed on delicate paper, making them susceptible to tears and creases. Condition is important and any damage to the image is likely to seriously affect the value of a poster. Professional restorers can correct many problems and can back them with linen.

- Beware of reproductions. Learn to recognise the difference in the print qualities of early and contemporary posters by visiting dealers and salesrooms. Later examples tend to be printed on thicker, paper with an image made up of pixels.

'AOA USA The Route of the Flagships', poster designed by Lewitt-Him, printed by W.R. Royle.

37.75in (96cm) high

£120-180   **ON**

'American Airlines to New York' poster designed by Edward McKnight Kauffer.

Modernist designer Edward McKnight Kauffer (1890-1954) is perhaps best known for his Art Deco poster designs for Shell. He worked in London from 1914-40, notably for Frank Pick of London Transport, returning to the US in 1940. His work has featured in many exhibitions, including at the Museum of Modern Art, New York, and the Victoria & Albert Museum, London.

c1950   39.25in (98cm) high

£450-550   **SWA**

'BEA, British European Airways', 1940s English poster, in very good condition.

39in (100cm) high

£300-400   **CL**

'For Better Travel by B.O.A.C.', poster designed by Abram Games (1914-96).

1952   30in (75cm) high

£300-500   **SWA**

'B. O. A. C. Flies to All 6 Continents', poster designed by Abram Games, printed by Baynard Press.

1952   40in (100cm) high

£350-450   **SWA**

'Fly BOAC, It's a Smaller World by Speedbird', 1950s British poster, designed by Beverly Pick.

39in (100cm) high

£100-200   **CL**

'Rome by Clipper, Pan American', 1950s American poster.

39in (100cm) high

£250-350   **CL**

A CLOSER LOOK AT AN AIRLINE POSTER

Founded in 1933 by the merger of three companies, Air France is one of the most desirable names in airline posters due to its superb designs.

This is typical of his style for the company, which usually incorporated maps. His posters showing maps of the world are highly sought after.

This poster was designed by Lucien Boucher (1889-1971), who designed many posters for Air France during the 1940s and 1950s.

Boucher had a Surrealist artistic background – here the wing not only represents flight, but also the shape of South America.

'Air France, South America', 1950s French poster, designed by Lucien Boucher.

39in (100cm) high

£300-400   **CL**

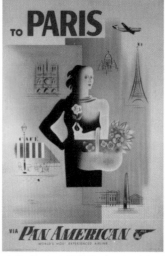

'To Paris via Pan American', 1950s French poster, designed by Jean Carlu.

Jean Carlu (1900-97) was the third of France's foremost poster designers during the 1920s and 1930s, after Adolphe Mouron 'Cassandre' and Paul Colin. He is known for his bright colours, strong geometric designs and minimal use of words to create dramatic, eye-catching posters. Cubism and Surrealism were strong influences. This example also shows styling typical of the 1950s. He designed for Perrier and Cinzano, as well as for the US government.

41in (104cm) high

£250-350   **CL**

'Round the World, Round the Clock via Pan American', 1950s American poster.

41in (104cm) high

£150-200   **CL**

'Seattle United Air Lines', 1960s American poster.

39in (100cm) high

£80-120   **CL**

'Fly by West African Airways Corporation', 1950s poster, by an anonymous designer.

30in (76cm) high

£180-220   **ON**

A CLOSER LOOK AT A RAILWAY POSTER

Designed by John Hassall in 1908, this poster, incorporating the 'Jolly Fisherman', is perhaps the most famous holiday railway poster ever printed.

Produced for the LNER, it exists in a number of versions. One features a child pulling the fisherman's scarf and another is in portrait format.

Later Skegness posters, such as BRER's 1958 version, have the addition of Skegness' famous pier in the background.

The poster was produced to promote Skegness to Londoners. In 1908, the town had 300,000 visitors, making it one of Britain's most popular holiday destinations.

'Skegness Is So Bracing, It's Quicker By Rail', designed by John Hassall, printed for the LNER by Waterlow & Sons Ltd London, mounted on linen.

Hassall (1868-1948) had never visited Skegness when he designed this poster, for which he received 12 guineas! The catchphrase is thought to have been developed by an unknown LNER (London & North Eastern Railway) employee.

50in (127cm) wide

£1,800-2,200   **ON**

'France, Normandy', 1950s English language French poster for French Railways, designed by Raoul Dufy.

Born in Normandy, Raoul Dufy (1877-1953) was a notable French painter and part of the 'Fauve' group. Meaning 'wild beast', they gained their nickname from their wild use of bright colour.

39in (99cm) high

£250-350   **CL**

'London's Offer', designed by Jan Lewitt (1907-91) and Jerzy Him (1900-82), printed by Baynard Press, London, for the London Underground.

Each arm holds an item symbolic of the various activities that people can participate in around London.

1938   40in (101.5cm) high

£300-400   **SWA**

'Service To Industry Steel', designed by Norman Wilkinson, published by RELMR, printed by Jordison, mounted on linen.

1949   50in (127cm) wide

£500-600   **ON**

'East Coast Frolics Travel Cheaply by L.N.E.R.', designed by Frank Newbould, lithographic print by Chorley & Pickersgill Ltd., published by LNER, unframed.

39.5in (100cm) high

£1,000-1,500   **L&T**

'Demountable Tanks', designed by Kenneth McDonough, published by RELMR, printed by Jordison.

1951   40.25in (102cm) high

£80-120   **ON**

'Bata', 1950s Swiss footwear advertising poster, designed by Birkhauser.

51in (128cm) high

£200-250   **CL**

'Macy's', anonymous American advertising poster.

1938   *33in (82.5cm) high*

£60-80   **SWA**

A CLOSER LOOK AT AN ADVERTISING POSTER

Beginning his poster work in 1899, Cappiello (1875-1942) became one of the most revered and revolutionary 20thC poster designers.

As well as the 'unnecessary' gentlemen's bodies being out of the design, Cappiello's clever design skills show in the reason for gentlemen removing their hats – for a lady, who is also unseen.

This design for a French hat maker honours Surrealist artist René Magritte, who famously painted bowler-hatted men from 1927.

The yellow gloved hand is unusual and hints at the Dandies or show performers of the day, adding a louche but theatrical aspect.

'Mossant', designed by Leonetto Cappiello, printed by Edimo, Paris.

1938   *62.5in (156cm) high*

£1,200-1,800   **SWA**

'Galeries Lafayette', 1980s French poster for the English market, showing an elegant Parisienne, dressed and with a haircut in the style of the day.

66in (167.5cm) high

£150-200   **CL**

'Familistère', designed by Leon Dupin, printed by Joseph-Charles, Paris.

1928   *55in (137.5cm) high*

£500-600   **SWA**

'Thonet Seatings Greeting', 1970s American Christmas poster.

Austrian company Thonet (est. 1819) produced fine quality chairs made from bent beech wood from 1859 and, later, chromed metal tubing.

41in (104cm) high

£120-180   **CL**

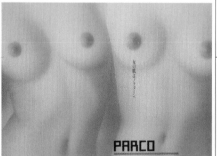

'Parco', by an unknown designer, for a Japanese Department store.

c1975   *40.5in (101cm) high*

£250-350   **SWA**

'Chanel No. 5', American advertising poster, artwork designed by Andy Warhol.

Andy Warhol's (1928-87) 1985 screenprints were produced in four colours, and were used for the perfume's 75th Anniversary in 1996.

1996   *68in (27cm) high*

£120-180   **CL**

'Écoutez La Voix Du Monde', French radio advertising poster designed by René Ravo (1904-98), printed by Réunies, Paris.

c1935   *46.25in (115.5cm) high*

£900-1,000   **SWA**

'Hora Cine Dial', 1930s Spanish advertising poster designed by Kras for Cabouli & Villaro.

                          39in (100cm) high

£400-500   **CL**

A CLOSER LOOK AT AN IPOD POSTER

The use of a strongly coloured background is unusual, Apple usually choose white.

The iPod has revolutionized the way we listen to music and has become the 'must-have' for all ages of music lovers.

Rumour has it that Apple demand all advertising is sent back to them for recycling – as the product and campaign is so iconic, examples may become sought-after and collectable.

It is typical of Apple's approach to advertising, showing a young person dancing to music and clearly holding an iPod – encapsulating both brand and lifestyle.

'iPod', American silhouette advertising poster for Apple Computers.

This campaign was produced in myriad colours with people of many races and nationalities. The lack of detail and simple, striking colours work well, leaving the iPod shown in its real-life white. This is one of the more appealing versions.

c2003   *36in (91.5cm) high*

£50-60   **CL**

'You'll See – Murphy Television', rare and early poster designed by Frederic Henri Kay Henrion (1914-90).

1950   *22.5in (56cm) high*

£280-320   **SWA**

'Olympia Portable', 1930s French advertising poster.

                    45in (115cm) high

£200-300   **CL**

'Olivetti Graphika', Italian adverting poster designed by Giovanni Pintori (b.1912), printed by N. Moneta, Milan.

c1958   *27.5in (69cm) high*

£400-500   **SWA**

'Bissell's Cyco-Bearing Carpet Sweeper', American Christmas advertising lithographic poster, by Michigan Litho. Company, Grand Rapids.

                    50in (127cm) high

£1,000-1,500   **JDJ**

'iPod', American advertising poster for Apple Computers.

c2003   *36in (91.5cm) high*

£30-40   **CL**

'Papier à Cigarettes Job', 1900s French advertising poster for Job cigarettes designed by Edgard Mascence.

22in (56cm) high

£250-350   **CL**

'Fumar el Papel Job', 1900s Spanish advertising poster for Job cigarettes designed by A. Villa.

22in (56cm) high

£150-250   **CL**

'Marlboro', 1980s American advertising poster.

22in (56cm) high

£15-25   **CL**

'Marlboro', 1980s American advertising poster.

22in (56cm) wide

£15-25   **CL**

'The New Yorker', 1970s American advertising poster, designed by R.O. Blechman.

40in (101cm) high

£100-150   **CL**

'The New Yorker', 1950s American Christmas advertising poster.

46in (117cm) high

£200-300   **CL**

'It's Spring! And Life is Wonderful!', American LIFE magazine advertising poster, designed by R.M.

c1963   *43.75in (109cm) wide*

£250-350   **SWA**

'Le Parisien', French advertising poster, designed by Phili.

c1946   *63in (160cm) high*

£700-900   **CL**

'Cacao Lhara', designed by Jules Cheret, printed by Chaix, Paris.

Jules Cheret (1836-1932) is a notable early poster artist, who contributed to the development of the advertising poster is huge. Executed in the Art Nouveau style, his designs also capture the 'laissez-faire' attitude of Belle Epoque Paris.

1893   97in (242.5cm) high

£800-1,200   **SWA**

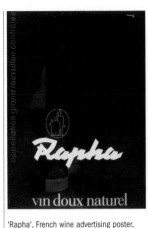

'Rapha', French wine advertising poster, designed by Charles Loupot (1892-1962), printed by I.C.A., Paris.

1958   31in (77.5cm) high

£600-700   **SWA**

'Volg Traubensaft', German grape juice advertising poster, designed by Josef Müller-Brockmann (1914-96), printed by A. Trub & Co., one in a series for a brand of grape juice.

c1952   50in (125cm) high

£250-350   **SWA**

'Phillips Bicycles Renowned The World Over', anonymous printed advertisement.

27.25in (69cm) high

£350-450   **ON**

'Teinturerie Du Point Noir', designed by Leon Dupin, printed by Joseph-Charles, Paris.

1934   55in (137.5cm) high

£350-450   **SWA**

'Humber', British bicycle advertising poster designed by French poster designer Clouet.

Humber Bicycles (1898-1976) must have given a truly 'heavenly' ride! It's the superb design and printing quality of this poster, as well as its age and style, that makes it so valuable.

c1900   63in (160cm) high

£800-1,200   **CL**

'Hangi Daitokan', designed by Tadanori Yokoo (b.1936), to advertise a book by Tatsumi Hijikata, reusing an old poster design, central calligraphy by writer Yukio Mishima.

1970   42.75in (107cm) high

£1,500-2,000   **SWA**

'For You from Britain', 1960s British advertising poster designed by Eileen Evans.

This poster promoted Britain's innovative modern design during the 1960s, from the 'Mini' to glass, fabric and metalware.

39in (99cm) high

£70-100   **ON**

'The London Group – Exhibition of Modern Art', designed by Edward McKnight Kauffer (1890-1954), printed by Dangerfield, London, using two colours.

1919   *29.75in (74cm) high*

£800-1,200   **SWA**

A CLOSER LOOK AT AN EXHIBITION POSTER

The image shows Hamilton's iconic collage "Just What Is It that Makes Today's Home so Different, so Appealing?" which is considered to be the first true piece of Pop Art.

It shows 'new' domestic appliances of the 1950s such as a vacuum cleaner, tape player and television, as well as canned foods and other references to the new popular and consumerist culture.

It was initially designed for the poster and catalogue of the exhibition 'This Is Tomorrow' at the Whitechapel Gallery, London in 1956

This poster was produced in the 1970s when Hamilton was internationally famous and enjoying many retrospectives.

'Just What Is It...?', designed by Richard Hamilton (b.1922).

1976   *30in (75cm) high*

£600-800   **SWA**

'Buy American Art/Art Week', small silk screen poster designed by Joseph Binder (1898-1972), printed by New York City W.P.A. Project.

1940   *12in (30cm) high*

£600-700   **SWA**

'Moderne Kunst aus USA', designed by Karl Oscar Blasé (b.1925).

1955   *33in (82.5cm) high*

£120-180   **SWA**

'Bauhaus Exhibition 1968, designed by Herbert Bayer.

1968   *25in (66cm) high*

£70-100   **CL**

'Guggenheim Museum', designed by Malcolm Grear.

This was produced as a set of four posters.

c1970   *33in (82.5cm) high*

£250-350   **SWA**

'Rokuo Taninchi's Exhibition', by Tadanori Yokoo.

This was produced for the retrospective of painter and illustrator Rokuo Taninchi's work.

1981   *40.5in (101cm) high*

£350-450   **SWA**

'Robert Mapplethorpe', designed by Robert Mapplethorpe.

1988   *33in (91cm) high*

£60-80   **CL**

'Bygge og Bolig', Danish exhibition poster, artwork by I.B. Anderson.

Produced for an exhibition of Danish construction and housing, the impactful design is quintessentially of its period. It has strong Art Deco and Bauhaus elements in both the pictorial design and use of font.

1929   33in (80cm) high

£1,800-2,200   **CLG**

'International Industries Fair Brussels 1939', anonymous designer, printed by Creations Brussels, tears and folds.

1939   39.75in (101cm) wide

£80-120   **ON**

'International Society for Contemporary Music XVII Festival Krakow Poland 1939', designed by Osiecki and printed for Polish State Railways by W. Glowczewski.

1939   39.75in (101cm) wide

£80-120   **ON**

'Leipzig Fair, 1951', German exhibition poster.

1951   33in (80cm) high

£70-100   **CL**

'Ulster Farm and Factory', Irish exhibition poster, produced to promote regional activities during the Festival of Britain in 1951.

Regional promotions can be rare as fewer examples were produced than for events in London, the centre of the exhibition.

1951   29in (73.5cm) high

£60-80   **CL**

'Jens Olsens Verdens ur Københavns Rädhus', Danish poster designed by Aage Rasmussen.

Aage Rasmussen designed this poster to advertise Jens Olsen's (1872-1945) astronomical clock in Copenhagen's town hall. Designed by 1932, and with work beginning in 1943, the clock was completed and opened in December 1955. Rasmussen is a noted Danish poster artist who also worked for Danish railways and produced designs promoting Denmark as a tourist destination.

1957   39in (100cm) high

£50-60   **CL**

'Foire Internationale de Bordeaux', French exposition poster, artwork by Roger Varenne.

1959   39in (100cm) high

£100-150   **CL**

'Carnaval de Nice', 1950s French poster designed by Jean Luc.

39in (100cm) high

£120-180   **CL**

COLLECTORS' NOTES

■ There are many shapes and sizes of poster available, ranging from small glossy stills to massive 24-sheet bill posters. The most popular, and usually the most valuable, are the US one sheet (27in by 41in) and the British quad (30in by 40in) sizes. The most collectable Polish posters are those in A1 format (23in by 33in).

■ As prices for American and British posters rise exponentially, collectors have developed ever greater interest in movie paper from eastern European countries such as the Czech Republic and Poland.

■ The Golden Age of Polish poster design was from c1955-65, following the alleviation of restrictive government policies regarding art and graphic representation.

■ The state monopoly on film distribution and marketing created a climate in which Polish artists and their personal interpretations of the iconography of film could flourish.

■ Polish posters now enjoy a reputation for innovative, striking and accomplished artwork. Collectors in this area are generally more interested in the artists than the film being depicted, unlike those who collect American or British posters. Masters such as Lucjan Jagodzinski are becoming hot property.

■ Although there is no generally recognised grading system for film posters, any form of folding, tearing or other damage will detract from value. Many valuable posters are backed with linen to better preserve them.

'Czas Apokalipsy' (Apocalypse Now), Polish film poster for the Francis Ford Coppala film, artwork by Waldemar Swierzy.

1981   39in (100cm) high

£180-220   **CL**

'Lala' (Big Baby Doll), Polish film poster for the Franco Giraldi Italian film, artwork by Andrzej Krajewski.

1971   33in (84cm) high

£70-90   **CL**

'Czarny Narcyz' (Black Narcissus), Polish poster for the Michael Powell film, artwork by Henryk Tomaszewski.

Henryk Tomaszewski was one of the three Polish artists and illustrators first commissioned by Film Polski (the State film distributor) to produce film posters in 1946. This rare, very early poster was re-issued in 1957.

1948   33in (84cm) high

£300-400   **CL**

'Kabaret' (Cabaret), Polish film poster for the Bob Fosse film, artwork by Wiktor Gorka.

This is one of the most well-known and desirable of all Polish film posters and is very rare. The frightening image of a 1930s Berlin singer superimposed into a Nazi swastika made up of stocking clad legs is not only highly dramatic but sums up the film perfectly.

1973   33in (80cm) high

£550-650   **CL**

'Bullitt', Polish film poster for the Peter Yates film, artwork by Marian Stachurski.

1971   33in (80cm) high

£180-220   **CL**

'Kabaret' (Cabaret), Polish film poster for the Bob Fosse film, artwork by Andrjez Pagowski.

1988   39in (100cm) high

£100-150   **CL**

'Kleopatra' (Cleopatra), Polish film poster for the Joseph L. Mankiewicz film, artwork by Eryk Lipinski.

This is a highly sought after poster design by a popular artist, as well as being for a popular film.

1968   33in (84cm) high

£250-350   **CL**

'Zbrodnia w klubie tenisowym' (Crime in the Tennis Club), Polish poster for the Franco Rossetti Italian film, artwork by Andrzej Krajewski.

1973   33in (84cm) high

£80-120   **CL**

'E.T., the Extra-Terrestrial', 1980s Polish film poster designed by Jakob Erol.

39in (100cm) high

£120-180   **CL**

'Diabel Wcielony' (Devil in the Flesh), Polish poster for the Claude Autant-Lara French film, designed by Jozef Roszczak.

1956   33in (84cm) high

£200-250   **CLG**

'Skrzypek na dachu' (Fiddler on the Roof), Polish film poster designed by Wieslaw Walkuski.

39in (100cm) wide

£80-120   **CL**

'Upior z Morrisville', (The Ghost from Morrisville), Polish poster for the Borivoj Zeman Czechoslovakian film, art work by Frantiszek Starowieyski.

1967   33in (84cm) high

£150-200   **CL**

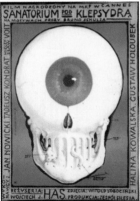

'Sanatorium pod Klepsydra', (The Hour-Glass Sanatorium), Polish poster for the Wojciech J. Has Polish film, artwork by Frantisek Starowieyski.

1973   33in (84cm) high

£120-180   **CL**

'Ludzie i Wilki' (Humans and Wolves), Polish poster for the Giuseppe De Santis film, artwork by Roman Cieslewicz.

1959   33in (84cm) high

£220-280   **CLG**

'Indiana Jones I Swiatynia Preznaczenia' (Indiana Jones and the Temple of Doom), Polish film poster for the Steven Spielberg film, artwork by Witold Dybowski.

1985	*39in (100cm) high*
£120-180	**CL**

A CLOSER LOOK AT A POLISH FILM POSTER

Jagodzinski (1897-1971) designed film posters between 1952 and 1958 and this is his most sought-after poster.

The style of the image and the colours are reminiscent of Toulouse Lautrec's poster designs – Lautrec designed posters when the real Moulin Rouge was at its peak.

It was produced during the 1950s, the 'golden age' of the Polish film poster.

Featuring an absinthe drinking man and a chorus girl, the design ties in with the 'Belle Epoque' Paris theme of the film.

'Moulin Rouge', 1950s Polish poster for the John Huston film, artwork by L. Jagodzinski.

Many experts still cite Jagodzinski's work as being under-valued.

1957	*33in (84cm) high*
£1,500-2,000	**CL**

'King Kong', Polish poster for the John Guillermin film, artwork by Jakob Erol.

1978	*50in (127cm) high*
£100-150	**CL**

'Miraz', (Mirage), Polish poster for the Edward Dmytryk film, artwork by Maciej Zbikowski.

1970	*33in (84cm) high*
£80-120	**CLG**

'Moby Dick', Polish poster for the John Huston film, artwork by Wiktor Gorka.

1961	*26in (66cm) high*
£120-180	**CL**

'Moj Wujaszek', (My Uncle), Polish poster for the Jacques Tati French film, artwork by Pierre Etaix.

1959	*33in (84cm) high*
£120-180	**CLG**

'SOS Titanic (A Night to Remember)', Polish film poster for the Roy Ward Baker film, artwork by Wojciech Zamecznik.

1961	*33in (84cm) high*
£200-250	**CL**

'Dawno Temu w Ameryce' (Once Upon a Time in America), Polish film poster for the Sergio Leone film, artwork by Jan Mlodozeniec.

1986	*39in (100cm) high*
£120-180	**CL**

'Gwiezdne Wojny' (Star Wars Episode IV: A New Hope), Polish film poster for the George Lucas film, artwork by Jakob Erol.

1980   39in (100cm) high

£250-350   **CL**

'Powrot Jedi' (Star Wars Episode VI: Return of the Jedi), Polish film poster, artwork by Witold Dybowski.

1984   39in (100cm) high

£120-180   **CL**

'Nieznajomi z Pociagu' (Strangers on a Train), Polish poster for the Alfred Hitchcock film, artwork by Witold Janowski.

1963   33in (84cm) high

£120-180   **CL**

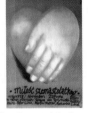

'Milosc Szesnastolatkow' (Teenage Love), Polish poster for the Herrmann Zschoche film, artwork by Jerzy Czeronawski.

1975   33in (84cm) high

£70-100   **CL**

'Wehikul Czasu' (The Time Machine), Polish film poster, artwork by Marian Stachurski.

This is deemed a classic example of the Polish poster.

1965   33in (84cm) high

£180-220   **CL**

'Tootsie', Polish film poster for the Sydney Pollack film, artwork by Wieslaw Walkuski.

1984   39in (100cm) high

£100-150   **CL**

'Wall Street', Polish film poster for the Oliver Stone film, artwork by Andrzej Pagowski.

1988   39in (100cm) high

£150-200   **CL**

'Zet i Dwa Zera' (A Zed and Two Noughts), Polish film poster for the Peter Greenaway film, artwork by Wiktor Sadowski.

1994   39in (100cm) high

£180-220   **CL**

FIND OUT MORE...

www.cinemaposter.com

'Blow-Up', 1960s Italian poster of the Michelangelo Antonioni film.

79in (200.5cm) high

£250-350 CL

'Diamonds Are Forever', American for the foreign market, three-sheet poster, with blue ink Dutch stamp, folded, minor holes, dated.

1971   74.75in (190cm) high

£120-180 SAS

'The Spy Who Loved Me', US one-sheet poster, folded, dated.

1977   41in (104cm) high

£60-90 SAS

'The Man with the Golden Gun', American one-sheet poster for the eastern hemisphere, folded, faded, pinholes.

1974   41in (104cm) high

£100-150 SAS

'Moonraker', UK three-sheet poster, dated.

1979   75in (190cm) high

£70-100 SAS

'Live And Let Die', US one-sheet poster, for the Eastern hemisphere, dated.

1973   41in (104cm) high

£100-150 SAS

'Café De Paris', French film poster, artwork by René Peron, printed by Baudin, Paris. 1938

62.5in (156cm) high

£700-900 SWA

'Genesúng', East German film poster, artwork by John Heartfield (1891-1968).

c1956   32.5in (80cm) high

£300-400 SWA

'Tundra', American film poster, artwork by Robert Igot, printed by S.E.G. of Paris.

62.75in (159.5cm) high

£650-750 SWA

COLLECTORS' NOTES

■ Original posters promoting concerts, 'be-ins' and other events from c1965 and into the 1970s are collected for their nostalgia value as well as their highly original and appealing artwork.

■ The core value of a poster or flyer is determined by the artist, design and quality of the paper and the printing process used. Silkscreen printing is more labour intensive than offset, and posters made this way are generally more valuable due to the shorter print runs.

■ Posters designed by prolific or cult artists will attract a premium, although any work produced in very large quantities will usually have a lower value. Advertisements for gigs at renowned venues or featuring iconic bands are particularly sought after.

A Family Dog 'Balloon' poster, FD35, for Daily Flash, Quicksilver Messenger Service and Country Joe & The Fish, at the Avalon Ballroom on November 18 and 19, 1966, artwork by Stanley Mouse and Alton Kelley, marked "San Francisco Poster Co".

21in (53.5cm) high

£120-180   **GAZE**

A Family Dog 'Earthquake' poster, FD21, for Bo Diddley and Big Brother & the Holding Company, on August 12 and 13 1966, by San Francisco Poster Co, artwork by Stanley Mouse.

£70-100   **GAZE**

'Sierra Club Wilderness Conference', psychedelic poster, by the San Francisco Poster Co., designed by Stanley Mouse and Alton Kelley.

1967   *20in (51cm) high*

£40-60   **GAZE**

A 1970s American psychedelic poster for 'Follies', designed by David Byrd.

38in (96.5cm) high

£70-100   **CL**

A 1960s American 'Are You Experienced' psychedelic poster.

This was also the title of Jimi Hendrix' first album, which catapulted him to fame.

35in (89cm) high

£70-80   **CL**

An American psychedelic poster, 'Gloves', designed by Peter Max.

1968   *36in (91cm) high*

£100-150   **CL**

An American psychedelic poster, 'From the Moon – Apollo 11', designed by Peter Max.

1969   *36in (91cm) high*

£70-100   **CL**

An American psychedelic poster, 'Visionaries at the East Hampton Gallery', designed by Peter Max.

This was the first exhibition of psychedelic art, and formed the basis of a book in 1968.

1967   *25in (66cm) high*

£50-60   **CL**

A 1970s Marvel Comics advertising poster, 'Silver Surfer: At Last I'm Free'.

33in (84cm) high

£70-100 CL

A 1970s Marvel Comics advertising poster, 'Namor the Submariner'.

33in (84cm) high

£80-120 CL

A 1970s Marvel Comics advertising poster, 'Thwoom!'.

33in (84cm) high

£70-100 CL

A 1970s Marvel Comics advertising poster, 'So Shall It Be – Odin & Hela'.

31in (78.5cm) high

£60-80 CL

An American neon psychedelic poster, 'Zeus', manufactured and distributed by Third Eye Inc. of New York.

1972 *33.5in (85cm) high*

£20-30 NOR

A 1970s American psychedelic poster, 'Acid Rider'.

£50-70 CL

A 1960s American marijuana related psychedelic poster, 'Crop Rotation Pays'.

This poster is based on Grant Wood's 1930 painting 'American Gothic', one of the most famous images in American art, which depicts the morally virtuous pastoral life in the American Midwest.

35in (89cm) high

£60-80 CL

A CLOSER LOOK AT A PSYCHEDELIC POSTER

This image is a conflation of two of Robert Crumb's most famous creations – 'Mr Natural', the dubious guru, and the 'Keep on Truckin' slogan.

This image lacks the cross-hatching characteristic of Crumb's own work, indicating that it is probably by another hand.

Crumb hit a low ebb in 1976 when a court ruling that 'Keep on Truckin' was public property coincided with a large bill for unpaid tax on royalties earned.

The laid back ethos encapsulated in Crumb's original 'Keep on Truckin' panels led to its enthusiastic adoption by the hippie movement.

An American neon poster, depicting 'Mr Natural', with velvet-like black areas, from an original design by Robert Crumb.

Long a counter-cultural hero, Robert Crumb has recently been embraced by the art establishment and his work has been exhibited at high profile galleries. Robert Hughes, art critic for 'Time' magazine, has famously called him the "Brueghel of the last half of the 20th century".

1971   35.5in (90cm) wide

£15-25   **NOR**

A 1970s Canadian psychedelic poster, 'Hair is Beautiful'.

33in (80cm) high

£70-90   **CL**

A 1960s American psychedelic poster, 'New San Francisco, Free City'.

33in (80cm) high

£60-80   **CL**

A 1970s Italian psychedelic poster, 'Cora Americano', designed by M. Lecourt.

33in (84cm) high

£80-120   **CL**

A 1970s American psychedelic poster, 'Psychedelic Cat', artwork by Joe Roberts Jr.

30in (76cm) high

£50-60   **CL**

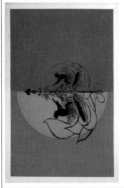

A 1960s American psychedelic poster, 'Psychedelic Surfers'.

40in (101.5cm) high

£100-140   **CL**

A 1960s American poster, 'Love', designed by Robert Indiana.

The use of short words in large colourful letters is typical of Pop artist Indiana's style. This, his most famous image, was created first for a Museum of Modern Art Christmas card in 1964, reused on a USPS stamp in 1973 and also for a sculpture in John F. Kennedy Plaza, Philadelphia.

29in (73.5cm) wide

£100-140   **CL**

DRURY LANE PANTOMIME

John Hassall, 'Bluebeard by Arthur Collins & J. Hickory Wood, Drury Lane Pantomime', printed by Waterlow, small tears.

John Hassall was born in 1868 in Walmer, Kent. After failing to get accepted into the Army on two occasions, he studied art in Antwerp and at Academie Julien, Paris, in 1894, and went on to become a full-time illustrator. As well as producing posters for a number of clients, the most famous perhaps 'The Jolly Fisherman' for the G.N.E.R, he also illustrated children's books. Hassall died in 1948.

30in (76cm) wide

£100-150 ON

John Hassall, 'Pontings Xmas Show, Dover to Calais Tube, Change at High Street Kensington'.

30in (76cm) high

£220-280 ON

William H. Barribal, 'The Palace, Airs and Graces', printed by David Allen, small tears.

30in (76cm) high

£40-60 ON

John Hassall, 'A Grand Concert will be held at the Albert Hall in aid of the Union Jack Club May 1910', printed by The Avenue Press, tears.

40.25in (102cm) high

£40-60 ON

John Hassall, 'Royal Naval & Military Tournament Olympia May to June', printed by Dobson Molle Ltd, tears and small losses to top margin.

40.25in (102cm) high

£50-70 ON

John Hassall, '"Oo-er" Savage Club Ball at the Royal Albert Hall June 1919', printed by Haycock & Cadle Ltd, tears to margin.

30in (76cm) high

£60-80 ON

John Hassall, 'Two Little Vagabonds by George Sims & Arthur Shirley from the Royal Princess's Theatre', printed by David Allen.

30in (76cm) high

£60-90 ON

John Hassall, 'The Whole Town's Talking', printed by David Allen.

30in (76cm) high

£80-100 ON

'The Man Who Wasted Gas!', designed by H.M. Bateman, issued by the Ministry of Fuel and Power, printed for HMSO by J. Weiner, fold.

15in (38cm) high

£35-45   **ON**

'It does matter: The Country pays for it, Don't waste Here- the fuel you save at Home!', designed by Fougasse, issued by Ministry of Fuel & Power, printed for HMSO by Stafford & Co Ltd, folds.

15in (38cm) high

£30-40   **ON**

'Waste Paper Still Wanted', designed by Eileen Evans, published by Ministry of Supply, printed for HMSO by Hubners Ltd.

28.75in (73cm) high

£18-22   **ON**

'No Llenceu Els Diaris', Spanish Catalan language poster, designed by Miguel, printed by Rieusset, Barcelona.

c1938   *39.25in (98cm) wide*

£350-450   **SWA**

'National Relief Fund two ways of fighting...', designed by John Hassall, printed by David Allen.

30in (76cm) high

£40-60   **ON**

'Buy a Share in America', designed by John Atherton, printed by US Government Printing Office.

Encouraging the public to buy war bonds was a common way of raising money for the war effort on both sides of the Atlantic.

1941   *28in (70cm) high*

£500-600   **SWA**

'Post Office Savings Bank', British wartime savings poster designed by Frederic Henri Kay Henrion (1914-90), printed by J. Howitt, Nottingham.

36in (90cm) wide

£700-900 SWA

GIVE IT YOUR BEST!

'Give it your Best!', American poster designed by Charles Coiner, printed by U.S. Government Printing Office.

Charles Coiner (1898-1989) is credited with bringing modern art to US advertising. This simple but striking poster promotes nationalistic support during wartime. In 1933, he also developed the blue eagle motif used by the National Recovery Administration.

1942 *28in (70cm) wide*

£300-400 SWA

'Never Was So Much Owed By So Many To So Few', published by HMSO, printed by Lowe & Brydone, folds and small tears.

Winston Churchill spoke this famous line after the decisive airborne Battle of Britain.

1940 *30in (76cm) high*

£280-320 ON

'The Freedom of the Seas from the Hun point of view', designed by David Wilson, printed by H. & C. Graham Ltd, folds.

15in (38cm) high

£120-180 ON

'VD May Ruin Your Career', 1940s-50s American poster.

22in (56cm) high

£100-150 CL

'For Victory, London's Transport No. 1 - 10,000,000 Passengers a Day', GPD 365/13/28.

19.25in (49cm) wide

£40-60 ON

'For Victory, The Fleet Air Arm: No. 3 - A "Seafire" fighter takes off'.

19.25in (49cm) wide

£80-120 ON

'A Cocoa Estate In Trinidad', RBD3, designed by Frank Newbould, issued by the Empire Marketing Board, printed by Johnson Riddle London, tears into image.

30in (76cm) wide

£50-70   ON

'The Market Gardens of the Tropics – Malayan Pineapples', RCB1, designed by Edgar Ainsworth, issued by the Empire Marketing Board, printed by Waterlow, London.

30in (76cm) wide

£100-150   ON

'Borneo Sago', RCB2, designed by Edgar Ainsworth, issued by The Empire Market Board, printed by Waterlow, London.

20in (51cm) high

£80-120   ON

'Outposts of Britain', designed by Edward McKnight Kauffer.

This series of four posters showed that the General Post Office could reach anywhere in Britain, even a remote Irish crofter's cottage.

1937   *25in (62.5cm) wide*

£450-550   SWA

'Outposts of Britain', designed by Edward McKnight Kauffer.

The use of broad areas of colour and a stylised font is typical of much of Edward McKnight Kauffer's (1890-1954) work.

1937   *25in (62.5cm) wide*

£450-550   SWA

'United Nations / For All Children a Safe Tomorrow – IF You Do Your Part', American poster.

c1949   *28in (70cm) high*

£220-280   SWA

'United Nations / "We the Peoples of the United Nations"' American poster, designed by Ladislav Sutnar.

Sutnar (1897-1976) also designed a wall at N.B.C. in the Rockefeller Center in 1946.

c1949   *28in (70cm) high*

£220-280   SWA

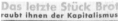

'Das Letzte Stück Brot', a German political poster, designed by John Heartfield.

Ernst Thalmann (1886-1944) was one of the founders of the German Communist Party, after whom songs were written and streets named in post-war East Germany. This pro-Communist poster, originally printed in 1932, explains that capitalism is stealing the last piece of bread from children.

c1970   *36.25in (90.5cm) high*

£600-800   SWA

'Tariff Reform Means Happier Dukes', political poster designed by Ernest Noble, published by the Liberal Publication Department.

1903-06   *19.75in (50cm) high*

£20-30   **PC**

'Cigarettes Cause Lung Cancer', designed by Reginald Mount, issued by Central Office of Information, printed by MMP Ltd.

1962-c1963   *30in (76cm) high*

£10-15   **ON**

'Smoking Pollutes...', 1970s American public health poster.

22in (59cm) high

£50-70   **CL**

'Oranges and Their Importance to Health', 1930s American public information poster.

22in (59cm) wide

£70-100   **CL**

'Ignorance = Fear, Silence = Death' 1980s American poster, designed by Keith Haring.

This is from a series of AIDS awareness posters designed by Haring and promoted by the 'ACT UP' group in the late 1980s. The pink triangle was used as a gay 'motif' during the 1970s and 80s – it was previously used by the Nazis to identify gay men, like the Star of David for the Jewish.

43in (109cm) wide

£120-180   **CL**

'Save the Products of the Land, Eat More Fish', 1910s American political poster, artwork by Charles L. Bull.

28in (71cm) high

£350-450   **CL**

'Wait Till It Stops' poster', designed by Zero-Hans Schleger, printed by Loxley.

A pioneer of Modernism, Schleger (1898-1976) uses strong lines and perspective, an eye reflecting a stop sign and different typefaces, (a hallmark of his work) to create a striking image warning of the dangers of getting on or off a tram or bus if still moving.

c1946   *29.75in (74cm) high*

£450-550   **SWA**

'Brands Hatch', 1960s English motor racing poster, designed and printed by Briscall Studios, Ashford, Kent.

30in (76cm) high

£70-90 CL

'Brands Hatch 1000Kms, September 18', full-colour English motor racing poster.

1983 *30in (76cm) high*

£20-30 SAS

'The R.A.C. British Grand Prix Silverstone', full-colour English motor racing poster, dated 10 July 1965.

When building a collection of motor racing posters, look for popular drivers, marques or teams at well-known tracks. An important or infamous race can also add value. Look for a visual sense of speed or for dramatic images of the cars themselves.

1965 *30in (76cm) high*

£120-180 SAS

'Motor Racing Goodwood', for formula 3 cars, historic and vintage racing by the British Automobile Racing Club.

1966 *30in (76cm) high*

£50-70 SAS

'Nürburgring, 1000-km-Rennen', full-colour German motor racing poster, dated 28 May.

1967 *33in (84cm) high*

£50-70 SAS

'Silverstone, Daily Express 23rd International Trophy Meeting', full-colour English motor racing poster.

1971 *30in (76cm) high*

£40-60 SAS

'Monaco 25/26 Mai 1968', French full-colour motor racing poster, illustration by Michael Turner, Edition J. Ramel-Nice.

23.5in (60cm) wide

£70-100 SAS

'24 Heures du Mans 13-14 Juin 1981', French motor racing poster, slight water damage.

1981

21in (53.5cm) wide

£80-120 AGI

'Emprunt Acier' poster, designed by Bernard Villemot, printed by R.L. Duphy, Paris.

This poster is typical of Villemot's (1911-89) work, being stylized and colourful with a plain background and painterly effect. Villemot also designed posters for high-end shoe shop Bally.

1964   31.5in (79cm) high

£200-300   **SWA**

'(God's Love We Deliver)', 1990s American Pop Art poster designed by Keith Haring.

       34in (85cm) high

£50-60   **CL**

'Enjoy Cocaine', 1970s American poster.

This design was developed in late 1970 by Gemini Rising Inc. and is said to have sold over 100,000 copies in two years. Coca-Cola took the company to court around 1972, claiming it damaged their brand. An injunction was granted by the court who found it was likely to tarnish Coca-Cola's 'wholesome' reputation and costly global advertising campaigns. Seen by many as parodying an American national icon, it also plays on the untrue rumour that Coca-Cola contains cocaine, which was said to be the reason why it was marketed as a 'pick-me-up' since its inception in 1886.

       33in (80cm) wide

£80-120   **CL**

'"Nonsense! There are no such things as--UHH!"', poster by an unknown designer.

1968   41in (102.5cm) high

£500-600   **SWA**

'Pays-Bas', Dutch poster designed by Libra Studio, printed by Kühn en Zoon, Rotterdam.

From a group of six posters, each promoting a different aspect of the Dutch economy, the Art Deco photo-montage style is highly desirable. Little is known about the design studio, and the series was aimed at use abroad.

1948   43in (107.5cm) high

£100-150   **SWA**

COLLECTORS' NOTES

■ Pot-lids form one of the earliest types of visually appealing packaging. Products include bear's grease (a hair product), toothpaste, and meat or fish paste. Blue and white printed pot-lids were introduced in the 1820s, with coloured examples appearing in the mid-1840s. Makers include F.R. Pratt, T.J. & J. Mayer and Brown-Westhead & Moore.

■ It is not possible to date pot-lids precisely as so many were produced over large periods of time, with no records remaining. Events depicted and certain makers' marks can help to date some pot-lids to within a date range, as can the form. Over 350 different images are known, many taken from watercolours by Jesse Austin.

■ Earlier lids, from before 1860, are usually flat and light in weight, with fine quality prints and often have a screw thread. Lids from 1860 to 1875 are heavier and have a convex top. Handle as many as possible to gain experience of weights and appearances.

■ Look for lids with good, strong colours, as faded, weak examples are worth considerably less. Chips to the flange and rim do not affect value seriously. Chips to the image, or restoration, can lower values by 50-75 per cent, even if well restored. Complex or coloured borders usually add value. Non-circular lids usually date from after the late 1870s.

■ Some collectors choose to collect by type. Two of the most popular are lids for bear's grease, or those depicting Pegwell Bay. Beware of reproductions. Run your finger over a lid and if you can feel the transfer, it is likely to be a later reproduction. Numbers given here relate to lid reference numbers in Mortimer's pot-lid reference book, listed at the end of this section.

A 'Bear's Grease Manufacturer' pot-lid, no. 3, no lettering, by the Mayer factory.

Although restored, this is an extremely rare lid, with less than ten thought to exist. Variants with advertising wording can be worth around 20 per cent more.

3.25in (8cm) diam

£3,000-4,000   **SAS**

An 'Alas! Poor Bruin' pot-lid, no. 1, with lantern, double line and dot border.

3.5in (8.5cm) diam

£120-180   **SAS**

A 'Bear Hunting' pot-lid, no. 4, with advertising for Ross & Sons Bear Grease at 119 & 120 Bishopsgate, blue-checkered border, hairline crack.

3.5in (9cm) diam

£500-600   **SAS**

A 'Shooting Bears' pot-lid, no. 13, no lettering.

3.25in (8cm) diam

£100-150   **SAS**

A 'The Ins' pot-lid, no. 15, fancy lettering, flange restored.

3.5in (8.5cm) diam

£350-450   **SAS**

A 'The Outs' pot-lid, no. 16, with fancy border, restored.

The fancy border makes this more valuable. Without the border, the value is around 20 per cent less. 'The Ins' is the partner lid and both are early, dating from before the 1860s.

3.5in (9cm) diam

£700-800   **SAS**

A 'Polar Bears' pot-lid, no. 18, lacks moon, gold line.

Produced in 1846, this is the earliest known coloured pot-lid pattern. The version with a moon in the sky is more valuable.

3.25in (8cm) diam

£300-400   **SAS**

A CLOSER LOOK AT A POT-LID

The pot-lid shows singer Jenny Lind, the 'Swedish Songbird', who came to England in 1847.

This version with J. Grossmith advertising is extremely rare. Under ten examples are thought to exist.

'Jenny Lind' was produced in two versions, one with just the floral border around the figure, of which around 25 examples are known.

A 'Jenny Lind' pot-lid, no. 180, advertising J. Grossmith & Co. 85 Newgate St. London, stained.

The manufacturer of this lid is not known.

Although stained, the great rarity and bright colours on this lid make it desirable and valuable.

3.5in (9cm) diam

£2,000-2,500 **SAS**

A Pratt 'Queen Victoria and Prince Consort' pot-lid, no. 167, oak leaves and acorn border.

5.5in (14cm) diam

£200-300 **SAS**

A Staffordshire 'Wellington with Cocked Hat' no. 183 potlid, with lettering pertaining to his birth and death, restored.

5in (13.5cm) diam

£500-600 **SAS**

A large 'Wellington with Clasped Hands' no. 184 pot-lid, with border.

The colours on this large example are particularly rich and the colour variation on the border is comparatively unusual.

4.75in (12cm) diam

£700-1,000 **SAS**

A Pratt 'The Blue Boy' pot-lid, no. 196.

This is taken from Gainsborough's famous painting. Look for a strong blue, rather than a greyish blue. The version with the 'seaweed' border and flange is the most valuable, and can fetch up to £1,000.

4.75in (12cm) diam

£55-65 **SAS**

A 'Little Red-Riding Hood' pot-lid, no. 200.

3in (7.5cm) diam

£90-100 **SAS**

A 'Windsor Castle or Prince Albert (Hare Coursing)' pot-lid, no. 176, produced by the Mayer factory, minor hairline crack.

4.25in (10.5cm) diam

£120-180 SAS

An 'Albert Memorial' pot-lid, no. 190.

A version with a carriage is also known, but is worth slightly less.

4in (10cm) diam

£80-120 SAS

A 'St. Paul's Cathedral' pot-lid, no. 238, probably by Brown-Westhead, Moore & Co.

4.25in (10.5cm) diam

£120-180 SAS

A 'Belle Vue Tavern' pot-lid, no. 29, flat lid, dark cliffs, no name on the inn.

There are a number of complex variations to this lid, including a domed or flat shape, small or large lettering, a name on the inn, the colour of the cliffs and the presence of a small pile of boulders on the beach.

3.5in (9cm) diam

£1,000-1,500 SAS

A Pratt 'Pegwell Bay, Established 1760' pot-lid, no. 32, with earlier sandy road and pathway design.

4in (10cm) diam

£40-60 SAS

A 'Walmer Castle' pot-lid, no. 45, with two horsemen, probably made by Cauldon.

4.25in (10.5cm)

£45-55 SAS

A 'Royal Harbour, Ramsgate' pot-lid, no. 50, probably by the Cauldon factory.

4in (10cm) diam

£70-90 SAS

A Pratt 'Hauling in the Trawl' pot-lid, no. 60.

Pratt produced this for Cross & Blackwell over many years, making it comparatively common. The pattern was copied from a drawing in the London Illustrated News, 6th March, 1847.

4.25in (11cm) diam

£60-80 SAS

A Pratt 'Letter from The Diggings' pot-lid, no. 131, with fancy border.

Look out for the ultra-rare versions of this lid with 'Valentine's Day' or a retailer's advertising wording.

5in (13cm) diam

£50-60   **SAS**

A Mayer 'The Boar Hunt' pot-lid, no. 288.

This was reissued up to the 1960s by Kirkhams. Early examples, such as this one, are rarer.

4.25in (10.5cm) diam

£450-550   **SAS**

A 'The Shepherdess' pot-lid, no. 279, produced by Bates, Brown-Westhead & Moore at the Cauldon factory.

4in (10cm) diam

£35-45   **SAS**

A Pratt 'Master of the Hounds' pot-lid, no. 295.

4.25in (10.5cm) d

£90-100   **SAS**

A 'Fair Sportswoman' pot-lid, no. 297, produced by Bates, Brown-Westhead & Moore at the Cauldon factory.

4.25in (10.5cm) d

£40-50   **SAS**

A Mayer or Pratt 'A Fix' pot-lid, no. 302, no border.

4.25in (11cm) diam

£150-250   **SAS**

A Pratt 'The Times' pot-lid, no. 307.

4.25in (10.5cm) diam

£50-60   **SAS**

A Pratt 'The Queen God Bless Her' pot-lid, no. 319, fancy border.

5in (12.5cm) diam

£45-55   **SAS**

A CLOSER LOOK AT A PRATT POT-LID

More common versions contain a verse of poetry in the design. —————

The extra white surround shows a late production. Earlier examples simply ———— have a black line.

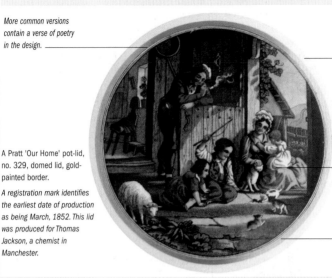

The reverse is stamped in red for "F.R. Pratt, Potters to HRH Prince Albert". This pot-lid, originally from the Pratt factory archives, is one of only two known examples, the other is not stamped.

A Pratt 'Our Home' pot-lid, no. 329, domed lid, gold-painted border.

A registration mark identifies the earliest date of production as being March, 1852. This lid was produced for Thomas Jackson, a chemist in Manchester.

This has a gold line and no title, also making it a ———— rare variation.

4.25in (10.5cm) diam

£4,500-5,500 **SAS**

A Pratt 'The Dentist' pot-lid, no. 331.

4.25in (10.5cm) diam

£120-180 **SAS**

A 'Xmas Eve' pot-lid, no. 323, double-lined border in black.

3.75in (9.5cm) diam

£350-450 **SAS**

A 'May Day Dancers and the Swan Inn' pot-lid, no. 324, probably designed by Jesse Austin for Bates, Brown-Westhead & Moore around 1860.

4.25in (10.5cm) diam

£60-80 **SAS**

A 'Children of Flora' pot-lid, no. 326, probably by the Cauldon factory.

4.75in (12cm) diam

£80-120 **SAS**

A Pratt 'The Village Wakes' pot-lid, no. 321, based on a Jesse Austin watercolour, with fancy border and bullnose rim.

Look out for the rare variation without two children, the dog and monkey, as this can fetch over 50 per cent more than this version.

4in (10cm) diam

£280-320 **SAS**

A Pratt 'The Poultry Woman' pot-lid, no. 338.

The presence of a wide gold band can fetch up to eight times the value of this example.

4.25in (10.5cm) diam

£120-180 **SAS**

FIND OUT MORE...

'Pot-Lids and Other Coloured Printed Staffordshire Wares', by K.V. Mortimer, published by Antique Collectors' Club, 2003.

COLLECTORS' NOTES

■ Powder compacts first became popular in the 1920s when it became acceptable for women to apply make-up in public. Earlier examples do exist, but they were not intended for use outside of the house.

■ Made to be seen, they are often highly decorative and reflect the fashions of the time. Early examples can be made of early plastics like Bakelite and often feature long tassels. Guilloché enamelled pieces with strong geometric Art Deco decoration are sought-after.

■ WWII halted the production of face powders and compacts, although late 1930s examples with a military theme were made for members of the armed forces to send back to their sweethearts. Post war production saw compacts become larger, with novelties, such as musical movements added. Compacts also became thicker as face powders moved from loose to solid.

■ As fashion changed powder compacts began to loose their appeal in the 1960s and were more or less obsolete by the 1980s.

■ Some cosmetic companies such as Estee Lauder and Yves St Laurent continue to make compacts as limited editions, often designed to hold solid perfume rather than powder.

■ Stratton and Kigu in England and Elgin in the US were the most prolific producers and collectors often concentrate on their compacts. Ideally compacts should retain their puffs and sifters, although they are not essential, but examples with cracked mirrors should be avoided, as they are difficult to replace. Any old powder should be carefully removed as it can damage the compact.

A 1920s yellow guilloché enamelled silver compact, possibly French, with silhouette of a lady under a tree, London silver import mark.

1923-24 — 1.75in (4.5cm) diam

£200-250 — **MGT**

A rare 1920s/30s Art Deco powder compact, with grinder and powder refill from underneath, unmarked.

The grater underneath the compact was used to 'shave' powder from the cake.

2.25in (5.5cm) diam

£120-180 — **MGT**

A Shildkraut cloisonné enamel powder compact, with floral top.

c1947 — 3in (7cm) diam

£25-35 — **SH**

A late 1950s Stratton 'Swan' Rondette shape powder compact, from the Water Birds series.

3.75in (9.5cm) diam

£20-30 — **MGT**

An early Stratton non-spill powder compact, with Art Deco decoration in red enamel and chrome.

c1934 — 3.75in (9.5cm) diam

£60-90 — **MGT**

An Elizabeth II coronation souvenir compact, by Le Rage.

1953 — 3.5in (9cm) diam

£40-60 — **MGT**

A Kigu 'Celestial' Flying Saucer shape powder compact.

This model was produced with and without a musical movement and also came in green and red.

c1951 — 2.5in (6.5cm) diam

£120-180 — **MGT**

A blue guilloché enamelled silver powder compact, with naval emblem, Birmingham hallmarks and makers mark "JWB".

1937   *3in (7.5cm) wide*

£80-120   **SH**

A 1960s Kigu Cherie shape powder compact, with enamelled butterfly top.

3in (7.5cm) long

£30-50   **MGT**

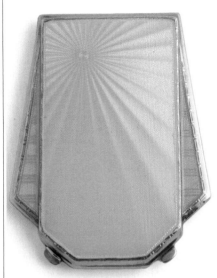

An Art Deco guilloché enamel and silver compact, London hallmarks.

1936-37   *3.5in (9cm) long*

£200-250   **MGT**

An early 1990s Yves St Laurent heavy gilt heart-shaped compact, embellished with green diamanté stones.

2.5in (6.5cm) wide

£60-80   **MGT**

A 1920s white metal 'tango' powder compact, with guilloché enamel cartouche and blush compartment.

A 'tango' compact comes with a wrist chain attached.

2in (5cm) diam

£60-90   **SH**

A 1930s American enamel-on-copper butterfly powder compact.

3in (7.5cm) wide

£30-40   **SH**

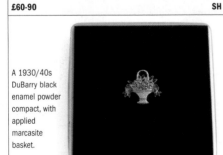

A 1930/40s DuBarry black enamel powder compact, with applied marcasite basket.

2.5in (6.5cm) wide

£35-45   **SH**

A 1920s Andre Duval 'postal telegraph' enamelled powder compact.

The value of this compact would have been higher if it didn't have a slight chip to the enamel.

3in (7.5cm) wide

£50-80   **SH**

POWDER COMPACTS

A 1920s faux tortoiseshell vanity, with inlaid diamanté pattern to top and bottom.

4in (10cm) long

£350-450   **MGT**

An American Platé Trioette bakelite powder compact, with lipstick in handle.

This was made in seven different colours – Ivory, Ebony, Cornelian, Tortoise, Briar Rose, Nile Green and Rueben Blue. The ivory and ebony are the easiest to find and the rose, green and blue are harder to find and are more desirable.

c1945

£80-120   **SH**

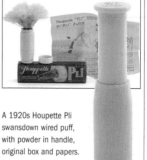

A 1920s Houpette Pli swansdown wired puff, with powder in handle, original box and papers.

Box 4in (10cm) high

£40-60   **SH**

A 1920s/30s bakelite powder compact, with horse racing scene, unmarked.

3in (7.5cm) diam

£30-50   **MGT**

A 1940s Coty 'Powder Puffs' plastic powder compact, designed by Lalique.

2.5in (6.5cm) diam

£25-35   **MGT**

A 1950s Kigu 'Bouquet' shape Lucite powder compact, with movable handle.

2.25in (5.5cm) diam

£60-90   **MGT**

A promotional Melody record powder compact, marked "Creation JD" on label.

3.5in (9cm) diam

£120-180   **MGT**

A French Bourjois 'Evening in Paris' blue plastic compact, with embossed Parisian scenes on a chrome lid.

c1938   *2.75in (7cm) wide*

£60-80   **MGT**

A CLOSER LOOK AT A SCHUCO COMPACT

German toy manufacturer Schuco are well known for their teddy bears and soft toys and in particular for their miniature bears.

This duck compact is a rare variation of the bear compacts and is very desirable.

These teddy bears also came concealing perfume bottles, powder compacts and lipsticks or manicure sets. They are all sought-after.

It came in a few different colourways, which are all of a similar value.

A rare 1920s Schuco duck compact, covered in jade velvet with orange felt feet and beak.

3.5in (9cm) high

£700-1,000   **MGT**

A 1930s Gwenda painted canvas powder compact, decorated with a kingfisher and with original puff and sifter.

3.25in (8cm) diam

£30-50   **SH**

A 1930s Gwenda tartan fabric-covered hexagonal compact, embroidered souvenir greeting, tartan pad.

2.25in (5.5cm)

£30-50   **MGT**

A 1950s zippered petit point on silk powder compact, probably German.

3in (7.5cm) wide

£20-30   **SH**

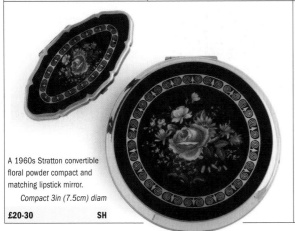

A 1960s Stratton convertible floral powder compact and matching lipstick mirror.

Compact 3in (7.5cm) diam

£20-30   **SH**

A fine petite point compact, depicting a courting couple with musician, black cloth base, no makers mark.

3.25in (8.5cm) diam

£40-60   **MGT**

POWDER COMPACTS

A 1940s Coty Air spun face powder 'Paris' box, sealed.

Powder boxes contain the loose powder used to refill a compact and are usually made from lithographed card. They were often made to match the company's own powder compacts such as this example. Examples should ideally be filled but unopened.

3.25in (8.5cm) diam

£15-20   **SH**

A 1920s Herbert Roystone 'Poudre L'Ame' powder box, sealed.

This American company offered a $1,000 reward if you could find a better face powder.

2.75in (7cm) diam

£35-45   **SH**

A 1930s Strange Music powder box, by Farel Destin.

2.5in (6.5cm) diam

£15-25   **SH**

A 1920s-30s French Houbigant powder box, sealed, with original card outer box.

3in (7.5cm) diam

£20-30   **SH**

A 1930s Luxor sample complexion powder box.

2in (5cm) wide

£12-18   **SH**

A 1930s French Mury, Paris 'Le Narcisse Bleu' powder box.

2.75in (7cm) diam

£30-40   **SH**

A 1920s Pompeian Beauty powder trial tin, with original puff.

1.5in (4cm) diam

£10-15   **SH**

A 1930s Princess Pat souvenir trial-size powder tin box.

1.75in (4.5cm) diam

£10-15   **SH**

A 1940s/50s Richard Hudnut 'Three Flowers' face powder, opened, with puff.

3.25in (8.5cm) diam

£25-35   **SH**

FIND OUT MORE...

Collector's Encyclopedia of Compacts, Carryalls and Face Powder Boxes Vols. I & II, by Laura Mueller, published by Collector Books, 1993 & 1997.

Vintage and Vogue Ladies' Compacts, by Roselyn Gerson, published by Collector Books, 2001.

British Compact Collectors' Club, PO Box 131, Woking, Surrey, GU24 9YR.

Compact Collectors, P.O. Box 40, Lynbrook, NY 11563, USA.

COLLECTORS' NOTES

■ Look for radios from the 1930s-50s, the golden age of the radio. It is the case that counts the most with shape and colour being key factors. Bright colours, produced in cast phenolic plastic known as Catalin, are usually the most desirable. Also look for hallmarks of the Art Deco or 1940s streamlined style. Makers' names also add interest, with FADA, Emerson, Motorola and EKCO among those being sought-after.

■ Examine all areas of a radio with your hands and eyes for damage such as chips and cracks, warping or burning caused by heat from valves. Original grille cloths and backs add desirability and missing or replaced knobs or grille parts reduce value. Radios can be restored to working order by qualified restorers but never plug a vintage radio into the mains without seeking advice from an electrician first. Also consider more modern transistor radios, as rare models or unusually designed examples can fetch high sums.

An International Radio Corp Kadette Jewel red Catalin radio, with clear Lucite fretwork style grille.

1934   8in (20cm) wide

£350-450   **CAT**

A Motorola Model 52 'Aero-Vane' alabaster Catalin radio, with tortoiseshell coloured Catalin vertical grille and knobs.

1939   9.5in (24cm) wide

£1,000-1,500   **CAT**

A Canadian Addison mottled red Catalin Model 5F radio, with yellow grille and knobs.

1940   12in (30cm) wide

£550-650   **CAT**

A very rare General Television Model 591 turquoise green and cream Catalin radio.

Only General Television and Motorola made radios in this colour, which is extremely rare.

1940   8.75in (22.5cm) wide

£3,500-4,500   **CAT**

An Emerson Model EP-375 indigo blue Catalin radio, with cream Catalin grille, knobs and handle.

1941   9.5in (24.5cm) wide

£1,200-1,800   **CAT**

A FADA 700 'Cloud' alabaster Catalin radio, with mottled red knobs and handle.

The 'Cloud' was available in at least five colours. The 'alabaster' here has discoloured to yellow over the years. With much effort, this can be polished away.

1946   10.5in (27cm) wide

£550-650   **CAT**

A Philco Model 49-501 brown bakelite Transitone radio.

Known as the 'Boomerang' this unforgettable radio has become an icon of Pop culture. Its futuristic and modern style typifies post-war spirit.

1949   11.5in (29cm) wide

£300-400   **CAT**

A Crosley Model 11-103 U 'Dynamic' bulls-eye style red tabletop radio, with sprayed-on colour.

1951   10.25in (26cm) wide

£120-180   **CAT**

A Philips 634 A four circuit receiver radio, with five valves.

1933

£350-450 ATK

An Emerson Model 744B black bakelite and white plastic radio.

1954 11.5in (29.5cm) wide

£250-350 CAT

A Daniel Weil transistor radio in clear PVC bag, printed "176".

Since designing this 'pop' style radio, Weil has worked for Alessi and Esprit amongst others. Weil is also responsible for designing the current 'Boots' (The Chemist) logo in 1985.

1981 10.75in (27.5cm) high

£100-150 WW

A CLOSER LOOK AT A SPARTON RADIO

Sparton made the most famous mirrored radios of the Art Deco period – during this time blue and other mirrored items were the height of fashion.

The clean lines, curving front and chromed back 'fins' give the radio its nickname name (sled) and impart a visual feeling of speed and movement. They are archetypally Art Deco in their look.

This was designed, or influenced by, renowned industrial designer Walter Dorwin-Teague who designed the circular blue mirrored 'Bluebird' and ultra-rare 'Nocturne' for Sparton in 1935.

The black areas are lacquered using a special mixture that gives a distinctive crystalline appearance – look closely as if this is not present, the radio has been refinished.

A Sparton Model 557 'Sled' radio, lacking back.

Sparton was the trade name used for the Sparks-Withington Company of Jackson, Michigan.

1936 17in (43cm) wide

£800-1,200 EG

A Decca model TPW70 radio, the circular burgundy and cream casing with integral speaker and tuning dial.

9.75in (25cm) diam

£70-100 ROS

A scarce Sony ICF-SW1S world-band receiver radio, in complete and working condition.

c1987

£100-150 ATK

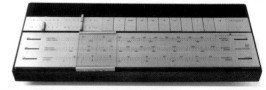

A Bang & Olufsen Beomaster 1900 programming section, with Bevoy S45 speakers and Beomaster 1200 stereo.

The Beomaster 1200 set, introduced in 1969, was designed by Industrial designer Jacob Jensen (b.1926). It set the trend for Bang & Olufsen's designs for years to come.

c1977 Stereo 20in (51cm) high

£70-100 GAZE

RAILWAYANA

COLLECTORS' NOTES

- Collectors focus on railway memorabilia from the last decades of the 19th century and the first half of the 20th century due to the scarcity of earlier pieces. Nostalgia is a key driver for much of the market, creating demand. The more demand, the higher the prices can be.

- Although many collect examples connected to the 'big four' companies (GWR, LMS, LNER and SR), all established in 1924, pieces connected to smaller lines from before 1910-20 are usually rare and much sought-after. While a standard GWR hand lamp may fetch around £40-60, one for the smaller Shropshire & Montgomery railway may fetch around £3,000.

- A totem is a sign hung on a platform, usually at each end, to indicate its name. Many were double-sided, attached together with brackets, but have been separated as single signs tend to fetch more individually than as a pair.

- Today market values are tending to steady after a period of rapid rises. Examples should be clean and in good condition so that they can be displayed. Other station signs are collected, with condition and the type of sign affecting value. Many can be found for under £100-300.

- Anything connected or physically attached to steam locomotives is of great interest and often great value. Nameplates are at the top of the tree, and can fetch tens of thousand of pounds. Shedplates and smoke box plates are becoming increasingly desirable and although prices are rising, they remain more affordable.

- Signs are commonly reproduced, so buy only from reputable auction houses or dealers. A common feature of reproductions is a slightly smaller size, as reproductions are cast from moulds taken from the originals. Definition of relief details may also be reduced. Also examine boltholes, which should be correctly placed and drilled to fit preset holes such as on a locomotive.

A rare BR(S) 'Gentlemen' light green enamel doorplate, in mint condition.

'Gentlemen' signs come on to the market rarely, although there were presumably as many of these as the more commonly found 'Ladies' sign. This may be due to theft by souvenir hunters or high jinks. Like 'Ladies' signs, most were thrown away, making them rarer still.

18in (45.5cm) wide

£400-500   **GWRA**

A BR(S) 'Ladies Room' dark green enamel doorplate.

18in (45.5cm) wide

£220-280   **GWRA**

A BR(S) 'Station Master' dark green enamel doorplate, with early, 'SR'-style lettering, very good condition with one repaired chip.

18in (45.5cm) wide

£280-320   **GWRA**

A BR(S) 'Private' light green enamel doorplate.

18in (45.5cm) wide

£200-300   **GWRA**

A BR(E) 'Parcels' enamel doorplate, single line, flangeless example in virtually mint condition.

£70-100   **GWRA**

A GWR 'Tickets' cast-iron doorplate, post grouping, flat border style, restored, bearing the casting number "B1" on rear.

£120-180   **GWRA**

A CLOSER LOOK AT A BRITISH RAIL TOTEM SIGN

Totems for Nottinghamshire, Derbyshire and Leicestershire stations tend to be more desirable as there are many totem collectors based in these regions.

Values depend on the size of the station, in terms of the number of platforms and hence the number of totems.

This totem is for a station that closed in June, 1966 – totems for closed stations are more desirable.

It is in mint condition, which attracts more interest from collectors, partly as it makes a more appealing display.

A BR(M) 'Welford & Kilworth' totem, virtually mint.

This totem was for an ex-LNWR station in Leicestershire between Market Harborough and Rugby.

£3,500-4,500   GWRA

A BR(M) 'Gospel Oak totem, one very small face chip, otherwise excellent.

Ex-LNWR station between Kentish Town and Willesden Junction.

£2,500-3,500   GWRA

A BR(M) 'Lichfield City' totem, a number of repairable face chips and a little mottling.

Ex-LNWR station between Walsall and Burton-on-Trent, also cross-city line from Birmingham New Street.

£350-450   GWRA

A BR(M) 'Wylde Green' totem, no face chips but a little mottling.

Ex-LNWR station between Birmingham New Street and Lichfield City.

£350-450   GWRA

A BR(S) 'Guildford' totem, light green, white flange variety.

Ex-LSWR station between Woking and Godalming.

£550-650   GWRA

A BR(S) 'Paddock Wood' totem, light green variety, with no face repairs or faults.

Ex-SECR station in Kent, between Tonbridge and Ashford.

£700-800   GWRA

A BR(S) 'St. Johns' dark green totem, white edge variety.

Ex-SECR station between New Cross and Chislehurst.

£550-650   GWRA

A BR(E) 'Bishops Stortford' totem.

This totem, for an ex-GER station between London Liverpool St. and Cambridge, has never been seen at auction before, with the rest apparently having been thrown away. The two sides of a totem are generally worth more when sold individually.

£6,500-7,500   GWRA

RAILWAYANA

A '3A' oval cast-iron shed plate, from Bescot station.

£150-200   **GWRA**

A CLOSER LOOK AT A SHEDPLATE

Shedplates were placed on the front of a locomotive, below the smoke box and denoted the home depot or 'garage' of the locomotive.

The number indicates the railway area, which is not necessarily a geographic area.

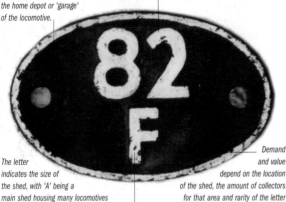

The letter indicates the size of the shed, with 'A' being a main shed housing many locomotives and letters lower down the alphabet being smaller regional sheds.

Demand and value depend on the location of the shed, the amount of collectors for that area and rarity of the letter – a smaller shed held fewer trains meaning fewer plates existed.

An '82F' shed plate.

This plate was at Weymouth from 1948-58, then the S&D Bath Green Park from 1958-66.

£350-450   **GWRA**

A '34F' oval cast-iron shed plate, old face re-painting, picked out in silver.

This plate was at Grantham from 1958 until 1963.

£220-280   **GWRA**

A '65A' oval cast-iron shed plate, restored long ago.

At Glasgow Eastfield station until 1973.

£100-150   **GWRA**

An '83D' alloy shed plate, some damage around the right side bolt hole.

Plymouth Laira until 1963 and then Exmouth Junction until 1967.

£150-200   **GWRA**

A '82A' oval alloy shed plate, in ex-locomotive condition, with original green paint, four hole variety as affixed to Hymeks and others.

At Bristol Bath Road until 1973. Compare the price of this plate, from a larger shed, to the plate from a smaller shed and numbered "82 F".

£100-150   **GWRA**

A '84A' oval alloy shed plate, and in ex-locomotive condition with the exception of polished numerals.

Plymouth Laira from 1963 until 1973.

£150-200   **GWRA**

An '85B' oval shed plate, white re-touched.

This plate was at Gloucester Horton Road.

£250-300   **GWRA**

A London Transport 'Chancery Lane' enamel target station sign.
Central Line station between St Paul's and Holborn.

£70-90 GWRA

A London Transport 'Chancery Lane', Central Line enamel frieze sign.

£55-65 GWRA

A London Transport 'St. Paul's', Central Line enamel frieze sign.

£80-120 GWRA

A London Transport 'Russell Square', Piccadilly Line enamel frieze sign.

£50-60 GWRA

An LMS & Bakerloo Joint 'Euston - Willesden' double-sided enamel train destination indicator, abbreviated station names on each end, some chipping, particularly to Willesden side.

£70-90 GWRA

A 'Brodick' carriage destination board, of substantial wooden construction, with metal, reinforcing ends and original white background with black lettering.
Believed to have been used on early boat trains to the Scottish Highlands & Islands.

35in (89cm) long

£25-35 GWRA

A BR 'Springburn - Clydebank East' maroon and cream wooden carriage board, with strengthened ends, ex-North British Railway route within Glasgow.

32in (81.5cm) wide

£80-120 GWRA

A London Transport District 'Metropolitan' line destination indicator, enamel with brass ends.
Most indicators are white on black backgrounds, making this colour combination unusual.

£60-80 GWRA

A BR(NE) enamel quad royal poster board heading.

Ex-Morley area.

£200-250 GWRA

A Midland Railway 'Booking Hall' enamel sign, white lettering on blue background, in original frame with wrought iron support bracket.

21in (53.5cm) wide

£150-200　　　　　　　　**GWRA**

A Midland Railway 'Beware Of Trains' sign, unrestored.

Items in original, unrestored ex-loco/station condition tend to generate more interest, partly as it gives buyers the choice whether to restore or not. Unrestored examples can also help with spotting replicas or reproductions in terms of levels of wear and grime.

£60-80　　　　　　　　**GWRA**

A Southern Railway 'Beware Of Trains' cast-iron sign, LSWR rounded corner pattern, restored.

£60-80　　　　　　　　**GWRA**

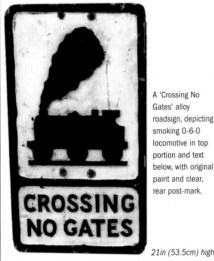

A 'Crossing No Gates' alloy roadsign, depicting smoking 0-6-0 locomotive in top portion and text below, with original paint and clear, rear post-mark.

21in (53.5cm) high

£200-250　　　　　　　　**GWRA**

A 'Level Crossing' alloy road sign, depicting single gate in top portion and text below, with original paint and clear, rear post-mark.

21in (53.5cm) high

£100-150　　　　　　　　**GWRA**

A 'Steep Hill' alloy road sign, complete with all reflectors, bears the maker's name "Gowshall Ltd".

£120-180　　　　　　　　**GWRA**

A GWR 'Danger' enamel sign.

£120-180　　　　　　　　**GWRA**

A GWR 'Gloucester Docks Arrangements In Case Of Fire' letterpress notice, on stiff card, describing the various actions to be taken, and naming the responsible persons with addresses, dated May 1899.

20in (51cm) high

£50-80　　　　　　　　**GWRA**

A '45272' smoke box number plate, neatly welded by BR, plate restored.

Ex-LMS Class 5 (Black Five) 4-6-0 Locomotive built 1936 by Armstrong Whitworth as works number 1327. A Bristol Barrow Road loco for many years but finally resident, and well known, at Saltley.

£450-550　　　　　　　　**GWRA**

A rare GWR Wright's patent coppertop three-aspect hand lamp, in original condition with main body stamped "GWR" and complete with brass plate "Wright's Patent".

Wright's Patent lamps are rarer and more valuable than the other many thousands of handlamps made for the GWR, most of which will fetch around £40-60. Firstly, its copper top dates it to before c1920. Secondly, although made to a GWR design by Wright, the company unusually inserted their own breather tube into the design, making it scarcer.

c1897

£400-500 GWRA

An L&YR three-aspect hand lamp, with square front and clear, bullseye lens, one side has company initials over which is stamped "RINGLEY ROAD", (between Salford and Bury), also stamped elsewhere "BURY ELD" (Electric Loco Department).

£280-320 GWRA

An M&GN three-aspect Midland pattern handlamp, with Midland Railway reservoir bearing an unmarked burner, stamped with the company initials and large rectangular plate stamped "976 F. Christian" and "M. & G.N.J.R.".

£220-280 GWRA

An LMS Dining Cars hand-beaten copper cooking pot, with double brass handles, bearing maker's name within a crest "Benham & Sons Ltd., 66 Wigmore Street, London", stamped beneath "LMS Dining Cars".

8in (20cm) diam

£180-220 GWRA

A GWR 'landmine' inkwell, stamped with initials.

£30-40 GWRA

A Manchester Sheffield & Lincoln Railway mahogany-cased receiving block instrument, bears ivorine plate 'Up Line' above the indicator panel which has 'Train On Line, Line Clear and Line Blocked' indicated, stamped on both sides of the roof, "M.S.L. Ry" and also on top of the back wooden board.

£180-220 GWRA

A GCR mahogany-cased fusee dial clock, with a good quality, early 20thC movement, the dial lettered "GCR 10102 J.J.Stockall & Sons Ltd., London", the rear of the dial lettered "18678 Willesden".

12in (30.5cm) diam

£1,000-1,500 GWRA

A Severn & Wye Railway station master's uniform cap, with GWR roundel badge.

This belonged to Dick Jones, Cinderford Station Master and was evidently his spare as it appears seldom, if ever, worn.

£30-50 GWRA

A Greek Railways alloy winged emblem.

Carried by the Hellenic State Railways Class LB 2-10-0 Locomotive number 960. Built by the North British Locomotive Company for wartime use in 1944, it was originally numbered a WD 736672. The loco was acquired by the North Yorkshire Moors Railway and runs with the name Vera Lynn. This particular plate came from a man who was involved in the repatriation of the locomotive.

£150-200 GWRA

COLLECTORS' NOTES

■ Music fans are always eager to acquire items with a connection to their idols. The Beatles, Elvis Presley and The Rolling Stones remain the most avidly collected artists in the rock and pop pantheon. It remains to be seen whether more recent acts such as Radiohead and Coldplay will enjoy the same longevity.

■ Signatures invariably increase the value of an album or concert ticket, but be aware that facsimile signatures and those done by assistants add little if any additional value.

■ Most records fetch low values as so many were made. Rare, often foreign, pressings, early versions and sleeve or label variations can fetch high sums.

■ Items owned, used and, ideally, played by big stars have the most cachet. Instruments, clothing and original lyric sheets can be worth a great deal of money if properly authenticated.

■ Some of the highest prices are paid for items relating to icons who died young and at the height of their careers, such as Jimi Hendrix, Janis Joplin and Jim Morrison. The rock mythology that surrounds these figures acts as a powerful draw for many enthusiasts.

■ Condition is generally very important – toys and games should be complete with original packaging and ephemera should be free from creases and tears as far as possible. Conversely, a guitar smashed on stage by The Who's Pete Townshend would be worth far more than an intact one he had used in private.

The Beatles, 'The Beatles featuring Tony Sheridan', stereo 8-track, CN8 2007, released by Contour Records, mounted with a picture of The Beatles including Pete Best.

c1962   14in (35.5cm) high

£20-30   **GAZE**

The Beatles, 'Please Please Me', mono LP, PMC 1202, released by Parlophone, with black and gold label.

1963

£80-120   **GAZE**

A CLOSER LOOK AT A SET OF BEATLES' AUTOGRAPHS

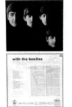

'Twist & Shout' was The Beatles' first EP, released in the UK on July 12th, 1963.

Beatles' signatures are among the most faked on the market, so look for a certificate of authenticity or have them approved by a recognised expert.

The historic place of this EP in The Beatles discography further enhances the value of this item.

One item with all four members' signatures is more valuable than four individually signed items.

The Beatles, 'Twist and Shout', mono EP, GEP 8882, released by Parlophone, signed on the reverse by all four members of the band.

1963

£700-800   **GAZE**

The Beatles, 'Twist and Shout', German EP, O 41560, released by Odeon, with green label.

c1963

£7-10   **GAZE**

The Beatles, 'With the Beatles', LP sleeve, the reverse with four signatures reading the Beatles' names, mounted and framed.

1963   25.25in (64m) high

£120-180   **GAZE**

The Beatles, 'A Hard Day's Night', stereo LP factory sample, PCS 3058, released by Parlophone, mounted with a ticket from the group's first American concert.

c1964

£50-70   **GAZE**

The Beatles, 'Please Mister Postman/ Money', Japanese single, EAR 20245, released by EMI.

1964

£15-25   GAZE

The Beatles, 'The Beatles' Second Album' American LP, ST 2080, released by Capitol Records.

1964

£30-50   GAZE

The Beatles, 'Help!', American film soundtrack LP, SMAS 2386, released by Capitol Records.

1965

£30-40   GAZE

The Beatles, 'The Beatles '65', American LP, ST-2228, released by Capitol Records.

1964

£15-25   GAZE

The Beatles, 'Yesterday', rare English first issue picture sleeve mono EP, GEP 8948, released by Parlophone.

c1966

£30-40   GAZE

The Beatles, 'The Ballad of John and Yoko', stock record, R5786, on black Parlophone label, possibly Swedish, with flower design sleeve.

c1969

£20-30   GAZE

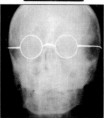

Plastic Ono Band, 'Cold Turkey', rare picture sleeve issue, Apple 1813, released by Apple Records.

c1969

£10-15   GAZE

John Lennon & The Plastic Ono Band, 'Unfinished Music No.2: Life With the Lions', EAS-80701, released by Zapple, with insert.

c1969

£50-80   GAZE

The Beatles, 'The Beatles Broadcasts', very rare bootleg picture disc LP, LK4450, released by Circuit Records, with die-cut cover.

1982

£40-60   GAZE

The Beatles, 'So Much Younger Then: Beatles BBC Sessions', picture disc, DC 7577-5, released by Democratic Records, from a limited edition set of five picture discs.

1983

£10-20   **GAZE**

A CLOSER LOOK AT A SIGNED JOHN LENNON BOOK

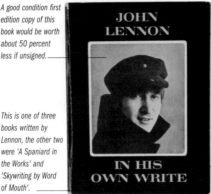

A good condition first edition copy of this book would be worth about 50 percent less if unsigned.

Being a first edition copy also makes this more desirable.

This is one of three books written by Lennon, the other two were 'A Spaniard in the Works' and 'Skywriting by Word of Mouth'.

The provenance from the original owner adds interest.

John Lennon, "In His Own Write", first edition, published by Jonathan Cape, signed by the author.

The original owner got this book signed at the Beatles concert, Ipswich Gaumont, 31st October 1964.

1964

£300-400   **GAZE**

An early 1960s Beatles poster, featuring Maureen Cleave interviewing The Beatles for the Evening Standard.

30in (76cm) high

£180-220   **SWO**

A 'The Beatles at Carnegie Hall' booklet, by Ralph Cosham and United Press International, printed by Hamilton Co. Ltd.

1964   *9.75in (25cm) high*

£10-15   **GAZE**

A magazine page with a portrait of John Lennon, with printed signature and mounted with a signed autograph book page, framed and glazed.

c1966

£100-150   **GAZE**

An Apple Corp original production sketch from 'The Yellow Submarine', featuring Fred, mounted with a factory sample film sound track stereo LP and cover.

1968   *42.25in wide*

£280-320   **GAZE**

A set of four Beatles colour printed publicity photographs, with facsimile signatures.

10.25in (26cm) high

£15-20   **GAZE**

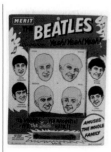

A 'The Beatles Magnetic Hair' carded game, by Merit, marked "©1964".

10.5in (26cm) high

£15-20   **GAZE**

A 1960s Beatles rug, in yellow, oranges and black, showing the four faces of the group.

34.5in (87.5cm) wide

£200-300   **GAZE**

A 1960s 'Paul McCartney' rubber doll, by Rosebud of England, with punched nylon hair.

7.25in (18.5cm) high

£30-50   **GAZE**

A set of four 1960s candy dishes, with gilt scalloped edges, each depicting one of The Beatles.

£180-220   **GAZE**

A framed proof etching by Pietro Psaier, titled 'The Fisherking, Rat Race John Lennon'.

20.5in (52cm) wide

£150-250   **GAZE**

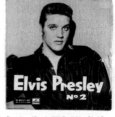

Elvis Presley, 'Rock 'N' Roll No.2', LP, CLP1105, released by HMV.

The poor condition of this album sleeve reduces its value. In excellent condition it could be worth around £500.

1957

£100-150   **GAZE**

Elvis Presley, 'Love Me Tender', soundtrack EP, HMV 7EG8199, released by HMV.

1957

£100-150   **GAZE**

Elvis Presley, 'All Shook Up', 45rpm single with purple and silver label and solid centre, HMV POP 359, released by HMV.

Look for the version with the removable centre, it can be worth over £100.

£15-20   **GAZE**

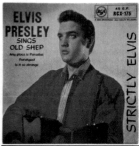

Elvis Presley, 'Strictly Elvis', EP, RCX 175, released by RCA.

1959

£15-25   **GAZE**

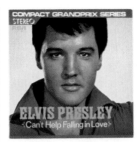

Elvis Presley 'Can't Help Falling In Love', Japanese 45 EP from the Compact Grandprix Series, with gatefold sleeve and orange label, RCA SRA-91, released by RCA.

1961

£25-35   **GAZE**

Elvis Presley, 'Tickle Me Vol. 2', mono soundtrack EP, RCX 7174, released by RCA.

1965

£15-25   **GAZE**

Elvis Presley, 'Greatest Hits', seven-disc box set, GELV-6A, released by Reader's Digest.

1978

£6-8   **GAZE**

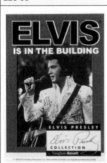

An 'Elvis Is In The Building' framed poster, from Vaughn-Bassett, produced to advertise a range of Elvis-inspired furniture, framed.

2002   35in (88cm) high

£30-50   **GAZE**

The Rolling Stones, 'The Rolling Stones', EP, DFE 8560, released by Decca.

1964

£10-15   **GAZE**

The Rolling Stones, 'Five by Five' EP, DFE 8590, released by Decca, mounted with a picture of the group, bearing signatures.

c1964   22in (56cm) high

£30-50   **GAZE**

A Rolling Stones US tour picture book programme, printed in the US.

1966

£40-60   **GAZE**

The Rolling Stones, 'Big Hits (High Tide and Green Grass)', LP with gatefold sleeve, TXS 101, released by Decca.

1967

£6-8   **GAZE**

The Rolling Stones, 'Flowers', rare Belgian LP with unique cover, SSS 120Y, released by Decca.

c1968

£30-50   **GAZE**

The Rolling Stones, 'Honky Tonk Women',
Japanese 45rpm single, TOP 1422,
released by the London label.

c1969

£20-30   **GAZE**

Mick Jagger, 'Just Another Night', 12in
single, TA 4722, released by CBS, bears
signature, framed with certificate of
authenticity.

1985   *21.5in (54.5cm) wide*

£50-70   **GAZE**

A 'Life With The Rolling Stones' newspaper,
from the Life With The Stars series, printed
by East Midlands Printers Ltd for Go
Magazine.

1964   *16in (40.5cm) high*

£10-20   **GAZE**

David Bowie, 'Man of
Words/Man of Music', rare
American LP, SR 61246,
released by Mercury.

c1969

£60-90   **GAZE**

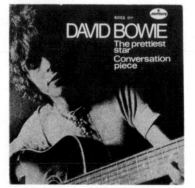

David Bowie, 'The Prettiest Star', rare Norwegian picture sleeve
single, MF1153, released by Mercury.

1970

£70-100   **GAZE**

David Bowie, 'Let's Talk', 1970s
Scandinavian 12in interview
picture disc, AR 30010,
released by NBC.

£6-8   **GAZE**

Kate Bush, 'The Kick Inside', American LP,
SW 17003, released by EMI America, with
rare cover.

c1978

£12-18   **GAZE**

Kate Bush, 'Wuthering Heights', German
7in picture sleeve, LC 0542, released by
EMI.

c1978

£5-8   **GAZE**

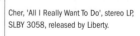

Cher, 'All I Really Want To Do', stereo LP,
SLBY 3058, released by Liberty.

1965

£7-10   **GAZE**

The Clash, 'Give 'Em Enough Rope', promotional LP, CBS 82431, released by CBS, lacks poster.

The addition of the original poster could make this album worth around £50.

1978

£20-30   GAZE

George Clinton, 'Martial Law', 12in single double pack, PRO-A-5998, released by Paisley Park Records, comprising a red vinyl 'X-Rated Deep Down & Dirty Mixes' disc and a green vinyl 'Clean' disc.

1993

£4-8   GAZE

Dave Clark Five, 'Glad All Over/I Know You' 45rpm single, DB 7154, released by Columbia, mounted with a photograph of the group and copy of an autograph book slip bearing signature.

c1963   19.75in (50cm) high

£30-50   GAZE

A Duran Duran publicity photograph, with facsimile signatures in silver.

10.75in (27.5cm) wide

£15-25   GAZE

Bryan Ferry and Roxy Music, 'Street Life - 20 Greatest Hits', 12in LP, EGCTV1, released by E.G., bears signature.

£10-15   GAZE

A reproduction 'Meet The Beat' Billy Fury show poster, for the Britannia Pier, Great Yarmouth, framed.

30in (76cm) high

£12-18   GAZE

A Genesis handbill, from the Knebworth Festival, other acts including Jefferson Starship and Tom Petty & the Heartbreakers.

1978   11.75in (30cm) high

£30-40   GAZE

Goldfrapp, 'Black Cherry', LP, LC 5834, released by Mute Records.

2003   12in (30.5cm) wide

£5-10   GAZE

A CLOSER LOOK AT A SIGNED GRATEFUL DEAD PICTURE

This is a well-known image and was taken by rock photographer Bill Seidemann for use in the band's eponymous double album released in 1971.

The value would have been greater if the image had not been cut down, losing half of Bill Kreutzman's signature.

The signatures of all the featured band members include Ron McKernan (Pig Pen) who was known for disliking autographs, making this a rare example.

The group disbanded in 1995 following the death of Jerry Garcia, but returned to touring in 2003 as 'The Dead'.

An extremely rare Grateful Dead publicity print, signed by all the members of the Grateful Dead's original five member line-up.
c1971

10.5in (27cm) wide

£2,500-3,000   **NOR**

Gun, 'Steal Your Fire', limited edition 12in record, AMY-885, released by A&M, with original metal badge and large poster.

c2002

£12-18   **GAZE**

Rolf Harris, 'Tie Me Kangaroo Down, Sport', 45rpm single, ZSP 59995, released by Epic, mounted with sleeve and slip of paper bearing autographed dedication and image, dated "12/3/63".

27.75in (70.5cm) high

£15-25   **GAZE**

A Jimi Hendrix Experience 'Axis: Bold as Love' songbook, published by A. Schroeder Music Publishing Co. Ltd.
1968

£25-35   **GAZE**

Jimi Hendrix, 'Purple Haze', rare Japanese picture sleeve 45rpm single, DP 1559, released by Polydor.

c1968

£30-50   **GAZE**

Jimi Hendrix, 'Sound Track Recordings From The Film Jimi Hendrix', Japanese two disc stereo LP with gatefold sleeve and obi strip, P 4621 2R, released by WEA, mint condition.
1973

£18-22   **GAZE**

An Iron Maiden printed glittery glass picture, with wooden frame.

19in (48.5cm) high

£40-50 NOR

A novelty postcard of a Life Guard, signed by members of the Jackson Five.

£200-300 ROS

A Led Zeppelin at Knebworth official programme.

1979 *11.75in (30cm) high*

£12-18 GAZE

A 'Led Zeppelin at Earls Court '75' official concert programme.

1975 *11.75in (30cm) high*

£15-20 GAZE

Led Zeppelin, 'Led Zeppelin', Italian LP, SM 3721, released by Joker, semi-legitimate recording of a 1971 BBC concert.

1974

£20-30 GAZE

Led Zeppelin, 'Trampled Underfoot', special limited edition 45rpm single, DC 1, released by Swan Song.

1975

£18-22 GAZE

A limited edition Jerry Lee Lewis poster, reading 'Springhill Salutes The Founders of Rock 'N' Roll', bearing signature, framed.

This poster was also available with an image of Elvis Presley.

22.75in (58cm) high

£40-60 GAZE

Little Angels, 'Boneyard', 12in picture disc, LTXP8, released by Polydor, signed by the five band members.

1991

£7-10 GAZE

Madonna, 'Crazy For You', picture disc, WOO8P, released by Sire Records.

1991 *11in (28cm) high*

£20-30 GAZE

Pink Floyd, 'See Emily Play', rare 1990s Spanish re-issue EP, EPL 14.377, released by EMI.

A photograph of Bob Marley, mounted with signed piece of paper, framed and glazed.

19.5in (49.5cm) high

£150-250 GAZE

A Roy Orbison black and white photograph, mounted with a signed autograph book page, framed and glazed.

18.5in (47cm) high

£80-120 GAZE

To differentiate between the reissue and the original, look at the upper left hand corner – the original will have the catalogue number listed there.

£100-150 GAZE

A run of five tickets for Pink Floyd's 'The Wall' concert, in Dortmund, dated 15th - 19th February.

1981 6.5in (16.5cm) high

£30-40 GAZE

Cliff Richard, 'Don't Stop Me Now', factory sample LP, S(C)X 6133, released by Columbia, Norrie Paramor signature stamp on sleeve.

Norrie Paramor was the UK recording director of EMI Columbia from 1952 until the late 1960s.

£30-40 GAZE

Cliff Richard with The Shadows, 'Wonderful Life', mono soundtrack LP, SX 1628, released by Columbia.

1964

£10-20 GAZE

Cliff Richard, 'Rock 'n' Roll Juvenile', 12in LP, EMC 3307, released by EMI Records, signed on the cover.

1979

£30-40 GAZE

Sex Pistols, 'The Great Rock 'n' Roll Swindle', soundtrack LP, VD 2510, released by Virgin.

This is the first version of the LP and contains the track 'Watcha Gonna Do About It'. The second version replaces it with 'I Wanna Be Me' and 'Who Killed Bambi' and is worth less than half of the original version.

1980

£25-35 GAZE

Sex Pistols, 'The Great Rock 'n' Roll Swindle', first issue Benelux film soundtrack LP, 70025, released by Virgin Records, with unique cover artwork.

1981

£40-60 GAZE

A Small Faces 'Pop '66' tour programme, printed by Hastings Printing Company, together with a ticket for Morecambe April 11th.

1966   10.5in (26cm) high

£70-90   **GAZE**

The Spencer Davis Group, 'The Second Album', TL 5295, released by Fontana.

1966

£10-15   **GAZE**

Screaming Lord Sutch, 'Lord Sutch and Heavy Friends' LP, 2400 008, released by Atlantic, with contributions from Jimmy Page, John Bonham and Jeff Beck.

1970

£40-60   **GAZE**

Tyrannosaurus Rex, 'A Beard of Stars', LP, SLRZ 1013, released by Royal Zonophone, with lyric sheet.

1970

£30-50   **GAZE**

Tyrannosaurus Rex, 'By The Light of A Magical Moon', rare 1960s German picture sleeve, released by Polydor.

£50-60   **GAZE**

A very rare Gene Vincent concert flyer, for Shrewsbury, July 1961, printed by Willonns (Printers) Ltd.

1961   10.25in (26cm) wide

£70-100   **GAZE**

A limited edition NME front sheet, featuring The Who, live at Leeds, from an edition of 1,300, with facsimile signatures, dated May 23rd, 1970.

30in (76cm) high

£60-90   **GAZE**

The Who, 'Substitute', 45rpm single, 591 001, released by Reaction, mounted with a picture of the band and an autograph book slip bearing signatures.

17.75in (45cm) wide

£40-60   **GAZE**

The Who, 'See Me, Feel Me', 33rpm EP, released by Polydor, with picture sleeve.

1970

£40-60　　　　　　　　GAZE

The Who, 'My Generation', LP, LAT 8616, released by Brunswick.

1965

£60-80　　　　　　　　GAZE

A John Entwistle's Art The Who – '2000' poster, signed by Entwistle, framed.

26in (66cm) high

£60-80　　　　　　　　GAZE

Yes, 'The White Album' LP, OF 722, released by Offshore, Holland.

1972

£25-35　　　　　　　　GAZE

A Stranglers 'Strangled – The Peevish Summer of 77' Summer Special booklet, published by Albion Leisure Services.

1977　　11.75in (30cm) high

£8-12　　　　　　　　GAZE

An Isle of Wight Festival weekend ticket.

1969　　6.75in (17cm) high

£30-50　　　　　　　　GAZE

A 5th National Jazz & Blues Festival official programme, at Richmond, featuring The Who and the Yardbirds.

This rare programme was made only for performers.

1965　　11.25in (28.5cm) high

£80-120　　　　　　　　GAZE

Three Isle of Wight Festival one day tickets, for the reserved enclosure.

1970　　　　　4.75in (12cm) long

£40-60　　　　　　　　GAZE

Frank Zappa 'Marvellous Stunner' limited edition multi-coloured LP, released by Angry Taxman Records, from an edition of 50.

£30-50　　　　　　　　GAZE

COLLECTORS' NOTES

- The development of transfer printing in the late 18th century, along with improved manufacturing and distribution methods in the 19th century, allowed royal commemorative ceramics to become more widely available. Many items were produced from the reign of Queen Victoria onwards.

- As the variety of items available is so vast, many collectors choose to collect pieces related to a single monarch or member of the Royal Family, or a single event in a monarch's life, such as a jubilee.

- The quality of an item is a key indicator to value, with those by well-known makers made from high quality materials and with fine decoration usually being the most valuable. Condition is also vital as so many

pieces were produced in large numbers. Always buy pieces in the best condition possible, as this will help values to remain constant or grow.

- As well as ceramics, many other different items have been produced to celebrate events such as coronations and jubilees. Some, such as biscuit tins, were special versions of usual items, while some were produced for the event itself. 'Ephemeral' card and paper items can be found regularly at affordable prices and can make a satisfying collection.

- With modern wares, look for limited editions made in very low numbers. Some collectors tend to prize items with photographic images while others prefer those with just coats-of-arms or ciphers.

A Spode Prince Regent's Royal Yacht plate.

This plate may be from the 'Royal George' yacht, built at Deptford in 1817.

c1817   9.75in (24.5cm) diam

£280-320   **SAS**

A King George III In Memoriam pearlware plate, repaired.

1820   6.75in (17cm) diam

£220-280   **SAS**

An A. Stephenson Queen Caroline commemorative pearlware nursery plate, titled 'Long Live Queen Caroline', the reverse with impressed mark.

1821   6.75in (17cm) diam

£350-450   **SAS**

A Princess Charlotte, Princess Royal In Memoriam cup and saucer, printed in black with her husband Prince Leopold grieving at an inscribed tomb.

Princess Charlotte was the eldest daughter of King George III.

1817

£100-150   **SAS**

An unusual Prince Frederick Duke of York In Memoriam cup and saucer, printed with a named tomb, cup stained.

Prince Frederick of Prussia was the second son of George III.

1827

£150-200   **SAS**

A Staffordshire Queen Victoria Proclamation pottery jug, printed in black with portraits, centred by name and dated 1837.

7.5in (19cm) high

£450-550   **SAS**

A Staffordshire Queen Victoria Proclamation pottery nursery plate, the centre printed in brown with a named and dated portrait.

1837   6.5in (16.5cm) diam

£250-350   **SAS**

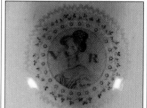

A Queen Victoria Coronation cup and saucer, printed with central portrait medallion of Victoria and with "VR" initials.

1837

£350-450 SAS

A CLOSER LOOK AT A QUEEN VICTORIA MUG

This was made to celebrate Queen Victoria's Coronation in 1837 at Westminster Abbey.

Of those produced, few survive due to the fragility of the material, therefore a minor chip to the foot will have little effect on its value.

Commemorative pieces from this period are very rare, as it is unlikely that many were made at the time.

This mug would have been given as a present and has been personalized with the inscription "A Present to Eliza", a common practice at the time.

A Queen Victoria commemorative earthenware mug, printed in black with half-length seated portraits of Queen Victoria and inscribed "A Present to Eliza", minor chip to foot.

The long-reigning Queen was extremely popular, and early commemorative pieces in her honour are sought-after by collectors of royal memorabilia.

1837-38

£800-900 SAS

A Queen Victoria and Prince Albert Royal Wedding earthenware nursery plate, the border moulded with the alphabet.

1840 5.25in (13cm) diam

£280-320 SAS

A Queen Victoria and Prince Albert porcelain mug, lined in pink lustre and printed in pink with green and yellow enamelled decoration.

c1847 3.25in (8cm) high

£30-40 SAS

An English Queen Victoria and Prince Albert commemorative porcelain mug, printed with Victoria seated upon a throne attended by Albert.

c1847

£70-100 SAS

A Queen Victoria and Prince Albert commemorative saucer, printed in pink and enamelled in green and yellow with a family scene, minor hairline crack.

c1850

£35-45 SAS

A Queen Victoria and Prince Albert commemorative cup and saucer, printed in pink and enamelled in colours with named portraits.

c1851

£70-100 SAS

A Queen Victoria Golden Jubilee quatrelobe pottery plate, printed in brown and enamelled in colours with a portrait.

1887

£70-90 SAS

A Doulton Lambeth Queen Victoria Golden Jubilee stoneware jug, decorated with applied white with Victoria upon her throne.

1887   *6.25in (15.5cm) high*

£100-150   **SAS**

A 'Balance of Payment' pottery plate, commemorating Queen Victoria's Golden Jubilee, printed in black, enamelled in colours and gilded.

1887

£80-120   **SAS**

An unusual Queen Victoria Golden Jubilee side plate, printed in black and lined in gilt.

1887

£40-50   **SAS**

A Plant Queen Victoria Golden Jubilee circular plate, printed in brown with a dated and inscribed portrait of the Queen.

1887

£70-100   **SAS**

A Minton Queen Victoria Golden Jubilee pottery teapot stand, printed with an inscribed portrait of the Queen.

1887   *8.25in (20.5cm) wide*

£100-150   **SAS**

A Queen Victoria Diamond Jubilee horse brass.

1897   *4in (10cm) high*

£7-10   **GAZE**

A Queen Victoria Diamond Jubilee brown-glazed rectangular pottery portrait tile, titled, dated and inscribed "A Queenly Woman, A Womanly Queen", framed.

1897   *10.5in (26.5cm) high*

£180-220   **SAS**

A Doulton Burslem Queen Victoria Diamond Jubilee tapering pottery beaker, printed in brown and decorated in colours.

1897

£100-150   **SAS**

A Queen Victoria Diamond Jubilee octagonal pottery plate, printed in black with an inscribed portrait within rod border, gilt rim.

1897

£35-45   **SAS**

ROYAL MEMORABILIA

A Queen Victoria Diamond Jubilee pottery mug, printed in brown and decorated in colours with portrait flanked by palaces, gilt rim.

1897

£35-45   SAS

A Queen Victoria Diamond Jubilee tapering pottery jug, printed in pale blue with dated young and old portrait medallions.

1897   *7.5in (19cm) high*

£60-80   SAS

A Coalport Queen Victoria Diamond Jubilee plate, with gilt rim, the reverse inscribed.

1897

£80-120   SAS

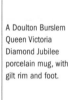

A Doulton Burslem Queen Victoria Diamond Jubilee porcelain mug, with gilt rim and foot.

1897

£180-220   SAS

A Queen Victoria Diamond Jubilee pottery side plate, printed in black with young and old portrait ovals.

1897

£25-35   SAS

A Samuel Barker Queen Victoria Diamond Jubilee plate, with a portrait of the Queen encircled by sporting vignettes, gilt rim.

1897   *9.25in (23cm) diam*

£50-70   SAS

A Queen Victoria Diamond Jubilee pottery mug, made for Harrods, printed with portrait of the Queen flanked by sporting vignettes.

1897

£70-100   SAS

A Scottish Queen Victoria Diamond Jubilee fluted pottery jug, printed with portrait of the Queen and named view of Osborne House.

1897   *6.75in (17cm) high*

£80-120   SAS

An Aynsley for Whiteley Queen Victoria Diamond Jubilee cup and saucer, printed with portraits, palaces, ships and flags, gilt rim.

1897

£70-100   SAS

A Queen Victoria Jubilee pottery jug, printed with a portrait oval and inscribed with dates of birth, coronation and marriage.

6.75in (17cm) high

£50-70 SAS

A Queen Victoria gift tin for troops in South Africa, containing six bars of Rowntree's chocolate in silver wrappers.

£150-200 W&W

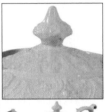

A Doulton Burslem Queen Victoria In Memoriam porcelain lobed dish, inscribed and lined in purple, gilt rim.

1901

£120-180 SAS

A Queen Victoria commemorative moulded terracotta plaque, the reverse with Pratt/Prince Albert stamp.

12.25in (30.5cm) high

£150-200 SAS

An unusual Prince Albert commemorative stoneware teapot and cover, moulded with floral cartouche and alternate jewelled shields, the underside impressed "Prince Albert", tiny rim chip.

c1840   3.5in (9cm) high

£120-180 SAS

A Prince Albert commemorative small earthenware cup and saucer, printed with the study of a lion, a named equestrian portrait and a Chinese figure.

c1845

£100-150 SAS

A Prince Albert small octagonal earthenware plate, with floral moulded border, printed with a named equestrian portrait.

c1847   3.5in (9cm) diam

£50-70 SAS

A Princess Victoria, Princess Royal and Prince Frederick Royal Wedding cup and saucer, enamelled in green and yellow with named portraits, the rims lined in blue.

See the George V section for a similar cup and saucer commemorating the wedding of Victoria's brother.

1858

£70-100 SAS

A Princess Victoria, Princess Royal and Prince Frederick Royal Wedding pottery jug, printed with named portraits flanked by flowers in colours.

1858   5.75in (14.5cm) high

£80-120 SAS

A Scottish Prince Albert Edward and Princess Alexandra Royal Wedding pottery jug, printed with portrait ovals centred by Prince of Wales' feathers.

1863   *9in (22.5cm) high*

£150-200   SAS

A Prince Albert Edward and Princess Alexandra Royal Wedding cup and saucer, printed in black with named wedding portraits, turquoise lined rims.

1863

£100-150   SAS

A James Beech Prince Albert Edward and Princess Alexandra Royal Wedding cup and saucer, printed with wedding portraits, gilt rim.

1863

£50-70   SAS

A King Edward VII and Queen Alexandra Silver Wedding cup and saucer, enamelled in colours with heraldic shield and flags, gilt rims.

1888

£80-120   SAS

Two miniature silver replica 'King Edward's Chairs', commemorating the accession of King Edward VII, one hallmarked for London, the other for Birmingham.

King Edward's Chair, commissioned by King Edward I in 1296, has been used in the coronation of all the British monarchs since 1308 with the exception of Queen Mary I.

1901   *Tallest 2.5in (6cm) high*

£150-200   SAS

A Hammersley King Edward VII Coronation oval plaque, moulded with head in profile and decorated in colours and gilt.

1902   *9.75in (25cm) high*

£80-120   SAS

A Royal Doulton King Edward VII and Queen Mary Coronation mug, inscribed on the reverse for the postponed coronation.

Pieces with the postponed 1902 coronation date are rarer and can be worth twice as much.

£30-50   SAS

A King Edward VII In Memoriam pottery jug, printed with a dated and inscribed portrait in colours.

Despite his popular reign, ceramic pieces recording Edward's death are rare.

1910   *8.25in (20.5cm) high*

£30-50   SAS

A German Prince George, Duke of York and Princess May (Mary) Royal Wedding porcelain cup and saucer, printed with named portraits, lined in gilt.

1893

£35-45   **SAS**

An unusual Prince George, Duke of York and Princess May (Mary) Royal Wedding cup and saucer, printed with three-quarter length portrait and entitled "Princess May, HRH Duke of York".

1893

£70-100   **SAS**

A Prince George and Princess Mary, Duke and Duchess of Cornwall lobed plate, commemorating their visit to Canada in 1901.

1901   *8.5in (21.5cm) high*

£40-60   **TYA**

A Royal Crown Derby King George V and Queen Mary Coronation miniature loving cup.

1911   *1.5in (4cm) high*

£100-150   **SAS**

A Copeland Spode for Usher's King George V and Queen Mary Coronation pottery bottle and crown stopper, moulded in white with portraits within flag cartouche on a green ground.

1911   *13.75in (35cm) high*

£50-70   **SAS**

A Wedgwood King George V and Queen Mary Coronation plate, printed all over in blue and inscribed on the reverse, gilt rim.

An identical plate was produced for Edward VII.

1911

£80-120   **SAS**

A Royal Doulton King George V Coronation porcelain beaker, decorated in gilt and printed in sepia with portrait ovals.

1911

£220-280   **SAS**

A Royal Doulton King George V Coronation pottery plate, printed with portrait oval within a border detailing the Empire.

1911

£40-60   **SAS**

A MacIntyre for Derry & Tom King George V Coronation small vase, enamelled in colours and gilded with an escutcheon flanked by flags.

1911   *5.25in (13cm) high*

£50-70   **SAS**

A Royal Doulton George V Coronation stoneware waisted cup, applied in white with a shield and inscribed in brown.

1911   *4in (10cm) high*

£50-80   **SAS**

A King George V and Queen Mary Coronation squat pottery jug, decorated with an inscribed shield by Raphael Tuck and inscribed "Ask for Worthington in Bottle".

1911   *5in (12.5cm) high*

£70-100   **SAS**

A King George V cup and saucer, commemorating his visit to the Widnes-Runcorn Transporter Bridge, with view of bridge, gilt rim.

1925

£100-150   **SAS**

A King George V and Queen Mary Silver Jubilee beaker, with gilt rim.

1935   *4.25in (11cm) high*

£3-5   **GAZ**

A Paragon King George V and Queen Mary Silver Jubilee plate, decorated in coloured enamels and gilt within a moulded border.

1935   *9.5in (24cm) diam*

£70-100   **SAS**

A Royal Doulton King George V In Memoriam loving cup, titled 'A Royal Exemplar'.

1936   *5in (12.5cm) high*

£45-55   **SAS**

A Royal Doulton King George V and Queen Mary Coronation porcelain boat-shaped dish, printed in colours with a portrait of the Queen, gilt rim.

1911   *13.25in (33.5cm) wide*

£35-45   **SAS**

A signed Royal presentation photographic portrait of Queen Mary, signed in pencil and also "Mary .R." in ink on the mount.

1936   *9.75in (25cm) high*

£100-150   **ROS**

A Cauldon Princess Mary, Princess Royal and Henry, Viscount Lascelles Royal Wedding cup and saucer, the reverse inscribed with details of the presentation of a similar service.

1922

£60-80   **SAS**

A Wedgwood cup and saucer, commemorating the visit of Mary, Princess Royal to the Royal Scots regiment, printed in blue with the regimental crest.

The Princess Royal was Colonel-in-Chief of the Royal Scots regiment from 1918.

1930

£70-100   **SAS**

WITH MANY THANKS FOR YOUR
HELP DURING MY TOUR
IN CANADA

A signed photographic print of Prince Edward, Prince of Wales, with printed mount "With many thanks for your help during my tour in Canada", signed in ink dated 1919, framed and glazed.

7.5in (19cm) high

1919

£50-70   **CLV**

A CLOSER LOOK AT A ROYAL CROWN DERBY CUP

This unusual twin-handled cup is in excellent condition.

Commemorative porcelain of this quality from this era is rarely seen and therefore commands a premium.

Royal Crown Derby has been producing richly decorated porcelain items since 1876 and continues today. A link with a well-known and prestigious company such as Royal Crown Derby will add value to the piece.

Edward VIII abdicated the throne before his coronation could take place. This meant that few pieces commemorating his short reign were made, making this finely produced example very rare, and sought-after by collectors.

An unusual Royal Crown Derby King Edward VIII cup on spreading foot, with sepia portrait on a pale blue reserve within shield-shaped cartouche.
1937   *4.5in (11.5cm) high*

£1,500-2,000   **SAS**

A rare Gladstone China cup and saucer, commemorating the visit of Prince Edward, Prince of Wales to Hastings, printed with a military portrait, gilt lining rubbed.
1927

£180-220   **SAS**

A Crown Devon coffee can and saucer, commemorating the visit of Prince Edward, Prince of Wales to Buenos Aires, with a named portrait, turquoise-lined border.
1931

£100-150   **SAS**

A small Crown Staffordshire King Edward VIII Coronation quatrelobe dish, printed with a sepia portrait oval.
1936   *5in (12cm) wide*

£120-180   **SAS**

A Crown Devon King Edward VIII musical pottery tankard, with portrait oval, the reverse inscribed with abdication, plays "Here's a Health unto his Majesty".
1936   *6.5in (16cm) high*

£80-120   **SAS**

A Wedgwood Edward VIII blue jasperware tapering jug.
1937   *5.25in (13.5cm) high*

£80-120   **SAS**

A Japanese King Edward VIII small porcelain coffee cup and saucer, printed in black with a named portrait, lined in gilt.
1937

£40-60   **SAS**

A King George VI & Queen Elizabeth Coronation mug.

1937

£5-10 GAZE

A King George VI and Queen Elizabeth Coronation trio set and teapot.

1937 *Plate 6.5in (16.5cm) diam*

£15-25 GAZE

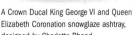

A Crown Ducal King George VI and Queen Elizabeth Coronation snowglaze ashtray, designed by Charlotte Rhead.

c1937 *3.5in (9cm) wide*

£50-60 H&G

A Paragon King George VI and Queen Elizabeth Coronation loving cup, from a limited edition of 1,000, numbered on the base.

1937 *4.25in (11cm) high*

£150-200 SAS

A Shelley King George VI and Queen Elizabeth Coronation porcelain loving cup, printed with portraits in sepia.

c1937 *3.5in (8.5cm) high*

£60-80 SAS

A Grimwades King George VI and Queen Elizabeth Coronation musical pottery mug, moulded with superimposed portraits, playing the National Anthem.

1937 *6.5in (16cm) high*

£100-150 SAS

A Paragon King George VI and Queen Elizabeth Coronation plate, decorated in bright colours and gilt.

1937

£50-70 SAS

A Royal Doulton King George VI and Queen Elizabeth Coronation porcelain beaker, printed with a superimposed portrait medallion.

1937

£250-300 SAS

A Royal Crown Derby King George VI and Queen Elizabeth Coronation mug, with portrait medallions and monograms.

1937 *3.5in (9cm) high*

£400-500 SAS

A Shelley King George VI and Queen Elizabeth Coronation porcelain loving cup, printed with portraits including the Princesses.

c1937   *3.5in (9cm) high*

£150-200   **SAS**

A pair of Royal Crown Derby King George VI and Queen Elizabeth small square dishes, each printed in sepia with a named and dated portrait, gilt rims.

1937   *3in (7.5cm) wide*

£120-180   **SAS**

A Royal Crown Derby limited edition footed bowl, commemorating the visit of King George VI and Queen Elizabeth to America, from an edition of 3,000.

1939   *5in (12cm) high*

£450-550   **SAS**

A limited edition Royal Doulton 'The Queen Mother' figure, HN3944, designed by Alan Maslankowski, from an edition of 5,000, no certificate.

1997   *10.5in (26.5cm) high*

£100-150   **PSA**

A limited edition Royal Doulton 'H.M. Queen Elizabeth The Queen Mother' figure, HN4086, designed by Alan Maslankowski, from an edition of 2,000, commemorating her 100th birthday, with certificate.

2000   *9in (23cm) high*

£120-180   **PSA**

A Crown Ducal dish, with a sepia portrait of Princess Margaret, named in gilt within a black, red and gilt dotted border.

c1933   *5in (12cm) diam*

£100-150   **SAS**

An unusual pair of Crown Ducal Princess Elizabeth and Princess Margaret commemorative dishes, printed with named portraits in sepia.

c1933   *6.75in (17cm) high*

£180-220   **SAS**

An Aynsley Queen Elizabeth II Coronation plate, the reverse inscribed in gilt.

1953   *10.75in (27cm) diam*

£150-200   **SAS**

An Aynsley Queen Elizabeth II Coronation plate, the reverse inscribed in gilt.

1953   *10.5in (26.5cm) diam*

£120-180   **SAS**

A CLOSER LOOK AT A QUEEN ELIZABETH II COMMEMORATIVE CUP

The box and booklet make the piece desirable, but do not have a great effect on the value.

Mugs can be found without the limited edition mark. Unnumbered examples are still valuable, but marked versions command a much higher price.

It is by a fine maker and is of excellent quality, making it highly desirable.

The limited editions of small numbers are more generally more sought-after and tend to keep their value better.

A rare Royal Crown Derby Queen Elizabeth II Coronation loving cup, from a limited edition of 250, with original box and booklet.
c1953

4in (10cm) high

£400-500 H&G

A Burleigh Queen Elizabeth II Coronation earthenware loving cup.
c1953   3.25in (8cm) high

£60-80 H&G

A Kaiser Queen Elizabeth II Silver Jubilee silhouette vase, the profile of the Queen and the Duke of Edinburgh formed by the shape of the vase.
c1977   8in (20cm) high

£180-220 H&G

A limited edition Paragon Queen Elizabeth II Coronation loving cup, from an edition of 1,000, with original certificate.

A similar example was made to celebrate the silver wedding anniversary of Queen Elizabeth and Prince Philip, with silver handles.

c1953   4.75in (12cm) high

£300-400 H&G

A limited edition Coalport Queen Elizabeth II Silver Jubilee urn and cover, from an edition of 200, painted with a scene of The Mall, numbered on the base.

1978
11.5in (25cm) high

£150-200 SAS

A limited edition Capo di Monte 'H.R.H. The Queen' figure, designed by Bruno Merli, with silver jubilee certificate.
c1973   15.5in (38.5cm) high

£100-150 SAS

A limited edition Royal Doulton 'H.M. Queen Elizabeth II' figurine, HN3440, designed by Peter Gee, from an edition of 3,500, with certificate and box.
1992

£120-180 SAS

A limited edition Capo di Monte 'H.R.H. Prince Charles' figurine, commemorating his investiture, with certificate.

1969   *15in (37.5cm) high*

£100-150   **SAS**

A Prince Charles and Lady Diana Spencer Royal Wedding caddy spoon, maker's mark "DSS London", in original fitted box.

c1981   *2.75in (7cm) long*

£70-100   **WW**

A Derek Fowler Studio Prince Charles and Lady Diana Spencer Royal Wedding ceramic night light.

1981   *8.5in (11.5cm) high*

£35-45   **DH**

A limited edition Poole Pottery Prince Charles and Lady Diana Spencer Royal Wedding plate, from an edition of 2,000.

1981

£20-30   **C**

A Caverswall Prince Charles and Lady Diana Spencer Royal Wedding square casket and cover, from a limited edition of 250.

1981   *12.5in (32cm) high*

£200-300   **SAS**

A Royal Worcester Prince Charles and Lady Diana Spencer Royal Wedding urn and cover, from a limited edition of 750, modelled with Prince of Wales' feathers.

9in (23cm) high

£120-180   **SAS**

A Spode Prince Charles and Lady Diana Spencer Royal Wedding large chalice and cover, from a limited edition of 500, decorated with enamels and gilt, with certificate.

1981   *12.75in (32.5cm) high*

£100-150   **SAS**

A Poole Pottery Queen Elizabeth II commemorative tile, in a wooden surround.

£20-30   **C**

A late 19thC small brass microscope, probably American, with partial lacquer, pull-tube and stage focusing, on green-painted cast iron base.

8in (20cm) high

£30-50 — **EG**

An early 20thC microscope, by Gundlach-Manhattan, Optical Co., Rochester, New York, with pull-tube, rack and micrometer focusing, lacquered-brass bodytube, circular stage with wheel stops, and plano/concave mirror, mounted on twin-pillar support to Y-shaped shoe, in mahogany case.

10.25in (26cm) high

£180-220 — **EG**

A mid-19thC German, Oberhauser-type drum microscope, lacquered-brass with pull-tube focusing, detached, bull's-eye condenser, micrometer stage adjustment, wheel stops and reflector in drum, on circular base, with accessories in fitted mahogany case.

8.25in (21cm) high

£120-180 — **EG**

A brass drum microscope, by J.H. Steward, London, with three objectives and accessories in a mahogany box.

c1850   7.25in (18cm) high

£120-180 — **ATK**

A 'Prof. Fuller's Calculating Slide Rule' logarithmic spiral calculator, manufactured and distributed by W.F. Stanley & Co. Ltd., London, with mahogany handle, side ends and original case, brass fittings, no support, original 32-page instruction manual.

c1925   18in (45.5cm) long

£200-300 — **ATK**

An early logarithmic 'Fuller's Spiral slide rule', with mahogany handle, dated.

1889

£150-200 — **ATK**

A German orbit tellurium, by Columbus of Berlin, made for the Scandinavian market, with later electrical fittings.

A tellurium demonstrated the Sun and Earth system.

c1920   20in (50cm) long

£400-600 — **ATK**

A mid-20thC Curta Type I calculator, with original plastic box, shipping carton and two manuals, mint condition.

This example fetched such a high value as it is unusually totally complete and is in truly mint condition.

£600-900 — **ATK**

A 19thC English demonstration compass, with printed rose, iron needle and mahogany frame with glazed top.

9in (23cm) diam

£70-100 — **EG**

SCIENTIFIC INSTRUMENTS

An American brass circumferentor, by William James Young, Philadelphia, magnetic compass surrounded by a divided circle, and equipped with fixed sights, with original wooden case.

c1850   14.25in (35.5cm) long

£300-500   ATK

A brass pantograph, by Thomas Rowley, Brighton, with ceramic casters, in shaped mahogany case.

A pantograph (developed by Christoph Scheiner in c1603-c1605) was used for enlarging or reducing the scale of maps when copying them.

c1840   21in (53.5cm) wide

£100-150   EG

An early 20thC paper micrometer, by Schopper, Leipzig, with silvered dial, operating lever and foot, agent's label of "Foreign Paper Mills, New York" and cast iron base with gilt decoration.

This is used for measuring the thickness of paper.

11in (28cm) high

£100-150   EG

An early American Abbott 'Automatic Check Punch' cheque protection device, very good condition.

c1890

£280-320   ATK

A CLOSER LOOK AT A PERPETUAL FOUNTAIN

This fountain was based on Greek engineer Hero's (10-70 AD) famous mechanical fountain, but used revolving reservoirs to provide perpetual movement.

The water pressure from, and weight of the water in, the revolving reservoirs aimed to cause the fountain to spray and the reservoirs to revolve in perpetuity.

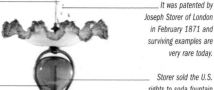

It was patented by Joseph Storer of London in February 1871 and surviving examples are very rare today.

Storer sold the U.S. rights to soda fountain maker John Tufts of Boston, who made them until the early 1900s.

A 'Storer's Patent Perpetual Fountain', manufactured and distributed by J. Defries & Sons, London.

These ornamental table fountains would often contain scented water, so that as the fountain sprinkled, the room's air was delicately fragranced.

1871-1900s   20in (50cm) high

£1,500-2,500   ATK

A large Wimshurst's pattern electrostatic generator.

The foil strips and glass rubbed against the wire brushes, generating static electricity.

20in (50cm) high

£800-1,000   ATK

A telegraph key and sounder, by Manhattan Electrical Supply Co., 20 ohm, with steel lever and twin binding posts on mahogany base.

7in (18cm) wide

£50-80   EG

COLLECTORS' NOTES

■ Although sewing is no longer seen as a fashionable pastime, sewing tools are a popular collecting area.

■ A number of patents for sewing machines were granted around the turn of the 19th century. The first useable machine was patented by French tailor Barthelemy Thimonnier in 1830. Elias Howe and later Isaac Merritt Singer added improvements and Singer's name has become synonymous with sewing machines today.

■ The majority of sewing machines can be collected relatively inexpensively, especially Singer machines. Early examples, made for only a short period of time are more sought-after and valuable.

■ Metal thimbles were made from the mid-18th century and production peaked in the 19th century when sewing was popular. Many were made as souvenir or commemorative pieces. Look for decorative or named examples and those made of precious metal, but be aware that before the 1870s hallmarks were not required on such small items.

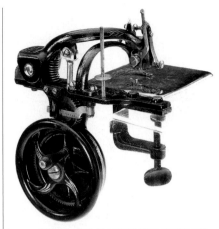

An unusual American Beckwith sewing machine, complete with accessories, manual and original spare needles.
c1875

£1,200-1,800   **ATK**

A very rare French 'L'Incomparable' sewing machine, retailed by Rumpf of Paris, complete with foot pedal, table clamp and original wooden box.
c1890

£650-750   **ATK**

A Wilcox & Gibbs domestic sewing machine, marked "W&G" and with patent date "17 April 1883".
c1884

£140-200   **ATK**

An English cast-iron domestic sewing machine, by Jones.
c1890

£70-90   **ATK**

An unmarked cast-iron sewing machine, probably German.
c1895

£150-250   **ATK**

A 'The Nelson' domestic sewing machine, probably German, retailed in London by the American Sewing Machine Co.
c1900

£70-100   **ATK**

An English 'Ideal' sewing machine by Salters.
c1910

£70-90   **ATK**

A Müller 12 toy sewing machine, by Müller of Berlin, complete and in good condition.
c1935

£350-450   **ATK**

SEWING

A metal thimble, commemorating Queen Victoria's coronation, reading "Long Live Queen Victoria", lacks glass or stone at top.

c1837

£50-70   **CBE**

A silver-plated thimble, commemorating the Silver Jubilee of King George and Queen Mary.

c1935

£35-45   **CBE**

An early 20thC French silver novelty thimble, reading "BONNE ANNEE", with French control marks.

£45-55   **CBE**

A tartanware needle book, printed with the 'Stuart' tartan.

2.25in (5.5cm) high

£50-70   **WW**

An early 20thC German thimble, by Gabler, with enamelled band of a landscape scene.

Gabler, which closed in 1963, made many enamelled thimbles. It can be recognised by the eight-pointed star motif at the crown of the thimble.

£35-45   **CBE**

A Japanese blue felt plush elephant tape measure.

2.25in (5.5cm) high

£20-40   **SOTT**

A 19thC rosewood sewing compendium, the turned handle with reel support, a pair of pin cushions flanking a thimble, above a frieze drawer.

5in (12.5cm) high

£150-250   **WW**

A WWI period 'Red Cross' pin cushion, by C.S. Green and Co. of Birmingham.

1914   *3.5in (9cm) diam*

£220-280   **WW**

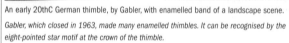

COLLECTORS' NOTES

■ The excitement, inherent danger and historical importance of space travel have helped make space memorabilia a rapidly growing area over the past ten years.

■ Flown memorabilia is the most sought-after, with unique items used on lunar missions being the 'holy grail' for many collectors. NASA does not allow items to be taken into space solely to increase their value, meaning numbers are limited.

■ Commemorative pieces are more affordable and varied with autographs and patches being a good start, as so many were produced. Focus on one program, or type such as pre-shuttle missions like Apollo or Gemini, or shuttle missions (STS).

■ Certain objects with astronauts' signatures, such as baseballs, can be rare. Many astronauts still sign today, some for a fee. The autographs of those that no longer sign can rise in value, particularly if the astronaut is especially notable.

■ The condition of flown items, especially equipment, can be poor with signs of wear and use. This is not unexpected and rarity and importance to a mission take precedence over condition.

■ Mass-produced memorabilia should be bought in as close to mint condition as possible. Always try to ensure an autograph comes with a certificate of authenticity, even if obtained personally.

An Apollo 7 Beta cloth crew patch, without cutting lines.

1968   *9in (23cm) wide*

£70-100   **AGI**

A rare flown Apollo 11 crew-signed Beta emblem, made of teflon-coated fibreglass, signed by Neil Armstrong and Buzz Aldrin and signed and inscribed by Michael Collins with: "Carried to the Moon aboard Apollo XI, July 1969.", together with a letter from Michael Collins.

Apollo 11 crew signed items are very desirable but an item flown to the Moon having their signatures is perhaps the ultimate autograph collectable from this mission. The American Eagle and mission importance make this an iconic emblem.

1969   *6in (15cm) wide*

£22,000-28,000   **SWA**

A flown to lunar surface Apollo 15 mission patch, carried by Dave Scott, with "XV" stitched in silver, in its flight bag with original tape.

1971

£3,000-4,000   **AGI**

A flown Gemini GT-10 crew patch, together with a handwritten certificate of authenticity.

1966   *3in (7.5cm) wide*

£1,800-2,200   **AGI**

An extremely rare STS 51L mission patch, together with a crew patch decal.

STS stands for 'Space Transportation System' and refers to the Shuttle. This patch was given to Bob Overmyer by crew member Dick Scobee.

1993

£80-120   **AGI**

A Spacepex Beta cloth patch, distributed at the Manned Spacecraft Center Stamp Club stamp show, "Commemorating Ten Years of U.S. Manned Space Flight, May Fifth, 1961/1971".

1971   *8in (20cm) wide*

£30-40   **AGI**

A flown Gemini GT-11 Richard Gordon Jr. U.S. Navy patch.

£3,000-4,000   **AGI**

SPACE MEMORABILIA

A flown Apollo 11 'United Nations' silk flag, inscribed "Carried to the Moon aboard Apollo XI, Michael Collins" at the bottom, together with a NASA certificate of authenticity signed "Michael Collins".

c1969   *12in (30.5cm) high*

£3,000-4,000   **AGI**

A flown Apollo 11 US silk flag, on a presentation certificate inscribed: "This Flag travelled to the Moon with Apollo 11, the first manned lunar landing. July 20, 1969", unsigned.

1969   *12in (30.5cm) high*

£8,000-12,000   **AGI**

A flown Apollo 16 United States flag, signed by Charles Duke and inscribed: "This flag—Flown to the Lunar Surface Aboard the Lunar Module "Orion" April 20, 1972. Charles M. Duke, Jr. Apollo 16 LMP", mounted on a NASA certificate.

1972   *12in (30.5cm) high*

£5,000-6,000   **SWA**

An extra large flown US silk flag, inscribed and signed by Tom Stafford with: "Flown to the Moon on Apollo X, May 1969, Tom Stafford", with a typed letter signed by Stafford providing additional flight details.

1969 Apollo mission flown flags of this size are extremely rare as they are both heavy and large, taking the space of ten 4in x 6in flags.

1969   *18in (47.5cm) wide*

£10,000-15,000   **SWA**

A CLOSER LOOK AT A FLOWN FLAG

This flag was flown on the first manned lunar landing mission, arguably the most important space mission.

It is from Aldrin's personal collection, adding to its desirability.

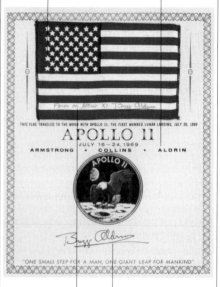

It is signed and inscribed by Buzz Aldrin, one of the first two men to walk on the moon.

It is attractively mounted on a NASA certificate, which is also signed by Aldrin, making it a superb display piece.

A flown United States flag, inscribed and signed by Buzz Aldrin with: "Flown on Apollo XI, Buzz Aldrin", with an NASA certificate reading "This flag travelled to the Moon with Apollo 11, the first manned lunar landing, July 20, 1969" and "Apollo 11, July 16-24, 1969".

1969   *12in (30.5cm) high*

£14,000-16,000   **SWA**

A flown United States flag, carried to the Moon on Apollo 14 in the Command Module "Kitty Hawk", inscribed and signed by Mitchell with: "Flown to the Moon--Apollo 14, Edgar Mitchell".

1971

£5,000-7,000   **SWA**

A flown Texas state flag, carried to the Moon on Apollo 14 in the Command Module "Kitty Hawk", inscribed and signed by Dr. Mitchell with: "Flown to the Moon aboard Kitty Hawk on Apollo 14, Edgar Mitchell, LMP".

1971

£2,000-3,000   **SWA**

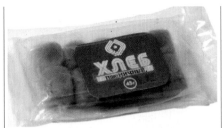

A Russian flight-ready 'Loaf of Bread', consisting of 10 thimble-sized mini-loaves, vacuum-wrapped.

3in (7.5cm) wide

£30-40   AGI

A Mercury Program freeze-dried strawberry cereal cube, mounted in a clear Lucite block.

1961-64   Block 2in (5cm) high

£120-180   AGI

A flown Apollo 12 spoon, engraved "Richard F. Gordon Apollo 12 CMP".

c1969

£1,500-2,000   AGI

A CLOSER LOOK AT A TOOTHBRUSH

Toothbrushes are a rare and highly personal item.

This was one of only two toothbrushes taken to the lunar surface by Aldrin and Armstrong.

It was transferred as part of the 'Oral Hygiene' kit from the Command Module to the Landing Module and is complete with its protective case.

It was owned by Buzz Aldrin, the second man to walk on the moon, adding to its value.

A flown Apollo 11 "Tooth Tip" toothbrush and button fastening storage sleeve, model S-19, made by Lactona for NASA/MSC, the sleeve with blue velcro patch and flight designation for the Lunar Module Pilot (LMP), with a typed letter signed by Aldrin.

c1969   *8in (20cm) long*

£10,000-15,000   SWA

A flown Apollo 12 mechanical pencil, carried by Richard F. Gordon.

c1969

£2,000-3,000   AGI

An unusual Apollo "Lunar Rock Storage Container", the two-part polished stainless steel containment vessel secured by three screws through the bottom, marked "45" on both pieces.

1965-73   2.75in (7cm) long

£400-600   AGI

A Mercury orange-flavoured drink, in its original intact NASA plastic bottle.

1961-64   3in (7.5cm) high

£200-300   AGI

A Mercury pilot survival kit, made by the ACR Electronics Corp in New York for NASA during the Gemini Program; contents include a signal mirror, fish hook and line, siren whistle, fire starters, flashlight, with label reading "Model 4H-1, Ser No. 5058, Name Combination Survival Light, Cont No. NAS9-5294, Part No. 20538, Date 3.4.66".

1966

£300-400   AGI

A Mercury Capsule savings bank, marked "Space Capsule" on one side and "United States" on the other.

4.5in (11.5cm) high

£120-180 AGI

A Mercury MR-6 'Friendship 7' black ceramic cookie jar, reading "Friendship 7" on one side and "United States" on the other, a small chip on the bottom.

The proposed Autumn 1961 Mercury MR-6 manned flight was cancelled in July of that year, and never took place.

c1961 11in (28cm) high

£500-700 AGI

An Apollo lunar module model, made for the Grumman Aerospace Corp.

The ascent stage is detachable from the descent stage, as with the actual vessel.

1969 8in (20cm) high

£1,200-1,800 SWA

An Apollo 8 painted cast iron money bank, marked "Borman, Lovell, Anders" on one side.

c1968

£50-80 AGI

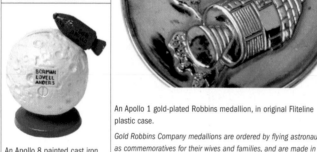

An Apollo 1 gold-plated Robbins medallion, in original Fliteline plastic case.

Gold Robbins Company medallions are ordered by flying astronauts as commemoratives for their wives and families, and are made in strictly limited numbers. The original Apollo 1 mission (previously named AS-204) crew were tragically killed in a training exercise fire.

c1967 1.25in (3cm) diam

£500-700 AGI

An Apollo 11 souvenir brass bowl, featuring the lunar landing and takeoff, the Apollo 11 emblem, and reading "For your contribution to the first manned lunar landing 1969, NASA MSC".

c1969 4.75in (12cm) diam

£50-80 AGI

A sterling silver Robbins STS 107 medallion, in its original case with astronaut's names and dates on the reverse.

Not all Robbins medallions were flown. This example is a restrike, made to commemorate the 2003 Columbia Space Shuttle tragedy. The dates are die-cut, rather than engraved after flying.

£200-300 AGI

An Apollo 15 David Scott signed Rawlings baseball, inscribed "Dave Scott Apollo 15 CDR".

David Scott decided not to autograph baseballs a number of years ago, making this one of the few available. Buzz Aldrin also does not sign baseballs.

£2,000-3,000 AGI

An Apollo 17 coffee mug, with the official Apollo 17 logo below the inscription "The Beginning!".

c1972

£120-180 AGI

An STS 7 Sally Ride signed official NASA photograph.

Ride became the first American woman in space in 1983, on board a space shuttle. The Shuttle was first seen in 1976 and undertook its first mission in space in 1981.

10in (25.5cm) high

£30-40   **AGI**

A Mercury MR-6 John Glenn signed official NASA lithograph, minor edge bends/faults.

10in (25.5cm) high

£30-40   **AGI**

An Apollo 7 Walter Cunningham signed NASA colour lithograph, inscribed "To Bobby, Study Hard".

10in (25.5cm) high

£30-40   **AGI**

An Apollo 17 Ron Evans signed photograph of the American flag on the lunar surface, mounted on white matt board.

12in (30.5cm) high

£100-150   **AGI**

A complete set of Mercury 7 astronaut autographs, comprising Scott Carpenter, Gordon Cooper, John Glenn, Virgil Grissom, Wally Schirra, Alan Shepard and Deke Slayton, signed on an RCA Photo Lab/Patrick AFB publicity glossy photo.

£3,000-4,000   **AGI**

An STS 107 signed official NASA lithograph, signed by all crew members, comprising Dave Brown, Rick Husband, Laurel Clark, Kalpana Chawla, Mike Anderson, Willie McCool and Ilan Ramon, with biographies printed on the reverse side.

STS 107 was the catastrophic final flight for the space shuttle Columbia, which broke up upon re-entry on February 1st, 2003 with the tragic loss of all on board.

2003   *10in (25.5cm) wide*

£10,000-15,000   **SWA**

A Gemini GT-06 Wally Schirra and Tom Stafford signed NASA reprint photo.

10in (25.5cm) wide

£70-100   **AGI**

A Mercury MA-8 Wally Schirra signed copy of "The Astronauts, Pioneers in Space", published by Golden Book Press and the Editors of Life Magazine.

1961

£30-40   **AGI**

Three Apollo 11, 12, and 14 Traverses charts, illustrating the lunar EVAs (moon walks) from the first three lunar landings.

1969-71

£3,000-4,000   **SWA**

COLLECTORS' NOTES

■ Russian space memorabilia is generally less popular than American and as such usually less valuable. Cosmonauts were allowed to take pieces home after flights, whereas American astronauts were not, or were only allowed a limited numbers of items.

■ Although Americans were the first to land on the Moon, Russian Yuri Gagarin was the first man in space in Vostok I on April 12th 1961, so much memorabilia focuses on this legendary character.

■ Russian space programmes are also comparatively less well known and the language barrier makes it hard to understand them, or how a flown piece fits in to a mission.

■ Despite this, posters with their bold and striking artwork and colours, and memorabilia from the earliest years of space travel during the early 1960s are popular.

A Russian 'Glory to the Soviet People, People of Heroes' poster, depicting a revolutionary soldier and a cosmonaut, printed in Leningrad in a quantity of 185,000, some folds and edge faults.
1962   *37in (94cm) wide*
£280-320   **AGI**

A Russian 'Country of October - Country of Cosmonauts'.
1977   *33in (84cm) high*
£400-600   **SWA**

A Vostok 1 Yuri Gagarin signed picture postcard.
£120-180   **AGI**

A Russian 'To the Courage, Labour, Mind of the Russian People - Glory!' poster, showing Yuri Gagarin in front of Earth, his flight path marked as a white ring.
1962   *33in (84cm) high*
£400-600   **SWA**

Konstantin Eduardovitch Tsiolkovsky, "The Road to the Stars", USSR Academy of Science, 351pp., Russian-language hardback with dust jacket, the science-fiction anthology including "On the Moon", "Dreams about Earth and Sky", "On the Planet Vesta".
1960
£30-40   **AGI**

Evgeny Ryabchikov, "Pilot of the Star Ship", published by The Printing House of Children's Literature of the Department of Education, 48pp., minor faults.
This was the first hardcover book about Gagarin published in the USSR.
1961
£50-80   **AGI**

Yuri Gagarin, "My Blue Planet", 239pp., signed by the author, Russian-language hardback with dust jacket, some wear to dust jacket.
This book is hard to find, particularly with the dust jacket.
£220-280   **AGI**

An 'Order for Conquering Space' enamelled award, set with four artificial diamonds.
This is a new decoration from the Russian Republic rather than from the older Soviet times, but it is still awarded with care and respect.
2in (5cm) wide
£40-60   **AGI**

A Russian 'ASTP' enamelled press badge.

Distributed to Soviet journalists that attended the Soyuz 19 launch, prior to its docking with Apollo.

1975   3in (7.5cm) high

£80-120   AGI

A Mir programme Soyuz TM-6 presentation enamelled plaque, presented to dignitaries after the flight by the Russians in honour of the first Russian-Afghan space flight.

1988   3.5in (9cm) high

£120-180   AGI

A bronze wall hanging, depicting a cosmonaut, a Sputnik and a rocket.

10in (25.5cm) high

£120-180   AGI

A Russian lithographed tin container, featuring space dogs "Belka and Strelka" surrounded by stars, minor rubs.

These were the first living creatures to be sent into space and returned safely to Earth. Travelling on Sputnik 5, they spent a day in orbit on August 19th 1960 and were accompanied by 40 mice, two rats and some plants. One of Strelka's six post-adventure puppies was presented to President Kennedy's daughter as a gift by President Kruschev.

c1960   6in (15cm) diam

£100-150   AGI

A Sputnik music box, with engraved inscription "To Lev Stepanovich on his birthday from his co-workers. January 11, 1963".

This was presented to the 37-year-old Cosmonaut Stepanovich by his fellow cosmonauts.

c1963   7in (18cm) long

£50-80   AGI

A Vostok 1 Yuri Gagarin and Gherman Titov signed photo of them at a parade.

8in (20cm) high

£120-180   AGI

A Vostok 1 Yuri Gagarin and Valentina Tereshkova signed Russian 3k postcard, with a red 1964 commemorative cancel.

Valentina Tereshkova became the first woman in space in 1963, orbiting the world 48 times in Vostok 6.

1964

£100-150   AGI

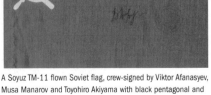

A Soyuz TM-11 flown Soviet flag, crew-signed by Viktor Afanasyev, Musa Manarov and Toyohiro Akiyama with black pentagonal and octagonal MIR on-board hand-stamps, with Russian-language certificate of authenticity.

1990   5.5in (14cm) wide

£120-180   AGI

COLLECTORS' NOTES

- Apart from cricket bats having been curved rather than straight before the mid-18th century, cricket equipment has seen very few changes. As a result it is the personal association or historical importance of a piece that dictates interest and value, but firm provenance is required. Items bearing signatures or ones that which were used in notable matches are typical examples.

- In general, the more notable the player, or the more historically important the event, the greater the value. Notable players to look out for include Geoffrey Boycott (b.1940), Gary Sobers (b.1936), Don Bradman (1908-2001) and the legendary and instantly recognisable Dr. W.G. Grace (1848-1915), but even items connected to modern players or important recent events can fetch high sums.

- Most memorabilia dates from the mid-19th century onwards and ceramics, accessories, tickets, programmes and photographs are popular, adding variety to a collection. 'Wisden Cricketer's Almanac', published annually since 1864, continues to form the bulk of many collections. Early examples can be rare due to low numbers of surviving copies.

A Wisden 'Cricketer's Almanac', 77th edition, with original cloth covers and slight bowing to the spine.

Only 8,000 copies of Wisden were printed in this year.

1940

£220-280   **MM**

A Wisden 'Cricketer's Almanac', 82nd edition, with original cloth covers.

Only 1,500 copies of Wisden were printed in this year.

1945

£150-200   **MM**

A Wisden 'Cricketer's Almanac', 86th edition, with original hard cover, some wear to hinges.

1949

£50-80   **MM**

A Wisden 'Cricketer's Almanac', with original hard cover, complete with dust jacket.

1970

£40-60   **MM**

A rare Headingley Leeds Cricket, Football & Athletic Co. members ticket and booklet.

This was for the first full season (1891-92) of rugby and cricket played by Leeds St. John at the Headingley ground.

£100-150   **MM**

An autographed team sheet for the 1968 Australian cricket team on tour, and a similar sheet for the 1961 touring team.

10.5in (26.5cm) high

£80-120   **GORL**

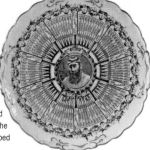

A Dr. W.G. Grace commemorative plate, by Coalport, printed in blue and decorated in gilt, the reverse with inscribed detail.

1895   *9in (23cm) diam*

£1,000-1,500   **SAS**

An earthenware plate, the centre printed in black with a scene entitled 'Cricket', the border moulded with flowers and foliage decorated in red and green enamels and underglaze in blue.

c1860   7.25in (18.5cm) diam

£220-280   **SAS**

A rare Hampshire County Cricket Club championship commemorative bone china plate, by Coalport, from an edition of 1,500.

1973   *10.5in (26.5cm) diam*

£15-20   **MM**

A Geoffrey Boycott 'Century of Centuries' commemorative bone china plate, by Coalport, with facsimile autograph to base, from an edition of 1,500, boxed.

1977   *9in (23cm) diam*

£30-40   **MM**

A Tom Richardson heart-shaped pottery dish, by MacIntyre, printed in brown with a named portrait of the famed fast bowler.

c1895   *3.75in (9.5cm) wide*

£350-450   **SAS**

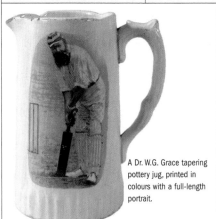

A Dr. W.G. Grace tapering pottery jug, printed in colours with a full-length portrait.

£650-750   **SAS**

A novelty cricket teapot, by Richard Partington Designs of Whitstable in Kent, issued in conjunction with The Cricketer magazine.

1991   *8.5in (21.5cm) high*

£8-12   **MM**

An extremely rare Victorian ebonite vesta case, in the shape of a book with embossed golfing and cricketing scenes to the sides.

c1890   *2in (5cm) long*

£350-450   **MM**

A silver cricket bat shaped fruit knife, with Sheffield hallmarks.

1913   *5.5in (14cm) long open*

£180-220   **MM**

A pair of 19thC skeleton cricket pads.

26in (66cm) high

£150-200   **MSA**

Murray Urquhart, 'Portrait of Sebastian E.F. Snow as a Young Cricketer', inscribed and dated 1939, oil on canvas.

23.5in (60cm) high

£650-750   **L&T**

COLLECTORS' NOTES

- Football programmes form the backbone of many football memorabilia collections, as many can be picked up for only a few pounds, while rare examples can reach into the thousands.

- Generally earlier programmes are higher in value than later ones, with pre-WW1 always sought-after and pre-1900 very rare indeed. Later programmes, from the last forty years or so, start from a couple of pounds, making them accessible even to young collectors.

- Other programmes that fetch a premium are Cup Finals, international matches and early foreign matches. Perhaps surprisingly, programmes from the 1966 World Cup final between England and West Germany are worth around a modest £50 as many

people kept them in good condition as souvenirs after the match.

- Manchester United is the most widely collected British team, with an international following. Their long-standing position at the top of the game, both at home and abroad, means there are plenty of programmes to choose from. Games featuring Sir Matt Busby's team and star players like Sir Bobby Charlton and George Best are desirable. Of particular interest to collectors are the programmes from either side of the tragic 1958 Munich air crash that killed eight of the 'Busby Babes'.

- Look for examples in good condition: early programmes in particular were printed on poor quality paper. Avoid those with handwritten notations, rips and tears.

A Fulham v Exeter City Division Three football programme, 7th May, 1932.

This is a desirable Championship-winning commemorative issue.

9in (23cm) high

£70-90　　　　　PC

A Wolverhampton Wanderers v Fulham Division One football programme, 17th Dec, 1949.

1949　　8.5in (22cm) high

£30-35　　　　　PC

A Newcastle United v Fulham Division One football programme, 11th Nov, 1950.

1950　　8.5in (22cm) high

£30-35　　　　　PC

A Manchester United v Fulham Division One football programme, 25th December, 1951.

1951　　9in (23cm) high

£30-40　　　　　PC

A Manchester United v Manchester City Division One football programme, 14th February, 1959.

1959　　9in (23cm) high

£5-8　　　　　PC

An Arsenal v Sheffield Wednesday Division One football programme, 8th August, 1962.

Arsenal's excellent footballing record and large fan base mean that their programmes are always collectable.

1962　　7in (18cm) high

£3-4　　　　　PC

A Leicester City v Manchester United FA Cup Final football programme, 25th May, 1963.

1963　　9in (23cm) high

£15-18　　　　　PC

An England v Rest of the World F.A. Centenary football programme, 23rd October, 1963.

1963   *9in (23cm) high*

£7-10   **PC**

A Newcastle United v Moscow Dynamo Friendly football programme, 22nd November, 1965.

1965   *8.5in (22cm) high*

£4-7   **PC**

An Everton v Sheffield Wednesday F.A. Cup Final football programme, 10th May, 1966.

1966   *9in (23cm) high*

£10-15   **PC**

A Chelsea v Tottenham Hotspur FA Cup Final football programme, 20th May 1967.

1967   *9in (23cm) high*

£10-12   **PC**

An Ajax v Real Madrid European Cup first round football programme, 29th August, 1967.

1967   *9.5in (24cm) high*

£3-5   **PC**

A Benfica v Manchester United European Cup Final football programme, 29th May 1968.

United won this match 4-0 and became the first English team to win the European Cup.

1968   *9in (23cm) high*

£4-7   **PC**

An England v Spain European Championship football programme, 3rd April 1968.

1968   *9in (23cm) high*

£3-4   **PC**

An England v Poland World Cup qualifier football programme, 17th October, 1973.

1973   *10in (25cm) high*

£4-7   **PC**

A World Cup official football programme, Mexico May/June 1970.

1970   *9in (23cm) high*

£10-15   **PC**

FIND OUT MORE...

'Famous Football Programmes', by John Litster, published by Tempus Publishing, 2002.

'The Supporters' Guide to Football Programmes 2004', by John Robinson (ed.), published by Soccer Books, 2003.

A scarce Manchester United team postcard, the reverse signed in ink by 13 players including Rowley, Griffiths, Bryant, Porter, Hall and Brown, some creases.

c1938   5.5in (14cm) wide

£320-380   **MM**

A Manchester United League Champions 1964/5 season official squad photograph, signed in the bottom autograph section by nine players including Law, Cantwell, Charlton, Stiles and Foulkes.

10in (25.5cm) wide

£100-150   **MM**

A Manchester United embroidered cloth badge, with the wording "Wembley 1958" and official club crest used during the 1958 FA Cup Final against Bolton Wanderers.

5.75in (14.5cm) high

£400-500   **WW**

A Football Association steward's enamel and brass badge, depicting the three lions crest to centre, complete with original fixing pin.

1936   1.5in (4cm) high

£70-100   **MM**

A Football Association steward's enamel and brass badge, complete with original fixing pin.

1935   1.5in (4cm) high

£80-120   **MM**

A zip-up kit bag, with wording to each side "World Cup 1966 West Germany" and sponsor's details "Barratts Sports Shoes", with letter of authenticity.

This bag was the property of Bert Trautmann (b.1923), a German national who played for Manchester City for 15 years as a goalkeeper and saw them through a number of FA Cups. Despite his skills as a goalkeeper, he was never called to play for the German National team.

1966   18.5in (47cm) wide

£350-450   **WW**

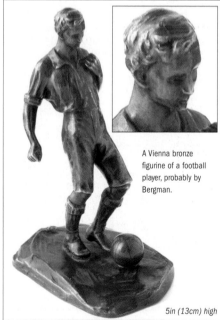

A Vienna bronze figurine of a football player, probably by Bergman.

5in (13cm) high

£500-600   **MSA**

A 1930s bronze figure of a football player, on a brown marble pedestal base.

9in (23cm) high

£280-320   **B**

A clay pipe, the bowl moulded with figures playing football, the underside as a boot kicking a ball.

c1860   8in (20cm) long

£100-150   **SAS**

COLLECTORS' NOTES

■ Golf is one of the oldest sports still played today, however, most of the memorabilia available today originates in the late 19th century.

■ Golf clubs and balls form the basis of many a collection with early, rare or high quality examples forming the upper part of the market. More modern clubs can still be collectable, yet affordable.

■ As well as playing equipment, there is a huge range of items carrying a golfing theme, including ceramics, metalware, artwork and books.

■ Ephemera produced for games and tournaments are also popular and come in a wide range of values. Those from very early or landmark games will be the most sought-after.

■ Women began playing golf in the early 20th century and the popularity of the game continues to grow. Memorabilia featuring women is harder to find and so can command a premium when it does appear.

A scarce Bramble pattern gutty golf ball, stamped "The Paxton's Brand 1898", wear to paint and some strike marks but retaining good shape.

1.75in (4.5cm) diam

£120-180   **MM**

A scarce 'Scotch Jenny Make' rubber dimple golf ball, made by the St Andrews Golf Co., some paint wear.

1.75in (4.5cm) diam

£50-70   **MM**

A scarce and unusual 'B. I.' hexagonal mesh pattern rubber core ball, with three strike marks.

c1910   *1.75in (4.5cm) d.*

£40-60   **MM**

A Blue Star paper-wrapped golf ball, complete with original label.

1.75in (4.5cm) diam

£40-60   **MM**

A Dunlop 'Goblin' No. 4 paper-wrapped golf ball, complete with original label.

1.75in (4.5cm) diam

£70-100   **MM**

A Dunlop 'Sixty-Five' No. 4 paper-wrapped golf ball, complete with original label.

1.75in (4.5cm) diam

£35-45   **MM**

A two-part cast iron cross-hatched golf ball press/mould.

3.75in (9.5cm) wide

£450-550   **MSA**

H.M. Bateman, "Adventures at Golf", new leather green and gilt spine, minor scuffing to corners.

1923   *11in (28cm) high*

£120-180   **MM**

Walter Camp & Lilian Brooks, "Drives and Puts: A Book of Golf Stories", first edition, published by L. C. Page, Boston, frontispiece of a woman golfer by H.C. Ireland.

1899

£450-550   **L&T**

Robert Marshall, "The Enchanted Golf Clubs", first edition, published by Frederick Stokes, New York, illustrated by Stuart Hay.

1920

£180-220   **L&T**

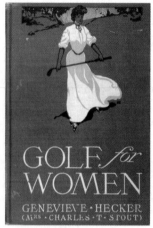

Genevieve Hecker, "Golf for Women", first edition, published by The Baker & Taylor Co., New York.

1904

£450-550   **L&T**

Clare Briggs, "Golf: The Book of a Thousand Chuckles - The Famous Golf Cartoons by Briggs", first edition, published by P. F. Volland, Chicago.

1916

£180-220   **L&T**

"How to Play the Old Course at St Andrew's and All About It", second edition, front cover loose.

1933   *6.5in (16.5cm) high*

£40-60   **MM**

Francis Bowler Keene, "Lyrics of The Links; Poetry, Sentiment and Humour of Golf", first edition, published by D. Appleton and Co., New York.

1923

£200-300   **L&T**

Miles Bantock, "On Many Greens: A Book of Golf and Golfers", first edition, published by Grosset & Dunlap, New York.

1901

£250-350   **L&T**

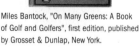

A programme from the 1949 Ryder Cup, played over Ganton Course in Scarborough on 16th and 17th September 1949, cover loose and some repairs.

1949   *10in (25.5cm) wide*

£150-200   **MM**

A scarred wooden head putter, by Alexander Patrick, Leven, horn insert to sole, lead counterweight, hickory shaft, wrapped soft leather grip.

Patrick was apprenticed to his cabinetmaker father, who also made clubs, and inherited the family business in 1866. He made clubs at the Royal Wimbledon Golf Club from 1886.

£350-450   **L&T**

A CLOSER LOOK AT A PUTTER

The 'Schenectady' was designed by engineer Arthur F. Knight and was named after his home town.

It was designed so that the hickory shaft met the aluminium head in the centre, rather than at one end.

In 1904, the year after it was launched, the 'Schenectady' helped Walter Travis become the first American to win the British Amateur Championship.

It was an extremely popular putter in the US, but was effectively banned by the Royal & Ancient Golf Club (of St. Andrews) Rules of Golf Committee because of its design.

An unusual 'Schenectady' type aluminium putter, stamped on the head "TRUPUT TRADEMARK F H AYRES LONDON", with original hickory shaft and sheepskin grip.
c1910   Head 3.75in (9.5cm) long

£250-300   **MSA**

An Eve smooth-faced putter, the back stamped with trademark, and further marked, "Left 10 degree, weight 8.5oz", hickory shaft, wrapped leather drip.

£80-120   **L&T**

A beech driving putter, by Robert Simpson, the scarred head with horn insert to sole, lead counterweight, hickory shaft, wrapped, white leather grip with silver band mount and cap, engraved initials.

£350-450   **L&T**

An early "Special Patent" wry-neck putter, by Willie Park, smooth face, long crimped hosel, hickory shaft, leather grip.

£180-220   **L&T**

A 'Premier' putter, by Robert Simpson, the iron head with mesh patterned face, the hickory shaft stamped with maker's name, wrapped leather grip.

£400-500   **L&T**

An unusual American centre-shafted Model AC putter, by Winter Dobson of Dallas, Texas, with Bakelite face and brass sale plate to base of head.
c1945   5in (12.5cm) long

£250-300   **MSA**

A cleek, by Robert Forgan & Son of St Andrews, showing the Prince of Wales feathers mark and maker's stamp to shaft.

39.5in (100.5cm) high

£45-55   **MM**

A smooth-faced cleek, by Carrick, Musselburgh, stamped "Carrick" and "X", long crimped hosel, hickory shaft, replacement wrapped leather grip.

£120-180   **L&T**

A driving iron, by Tom Morris, of St. Andrews, showing the later Tom Morris head and shoulder stamp mark.

39in (99cm) high

£35-45   **MM**

A Zenith jigger, by Tom Morris of St Andrews, with unusual Tom Morris colour transfer label to shaft inscribed "Open Champion 1861, 62, 64 & 67", together with the maker's autograph shaft stamp.

39in (99cm) high

£100-150   **MM**

A smooth-faced rut niblick, by G. Forrester, Elie & Earlsferry long hosel, hickory shaft, wrapped leather grip.

£300-350   **L&T**

A giant niblick, by James McDowell Turnberry, with a Spalding anvil cleek mark and punch dot facings, fitted with full length original leather grip.

37in (94cm) high

£120-180   **MM**

A persimmon head Sunday club, by J. & H. Scott, Elie, the fancy face head with stamped trademark.

£250-350   **L&T**

A John Letters walking stick golf club, the head bearing transfer trademark.

£220-280   **L&T**

A rare Prestwick golf scorer, made of nickel-plated brass and ivorine.

c1920s   *4in (10cm) wide*

£180-220   **MSA**

A rare Douglas Golf silver-plated patent 'Sand Tee', unused, in original maker's box priced 3/9d, with instructions and blue paper wrapper.

Box 3.25in (8.5cm) long

£850-950   **MM**

A 1920s golf score keeper, the leather wallet with leaves of ivorine set with revolving discs of numbers, the front stamped in gilt with a golf bag.

4.25in (11cm) high

£100-120   **MSA**

An American clear plastic and paper Strokmaster golf score keeper, made by Healthways of Los Angeles, California, with original box.

4.25in (11cm) high

£80-120   **MSA**

A rare Spalding golf clubs store display stand, the wooden easel-back piece having Spalding golf flag style sign at top, and containing a set of four unused Bobby Jones model woods, some light paint flaking.

c1960s

£200-300   **HA**

A 1920s Walker & Hall silver-plated nut dish, with squirrel on a twisted horizontal, supported by golf clubs.

8.25in (15cm) wide

£120-140   **MSA**

A three-piece EPNS condiment set, in the form of Bramble golf balls supported by golf clubs, with stamped registered number 604192 for 1912.

Salt 3.25in (8cm) high

£120-140   **MSA**

A set of three golf club-shaped pencils, in a papier-mâché golf bag-style case.

c1930s/40s

£60-80   **HA**

A pair of Hagenauer-style hand-painted brass golfing figures.

3in (7.5cm) high

£30-50 MM

A scarce Britains golfer lead figure, with grey jacket, plus-fours and peaked cap, brown socks and shoes, walking with golf club in right hand.

£70-80 W&W

A Continental hand-painted bisque figure of a golf caddy, probably Austrian.

c1910 *7in (18cm) high*

£240-280 MSA

A pair of green patinated bronze bookends, depicting a golfer and a diminutive caddy with bag of clubs, each on a variegated black/green marble base.

c1930 *largest 9.25 (23.5cm) high*

£700-800 L&T

A pair of Weller Dickens Ware pottery vases, of cylindrical form, each incised and polychrome, decorated with a golfer in a landscape, incised numerals "318/0" to the underside.

7.75in (19.5cm) high

£600-800 L&T

A Royal Doulton 'The Nineteenth Hole' plate, with printed and handpainted design of two gentlemen enjoying a post game drink.

c1925 *10.5in (26.5cm) diam*

£300-400 MSA

A Royal Doulton 'Picturesque Scenes' plate, 'Melrose Abbey, Killarney and Stratford', with a transfer scene of a golfer.

10.5in (26.5cm) diam

£250-350 MSA

A Tony Wood Studio ceramic dimple golf ball-shaped teapot, with a club handle and 18th flag mounted to the lid.

7.75in (19.5cm) high

£40-60 MM

COLLECTORS' NOTES

■ Motor car racing started almost as soon as the first motor car appeared, with the first race taking place in Paris, France in 1894. France continued to dominate motor racing into the beginning of the 20th century.

■ The first Grand Prix race took place in France in 1906. By 1934, 18 different countries were holding their own versions of the race, but it was not until 1946 that the various races were linked to create the Formula 1 world championship.

■ When it comes to memorabilia, Formula 1 is the most popular and usually the most valuable, although there are items for most budgets. Earlier pieces, particularly from exotic locations like Brazil or Monaco, are more desirable. Uniforms and parts from the actual cars occupy the high end of the market. Autographs, pins and patches are generally more affordable. Overall, the market has declined slightly making items comparatively affordable.

■ Popularity and current racing success affect value greatly. Ferrari, star driver Michael Schumacher and the late Ayrton Senna have a huge global following and anything connected to them is sought-after.

A Mika Hakkinen replica Corser racing helmet, from the 1999 Formula 1 season, the clear visor signed by the driver with a thick black pen, with a padded carrying bag.

£350-450　　　　**TCA**

A Damon Hill replica racing helmet, from the 1996 Formula 1 season, the dark visor signed and dated by the driver with a silver pen, with a padded carrying bag.

£550-650　　　　**TCA**

A Michael Schumacher replica racing helmet, from the 2000 Formula 1 season, the dark visor signed by the driver with a thick silver pen, with a padded carrying bag.

£600-700　　　　**TCA**

An Ayrton Senna replica Formula 1 racing helmet, with a padded carrying bag.

£350-450　　　　**TCA**

An official Renault/Elf helmet visor signed by Alain Prost, in black marker pen.

9in (23cm) wide

£50-60　　　　**MM**

A Gerhard Berger Ferrari Formula 1 racing suit, made in Italy by OMP, emblazoned with sponsors labels, "G. Berger" stitched in white.

£2,500-3,500　　　　**AGI**

A Damon Hill Formula 1 Williams Camel/Renault racing suit, emblazoned with sponsors labels, "Damon Hill Ox" stitched in the waistband and a Union Jack on the right knee.

1993-96

£2,000-3,000　　　　**AGI**

A Maserati 2000 brochure, with Italian language text and images of the racing car, engine, suspension and specifications.

1954

£250-300   **TCA**

A Michael Schumacher signed photograph, mounted with another photograph and Formula 1 career statistics.

22in (56cm) high

£120-180   **GAZE**

'Simply the Best', limited edition print by John Ketchell, from an edition of 250 showing the Ford GT40 that won Le Mans in 1969, mounted, framed and glazed.

23in (58.5cm) wide

£80-120   **TCA**

'Michael Schumacher', limited edition print by Juan Carlos Ferrigno, from an edition of 850 showing Schumacher in his Monaco winning 1997 Ferrari F310B.

21in (53.5cm) high

£100-150   **TCA**

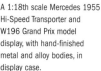

A 1:18th scale Mercedes 1955 Hi-Speed Transporter and W196 Grand Prix model display, with hand-finished metal and alloy bodies, in display case.

£1,200-1,800   **TCA**

A limited edition Marc Surer wind tunnel-type model car, from the 1980 Barclay Arrows Australian Grand Prix, signed on the body with marker pen.

42in (106.5cm) long

£500-700   **TCA**

A 1:12th scale Ferrari 1961 250 TR 61 model of the 1961 Le Mans winning 250 TR 61.

£1,500-2,000   **TCA**

A limited edition photographic print of Ayrton Senna, from an edition of 850, winning the 1993 Australian Grand Prix in the McLaren MP4/8, framed and glazed.

This was to be Senna's 41st and last Grand Prix win, as he died while competing in the 1994 San Marino Grand Prix.

32in (81.5cm) high

£60-80   **TCA**

An amusing French side plate, depicting an early motor racing scene, decorated with a blue edge maker's stamp to rear.

7.5in (19cm) diam

£25-35   **MM**

COLLECTORS' NOTES

■ Olympic memorabilia has been collected since the modern games started in 1896, but was mainly collected by people involved in the games, such as the participants and officials.

■ The first official piece of memorabilia released was a set of stamps for the 1896 games, issued by the organising committee to balance the event's budget. Olympic coins followed much later in 1951.

■ Lapel badges have been produced since the games restarted. They are an affordable way to start a collection and are usually easy to obtain, with participation medals forming the next step up the ladder. These medals were given to all the participants, officials and members of the International Olympic Committee, so numbers can be quite large.

■ Mascots are a relatively new marketing tool, the first being 'Schuss' – the unofficial mascot of the 1968 games, held in Grenoble. 'Waldi' the dachshund was the first official mascot and presided over the 1972 summer games at Munich.

■ Memorabilia from the earliest games tends to be the hardest to find, and so the most valuable, making more recent games a good place to start for collectors on a budget.

■ Look for pieces connected to countries that no longer 'exist', such as Eastern Germany or the Soviet Union, as historical interest can add to their value and desirability.

A scarce pewter goblet, relating to the 1912 Olympic games in Stockholm, with a raised acorn leaf design, stamped to base.

1912   3.5in (9cm) wide

£40-60   **MM**

A book commemorating the 1912 Olympics, entitled 'Den Femte Olympiade I Bild och Ord', including a piece on the British gold medal-winning football team.

1912   12in (30.5cm) wide

£70-100   **MM**

A 1928 Amsterdam Olympic commemorative plate, decorated in bright colours.

1928   11.5in (29cm) wide

£15-20   **SAS**

An official programme for the 1936 Winter Olympics, with official Olympic poster design to front cover.

1936   8.75 (22cm) wide

£30-50   **MM**

An official 1936 Berlin Olympics brass and white enamel lapel badge, reading "XI Olympiade Berlin", depicting the official games logo.

1936   1.25in (3cm) wide

£30-50   **MM**

An official 1936 Berlin Olympics competitor's medal, reading "XI Olympiade Berlin 1936", with the games logo to the reverse.

1936   2.75in (7cm) wide

£50-80   **MM**

A gold medal, reading "The 18th Olympic Games Tokyo 1964" to the front, with a Roman chariot scene to the rear, with original box.

2.25in (5.5cm) diam

£400-600   **MM**

A 1980 Moscow Olympics walking mug, by Carltonware.

1980   4.25in (11cm) high

£20-30   **SAS**

FIND OUT MORE...

www.collectors.olympic.org, The Olympic Collectors Commission, official collectors association.

COLLECTORS' NOTES

■ While rugby memorabilia doesn't yet have the same caché as football memorabilia, the sport has a long and distinguished history and can prove more affordable.

■ Many collections are based on a particular team and can include caps and shirts, official dinner menus, themed ceramics and metalware and signed photographs and autographs.

■ While earlier pieces are sought-after, memorabilia from England 2003 World Cup triumph will be desirable, even though much of it was mass produced.

■ The recent success of the English rugby team has raised the sport's image and may increase the number of collectors, and as a result, the value of memorabilia.

A Rugby World Cup 2003 England team display, comprising an action shot from the final of Martin Johnson and another of him with the Webb Ellis Cup mounted together with an autographed card.

21in (53.5cm) wide

£30-40   **MM**

A Rugby World Cup 2003 England team display, comprising an action shot from the final of Lawrence Dallaglio, mounted together with an autographed card.

21in (53.5cm) wide

£30-40   **MM**

An England Rugby squad signed photograph, depicting 28 players and officials, signed to mount by 23 in ink including Martin Johnson, Phil De Glanville, Mike Catt, Clive Underwood, Jeremy Guscott and Will Carling, framed and glazed.

1995   *20in (51cm) wide*

£80-120   **MM**

A red and black six-panelled University College Cork rugby cap, dated 1930-31, some fading.

University College Cork Rugby Football Club was founded in 1872 and is one of the oldest rugby clubs in the UK.

£60-80   **MM**

A red and blue six-panelled Irish Rugby velvet cap, dated 1913-1914, makers detail "W. Lairds Corn Mkt. Belfast" inside.

This cap was either awarded for playing for the Black Rock or Beckwith Rangers clubs.

£80-120   **MM**

A Gilbert official England rugby ball, signed in ink by 22 players including Jonny Wilkinson, Martin Johnson and Mike Catt.

£100-150   **MM**

A Gilbert 'Puntabout' brown leather rugby ball.

11in (28cm) long

£30-50   **MSA**

A replica England World Cup rugby shirt, signed in marker pen by 20 players including Will Carling, Martin Johnson, Jeremy Guscott and Phil De Glanville.

1999

£100-150   **MM**

A Baines Rugby trade card, titled 'Ye Olde Game', depicting a game in play in shield design.

£80-120   **MM**

COLLECTORS' NOTES

- Tennis originated as 'jeu de paume' in France 900 years ago, slowly gaining the use of gloves, then bats, and then rackets in the 16th century, to replace the palm (paume) of the hand. In 1874, Major Walter Clopton Wingfield developed 'Sphairistike', tennis' immediate forerunner.

- Rackets are a popular area. Changing shapes allow them to be dated to a period. Full size rackets were developed by the 1700s and had asymmetrical, lop-sided heads. By the early 1880s, this was replaced with a 'flat' top and designs gained a concave throat piece (i.e. curved towards the handle).

- During the 1890s the flat top began to be rounded off, and from 1900-1920s, heads became more oval in shape. Look out for early rackets made before the 1900s with unusual stringing designs and shaped handles and heads, as experimentation was common.

- The Wimbledon Championships began in 1877, moving to their present site in 1922. They were suspended during WWII. Early programmes, especially from the 1930s, are sought after.

- Cans of balls form an interesting collection. Unopened cans are more valuable – check that the coloured design goes all the way to the metal band at the top, rather than having a gap showing the opening strip has been torn off. Look at the artwork to discern the period of the can. Card was used during WWII due to a shortage of metal, and plastic was introduced in 1984.

- Novelty memorabilia is also appealing and collectable, with more jewellery and small items found than for other sports, perhaps due to the larger number of female players. Look for quality of design and materials and an early date, from 1880s-1930s.

A 1950s American Spalding 'Pancho Gonzales' endorsed tin tube of tennis balls.

Pancho Gonzales (1928-95) won the U.S. Championship 1947-48, dominated the professional circuit during the 1950s and played and won the longest ever Wimbledon match, lasting 5 hours and 12 minutes!

8in (20.5cm) high

£50-80　　　**MSA**

An early Dunlop 'The Service' blue lawn tennis ball tin, complete with four maker's unused balls including two fully paper-wrapped with original Dunlop labels, all stamped "Service".

1939-45　　11in (28cm) high

£150-200　　**MM**

A 1940s Dunlop Championship tin tube of tennis balls.

8in (20cm) high

£60-90　　**MSA**

An early Slazenger tin, with two used period balls, removable lid and retaining much original finish.

1900s-1910s

11in (28cm) high

£80-120　　**MM**

A Dunlop 'Fort' tennis ball box, complete with six unused balls, dated 1974.

8in (20.5cm) wide

£20-30　　**MM**

A 1930s Dunlop Warwick card box of six tennis balls, one with original paper wrapping.

8.25in (15cm) wide

£80-120　　**MSA**

A 'Kleenball' patent lawn tennis wooden hand ball cleaner, complete with bristle linings and unusual bowl-shaped body, with turned wooden handles.

4in (10cm) diam

£180-220　　**MM**

A rare Hammer Handle flat-top 14oz lawn tennis racket, by F.H. Ayres, handle stamped "Hammer Handle" in script and with reg'd number 37585.

c1880   27.5in (70cm) long

£280-320   **MSA**

A Bussey lawn tennis fishtail 'The Diamond' racket, with unusual grooved handle, with "GEO.G.BUSSEY & CO Ltd" and "THE DIAMOND" stampings.

c1895   27.25in (69cm) long

£280-320   **MSA**

A CLOSER LOOK AT A TENNIS RACKET

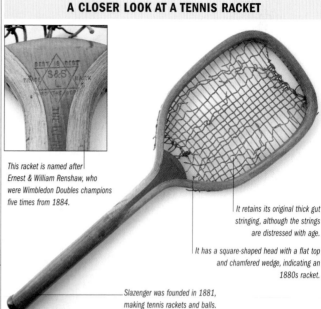

This racket is named after Ernest & William Renshaw, who were Wimbledon Doubles champions five times from 1884.

It retains its original thick gut stringing, although the strings are distressed with age.

It has a square-shaped head with a flat top and chamfered wedge, indicating an 1880s racket.

Slazenger was founded in 1881, making tennis rackets and balls.

An early Slazenger 'The Renshaw' racket.
c1888   27.25in (69.5cm) long

£300-500   **MSA**

An unmarked fishtail handle racket, stamped "12oz X".

c1905   27.25in (69cm) long

£100-150   **MSA**

A 1920s F.H. Ayres Tournament Model Davis Cup tennis racket, with transfers.

27.25in (69.5cm) long

£100-140   **MSA**

A 1920s American 'Wilding' open throat tennis racket, by Rawlins of St Louis.

27.25in (69cm) high

£70-100   **MSA**

A 1920s good Speedshaft 'Ultra Souple' tennis racket, with transfers, one in a shield reading "Darsonval Brevetee".

27in (68.5cm) high

£70-100   **MSA**

A 19thC mahogany racket press, with brass fitting and painted initials "J.E.B.".

13in (33cm) wide

£180-220   **MSA**

Three German Thuringian ceramic tennis figures, each with blue anchor mark to base.

1880s   *Tallest 4.75in (12cm) high*

£300-400   **MSA**

A Continental hand-painted ceramic tennis theme figurine, in the form of a spill vase, of a boy standing next to a tree trunk, unmarked.

5in (12.5cm) high

£70-100   **MSA**

A Victorian Denby-style stoneware loving cup with tennis motifs, handles mounted as greyhounds, marked.

8in (20.5cm) wide

£180-220   **WW**

An Austrian ceramic plate, with moulded design of a gentleman tennis player, with painted detailing.

c1880   *6in (15cm) diam*

£120-180   **MSA**

A Spode bone china figure of an Edwardian female tennis player, 'Alexandra', by Paula Shone, wearing a full-length tennis dress and boater, decorated with gold leaf highlights.

c1985   *9.5in (24cm) high*

£30-50   **WW**

A Clifton commemorative crested china miniature tennis racket, transfer-decorated.

c1900   *4in (10cm) high*

£30-50   **MSA**

A pair of early 20thC printed silk tennis theme lamp shades, with wire bulb grips.

4.25in (11cm) high

£200-300   **MSA**

£100-150   **MSA**

A Midwinter tennis theme oval plate, after a design by Shelley, with transfer-printed scene of children playing tennis and a hand-painted border, some wear to the transfer.

11.5in (29cm) wide

A Dean leather-bound lawn tennis measure, in exceptional condition with yellow paper label.

A worn example of the this would be worth under half this value.

c1900   *5.25in (13.5cm) diam*

£150-200   **MSA**

SPORTING MEMORABILIA

An American moulded composition wall clock, in the form of a tennis racket, fitted with a wind-up movement by the Lux Clock MFG Co Ltd of Waterbury, Conn, USA.

7.5in (19cm) long

£60-90   MSA

A rare S. Mordan & Co. silver slide action pencil, in the form of a Real Tennis racket.

The London firm of Sampson Mordan is well-known for its novelty-shaped pencils, which can be valuable, especially as they appeal also to writing equipment collectors.

c1880

£300-500   GORL

THE ART OF TENNIS
AND HOW TO PLAY IT
Showing the Various Strokes of the Game demonstrated by the Leading Players of England

1. The FOREHAND DRIVE
 By Miss JOAN AUSTIN
2. The BACKHAND DRIVE
 By Mr. J. D. P. WHEATLEY
3. The SERVICE
 By Mr. J. B. GILBERT
4. VOLLEYING
5. The LOB
 The SMASH
 By Mr. J. B. GILBERT
 Mr. J. D. P. WHEATLEY
6. TOP SPIN and CHOP
 By Miss K. COLYER
7. MIXED DOUBLES
 By Miss E. COLYER
 Miss JOAN AUSTIN
 Mr. J. B. GILBERT
 Mr. J. D. P. WHEATLEY
8. HINTS ON PRACTICE
 By Mr. L. A. GODFREE

SHOWING AT THIS CINEMA
Come and See the Game as it should be Played.

A 1920s 'The Art of Tennis and How To Play It' poster, by an anonymous designer and produced by the Parkstone Film Co. Lytham.

A small wooden tennis racket-shaped '25 Year Silver Anniversary' hand-held mirror.

13.5in (34.5cm) high

£120-180   MSA

A Victorian black jet brooch, in the form of a hand holding a racket with tennis ball.

2.25in (5.5cm) high

£50-80   WW

£200-250

30in (76cm) high

CL

A 20thC Wimbledon official member's bow tie.

4.5in (11.5cm) wide

£30-50   WW

A woven fabric and gilt and metal thread 'Tennis Club' blazer pocket badge.

3.5in (9cm) high

£20-30   MSA

A 1980s Snoopy tennis watch, on replaced strap.

£50-80   MSA

An original press photograph of Suzanne Lenglen (1899-1938).

Lenglen won 25 Grand Slam titles between 1919 and 1926.

c1925   *9in (23cm) high*

£40-60   WW

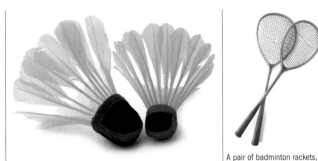

Two 19thC feather, blue velvet and pink woven ribbon badminton shuttlecocks.

Largest 5in (12.5cm) high

£200-300 **MSA**

A pair of badminton rackets, stamped "President" and "Army & Navy CTL".

c1900   26.5in (67.5cm) long

£80-100 **MSA**

CHRIS EUBANK

A signed Chris Eubank publicity postcard.

6in (15cm) high

£6-8 **LCA**

A note signed by Gene Tunney, inscribed "P.S. Tell your brother to stop picking on you".

James Joseph "Gene" Tunney was heavyweight boxing champion from 1926 to 1928.

5in (12.5cm) high

£70-90 **MM**

A mechanical boxing toy titled 'Time!', with two lithograph-on-paper board boxing figures operating when tabs are depressed, a few abrasions on the players.

c1911   10in (25.5cm) long

£40-60 **HA**

A bronze group of two men boxing, on a rectangular plinth with outswept marble base, some chips to base.

10.5in (27cm) high

£650-750 **DN**

A 1950s/60s John L. Sullivan figural advertising display piece, the painted metal statue on original base, marked "James Clark Distilling Co., NY" on back.

11in (28cm) high

£100-150 **HA**

A Joe Louis vs. Joe Walcott Championship program, from June 23, 1948, at Yankee Stadium.

£200-300 **HA**

A pair of Everlast 5403 burgundy leather boxing gloves, printed with Jack Dempsey's signature.

10in (25.5cm) long

£60-80 **VSC**

An unmarked wooden squash racket, stamped "6".

26.25in (66.5cm) long

£80-120   MSA

A small cream leather Five's ball, with red stitching, made from a single piece of cut leather.

£10-20   MSA

A 19thC brass croquet belt buckle, with applied brass hammers, ball and hoop.

1.75in (4.5cm) high

£100-120   MSA

An early sepia photograph of the Pembroke Collage Torpid rowing team, in oval mount with full crew details and college crest.

1868   16in (40cm) high

£80-120   MM

A mahogany snooker scoreboard, with original brass sliding rail and markers.

23in (58.5cm) wide

£30-40   MM

A pair of Royal Doulton tankards, relating to the 1937 Grand National, the coronation year, decorated with the coronation coach and the winning horse, 'Royal Mail'.

5.5in (14cm) high

£70-100   MM

A 1920s Eton St George's straw boater, by Ayres & Smith Ltd, decorated with silk flowers and with red ribbon and trim.

13.25in (33.5cm) long

£250-300   MSA

An enamel and white 'Rockets' annual member's badge with eight date bars 1950-57 attached.

The Rockets are a speedway motorcycling racing team now based at the Rye House stadium in Hertfordshire.

4in (10cm) long

£50-60   MM

A Dave Richter Philadelphia Flyers ice hockey home jersey, with a letter of authenticity from SCD Authentic.

1985-86

£250-350   HA

COLLECTORS' NOTES

■ Teddy bears are as valuable and desirable to collectors today as they were to the children that originally owned them. The maker, date and size are the primary indicators to value, followed by colour and other features such as facial expression and moving parts. Steiff is the most collectable name, holding the world record with 'Teddy Girl' selling for £110,000 in 1994. Fellow German makers Bing, Schuco and Hermann, English maker Farnell and US maker Ideal follow close behind.

■ Look at the shape of a bear as it can help you identify the maker, country of origin and most importantly, the date of manufacture. The face and limbs in particular can help with identifying the maker. Long limbs, a humped back, boot button eyes and a pronounced snout are early features to look for, as are mohair fur and hard, wood wool stuffing. As with any valuable collectable, reproductions do exist so learn how to spot the hallmarks.

■ As early bears by major makers become scarcer and more expensive, those from the mid-20th century by lesser known makers are growing in popularity. Much loved names such as Merrythought, Chad Valley and Chiltern are growing in value, particularly if in good condition. As before, consider the shape, material and stuffing, as post-war bears tend to be plumper in form, using synthetic and soft stuffing from the 1960s and 70s.

■ Bears that have been well played with and are now lacking their fur, and or have been repaired, are likely to be primarily of sentimental value. Modern limited edition bears, introduced to the collecting market in the 1970s by companies such as Steiff are likely to grow in value, but only if in mint condition with all their paperwork and box, if applicable.

■ Despite the dominance of well-known names and condition, 'eye appeal' is another primary consideration. Bears, even home-made ones, with the 'cute' factor will always appeal to collectors, especially if they date from around the mid-20th century.

A large blond mohair teddy bear, stuffed with wood wool stuffing, brown glass eyes, black stitched nose and three stitched claws to each foot.

A beige mohair teddy bear, with hump-backed body, long jointed limbs and neck, black button eyes, pointed snout, suede pads, and oilcloth nose, repair at neck, slight looseness to joints.

The triangular shape of his head and high placed arms suggest an American origin.

An American blond mohair teddy bear, with boot button eyes and stitched black wool nose and mouth.

1920-30 29.5in (74cm) high	c1918 21in (53.50cm) high	1906-08 11.5in (29cm) high
£100-200 WDL	**£250-350** JDJ	**£550-650** HGS

A light-brown teddy bear, with unusual joints, brown wool stitched nose, black card eyes, wood wool stuffing, fur worn away.

A gold mohair teddy bear, with glass eyes and brown stitched nose, stuffed with wood wool and with repaired paws, moth damage.

A blond mohair teddy bear, with wood wool stuffed body, with light brown glass eyes and a stitched pointed nose in black, repairs in leather to arms and feet pads.

An early English teddy bear, possibly by Farnell, blond plush fur with glass eyes, protruding stitched snout and jointed limbs, formerly with hump, worn.

c1915 12.5in (31cm) high	1930-40 28.75in (72cm) high	c1920 13.5in (34cm) high	c1925 23in (58.5cm) high
£70-90 WDL	**£80-120** WDL	**£120-180** WDL	**£550-650** GORL

A small pink and cream teddy bear, possibly French, with simple visible joints, stuffed with wood wool, growler not working, losses to colour.

c1920   12.5in (31cm) high

£40-60   **LAN**

A CLOSER LOOK AT A REPRODUCTION TEDDY BEAR

Although he has the form and wear of an old bear, suspicions are raised, starting with the unusual colour.

He is still very firmly stuffed, inconsistent with his age and the level of fur wear - it is doubtful he is old and has been re-stuffed.

His pads match his fur colour and are suspiciously intact - always smell suspect vintage bears as the odour of years of love and play cannot yet be faked!

The wear to his fur is uneven and inconsistent with play use - he is more 'play worn' around his eyes and snout than on the top of his head or on his arms or chest.

A brown teddy bear, with short mohair fur, small black eyes, black stitched nose, wood wool stuffed body and woven claws.

c1925   10in (25cm) high

£40-60   **WDL**

A late 20thC dark cinnamon teddy bear, with all the features of an early 20thC bear including hump, elongated, curved arms and long feet, boot button eyes, stitched nose and mouth.

                              17in (43cm) high

£20-30   **PC**

An early teddy bear, possibly English, with boot-button eyes, uniform fur loss, heavier on tummy.

c1920   20in (51cm) high

£280-320   **JDJ**

A large German or American beige plush teddy bear, with wood-wool filling, glass eyes, upright ears, stitched snout and claws, jointed limbs and felt pads.

c1920   32in (81.5cm) high

£180-220   **GORL**

A Steiff miniature blond mohair teddy bear, lacking button and tag, with jointed limbs, revolving head, black eyes and black stitched nose.

c1930   3.5in (9cm) high

£55-65   **WDL**

A Steiff blond mohair teddy bear, brown glass eyes, black stitched nose, wood wool stuffed body, with tag, but lacking button and label.

c1950   5.5in (14cm) high

£100-150   **WDL**

A German blond plush teddy bear, possibly by Gebrüder Hermann, wood wool stuffed, glass eyes, woven snout and disc joints.

20in (50cm) high

£150-250   **LAN**

A CLOSER LOOK AT A MERRYTHOUGHT BEAR

The Cheeky bear was introduced by Merrythought in 1957 and became very popular leading to many variations.

The pink fur is rare, he is more commonly found in blond. The fur is also mohair rather than acrylic, showing an earlier date.

He retains his original label, the shape and content of which helps to date him to between 1957-91 – examples are still made today.

He has bells in his ears, a typical feature of all Cheeky bears.

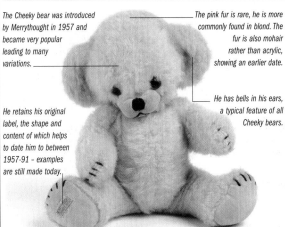

A rare Merrythought pink mohair Cheeky teddy bear, with velveteen snout.

c1960   14in (35.5cm) high

£300-400   **GAZE**

A 1950s Steiff teddy bear, wood wool-stuffed, with glass eyes, lacks button.

This post-war bear shows Steiff's new shape for their Original Teddy, launched in 1951. This form is also typical of other post war bears. He has a plumper body, a rounder face with ears placed closer together, shorter and straighter arms and a less pronounced muzzle. This is also the most common colour found.

18in (45cm) high

£150-250   **LAN**

A 1950s/60s teddy bear, with red tongue, slightly curled synthetic golden plush fur, brown glass eyes, unusual snail-shaped leather nose, long felt tongue, wood wool stuffed body.

15.25in (38cm) high

£25-35   **WDL**

A yellow and black teddy bear, wood wool stuffed, brown glass eyes, yellow and black stitched nose.

20in (50cm) high

£50-60   **WDL**

A black teddy bear, with short synthetic silk plush fur, light nose and ears, brown glass eyes, stuffed with wood wool, pink felt paws.

26in (65cm) high

£30-40   **WDL**

A Merrythought golden mohair Cheeky teddy bear, with velveteen snout, bells in ears and label to foot.

14in (35.5cm) high

£150-250   **GAZE**

TEDDY BEARS & SOFT TOYS

A Steiff small mohair teddy bear, with wood wool stuffing, brown stitched nose and light brown felt paws, one eye and button and tag missing.

7.5in (19cm) high

£35-45   **WDL**

A grey brown furry mohair teddy bear, pink paws and three stitched claws to each foot, black stitched nose, brown plastic eyes.

16in (40cm) high

£20-30   **WDL**

A yellow teddy bear, stuffed with wood wool, yellow artificial plush, brown eyes, black stitched nose, some wear.

24in (60cm) high

£8-12   **WDL**

A late 20thC Steiff mohair 'Classic 1920' reproduction teddy bear, with button and tag, disc-joints, glass eyes and growler.

16.5in (41cm) high

£50-80   **LAN**

A late 20thC Steiff Club 'Night' pink and black mohair teddy bear, with growler, button and label.

12in (30.5cm) high

£50-80   **GAZE**

A late 20thC Steiff Club 'Day' cream, pink and blue mohair teddy bear, with growler, button and label.

12in (30.5cm) high

£35-45   **GAZE**

A Merrythought large grey teddy bear.

c1965   *20in (51cm) high*

£20-30   **GAZE**

A Chiltern Toys plush teddy bear, with glass eyes, white paws and label.

This bear by one of Britain's best loved makers follows the washable synthetic fur bears designed by Wendy Boston and introduced in 1954.

c1960-67   *11in (28cm) high*

£12-18   **GAZE**

A 1980s-90s Steiff soft, unjointed teddy bear, with button and tag in ear.

12.5in (31.5cm) high

£15-25   **GAZE**

FIND OUT MORE...

Bears, *by Sue Pearson, published by De Agostini, 1995.*

Teddy Bear Encyclopedia, *by Pauline Cockrill, published by DK, 2001.*

COLLECTORS' NOTES

■ Soft toys pre-date teddy bears, with Margarete Steiff making soft animal-shaped pins as gifts in the 1890s. Steiff soon became the most famous name in teddy bears and also became prolific in making soft toys. Many collectors focus on one maker, or one animal, with cats and dogs being especially popular.

■ The 1920s to the 1950s was the golden age of the soft toy, before Far Eastern imports flooded the market. Pre-1920s soft toys are scarce. Steiff is the most popular and high quality maker, but also look for fellow German maker Schuco (Schreyer & Co), and Dean's, Chad Valley and Merrythought from England, the latter of whom included soft toys in their first catalogue from 1930. Such British toys currently offer great value for money by comparison.

■ Consider form, labels and material as these will help to date a soft toy – many, particularly by Steiff, were produced for long periods of time. Mohair and a hard stuffing will usually indicate an earlier example, but look for signs of age as Steiff still use these high quality materials today.

■ Look for bright, un-faded original colours and avoid buying damaged or dirty soft toys. Animals with concealed features, unusual outlandish creatures and nostalgia-filled characters are popular. As with teddy bears, do not ignore the 'cute' or 'amusement' factors as these often force a collector to add an appealing soft toy to their collections.

A late 20thC Steiff 'Snuffy' plush bunny, in grey and white, blue glass eyes, soft filling, with button, flag and mark.

4.5in (11cm) high

£15-20   LAN

A Merrythought novelty soft toy child's handbag, modelled as rabbit.

14in (35.5cm) high

£8-12   F

A 1950s Steiff 'Tessie' dog, with button, ribbon and original cardboard swing tag, light grey long mohair fur, pivotable head, red collar.

5.25in (13cm) high

£40-50   WDL

A Steiff 'Waldi' mohair dachshund, with boot button eyes, stuffed with wood wool and with Steiff ear button, minimal wear, but lacks tag.

10in (25cm) long

£12-18   LAN

A hard-filled mohair cow soft toy, possibly by Steiff, with felt udders, lacks one horn and both eyes.

9.75in (25cm) long

£12-18   GAZE

A 1960s Steiff 'Zedonk' giraffe soft toy, with button in ear.

15in (38cm) high

£25-35   GAZE

A 1960s Steiff koala bear, with pad nose, glass eyes and ear stud with raised "Steiff" logo, in mint condition with original fabric tag.

7in (18cm) high

£200-300   TCT

A Steiff life-size peacock soft toy, with moulded feet, felt and fur wings, yellow Steiff tag, button and hangtag, slight soiling, some restoration to beak.

31in (79cm) long

£300-500   JDJ

A Schuco miniature Yes/No monkey, with orange mohair plush.

The fine condition, the orange colour (the brighter, the better) and the Yes/No mechanism, that makes him shake or nod his head, make him this valuable. Look out for other examples that have concealed powder compacts and lipsticks within.

c1920

£300-400 BEJ

A Merrythought large dressed Golly, with internal bell and felt tailcoat.

19in (48cm) high

£120-180 PWE

A Wendy Boston Basil Brush soft toy, with voice box.

14in (35.5cm) high

£8-12 GAZE

A Gabrielle Designs 'Paddington Bear' glove puppet, with felt hat and duffel coat with wooden buttons.

12in (30.5cm) high

£20-30 GAZE

A 1970s Merrythought 'Jerry Mouse' velveteen soft toy, with tag and label.

Jerry was originally designed by deaf and dumb designer Florence Atwood, who used MGM's drawings as inspiration and was chief designer for Merrythought until 1949.

12in (30.5cm) high

£15-25 GAZE

A 1970s Pedigree 'Dougal' soft toy, from 'The Magic Roundabout', with rubber face.

11.5in (29cm) wide

£28-32 GAZE

A Ty 'Clubby III' Beanie, with tag reading "2000 Official Club".

This Beanie bear was only available from September 2000 until January 2001. To be of interest to serious collectors Beanie Babies and Buddies must be in mint condition, retaining their tags and any accessories, also in mint condition.

2000 *8.5in (21.5cm) high*

£6-8 GAZE

A Ty 'Princess' Beanie Baby, woven rose and tag reading "©1997".

This Beanie Baby was launched on October 29th 1997 and retired on 13th April 1999 with all of Ty's profits from the original sale going to the 'Diana, Princess of Wales Memorial Fund' to carry on the work of the late Princess.

1997 *8.5in (21.5cm) high*

£4-6 GAZE

COLLECTORS' NOTES

- Until the 1680s, workers would make tools themselves when the need arose. Around 1680-1700, decorative tastes changed and more complex forms and shapes became fashionable. As many new tools were needed, specialist toolmakers sprung up, making a growing range of tools for specific purposes.

- Commercial production began in earnest from c1700 and boomed during the Industrial Revolution. The 'golden age' of the tool lasted until the 1930s-40s and saw a vast number of tools being made. Planes are one of the most popular types to collect – look out for noted names such as Stanley and Norris. Each model is numbered and many collectors aim to collect as many of the models made by a company as possible.

- The Stanley market is dominated by the US and the benchmark currency is in dollars, so currency fluctuations can affect value. The Norris market, dominated by the UK, is similarly affected.

- Collectors also appreciate the design and skill that goes into making a tool. Materials and visual appearance add value, so look for added decorative features such as artistically carved handles and detailed metal plates.

- Specialist tools are another popular area. Tools for coopers (barrel makers), watchmakers, musical instrument makers and goldsmiths are good examples.

- Tools made for rarely practised tasks tend to be the most valuable. A large wooden plane used by a great many workers is unlikely to be of value, unless it is old (for example from the 18th century) and thus rarer.

- Tools in unused condition, and even retaining their original packaging, are generally more desirable and valuable. Missing pieces and damage, such as rust and woodworm, reduce value dramatically.

A Stanley 4 1/2 H plane, repainted, in very good condition.

The 'H' series of planes were heavier in weight and were made to satisfy overseas customer demand. As such, they are rarely found in the US and more often in the UK or Europe.

£200-300   **MUR**

A Stanley Victor No.20 black-japanned plane, in fine condition.

£80-120   **MUR**

A Stanley No.85 scraper, in fine condition.

£400-500   **MUR**

A Stanley No.113 compass plane, in fine condition.

£80-120   **MUR**

A Stanley 140 skew block plane, in very good condition.

£60-80   **MUR**

A Stanley 140 skew block plane, in fine condition.

£100-150   **MUR**

A rare patent Norris No.13 metal plane, rosewood infill, Ward & Payne parallel iron, in fine condition.

£500-600   **MUR**

A CLOSER LOOK AT A PLANE

This dovetailed plane is infilled with rosewood, denoting high quality.

Mitre planes are used for shooting end grains and are not common as the job was rarely executed, so fewer tools were made.

It has a maker's name – in this case it is Holtzapffel, the 'Rolls Royce' of tool-makers known for their fine quality ornamental turning tools.

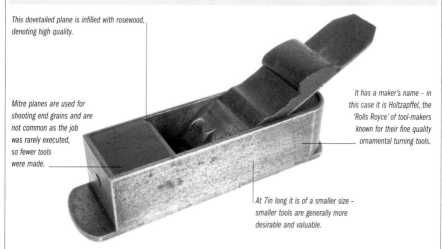

At 7in long it is of a smaller size – smaller tools are generally more desirable and valuable.

A very rare Holtzapffel mitre plane, dovetailed, with rosewood infill and replaced blade, in very good condition.

7in (18cm) long

£1,000-1,200   **MUR**

A scarce Norris No.20 gunmetal shoulder plane, with original iron, rosewood infill, in very good condition.

1.25in (3cm) wide

£300-400   **MUR**

A post-war Norris A5 smoothing plane.

The 'golden age' of the tool ended during the 1930s-1940s. However, some postwar tools are desirable, especially if by noted names and if few were made, making them rare. The value of this example is increased as it has hardly been used and still retains its box.

£500-600   **MUR**

A Record 08 plane, in virtually unused condition.

£120-180   **MUR**

A rare Mathieson smoothing plane, styled on the Stanley 4.5in plane, with rosewood handles, in very good condition.

£60-80   **MUR**

A scarce Preston No.118 block plane, in very good condition.

£80-120   **MUR**

A Scottish gunmetal smoothing plane, with heart and shield lever cap, in fine condition.

£280-320   **MUR**

An Ibbotson brass-plated brace, small chip to head.

£40-60   **MUR**

A CLOSER LOOK AT A BRACE

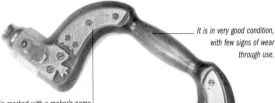

It is in very good condition, with few signs of wear through use.

It is marked with a maker's name – Pilkington are known for their quality tools but few braces were made, making this comparatively rare.

Pilkington braces were made for, and exported to, the American market.

It has unusual 'artistic' decorative brass plates, which adds interest and value.

A Robert Marples registered octagonal chuck plated brace, in very good condition.

£250-350   **MUR**

A rare Pilkington beech and brass brace, in very good condition.

£700-900   **MUR**

A rare Tillotson brace, with early Ultimatum-style chuck, small chip and crack to head.

£120-180   **MUR**

A Flather plated brace, with 'Eagle' button, for export to the US, in very good condition.

£120-180   **MUR**

An unused Tatham and Darracott brass-framed rosewood brace.

£700-900   **MUR**

A rare solid macassar ebony plated brace, hairline shrinkage crack to web, in very good to fine condition.

Although this is the basic shape and style for a brace, it is made from ebony rather than the standard beech. This indicates that it may have been a special, 'bespoke' request, or was made for exhibition at a trade fair.

£400-500   **MUR**

A very rare Gavin & Cromer's patent brace, with lignum vitae head.

This patent was granted in Eureka, Nevada on July 19, 1887. There are less than five known examples, this is the only one found with a lignum vitae head.

£30-40   **MUR**

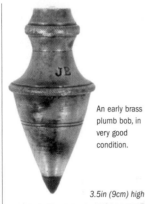

An early brass plumb bob, in very good condition.

3.5in (9cm) high

£80-120   **MUR**

A knurled brass plumb bob, in fine condition.

8.5in (21.5cm) long

£200-300   **MUR**

A steel-tipped brass plumb bob, decorated with an engraved brass spool, in very good condition.

3in (7.5cm) long

£250-350   **MUR**

A brass plumb bob, by Preston, with original Preston brass reel, in very good condition.

2.5in (6.5cm) high

£100-150   **MUR**

An early 19thC steel-tipped bronze plumb bob, in very good condition.

8.25in (21cm) high

£120-180   **MUR**

An iron plumb bob, knurled brass head, in very good condition.

6in (15cm) high

£50-70   **MUR**

An original 19thC ebony and ivory plumb bob, in very good condition.

£400-500   **MUR**

An early 19thC walnut plumb bob, with brass acorn bob, in very good condition.

£70-100   **MUR**

A 19thC plumb board, with bronze bob, in very good condition.

The Egyptians were the first civilisation recorded using a plumb bob to ensure that walls were vertical. The plumb board also allows good judgment of a horizontal against a vertical. The Industrial Revolution saw the decline of the widespread use of the plumb bob, and it was replaced in many situations by the spirit level.

12.5in (32cm) high

£120-180   **MUR**

A rare and tiny goldsmiths' hammer, with original handle, in fine condition.

Head 1.25in (3cm) long

£200-300 **MUR**

A watchmakers' hammer, with elaborate knurling to the head, in fine condition.

9in (23cm) long

£150-200 **MUR**

A violin makers' sounding post.

£25-35 **MUR**

An early 19thC jewellery anvil, in a dark oak base, in fine condition.

6in (15cm) long

£150-200 **MUR**

A 19thC brass wheel cutting tool, on a later mahogany stand.

£500-600 **GHOU**

An unusual coachmakers' plough, by Tremain, with snicker iron, in very good condition.

£120-180 **MUR**

A 19thC miniature adze, of unknown purpose, in very good condition.

An adze was used for woodworking (for example on a beam) to chip away slices of wood with an axe-like motion. The blade is thin and the edge is aligned horizontally to the shaft, unlike an axe.

13in (33cm) long

£70-100 **MUR**

A miniature coachbuilders' beech plow, with side handle and adjustable fence, marked "I. Rowland", in very good to fine condition.

3.5in (9cm) long

£700-900 **MUR**

A quality rosewood and brass double-bladed cutting gauge, for purling on violins and cellos, in very good condition.

£120-180 **MUR**

A late 18thC veterinary tail docker, iron bound and fruitwood, dated "1787", in fine condition.

This was used for the gruesome task of 'docking', or removing, an animal's tail.

£100-150 **MUR**

A rare brass back tenon saw, by Mathieson, marked on blade and handle escutcheons, in very good condition.

£55-65   **MUR**

An early Groves No.2 handsaw, with ten tines per inch, 1770 escutcheon, in fine condition.

£60-70   **MUR**

A brass and rosewood bevel, in very good condition.

4.5in (11.5cm) long

£180-220   **MUR**

A rare 18thC astragal cove wooden plane, by Richard Burman, in very good condition.

As well as being of an early date and bearing a maker's name, this is indicative of the 'new' tools that needed to be made to create the more complex shapes that became fashionable at this time. An astragal is a narrow, convex shape, often taking the form of beading.

10.5in (26.5cm) wide

£700-1,000   **MUR**

An Arts & Crafts architrave moulding plane, by Vincent, in very good to fine condition.

2.5in (6.5cm) wide

£80-120   **MUR**

A pair of brass trammels, by Preston, with double pencil holder, in very good condition.

Trammels allow the drawing of ellipses.

6.5in (16.5cm) long

£70-100   **MUR**

A Mathieson No.14C ebony spirit level, in fine condition.

10in (25.5cm) long

£200-300   **MUR**

A rare Fields triple-arm rule, boxwood with brass fittings, Hezzanitti patent mark and Hills patent no. 15A55, in fine condition.

£120-180   **MUR**

An original box of Rabone 1167 rules, complete with three unused rules, in fine condition.

£60-80   **MUR**

FIND OUT MORE...

The Ultimate Brace – A Unique Product of Victorian Sheffield, *by Reg Eaton, published by Erica Jane Publishing, 1989.*

Dictionary of Woodworking Tools, *by R.A. Salaman, published by Astragal Press, 1997.*

TOYS & GAMES

COLLECTORS' NOTES

■ Introduced by Mettoy Limited in 1956, Corgi Toys are still in production today.

■ They were an innovative company and were the first to add plastic windows and opening doors and boots to their cars, features that helped them compete against rivals Dinky.

■ Corgi are also well-known for their film- and TV-related toys, which include various James Bond vehicles, Batman, The Man from U.N.C.L.E. and Chitty Chitty Bang Bang.

■ Different variations and versions are sought after by collectors, and some examples were made for less than one year. Invest in a specialist price guide listing the various examples.

■ The original boxes and instructions will add to the value, but like the toys, they must be complete and in good condition to fetch the highest prices.

A scarce Corgi No. 201 Austin Cambridge, silver over metallic green, with two types of white wall over stickers, in original box.
1956-61

£180-220   **W&W**

A Corgi No. 255 Austin Motor School A60, dark blue, spun hubs, export issue, mint condition, in good although grubby carded box.
1964-68

£100-150   **VEC**

A Corgi No.224 Bentley Continental Sports Saloon, cream over green, red interior, spun hubs and another similar but black over silver, in excellent plus to mint condition, in good to very good condition carded boxes.
1961-65

£70-100 each   **VEC**

A Corgi No. 245 Buick Riviera, powder blue, red interior, wire wheels, slightly retouched, and another similar in gold, excellent condition, in good condition carded boxes.
1964-68

£50-80 each   **VEC**

BACK: A Corgi No. 235 Oldsmobile Super 88, metallic blue, red interior, spun hubs, excellent condition, in very good condition carded box.
1962-66

£30-40   **VEC**

FRONT: A Corgi No. 229 Chevrolet Corvair, blue, flat spun hubs, excellent condition, in very good condition carded box.
1961-66

£30-50   **VEC**

BACK: A Corgi No. 223 Chevrolet 'State Patrol' Police Car, black, lemon interior, flat spun hubs, excellent condition, in good to very good condition box.
1959-61

£70-100   **VEC**

FRONT: A Corgi No. 437 Superior Cadillac Ambulance, red, cream, spun hubs, slight wear to side decals, excellent condition.
1962-65

£80-120   **VEC**

BACK: A Corgi No. 220 Chevrolet Impala, blue, lemon interior, flat spun hubs, in very good to excellent condition, in good although grubby box.
1960-65

£40-60   **VEC**

FRONT: A Corgi No. 248 Chevrolet Impala, brown, cream, cast wheels, very good to excellent condition, in good although grubby carded box.
1965-67

£40-60   **VEC**

A Corgi No.314 Ferrari Berlinetta 250 Le Mans, red, with wire wheels, racing No. 4, and a No. 330 Porsche Carrera 6, white, red, and racing No. 60, excellent to mint condition, in excellent to near mint boxes.

1965-72

£70-100 each VEC

A Corgi No. 440 Ford Consul Cortina Super Estate Car, blue, spun hubs, excellent plus including inner pictorial stand, in very good condition outer picture box.

1966-69

£180-220 VEC

FRONT: A Corgi No. 217 Fiat 1800, pale pink, spun hubs, very good to excellent condition, in good although grubby box.

1960-63

£30-50

BACK: A Corgi No. 436 Citroen Safari 'Wildlife Preservation', yellow, brown and red luggage, slightly sun faded, very good to excellent condition, in good although grubby box.

1963-65

£60-90 VEC

A Corgi No. 313 Ford Cortina GXL 'Graham Hill', bronze, black roof, white interior, Whizzwheels, mint condition, in excellent window box complete with figure.

The yellow version of this car can be worth twice as much as the bronze or metallic blue examples.

1970-73

£100-150 VEC

A Corgi No. 233 Heinkel Trojan Economy Car, orange, lemon interior, spun hubs, with minimal marks, in good condition yellow and blue card box.

The metallic blue, turquoise and fawn versions of this car can be worth twice as much as any other colour.

1962-72

£50-80 LAN

FRONT: A Corgi No. 234 Ford Consul Classic, beige, salmon pink roof, lemon interior, spun hubs, excellent condition, in excellent condition carded box.

1961-65

£40-60

BACK: A Corgi No. 424 Ford Zephyr Estate Car, two-tone blue, flat spun hubs, excellent condition, in excellent condition carded box.

1961-65

£50-80 VEC

FRONT: A Corgi No. 259 Citroën Le Dandy Coupé, red, lemon interior, wire wheels, very good to excellent condition, in slightly grubby box.

1966-69

£50-80

BACK: A Corgi No. 241 Chrysler Ghia L64, light metallic blue, red interior, spun hubs, very good to excellent condition, in good although slightly grubby box.

1963-69

£30-50 VEC

A Corgi No. 214 Ford Thunderbird hardtop, light green, cream roof, flat spun hubs and a No. 215 Ford Thunderbird Open Sports Car, white, silver and blue interior, spun hubs, very good plus to excellent condition, in good to good plus carded boxes.

1959-65

£40-60 each VEC

A Corgi No.302 Hillman Hunter, blue, white roof and matt black bonnet, with kangaroo and equipment, very good condition, boxed.

1969-72

£100-150   **CHEF**

A Corgi No. 238 Jaguar Mark 10, mid-blue, red interior, spun hubs, missing one tyre, otherwise good plus, and another similar but silver, in very good condition, both in good carded boxes.

1962-67

£50-80 each   **VEC**

A Corgi No. 438 Land Rover, green, light beige plastic canopy, spun hubs, mint condition, in excellent blue and yellow carded box.

1963-77

£120-180   **VEC**

A Corgi No. 318 Lotus Elan 'I've Got a Tiger in My Tank', blue, black interior, spun hubs, figure, racing No. 6 decals applied, near mint condition, in carded box.

This is the cheapest variation of the open-top Lotus Elan, despite having a shorter production period. Other versions can be worth around twice as much.

1965-67

£120-180   **VEC**

A Corgi No. 324 Marcos 1800GT, white, red interior, wire wheels, racing number, near mint condition, decals applied, in good condition carded box.

1966-69

£40-60   **VEC**

Two Corgi No. 393 Mercedes Benz 350SLs, one dark blue, pale blue interior, spoked wheels, and another similar with dish wheels, near mint to mint condition, in excellent condition boxes.

1972-79

£50-80 each   **VEC**

Two Corgi No. 282 Whizzwheels Mini Coopers, one white, and a 'Rally Monte Carlo', yellow, roof rack, excellent to mint.

'Whizzwheels' spun faster than the standard wheels. They are a variation rising in value.

1971-74

£30-50 each   **VEC**

A Corgi No. 249 Morris Mini-Cooper, black, red roof, lemon interior with wickerwork panels, excellent condition, box partly cut-up.

1965-69

£60-90   **LAN**

A Corgi No. 227 Morris Mini Cooper 'Competition Model', primrose yellow, white roof and bonnet, Union Jack and chequered flag decals, racing number "3", excellent condition, slight mark to roof, fair condition but complete, in carded box.

1962-65

£180-220   **VEC**

A scarce Corgi No. 330 Porsche Carrera 6, white, red, blue, cast wheels, racing number "1", excellent condition, slight glue marks around lights, in excellent condition carded box, slight graffiti marks on end flaps.

1967-69

£40-60 VEC

A Corgi 'Tour de France' Renault 16, from Gift Set 13, white with black roof and bonnet, with 'Tour de France' and 'Paramount' decals and 35mm camera, lacks cameraman, cyclist and box.

1968-72

£70-100 ATK

BACK: A Corgi No. 252 Rover 2000 Saloon, steel blue, red interior, spun hubs, near mint to mint condition, in excellent condition blue and yellow carded box.

1963-66

£50-80 VEC

FRONT: A Corgi No. 424 Ford Zephyr Estate, two-tone blue, flat spun hubs, near mint to mint condition, in excellent condition carded box.

1961-65

£50-80 VEC

A Corgi No. 275 Rover 2000 TC, green, white interior, Golden Jack take-off wheels, mint condition, in excellent condition window box.

'Golden Jacks' was a jacking system, built into the car, which were used with the 'Take-Off' wheels.

1968-70

£100-150 VEC

A Corgi No. 315 Simca 1000 'Competition Model', chrome finish, spun hubs, red interior, mint condition, in good condition carded box.

The metallic blue version can be worth up to three times as much as this example.

1964-66

£60-90 VEC

An early Corgi No.204 Rover 90, in mid-grey with spun wheels, boxed.

1956-61

£70-100 W&W

A Corgi VW No. 256 'East African Safari Car', red with "18" decals to sides, complete with rhinoceros on inner display packaging, in original box, some damage.

1965-68

£120-180 W&W

A Corgi No.492 Volkswagen Beetle police car, dark green and white Polizei livery, boxed.

1966-69

£80-120 W&W

A unique Corgi promotional 'World Cup Bid 2006 FA' FX4 taxi, a pre-production model with a special livery, complete with a letter from Susan Pownall, manager of the Corgi collectors' club, won in a competition in 1999.

1999

£120-180 W&W

TOYS & GAMES

A Corgi No. 267 'Batman' Batmobile, gloss black, with sealed secret instructions, one rocket only, near mint condition, in very good condition pictorial card box.
1966-67

£280-320   **GAZE**

A Corgi No. 266 'Chitty Chitty Bang Bang', with four character figures, incorrectly fitted steering wheel, missing front grille, boxed, re-cellophaned.
1968-72

£180-220   **VEC**

A CLOSER LOOK AT A CORGI TOY

These toys appeal to Beatles collectors as well as Corgi collectors.

Film- and TV-related Corgi toys are some of the most sought-after.

This example has two red hatches, and is slightly more desirable than the version with one white and one yellow. The variation with one red and one white hatch can be worth a third as much as this one.

The toy should be complete with the figures John, Paul, George and Ringo, and in an undamaged picture box.

A Corgi No. 803 'The Beatles' Yellow Submarine, red front and rear hatches, very good condition, although slightly retouched, inner plastic tray is excellent plus, outer box re-cellophaned and slight tears to end flaps.
1970-71

£180-220   **VEC**

A Corgi No. 270 'James Bond' Aston Martin DB5, front and rear number plate decals applied, one side bumper broken.
1968-76

£220-280   **VEC**

A Corgi No. 336 'James Bond' Toyota 2000GI, with red aerial, two figures, secret instruction pack, missing badge, boxed.
1967-69

£280-320   **VEC**

A Corgi No. 261 'James Bond' Aston Martin DB5, bronze, red interior, wire wheels, secret instruction pack containing leaflet, spare bandit figure, lapel badge and a 'Corgi Toys Model Car Makers to James Bond' colour leaflet, excellent condition, including inner pictorial, stand outer blue and yellow picture box in very good condition.
1965-69

£300-400   **VEC**

A Corgi No. 277 'Monkees' Monkeemobile, cast wheels, red, white roof, near mint, in excellent although slightly grubby window box, with plastic 'Monkees' Guitar.
1968-72

£200-300   **VEC**

A Corgi No. 258 'The Saint's' Volvo P1800, white, red interior, spun hubs, excellent condition, in excellent condition carded box.
1965-68

£200-300   **VEC**

A CLOSER LOOK AT A CORGI GIFT SET

Corgi Gift Sets are popular with collectors and can fetch more than the individual pieces together.

Look for the variation that contains a green Bentley as it is worth around 20 per cent more.

The two cars were only available as a gift set, and were not sold separately.

All the accessories and internal packaging should be present and in good condition to fetch the best price.

A Corgi Gift Set No.40 'The Avengers', comprising 'John Steed's' Bentley, red and black, with wire wheels and, 'Emma Peel's' Lotus, white and black, with figure and three umbrellas, very good to near mint condition, in good to very good stand and box.

1966-69

£300-500   **VEC**

A Corgi Gift Set No.12 Chipperfields Crane Truck and Cage, with animals, excellent condition, in good condition box.

1961-64

£280-320   **GAZE**

A Corgi Gift Set No.21 ERF Dropside Lorry and Platform Trailer, with milk churns, no decorative accessories, very good condition, in very good condition box.

1962-66

£50-80   **GAZE**

A Corgi Gift Set No. 4 Bristol Ferranti Bloodhound Guided Missile Set, containing a Bloodhound guided missile with launching ramp, loading trolley and RAF Land Rover, in original box with inner packaging, some age wear to box, paint chips.

1958-60

£280-320   **W&W**

A Corgi Gift Set No.5 Racing Car Set, comprising a No.150 Vanwall, red, flat spun hubs; a No.151 Lotus XI, blue, racing number 3 and a No.152 BRM Grand Prix Car, turquoise, racing number 7, good to excellent condition, in good although grubby inner polystyrene packing and fair condition but complete all-carded box.

1959-60

£180-220   **VEC**

A Corgi No. GS30 Grand Prix Gift Set, including Surtees TS9, Lotus John Player Special, Yardley McLaren, overall conditions are near mint to mint in good box, missing original shrink wrap.

1973

£80-120   **VEC**

A Corgi Gift Set No.2 Land Rover and Pony Trailer, green Land Rover, beige tin canopy, and red trailer with brown horse, excellent condition, with excellent condition inner card and very good condition outer blue and yellow picture box.

1958-68

£200-300   **VEC**

A Corgi Gift Set No.37 Lotus Racing Team, comprising a No. 490 Volkswagen breakdown van and trailer, a No.155 Lotus Climax racing car, a No.318 Lotus Elan coupé, a No.319 Lotus Elan S2, an Elan chassis, boxed, minor wear.

1966-69

£300-400   **W&W**

A Corgi No. 404 Bedford Dormobile Personnel Carrier, cerise, flat spun hubs, in very good condition, in fair but complete all-carded blue box.

1956-62

£50-80 VEC

A Corgi No. 403 'Daily Express' Bedford Van, blue, flat spun hubs, excellent condition, in good although grubby all-carded blue box.

1956-60

£50-80 VEC

A Corgi No.1121 Chipperfields Circus Crane Truck, red with blue lettering, with light grey crane jib, in earlier lidded box, some damage.

1960-62

£120-180 W&W

BACK: A Corgi No. 464 'County Police' Commer Van, metallic blue, red interior, spun hubs, good condition, in very good condition box.

1967-68

£40-50 VEC

FRONT: A Corgi No. 465 Commer Pick-up, yellow, red, spun hubs, in very good condition, including blue and yellow carded box.

1963-66

£30-40 VEC

A Corgi No.420 Ford Thames 'Airborne' Caravan, finished in two-tone lilac with beige interior and spun wheels, in original box.

Other colourways of this model are worth up to half the value of this colourway.

£100-150 W&W

A Corgi No. 66 Massey-Ferguson '165' Tractor, red, white, grey, mint condition, in good carded box.

1966-72

£70-100 VEC

A Corgi No. 447 'Wall's Ice Cream' Van, cream and blue Ford Thames, with salesman, lacks boy, very good condition, in fair condition box with leaflet.

1965-66

£100-150 GAZE

FRONT: A Corgi No. 458 ERF Tipper, red, yellow, spun hubs, near mint condition, in good condition plain carded box.

1958-66

£40-50 VEC

BACK: A Corgi No. 470 Forward Control Jeep, pale green, grey plastic canopy, spun hubs, excellent condition, roof is badly faded, in good condition carded box.

1965-72

£30-35 VEC

14 boxes of Corgi spare tyres, comprising four C1449, four 1250 and six 1451.

1961-71

£40-60 GAZE

COLLECTORS' NOTES

■ Dinky toys were released as accessories to Hornby's model railways in 1931, taking on the name 'Dinky' in 1934, just after the first cars were produced. The 1930s became one of Dinky's most important decades, and the same is true for collectors today.

■ Supertoys were introduced in 1947, and Speedwheels in 1969, in response to Mattel's 'Hotwheels' brand. The factory closed in 1979. The name was taken over by Matchbox in 1987 but was dropped in 2001.

■ Condition and variations are vitally important. To fetch the highest values, toys must be undamaged and in as near to shop-sold condition as possible. If the paintwork is worn, do not repaint it.

■ Boxes are very important and can double the value. The box itself should also be in excellent condition. Collectors use terms such as 'good', 'excellent' and 'mint' to describe the condition of the toy and box.

■ Variations can be valuable: look closely at colour, the transfer, wheels and other details, such as national variations. All comparative values shown for variations are for items in similar condition to the one pictured.

A Hornby Dinky 22 Series tractor, yellow, blue, red wheels, no hook, good condition.

Although not strictly a car, this is from the earliest series of Dinky Toys, originally produced as Meccano Model Miniatures and as accessories to Hornby train sets.

1933-40

£300-500 VEC

A Dinky No. 38B Sunbeam Talbot, light blue with grey tonneau, in very good condition.
1947-49

£300-500 SAS

A Dinky No. 36C Humber Vogue, with driver and footman, blue, excellent condition, with small glue repair to one mudguard.

The all-over blue colour was only produced with figures. Both the excellent condition and fact that this model is complete with both its tin figures account for the high value.

1937-41

£1,200-1,800 SAS

A Dinky No. 110 Aston Martin DB3 sportscar, light green with red hubs, competition number 22, excellent, with small chip to drivers helmet.

This is the most valuable colour variation for this car. The grey and a darker green version is worth roughly 50 per cent of this variation's value.

c1956

£200-300 SAS

A Dinky No. 167 A.C. Aceca Coupé, grey and red with windows and spun alloy hubs, in good condition box with grey end-spot.

To compete with the newly released Corgi toys with windows, this box advertises the fact that this model too has windows.

1958-60

£280-320 SAS

A rare South African Dinky No. 112 Austin Healey Sprite Mk II, lilac, excellent condition, in very good condition Afrikaans box.

1961-66

£600-900 SAS

A 1960s French Dinky No. 559 Ford Taunus 17M, light metallic bronze, red interior, excellent condition, slight flatting to one tyre, in fair condition box.

A Dinky No. 195 Jaguar 3.4 Mk II Saloon, maroon, excellent condition, in fair condition box, with red end-spot.

Look out for the rare South African issues produced in red, cream and light sky blue, which can be worth over five times the value of this British edition.

A Dinky No. 195 Jaguar 3.4 Saloon, grey, excellent condition, in fair condition box, with grey end-spot.

1961-71

£50-80   **VEC** | **£100-150**   **SAS** | **£120-180**   **SAS**

A Dinky No. 265 USA Plymouth Taxi, very good condition, in fair condition box, end flap taped.

£100-150   **SAS**

This South African Dinky No. 113 MGB Sportsmotor, ivory, excellent condition, in very good condition Afrikaans box.

This ivory South African issue variation is very rare, having been produced in 1966 only, and is worth up to ten times the value of the British version.

A Dinky No. 268 Renault Dauphine minicab, red body with Meccano, Kenwood, Britax and other decals, in original box.

£500-700   **SAS** | **£180-220**   **W&W**

A Spanish Dinky No. 1450 Simca 1100 Police Car, black and white, excellent condition, in good condition box.

A Dinky No. 145 Singer Vogue, excellent condition, in good condition box.

Look out for the rare lemon yellow body shown on the box, which can be worth up to 10 times the value of this colour.

1962-67

An Italian Dinky No. 12 Volvo 265 DL Estate, orange, with applied gold "Made to Dinky Specifications in Italy" label, excellent condition, in very good condition box.

1979-80

£70-100   **SAS** | **£100-150**   **SAS** | **£30-40**   **SAS**

A Dinky No. 903 Foden Flat Truck, with tailboard, second-type cab, mid-blue cab and chassis, fawn back, mid-blue Supertoy hubs, riveted back, excellent condition, in excellent condition box, a tiny amount of edge ware to box.

1957-60

£70-100 VEC

A Dinky No. 502 Foden Flat Truck, first-type cab, blue cab and chassis, red back and side flash, mid-blue ridged hubs, good condition, some marks to wheel arches, in excellent condition box, some stains caused by rusting to staples.

1948-52

£300-500 VEC

A French Dinky No. 36A Willeme Log Lorry, orange cab, yellow trailer and hubs, log load, excellent condition, in excellent condition box.

£120-180 VEC

A Dinky No. 935 Leyland Octopus Flat Truck, with chains, mid-green cab and chassis, light grey back and band around cab, red plastic hubs, excellent condition, minor chipping and slight protrusion to flatbed.

If this model retained its box and was in better condition, the value would have been higher. Look out for the valuable variation of the 935 with a blue cab, yellow flash and grey flatbed.

1964-66

£220-280 VEC

A Dinky No. 513 Guy Flat Truck with tailboard, first type cab, grey, black chassis and mudguards, black ridged wheels, excellent condition, small chip to front right-hand mudguard, in good condition, buff box, split to one end and label attached to one end.

Dark blue rather than black chassis, guards and hubs can more than double the value of this model.

1947-48

£220-280 VEC

A Dinky No. 34B Royal Mail Van, red and black, excellent condition.

1938-47

£280-320 SAS

A Dinky No. 514 Guy Van 'Slumberland', first-type cab, good condition, with box.

The yellow 'Weetabix' Guy Van is the most valuable of this type, and can fetch up to five times more than the 'Slumberland'.

1950-52

£180-220 VEC

A Dinky No. 454 Trojan Van 'Cydrax', mid-green including ridged wheels, roof slightly sunfaded, in good condition box, repair to end flaps and slight graffiti.

1957-59

£100-150 VEC

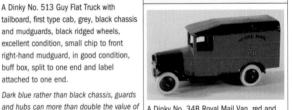

A scarce Dinky No. 280 South African issue Delivery Van, khaki green including ridged hubs, complete with original treaded tyres, good condition.

£300-400 VEC

A Dinky No. 471 Austin Nestlé's van, red body with yellow and beige wheel hubs, Nestlé's decals in gold to the sides, in original box, some wear.

1955-60

£80-120 W&W

A Dinky No. 152B Reconnaissance Car, with black tyres, in good condition.

1937-41

£30-40   SAS

A Dinky No. 151B Transport Wagon with Driver, with white tyres, in good condition.

1937-41

£40-60   SAS

A 1930s Dinky Searchlight Lorry, military green, smooth hubs, painted camouflage stripes and small repair to searchlight, fair condition.

£120-180   VEC

A 1960s French Dinky No. 818 Camion Berliet Tous Terrains, in matt olive green, complete with tin tilt, boxed.

Production of Dinky toys in France began around the same time as in the UK and ended in 1972.

£100-150   W&W

A Dinky No. 688 Field Artillery Tractor, with windows and plastic hubs, excellent condition with minor bonnet transfer embellishment, in good condition box.

1968-70

£50-80   SAS

A 1960s French Dinky No. 820 Renault Ambulance, with windows and concave hubs, excellent condition, in very good condition box.

£120-180   SAS

A French Dinky No. 890 Tank Transporter, military green, ridged hubs, good condition, in good condition plain blue and white striped box, complete with inner packing.

£120-180   VEC

A Dinky 152A Light Tank, gloss with black rubber wheels, in good condition.

1937-41

£40-60   SAS

A Dinky No. 152 Royal Tank Corp Light Tank Gift Set, containing Light Tank, Reconnaissance Car and Austin Open Tourer, military green, good condition, in fair condition box.

Gift sets are hard to find complete with their original models and packaging as they were usually opened and played with.

1937-41

£180-220   VEC

A Dinky No. 100 Thunderbirds Lady Penelope's FAB1, luminous pink, with Lady Penelope and Parker figures and front rocket, in original box, losses.

The luminous pink variation is more desirable than the standard pink body also shown on this page.

1967-75

£300-400 W&W

A Dinky No. 100 Thunderbirds Lady Penelope's FAB 1, pink including roof slides, missile and harpoons, excellent, slight discolouration to bare metal parts and has been re-touched in places, inner pictorial tray is good, including outer picture box.
1967-75

£120-180 VEC

A Dinky No. 352 UFO Ed Straker's Car, gold finish, silver engine cover, blue interior, cast wheels mint in good box.
1971-75

£100-150 VEC

A Dinky No. 104 Captain Scarlet Spectrum Pursuit Vehicle, seat and figure attached to door, with leaflet and box.

The earlier variation where the seat and figure is not attached to the door is usually worth slightly more.

1973-75

£80-120 GAZE

A Dinky No. 108 Joe 90 Sam's Car, red, yellow interior, silver rear engine cover, cast wheels, near mint condition, including inner pictorial stand, in excellent condition outer picture box.

Red is one of the most desirable and valuable colours. Surprisingly it is worth slightly more than the silver-grey version that appeared in the TV series.

£200-250 VEC

A Dinky No. 106 The Prisoner Mini Moke, white, brown side steps, excellent condition, in good condition picture box.
1967-70

£180-220 VEC

A Dinky No. 103 Captain Scarlet Spectrum Patrol Car, red, white base and aerial, cast spun hubs, near mint in good box.
1968-75

£180-220 VEC

A Dinky No.354 The Pink Panther's Jet Car, excellent condition, on excellent condition card.
1977-79

£40-60 SAS

A Dinky No.357 Star Trek Klingon Battle Cruiser, excellent condition, box with small fracture to cellophane.
1977-80

£30-50 SAS

A pre-war Dinky No. 62m Airspeed Envoy, green, red propellers, G-A ENA, excellent condition.

Dinky began making aircraft just before the start of WWII and today the market is strong and brisk. Post-war, they focused on making models of the new commercial airliners and jet planes. Pre-war models are particularly prone to degradation of the metal on parts such as wings, known as 'fatigue', which leads to 'sagging'.

1938-41

£180-220 VEC

A French pre-war Dinky No. 60D Breguet Corsair, red, green wing edges, propeller and undercarriage, good condition.

£150-200 VEC

A pre-war Dinky No. 60r Empire Flying Boat 'Caledonia', silver, red propellers, red plastic roller, G-A DHM, good condition, no visible signs of fatigue.

1937-40

£120-180 VEC

A Dinky No. 60r Empire Flying Boat 'Cambria', silver, red propellers, red plastic roller, G-A DUV, good condition, slight warpage to wings and minor fatigue, in good condition blue box.

1937-40

£180-220 VEC

A Dinky No. 62w Imperial Airways Liner 'Frobisher', silver, red propellers, gliding pin hole, G-A FDK, excellent condition, in excellent condition box complete with leaflet.

1939-41

£300-500 VEC

A CLOSER LOOK AT A DINKY FLYING BOAT

This was the first 'Supertoys' plane model produced.

It was produced for a short period only, and production began less than two years after the war had ended.

It is in excellent condition and complete with its own labelled box, which is also in good condition.

It shows no sign of metal fatigue, a degradation of the metal associated with pre-war Dinky planes.

A Dinky No.701 Shetland Flying Boat, 'G-A GVD' in silver with black propellers and box.

1947-49

£600-900 VEC

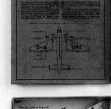

A Dinky No. 62n Junkers JU90 Airliner, silver, red propellers, two replacement propellers D-A URE, fair condition, in good condition but sunfaded box.

1938-41

£200-250 VEC

A Dinky No. 999 The Police DH Comet Airliner, silver, white, blue, G-ALYX, near mint condition, in good condition blue and white striped box, complete with inner packing, slight tear mark to top of lid.

1955-65

£100-150   **VEC**

A Dinky No. 62t Armstrong Whitworth Whitley Bomber, camouflage with gliding pin and leaflet, good condition, in excellent condition box, slightly sunfaded.

The dark camouflage colourway with yellow, rather than purely red and blue, RAF wing roundels is the most desirable and valuable variation.

1939-41

£300-350   **VEC**

A French Dinky No. 60c Super G Constellation Lockheed 'Air France', silver-grey, silver propellers, F-B HBX, excellent condition, in good condition box, slightly crushed and split to one edge.

£180-220   **VEC**

A French Dinky No. 891 Caravelle 'Air France', silver, blue, white, F-B GNY, near mint condition, box in good condition complete with inner packing.

£120-180   **VEC**

A Dinky 702 BOAC DH Comet Airliner, with packing piece, good condition, in fair condition box.

1954-55

£40-60   **SAS**

A 1960s French Dinky Vautour, silver, French rosettes to wings, near mint condition, in excellent condition box, slight tear mark to one end.

£100-150   **VEC**

A French Dinky No. 60A Mystere, silver, French rosettes to wings, near mint condition, in excellent condition box.

£80-120   **VEC**

A French Dinky No. 60D Sikorsky Helicopter, white, black, blue, excellent condition, in box, complete with inner packing, V-shape cut mark to one end flap.

£80-120   **VEC**

A Dinky 732 red Bell Police Helicopter, excellent condition, in excellent condition box.

1974-80

£30-40   **SAS**

FIND OUT MORE...

Ramsey's British Diecast Model Toys, by John Ramsey, 9th Edition, published by Swapmeet Publications, 2001.

The Great Book of Dinky Toys, by Mike & Sue Richardson, published by New Cavendish Books, 2000.

The Great Book of Corgi, by Marcel R. Van Cleemput, published by New Cavendish Books, 2001.

COLLECTORS' NOTES

- Tri-ang produced their Spot-On range from 1959 to 1967, in direct competition with Dinky and Corgi.

- The name comes from the fact that all the models were made to exactly 1:42 scale, making them closer to models than toys.

- The range consisted of over 100 different models and including buildings and road signs, which were all at the same 1:42 scale.

- Production ended when Tri-ang bought Dinky in 1967.

- As they were only made for a short period of time, all the Spot-On models are collectable, particularly the commercial vehicles and presentation and gift sets.

- As with all die-cast model cars, condition, rare or unusual variations and the original box and paperwork all have a dramatic effect on value.

A scarce Tri-ang Spot-On No.211 Austin Seven Mini, light grey, red interior, excellent condition.

1963

£300-500   **VEC**

A Tri-ang Spot-On No.101 Armstrong-Siddeley 236 Sapphire, pink, black roof, cream interior, excellent condition, in good condition box, complete with leaflet.

1959

£180-220   **VEC**

A Tri-ang Spot-On No.118 BMW Isetta, green, cream interior, near mint in fair box, incorrect colour spot and sellotape repair to one end.

1960

£80-120   **VEC**

A Tri-ang Spot-On No. 215 Daimler Dart SP250, red, cream interior, excellent condition, in fair condition box.

1961

£100-150   **VEC**

A Tri-ang Spot-On No. 120 Fiat Multipla, pale blue, white interior, good plus in fair box.

1960

£50-80   **VEC**

A Tri-ang Spot-On No. 131 Goggomobile Super Regent, salmon pink, cream interior, slightly sunfaded, excellent condition, the box with sellotape repair to one end.

1960

£70-100   **VEC**

A Tri-ang Spot-On No. 112 Jenson 541, metallic blue-green, cream interior, excellent condition, slight mark to roof, in excellent condition box.

1960

£150-200   **VEC**

A Tri-ang Spot-On No.100sl Ford Zodiac, in yellow and beige, with battery powered lights, boxed, some damage and chipping.

1959

£30-50   **W&W**

A Tri-ang Spot-On No. 104 M.G. 'MGA' Sports Car, red, grey interior, good condition, in poor condition box.

1959

£100-150 VEC

A Tri-ang Spot-On No.119 Meadows Frisky, dark blue-green, black roof, blue interior excellent plus in excellent box.

1960

£100-150 VEC

A Tri-ang Spot-On No. 166 Renault Floride, pale blue, red interior, good condition, in good condition box, sellotape repairs to both ends.

£60-90 VEC

A Tri-ang Spot-On No.191/1 Sunbeam Alpine, with hard top, red, white roof, white interior, excellent condition, in poor condition box.

1963

£80-120 VEC

1963

£300-400 VEC

A Tri-ang Spot-On No.195 VW Beetle Rally Car, red, white interior, driver, racing number "23", flags to bonnet, roof light and spare wheel to roof, excellent condition, in good condition box, missing one inner end flap.

A scarce Tri-ang Spot-On Presentation Set A, comprising five cars including a Jaguar 3.4, a Bentley sports saloon, a Triumph TR3, a BMW Isetta and an Austin A40 Farina, boxed with inserts, some wear and minor chipping.

1960

£300-400 W&W

A scarce Tri-ang 'Mini Hi-Way' series Rover service truck, red, with yellow jib, metal lever and hook, and white plastic interior, boxed.

£40-60 W&W

A scarce Tri-ang 'Mini Hi-Way' series military Land Rover, olive green, with detachable roof and white plastic interior, boxed.

£40-60 W&W

A scarce Tri-ang Spot-On No. 207 Wadham Morris ambulance, cream, complete with patient on stretcher, boxed with data sheet.

Look for the white example decorated with red crosses, which can be worth 30% more than this version.

1964

£280-320 W&W

A Tri-ang Spot-On No.315 'Glass and Holmes' Window Cleaner's Van, pale blue, white interior, driver, ladders to roof, in excellent condition, in very good condition box, and labels attached to both ends.

1965

£150-200 VEC

A Tri-ang Spot-On No. 122 'United Dairies' Milk Float, red, white, excellent condition, in excellent condition box, slight tear mark.

1961

£100-150 VEC

A scarce Tri-ang Spot-On No. 271 Express Dairy Milk Float, dark blue and white livery, complete with crates and milkman, boxed with data sheet.

1965

£60-90 W&W

A Tri-ang Minic single-decker bus, destination Dorking, green, excellent condition, in very good condition box.

£300-400 SAS

A scarce Tri-ang Spot-On London Transport Routemaster double decker bus, red, with Ovaltine advertising on the sides, second-type radiator, "LBL 100" numberplates, boxed with data sheet, some damage.

The version with the first-type, moulded radiator is worth approximately the same as this.

1963

£200-300 W&W

A Tri-ang Spot-On 110/3d AEC Mammoth Major, with 10 oil drums, fair condition with some minor chipping, in poor condition box.

1962

£180-220 SAS

A Tri-ang Spot-On No.111a/1 Ford Thames Trader, in maroon and cream British Railways livery, boxed with data sheet.

1959

£220-280 W&W

A scarce Tri-ang Spot-On 106a/0c Austin Articulated Flatbed Lorry, blue and silver livery, complete with a crate load containing a turquoise MGA, boxed with packing, some wear.

1960

£300-400 W&W

A 1961 Tri-ang Spot-On No.135 14ft GP Sailing Dinghy and Trailer, good condition, missing mast and rudder board.

£30-50 VEC

COLLECTORS' NOTES

■ Model trains were first produced in the 1850s, but forms tended to be stylized, bulky and rather unrealistic. By the 1890s, German makers such as Märklin (est. 1859) and Gebrüder Bing (1863-1933) had introduced more realistic trains made from tinplate, with clockwork or steam mechanisms. Many of these were exported to the US and other European countries, with the two world wars temporarily stopping exports.

■ The first model trains for adult enthusiasts were developed in the 1900s. These were commonly made from tinplate, propelled by clockwork and hand-painted to mimic the liveries of real train operators. Large, well-detailed examples of engines and stock in fine condition are desirable and fetch a premium. Railway accessories from this period, such as stations, are highly prized and certain lamps and other small accessories can be rare and valuable, despite their size.

■ Märklin introduced gauge sizes in 1891. The larger gauges of I, II and III were replaced by 1910 with the smaller gauge 0 as demand for smaller trains grew. The 0 gauge itself was replaced in 1954 with the smaller 00 gauge, and the H0 gauge appeared in 1948.

■ Hornby began making trains in 1920. Its 'Dublo' is highly collectable. Look out for mint, boxed examples as these continue to rise in value. Sets from the 1950s-60s, such as those by Triang, are now worth looking out for if in mint condition with their boxes. These are still reasonably priced, but may rise in value in the future.

■ Condition is of paramount importance, particularly for later trains as they were made to be played with. Collectors therefore seek out examples in the best condition possible as well as rarities and much loved favourites.

A Märklin 0 gauge A-1 steam locomotive with tender, hand-painted in green, movement in working order.

£1,800-2,200   **LAN**

A Märklin 0 gauge B-1 steam locomotive.

The cow catcher on the engine indicates that this train was made for the US market.

12.5in (31cm) long

£2,500-3,500   **LAN**

A Märklin 1 gauge B-1 steam locomotive with a 2-A tender, movement in working order, hand-painted in black, three imitation headlights, hairline cracks to finish.

£800-1,200   **LAN**

A Märklin 2 gauge train set, with B-movement 1022 BN, comprising a 2-A tender, a luggage car and an open goods car with cast iron wheels, two figures, six straight and two half-straight tracks, brake track and buffer, in original box.

It is unusual to find the original box, and the cover picture is rare.

5.75in (14.5cm) wide

£2,500-3,500   **LAN**

A Märklin 0 gauge clockwork 4-4-2 Great Northern Railway Atlantic locomotive and tender, in green painted finish with white and black lining, for the English Market.

16in (41cm) long

£1,000-1,500   **F**

Two Märklin H0 gauge electrical locomotives and tenders, both of black cast iron and plastic, one locomotive signed "DB 18 478", together with a four axle tender, the other signed "DC 23015", marked "Made in Western Germany".

10in (25cm) long

£100-150   **WDL**

A Märklin 0 gauge 'R 890' locomotive, with tender, of black lacquered sheet metal, on two axles, missing key.

10.5in (26cm) long

£100-150   **WDL**

A rare Märklin 1 gauge 1912 carriage, hand-painted in green, with 2-A tinplate wheels.

A rare Märklin 0 gauge 1825 'Alpine Summer Carriage', hand-painted in yellow, with cast iron wheels and ball hitch.

Note the fine detailing that Märklin was known for, including the tied back curtains.

6.75in (17cm) long | c1904

5.25in (13cm) long

£650-750   **LAN** | **£1,500-2,500**   **LAN**

A Märklin 0 gauge P.R.R. carriage, hand-painted in blue, 2-A, old paint, some wear.

A Märklin 0 gauge 1828 ambulance, hand-painted in grey, with tinplate wheels, interior decoration furnace and two opening doors, some wear.

4.5in (11cm) long

5.25in (13cm) long

£850-950   **LAN** | **£800-900**   **LAN**

A Märklin 1 gauge 1828 ambulance, hand-painted in grey, 2-A tinplate wheels, two opening doors, with complete interior decoration, without figures.

A Märklin 1-gauge Emperor's coach 1841, hand-painted in green, with crown, 4-A cast iron wheels, four opening doors, with interior decoration, some wear.

Stock from the Imperial (or Royal) train is extremely desirable.

8.75in (22cm) long | c1909

10.75in (27cm) long

£450-550   **LAN** | **£1,500-2,000**   **LAN**

A Märklin 0 gauge 1828 P ambulance, hand-painted in grey, with tinplate wheels, interior decoration, stretchers and two opening doors, roof restored, figures missing.

A Märklin 0 gauge "Rheingold" 4-A dining car, chromolithographed in purple and cream, with four opening doors, tinplate wheels, interior decoration, seven people in the carriage.

A Märklin 0 gauge 1858 crane car, hand-painted in blue, with cast iron wheels, with chain and ball hook.

6.5in (16cm) long | 9.75in (24.5cm) long | 4in (10cm) long

£200-300   **LAN** | **£550-650**   **LAN** | **£450-550**   **LAN**

A modern Lionel 907 diecast 4-8-2 locomotive, with a 12-wheel Texas & Pacific tender.

£200-300 JDJ

A modern Lionel 2044 4-6-2 locomotive, with a Spokane, Portland & Seattle RY tender.

£80-120 JDJ

A Lionel 763 R locomotive, with 263 W oil tender, in gunmetal grey, slight chipping to frame.

£750-850 JDJ

A 1970s Lionel No. 3 General engine and tender, with original box.

£30-40 JDJ

A modern Lionel 8960 SP locomotive, an 8961 GP locomotive and four SP freight cars.

£60-80 JDJ

A modern Lionel 490 4-6-4 Chesapeake & Ohio locomotive, with 12-wheel tender.

£350-450 JDJ

A clockwork Hornby No. 1 special tender 0-4-0 locomotive, with a four-wheel tender, in early 1930s LMS maroon livery, RN8712.

£120-180   **W&W**

A clockwork Hornby Series 1185 4-4-0 locomotive and tender, in LMS livery, fair condition, some wheels replaced.

£180-220   **SAS**

A electric Hornby O gauge 4-4-2 No. 2 special tank locomotive, in green Southern Railway livery, RN 2091.

£80-120   **W&W**

A clockwork Hornby O gauge 4-4-2 locomotive in maroon LMS livery, RN 6954, black smoke box and cab roof top.

£180-220   **W&W**

A Hornby OO-gauge 4-6-0 Black Five locomotive, in LMS livery, with original box.

Box 13in (33cm) long

£40-60   **F**

A Hornby-Dublo two-rail 2226 City of London locomotive and tender, with box, very good condition.

£120-180   **SAS**

A Hornby-Dublo two-rail 2235 Barnstaple locomotive and tender 34005, with box, excellent condition.

£150-200   **SAS**

A Hornby-Dublo two-rail 2250 SR Electric Motor Coach Brake, lacks two axle guards, with box, very good condition.

£220-300   **SAS**

A Bing 1 gauge B-steam locomotive, with mismatched tender, hand-painted, slight damage to driver's cab and chimney.

£600-700 LAN

A Bing 1 gauge 2-B steam locomotive, with mismatched 3-A tender, spirit-operated, missing lanterns, some wear and cracks to finish.

£1,500-2,000 LAN

A rare Bing English 4-gauge locomotive 17592, with a 3-A tender, hand-painted in red and brown, inscribed "2631 MR", restored, one puffer of tender missing.

£3,500-4,500 LAN

A clockwork Bing 0 gauge locomotive, black lacquered tinplate, two lanterns missing, together with a triple axle tender.

c1920

£220-280 WDL

A Bing 1 gauge 2-B spirit locomotive 7094, together with a carriage and a luggage car, with interior decoration, in LSWR livery, some wear, replaced burner.

11.5in (29cm) long

£4,000-5,000 LAN

A rare Bing 0 gauge 2-A mobile workshop with crane, hand-painted in grey, with tinplate wheels and two sliding doors, together with a standing brakesman house.

5.25in (13cm) long

£800-900 LAN

One of a pair of Bing 0 gauge luggage carriages, of polychrome lithographed tinplate, with two axles, inscribed "Baggage 520", together with a Bing postal carriage with four small doors.

c1925 *4.25in (10.5cm) long*

£70-100 WDL

A scarce Bonds 0 gauge 0-6-0 tank locomotive, dockland style, with a hand-built tinplate body on three rail electric mechanism, finished in deep yellow, inscribed "Bonzone" to tank sides and "No 1" to can sides, minor marking and wear.

£200-250 W&W

A Bassett-Lowke clockwork 4-4-0 locomotive, with red lining, inscribed "41109", in excellent condition, lacks handrails and front wheels.

£150-200 SAS

A Bassett Lowke three-rail electric 4-6-2 locomotive and tender, in green LNER livery, parts overpainted and renamed 'Spearmint', good condition.

£550-650 SAS

A Bassett Lowke O gauge 4-4-0 freelance clockwork Duke of York locomotive and six-wheel tender, RN1927, with key, restored.

£150-250 W&W

A Tri-Ang Railways OO gauge RS37 set, comprising a Davy Crocket locomotive and two coaches, with box, damaged.

£100-150 W&W

A Tri-Ang Railways OO gauge R3F Southern EMU two car set.

£150-200 W&W

A Triang R23 Operating Royal Mail Coach Set, excellent condition, with box.

£35-45 SAS

A Tri-Ang Hornby Inter City R644A set, comprising an E3001 locomotive and three coaches with lights, boxed.

£100-150 W&W

A Wren OO gauge 4-6-0 Devizes Castle locomotive and tender, RN 7002, in green GW livery, in original box, minor marks.

£150-200 W&W

A Wrenn OO gauge 2-6-4 4MT standard tank, finished in GWR matt green, "RN 8230" plate to bunker sides, with paperwork, minor wear, in original box.

£120-180 W&W

A Wrenn W2207 SR 0-6-0 tank locomotive, 1127, excellent condition, with box.

£50-70 SAS

A Bing street lamp, hand-painted in red, few rusty spots.

8.5in (21cm) high

£70-100   LAN

A Märklin arch street lamp, hand-painted in blue, electrified.

8in (20cm) high

£80-120   LAN

Two tinplate and cast iron double-arch street lamps, painted in blue, electrified, one bulb missing, minimal wear.

10.5in (26.5cm) high

£80-120   LAN

A Märklin 0 gauge 2338 signal, hand-painted tinplate, some wear.

7.75in (19.5cm) high

£20-30   LAN

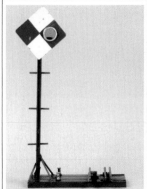

A Bing French signal, variable gauge, of hand-painted tinplate, bulb missing, wear.

10.5in (26.5cm) high

£20-40   LAN

A Märklin 0 gauge city train station 2035 B, with a marquee, hand-painted, with imitation clock, some wear.

Large, hand-painted stations by Märklin were expensive when first sold. Examples in excellent condition are in great demand due to their quality and rarity, leading to high prices.

23.25in (58cm) wide

£1,500-2,000   LAN

A small Märklin signalman's house, electrified inside, with shuttered windows, black fence and gate, signal missing, removable "Halt" sign, marked "Märklin Germany".

c1930   7.25in (18cm) wide

£120-180   WDL

A Bing buffet house, of hand-painted tinplate, with two imitated lamps, opening door and bar.

5.75in (14.5cm) wide

£450-550   LAN

A rare Märklin 2208 shooting stand, hand-painted.

12in (30cm) high

£300-400   LAN

A Bing tinplate ticket machine, hand-painted in yellow and red on a green base, signed "Fahrkarten – Direkte Zugverbindungen", ('Tickets – Direct Connections'), containing colourful cardboard tickets, marked "Bing".

c1925   7.5in (19cm) high

£120-180   WDL

COLLECTORS' NOTES

■ Tinplated steel had overtaken wood as a material for toys by the mid-19th century. Tinplate was less costly to produce and could be fashioned with more intricate details. Germany was the centre of production with the US producing toys from the mid-to late 19th century onwards. Germany's most notable makers included Marklin (founded 1856), Gebrüder Bing (1863-1933), and Lehmann (founded 1881). US makers included Louis Marx (1896-1982) and Ferdinand Strauss (c1914-42).

■ Tinplate from the 19th and early 20th century was generally hand-painted, before the introduction of transfer-printed 'lithography', and is generally very desirable. Hand-painted examples can be discerned by a more uneven surface and the presence of brush marks. Lithographed examples have a smooth, often shiny, surface with no brushmarks and usually have finer detailing.

■ After WWII, the Far East took over, with production initially being focused in Japan, followed by China from the late 1960s onwards. Toys became brighter in colour and more 'novelty' in theme, with 'mystery' actions involving sounds, light and movement. In the West, diecast toys and plastic toys had taken over the market since their introduction in the 1930s and 1950s respectively.

■ Many Japanese examples combine tinplate with plastic. Many are still affordable compared to their earlier cousins, but prices are rising, especially if in mint, working condition with original boxes. Transport toys, including cars, boats and planes are among the most popular toys with collectors, especially if large, early, finely detailed or by major makers. Avoid examples that display rust, splits or missing parts as these are virtually impossible to restore satisfactorily.

A scarce tinplate clockwork tipping lorry, in the Mettoy Wells style, with simple steering system and driver.

9.75in (25cm) wide

£250-300   **W&W**

A German Hausser tinplate pick-up truck, movement in working order, one opening door, steering wheel missing, few marks.

12in (30cm) wide

£700-900   **LAN**

A rare French C.R. Rossignol lithographed tinplate clockwork Renault petrol tank wagon, with simple steering system, one gear shaft missing.

£80-120   **W&W**

A Distler chromolithographed Dapolin truck 5881, with driver and electrical lighting, movement in good working order.

11.25in (28cm) long

£1,500-2,000   **LAN**

A Minic tinplate clockwork model 'Minic Transport Express' service box van.

5.5in (14cm) long

£40-60   **F**

A Schuco 'Constructions' fire engine, no.6080, lacks crew, accessories and hood ornament.

This fire engine was made in three versions between 1956-67. This is the earliest version with Schuco transfers on the doors. Later versions had moulded wording and less accessories. The Schuco Constructions range was made from 1949-67.

c1958   *10.75in (27cm) long*

£1,500-2,000   **LAN**

A rare early 1900s German Ernst Plank town sedan car, with lift-up access interior, two holes to seats for missing figures.

£120-180   **W&W**

A 1930s American Marx printed tinplate clockwork 'Old Jalopy' limousine.

7.25in (18.5cm) long

£60-80   **PWE**

An American hand-painted tinplate Hill Climber delivery truck, with "J.L. Kessner Co. Sixth Ave 22nd & 23rd Sts" transfer.

c1910   *11in (28cm) wide*

£150-250   **PWE**

A Mettoy tinplate clockwork model mechanical racing car, in original box.

Box 11in (28cm) wide

£180-220   **F**

A scarce 1950s Mettoy 'Sparking Racer', 'push 'n' go' mechanism with sparking action, in original box.

£80-120   **W&W**

A Schuco Studio toy car, with original box and paperwork, including salesman's instructions.

c1935   *Box 5.5in (14cm) long*

£40-60   **CA**

A 1950s Schuco limousine, No. 1010, movement in working order, with instructions, keys and original box.

£70-100   **LAN**

A 1960s Japanese Yoneszawa battery-operated tinplate mystery action taxi cab, mint and boxed.

8.75in (22.5cm) long

£25-35   **PWE**

A Masudaya (TM Modern Toys) battery-operated tinplate Super Patrol Man, boxed with packaging.

9in (23cm) wide

£120-180   **W&W**

A Tipp & Co. lithographed tinplate airplane no.60, with retractable undercarriage, movement in working order, electrified.

11.5in (29cm) long

£300-400   **LAN**

A scarce French Joustra Super G Constellation battery-powered tinplate airliner, in Air France blue livery.

19in (48cm) wide

£120-180   **W&W**

A Tipp & Co. painted tinplate propeller biplane, type '1424', removable wings, decorative foil stripes and numbers affixed.

14.75in (37cm) long

£50-80   **WDL**

A Lehmann chromolithographed tinplate airplane He 111 no.831, with accessories and instructions, renewed HK-emblem, original box.

£300-400   **LAN**

A Tri-Ang 'Frog' Mark IV interceptor fighter, in Belgian flying colours, with original orange box.

Box 11in (28cm) long

£60-80   **GORL**

A Günthermann lithographed tinplate water plane 1069, movement in working order, elevator replaced.

12in (30cm) long

£350-450   **LAN**

A 1950s Japanese Bandai 'Space Bus' lithographed tinplate toy, battery-operated via remote control.

£80-120   **W&W**

A CLOSER LOOK AT A MARX ZEPPELIN

The 'MAR' and 'X' in a circle logo identifies it as having been made by notable US maker Louis Marx (1919-79).

For a hollow, tinplate pull-along toy, it is in excellent condition with no dents or scratches and is complete with its wheels and engines.

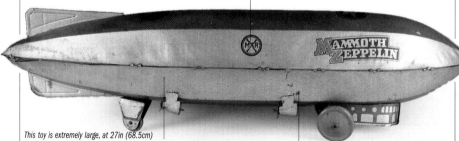

This toy is extremely large, at 27in (68.5cm) long – zeppelins are also a scarce and sought-after tinplate toy, especially in visually impressive sizes.

It dates from the 1930s, before WWII and the tragic Hindenburg disaster in 1937, when the heyday of airships as a mode of transatlantic transport ended.

A large Marx Zepplin tinplate toy, with four facsimile prop motors at side, on three tin wheels with suspended gondola at front, no dents or scratches.

27in (68.5cm) high

£350-450   **JDJ**

A German printed tinplate and metal clockwork boy on a tricycle, with bell.

9in (22.5cm) high

£350-450 PWE

A rare large Japanese 'Harley Davidson' police motorbike, chromolithographed tinplate, some wear.

12.25in (31cm) long

£800-1,200 LAN

A scarce 1950s Japanese Usagiya 'Rabbit' friction-driven lithographed tinplate motorcycle and side car, with original box.

£400-500 W&W

An American Marx lithographed tinplate coast-to-coast Greyhound bus, with wind-up action, in very good condition.

10in (25.5cm) long

£300-400 BER

An Arnold chromolithographed tinplate armoured scout car 562, with driver, movement in good order.

10in (25cm) long

£450-550 LAN

A scarce early German tinplate penny toy, in the style of an ocean liner.

Penny toys are small tinplate toys that were often sold by street vendors, reaching the height of their popularity around 1900-10. Look for well modelled and detailed examples, as well as popular themes, such as cars. Condition is also paramount for high value.

4.5in (11.5cm) wide

£100-150 W&W

An American Louis Marx tinplate 'Hee Haw' balky mule cart, with wind-up action.

10.5in (27cm) long

£150-200 PWE

A German Lehmann tinplate balky mule cart, for the American market, lacks the back of the cart.

8in (20cm) long

£220-280 PWE

An Arnold tinplate boy on a sledge, made in US Zone Germany, with clockwork motor.

c1950

£60-80   **W&W**

An Arnold clockwork tinplate porter, made in US Zone Germany, in original box.

c1950

£80-120   **W&W**

A 1950s Japanese T.P.S. clockwork mechanical 'Suzy Bouncing Ball' toy, lithographed tinplate with plastic head and fabric skirt, in original box.

Box 5.75in (14.5cm) wide

£25-35   **GAZE**

A scarce 1950s Japanese T.P.S. tinplate clockwork 'Mechanical Happy the Violinist', with original clothes and box.

9in (23cm) high

£250-350   **W&W**

A Mattel tinplate mechanical musical Jack-In-The-Box, in original box.

c1968   *6.25in (16cm) wide*

£40-50   **F**

An early 20thC Gunthermann clockwork tortoise, lacks boy rider to top of shell, some wear to legs.

10.5in (26.5cm) long

£120-180   **W&W**

A rare, early American hand-painted tin jockey on an oversized dog pull-along toy, by George W. Brown & Co.

Brown, of Forestville, Connecticut, manufactured toys from 1856-80 and was the first maker to employ clockwork mechanisms. He is known for his boats, vehicles and animals in hand-painted tin. In 1868, he merged with J. & E. Stevens.

c1878   *10in (25.5cm) long*

£1,200-1,800   **AMJ**

A 1920s Lehmann tinplate clockwork climbing monkey, gripping a rope that moves him up and down.

£150-200   **TCA**

A Chad Valley lithographed tin drum, with sticks.

c1950   *8.75in (22cm) high*

£10-15   **GAZE**

COLLECTORS' NOTES

■ The majority of space-themed toys traded today were originally made in Japan during the 1950s and 60s. American and Russian models are also available. They reflect the mood of their age, especially the preoccupation with the space race.

■ Yonezawa, Nomura and Masudaya are among the biggest names on the market. Many companies that made these toys have fallen into obscurity, and are now identified only by their stamped initials.

■ The most serious form of damage found on tinplate toys is rust. Even small amounts of rust visible on the surface of a toy can be indicative of an ongoing corrosion problem. Battery leaks will also wreak havoc on metal toys and are extremely hard to rectify.

■ Missing parts can be replaced but are often hard to source. Many collectors are, however, happy to purchase toys that are not in full working order. Repainting invariably detracts from the original aesthetic of a toy and should be avoided.

■ Toys complete with boxes will command a premium, particularly if the box is in good condition. The science fiction inspired designs on these boxes hold great appeal for collectors.

■ More and more toys were made from plastic from the late 1960s onwards. This proved a cheaper and more child-friendly alternative to tinplate, eventually replacing it completely. Collectors are increasingly interested in early plastic space toys.

A Rosko Toy 'Rocket Man' battery operated robot, made in Japan by Alps, remote control, complete with original box with legend.

The box illustration depicts the spaceman with a NASA insignia on his helmet beneath his armour, however on the actual toy this has been obliterated by the addition of a small lamp.

15in (38cm) high

£1,500-2,000 **RSJ**

A CLOSER LOOK AT A ROBOT

This is of a large size, which is typical of the 1950s and 1960s as sizes increased.

It is one of the popular 'Gang of Five' skirted toy robots produced by Masudaya, the others include Robot the Robot, Machine Man, Radicon Robot and Target Robot.

It's nickname 'Train Robot' comes from the train-like sound it makes.

It boasts a mystery 'bump-n'-go' action, with swinging arms and flashing eyes and ears. These actions appeal greatly to collectors. The more the better!

A 1950s Japanese giant Sonic 'Train' battery operated robot, by Masudaya, made by Trademark Toys.

4.5in (37cm) high

£2,000-2,500 **RSJ**

A 1950s Japanese 'Space Man Robot' tinplate astronaut, by Daiya, some wear and faulty switch.

14in (35.5cm) high

£200-300 **W&W**

A 1960s Japanese 'Super Astronaut' tinplate robot, by S.H. Horikawa, boxed, some wear, in working order.

£60-80 **W&W**

A Japanese 'Answer Game' calculating battery operated tinplate robot, by Ichida, with blinking eyes, and a disc revolving in his head.

14in (36.5cm) high

£550-650 **ATK**

A Marx Toys plastic and tinplate wind-up walking 'Son of Garloo', made in Hong Kong, with original medallion and box.

6in (15cm) high

£180-220   **RSJ**

A scarce West German 'Dux Astroman' battery-powered plastic spaceman figure, by Markes & Co, boxed.

c1955

£300-400   **W&W**

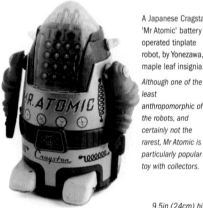

A Japanese Cragstan 'Mr Atomic' battery operated tinplate robot, by Yonezawa, maple leaf insignia.

Although one of the least anthropomorphic of the robots, and certainly not the rarest, Mr Atomic is a particularly popular toy with collectors.

9.5in (24cm) high

£1,200-1,800   **RSJ**

A Japanese 'Planet' clockwork robot, by Yoshia, with walking mechanism, tin with plastic hands, minor paint wear to back.

1960   8.75in (22cm) high

£150-200   **ATK**

A Japanese tinplate and plastic battery operated 'Docking Robot', by Daiya, boxed, minor wear, in working order.

16in (40.5cm) high

£50-70   **W&W**

A Japanese tinplate and plastic 'Apollo 11 Eagle NASA Lunar Module', by DSK Daishin Kogyo Co., battery powered, boxed, in working order.

c1970

£50-70   **W&W**

A Japanese 'United States Space Capsule', by S.H. Horikawa, Spanish export version, battery powered, boxed, minor wear, in working order.

£50-80   **W&W**

A Japanese TM Modern Toys battery powered 'Space Ship X5', boxed, some wear, in working order.

£40-60   **W&W**

A Japanese large lithographed tinplate 'Atom Jet', by Yonezawa, friction-powered, missing windscreen, one new break light.

This is the largest Japanese tin toy car made in the 1950s.

c1950   26.5in (66cm) long

£750-850   **ATK**

A Japanese battery operated plastic and tinplate 'Space Rocket Saturn X5', by Alps, boxed, some wear, in good working order.

11.5in (29cm) long

£70-100 **W&W**

A 1970s Japanese TM Modern Toys battery powered 'Space Ranger No 3', boxed, in working order.

A Japanese battery powered tinplate 'Sky Patrol', by TN.

13in (33cm) long

£50-70 **W&W** | **£150-250** **W&W**

A scarce 1950s Marx 'Tom Corbett Space Cadet 2' space ship, motor in working order.

12.5in (32cm) high

£70-100 **W&W**

A scarce Tri-Ang Minic 'push and go' tinplate Space Cruiser, in a colourful original box.

10.25in (26cm) long

£120-180 **W&W**

A Pepys Party Games 'Dan Dare – A Treasure Hunt in Space Ships', boxed.

£30-40 **SAS**

A 1960s 'Dan Dare Planet Gun' by Merit, with three spinning missiles, boxed.

The box and missiles are hard to find.

Box 10.5in (26.5cm) wide

£50-70 **GAZE**

A 'Dan Dare, Pilot of the Future' pop up, by Juvenile Productions Ltd.

1953   10.5in (26.5cm) wide

£60-80 **GAZE**

A 'Dan Dare Planet Gun', by Merit, complete and boxed.

c1953   Box 10.75in (27.5cm) wide

£120-180 **GAZE**

TOYS & GAMES

A Schuco novelty perfume bottle, in the form of a plush fabric monkey, with removable head revealing a glass tube insert.

c1920s   *4in (10cm) high*

£250-350   **RDL**

A Schuco ragged plush monkey, 'Schnico 183', with moving head, movement in working order, some wear.

8.75in (22cm) high

£150-250   **LAN**

A CLOSER LOOK AT A SCHUCO FIGURE

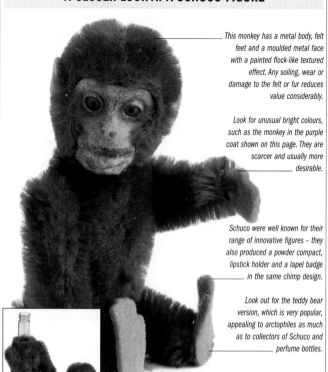

This monkey has a metal body, felt feet and a moulded metal face with a painted flock-like textured effect. Any soiling, wear or damage to the felt or fur reduces value considerably.

Look for unusual bright colours, such as the monkey in the purple coat shown on this page. They are scarcer and usually more desirable.

Schuco were well known for their range of innovative figures – they also produced a powder compact, lipstick holder and a lapel badge in the same chimp design.

Look out for the teddy bear version, which is very popular, appealing to arctophiles as much as to collectors of Schuco and perfume bottles.

A 1920s Schuco novelty perfume bottle, in the form of a plush fabric monkey, with a glass tube insert, some wear to face.

5in (12.5cm) high

£200-300   **RDL**

A Schuco dancing figure of a piglet, playing the violin in a sailor's outfit, movement in working order, lacks violin, some wear.

£80-120   **LAN**

A Schuco monkey sailor figure.

c1925   *4.5in (11.5cm) high*

£70-100   **B&H**

A Schuco dancing figure of a Dutch boy with violin, movement in working order.

5.5in (14cm) high

£150-250   **LAN**

A Schuco clown with violin, movement in working order, some wear.

£120-180   **LAN**

COLLECTORS' NOTES

- The first metal soldiers were flat Zinnfiguren manufactured in Germany in the 18th century. One of the first companies to make three-dimensional figures was Paris-based Lucotte.

- William Britain Junior revolutionised the industry in 1893 when he patented his hollow casting process, allowing for the economic manufacture of large numbers of figures.

- Figures with good detail are generally more desirable. Britains soldiers in particular are popular for the authenticity of their uniforms.

- After the First World War many manufacturers found that the buying public did not want lead soldiers and

began to make civilian models instead, such as farm and zoo sets.

- Oxidation is a common problem with lead figures, and, if left unchecked, can destroy fine details and ruin painted finishes, decimating the value of a figure.

- Check figures for lumps and small areas of repainting. This could be a sign of customisation, whereby a figure is amended by replacing its head or making other changes.

- In 1966 the use of lead in children's toys was banned due to its toxicity. Some manufacturers switched to producing plastic figures, and the market for these is growing steadily.

A Britains Hunt in Full Cry set, including three huntsman and four ladies riding side-saddle, 10 chasing hounds and a fox, in good condition.

£400-500　　　　**CHEF**

A Britains Hunt Series The Meet set 1446, mounted huntsman, foot huntsman and huntswoman, together with six hounds, all very good condition.

£80-120　　　　**VEC**

A Britains North American Indians set 208, comprising four mounted and seven foot Indians in various poses, one tomahawk broken, the box with illustrated label, one lid corner repaired.

£300-350　　　　**VEC**

A Britains Prairie Schooner set 2034, comprising green wagon, red wheels, white tin tilt, four-horse team, driver with wife, excellent condition, the box with illustrated label, four lid corners torn.

£450-550　　　　**VEC**

Five Britains Knights of Agincourt Foot Knights, various poses, one shield missing, minor paint loss.

£120-180　　　　**VEC**

A Britains Miss Dorothy Paget Racing Colours, excellent condition, in very good condition box.

£300-400　　　　**VEC**

Four Britains American Girl Scouts figures from set 238, in brown uniforms and hats, black stockings, excellent condition.

£220-280　　　　**VEC**

A Britains Painters and Ladder set 1495, comprising two painters with ladder, and a painter with brush, excellent condition, in very good condition box with illustrated label, no insert card.

£400-500　　　　**VEC**

A Britains Royal Artillery Gunners set 313, in original damaged yellow front Whisstock box.

c1928

£100-150   **W&W**

A Britains African Warriors Zulus Running set 147, comprising eight figures on square beige top bases, with knobkerries or spears to moving right arm, in original box with tie card.

c1948

£100-150   **W&W**

A CLOSER LOOK AT A BRITAINS SET

This is one of only five or six examples of this set to have come on to the market.

The completeness of the set, the excellent condition of the pieces and the original box help increase the value.

It is more commonly seen as a British Mountain Battery.

Many collectors focus entirely on Britains figures, due to their high quality, accuracy and attention to detail.

A rare Britains Indian Mountain Battery, review order, No 2013, with soldiers and mules, boxed.

£1,800-2,200   **W&W**

A Britains Argentine Horse Grenadiers set 217, comprising four men with lances, post war painting, in original box.

£60-80   **W&W**

A Britains RAMC 4 horse wagon set 145, with a matt wagon, canvas tilt, collar harness and twisted wire traces, also two stretcher bearers, stretcher, two lying wounded and a nurse in field grey dress with a red cape.

Wagon 11in (28cm) long

£70-90   **W&W**

A Royal Corps of Signals dispatch riders set 1791, comprising four riders on motorcycles, the motorcycles with silver exhaust pipes, on original card in original box.

£180-220   **W&W**

A scarce Hugar for Britains wooden guard hut, in embossed plywood, wire glazed window, a "Join a Yorkshire Regiment" poster to front, some woodworm holes.

5in (12.5cm) wide

£150-200   **W&W**

A scarce Britains Army Staff car set 1448, with plastic tyred wheels, removable officer passenger and driver casting, with original box with picture lid.

4.25in (10.75cm) long

£180-220   **W&W**

A Taylor & Barrett Llama Ride, comprising of two wheeled cart, four children, llama and keeper, all very good condition, in original box with illustrated label.

£180-220　　　　**VEC**

A Taylor & Barrett Wild West Wagon, yellow, red wheels, canvas tilt, driver and two seated women passengers, together with a cowgirl on horseback.

£120-180　　　　**VEC**

A Taylor & Barrett Brewers Dray, comprising four wheeled dray, grey horse, seat, driver with whip, end broken, Watney's sign replaced, loading ladder and five barrels, some repainting.

£120-180　　　　**VEC**

A Taylor & Barrett window cleaner, with cart, ladder and bucket, and a bread cart, yellow, red wheels, cream roof, delivery man and basket, both in very good condition.

£150-200　　　　**VEC**

A Taylor & Barrett donkey ride, two donkeys, two donkeys colts, tethering post with sign, child rider and keeper, together with two parrots on grey stand, all very good condition.

£120-180　　　　**VEC**

A Taylor & Barrett A.F.S. pump, with hose and two frogmen, blue suits, green helmets, together with chimps tea party, white table, three chairs, three chimpanzees, all good to very good condition.

£150-200　　　　**VEC**

A Taylor & Barrett donkey ride, comprising donkey hut, two donkey stands with '2d all the way' signs, two donkeys, three donkeys colts, one child rider, keeper, mainly good to very good condition.

£180-220　　　　**VEC**

Three Taylor & Barrett Air Raid Precautions figures, man carrying two buckets, woman with bucket and stirrup pump, and woman holding hose, all very good condition.

£100-150　　　　**VEC**

An F.G. Taylor & Sons costermonger's donkey cart set, complete with walking costermonger holding a cauliflower and a basket, two bunches of bananas, two turnips, two carrots and a marrow, good condition, unboxed.

£80-120　　　　**DN**

A rare 1930s Crescent deep sea diver, part of set NN692, with a grey dive suit, gold-painted removable helmet, elastic airline and air distribution set finished in red, tools missing.

Although part of a larger set, this figure is hard to find with the helmet and air distribution set as they were often lost.

A Crescent Cowboys and Indians display set, comprising of 11 figures, all very good in poor illustrated box, old repairs and tears to lid.

£50-70   W&W | **£70-100**   VEC

A Crescent Farm Animals set, nine animals, feeding trough, farm girl with bucket, farmer with pitchfork, in illustrated box, corners torn, one lid edge partially missing.

A collection of Crescent Civilian issue figures, including seat with grandma and grandad, milkmaid, nurse, woman customer, man with oilcan, farm girl with bucket, kneeling nurse, porter, woman shopper, farmer with broken pitchfork, milkmaid with stool and gorilla, all in mainly good condition.

£30-50   VEC | **£50-80**   VEC

A John Hill four-wheeled cattle float, grey with red wheels, includes seated drover and brown horse, in very good condition.

Five John Hill wedding figures, comprising vicar, bride, groom, bridesmaid, further bride figure in blue, no detail painted, some paint loss to bride in white.

£80-120   VEC | **£100-150**   VEC

A John Hill miniature hunting series, comprising huntsman standing beside horse, mounted huntsman, mounted huntswoman, huntswoman standing with hound, three hounds, in illustrated box.

Six John Hill racehorses with jockeys, in various colours, one head broken, one horse's leg broken.

£180-220   VEC | **£50-80**   VEC

COLLECTORS' NOTES

▪ Action Man was first issued by UK toy manufacturer Palitoy in 1966. It was essentially a repackaged 'G.I. Joe' action figure, which was licensed to Palitoy by Hasbro in the US.

▪ The first figures had a 12-jointed body and came with moulded, hard plastic heads with painted hair and features. They were titled 'Action Soldier', 'Action Sailor' and 'Action Pilot'.

▪ The range was expanded to include foreign military uniforms. The popular 'Famous British Uniforms' series featured highly detailed and accurate ceremonial uniforms from British regiments. The first non-military figure was added in 1968.

▪ Palitoy developed a number of innovations that made their way back across the Atlantic and were taken up by Hasbro. These included more realistic 'flock' hair, introduced in 1970, and 'gripping' hands from 1973.

▪ A new body, which can be identified by the blue moulded plastic underpants, was modelled in 1978. It was used until the range was discontinued in 1984. The uniforms and accessories were also modified and collectors look for complete outfits that correspond to the figures.

▪ Each Action Man came with a number of loose accessories, many of which were lost or damaged through play. These can make a huge difference to the value of a figure, though reproduction replacements are being made today.

▪ The traditional military uniforms from the 1960s and 1970s, in particular the 'Ceremonials', are the most sought after.

▪ Most of the examples shown here are complete, or near to complete. Incomplete examples will be less valuable.

A 1970s Action Man 'Soldier' figure, by Palitoy, slightly faded, boxed, with literature.

Box 12in (30.5cm) high

£80-120   **GAZE**

A 1970s Action Man 'Action Soldier' figure, by Palitoy, faded, lacks machine gun, boxed.

Box 12in (30.5cm) high

£80-120   **GAZE**

A CLOSER LOOK AT AN ACTION MAN

The Talking Commander figure was released in 1968. It spoke eight phrases, which could be selected by pulling the cord in his back to different lengths.

The original box and product sheet adds to the value of the figure.

Gripping hands were introduced in 1973 and proved so successful that Hasbro took up the feature for use in the 'G.I. Joe' figure.

While he retains his beret, belt and holster, his pistol is missing, reducing his value.

An Action Man 'Commander' talking figure, by Palitoy, with gripping hands, lacks firearm.

c1973   *Box 12in (30.5cm) high*

£100-150   **GAZE**

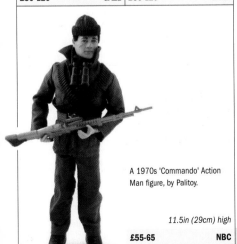

A 1970s 'Commando' Action Man figure, by Palitoy.

11.5in (29cm) high

£55-65   **NBC**

A 1980s 'Royal Hussars' Action Man figure, by Palitoy.

The Royal Hussars was the last figure added to the 'Ceremonial' series in 1979 and is considered to be the rarest.

11.5in (29cm) high

£100-150   **NBC**

A 'Grenadier Guard' Action Man figure, by Palitoy.

1970   *11.5in (29cm) h*

£60-80   **NBC**

A 1970s '17th/21st Lancers' Action Man figure, by Palitoy.

The regiment itself asked Palitoy to add its uniform to the Action Man range.

11.5in (29cm) high

A 1970s 'Army Medic' Action Man figure, by Palitoy.

11.5in (29cm) high

£60-70   **NBC**

A 1970s 'Mountain Rescue' Action Man figure, by Palitoy.

11.5in (29cm) high

£60-70   **NBC**

£120-180   **NBC**

A 1970s 'Mountain & Arctic Warfare' Action Man figure, by Palitoy.

11.5in (29cm) high

£60-80   **NBC**

A 1960s 'Ski Patrol' Action Man figure, by Palitoy, with bear motif on uniform.

11.5in (29cm) high

£70-110   **NBC**

A 1960s 'Scramble Pilot' Action Man figure, by Palitoy.

11.5in (29cm) high

£70-100   **NBC**

A 1960s 'Air Police' Action Man figure, by Palitoy, with rare grey field telephone.

11.5in (29cm) high

£100-150   **NBC**

A 1960s 'Australian Jungle Fighter' Action Man figure, by Palitoy.

11.5in (29cm) high

£70-100　　　　**NBC**

A 'Royal Canadian Mounted Police' Action Man figure, by Palitoy, with 'Brutus' police dog figure.

The Mountie Action Man figure was not available for purchase, it could only be obtained by collecting 'stars' from the packaging of other figures and sending away for it.

1970　　　11.5in (29cm) high

£60-80　　　　**NBC**

A 1980s 'Luftwaffe Pilot' Action Man figure, by Palitoy, with rare goggles.

11.5in (29cm) high

£70-100　　　　**NBC**

A 1980s 'German Panzer Captain' Action Man figure, by Palitoy.

11.5in (29cm) high

£60-80　　　　**NBC**

A 1970s 'Camp Kommandant' Action Man figure, by Palitoy, lacks rare baton.

11.5in (29cm) high

£40-60　　　　**NBC**

A 1970s 'French Foreign Legion' Action Man figure, by Palitoy, with rare blue sash and bayonet.

11.5in (29cm) high

£70-100　　　　**NBC**

A 1980s 'Afrika Corp' Action Man figure, by Palitoy.

Flock hair replaced the moulded hair in 1970 and was produced in blond and black. It wears well and examples in good condition are not too hard to find.

11.5in (29cm) high

£80-120　　　　**NBC**

A 1960s 'Russian Infantryman' Action Man figure, by Palitoy, with rare tripod for the machine gun.

11.5in (29cm) high

£70-100　　　　**NBC**

A 1960s/70s 'US Military Police' Action Man figure, by Palitoy, with rare arm band.

11.5in (29cm) high

£60-80   **NBC**

A 1960s 'Paratrooper - US' Action Man figure, by Palitoy.

Heads were initially made of hard plastic with painted hair and eyebrows in black, brown, blond, and auburn, which were prone to wearing off. A transitional softer plastic head was produced before the hair was changed to flock.

11.5in (29cm) high

£100-140   **NBC**

A 1980s 'US Paratrooper' Action Man figure, by Palitoy.

11.5in (29cm) high

£70-90   **NBC**

A CLOSER LOOK AT AN ACTION MAN

Captain Zargon was part of the Space Rangers series, which included the Space Ranger Captain, Patroller and ROM the Space Knight.

The range was introduced in response to the craze for all things space-related, brought about by the release of Star Wars in 1977.

The laser sword is missing, but the figure does retain the visor, which was also produced in red and clear plastic.

Many collectors see this series as the beginning of the end for Action Man, who was unable to compete with Star Wars figures, ironically also made by Palitoy.

A 'Captain Zargon, Space Pirate' Action Man figure, by Palitoy, boxed with Star Awards card and product sheet.
c1980

11.5in (29cm) high

£30-40   **MHC**

A 1970s 'Deep Sea Diver' Action Man figure, by Palitoy, in Sea Wolf submarine.

Figure 11.5in (29cm) high

£50-70 Submarine: £20-30   **NBC**

A 1960s 'Astronaut' Action Man figure, with space capsule.

Figure 11.5in (29cm) high

£60-80 Capsule: £25-35   **NBC**

FIND OUT MORE...

www.actionman.com, *official company website.*

www.vintageaction.com, *collectors website.*

Action Man: The Official Dossier, *by Ian Harrison, published by Collins, 2003.*

STAR WARS 549

TOYS & GAMES

COLLECTORS' NOTES

- Star Wars figures have been issued by different companies in many countries worldwide. The most commonly found vintage toys are those made for the US and UK markets by Kenner and Palitoy respectively. More recently, figures have been distributed by Hasbro.

- The first figures could not be manufactured in time for the 1977 Christmas season, so Kenner instead issued the 'Early Bird' package with coupons redeemable against the first four figures, including Luke and Leia. These packs can now fetch up to £200.

- Figures and vehicles associated with the first three Star Wars films will generally be more valuable than later issues. Packaging with the original 'Star Wars' logo adds the most value to a toy, especially if combined with a '12-back' reverse design, so called because it depicts the 12 figures that were available at the time.

- The 1985 'Power of the Force' set of 37 figures was issued in limited numbers due to a drop in demand. Today, card-backed examples of these figures are among the most sought-after and the coins included in the original packaging also do a brisk trade.

- The highest prices are reserved for rare variations such as the vinyl-caped Jawa, Boba Fett with rocket-firing backpack and the original 'Power of the Force' issue of the Anakin Skywalker figure. Even these must be complete with original packaging to realise their full value, and fakes are known to exist.

A CLOSER LOOK AT A STAR WARS ACTION FIGURE

This is an early version of one of the first 12 figures released by Kenner in 1979.

Early examples of this figure were produced with a vinyl cape. Executives felt that, together with the figure's diminutive size, this did not represent good value for money and the cape was therefore changed to cloth.

Beware of fake vinyl capes, which are often cut down from 'Ben Kenobi's' cape. The material should be the same colour as the figure's face.

This figure is on a '12-back' card, the first form of packaging that carried illustrations of the first 12 figures on the back. The same figure on a later '20-back' card is worth less than this example.

A Star Wars 'Ben (Obi-Wan) Kenobi' large action figure, by Kenner, mint and boxed.

These large sized (12in) action figures were only issued for two years and are scarce.

c1980   figure 12in (30.5cm) high

£180-220   NOR

A Star Wars 'Jawa' carded action figure, by Kenner, with vinyl cape, on '12-back' card.

If the proof of purchase token at the bottom right hand corner of this card were still intact it could be worth £1,500-2,500.

c1978

£750-850   NOR

A Star Wars – The Empire Strikes Back 'Imperial TIE Fighter Pilot' action figure.
c1982

£50-80   W&W

A Star Wars – Return of the Jedi 'AT-AT Commander' action figure, by Kenner, on '65-back' card.
c1982

£22-28   W&W

A Star Wars – Return of the Jedi 'Bib Fortuna' action figure, by Kenner.
c1983

£18-22   W&W

A Star Wars – Return of the Jedi 'Gamorrean Guard' action figure, by Kenner, on '77-back' card.
c1983

£12-18   W&W

A Star Wars – Return of the Jedi tri-logo 'Imperial Stormtrooper – Hoth Battle Gear' action figure, by Kenner, on '70-back' card.

c1980

£25-35   **W&W**

A Star Wars – Return of the Jedi 'Biker Scout' action figure, by Kenner.

c1983

£20-30   **W&W**

A Star Wars – Return of the Jedi 'C-3PO' action figure, by Palitoy, incorrectly sealed on a 'Death Star Droid' tri-logo card.

This error variation is undoubtedly unusual but is of limited appeal to collectors.

c1983

£20-25   **W&W**

A Star Wars – Return of the Jedi 'Emperor's Royal Guard' action figure, by Kenner, on '77-back' card.

c1983

£20-30   **W&W**

A Star Wars – Return of the Jedi 'Klaatu' action figure, by Kenner.

Klaatu and his comrades Barada and Nikto are members of Jabba's entourage. Their names are a homage to the film 'The Day the Earth Stood Still' in which they were used as an order to stop Gort, a giant robot, from destroying Earth.

c1983

£15-20   **W&W**

A Star Wars – Return of the Jedi 'Logray – Ewok Medicine Man' action figure, by Kenner, on '77-back' card.

c1983

£15-30   **W&W**

A Star Wars – Return of the Jedi tri-logo 'Squid Head' action figure, by Palitoy, bubble pack opened.

Squid Head was renamed 'Tessek' for the second edition of Power of the Force figures.

c1983

£12-18   **W&W**

A Star Wars – Return of the Jedi 'Weequay' action figure, by Palitoy, incorrectly sealed on a 'Warok' tri-logo card.

c1983

£10-15   **W&W**

A Star Wars – The Power of the Force second edition 'Chewbacca as Boushh's Bounty' action figure, by Kenner, with Bowcaster, on green 'Freeze Frame' header card.

c1997   9in (23cm) high

£5-7   **W&W**

A Star Wars – The Power of the Force second edition 'Luke Skywalker' action figure, by Kenner, with blast shield helmet and lightsaber, on green 'Freeze Frame' header card.

c1997   9in (23cm) high

£5-7   **W&W**

A Star Wars – Return of the Jedi 'Ewok' action figure triple pack, by Kenner, containing 'Logray', 'Wicket' and 'Paploo'.

c1984   box 5in (12.5cm) high

£70-90   **KF**

A Star Wars Special Edition 300th figure 'Boba Fett' action figure, by Hasbro, with rocket-firing backpack.

This special edition commemorates the first Boba Fett figure that was designed with a rocket-firing backpack. It was considered too dangerous for children and was never properly issued, making it very rare today.

c2000   8in (20cm) high

£12-18   **W&W**

A Star Wars – The Power of the Force second edition 'Oola & Salacious Crumb' action figure twin pack, by Kenner.

This pack was an Official Star Wars Fan Club exclusive.

c1998   5.5in (14cm) high

£10-15   **W&W**

A Star Wars – The Power of the Force second edition 'Purchase of the Droids' 'Cinema Scenes' triple pack, by Kenner, containing 'Uncle Lars Owen', 'Luke Skywalker' and 'C-3PO', in green box.

All of the 'Cinema Scenes' sets contain at least one exclusive figure, in this case 'Uncle Lars Owen'.

c1998   10.5in (26.5cm) wide

£7-9   **W&W**

A Star Wars – The Power of the Force second edition 'Death Star Escape' 'Cinema Scenes' triple pack, by Kenner, containing 'Chewbacca', 'Han Solo' and 'Luke Skywalker' in Stormtrooper outfits.

This set was released exclusively through Toys 'R' Us. The Han Solo figure had previously been available via a Froot Loops mail-in offer.

c1997   10.5in (26.5cm) wide

£22-28   **W&W**

A Star Wars – The Power of the Force second edition 'Darth Vader' action figure, by Kenner, with short lightsaber, on multi-language red header card.

Look for the transitional version of this figure which has a short lightsaber and a long slot in the packaging. It can be worth three times more than this version.

c1996   9in (23cm) high

£7-9   **W&W**

AGES 4 & UP

A Star Wars – Episode 1 'Adi Gallia' carded action figure, by Hasbro.

c1998   *9in (22.5cm) high*

£6-8   KF

A Star Wars – Episode 1 'Anakin Skywalker' carded action figure, by Hasbro.

c1998   *9in (22.5cm) high*

£3-4   KF

A Star Wars – Episode 1 'Destroyer Droid' carded action figure, by Hasbro.

c1998   *9in (22.5cm) high*

£4-5   KF

A Star Wars – Episode 1 'OOM-9' carded action figure, by Hasbro.

c1998   *9in (22.5cm) high*

£4-6   KF

A Star Wars – Episode 1 'Obi-Wan Kenobi' carded action figure, by Hasbro.

c1998   *9in (22.5cm) high*

£3-4   KF

A Star Wars – Episode 1 'Qui-Gon Jinn' carded action figure, by Hasbro.

c1998   *9in (22.5cm) high*

£3-4   KF

A Star Wars – Episode 1 'Ric Olié' carded action figure, by Hasbro.

c1998   *9in (22.5cm) high*

£3-5   KF

A Star Wars – Episode 1 'Senator Palpatine' carded action figure, by Hasbro.

c1998   *9in (22.5cm) high*

£5-7   KF

A Star Wars – Attack of the Clones 'Jar Jar Binks (Gungan Senator)' carded action figure, by Hasbro.

c2002   *9in (22.5cm) high*

£4-6   KF

A Star Wars 'Walrus Man' action figure.

c1979　　　　3.75in (9.5cm) high

£7-8　　　　　　　　　　**KF**

A CLOSER LOOK AT A STAR WARS VEHICLE

This was one of the most expensive vehicles produced by Kenner for the Star Wars line and few were sold at the time.

This toy was initially issued in a Star Wars box, and later re-issued by Kenner Canada in bi-lingual Empire Strikes Back packaging. Boxed examples are extremely hard to find.

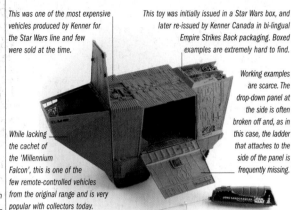

Working examples are scarce. The drop-down panel at the side is often broken off and, as in this case, the ladder that attaches to the side of the panel is frequently missing.

While lacking the cachet of the 'Millennium Falcon', this is one of the few remote-controlled vehicles from the original range and is very popular with collectors today.

A rare Star Wars remote-controlled 'Jawa Sandcrawler', the remote control console lacking its battery cover.

A boxed example of this toy could be worth up to £500.

c1979　　　　　　　16.5in (42cm) long

£150-200　　　　　　　　　　**KNK**

A Star Wars – Return of the Jedi 'Ree-Yees' action figure.

c1983　　　　3.75in (9.5cm) high

£4-6　　　　　　　　　　**KF**

A Star Wars – Return of the Jedi 'Nien Nunb' action figure.

c1983　　　　3.75in (9.5cm) high

£5-7　　　　　　　　　　**KF**

An unusual set of three Star Wars figures, comprising 'C-3PO', 'B-Wing Pilot' and 'Emperor Palpatine', in generic packaging.

This unusual set does not cite Star Wars on the packaging. These figures may have been bought as surplus stock and repackaged.

　　　　　　9.75in (25cm) wide

£20-40　　　　　　　　　　**W&W**

A Star Wars – The Empire Strikes Back 'CAP-2 Captivator' mini-rig, by Palitoy, boxed.

A slightly more valuable version of this toy has a yellow sticker on the packaging and included a free 'Bossk' action figure.

c1982

£12-18　　　**W&W**

A Star Wars – Return of the Jedi 'Imperial Shuttle' vehicle, by Palitoy, boxed.

c1983　　　　18in (45.5cm) high

£180-220　　　　　　　　　　**W&W**

A Star Wars Micro Collection 'Death Star Escape' action playset, by Kenner.

c1982 7in (18cm) wide

£30-40 W&W

A Star Wars die-cast 'Y-Wing Fighter', by Palitoy, boxed, in mint condition.

Die-cast vehicles were issued in boxes and on card blister packs. The boxed versions are much more desirable. Some of the boxed versions of the Y-Wing were issued with special backgrounds and these can be worth nearly three times as much as this example.

1978-80 10.5in (26.5cm) wide

£50-80 W&W

A Star Wars Micro Collection 'Hoth Ion Cannon' action play set, by Kenner, boxed.

c1982 7in (18cm) wide

£15-25 W&W

A Star Wars Micro Collection 'Hoth Generator Attack' action play set, by Kenner, boxed.

c1982 7in (18cm) wide

£12-18 W&W

A Star Wars Micro Machines 'C-3PO/Cantina' transforming action set, by Kenner, boxed.

c1994 11in (28cm) wide

£8-10 W&W

A Star Wars Micro Machines Space 'Rebel Pilot/Hoth' transforming action set, by Kenner, boxed.

c1994 11in (28cm) wide

£8-12 W&W

A Star Wars – The Power of the Force second edition Wonder World set, by Kenner, boxed.

c1995 12.25in (31cm) wide

£4-5 W&W

A Star Wars – The Power of the Force second edition Micro Machines Space 'Planet Tatooine' playset, by Ideal, boxed.

c1995

£6-8 W&W

A Star Wars – Power of the Force second edition 'Speeder Bike', by Kenner, with 'Princess Leia Organa' in Endor gear, with moss air-brushed rocks, boxed.

c1997 9in (23cm) wide

£8-12 W&W

A Star Wars Micro Machines Action Fleet 'Ronto' Battle Pack, by Ideal, in sealed, multi-language bubble pack.

c1997   9.5in (24cm) high

£4-6   **W&W**

A Star Wars Micro Machines Action Fleet 'Dewback' Battle Pack, by Ideal, in sealed, multi-language bubble pack.

9.5in (24cm) high

£4-6   **W&W**

A Star Wars – The Power of the Force second edition electronic 'Talking C-3PO Carry Case', by Kenner, boxed.

1995-99   19in (48.5cm) high

£10-15   **W&W**

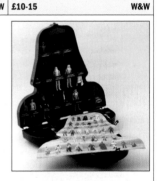

A Star Wars 'Darth Vader' Collector's Case, by Kenner, designed to hold 31 figures and containing 26 figures including 'Boba Fett', 'Han Solo', 'R2-D2', 'Ben Kenobi', 'Leia Organa', and others together with an insert depicting 79 characters from the films.

c1980   14.5in (37cm) high

£50-80   **W&W**

A Star Wars record tote bag, by Disneyland Vista Records.

c1982   7.75in (19.5cm) high

£7-10   **BH**

A Star Wars 'Chewbacca Bandolier Strap', by Kenner, to hold 10 figures, with two containers for accessories.

c1983   33in (84cm) long

£4-8   **W&W**

A limited edition Star Wars Coca Cola glass, for Burger King, picturing Darth Vader, Grand Moff Tarkin and a Stormtrooper.

5.5in (14cm) high

£1-2   **BH**

COLLECTORS' NOTES

■ The origins of the game of chess are uncertain, but it is possible that it developed from a 6th century Indian game called 'Chaturanga', although a similar game evolved in China in the 2nd century BC. The game, as it is played today, uses rules set down in the late 15th century in Italy.

■ The style and design of the boards and pieces has changed over the years as well as the rules. The 'Staunton' set, designed by Nathaniel Cook in 1849, was endorsed by famous player Howard Staunton and bears his name. It is one of the most popular designs and is the official set of the World Chess Federation.

■ The majority of chess sets on the market date from the 18thC and later and, although some earlier examples can be found, they tend to be at the high end of the market. As chess is such an international game, sets were manufactured and exported by a number of countries, each with their own style. These include India, China, Germany and Austria.

■ Sets should be complete and undamaged with the quality, intricacy of carving or manufacture and the materials used also important factors. The inclusion of a chessboard is not important and traditionally they were sold separately to the chess pieces.

■ The market continues to grow with lively internet-based trading. Older, good quality sets are becoming harder to find as demand increases and, as a result, more standard and commonplace sets are rising in value. 'Staunton' sets are doing particularly well at present.

An English 'green-stained' bone barleycorn chess set.

English barleycorn sets are more normally stained red. Green staining is usually associated with chess sets from India.

c1850   *king 4.5in (11.5cm) high*

£300-400   **BLO**

An English ivory chess set.

c1870   *king 3.25in (8cm) high*

£120-180   **BLO**

A mid-19thC English 'Old English' pattern ivory chess set, in a later wooden box with a sliding lid.

c1850   *king 2.25in (6cm) high*

£1,000-1,500   **BLO**

A 19thC Jacques Staunton boxwood and ebony weighted chess set, the white king signed "Jacques London", in a mahogany box.

king 3.5in (9cm) high

£650-750   **BLO**

A Silette Catalin Art Deco style chess set, by Grays of Cambridge, in a wooden box with a sliding lid.

c1925   *king 2.75in (7cm) high*

£180-220   **BLO**

An English aluminium 'aircraft' chess set, made of turned aluminium mechanical parts.

Sets such as these were made from the surplus aluminium stocks left over from aircraft manufacture during WWII.

c1948   *king 3.25in (8cm) high*

£400-500   **BLO**

A US Presidential plastic figural chess set, designed by Alexander Silvery of Graz, Austria.

1972   *king 7in (18cm) high*

£50-80   **BLO**

A 19thC 'Tenniel' pattern bone chess set, the green felt bases probably replaced, in a wooden box with a sliding lid.

The pieces are carved in the style of Sir John Tenniel's (1820-1914) illustrations for Lewis Carroll's 'Alice Though The Looking Glass', which famously included chess pieces among the characters.

king 2.75in (7cm) high

£350-450 BLO

A first version Augarten porcelain figural chess set, Vienna, designed by Mathilde Jaksch-Szendro, with "Vienna" mark on the base.

c1929 king 3.25in (8cm) high

£700-800 BLO

Five German 'Reynard the Fox' carved ivory chess pieces, after the illustrations of Wilhelm von Kaulbach, Erbach, all raised on ebony pedestal bases.

3.25in (8.5cm) high

£220-280 BLO

A 20thC 'Reynard the Fox' figural chess set, in a fitted presentation case.

king 4.25in (11cm) high

£450-550 BLO

A mid-20thC European carved ivory 'Egyptology' chess set, in a wooden box.

Despite being relatively modern, this set is well carved in ivory with a popular Egyptian theme.

king 3.25in (8cm) high

£6,000-8,000 BLO

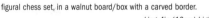

A 20thC Bohemian 'Royal Dux' type porcelain figural chess set.

king 4.25in (11cm) high

£250-350 BLO

An early to mid-20thC German carved wood and glass-mounted figural chess set, in a walnut board/box with a carved border.

king 4in (10cm) high

£450-550 BLO

A 20thC German 'Nutcracker' Christmas-themed painted wooden chess set, in a painted wooden box.

king 3.25in (8.5cm) high

£180-220 BLO

An early 1970s British politicians resin figural chess set, the red side as Labour, the blue side as Conservatives, the king shown.

king 5in (12cm) high

£350-450 BLO

A CLOSER LOOK AT A CHESS SET

The set was officially known as 'The Reds vs The Whites', but became known as 'The Communists vs The Capitalists'.

The use of boats as rooks is a typical feature of Russian chess sets.

This set was in production from 1920 until 1939 and depicts the 'evils' of the Capitalist State.

The Communist pieces are shown as either soldiers of the Red Army or healthy agrarian or industrial workers.

The Capitalist king is portrayed as the grisly figure of Death holding a human thighbone as his sceptre, while the pawns are workers bound up in the chains of slavery.

A Soviet Propaganda 'Communists vs Capitalists' porcelain chess set, Lomonosov State Factory, Leningrad, designed by Natalia Danko (1892-1942) and Yelena Danko (1898-1942).

1923-28   *king 4.25in (11cm) high*

£8,000-12,000   **BLO**

A 19thC Chinese export Staunton-style ivory chess set, Cantonese.

Although this set is clearly derived from the Staunton style pioneered by Jacques, the style of both the knight and the flat, angular-type carving of the screws reveal that it is, in fact, Cantonese.

king 2.75in (7cm) high

£220-280   **BLO**

A late 20thC Chinese hardstone figural chess set, Hong Kong.

king 1.5in (4cm) high

£180-220   **BLO**

A late 19thC Sumatran carved wooden 'Deity' chess set.

king 4in (10cm) high

£450-550   **BLO**

A 20thC Indian enamel and silver-coloured metal king chess piece, Jaipur, in the form of an elephant with howdah and parasol.

4in (10cm) high

£150-200   **BLO**

A 1950s northern Indian Islamic ivory chess set, with a wooden board/box with squares in ebony and ivory.

king 1.75in (4.5cm) high

£550-650   **BLO**

FIND OUT MORE...

Master Pieces: The Architecture of Chess, by Gareth Williams, published by Viking Press and Apple Press, 2000.

Musée International de Jeu d'Eche (The International Museum of Chess), Chateau de Clairvaux, 86140 Scorbe-Clairvaux, France.

US Chess Hall of Fame & Museum. US Chess Centre, 1501 M Street NW, Washington DC, 20005, USA.

A Lenormano card game, by Stralsund (North-east Germany), tax stamp "Deutsches Reich No. 4, 30Pf.", in a original cardboard box.

£8-12　　　　　　**WDL**

A German 'Schach – Dame und Mühle' army field games set, including a set of embossed card chess counters and a folding board, boxed.

c1942

£60-80　　　　　　**BLO**

A Spears 'Enid Blyton's Noddy Theatre' game, boxed.

Box 15.5in (39.5cm) wide

£100-150　　　　　　**GAZE**

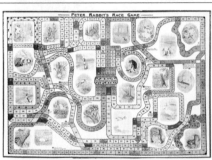

A Peter Rabbit Race board game, published by Frederick Warne & Co, London, complete with board, die, rule sheet and cast metal figural counters, boxed.

This is the favoured first edition of the game, which came with metal figures made by the toy soldier manufacturer Johillco. It is in excellent and complete condition, hence its high value.

c1925　　　　　*Board 29.5in (75cm) wide*

£400-500　　　　　　**BLO**

A Subbuteo table soccer game, Continental Club edition, with catalogue for 1971-72.

Box 18in (45.5cm) wide

£30-40　　　　　　**GAZE**

A Relum table soccer board game, made in Hungary, boxed.

Box 20.5in (52cm) wide

£12-18　　　　　　**GAZE**

An Ideal 'Battling Tops' game, complete.

14in (35.5cm) wide

£35-40　　　　　　**DTC**

An Ideal 'Poppin Hoppies' game.

c1968　　　　*18.5in (47cm) high*

£30-40　　　　　　**DTC**

A 'Twiggy' game, by MB Games.

The object of the game is to cover Twiggy's face with matching cards.

c1967　　　　*19in (48.5cm) wide*

£60-70　　　　　　**NOR**

TOYS & GAMES

An Atari VCS 2600 games console, with two games and a joystick.

c1977   10.5in (267cm) wide

£40-50   **PC**

An Interton Electronic Video 3000 game console, by Grundig, retailed by Dixons.

c1978   12.5in (31.5cm) wide

£30-40   **PC**

A Merlin 'Tic-Tac-Toe' game, by Parker Bros., made in Germany.

c1978   Box 10.25in (26cm) long

£25-35   **DTC**

A CLOSER LOOK AT A NINTENDO GAME

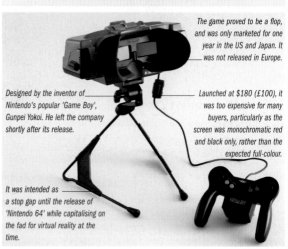

The game proved to be a flop, and was only marketed for one year in the US and Japan. It was not released in Europe.

Designed by the inventor of Nintendo's popular 'Game Boy', Gunpei Yokoi. He left the company shortly after its release.

Launched at $180 (£100), it was too expensive for many buyers, particularly as the screen was monochromatic red and black only, rather than the expected full-colour.

It was intended as a stop gap until the release of 'Nintendo 64' while capitalising on the fad for virtual reality at the time.

A Nintendo 'Virtual Boy' 3-D game system.

c1995

£100-150   **HLJ**

A Mattel 'Armor Battle' hand-held game.

c1978   3.5in (9cm) wide

£20-30   **HLJ**

A Sega Game Gear set, complete with box and accessories.

c1992   8in (20cm) wide

£60-80   **PC**

A Texas Instruments 'Speak & Math'.

One of three popular teaching games released by Texas Instruments that included 'Speak & Spell' and 'Speak & Read'.

c1987   Box 15.5in (39.5cm) long

£25-35   **DTC**

A Rolex WWI military silver wristwatch, with 15-jewel movement.

Rolex was registered in July 1908 by Hans Wilsdorf of Wilsdorf & Davies in London. Founder Wilsdorf started his own wristwatch factory predicting that the wristwatch would overtake the pocket watch for reasons of convenience and fashion. His speculation paid off and by the 1920s the wristwatch had indeed done so. Their more subtle, less 'heavy' watches from the 1950s, particularly in gold, are currently popular with collectors and those choosing to wear them.

1.5in (3.5cm) diam

£400-500 GHOU

A Rolex ladies' silver half-hunter-style wristwatch, with 15-jewel movement.

The 'half-hunter' style reveals the derivation of the earliest wristwatches from pocket watches. 'Half-hunter' pocket watches had an hinged opening metal case over the face with a smaller circular viewing aperture.

1in (3cm) diam

£350-450 GHOU

A 1950s Rolex 'Oyster Perpetual' 18ct gold gentleman's wristwatch.

1.5in (3.5cm) diam

£1,500-2,000 GHOU

A 1950s Rolex 'Oyster Perpetual Datejust' 18ct gold gentleman's wristwatch, with 25-jewel movement.

Among other developments, Rolex are known for their waterproof 'Oyster' case, developed in 1926 and successfully tested as a publicity stunt by cross-Channel swimmer Mercedes Gleitze in 1927. A clever advertising campaign with shop window displays of a Rolex Oyster in an aquarium created huge brand awareness. The 'Perpetual' automatic movement was developed in 1931 to make the watch yet more hermetic, and the automatic date 'Datejust' in 1945.

1.5in (3.5cm) diam

£1,800-2,200 GHOU

A Rolex 'Oysterdate Precision' gentleman's stainless steel wristwatch.

1.5in (3.5cm) diam

£400-600 GHOU

A Rolex 'Oyster Perpetual' stainless steel gentleman's wristwatch.

1.5in (3.5cm) diam

£400-600 GHOU

A Rolex 'Oysterdate Precision' gentleman's stainless steel bracelet wristwatch.

1.5in (3.5cm)

£500-700 GHOU

A Rolex 'Oyster Perpetual' ladies' gold and steel bracelet wristwatch.

1in (2.5cm) diam

£600-800 GHOU

A Rolex 'Oyster Perpetual GMT Master' stainless steel gentleman's bracelet wristwatch.

The GMT Master was released in 1955 and was innovative as it allowed the wearer to read the time in any two time zones.

1.75in (4.5cm) diam

£1,000-1,500   **GHOU**

An Omega military stainless steel wristwatch.

Military watches typically have black faces, to avoid bright reflections, and a durable, inexpensive stainless steel casing. Many will also bear military markings.

1.5in (3.5cm) diam

£300-500   **GHOU**

An Omega military stainless steel wristwatch, with 15-jewel movement.

1.5in (3.5cm) diam

£280-320   **GHOU**

An Omega 'Seamaster' automatic stainless steel gentleman's wristwatch, with 17-jewel movement.

The Seamaster was released in 1948 and is noted for its precision and reliability at sea. In 1993, a model was produced that can function at 1,000 feet (305 meters) beneath sea level. James Bond, played by Pierce Brosnan, in 'Goldeneye' and 'Tomorrow Never Dies' also used a Seamaster Professional Diver's watch, albeit one dramatically modified by Q!

1.25in (3.5cm) diam

£220-280   **GHOU**

A 1970s Omega 'Chronostop' gentleman's stainless steel wristwatch, with 17-jewel movement.

1.5in (3.5cm) diam

£220-280   **GHOU**

An Omega Constellation chronometer automatic gold-plated and stainless steel gentleman's wristwatch.

1.5in (3.5cm) diam

£220-280   **GHOU**

An Omega 'Speedmaster' professional chronograph gentleman's bracelet watch, together with papers and box.

Omega was founded in 1848 in Switzerland by Louis Brandt. It is renowned for its precision and reliability and has been the official timekeeper for 21 Olympic Games. The 'Speedmaster' is one of Omega's key watches and is the only watch to have passed NASA's stringent tests allowing it to be used on space missions, including one to the Moon. Look out for examples with commemorative moon landing engravings, which can fetch £600 or more.

1972   *1.75in (4cm) diam*

£600-800   **GHOU**

An Omega 'Seamaster Memomatic' alarm gentleman's stainless steel bracelet wristwatch, with 19-jewel movement.

1.5in (4cm) diam

£300-500   **GHOU**

A CLOSER LOOK AT A BOREL WRISTWATCH

A 1970s Buler manual wristwatch, deep red plastic bezel, with red dial, clear back, on original red plastic strap.

Face 1.5in (4cm) wide

£30-50   **SEVW**

Ernest Borel, founded in 1859, in Switzerland, is notable for its innovation and avant-garde designs, particularly in the 1950s and 1960s.

The Cocktail watch is one of their most popular, and can be found with five designs including the star (shown here), a flower, a sun, arrows and a wheel.

The dial moves around as time passes, creating a 'kaleidoscopic' optical effect. Ladies' watches were made in different colours.

It was sold in all parts of the Caribbean but not widely on the US mainland, or in the UK, so you had to travel or be given it as a gift to have one.

A 1950s/60s Ernest Borel men's 'Cocktail' watch, with skeleton display back and 17-jewel movement.

£120-180   **ML**

A Bulova 'flip top' photo wristwatch, with 17-jewel movement and gold-filled case.

The face and bezel of the watch flips up to reveal a space for a small photograph underneath.

c1940

£200-300   **ML**

A Bulova gold-filled doctor's watch, with three registers and 12-jewel movement.

This watch with three dials or 'registers' is rare.

1.75in (4.5cm) high

£500-700   **ML**

A 1930s Elgin sterling silver wristwatch, with hand-painted porcelain dial.

This watch uses a pocket watch movement.

£120-180   **ML**

An early 1920s Elgin two-tone gold-filled wristwatch, with 15-jewel movement and Art Deco enamelled details on the case.

£200-300   **ML**

A Gruen 'Precision' 14ct gold rectangular curved wristwatch, with 17-jewel movement, the back dated "8/16/26".

c1926   *1.5in (3.5cm) long*

£220-280   **GHOU**

A CLOSER LOOK AT AN ELGIN WRISTWATCH

The almost 'digital' readout, known as a jump hour, was called a 'Direct Reader' by Elgin.

The style of the case with its fin-like chevron form not only sums up a style of the age, but also mimics the hands of a watch at ten minutes to two.

A Hamilton Flight II asymmetric wristwatch, with 22-jewel movement, gold-filled case and sterling silver dial.

The shape of the case as well as the material it is made from make this watch very desirable. During the 1990s it was re-released due to demand.

1961

£1,200-1,800   ML

'Lord Elgin' denoted higher-end watches by Elgin, as shown by the 23-jewel movement – high quality movement jump hour watches are scarce.

This was the style of watch worn by Elvis Presley, although the case on his model was square.

A Lord Elgin 'Chevron' jump hour or 'Direct Reader' watch, with 23-jewel movement and gold-filled case, together with its original flex gold-filled metal band.

The inclusion of the original metal band makes this more desirable.

c1958

£180-220   ML

A Harwood 'Harwood Automatic' first production automatic wristwatch, with 15-jewel movement and stainless steel case.

Harwood was the first company to produce automatic wristwatches, from around 1926-28. Note the lack of a side winding and setting knob on the bezel. John Harwood had noticed the unreliability of watches in the trenches of WWI, identifying the hole around the winding stem to be the point of entry for dust and moisture etc. By removing this and placing the setting mechanism inside, he began to develop the idea of a self-winding watch. He had designed the mechanism by 1922 and had registered it a few years later. Watches based on his innovative design are still being made.

c1928

£200-300   ML

An Illinois Watch Co 14ct gold cased gentleman's wristwatch.

1in (2.5cm) long

£280-320   GHOU

A 1930s Illinois Watch Co 'Manhattan' or 'New Yorker' white gold-filled gentleman's wristwatch, with engraved and signed case, two-tone dial with radium numbers.

Founded in 1870 in Springfield, Illinois, and releasing its first watch (The Stuart) in 1872, the company became known as the Illinois Watch Company in 1885. During the late 1920s it was bought out by Hamilton and produced watches for them until 1932 when the last true Illinois watch was produced. After that, all Illinois watches were produced in Hamilton factories.

£200-300   ML

A 1940s/50s Ingersoll Walt Disney Productions Mickey Mouse watch, with chrome-plated case, in very good working condition.

This watch originally sold for $3.95, and the value is largely dependent on whether or not it works, as the movement is hard to fix.

£80-120   ML

An International Watch Co. 18ct gold mid-size wristwatch.

1in (2.5cm) diam

£280-320   **GHOU**

A 1960s Jaeger 'Le Coultre' automatic gentleman's stainless steel wristwatch.

1.5in (3.5cm) diam

£400-500   **GHOU**

A Longines 'Flagship' 18ct gold automatic gentleman's wristwatch.

c1970   *1.5in (3.5cm) diam*

£280-320   **GHOU**

A rare late 1950s/60s Longines gold-filled asymmetrical gentleman's wristwatch, unusually designed dial with starburst.

£220-280   **ML**

A Movado triple calendar stainless steel gentleman's wristwatch, boxed.

1.5in (3.5cm) diam

£280-320   **GHOU**

A 1940s Girard Perregaux stainless steel gentleman's wristwatch, with 17-jewel movement and rare day, month and date dial.

£200-250   **ML**

A Piaget 18ct gold gentleman's wristwatch, with 18-jewel movement.

1.25in (3cm) diam

£800-1,200   **GHOU**

A 1970s Sicura Chrono 2 wristwatch, steel bezel, black dial, date function, original steel bracelet.

Face 1.75in (4.5cm) wide

£100-150   **SEVW**

A Tag Heuer 'Super Professional' automatic gentleman's steel bracelet wristwatch.

1.75in (4.5cm) diam

£220-280   **GHOU**

A Tissot Bruce McLaren automatic gentleman's stainless steel bracelet wristwatch.

1.75in (4.5cm) diam

£200-250   **GHOU**

A 1970s Tudor 'Oyster Prince Date-Day' stainless steel gentleman's wristwatch, the day and date apertures with Spanish text.

Tudor is a sub-brand of Rolex and hence many Tudor watches bear stylistic resemblances to Rolex watches.

1.5in (3.5cm) diam

£400-500   **GHOU**

A CLOSER LOOK AT A MOVADO POCKET WATCH

Known as the 'Ermeto', this style of watch was released by Movado in 1926 and remained popular until the 1940s.

This example is more valuable as the crocodile skin covering is in excellent condition and the face has a moonphase and day, date and month. Look out for cases with enamel, precious metals or lacquered decoration.

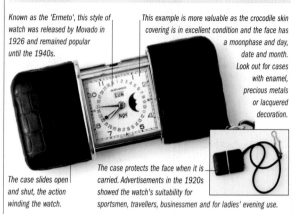

The case slides open and shut, the action winding the watch.

The case protects the face when it is carried. Advertisements in the 1920s showed the watch's suitability for sportsmen, travellers, businessmen and for ladies' evening use.

A Movado steel-cased travelling watch.

These effectively became the predecessor of the travelling alarm clock, as they had a bracket on the back to allow them to stand up and be viewed from bed.

c1930   Case 2in (5cm) wide

£400-600   **F**

A 1920s Waltham 18ct gold gentleman's wristwatch, with 15-jewel movement.

1.25in (3.5cm) diam

£200-250   **GHOU**

A Waltham 'jump hour' or 'direct read' gold-filled gentleman's wristwatch, signed "Waltham".

It is very unusual for this watch to be signed.

c1930

£150-250   **ML**

A Waltham 14ct yellow gold gentleman's open-face pocket watch, engraved "JAC" monogram.

1.75in (4.5cm) diam

£60-80   **DAW**

A Canadian gold-filled pocket watch, by James Thomson of Bracebridge, the case marked "A.W.C. Co."

c1915   1.5in (4cm) wide

£50-80   **TAB**

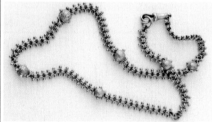

A gold mesh-link albert chain, with fancy ball spacers.

One end of an Albert would hold a pocket watch and the other a winding key, pencil or similar useful small object. The watch and item were put in waistcoat pockets, with the chain being pulled through one of the waistcoat buttonholes across the front of the waistcoat. They are seldom used now.

£180-220   **F**

COLLECTORS' NOTES

- The first range of Swatch watches was released in 1983. These 12 models were plain, quartz wristwatches, almost unrecognisable compared to today's brightly coloured, heavily designed models. Since then, the company has released two new collections each year.

- They were cheaply produced, having only 51 components, and were marketed at an affordable price, although later limited editions were issued at a higher price. They proved extremely popular and by 1984 over one million units had been produced.

- A number of designers and artists worked with Swatch including Keith Haring, Kiki Picasso, Vivienne Westwood and Christian Lacroix. Today their models are some of the most sought-after by collectors.

- Interest in collecting Swatches reached a peak in the early 1990s. While the market is not as strong as it once was, there is a smaller but stable marketplace for discontinued and limited edition models and a number of dedicated websites and internet auctions.

- Watches in mint, unworn condition, with the original packaging and paperwork are the most desirable and will hold their value better.

- Check the strap is original and correct for the model, as a replaced strap can reduce the value by half. Straps are also easily marked by the buckle, reducing the value, however, there are methods for removing bends.

A Swatch first series wristwatch, GB 402, with date function.

This was also made with a day and date function, model GB 702, which is worth about the same amount.

1983

£150-200 ML

A Swatch first series wristwatch, GB 103, with black strap.

Early examples were plain in comparison to later models and this was one of the most decorative watches made in the first year of production.

1983

£250-350 ML

A Swatch 'Don't Be Too Late' wristwatch, GA 100, from the Memphis series, with original packaging.

1984

£250-350 ML

A Swatch 'Stormy Weather' wristwatch, GV 100, from the Dream Waves series.

Look for the rare version without the Swatch logo at '12', worth about double the normal version.

1989

£70-100 ML

A Swatch 'Nicholette' ladies wristwatch, LB 105, from the Plaza series, with black strap.

This model was relaunched in 1987.

1985

£80-120 ML

A Swatch 'Chrono-Tech' wristwatch, GB 403, from the Aspen series.

This was remade in 1985.

1984

£120-180 ML

A Swatch 'Pinstripe' wristwatch, GA 102, from the Carlton series.

1985

£80-120 ML

A Swatch 'Gamela' ladies wristwatch, LG 102, from the Blue Nile series.

1986

£70-100 ML

A CLOSER LOOK AT A 'JELLY FISH' SWATCH

The original version was designed by artist Maryse Schmid and was first issued in 1984. Swatch states that only 200 examples were produced.

The metal dial ring was added to the 1985 version, which is worth double this version.

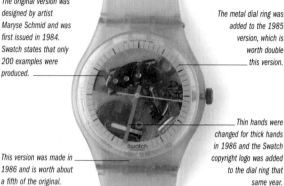

This version was made in 1986 and is worth about a fifth of the original.

Thin hands were changed for thick hands in 1986 and the Swatch copyright logo was added to the dial ring that same year.

A Swatch 'Jelly Fish' wristwatch, GK 100.

The clear plastic strap and case turns yellow and then brown over time.

1986

£120-180 ML

A Swatch 'Nine to Six' wristwatch, GB 117, from the Neo Geo series.

1987

£25-35 ML

A Swatch 'Marmorata' wristwatch, GB 119, from the Blake's series.

1987

£25-35 ML

A Swatch 'Needles' wristwatch, GB 408, from the Signal Corps series.

1988

£25-35 ML

A Swatch 'Sandy Mountains' wristwatch, GG 105, from the Dream Waves series, with replaced textured green strap.

With the correct strap, this watch would be worth at least twice as much.

1989

£30-50 ML

A Swatch 'Tango Azul' wristwatch, GX 401, from the Buenos Aires series, with blue leather strap.

1989

£70-100 ML

A Swatch 'Sun Lady' ladies wristwatch, LB 125, from the True Stories series.

1989

£35-45 ML

A Swatch 'Cosmesis' wristwatch, GM 103, from the Mendini's series.
1990

£20-40   ML

A Swatch 'Hacker's Reward' wristwatch, GK 122, from the Alu Cosmos series.
1990

£15-25   ML

A Swatch 'Patchwork' Pop wristwatch, PWB 150, from the Dancing Art series, with fabric strap.
1990

£70-100   ML

A Swatch 'Reflector' wristwatch, GK 130, from the Bright Flags series, with textured yellow strap.
1991

£40-50   ML

A Swatch 'Stalefish' wristwatch, GG 113, from the Cold Fever series.
1991

£40-50   ML

A Swatch 'Sappho' ladies' wristwatch, LV 101, from the Lovefrieze series, with decorated strap.
1991

£40-60   ML

A Swatch 'C.E.O.' wristwatch, GX 709, from the Grande Capo series, with blue leather strap.
1992

£50-70   ML

A Swatch 'Cappuccino' wristwatch, GG 121, from the Sunday Brunch series.

This was designed by artist Jennifer Morla and was sold with a 'Sunday Brunch' cup. It was also available as a 'Maxi'.
1993

£30-40   ML

A Swatch 'Alabama' chronograph, SCN 105/106.
1993

£50-70   ML

A Swatch 'IOC 100' wristwatch, SCZ 101, from the Olympic series, commemorating 100 years of the International Olympic Committee.
1994
£40-50   ML

A Swatch 'Ramarro' automatic wristwatch, SAK 111, from the Automatic series, with green leather strap.
1994
£40-50   ML

A Swatch 'Cigar' wristwatch, GK 250, from the 1,000 Years series, with 'cigar' strap.
1997
£30-40   ML

A Swatch 'Atlanta Laurels' wristwatch, GZ 145, from the Honor & Glory series commemorating the 1996 Atlanta Olympics, with original packaging.
1995
£60-80   ML

A limited edition Swatch 'Light Tree' Pop wristwatch, GZ 152, from the Christmas series and an edition of 20,000, with LED-tipped fronds, contained in a red Christmas bauble, and original card box.
1996
£100-150   ML

A limited edition Swatch 'Stripp' Scuba 200 wristwatch, SDN 120, designed by Andrea Arrigoni, with extra costumes to dress the spaceman, with original box and packaging.
1996
£30-50   ML

A Swatch 'Centipede' wristwatch, GG 143, from the Comic Hour series.
Designed by the artist Jamie Hewlett, who is better known for his 'Tank Girl' comic series and for his work with the band Gorillaz.
1997
£30-40   ML

Two late 1980s Swatch Guard Too watch guards, mint and boxed.
£4-5   ML

A Swatch clear plastic replacement watch strap.
1995-6   6.75in (17.5cm) high
£15-25   ML

FIND OUT MORE...

www.swatch.com – Official company and collectors' club website.

W.B.S. Collector's Guide for Swatch Watches, *by Wolfgang Schneider, published by W B S Marketing, October 1992.*

Almost Everything You Need to Know About Dealing & Collecting Swatch Watches, *by Roy Ehrhardt, Larry Ehrhardt, published by Heart of America Pr, October 1996.*

COLLECTORS' NOTES

■ Wedding collectables have grown in popularity over the past few years. Most of the items collected comprise the many forms of bride and groom wedding cake tops (known as 'toppers' in the US). Other themed items bulk out and add variety to a collection. Look for salt and pepper shakers and bride and groom dolls by companies such as Madame Alexander and Peggy Nisbet.

■ Consider the material, plastic is more likely to have been used from the 1940s/50s onwards, with bisque being used from the 1920/30s and other ceramics from the 1920s-50s. The complexity, quality and age of the piece will have an effect on value, with better made, earlier pieces from the 1920s fetching higher prices.

■ Examine clothing as styles of wedding dresses can help to date a piece, as can the hairstyles and general appearance of a piece. As a groom's morning dress or tuxedo has remained largely unchanged, this is usually not worth considering. However, look out for grooms wearing other clothes such as army or navy dress uniforms as these are very desirable.

A 1930s German bride and groom painted ceramic salt and pepper set, stamped "GERMANY" on the base.

2.5in (6.5cm) high

£30-40   **DAC**

A 1920s Kewpie-style bisque bride and groom, with crêpe paper clothing, wire-jointed arms and cardboard pads.

These were probably made for the top of a wedding cake. Look out for more accurate Kewpie wedding dolls as these are sought-after, often fetching over £60-80.

3in (7.5cm) high

£25-35   **DAC**

A 1950s small bisque fabric and netting dancing bride and groom.

3.25in (8cm) high

£15-25   **DAC**

A 1930s painted plaster cake top of an elegant, elongated bride and groom.

6.75in (17cm) high

£25-35   **DAC**

A 1950s painted plaster wedding cake top with glass dome, the base moulded "Our Wedding Day".

3.5in (9cm) high

£25-35   **DAC**

A 1940s cake top, made from plaster, wire, netting, fabric flowers and ribbon.

8.5in (21.5cm) high

£15-25   **DAC**

A 1940s painted plaster, wire-framed, card, material and ribbon wedding cake top.

8.5in (22cm) high

£40-60   **DAC**

WEIRD & WONDERFUL

An unusual late 19thC iron animal trap.

£70-100   **MUR**

A 17thC iron dog collar.

Dog collars are often mistaken for early 19thC slave collars, albeit less spikey examples. This early example has spikes to protect the dog's neck from attack by wolves.

20in (51cm) long

£70-90   **ANAA**

An unusual late 19thC iron animal trap.

£40-50   **MUR**

An unmarked metal grip, with internal row of spikes and restricted scissor type action.

Some objects were made for a specific use that has since fallen out of favour, or has become obsolete. Despite the opinions of a number of experts, nobody has yet identified this tool. If you know what is, please write in to the address at the front of the book. the first correct answer wins copy of next year's book!

5in (12.5cm) long

NPA   **PC**

A brass and steel hat measure, in very good condition.

£50-80   **MUR**

A horn from a German mine, salvaged by Lieutenant W.J. Carver of the Royal Naval Volunteer Reserve in 1918, mounted with descriptive plaque.

The horn was a trigger on German sea mines used extensively during WWI. A mine filled with around 500lbs of explosive would be anchored to the seabed with a wire, and covered with screw-in 'horns'. Any passing ship touching one of these horns would complete a circuit and cause the mine to explode. This example would probably have been unscrewed from a live mine.

c1918

£70-100   **BA**

A rare original US patent mouse trap, by Christopher Lang of Newark, Ohio, together with a copy of the patent of May 23, 1871.

This is one of the rarest mouse traps ever made.

1871

£250-350   **ATK**

A stilton cheese spoon, with ivory and silver handle, in very good condition.

£60-80   **MUR**

A late 19thC French painted canvas and carved wood ventriloquist dummy's head, with glass eyes.

9in (23cm) high

£300-400　　　　　　　　　　　**ANAA**

A highly realistic fairground horror show painted rubber severed hand.

6.75in (17cm) long

£8-12　　　　　　　　　　　**ANAA**

A collegiate skull porcelain tankard, the metal lid with porcelain inlay and dedication, dated.

The skull is a popular 'memento mori', a reminder of the passing of life and eventual death.

1900　　　　*6in (15cm) high*

£180-220　　　　　　　　　**WDL**

A mid-19thC German commemorative or souvenir bisque model of Chang and Eng, the Siamese twins, impressed on base "Siam Willinc".

Chang and Eng were born in Siam (now Thailand) in 1811 and were the source of the term 'Siamese Twins'. After being 'discovered' by an English merchant, they travelled in Europe and the USA extensively, taking part in many shows. They eventually settled in North Carolina, assumed the surname 'Bunker', married two sisters and fathered 21 children between them (no pun intended). They died aged 63 in 1874.

3.25in (8.5cm) high

£40-50　　　　　　　　　　　**ANAA**

A wooden auctioneer's gavel, with commemorative stamp for Phillips' the Auctioneers bicentenary celebrations 1796-1996 and original box.

1996　　　*4in (10cm) long*

£12-18　　　　　　　　　　　**GORL**

A set of 1930s 'square-dance band' carved and painted wooden figures, base and box stamped "Made in Japan".

Each figure is delicately hand-carved and painted and appears to have no specific use apart from being tiny decorative objects. They are also found in different dance types.

Box 5.5in (14cm) wide

£70-90　　　　　　　　　　　**SM**

A rare set of four brown leather pony or donkey tennis lawn boots, with straps and stamped flower motifs.

These were worn by ponies pulling lawnmowers across lawns and lawn tennis courts to stop their hooves ruining the turf.

Each 4.75in (12cm) high

£180-220　　　　　　　　　　　**MSA**

GLOSSARY

A

Acid etching A technique using acid to decorate glass to produce a matt or frosted appearance.

Albumen print Photographic paper is treated with egg white (albumen) to enable it to hold more light-sensitive chemicals. After being exposed to a negative, the resulting image is richer with more tonal variation.

Applied Refers to a separate part that has been attached to an object, such as a handle.

B

Baluster A curved form with a bulbous base and a slender neck.

Base metal A term describing common metals such as copper, tin and lead, or metal alloys, that were usually plated in gold or silver to imitate more expensive and luxurious metals. In the US, the term 'pot metal' is more commonly used.

Bisque A type of unglazed porcelain used for making dolls from c1860 to c1925.

Boards The hard covers of a book.

Brassing On plated items, where the plating has worn off to reveal the underlying base metal.

C

Cabochon A large, protruding, polished, but not faceted, stone.

Cameo Hardstone, coral or shell that has been carved in relief to show a design in a contrasting colour.

Cameo glass Decorative glass made from two or more layers of differently coloured glass, which are then carved or etched to reveal the colour beneath.

Cartouche A framed panel, often in the shape of a shield or paper scroll, which can be inscribed.

Cased Where a piece of glass is covered with a further layer of glass, sometimes of a contrasting colour, or clear and colourless. In some cases the casing will be further worked with cutting or etching to reveal the layer beneath.

Charger A large plate or platter, often for display, but also for serving.

Chromolithography A later development of 'lithography', where a number of printing stones are used in succession, each with a different colour, to build up a multi-coloured image.

Composition A mixture including wood pulp, plaster and glue used as a cheap alternative to bisque in the production of dolls' heads and bodies.

Compote A dish, usually on a stem or foot, to hold fruit for the dessert course.

Craze/Crazed/Crazing A network of fine cracks in the glaze caused by uneven shrinking during firing. It also describes plastic that is slowly degrading and has the same surface patterning.

Cuenca A technique used for decorating tiles where moulded ridges separate the coloured glazes, like the 'cloisonne' enamelling technique.

Cultured pearl A pearl formed when an irritant is artificially introduced to the mollusc.

D

Damascened Metal ornamented with inlaid gold or silver, often in wavy lines. Commonly found on weapons or armour.

Dichroic Glass treated with chemicals or metals that cause it to appear differently coloured depending on how it is viewed in the light.

Diecast Objects made by pouring molten metal into a closed metal die or mould.

Ding A very small dent in metal.

E

Earthenware A type of porous pottery that requires a glaze to make it waterproof.

Ebonized Wood that has been blackened with dye to resemble ebony.

E.P.N.S. Found on metal objects and standing for 'electroplated nickel silver', meaning the object is made from nickel which is then electroplated with silver.

F

Faience Earthenware that is treated with an impervious tin glaze. Popular in France from the 16th century and reaching its peak during the 18th century.

Faceted A form of decoration where a number of flat surfaces are cut into the surface of an object such as a gem or glass.

Faux A French word for 'false'. The intention is not to deceive fraudulently but to imitate a more costly material.

Finial A decorative knob at the end of a terminal, or on a lid.

Foliate Leaf and vine motifs.

G

Guilloché An engraved pattern of interlaced lines or other decorative motifs, sometimes enamelled over with translucent enamels.

H

Hallmark The series of small stamps found on gold or silver that can identify the maker, the standard of the metal and the city and year of manufacture. Hallmarks differ for each country and can consist only of a maker's or a city mark. All English silver made after 1544 was required to be fully marked.

IJKL

Incised Applied to surface decoration or a maker's mark that has been scratched into the surface of an object with a sharp instrument.

Inclusions Used to describe all types of small particles of decorative materials embedded in glass.

Iridescent A lustrous finish that subtly changes colour depending on how light hits it. Often used to describe the finish on ceramics and glass.

Lithography A printing technique developed in 1798 and employing the use of a stone upon which a pattern or picture has been drawn with a grease crayon. The ink adheres to the grease and is transferred to the paper when pressed against it.

MNO

Millefiori An Italian term meaning 'thousand flowers' and used to describe cut, multi-coloured glass canes which are arranged and cased in clear glass. When arranged with the cut side facing the exterior, each circular disc (or short cane) resembles a small flower.

Mint A term used to describe an object in unused condition with no signs of wear and derived from coinage. Truly 'mint' objects will command a premium.

Mount A metal part applied to an object made of ceramic, glass or another material, with a decorative or functional use.

Nappy A shallow dish or bowl with a handle used for drinking.

Opalescent An opal-like, milky glass with subtle gradations of colour between thinner more translucent areas and thicker, more opaque areas.

P

Paisley A stylized design based on pinecones and foliage, often with added intricate decoration. It originated in India and is most often found on fabrics, such as shawls.

Paste (jewellery) A hard, bright glass cut the same way as a diamond and made and set to resemble them.

Patera An oval or circular decorative motif often with a fluted or floral centre. The plural is 'paterae'.

Piqué A decorative technique where small strips or studs of gold are inlaid onto ivory or tortoiseshell on a pattern and secured in place by heating.

Pontil A metal rod to which a glass vessel is attached when it is being worked. When it is removed it leaves a raised disc-shaped 'pontil mark'.

Pot metal Please see 'Base metal'.

Pounce pot A small pot made of wood (treen), silver or ceramic. Found on inkwells or designed to stand alone, it held a gum dust that was sprinkled over parchment to prevent ink from spreading. Used until the late 18th century.

Pressed (Press moulded) Ceramics formed by pressing clay into a mould. Pressed glass is made by pouring molten glass into a mould and pressing it with a plunger.

R

Reeded A type of decoration with thin raised, convex vertical lines. Derived from the decoration of classical columns.

Relief A form of moulded, pressed or carved decoration that protrudes above the surface of an object. Usually in the form of figures of foliate and foliage designs, it ranges in height from 'low' to 'high'.

Repoussé A French term for the raised, 'embossed' decoration on metals such as silver. The metal is forced into a form from one side causing it to bulge.

S

Sgraffito An Italian word for 'little scratch' and used to describe a decorative technique where the outer surface of an object, usually in glazed or coloured ceramic, is scratched away in a pattern to reveal the contrasting coloured underlying surface.

Sommerso Technique developed in Murano in the 1930s. Translates as 'submerged' and involves casing one or more layers of transparent coloured glass within a layer of thick, clear, colourless glass.

Stoneware A type of ceramic similar to earthenware and made of high-fired clay mixed with stone, such as feldspar, which makes it non-porous.

T

Tazza A shallow cup with a wide bowl, which is raised up on a single pedestal foot.

Tooled Collective description for a number of decorative techniques applied to a surface. Includes engraving, stamping, punching and incising.

V

Vermeil Gold-plated silver.

Vesta case A small case or box, usually made from silver, for carrying matches.

W

White metal Precious metal that is possibly silver, but not officially marked as such.

Y

Yellow metal Precious metal that is possibly gold, but not officially marked as such.

INDEX TO ADVERTISERS

CLIENT	PAGE NO.
Dorling Kindersley	82
Live Auctioneers	91
Dorling Kindersley	109

Fragile Design	271
The Prop Store, London	283
Auction Team Köln	463
Wallis & Wallis	531

KEY TO ILLUSTRATIONS

Every collectable illustrated in DK Collectables Price Guide 2006 by Judith Miller has a letter code that identifies the dealer or auction house that sold it. The list below is a key to these codes. In the list, auction houses are shown by the letter A and dealers by the letter D. Some items may have come from a private collection, in which case the code in the list is accompanied by the letter P. Inclusion in this book in no way constitutes or implies a contract or a binding offer on the part of any of our contributors to supply or sell the goods illustrated, or similar items, at the prices stated.

AAC (A)
Alderfer Auction Company
501 Fairground Road,
Hatfield, PA 19440, USA
Tel: 001 215 393 3000
info@alderferauction.com
www.alderferauction.com

AB (A) (D)
Auction Blocks
The Auction Blocks,
P.O. Box 2321, Shelton, CT
06484, USA
Tel: 001 203 924 2802
auctionblocks@aol.com
www.auctionblocks.com

ABAA (D)
Abacus Antiques
No longer trading

ABIJ (D)
Aurora Bijoux
Tel: 001 215 872 7808
aurora@aurorabijoux.com
www.aurorabijoux.com

ADE (D)
Art Deco Etc
73 Upper Gloucester Road,
Brighton, Sussex BN1 3LQ
Tel: 01273 329 268
Mob: 07971 268 302
johnclark@artdecoetc.co.uk

AG (D)
Antique Glass at Frank Dux Antiques
33 Belvedere
Bath BA1 5HR
Tel: 01225 312 367
m.hopkins@antique-glass.co.uk
www.antique-glass.co.uk

AGI (A)
Aurora Galleries International
30 Hackamore Lane, Suite 2,
Bell Canyon, CA 91307 USA
Tel: 001 818 884 6468
vcampbell@auroraauctions.com
www.auroragalleriesonline.com

AGO (D)
Anona Gabriel
Otford Antiques Centre,
26-28 High Steet, Otford,
Sevenoaks,
Kent TN15 9DF
Tel: 01959 522 025
info@otfordantiques.co.uk

AGR (D)
Adrian Grater
Georgian Village, Camden
Passage, London N1
Tel: 0208 579 0357
adriangrater@tiscali.co.uk

AL (D)
Andrew Lineham Fine Glass
PO Box 465,
Chichester, PO18 8WZ
Tel: 01243 576 241
Mob: 07767 702 722
andrew@antiquecolouredglass.com
www.antiquecolouredglass.com

AMJ (D)
American Jazz
Box 302 Ossining
NY 10562, USA
Tel: 001 914 762 5519
amjazz@optonline.net

ANAA (D)
Anastacia's Antiques
617 Bainbridge Street,
Philadelphia, PA 19147 USA
Tel: 001 215 928 0256

ART (D)
Artius Glass
Street, Somerset BA16 0AN
Tel: 01458 443694
Mob: 07860 822666
Wheeler.Ron@ic24.net
www.artiusglass.co.uk

ATK (A)
Auction Team Köln
Postfach 50 11 19, Bonner Str.
528-530, D-50971 Cologne,
Germany
Tel: 00 49 221 38 70 49
auction@breker.com
www.breker.com

B&H (A)
Burstow & Hewett
Lower Lake, Battle, East Sussex,
TN33 0AT
Tel: 01424 772374
auctions@burstowandhewett.co.uk
www.burstowandhewett.co.uk

B (A)
Dreweatt Neate, Tunbridge Wells
Auction Hall, The Pantiles,
Tunbridge Wells,
Kent TN2 5QL
Tel: 01892 544 500
tunbridgewells@dnfa.com
www.dnfa.com

BA (D)
Branksome Antiques
370 Poole Road, Branksome,
Poole,Dorset BH12 1AW
Tel: 01202 763 324

BAD (D)
Beth Adams
Unit G043/4, Alfies Antique
Market, 13 Church Street,
Marylebone, London NW8 8DT
Mob: 07776 136 003
www.alfiesantiques.com

BB (D)
Barbara Blau
South Street Antiques Market
615 South 6th Street,
Philadelphia,
PA 19147-2128 USA
Tel: 001 215 739 4995/592
0256
bbjools@msn.com

BBR (A)
BBR Auctions
Elsecar Heritage Centre,
Nr Barnsley,
South Yorkshire, S74 8HJ
Tel: 01226 745156
www.onlinebbr.com

BEJ (D)
Bébés et Jouets
c/o Lochend Post Office,
165 Restalrig Road,
Edinburgh EH7 6HW
Tel: 0131 332 5650
bebesjouets@tiscali.co.uk

BEL (A)
Belhorn Auction Services
PO Box 20211, Columbus, OH
43220, USA
Tel: 001 614 921 9441
auctions@belhorn.com
www.belhorn.com

BER (D)
Bertoia Auctions
2141 Demarco Drive, Vineland
NJ 08360 USA
Tel: 001 856 692 1881
toys@BertoiaAuctions.com
www.bertoiaauctions.com

BEV (D)
Beverley
30 Church Street,
London NW8 8EP
Tel: 020 7262 1576
www.alfiesantiques.com

BGD (A)
Boisgirard et Associés, SVV
1, rue de La Grange-Batelière,
75009 Paris, France
Tel: 00 33 1 47 70 81 36
boisgirard@club-internet.fr
www.boisgirard.com

BGL (D)
Block Glass Ltd
blockglss@aol.com
www.blockglass.com

BH (D)
Black Horse Antique Showcase
2222 North Reading Road,
Denver PA, 17517 USA
Tel: 001 717 335 3300
www.antiques-showcase.com

BIB (D)
Biblion
1-7 Davies Mews,
London W1K 5AB
Tel: 020 7629 1374
info@biblion.com
www.biblion.com

BLO (A)
Bloomsbury Auctions
Bloomsbury House, 24 Maddox
Street, London W1 S1PP
Tel: 020 7495 9494
info@bloomsburyauctions.com
www.bloomsburyauctions.com

BR (D)
Beyond Retro
110-112 Cheshire Street,
London E2 6EJ
Tel: 020 7613 3636
sales@beyondretro.com
www.beyondretro.com

BRB (D)
Bauman Rare Books
535 Madison Avenue, New York,
NY10022 USA
Tel: 001 212 751 1011
brb@baumanrarebooks.com
www.baumanrarebooks.com

BRI (A)
Brightwells Fine Art
Fine Art Saleroom, Easters
Court, Leominster,
Herefordshire HR6 0DE
Tel: 01568 611 122
fineart@brightwells.com
www.brightwells.co.uk

BY (D)
Bonny Yankauer
bonnyy@aol.com

C (A)
Cottees
The Market, East Street,
Wareham, Dorset BH20 4NR
Tel: 01929 552 826
auctions@cottees.fsnet.co.uk
www.auctionsatcottees.co.uk

CA (A)
Chiswick Auctions
1 Colville Road,
London W3 8BL
Tel: 020 8992 4442
sales@chiswickauctions.co.uk
www.chiswickauctions.co.uk

CARS (D)
C.A.R.S. of Brighton
4/4a Chapel Terrace Mews,
Kemptown, Brighton,
Sussex BN2 1HU
Tel: 01273 622 722
cars@kemptown-
brighton.freeserve.co.uk
www.eurosurf.com/Cars

CAT (D)
CatalinRadio.com
Tel: 001 419 824 2469
steve@catalinradio.com
www.catalinradio.com

CBE (P)
Christina Bertrand
tineke@rcn.com

CGPC (P)
Cheryl Grandfield Collection

CHEF (A)
Cheffins
Clifton House, 1&2 Clifton
Road, Cambridge CB1 7EA
Tel: 01223 213 343
fine.art@cheffins.co.uk
www.cheffins.co.uk

CHS (D)
China Search
P.O. Box 1202, Kenilworth,
Warwickshire CV8 2WW
Tel: 01926 512 402
helen@chinasearch.co.uk
www.chinasearch.co.uk

CL/CLG (D)
Chisholm Larsson
45 8th Avenue, New York NY
10011 USA
Tel: 001 212 741 1703
info@chisholm-poster.com
www.chisholm-poster.com

CLV (A)
Clevedon Salerooms
The Auction Centre, Kenn Road,
Kenn, Clevedon,
Bristol, BS21 6TT
Tel: 01934 830 111
Fax: 01934 832 538
info@clevedonsalerooms.co.uk
www.clevedon-salerooms.com

COB (D)
Cobwebs
78 Old Northam Road,
Southampton SO14 0PB
Tel: 02380 227 458
www.cobwebs.uk.com

CRIS (D)
Cristobal
26 Church Street,
London NW8 8EP
Tel: 020 7724 7230
steven@cristobal.co.uk
www.cristobal.co.uk

CVS (D)
Cad Van Swankster at The Girl
Can't Help It
Alfies Antiques Market,
Stand G100 & G90 & G80,
13-25 Church Street,
Marylebone, London NW8 8DT
Tel: 020 7724 8984
cad@sparklemoore.com

DAC (D)
Dynamite Antiques &
Collectibles
eb625@verizon.net

DAW (A)
Dawsons Auctioneers &
Appraisers, now trading as
Dawson & Nye
128 American Road, Morris
Plains, NJ 07950, USA
Tel: 001 973 984 6900
info@dawsons.org
www.dawsons.org

DC (P)
Dust Collectors

DD (D)
Decodame.com
853 Vanderbilt Beach Road,
PMB 8, Naples FL34108 USA
Tel: 001 239 514 6797
info@decodame.com
www.decodame.com

DETC (D)
Deco Etc
122 West 25th Street
New York, NY 10001 USA
Tel: 001 212 675 3326
deco_etc@msn.com
www.decoetc.net

DH (D)
Huxtins
david@huxtins.com
www.huxtins.com

DMI (P)
David Midgley
dgmidgley@yahoo.co.uk

DN (A)
Dreweatt Neate
Donnington Priory Salerooms,
Donnington, Newbury, Berkshire
RG14 2JE
Tel: 01635 553 553
donnington@dnfa.com
www.dnfa.com/donnington

DRA (A)
David Rago Auctions
333 North Main Street,
Lambertville, NJ 08530 USA
Tel: 001 609 397 9374
info@ragoarts.com
www.ragoarts.com

DSC (D)
British Doll Showcase
squibbit@ukonline.co.uk
www.britishdollshowcase.co.uk

DTC (D)
Design20c
Tel: 0794 609 2138
sales@design20c.co.uk
www.design20c.com

EAB (D)
Anne Barrett
Otford Antiques & Collectables
Centre,
28-28 High Street, Otford, Kent
TN15 9DF
Tel: 01959 522 025
info@otfordantiques.co.uk
www.otfordantiques.co.uk

ECLEC (D)
Eclectica
2 Charlton Place, Islington,
London N1
Tel: 020 7226 5625
liz@eclectica.biz
www.eclectica.biz

EG (A)
Edison Gallery
Tel: 001 617 359 4678
glastris@edisongallery.com
www.edisongallery.com

EOH (D)
The End of History
548 1/2 Hudson Street,
New York, NY 10014 USA
Tel: 001 212 647 7598

EPO (D)
Elaine Perkins
Otford Antiques & Collectables
Centre,
28-28 High Street, Otford,
Kent TN15 9DF
Tel: 01959 522 025
info@otfordantiques.co.uk
www.otfordantiques.co.uk

ERI (D)
Eri Jones
Otford Antiques & Collectables
Centre,
28-28 High Street, Otford,
Kent TN15 9DF
Tel: 01959 522 025
info@otfordantiques.co.uk
www.otfordantiques.co.uk

EVL (D)
Eve Lickver
P.O. Box 1778 San Marcos CA
92079, USA
Tel: 001 760 761 0868

EWC (P)
Emma Wilson Collection
Tel: 07989 493 831

F (A)
Fellows & Sons
Augusta House, 19 Augusta
Street, Hockley, Birmingham
B18 6JA
Tel: 0121 212 2131
info@fellows.co.uk
www.fellows.co.uk

FD (D)
Fragile Design
8 Lakeside,
The Custard Factory, Digbeth,
Birmingham B9 4AA, UK
Tel: 0121 693 1001
info@fragiledesign.com
www.fragiledesign.com

FJA (D)
Feljoy Antiques
Shop 3, Angel Arcade, Camden
Passage, London N1 8EA
Tel: +44 (0)20 7354 5336
Joy@feljoy-antiques.demon.co.uk
www.chintznet.com/feljoy/

FRE (A)
Freeman's
1808 Chestnut Street,
Philadelphia, PA 19103 USA
Tel: 001 215 563 9275
info@freemansauction.com
www.freemansauction.com

GAZE (A)
Thos. Wm. Gaze & Son
Diss Auction Rooms. Roydon
Road, Diss, Norfolk IP22 4LN
Tel: 01379 650 306
sales@dissauctionrooms.co.uk
www.twgaze.com

GC (P)
Graham Cooley Collection
Mob: 07968 722 269
graham.cooley@metalysis.com

GCL (D)
Claude Lee
The Ginnel Antiques Centre,
off Parliament Street, Harrogate,
North Yorks HG1 2RB
Tel: 01423 508 857
info@theginnel.com
www.redhouseyork.co.uk

GEW (D)
Eileen Wilson at The Ginnel
The Ginnel Antiques Centre,
off Parliament Street,
Harrogate, North Yorks HG1 2RB
Tel: 01423 508 857
info@theginnel.com
www.redhouseyork.co.uk

GGRT (D)
Gary Grant Choice Pieces
18 Arlington Way,
London EC1R 1UY
Tel: 020 7713 1122

GHOU (D)
Gardiner Houlgate
Bath Auction Rooms,
9 Leafield Way, Corsham,
Nr Bath, SN13 9SW
Tel: 01225 812 912
auctions@gardiner-
houlgate.co.uk
www.gardinerhoulgate.co.uk

GL (D)
Gary Lickver
P.O. Box 1778, San Marcos, CA
92079 USA
Tel: 001 760 744 5686

GORL (A)
Gorringes, Lewes
15 North Street, Lewes, East
Sussex, BN7 2PD
Tel: 01273 472 503
clientservices@gorringes.co.uk
www.gorringes.co.uk

GORW (A)
Gorringes, Worthing
44/46 High Street
Worthing
West Sussex BN11 1LL
clientservices@gorringes.co.uk
www.gorringes.co.uk

GROB (D)
Geoffrey Robinson
Stand GO77-78 & GO91-92,
Alfies Antiques Market,
13-25 Church Street,
London, NW8 8DT
Tel: 020 7723 0449
www.alfiesantiques.com

GWRA (A)
Gloucestershire
Worcestershire Railway
Auctions
Tel: 01684 773 487
01386 760 109
www.gwra.co.uk

H&G (D)
Hope and Glory
131A Kensington Church
Street, London W8 7LP
Tel: 020 7727 8424

HA (A)
Hunt Auctions
75 East Ulwchlan Avenue, Suite
130, Exton, PA 19341 USA
Tel: 001 610 524 0822
info@huntauctions.com
www.huntauctions.com

HGS (D)
Harper General Store
10482 Jonestown Road,
Annville, PA 17003 USA
Tel: 001 717 865 3456
lauver5@comcast.com
www.harpergeneralstore.com

HH (P)
Holiday Happenings

HLJ (D)
Hugo Lee-Jones
Tel: 01227 375 375
Mob: 07941 187 2027
electroniccollectables@hotmail.com

JDJ (A)
James D Julia Inc
P.O. Box 830, Fairfield, Maine
04937 USA
Tel: 001 207 453 7125
jjulia@juliaauctions.com
www.juliaauctions.com

JJ (D)
Junkyard Jeweler
sales@junkyardjeweler.com
www.junkyardjeweler.com

JL (D)
Eastgate Antiques
Alfies Antiques Market,
Stand S007/009,
13-25 Church Street,
London NW8 8DT
Tel: 01206 822712
info@alfiesantiques.com

KAU (A)
Auktionhaus Kaupp
Schloss Sulzburg, Hauptstrasse
62, 79295 Sulzburg, Germany
Fax: 00 49 7634 5038 50
auktionen@kaupp.de
www.kaupp.de

KF (D)
Kari Flaherty Collectables
Tel: 02476 445 627
kfckarl@aol.com
www.kfcollectables.co.uk

KNK (D)
Kitsch-N-Kaboodle
South Street Antiques Market,
615 South 6th Street,
Philadelphia,
PA 19147-2128 USA
Tel: 001 215 382 1354
kitschnkaboodle@yahoo.com

L (D)
Luna
23 George Street,
Nottingham NG1 3BH
Tel: 0115 924 3267
info@luna-online.co.uk
www.luna-online.co.uk

L&T (A)
Lyon and Turnbull Ltd.
33 Broughton Place,
Edinburgh EH1 3RR
Tel: 0131 557 8844
info@lyonandturnbull.com
www.lyonandturnbull.com

LAN (A)
Lankes
Triftfeldstrasse 1, 95182,
Döhlau Germany
Tel: +49 (0)928 69 50 50
info@lankes-auktionen.de
www.lankes-auktionen.de

LB (D)
Linda Bee
Stand L18-21, Grays Antique
Market, 58 Davies Street,
London W1Y 2LP
Tel: 020 7629 5921
lindabee@grays.clara.net
www.graysantiques.com

LC (A)
Lawrence's Fine Art
Auctioneers
The Linen Yard, South Street,
Crewkerne, Somerset TA18 8AB
Tel: 01460 73041
enquiries@lawrences.co.uk
www.lawrences.co.uk

LCA (D)
Lights, Camera, Action
6 Western Gardens, Western
Boulevard, Aspley,
Nottingham, HG8 5GP
Tel: 0115 913 1116
nick.straw@lca-autographs.co.uk
www.lca-autographs.co.uk

LG (D)
Legacy
No longer trading

LOB (D)
Louis O'Brien
Tel: 01276 32907

MA (D)
Manic Attic
Alfies Antiques Market,
Stand S48/49,
13 Church Street,
London NW8 8DT
Tel: 020 7723 6105
manicattic@alfies.clara.net

MC (D)
Metropolis Collectibles, Inc.
873 Broadway, Suite 201, New
York, NY 10003, USA
Tel: 001 212 260 4147
orders@metropoliscomics.com
www.metropoliscomics.com

MGT (D)
Mary & Geoff Turvil
Vintage Compacts, Small
Antiques & Collectables
Tel: 01730 260 730
mary.turvil@virgin.net

MHC (P)
Mark Hill Collection
Mob: 07798 915 474
stylophile@btopenworld.com

MHT (D)
Mum Had That
info@mumhadthat.com
www.mumhadthat.com

MI (D)
Mood Indigo
181 Prince Street, New York, NY
10012, USA
Tel: 001 212 254 1176
info@moodindigonewyork.com
www.moodindigonewyork.com

MILLB (D)
Million Dollor Babies
Tel: 001 518 885 7397

ML (D)
Mark Laino
South Street Antiques Market,
615 South 6th Street,
Philadelphia, PA 19147-2128
Tel: 001 215 739 4995

MM (A)
Mullock Madeley
The Old Shippon, Wall-under-
Heywood, Church Stretton,
Shropshire SY6 7DS
Tel: 0169 477 1771
info@mullockmadeley.co.uk
www.mullockmadeley.co.uk

MSA (A)
Manfred Schotten Antiques
109 Burford High Street,
Burford, Oxfordshire OX18 4RH
Tel: 01993 822 302
enquiries@schotten.com
www.schotten.com

MTS (D)
The Multicoloured Time Slip
Unit S002, Alfies Antiques
Market, 13-25 Church Street,
London NW8 8DT, UK
Mob: 07971 410 563
dave_a_cameron@hotmail.com

MUR (D)
Tony Murland Auctions
78 High Street, Needham
Market, Suffolk, IP6 8AW
Tel: 01449 722 992
tony@antiquetools.co.uk
www.antiquetools.co.uk

NAI (D)
Nick Ainge
Tel: 01832 731063
Mob: 07745 902343
nick@ainge1930.fsnet.co.uk
decoseek.decoware.co.uk

NBC (D)
Nick Batt Collection
Tel: 020 8455 0719

NOR (D)
Neet-O-Rama
93 West Main Street,
Somerville, NJ 08876 USA
Tel: 001 908 722 4600
www.neetstuff.com

NPC (P)
No Pink Carpet
Tel: 01785 249 802
www.nopinkcarpet.com

ON (A)
Onslows
The Coach House, Manor Road,
Stourpaine, Dorset, DT11 8TQ
Tel: 01258 488 838
enquiries@onslows.co.uk
www.onslows.co.uk

P&I (D)
Paola & Iaia
Unit S057-58, Alfies Antiques
Market, 13-25 Church Street,
London NW8 8DT
Tel: 07751 084 135
paolaeiaialondon@hotmail.com

PC (P)
Private Collection

PCC (P)
Peter Chapman Collection
pgcbal1@supanet.com

PSA (A)
Potteries Specialist Auctions
271 Waterloo Road, Cobridge,
Stoke-on-Trent ST6 3HR
Tel: 01782 286 622
enquiries@potteriesauctions.com
www.potteriesauctions.com

PSI (D)
Paul Simons
5 Georgian Village, Islington,
London N1
Mob: 07733 326 574
pauliobanton@hotmail.com

PSL (D)
The Propstore of London
Great House Farm, Chenies,
Rickmansworth, Herts WD3 6EP
Tel: 01494 766 485
steve.lane@propstore.co.uk
www.propstore.co.uk

PWE (A)
Philip Weiss Auction Galleries
1 Neil Court, Oceanside,
NY 11572, USA
Tel: 001 516 594 073
info@philipweissauctions.com
ww.philipweissauctions.com

RDL (A)
David Rago/Nicholas Dawes
Lalique Auctions
333 North Main Street,
Lambertville, NJ 08530 USA
Tel: 001 609 397 9374
Fax: 001 609 397 9377
info@ragoarts.com
www.ragoarts.com

REN (D)
Rennies Seaside Modern
47 The Old High Street,
Folkestone, Kent CT20 1RN
info@rennart.co.uk
www.rennart.co.uk

RETC (D)
Retro Etc
13-14 Market Walk, Market
Square, Old Amersham,
Bucks HP7 0DF
Tel: 07810 482900
info@retroetc.com
www.retroetc.com

ROS (A)
Rosebery's
74-76 Knight's Hill, West
Norwood, London SE27 0JD
Tel: 020 8761 2522
auctions@roseberys.co.uk
www.roseberys.co.uk

RP (D)
Rosie Palmer
Otford Antiques & Collectable
Centre, 26-28 High Street,
Otford, Kent TN15 9DF
Tel: 01959 522 025
info@otfordantiques.co.uk
www.otfordantiques.co.uk

ROW (A)
Rowley Fine Arts
8 Downham Road, Ely,
Cambridge CB6 1AH
Tel: 01353 653020
www.rowleyfineart.com

RSJ (D)
Roger & Susan Johnson
Tel: 001 940 686 5686
czarmann@aol.com

RWA (D)
Richard Wallis Antiks
Tel: 020 8529 1749
info@richardwallisantiks.co.uk
www.richardwallisantiks.com

SAS (A)
Special Auction Services
Kennetholme, Midgham,
Nr. Reading, Berkshire, RG7 5UX
Tel: 0118 971 2949
commemorative@aol.com
www.invaluable.com/sas

SCG (D)
Gallery 1930 Susie Cooper
18 Church Street, Marylebone,
London NW8 8EP
Tel: 020 7723 1555
gallery1930@aol.com
www.susiecooperceramics.com

SEVW (D)
70s Watches
graham@gettya.freeserve.co.uk
www.70s-watches.com

SH (D)
Sara Hughes Vintage Compacts,
Antiques & Collectables
Mob: 0775 9697 108
sara@sneak.freeserve.co.uk
http://mysite.wanadoo-
members.co.uk/sara_compacts/

SI (D)
Da Silva Interiors
Stand G095, Alfies Antiques
Market, 13 Church Street,
London NW8 BDT
Tel: 020 7723 0449
dasilvainteriors@hotmail.com
www.alfiesantiques.com

SK (A)
Skinner, Inc.
The Heritage on the Garden
63 Park Plaza, Boston, MA
02116 USA
Tel: 001 617 350 5400
also at
357 Main Street, Bolton, MA
01740, USA
Tel: 001 978 7796 241
www.skinnerinc.com

SM (D)
Sparkle Moore at The Girl
Can't Help It
Alfies Antiques Market, Stand
G100 & G90 & G80, 13-25
Church Street, Marylebone,
London NW8 8DT
Tel: 020 7724 8984
sparkle@sparklemoore.com
www.sparklemoore.com

SOTT (D)
Sign of the Tymes
Mill Antiques Center,
12 Morris Farm Road,
Lafayette, NJ 07848 USA
Tel: 001 973 383 6028
jhap@nac.net
www.millantiques.com

SSC (P)
Sue Scrivens Collection

STC (D)
Seaside Toy Center
Joseph Soucy
179 Main St, Westerly, RI
02891 USA
Tel: 001 401 596 0962

STE (D)
Cloud Glass
info@cloudglass.com
www.cloudglass.com

SUM (D)
Sue Mautner Costume
Jewellery
No longer trading.

SWA (D)
Swann Galleries Image Library
104 East 25th Street, New York,
NY 10010 USA
Tel: 001 212 254 4710
swann@swanngalleries.com
www.swanngalleries.com

SWO (A)
Sworders
14 Cambridge Road, Stansted
Mountfitchet, Essex, CM24 8BZ
Tel: 01279 817 778
auctions@sworder.co.uk
www.sworder.co.uk

TA (A)
333 Auctions LLC
333 North Main Street,
Lambertville, NJ 08530 USA
Tel: 001 609 397 9374
info@ragoarts.com
www.ragoarts.com

TAB (D)
Take-A-Boo Emporium
1927 Avenue Road, Toronto,
Ontario M5M 4A2 Canada
Tel: 001 416 785 4555
swinton@takeaboo.com
www.takeaboo.com

TCA (A)
Transport Car Auctions
14 The Green, Richmond,
Surrey TW9 1PX
Tel: 020 8940 2022
oliver@tc-auctions.com
www.tc-auctions.com

TCM (D)
Twentieth Century Marks
Whitegates, Rectory Road,
Little Burstead, Nr Billericay,
Essex CM12 9TR
Tel: 01268 411 000
Mob: 07831 778 992 /
07788 455 006
info@20thcenturymarks.co.uk
www.20thcenturymarks.co.uk

TCS (D)
The Country Seat
Huntercombe Manor Barn,
Nr Henley on Thames,
Oxon RG9 5RY
Tel: 01491 641349
info@whitefriarsglass.com
www.whitefriarsglass.com

TCT (D)
The Calico Teddy
Tel: 001 410 433 9202
calicteddy@aol.com
www.calicoteddy.com

TDG (D)
The Design Gallery
5 The Green, Westerham,
Kent TN16 1AS
Tel: 01959 561 234
sales@designgallery.co.uk
www.designgallery.co.uk

TGM (D)
The Glass Merchant
Tel: 07775 683 961
as@titan98.freeserve.co.uk

TP (D)
Tenth Planet
Unit 37a, Vicarage Field
Shopping Centre, Ripple Road,
Barking, Essex IG11 8DQ
Tel: 020 8591 5357
sales@tenthplanet.co.uk
www.tenthplanet.co.uk

TR (D)
Terry Rodgers & Melody LLC
30 & 31 Manhattan Art &
Antique Center,
1050 2nd Avenue,
New York, NY 10022 USA
Tel: 001 212 758 3164
melodyjewelnyc@aol.com

TYA (D)
Yank Azman
Toronto Antiques Centre, 276
King Street West, Toronto,
Ontario, M5V 1J2 Canada
Tel: 001 416 260 5662
yank@yank.ca
www.antiquesformen.com

VE (D)
Vintage Eyeware of New York,
USA
Tel: 001 646 319 9222

VEC (A)
Vectis Auctions Ltd
Fleck Way, Thornaby, Stockton
on Tees TS17 9JZ
Tel: 01642 750 616
admin@vectis.co.uk
www.vectis.co.uk

VET (D)
Vetro & Arte Gallery
Calle del Cappeller 3212,
Dorsoduro, Venice 30123 Italy
Tel: +39 (0)41 522 8525
contact@venicewebgallery.com
www.venicewebgallery.com

VSC (D)
Vintage Sports Collector
3920 Via Solano, Palos Verdes
Estates, CA 90274 USA
Tel: 001 310 375 1723

VZ (A)
Von Zezschwitz
Friedrichstrasse 1a, 80801
Munich, Germany
Tel: 00 49 89 38 98 930
www.von-zezschwitz.de

W&W (A)
Wallis & Wallis
West Steet Auction Galleries,
Lewes, East Sussex BN7 2NJ
Tel: 01273 480 208
auctions@wallisandwallis.co.uk
www.wallisandwallis.co.uk

WAC (D)
What A Character!
hugh@whatacharacter.com
bazuin32@aol.com
www.whatacharacter.com

WDL (D)
Kunst-Auktionshaus Martin
Wendl
August-Bebel-Straße 4, 07407
Rudolstadt, Germany
Tel: 011 49 3672 424 350
www.auktionshaus-wendl.de

WW (A)
Woolley & Wallis
51-61 Castle Street, Salisbury,
Wiltshire SP1 3SU
Tel: 011 44 172 424 500
www.woolleyandwallis.co.uk

ZDB (D)
Zardoz Books
20 Whitecroft, Dilton Marsh,
Westbury, Somerset BA13 4DJ
Tel: 01373 865 371
www.zardozbooks.co.uk

DIRECTORY OF SPECIALISTS

If you wish to have any item valued, it is advisable to contact the dealer or specialist in advance to check that they will carry out this service and whether there is a charge. While most dealers will be happy to help you with an enquiry, do remember that they are busy people. Telephone valuations are not possible. Please mention the DK Collectables Price Guide 2006 by Judith Miller when making an enquiry.

ADVERTISING

Huxtins
david@huxtins.com
www.huxtins.com

ANIMATION ART

Animation Art Gallery
13-14 Great Castle St, London
W1W 8LS
Tel: 020 7255 1456
Fax: 0207 436 1256
gallery@animaart.com
www.animaart.com

ART DECO

Art Deco Etc
73 Gloucester Road, Brighton,
Sussex, BN1 3LQ
Tel: 01273 329 268
johnclark@artdecoetc.co.uk

AUTOGRAPHS

Lights, Camera Action
6 Western Gardens, Western
Boulevard, Aspley, Nottingham,
HG8 5GP, UK
Tel: 0115 913 1116
Mob: 07970 342 363
nick.straw@lca-
autographs.co.uk
www.lca-autographs.co.uk

AUTOMOBILIA

C.A.R.S. of Brighton
4/4a Chapel Terrace Mews,
Kemptown, Brighton, Sussex
BN2 1HU, UK
Tel: 01273 622 722
Fax: 01273-601960
cars@kemptown-
brighton.freeserve.co.uk
www.eurosurf.com/Cars

BOOKS

Biblion
1-7 Davies Mews, London W1K
5AB
Tel: 020 7629 1374
info@biblion.com
www.biblion.com

Zardoz Books
20 Whitecroft, Dilton Marsh,
Westbury, Somerset BA13 4DJ
Tel: 01373 865 371
www.zardozbooks.co.uk

BONDS & SHARES

Intercol
43 Templar's Crescent, Finchley,
London N3 3QR
Tel: 020 8349 2207
sales@intercol.co.uk
www.intercol.co.uk

CERAMICS

Beth Adams
Unit GO43/4, Alfies Antique
Market, 13 Church Street,
Marylebone, London NW8 8DT
Mob: 07776 136 003
www.alfiesantiques.com

Nick Ainge
Tel: 01832 731 063
Mob: 07745 902 343
nick@ainge.co.uk
decoseek.decoware.co.uk

Beverley
30 Church Street,
London NW8 8EP, UK
Tel: 020 7262 1576
www.alfiesantiques.com

China Search
P.O. Box 1202, Kenilworth,
Warwickshire CV8 2WW
Tel: 01926 512 402
Fax: 01926 859 311
helen@chinasearch.uk.com
www.chinasearch.uk.com

Eastgate Antiques
S007/009, Alfies Antique
Market, 13 Church St,
Marylebone, London NW8 8DT
Tel: 0207 258 0312
info@alfiesantiques.com
www.alfiesantiques.com

Feljoy Antiques
Shop 3, Angel Arcade, Camden
Passage, London N1 8EA
Tel: 020 7354 5336
Fax: 020 7831 3485
joy@feljoy-antiques.demon.co.uk
www.chintznet.com/feljoy

Adrian Grater
Georgian Village, Camden
Passage,London N1
Tel: 020 8579 0357
adriangrater@tiscali.co.uk

Susie Cooper at Gallery 1930
18 Church St, London NW88EP
Tel: 020 7723 1555
Fax: 020 7735 8309
gallery1930@aol.com
www.susiecooperceramics.com

Gary Grant Choice Pieces
18 Arlington Way, London
EC1R1UY
Tel: 020 7713 1122

Gillian Neale Antiques
P.O. Box 247, Aylesbury
HP201JZ
Tel: 01296 423754
Fax: 01296-334601
gillianneale@aol.com
www.gilliannealeantiques.co.uk

Louis O'Brien
Tel: 01276 32907

Mad Hatter
Admiral Vernon Antiques
Market, Unit 83, 141-149
Portobello Rd, London W11
Tel: 020 7262 0487
madhatter.portobello@virgin.net

Rick Hubbard Art Deco
3 Tee Court, Bell St, Romsey,
Hampshire SO518GY
Tel: 01794 513133
www.rickhubbard-artdeco.co.uk

Geoffrey Robinson
Stand GO77-78 & GO91-92,
Alfies Antiques Market, 13-25
Church Street, London, NW8 8DT
Tel: 020 7723 0449
unknown@unknown.com
www.alfiesantiques.com

Rogers de Rin
76 Royal Hospital Rd, Paradise
Walk, London SW34HN
Tel: 020 7352 9007
Fax: 020 7351 9407
rogersderin@rogersderin.co.uk
www.rogersderin.co.uk

Sue Norman
Antiquarius, Stand L4, 135
King's Rd, London SW34PW
Tel: 020 7352 7217
sue@sue-norman.demon.co.uk
www.sue-norman.demon.co.uk

CIGARETTE CARDS

Carlton Antiques
43 Worcester Road, Malvern,
Worcestershire WR14 4RB
Tel: 01684 573 092
dave@carlton-antiques.com
www.carlton-antiques.com

COINS

Intercol
43 Templar's Crescent, Finchley,
London N3 3QR
Tel: 020 8349 2207
sales@intercol.co.uk
www.intercol.co.uk

COMICS

Book & Comic Exchange
14 Pembridge Rd, London W11
Tel: 020 7229 8420

The Book Palace
Bedwardine Road, Crystal
Palace, London SE19 3AP
Tel: 020 8768 0022
Fax: 020 8768 0563
www.bookpalace.com

COMMEMORATIVE WARE

Hope & Glory
131a Kensington Church St,
London W87LP
Tel: 020 7727 8424

Recollections

5 Royal Arcade, Boscombe,
Bournemouth, Dorset BH14BT
Tel: 01202 304 441

Susan Rees
Tel/Fax: 01582 715 555

COSTUME & ACCESSORIES

Beyond Retro
110-112 Cheshire St, London
E2 6EJ
Tel: 020 7613 3636
sales@beyondretro.com
www.beyondretro.com

**Cad van Swankster at The Girl
Can't Help It**
Alfies Antiques Market, Stand
G100 & G90 & G80, 13-25
Church St, London NW88DT
Tel: 020 7724 8984
cad@sparklemoore.com

Cloud Cuckoo Land
6 Charlton Place, London, N1
Tel: 020 7354 3141

Decades
20 Lord St West, Blackburn
BB2 1JX
Tel: 01254 693320

Fantiques
Tel: 020 8840 4761
paula.raven@ntlworld.com

Linda Bee
Grays Antiques Market, 1-7
Davies Street, London, W1Y 2LP
Tel/Fax: 020 7629 5921
www.graysantiques.com

Old Hat
66 Fulham High St, London
SW63LQ
Tel: 020 7610 6558

**Sparkle Moore at The Girl
Can't Help It**
Alfie's Antiques Market, Shop
G100 & G90 & G80, 13-25
Church St, London NW8 8DT
Tel: 020 7724 8984
sparkle.moore@virgin.net
www.sparklemoore.com

Vintage Modes
Grays Antiques Market, 1-7
Davies Mews, London W1Y 5AB
Tel: 020 7409 0400
info@vintagemodes.co.uk
www.vintagemodes.co.uk

Vintage to Vogue
28 Milsom Street, Bath, Avon
BA1 1DG
Tel: 01225 337 323

COSTUME JEWELLERY

Cristobal
26 Church St, London NW8
8EP
Tel: 020 7724 7230
steven@cristobal.co.uk
www.cristobal.co.uk

Eclectica
2 Charlton Place, Islington,
London N1
Tel/Fax: 020 7226 5625
liz@eclectica.biz
www.eclectica.biz

Richard Gibbon
34/34a Islington Green,
London N1 8DU
Tel: 020 7354 2852
neljeweluk@aol.com

Ritzy
7 The Mall Antiques Arcade,
359 Upper Street, London N1
0PD
Tel: 020 7704 0127

William Wain at Antiquarius
Stand J6, Antiquarius, 135
King's Road, London SW3 4PW
Tel: 020 7351 4905
w.wain@btopenworld.com

DOLLS

Bébés & Jouets
c/o Lochend Post Office, 165
Restalrig Road, Edinburgh EH7
6HW, UK
Tel: 0131 332 5650
bebesjouets@tiscali.co.uk

British Doll Showcase
squibbit@ukonline.co.uk
www.britishdollshowcase.co.uk

Sandra Fellner
A18-A19 and MB026, Grays
Antique Market
Tel: 020 8946 5613
sandrafellner@blueyonder.co.uk
www.graysantiques.com

Victoriana Dolls
101 Portobello Rd, London
W112BQ
Tel: 01737 249 525
Fax: 01737 226 254
heather.bond@totalserve.co.uk

Yesterday Child
1 Angel Arcade,
118 Islington High St London
N1 8EG
Tel: 020 7354 1601

FIFTIES, SIXTIES & SEVENTIES

Twentieth Century Marks
Whitegates, Rectory Road,
Little Burstead, Nr Billericay,
Essex CM12 9TR
Tel: 01268 411 000
info@20thcenturymarks.co.uk
www.20thcenturymarks.co.uk

Design20c
Tel: 01276 512329 / 0794
609 2138
sales@design20c.co.uk
www.design20c.com

Fragile Design
8 Lakeside,
The Custard Factory, Digbeth,
Birmingham B9 4AA, UK
Tel: 0121 693 1001
info@fragiledesign.com
www.fragiledesign.com

Luna
23 George Street, Nottingham
NG1 3BH, UK
Tel: 0115 924 3267
info@luna-online.co.uk
www.luna-online.co.uk

Manic Attic
Alfie's Antiques Market, Stand
S48/49, 13-25 Church St,
London NW8 8DT
Tel: 020 7723 6105
manicattic@alfies.clara.net

The Multicoloured Timeslip
Unit S002, Alfies Antiques
Market, 13-25 Church Street,
London NW8 8DT, UK
Mob: 07971 410 563
d_a_cameron@hotmail.com

Retro Etc
13-14 Market Walk, Market
Square, Old Amersham,
Bucks HP7 0DF
Tel: 07810 482900
info@retroetc.com
www.retroetc.com

FILM & TV

The Prop Store of London
Great House Farm, Chenies,
Rickmansworth, Herts WD3 6EP
Tel: 01494 766 485
steve.lane@propstore.co.uk
www.propstore.co.uk

GENERAL

Alfie's Antiques Market
13-25 Church St, London
NW88DT
Tel: 020 7723 6066
info@alfiesantiques.com
www.alfiesantiques.com

Bartlett St Antiques Centre
5-10 Bartlett St, Bath BA12QZ
Tel: 01225 466689
Monday to Saturday (excluding
Wednesday)

Bermondsey Market
Crossing of Long Lane &
Bermondsey St, London SE1
Tel: 020 7351 5353
Every Friday morning from 5am

Brackley Antique Cellar
Drayman's Walk, Brackley,
Northamptonshire NN13 6BE
Tel: 01280 841 841

Camden Passage Market
Camden Passage, Islington,
London N1
Every Wednesday morning

The Ginnel Antiques Centre
Off Parliment St, Harrogate,
North Yorkshire HG1 2RB
Tel: 01423 508 857
info@theginnel.com
www.redhouseyork.co.uk

Great Grooms at Hungerford
Riverside House, Charnham St,
Hungerford,
Berkshire RG17 0EP
Tel: 01488 682 314
Fax: 01488 686677
antiques@great-grooms.co.uk
www.great-grooms.co.uk

Heanor Antiques Centre
11-3 Ilkeston Rd, Heanor,
Derbyshire
Tel: 01773 531 181
sales@heanorantiquescentre.co.uk
www.heanorantiquescentre.co.uk

Heskin Hall Antiques
Heskin Hall, Wood Lane,
Heskin, Chorley,
Lancashire PR7 5PA
Tel: 01257 452 044

Otford Antiques and Collectors Centre
26-28 High St, Otford,
Kent TN15 9DF
Tel: 01959 522 025
Fax: 01959 525858
info@otfordantiques.co.uk
www.otfordantiques.co.uk

Portobello Rd Market
Portobello Rd, London W11
Every Saturday from 6am

Potteries Antique Centre
271 Waterloo Rd, Cobridge,
Stoke-on-Trent ST6 3HR
Tel: 01782 201 455
Fax: 01782 201518
www.potteriesantiquecentre.com

The Swan Antiques Centre
High Street Tetsworth, nr Thame,
Oxfordshire OX9 7AB
Tel: 01844 281777
Fax: 01844 281770
antiques@theswan.co.uk
www.theswan.co.uk

Woburn Abbey Antiques Centre
Woburn Abbey, Woburn,
Bedfordshire MK179WA
Tel: 01525 290 333
www.woburnantiques.co.uk

GLASS

Andrew Lineham Fine Glass
Tel/Fax: 01243 576 241
Mob: 07767 702 722
andrew@antiquecolouredglass.com
www.antiquecolouredglass.com

Antique Glass at Frank Dux Antiques
33 Belvedere, Lansdown Road,
Bath, Avon BA1 5HR
Tel/Fax: 01225 312 367
www.antique-glass.co.uk

Francesca Martire
Stand F131-137, First Floor,
13-25 Alfies Antiques Market,
13 Church St, London NW8ORH
Tel: 020 7724 4802
www.francescamartire.com

Jeanette Hayhurst Fine Glass
32A Kensington Church St.,
London W8 4HA
Tel: 020 7938 1539

Mum Had That
info@mumhadthat.com
www.mumhadthat.com

Nigel Benson 20th Century Glass
Mob: 07971 859 848
nigel@20thcentury-glass.com
www.20thcentury-glass.com

No Pink Carpet
Tel: 01785 249 802
www.nopinkcarpet.com

Cloud Glass
info@cloudglass.com
www.cloudglass.com

KITCHENALIA

Appleby Antiques
Geoffrey Vans' Arcade, Stand
18, 105-107 Portobello Rd,
London W11
Tel/Fax: 01453 753 126
mike@applebyantiques.net
www.applebyantiques.net

Below Stairs of Hungerford
103 High Street, Hungerford,
Berkshire,RG17 0NB
Tel: 01488 682 317
Fax: 01488 684294
hofgartner@belowstairs.co.uk
www.belowstairs.co.uk

Ken Grant
F109-111 Alfies Antiques
Market, 13-25 Church Street,
Marylebone, London NW8 8DT
Tel: 020 7723 1370
k-grant@alfies.clara.net

Ann Lingard
18-22 Rope Walk, Rye,
Sussex TN31 7NA
Tel: 01797 233 486

MECHANICAL MUSIC

Terry & Daphne France
Tel: 01243 265 946
Fax: 01243 779 582

The Talking Machine
30 Watford Way, London
NW4 3AL
Tel: 020 8202 3473
Mob: 07774 103 139
talkingmachine@gramophones.n
direct.co.uk
www.gramophones.ndirect.co.uk

PAPERWEIGHTS

Sweetbriar Gallery Ltd
56 Watergate Street
Chester, Cheshire, CH1 2LA
Tel: 01244 329249
sales@sweetbriar.co.uk
www.sweetbriar.co.uk

PENS & WRITING

Battersea Pen Home
PO Box 6128,
Epping CM16 4CG
Tel: 01992 578 885
Fax: 01992 578 485
orders@penhome.com
www.penhome.com

Henry The Pen Man
Admiral Vernon Antiques
Market, 141-149 Portobello Rd,
London W11
Tel: 020 8530 3277
Saturdays only

PLASTICS

Paola & Iaia
Unit SO57-58, Alfies Antiques
Market, 13-25 Church Street,
London NW8 8DT, UK
Tel: 07751 084 135
paolaeiaialondon@hotmail.com

POSTERS

At The Movies
28 Hyde Park Gardens, London
W2
Tel: 07770 777 411
info@atthemovies.co.uk
www.atthemovies.co.uk

Barclay Samson
By appointment only
Tel: 020 7731 8012
richard@barclaysamson.com
www.barclaysamson.com

DODO
Stand F073/83/84,13-25
Church Street, Marylebone,
London NW8 8DT
Tel: 020 7706 1545
www.dodoposters.com

The Reelposter Gallery
72 Westbourne Grove,
London W2 5SH
Tel: 020 7727 4488
Fax: 020 7727 4499
info@reelposter.com
www.reelposter.com

Rennies
47 The Old High Street,
Folkestone, Kent CT20 2RN
Tel: 01303 242427
info@rennart.co.uk
www.rennart.co.uk

POWDER COMPACTS

**Sara Hughes Vintage Compacts,
Antiques & Collectables**
Mob: 0775 9697 108
sara@sneak.freeserve.co.uk
http://mysite.wanadoo-
members.co.uk/sara_compacts/

Mary & Geoff Turvil
Vintage Compacts, Small
Antiques & Collectables
Tel: 01730 260 730
mary.turvil@virgin.net

RADIOS

On the Air Ltd
The Vintage Technology Centre,
Hawarden, Deeside CH5 3DN
Tel/Fax: 01244 530 300
info@vintageradio.co.uk
www.vintageradio.co.uk

ROCK & POP

Beatcity
PO Box 229, Chatham,
Kent ME5 8WA
Tel/Fax: 01634 200 444
www.beatcity.co.uk

More Than Music
PO Box 2809,
Eastbourne,
East Sussex BN21 2EA
Tel: 01323 649 778
morethnmus@aol.com
www.mtmglobal.com

Tracks
PO Box 117, Chorley,
Lancashire PR6 0UU
Tel: 01257 269 726
Fax: 01257 231340
sales@tracks.co.uk
www.tracks.co.uk

SCIENTIFIC & TECHNICAL, INCLUDING OFFICE, OPTICAL

Arthur Middleton Antiques
50 Whitehall Park, Archway,
London N19 3TN
Tel: 020 7281 8445
www.antique-globes.com

Branksome Antiques
370 Poole Rd, Branksome,
Dorset BH12 1AW
Tel: 01202 763 324

Cobwebs
78 Old Northam Rd,
Southampton SO14 0PB
Tel/Fax: 02380 227 458
www.cobwebs.uk.com

Early Technology
Monkton House, Old
Craighall,Musselburgh,
Midlothian EH21 8SF
Tel: 0131 665 5753
michael.bennett-levy@virgin.net
www.earlytech.com

Stuart Talbot
PO Box 31525,
London W11 2XY
Tel: 020 8969 7011
talbot.stuart@talk21.com

SMOKING

Richard Ball
richard@lighter.co.uk

Tagore Ltd
c/o The Silver Fund, 1 Duke of
York Street, London SW1Y 6JP
Tel: 07989 953 452
tagore@grays.clara.net

Tom Clarke
Admiral Vernon Antiques
Centre, Unit 36,
Portobello Rd, London W11
Tel: 020 8802 8936

SPORTING MEMORABILIA

Manfred Schotten
109 High St,
Burford,
Oxfordshire OX18 4RH
Tel: 01993 822 302
Fax: 0 1993 822055
enquiries@schotten.com
www.schotten.com

Old Troon Sporting Antiques
49 Ayr St,
Troon KA10 6EB
Tel: 01292 311 822

Simon Brett
Creswyke House,
Moreton-in-Marsh GL56 0LH
Tel: 01608 650 751

Warboys Antiques
St. Ives, Cambridgeshire
Tel: 01480 463891
Mob: 07831 274774
johnlambden@sportingantiques
.co.uk
www.sportingantiques.co.uk

TOYS & GAMES

Automatomania
Logie Steading, Forres, Moray
IV36 2QN, Scotland
Tel: 01309 694 828
Mob: 07790 71 90 97
www.automatomania.com

**Collectors Old Toy Shop &
Antiques**
89 Northgate, Halifax, West
Yorkshire HX1 1XF
Tel: 01422 360 434
collectorsoldtoy@aol.com

Colin Baddiel
B24-B25, Grays Antique
Market, 1-7 Davies Mews,
London W1K 5AB
Tel: 020 7408 1239
Fax: 020 7493 9344
toychemcol@hotmail.com
www.colinsantiquetoys.com

Donay Games
Tel: 01444 416 412
info@donaygames.co.uk
www.donaygames.com

Garrick Coleman
75 Portobello Rd,
London W11
Tel: 020 7937 5524
Fax: 0207 937 5530
www.antiquechess.co.uk

Hugo Lee-Jones
Tel: 01227 375 375
Mob: 07941 187 2027
electroniccollectables@hotmail.com

Intercol
43 Templars Crescent, Finchley,
London N3 3QR
Tel: 020 8349 2207
Mob: 077 68 292 066
sales@intercol.co.uk
www.intercol.co.uk

Karl Flaherty Collectables
Tel: 02476 445 627
kfcollectables@aol.com
www.kfcollectables.com

**Sue Pearson Dolls & Teddy
Bear**
18 Brighton Square, 'The
Lanes', Brighton, East Sussex
BN1 1HD
Tel: 01273 774851
info@suepearson.co.uk
www.suepearson.co.uk

The Vintage Toy & Train Shop
Sidmouth Antiques &
Collectors' Centre,
All Saints' Rd,
Sidmouth EX10 8ES
Tel: 01395 512 588

Wheels of Steel (Trains)
Gray's Mews Antiques Market,
B10-B11, 58 Davies St,
London W1K 5LP
Tel: 020 7629 2813
wheelsofsteel@grays.clara.net
www.graysantiques.com

Pauline Parkes
Windsor House
Tel: 01608 650 993

Polly de Courcy-Ireland
PO Box 29,
Alresford,
Hampshire SO249WP
Tel: 01962 733 131

Susan Shaw Period Pieces
Saffron Walden, Essex
Tel: 01799 599217

WATCHES

Kleanthous Antiques
144 Portobello Rd,
London W11 2DZ
Tel: 020 7727 3649
antiques@kleanthous.com
www.kleanthous.com

70s Watches
graham@gettya.freeserve.co.uk
www.70s-watches.com

The Watch Gallery
1129 Fulham Road, London
SW3 6RT
Tel: 020 7581 3239

DIRECTORY OF AUCTIONEERS

This is a list of auctioneers that conduct regular sales. Auctioneers who wish to be listed in this directory for our next edition, space permitting, are requested to email info@thepriceguidecompany.com by 1st February 2005.

LONDON

Bloomsbury Auctions
Bloomsbury House, 24 Maddox Street, London W1 S1PP
Tel: 020 7495 9494
Fax: 020 7495 9499
www.bloomsbury-book-auct.com

Bonhams
101 New Bond St,
London W1S 1SR
Tel: 020 7629 6602
Fax: 020 7629 8876
www.bonhams.com

Christies (South Kensington)
85 Old Brompton Rd,
London SW7 3LD
Tel: 020 7581 7611
Fax: 020 7321 3311
info@christies.com
www.christies.com

Rosebery's
74-76 Knights Hill, West Norwood, London SE27 0JD
Tel: 020 8761 2522
Fax: 020 8761 2524

Sotheby's (Olympia)
Hammersmith Rd,
London W14 8UX
Tel: 020 7293 5555
Fax: 020 7293 6939
www.sothebys.com

BEDFORDSHIRE

W. & H. Peacock
The Auction Centre,
26 Newnham St,
Bedford MK40 3JR
Tel: 01234 266366
Fax: 01234 269082
www.peacockauction.co.uk
info@peacockauction.co.uk

BERKSHIRE

Dreweatt Neate
Donnington Priory,
Donnington, Nr. Newbury,
Berkshire RG14 2JE
Tel: 01635 553553
Fax: 01635 553599
auctions@dnfa.com
www.dnfa.com

Law Fine Art Ltd
Firs Cottage, Church Lane,
Brimpton,
Berkshire RG7 4TJ
Tel: 0118 971 0353
Fax: 0118 971 3741
info@lawfineart.co.uk
www.lawfineart.co.uk

Special Auction Services
The Coach House,
Midgham Park,
Reading,
Berkshire RG7 5UG
Tel: 01189 712 949
Fax: 01189 712 420
commemorative@aol.com

BUCKINGHAMSHIRE

Amersham Auction Rooms
125 Station Rd, Amersham,
Buckinghamshire HP7 0AH
Tel: 08700 460606
Fax: 08700 460607
info@amershamauctionrooms.co.uk
www.amershamauctionrooms.co.uk

CAMBRIDGESHIRE

Cheffins
Clifton House, 1&2 Clifton Road, Cambridge CB1 7EA
Tel: 01223 213 343
Fax: 01223 271 949
fine.art@cheffins.co.uk
www.cheffins.co.uk

CHANNEL ISLANDS

Martel Maides Ltd.
The Old Bank, 29 High Street,
Channel Islands GY1 2JX
Tel: 01481 713463
Fax: 01481 700337
sales@martelmaides.co.uk
www.martelmaides.co.uk

CHESHIRE

Bonhams (Chester)
New House, 150 Christleton Road, Chester, Cheshire CH3 5TD
Tel: 01244 313 936
Fax: 01244 340 028
www.bonhams.com

Bob Gowland International Golf Auctions
The Stables, Claim Farm,
Manley Rd Frodsham,
Cheshire WA6 6HT
Tel/Fax: 01928 740668
bob@internationalgolfauctions.com
www.internationalgolfauctions.com

CLEVELAND

Vectis Auctioneers
Fleck Way Thornaby, Stockton-on-Tees, Cleveland TS17 9JZ
Tel: 01642 750616
Fax: 01642 769478
www.vectis.co.uk

CORNWALL

W. H. Lane & Son
Jubilee House, Queen Street,
Penzance TR18 4DF
Tel: 01736 361447
Fax: 01736 350097
info@whlane.co.uk

David Lay FRICS
The Penzance Auction House
Alverton, Penzance TR18 4RE
Tel: 01736 361414
Fax: 01736 360035
david.lays@btopenworld.com

CUMBRIA

Mitchells Fine Art
Auctioneers, Station Road,
Cockermouth, Cumbria CA13 9PZ
Tel: 01900 827800
Fax: 01900 828073
info@mitchellsfineart.com
www.mitchellsfineart.com

Penrith Farmers' & Kidds
Skirsgill Saleroom, Skirsgill,
Penrith, Cumbria CA11 0DN
Tel: 01768 890781
Fax: 01768 895058
info@pfkauctions.co.uk
www.pfandk.co.uk

DERBYSHIRE

Bamfords Ltd
The Old Picture Palace,
133 Dale Road, Matlock,
Derbyshire DE4 3LT
Tel: 01629 574460
www.bamfords-auctions.co.uk

DEVON

Bearne's
St Edmund's Court,
Okehampton St, Exeter,
Devon EX4 1LX
Tel: 01392 207000
Fax: 01392 207007
enquiries@bearnes.co.uk
www.bearnes.co.uk

Bonhams
Dowell St, Honiton, Devon
EX14 1LX
Tel: 01404 41872
Fax: 01404 43137
honiton@bonhams.com
www.bonhams.com

Charterhouse
The Long Street Salerooms,
Sherborne, Dorset DT9 3BS
Tel: 01935 812277
Fax: 01935 389387
enquiry@charterhouse-auctions.co.uk
www.charterhouse-auctions.co.uk

HY Duke & Sons
Weymouth Avenue, Dorchester,
Dorset DT11QS
Tel: 01305 265080
Fax: 01305 260101
enquiries@dukes-auctions.co.uk
www.dukes-auctions.co.uk

Onslows
The Coach House, Manor Road,
Stourpaine DT11 8TQ
Tel/Fax: 01258 488 838
www.onslows.co.uk

Semley Auctioneers
Station Rd, Semley, Nr
Shaftesbury, Dorset SP7 9AN
Tel: 01747 855122
Fax: 01747 855222
semley.auctioneers@btinternet.com
www.semleyauctioneers.com

ESSEX

Ambrose
Ambrose House, Old Station
Rd, Loughton, Essex IG10 4PE
Tel: 020 8502 3951
Fax: 020 8532 0833
info@ambroseauction.co.uk
www.ambroseauction.co.uk

Sworder & Sons
14 Cambridge Rd, Stansted
Mountfitchet, Essex CM24 8DE
Tel: 01279 817778
Fax: 01279 817779
auctions@sworder.co.uk
www.sworder.co.uk

GLOUCESTERSHIRE

BK
The Tithe Barn, Southam,
Cheltenham,
Gloucestershire GL52 3NY
Tel: 01242 573904
Fax: 01242 224463
www.bkonline.co.uk

Dreweatt Neate (Formerly Bristol Auction Rooms)
Bristol Salerooms, St. John's
Place, Apsley Road, Clifton,
Bristol BS8 2ST
Tel: 0117 973 7201
Fax: 0117 973 5671
bristol@dnfa.com
www.dnfa.com/bristol

Cotswold Auction Co.
Chapel Walk Saleroom,
Chapel Walk, Cheltenham,
Gloucestershire GL50 3DS
Tel: 01242 256363
Fax: 01242 571734
info@cotswoldauction.co.uk
www.cotswoldauction.co.uk

Mallams Fine Art Auctioneers and Valuers
26 Grosvenor Street,
Cheltenham GL52 2SG
Tel: 01242 235712
Fax: 01242 241943
cheltenham@mallams.co.uk
www.mallams.co.uk/fineart

HAMPSHIRE

Andrew Smith & Son
The Auction Rooms, Manor
Farm, Itchen Stoke, nr.
Winchester SO24 0QT
Tel: 01962 735988
Fax: 01962 738879
auctions@andrewsmithandson.com

Jacobs and Hunt Fine Art Auctioneers
Lavant Street, Petersfield GU32 3EF
Tel: 01730 233 933
Fax: 01730 262 323
auctions@jacobsandhunt.co.uk
www.jacobsandhunt.co.uk

HEREFORDSHIRE

Brightwells
The Fine Art Saleroom,
Ryelands Rd, Leominster,
Herefordshire HR68NZ
Tel: 01568 611122
Fax: 01568 610519
fineart@brightwells.com
www.brightwells.com

HERTFORDSHIRE

Tring Market Auctions
Brook Street, Tring HP23 5EF
Tel: 01442 826 446
Fax: 01442 890 927
sales@tringmarketauctions.co.uk
www.tringmarketauctions.co.uk

ISLE OF WIGHT

Ways, The Auction House,
Garfield Rd, Ryde,
Isle of Wight PO33 2PT
Tel: 01983 562255
Fax: 01983 565108
www.waysauctionrooms
.fsbusiness.co.uk

KENT

Dreweatt Neate (Formerly Bracketts)
Tunbridge Wells Saleroom, The
Auction Hall, The Pantiles,
Tunbridge Wells, Kent TN2 5QL
Tel: 01892 544500
Fax: 01892 515191
tunbridgewells@dnfa.co.uk
www.dnfa.com/tunbridgewells

Gorringes
15 The Pantiles, Tunbridge Wells
TN2 5TD
Tel: 01892 619 670
Fax: 01892 619 671
auctions@gorringes.co.uk
www.gorringes.co.uk

LANCASHIRE

Capes Dunn & Co.
The Auction Galleries, 38
Charles St, Manchester,
M1 7DB
Tel: 0161 273 1911
Fax: 0161 273 3474

LEICESTERSHIRE

Gilding's
Roman Way Market,
Harborough, LE16 7PQ
Tel: 01858 410414
Fax: 01858 432956
sales@gildings.co.uk
www.gildings.co.uk

Tennants Co. (Formerly Heathcote Ball & Co)
Millhouse, South Street,
Oakham, Rutland LE15 6BG
Tel: 01572 724 66
Fax: 01572 72 4422
oakham@tennants-ltd.co.uk
www.tennants.co.uk

LINCOLNSHIRE

Golding Young & Co.
Old Wharf Rd, Grantham,
Lincolnshire NG31 7AA
Tel: 01476 565118
Fax: 01476 561475
enquiries@goldingyoung.com
www.goldingyoung.com

MERSEYSIDE

Cato, Crane & Co
6 Stanhope St,
Liverpool L8 5RE
Tel: 0151 709 5559
Fax: 0151 707 2454
www.cato-crane.co.uk

NORFOLK

Gaze and Son
Diss Auction Rooms, Roydon
Road, Diss IP22 4LN
Tel: 01379 650306
Fax: 01379 644313
sales@dissauctionrooms.co.uk
www.twgaze.com

Keys Auctioneers & Valuers
Aylsham Salerooms, Palmers
Lane, Aylsham, Norfolk NR11
6JA
Tel: 01263 733195
www.keysauctions.co.uk

Knights Sporting Auctions
The Thatched Gallery,
The Green, Aldborough,
Norwich, Norfolk NR11 7AA
Tel: 01263 768488
Fax: 01263 768788
www.knights.co.uk

NOTTINGHAMSHIRE

Mellors & Kirk Fine Art Auctioneers
Gregory Street, Nottingham,
Nottinghamshire NG7 2NL
Tel: 0115 9790000
Fax: 0115 9781111
enquiries@mellors-kirk.com
www.mellors-kirk.co.uk

Dreweatt Neate (Formerly Neales)
Nottingham Salerooms, 192
Mansfield Road, Nottingham
NG1 3HU
Tel: 0115 962 4141
Fax: 0115 969 3450
fineart@neales-auctions.com
www.dnfa.com/neales

T Vennett-Smith Auctioneers and Valuers
11 Nottingham Road, Gotham,
Nottingham NG11 0HE
Tel: 0115 9830541
Fax: 0115 9830114
info@vennett-smith.com
www.vennett-smith.com

OXFORDSHIRE

Mallams
Pevensey House, 27 Sheep St,
Bicester, Oxfordshire OX6 7JF
Tel: 01869 252901
Fax: 01869 320283
bicester@mallams.co.uk
www.mallams.co.uk

Mallams (Oxford)
Bocardo House, 24a St.
Michaels Street, Oxford,
OX1 2EB
Tel: 01865 241358
Fax: 01865 725483
oxford@mallams.co.uk
www.mallams.co.uk

Soames Country Auctions
Pinnocks Farm Estate,
Northmoor, Witney OX8 1AY
Tel: 01865 300626
soame@email.msn.com
www.soamesauctioneers.co.uk

SHROPSHIRE

Halls Fine Art
Welsh Bridge, Shrewsbury SY3
8LA
Tel: 01743 231 212
Fax: 01743 271 014
FineArt@halls.to
www.hallsgb.com

Walker Barnett & Hill
Cosford Auction Rooms,
Long Lane, Cosford,
Shropshire TF11 8PJ
Tel: 01902 375555
Fax: 01902375566
www.walker-barnett-hill.co.uk

Mullock Madeley
The Old Shippon,
Wall-under-Heywood,
Nr Church Stretton,
Shropshire SY6 7DS
Tel: 01694 771771
Fax: 01694 771772
info@mullockmadeley.co.uk
www.mullock-madeley.co.uk

SOMERSET

Clevedon Salerooms
The Auction Centre, Kenn Road,
Kenn, Clevedon, North
Somerset BS21 6TT
Tel: 01934 830 111
Fax: 01934 832 538
info@clevedon-salerooms.com
www.clevedon-salerooms.com

Gardiner Houlgate
The Bath Auction Rooms,
9 Leafield Way,
Corsham, Bath,
Somerset SN139SW
Tel: 01225 812912
Fax: 01225 811777
auctions@gardiner-houlgate.co.uk
www.invaluable.com/gardiner-houlgate

Lawrence's Fine Art Auctioneers Ltd
South St, Crewkerne,
Somerset TA18 8AB
Tel: 01460 73041
Fax: 01460 74627
enquiries@lawrences.co.uk
www.lawrences.co.uk

STAFFORDSHIRE

Potteries Specialist Auctions
271 Waterloo Rd, Cobridge,
Stoke-on-Trent,
Staffordshire ST6 3HR
Tel: 01782 286622
Fax: 01782 213777
www.potteriesauctions.com

Richard Winterton
School House Auction Rooms,
Hawkins Lane, Burton-on-Trent,
Staffordshire DE14 1PT
Tel: 01283 511224

Wintertons
Lichfield Auction Centre
Fradley, Lichfield, WS13 8NF
Tel: 01543 263256
Fax: 01543 415348
enquiries@wintertons.co.uk
www.wintertons.co.uk

SUFFOLK

Diamond Mills
Orwell Hall, Orwell Rd,
Felixstowe, Suffolk IP11 7BL
Tel:01473 218 600
diamondmills@btconnect.com
www.diamondmills.co.uk

Neal Sons & Fletcher
26 Church St,
Woodbridge,
Suffolk IP12 1DP
Tel: 01394 382263
Fax: 01394 383030
enquiries@nsf.co.uk
www.nsf.co.uk

SURREY

Barbers
The Mayford Centre,
Smarts Heath Rd,
Woking, Surrey GU22 0PP
Tel: 01483 728939
Fax: 01483 762552
www.thesaurus.co.uk/barbers

Clark Gammon
The Guildford Auction Rooms,
Bedford Road, Guildford, Surrey
GU1 4SJTel: 01483 880915
Fax: 01483 880918
fine.art@clarkegammon.co.uk
www.clarkgammon.co.uk

Ewbank Auctioneers
The Burnt Common Auction
Rooms, London Rd,
Send, Woking,
Surrey GU23 7LN
Tel: 01483 223101
Fax: 01483 222171
www.ewbankauctions.co.uk

Dreweatt Neate (Formerly Hamptons)
Baverstock House, 93 High
Street, Godalming GU7 1AL
Tel: 01483 423 567
Fax: 01483 426 392
godalming@dnfa.com
www.dnfa.com/godalming

EAST SUSSEX

Burstow & Hewett
Lower Lake, Battle,
East Sussex TN33 0AT
Tel: 01424 772 374
www.burstowandhewett.co.uk

Dreweatt Neate (Eastbourne)
46-50 South St,
Eastbourne,
East Sussex BN214XB,
Tel: 01323 410419
Fax: 01323 416540
eastbourne@dnfa.com
www.dnfa

Gorringes
Terminus Rd, Bexhill-on-Sea,
East Sussex TN39 3LR
Tel: 01424 212994
Fax: 01424 224035
www.gorringes.co.uk

Gorringes
15 North St, Lewes,
East Sussex BN7 2PD
Tel: 01273 472503
Fax: 01273 479559
www.gorringes.co.uk

Raymond P. Inman
The Auction Galleries, 98A
Coleridge Street, Hove BN3 5
AA
Tel: 01273 774777
Fax: 01273 735660
r.p.inman@talk21.com
www.invaluable.com/raymondin
man

Wallis & Wallis
West St Auction Galleries,
Lewes, East Sussex BN72NJ
Tel: 01273 480208
Fax: 01273 476562
auctions@wallisandwallis.co.uk
www.wallisandwallis.co.uk

TYNE & WEAR

Anderson and Garland
Anderson House, Crispin Court,
Newbiggin Lane, Westerhope,
Newcastle upon Tyne NE5 1BF
Tel: 0191 430 3000
andersongarland@aol.com
www.andersonandgarland.com

Corbitts
5 Mosley St, Newcastle-upon-
Tyne, Tyne and Wear NE1 1YE
Tel: 0191 232 7268
Fax: 0191 261 4130
collectors@corbitts.com
www.corbitts.com

WARWICKSHIRE

Locke & England
18 Guy Street, Leamington Spa
CV32 4RT
Tel: 01926 889100
Fax: 01926 470608
valuers@leauction.co.uk
www.leauction.co.uk

WEST MIDLANDS

Bonhams, Knowle
The Old House,
Station Rd, Knowle,
Solihull, B930HT
Tel: 01564 776151
Fax: 01564 778069
knowle@bonhams.com
www.bonhams.com

Fellows & Sons
Augusta House,
19 Augusta St, Hockley,
Birmingham,
West Midlands B186JA
Tel: 0121 212 2131
Fax: 0121 212 1249
info@fellows.co.uk
www.fellows.co.uk

WEST SUSSEX

John Bellman
New Pound Wisborough Green,
Billingshurst,
West Sussex RH14 0AZ
Tel: 01403 700858
Fax: 01403 700059
enquiries@bellmans.comuk
www.bellmans.co.uk

Denhams
The Auction Galleries,
Warnham, Nr Horsham,
West Sussex RH123RZ
Tel: 01403 255699
Fax: 01403 253837
enquiries@denhams.com
www.denhams.com

Rupert Toovey
Spring Gardens, Washington,
West Sussex, RH20 3BS,
Tel: 01903 891955
auctions@rupert-toovey.com
www.rupert-toovey.com

WILTSHIRE

Finan & Co
The Square, Mere,
Wiltshire BA12 6DJ
Tel: 01747 861411
Fax: 01747 861944
post@finanandco.co.uk
www.finanandco.co.uk

Henry Aldridge & Sons
The Devizes Auctioneers,
Unit 1, Bath Rd Business
Centre, Devizes,
Wiltshire SN10 1XA
Tel: 01380 729199
Fax: 01380 730073
www.henry-aldridge.co.uk

Woolley & Wallis
51-61 Castle St,
Salisbury,
Wiltshire SP1 3SU
Tel: 01722 424500
Fax: 01722 424508
enquiries@woolleyandwallis.co.uk
www.woolleyandwallis.co.uk

WORCESTERSHIRE

Andrew Grant
St Mark's House,
St Mark's Close,
Cherry Orchard,
Worcester WR5 3DJ
Tel: 01905 357547
Fax: 01905 763942
fine.art@andrew-grant.co.uk
www.andrew-grant.co.uk

**Gloucestershire Worcestershire
Railwana Auctions**
'The Willows',
Badsey Rd, Evesham,
Worcestershire WR117PA
Tel: 01386 760109
www.gwra.co.uk

Phillip Serrell
The Malvern Saleroom,
Barnards Green Rd, Malvern,
Worcestershire WR143LW
Tel: 01684 892314
Fax: 01684 569832
www.serrell.com

EAST YORKSHIRE

Dee, Atkinson & Harrison
The Exchange Saleroom,
Driffield,
East Yorkshire YO25 6LD
Tel: 01377 253151
Fax: 01377 241041
exchange@dee-atkinson-
harrison.co.uk
www.dahauctions.com

NORTH YORKSHIRE

David Duggleby
The Vine St Salerooms,
Scarborough,
North Yorkshire YO11 1XN
Tel: 01723 507111
Fax: 01723 507222
www.davidduggleby.com

Tennants
The Auction Centre, Leyburn,
North Yorkshire DL8 5SG
Tel: 01969 623780
Fax: 01969 624281
enquiry@tennants-ltd.co.uk
www.tennants.co.uk

SOUTH YORKSHIRE

A. E. Dowse & Sons
Cornwall Galleries, Scotland
Street, Sheffield S3 7DE
Tel: 0114 2725858
Fax: 0114 2490550
aedowes@aol.com
www.aedowseandson.com

BBR Auctions
Elsecar Heritage Centre,
5 Ironworks Row, Wath Rd,
Elsecar, Barnsley,
South Yorkshire S748HJ
Tel: 01226 745156
Fax: 01226 361561
www.onlinebbr.com

Sheffield Railwana
43 Little Norton Lane,
Sheffield, S8 8GA
Tel: 0114 274 5085
ian@sheffrail.freeserve.co.uk
www.sheffieldrailwayana.co.uk

WEST YORKSHIRE

Andrew Hartley Fine Arts
Victoria Hall Salerooms, Little
Lane, Ilkle,
West Yorkshire, LS29 8EA
Tel: 01943 816363
info@andrewhartleyfinearts.co.uk
www.andrewhartleyfinearts.co.uk

SCOTLAND

Bonhams Edinburgh
65 George St,
Edinburgh EH2 2JL
Tel: 0131 225 2266
Fax: 0131 220 2547
edinburgh@bonhams.com
www.bonhams.com

Loves Auction Rooms
52-54 Canal St, Perth,
Perthshire, PH2 8LF
Tel: 01738 633337
Fax: 01738 629830

Lyon & Turnbull
33 Broughton Place,
Edinburgh EH1 3RR
Tel: 0131 557 8844
Fax: 0131 557 8668
info@lyonandturnbull.com
www.lyonandturnbull.com

Lyon & Turnbull
4 Woodside Place,
Glasgow G3 7QF
Tel: 0141 353 5070
Fax: 0141 332 2928
info@lyonandturnbull.com
www.lyonandturnbull.com

**Thomson, Roddick & Medcalf
Ltd.**
44/3 Hardengreen Business
Park, Eskbank, Edinburgh,
Midlothian EH22 3NX
Tel: 0131 454 9090
Fax: 0131 454 9191
www.thomsonroddick.com

WALES

Bonhams Cardiff
7-8 Park Place, Cardiff,
Glamorgan CF10 3DP
Tel: 02920 727 980
Fax: 02920 727 989
cardiff@bonhams.com
www.bonhams.com

Peter Francis
Curiosity Salerooms, 19 King
St, Carmarthen, South Wales
Tel: 01267 233456
Fax: 01267 233458
www.peterfrancis.co.uk

Welsh Country Auctions
2 Carmarthen Road, Cross
Hands, Llanelli,
Carmarthenshire SA14 6SP
Tel: 01269 844428
Fax: 01269 844428
enquiries@welshcountryauctions
.com
www.welshcountryauctions.com

IRELAND

HOK Fine Art
4 Main St, Blackrock, Co
Dublin, Ireland
Tel: 00 353 1 2881000
fineart@hok.ie
www.hokfineart.com

Mealy's
The Square, Castlecomer,
County Kilkenny, Ireland
Tel: 00 353 56 41229
/41413
Fax: 00 353 56 41627
info@mealys.com
www.mealys.com

APPENDICES

CLUBS, SOCIETIES & ORGANISATIONS

ADVERTISING

Antique Advertising Signs
The Street Jewellery Society, 11
Bowsden Ter, South Gosford,
Newcastle-Upon-Tyne NE3 1RX

AUTOGRAPHS

Autograph Club of GB
gregson@blueyonder.co.uk
www.acogb.co.uk

BAXTER PRINTS

The New Baxter Society
c/o Reading Museum & Art
Gallery, Blagrave St, Reading,
Berkshire RG1 1QH
baxter@rpsfamily.demon.co.uk
www.rpsfamily.demon.co.uk

BANK NOTES

**International Bank Note
Society**
43 Templars Crescent, London,
N3 3QR

BOOKS

The Enid Blyton Society
93 Milford Hill, Salisbury,
Wiltshire SP1 2QL
Tel: 01722 331937
www.enidblytonsociety.co.uk

The Followers of Rupert
www.see.ed.ac.uk/~afm/followers

BOTTLES

Old Bottle Club of Great Britain
2 Strafford Avenue,
Elsecar, Nr Barnsley,
South Yorkshire S74 18AA
Tel: 01226 745 156

CERAMICS

**Carlton Ware Collectors'
International**
The Carlton Factory Shop,
Copeland St, Stoke-upon-Trent,
Staffordshire ST4 1PU
Tel: 01782 410 504
cwciclub@aol.com
www.lattimore.co.uk/deco/carlt
on.htm

Chintz World International
Tel: 01525 220272
Fax: 01525 222442
www.chintzworld-intl.com

Clarice Cliff Collectors' Club
Fantasque House, Tennis Drive,
The Park, Nottingham NG7 1AE
www.claricecliff.com

Goss Collectors' Club
Tel: 01159 300 441
www.gosschina.com

**Hornsea Pottery Collectors' &
Research Society**
128 Devonshire St, Keighley,
West Yorkshire BD21 2QJ
hornsea@pdtennant.fsnet.co.uk
www.easyontheeye.net/hornsea
/society.htm

M.I. Hummel Club (Goebel)
Porzellanfabrik, GmbH & Co. KG,
Coburger Str.7, D-96472
Rodental, Germany
Tel: +49 (0) 95 63 72 18 03
Fax: +49 (0) 95 63 9 25 92

Keith Murray Collectors' Club
Fantasque House, Tennis Drive,
The Park, Nottingham NG7 1AE
www.keithmurray.com

Lorna Bailey Collectors' Club
Newcastle Street,
Dalehall, Burslem,
Stoke-on-Trent ST6 3QF
Tel: 01782 837 341

Mabel Lucie Attwell
Abbey Antiques,
63 Great Whyte, Ramsey,
Huntingdon PE26 1HL
Tel: 01487 814753

Moorcroft Collectors' Club
Sandbach Rd, Burslem,
Stoke-on-Trent,
Staffordshire ST6 2DQ
Tel: 01782 820500
Fax: 01782 820501
cclub@moorcroft.com
www.moorcroft.com

Pendelfin Family Circle
Cameron Mill,
Howsin St, Burnley,
Lancashire BB10 1PP
Tel: 01282 432 301
www.pendelfin.co.uk

Poole Pottery Collectors' Club
The Quay, Poole,
Dorset BH15 1RF
Tel: 01202 666200
Fax: 01202 682894
www.poolepottery.co.uk

**Potteries of Rye Collectors'
Society**
22 Redyear Cottages,
Kennington Rd, Ashford,
Kent TN24 0TF
barry.buckton@tesco.net
www.potteries-of-rye-society.co.uk

**Royal Doulton International
Collectors' Club**
Minton House,
London Rd,
Stoke-on-Trent,
Staffordshire ST47QD
Tel: 01782 292292
Fax: 01782 292099
enquiries@royal-doulton.com
www.royal-doulton.com/collectables

**Royal Winton International
Collectors' Club**
Dancers End, Northall,
Bedfordshire LU6 2EU
Tel: 01525 220 272
Fax: 01525 222 442

The Shelley Group
38 Bowman Road,
Norfolk,
Norwich NR4 6LS
shelley.group@shelley.co.uk
www.shelley.co.uk

Susie Cooper Collectors' Group
Panorama House,
18 Oaklea Mews,
Aycliffe Village,
County Durham DL5 6JP
www.susiecooper.co.uk

The Sylvac Collectors' Circle
174 Portsmouth Rd, Horndean,
Waterlooville, Hampshire
admin@sylvacclub.com
www.sylvacclub.com

Novelty Teapot Collectors' Club
Tel: 01257 450 366
vince@totallyteapots.com
www.totallyteapots.com

**Official International Wade
Collectors' Club**
Royal Works, Westport Rd,
Stoke-on-Trent, Staffs ST6 4AP
Tel: 01782 255255
Fax: 01782 575195
club@wade.co.uk
www.wade.co.uk

**Royal Worcester
Collectors' Society**
Severn Street,
Worcester, WR1 2NE
Tel: 01905 746 000
sinden@royal-worcester.co.uk
www.royal-worcester.co.uk

CIGARETTE CARDS

Cartopulic Society of GB
7 Alderham Avenue, Radlett,
Herts WD7 8HL

COINS

British Numismatic Society
c/o The Warburg Institute,
Woburn Square,
London WC1H 0AB
www.britnumsoc.org

Royal Numismatic Society
c/o The British Museum,
Dept of Coins and Medals,
Great Russell Street,
London WC1B 3DG
Tel: 020 7636 1555
RNS@dircon.co.uk
www.users.dircon.co.uk/~rns

COMMEMORATIVE WARE

**Commemorative Collectors'
Society**
The Gardens,
Gainsborough Rd, Winthorpe,
nr Newark NG24 2NR
Tel: 01636 671377
chris@royalcoll.fsnet.co.uk

COMICS

**Association of Comic
Enthusiasts**
L'Hopiteau, St Martin du
Fouilloux 79420, France
Tel: 00 33 549 702 114

Comic Enthusiasts Society
80 Silverdale, Sydenham,
London SE26 4SJ

COSTUME & ACCESSORIES

**British Compact
Collectors' Club**
PO Box 64, Woking,
Surrey GU24 9YR

Costume Society
St. Paul's House, Warwick Lane,
London EC4P 4BN
www.costumesociety.org.uk

Hat Pin Society of GB
PO Box 74, Bozeat,
Northamptonshire NN29 7UD

DISNEYANA

Walt Disney Collectors' Society
c/o Enesco, Brunthill Road,
Kingstown Industrial Estate,
Carlisle CA3 0EN
Tel: 01228 404 062
www.wdccduckman.com

DOLLS

Barbie Collectors' Club of GB
117 Rosemount Avenue, Acton,
London W3 9LU
wdl@nipcus.co.uk'

British Doll Collectors Club
'The Anchorage', Wrotham Rd,
Culverstone Green, Meopham,
Kent DA13 0QW
www.britishdollcollectors.com

Doll Club of Great Britain
PO Box 154, Cobham, Surrey
KT11 2YE

**The Fashion Doll Collectors'
Club of GB**
PO Box 133, Lowestoft,
Suffolk NR32 1WA
Tel: 07940 248127
voden@supanet.com

FILM & TV

**James Bond 007 Fan Club
&Archive**
PO Box 007,
Surrey KT15 IDY
Tel: 01483 756007

**Fanderson - The Official Gerry
Anderson Appreciation Society**
2 Romney Road,
Willesborough, Ashford,
Kent TN24 0RW

GLASS

The Carnival Glass Society
P.O. Box 14, Hayes,
Middlesex UB3 5NU
www.carnivalglasssociety.co.uk

The Glass Association
1, White Knobs Way
Caterham, Surrey CR3 6RH
geoffcctim@btinternet.com
www.glassassociation.org.uk

Isle of Wight Studio Glass
Old Park, St Lawrence, Isle of
Wight, PO38 1XR
www.isleofwightstudioglass.co.uk

APPENDICES

Pressed Glass Collectors' Club
4 Bowshot Close, Castle
Bromwich B36 9UH
Tel: 0121 681 4872
www.webspawner.com/users/
pressedglass

KITCHENALIA

National Horse Brass Society
2 Blue Barn Cottage,
Blue Barn Lane,
Weybridge,
Surrey KT13 0NH
Tel: 01932 354 193

**The British Novelty Salt &
Pepper Collectors Club**
Coleshill,
Clayton Road, Mold,
Flintshire CH7 15X

MARBLES

Marble Collectors Unlimited
P.O. Box 206
Northborough,
MA 01532-0206 USA
marblesbev@aol.com

MECHANICAL MUSIC

**Musical Box Society of
Great Britain**
PO Box 299,
Waterbeach,
Cambridge CB4 4PJ

**The City of London
Phonograph and Gramophone
Society**
2 Kirklands Park,
Fyfe KY15 4EP
Tel: 01334 654 390

METALWARE

Antique Metalware Society
PO Box 63, Honiton,
Devon EX14 1HP
amsmemsec@yahoo.co.uk

MILITARIA

Military – Crown Imperial
37 Wolsey Close, Southall,
Middlesex UB2 4NQ

Military Historical Society
National Army Museum,
Royal Hospital Rd,
London SW3 4HT

**Orders & Medals Research
Society**
123 Turnpike Link,
Croydon CR0 5NU

PAPERWEIGHTS

Paperweight Collectors Circle
P.O. Box 941,
Comberton,
Cambridgeshire CB3 7GQ
Tel: 02476 386 172

PENS & WRITING

The Writing Equipment Society
wes.membershipsec@virgin.net
www.wesoc.co.uk

PERFUME BOTTLES

**International Perfume Bottle
Association**
396 Croton Road, Wayne,
PA 19087 USA
www.ipba-uk.co.uk

PLASTICS

Plastics Historical Society
31a Maylands Drive,
Sidcup, Kent DA14 4SB
mail@plastiquarian.com
www.plastiquarian.com

POSTCARDS

**The Postcard Club of Great
Britain**
34 Harper House,
St. James' Crescent,
London SW9 7LW

POTLIDS

The Pot Lid Circle
Keith Mortimer
Tel: 01295 722 032

QUILTS

**The Quilters' Guild of the
British Isles**
Room 190,
Dean Clough, Halifax,
West Yorks 3HX 5AX
Tel: 01422 347 669
Fax: 01422 345 017
info@quiltersguild.org.uk
www.quiltersguild.org.uk

RADIOS

**The British Vintage
Wireless Society**
59 Dunsford Close,
Swindon,
Wiltshire SN1 4PW
Tel: 01793 541 634
www.bvws.org.uk

RAILWAYANA

Railwayana Collectors Journal
7 Ascot Rd, Moseley,
Birmingham B13 9EN

SCIENTIFIC, TECHNICAL & MEDICAL INSTRUMENTS

Scientific Instrument Society
31 High St,
Stanford in the Vale,
Farringdon SN7 8LH
www.sis.org.uk

SEWING

**International Sewing Machine
Collectors' Society**
www.ismacs.net

The Thimble Society
1107 Portobello Rd,
London W11 2QB
antiques@thimblesociety.co.uk
www.thimblesociety.co.uk

SMOKING

Lighter Club of Great Britain
Richard Ball
richard@lighter.co.uk

SPORTING

**International Football Hall of
Fame**
info@ifhof.com, www.ifhof.com

British Golf Collectors Society
anthonythorpe@ntlworld.com
www.britgolfcollectors.wyenet.co.uk

STAMPS

Postal History Society
60 Tachbrook Street,
London SW1V 2NA
Tel: 020 7545 7773
john.scott@db.com

Royal Mail Collectors' Club
Freepost, NEA1431,
Sunderland, SR9 9XN

STANHOPES

The Stanhope Collectors' Club
jean@stanhopes.info
www.stanhopes.info

TEDDY BEARS & SOFT TOYS

British Teddy Bear Association
PO Box 290
Brighton, Sussex
Tel: 01273 697 974

**Merrythought International
Collectors' Club**
Ironbridge, Telford,
Shropshire TF8 7NJ
Tel: 01952 433 116

Steiff Club Office
Margaret Steiff GmbH,
Alleen Strasse 2, D-89537
Giengen/Brenz, Germany

TOYS

Action Man Club
PO Box 142,
Horsham, RH13 5FJ

The British Model Soldier Society
44 Danemead, Hoddesdon,
Hertfordshire EN119LU
www.model.soldiers.btinternet.co.uk

Corgi Collectors' Club
PO Box 323, Swansea, Wales
SA1 1BJ

Hornby Collectors Club
PO Box 35, Royston,
Hertfordshire SG8 5XR
Tel/Fax: 01223 208 308
hsclubs.demon.co.uk
www.hornby.co.uk

**The Matchbox Toys
International Collectors'
Association**
P.O. Box 120, Deeside,
Flintshire CH5 3HE
kevin@matchboxclub.com
www.matchboxclub.com

**Historical Model Railway
Society**
59 Woodberry Way,
London E4 7DY

**The English Playing Card
Society**
11 Pierrepont St, Bath,
Somerset BA1 1LA
Tel: 01225 465 218

Train Collectors' Society
P.O. Box 20340,
London NW11 6ZE
Tel: 020 8209 1589
tcsinformation@btinternet.com
www.traincollectors.org.uk

**William Britain
Collectors Club**
P.O. Box 32,
Wokingham RG40 4XZ
Tel: 01189 737080
Fax: 01189 733947
ales@wbritaincollectorsclub.com
www.britaincollectorsclub.com

WATCHES

**British Watch & Clock
Collectors' Association**
5 Cathedral Lane, Truro,
Cornwall TR1 2QS
Tel 01872 264010
Fax 01872 241953
tonybwcca@cs.com
www.timecap.com

COLLECTING ON THE INTERNET

■ The internet has revolutionised the trading of collectables. Compared to a piece of furniture, most collectables are easily defined, described and photographed. Shipping is also comparatively easy, due to average size and weight. Prices are also generally more affordable and accessible than for antiques and the Internet has provided a cost effective way of buying and selling, away from the overheads of shops and auction rooms. Many millions of collectables are offered for sale and traded daily, with sites varying from global online marketplaces, such as eBay, to specialist dealers' websites.

■ When searching online, remember that some people may not know how to accurately describe their item. General category searches, even though more time consuming, and even purposefully misspelling a name, can yield results. Also, if something looks too good to be true, it probably is. Using this book to get to know your market visually, so that you can tell the difference between a real bargain and something that sounds like one, is a good start.

■ As you will understand from buying this book, colour photography is vital – look for online listings that include as many images as possible and check them carefully. Beware that colours can appear differently, even between computer screens.

■ Always ask the vendor questions about the object, particularly regarding condition. If there is no image, or you want to see another aspect of the object – ask. Most sellers (private or trade) will want to realise the best price for their items so will be more than happy to help – if approached politely and sensibly.

■ As well as the 'e-hammer' price, you will probably have to pay additional transactional fees such as packing, shipping and possibly regional or national taxes. It is always best to ask for an estimate for these additional costs before leaving a bid. This will also help you tailor your bid as you will have an idea of the maximum price the item will cost if you are successful.

■ In addition to well-known online auction sites, such as eBay, there are a host of other online resources for buying and selling, such as fair and auction date listings.

INTERNET RESOURCES

Live Auctioneers
www.liveauctioneers.com
info@liveauctioneers.com
A free service which allows users to search catalogues from selected auction houses in Europe, the USA and the United Kingdom. Through its connection with eBay, users can bid live via the Internet into salerooms as auctions happen. Registered users can also search through an archive of past catalogues and receive a free newsletter by email.

invaluable.com
www.invaluable.com
sales@invaluable.com
A subscription service which allows users to search selected auction house catalogues from the United Kingdom and Europe. Also offers an extensive archive for appraisal uses.

The Antiques Trade Gazette
www.atg-online.com
The online version of the UK trade newspaper, comprising British auction and fair listings, news and events.

Maine Antiques Digest
www.maineantiquesdigest.com
The online version of America's trade newspaper including news, articles, fair and auction listings and more.

La Gazette du Drouot
www.drouot.com
The online home of the magazine listing all auctions to be held in France at the Hotel de Drouot in Paris and beyond. An online subscription enables you to download the magazine online.

Auctionnet.com
www.auctionnet.com
Simple online resource listing over 500 websites related to auctions online.

AuctionBytes
www.auctionbytes.com
Auction resource with community forum, news, events, tips and a weekly newsletter.

Auction.fr
www.auction.fr
Online database of auctions at French auction houses. A subscription allows users to search past catalogues and prices realised.

Auctiontalk
www.internetauctionlist.com
Auction news, online and offline auction search engines and live chat forums.

Go Antiques/Antiqnet
www.goantiques.com
www.antiqnet.com
An online global aggregator for art, antiques and collectables dealers who showcase their stock online, allowing users to browse and buy.

eBay
www.ebay.com
Undoubtedly the largest and most diverse of the online auction sites, allowing users to buy and sell in an online marketplace with over 52 million registered users. Collectors should also view eBay Live Auctions (www.ebayliveauctions.com) where traditional auctions are combined with realtime, online bidding allowing users to interact with the saleroom as the auction takes place.

INDEX

APPENDICES

INDEX